Advance Praise for Cops Across Borders

"I am extremely impressed with Professor Nadelmann's work. This is a rich and detailed account of a neglected chapter in the history of criminal justice and in American history generally. I found it extraordinarily illuminating. I don't think any student of social history, diplomatic history, or legal history can ignore this book, which sheds so much light on a wide variety of important policy issues, including, very notably, drug enforcement policy. It deserves a wide readership."   —Lawrence M. Friedman, Stanford Law School

"Ethan Nadelmann, who has become widely known as an advocate of drug legalization, proves in this book that he is an important scholar of international law enforcement. By casting his study of law enforcement across the borders, he has broken new criminological ground. Nadelmann's study of the development of the tangled, tight, and problematic relationship between U.S. foreign policy and U.S. law enforcement will enlighten, and even fascinate, students in both areas."
                    —Jerome H. Skolnick, University of California, Berkeley

"Like a meteorite, Ethan Nadelmann has burst upon the academic scene bringing light, heat, and deep impressions. *Cops Across Borders* opens up a new field of inquiry and must be read by anyone concerned with U.S. foreign policy and criminal justice."   —Gary T. Marx, University of Colorado

"Nadelmann's outstanding book illuminates with impressive detail a dimension of security policy about which we know far too little, the international activities of national police forces. This book opens up a new area of research for students of international relations."
                    —Peter Katzenstein, Cornell University

"Ethan Nadelmann's book, *Cops Across Borders*, opens broad new ground both in the study of policing and in the field of international relations. Combining the two, he provides for the first time a picture of the newest frontier of U.S. law enforcement. The book is a very valuable addition to two fields of study."   —Philip B. Heymann, U.S. Deputy Attorney General

"Ethan Nadelmann has produced a remarkable piece of scholarship. Blending the study of international relations and criminal justice within a long-term historical framework, *Cops Across Borders* casts important new light on U.S. foreign policy, the war on drugs, and likely claims to U.S. hegemony in the emerging post–Cold War international arena."
                    —Peter H. Smith, University of California, San Diego

COPS ACROSS BORDERS

COPS ACROSS

Ethan A. Nadelmann

BORDERS

The Internationalization of
U.S. Criminal Law Enforcement

The Pennsylvania State University Press
University Park, Pennsylvania

Library of Congress Cataloging-in-Publication Data

Nadelmann, Ethan Avram.
    Cops across borders : the internationalization of U.S. criminal
law enforcement / Ethan A. Nadelmann.
        p.   cm.
    Includes bibliographical references and index.
    ISBN 0-271-01094-0 (cloth : acid-free paper)
    ISBN 0-271-01095-9 (paper : acid-free paper)
    1. Transnational crime—History. 2. Law enforcement—United
States—History. 3. Law enforcement—International cooperation—
History. I. Title.
HV6252.N33   1993
363.2'0973—dc20   93–1305
                                                              CIP

Published by The Pennsylvania State University Press,
Suite C, Barbara Building, University Park, PA 16802-1003

To my mother,
Judith Wolpert Nadelmann
and
to the memory of my father,
Rabbi Ludwig Nadelmann
(1928–1986)

The laws of this country take no notice of crimes committed out of their jurisdiction. The most atrocious offender coming within their pale is received by them as an innocent man, and they have authorized no one to seize and deliver him. The evil of protecting malefactors of every dye is sensibly felt here as in other countries, but until a reformation of the criminal codes of most nations, to deliver fugitives from them would be to become their accomplice—the former, therefore, is viewed as the lesser evil.

—U.S. Secretary of State Thomas Jefferson
September 1793

Often more than 50 percent of my day is devoted to some matter relating to our international involvement in fighting drug trafficking, money laundering, international organized crime and business fraud, environmental depredations, terrorism or espionage.

—U.S. Attorney General Richard Thornburgh
August 8, 1989

Contents

Preface

This is a book about the internationalization of U.S. criminal law enforcement. It examines how and why U.S. law enforcement officials have extended their efforts beyond American borders, how they have dealt with the challenges confronting them, and why their efforts have proved more or less successful. These efforts date back to the nation's origins. They proliferated following World War II. And they have increased dramatically in frequency, scope, and intensity since the early 1970s. Police and prosecutors who rarely if ever pursued their investigations abroad or sought evidence from foreign jurisdictions now do so with increasing frequency. Federal regulatory agencies that traditionally perceived their responsibilities and turf entirely in domestic terms now focus increasing attention on transnational interactions. Diplomats who hardly gave a second thought to criminal matters now often find them high among their assigned priorities. And legislators on Capitol Hill who typically identified crime as a local concern now focus much more of their rhetoric and law-making on criminals beyond American borders. Never before have U.S. foreign policy and U.S. criminal justice been so deeply entangled.

This book represents the first significant engagement of two scholarly disciplines—U.S. foreign policy and criminal justice—that have had remarkably little to do with one another. The vast majority of criminal justice scholars have extended their attention no further than their nations' borders; the few exceptions are those who have analyzed and compared foreign criminal justice systems.[1] Among students of U.S.

1. See in particular the work of David Bayley: *Patterns of Policing: An International Comparative Perspective* (New Brunswick, N.J.: Rutgers University Press, 1985); *Forces of*

foreign policy, some have focused their attention on domestic influences, but almost no one has paid much attention to issues of crime and law enforcement. Even as scholarly analyses of U.S. international drug control policy have proliferated in recent years, few have focused on the criminal justice dimensions of that policy. Whatever arguments might once have justified this disengagement of the two disciplines can no longer be sustained. The interpenetration of foreign policy and criminal justice institutions and concerns have simply become too substantial to be ignored by scholars any longer.

People, products, money, information, ideas, and cultures transcend national borders today with an ease, and at a pace and volume, unprecedented in human history. At the same time, the United States and most other governments have assumed increasing responsibilities for enforcing food, drug, and consumer safety laws, policing the securities and commodities markets, protecting the environment, enforcing patent and copyright laws, collecting taxes, and protecting the general welfare of their citizens—all of which require increasing extraterritorial vigilance. This trend is not, to be sure, irreversible, but so long as it continues it will present a basic challenge to the state: how to control growing domains of transnational activities that either ignore or take advantage of national borders when the powers of the state remain powerfully circumscribed by the political, geographical, and legal limitations that attend notions of national sovereignty?

Among the principal responses of the United States and other governments to this challenge has been the internationalization of their criminal justice laws, policies, capabilities, and institutions. International criminal law enforcement can be understood as both the extraterritorial extension of criminal justice activities normally performed within a single jurisdiction and as the criminal justice dimension of foreign policy institutions and activities designed to protect and advance a state's national interests. It can be viewed, more broadly, as an essential component of states' unceasing efforts to control their borders and, by extension, their municipal realms. And it can be seen, more contempo-

---

Order: *Policing Modern Japan* (Berkeley and Los Angeles: University of California Press, 1991); "The Police and Political Change in Comparative Perspective," *Law and Society Review* 6 (1971), 91–112; and *The Police and Political Development in India* (Princeton: Princeton University Press, 1969). See also R. I. Mawby, *Comparative Policing Issues: The British and American System in International Perspective* (Boston: Unwin Hyman, 1990).

raneously, as part and parcel of the increasingly complex and multi-dimensional interdependence of states and societies today.

The broader relevance of this study stems primarily from its analysis of how municipal control systems respond to the demands of internationalization. Criminal justice systems in most countries evolve with little consideration of the need to interact with foreign systems. They may be influenced by foreign models, but they are almost entirely concerned with the control of municipal societies. The internationalization of crime and law enforcement thus places demands upon criminal justice systems to which they are generally ill suited to respond. Criminal justice systems are not, however, the only municipal control systems to have faced the challenges of internationalization. Therein lie the broader implications of this study.

The Evolution of This Study

When I began this study in 1983, my intent was to examine the evolution of U.S. international drug control policies. I conceived of the project as both an exercise in diplomatic history and a critical examination of the means employed to carry out those policies. I knew that the U.S. Drug Enforcement Administration (DEA), with its global operations and more than two hundred agents stationed abroad, would constitute part of the story, but I imagined my focus would be on the role played by the U.S. State Department.

As I pursued the study, however, my interest gradually shifted from the focus on diplomacy. To be sure, despite a number of fine studies of prewar U.S. drug control diplomacy,[2] no one had attempted (nor has yet attempted) a comprehensive analysis of subsequent developments in this area. But I remained reluctant to make that the focus of my research, for a number of reasons. It seemed to me that much of what was theoretically interesting about the nature and challenges of U.S. drug control diplomacy had apparently already been thoroughly analyzed by scholars of U.S. human rights diplomacy and other analogous dimen-

2. Arnold Taylor, *American Diplomacy and the Narcotics Traffic, 1900–1939* (Durham, N.C.: Duke University Press, 1969); William O. Walker III, *Drug Control in the Americas* (Albuquerque: University of New Mexico Press, 1981); and Peter D. Lowes, *The Genesis of International Narcotics Control* (Geneva: Librairie Droz, 1966).

sions of U.S. foreign policy.[3] I also increasingly realized that the "successes" and "failures" of U.S. international drug control efforts had relatively little impact on illicit drug abuse in the United States—a diplomatic analysis to show why was not needed.[4] But most important, while examining the activities of the DEA overseas, I stumbled onto a vein of inquiry so rich that it rapidly came to absorb all my attention. The more interesting questions, I discovered, concerned not how diplomats and other political authorities dealt with the international aspects of drug control but rather how law enforcement officials dealt with international matters.

My focus therefore shifted from examining the international drug control efforts of the United States as a subset of American foreign policy to examining them from the context of international law enforcement. The DEA became the focal point of an analysis that sought to shed light not just on the nature and challenges of international drug control but also on all criminal justice efforts evidencing an international dimension. The American drug enforcement agency, with its representatives in some sixty foreign cities around the world, was a unique phenomenon in the annals of both international relations and policing, but as I looked for and found both historical and contemporary analogues to the DEA, I realized that there was nothing particularly unique about the basic functions of the agency and the challenges confronting it. Historical parallels and antecedents abounded both within and without the United States, dating back to the origins of the American republic and beyond. The DEA's agents were not the only ones to travel overseas, to station representatives abroad, or even to operate undercover and recruit informants in foreign countries. The basic challenges of interacting with foreign law enforcement officials, deciphering foreign law enforcement systems, and generally operating in foreign political and legal environments beholden to very different criminal laws, procedures, and other norms were familiar not just to other police agents but also to the government attorneys charged with extradition and other mutual legal assistance tasks. I found, in short, a universe of governmental activity at the intersection of criminal justice and international

3. See, e.g., Lars Schoultz, *Human Rights and United States Policy Toward Latin America* (Princeton: Princeton University Press, 1981).

4. See my analyses in "International Drug Trafficking and U.S. Foreign Policy," *Washington Quarterly* 8 (1985), 87–104; and in "U.S. Drug Policy: A Bad Export," *Foreign Policy* 70 (1988), 83–108.

relations that had yet to be subjected to systematic scholarly examination.

My study of U.S. international law enforcement activities was further stimulated and complicated by the rapid expansion and transformation of those activities during the 1980s. This reassured me that the subject was indeed of increasing importance, but it also required persistent attention to new developments. As I scoured the scholarly literature during the mid-1980s for discussions of transnational crime and international law enforcement, I found strikingly little, so I set out to talk with those involved in international law enforcement activities. Between January 1984 and June 1990, I interviewed approximately three hundred individuals: DEA, FBI, IRS, Secret Service, and customs agents; U.S. marshals; CIA analysts; Justice, Treasury, and State Department officials; Congressional staff; Interpol employees; foreign police; and other government officials, as well as knowledgeable attorneys, journalists, and other experts. A majority of these interviews were conducted in 1984 and 1985 in Washington, D.C., Miami, and New York City, as well as during two international trips: the first in January 1985 to Jamaica, Panama, Ecuador, Peru, Chile, Argentina, and Bolivia; the second in May and June 1985 to France, Belgium, the Netherlands, Germany, Switzerland, Austria, Italy, and Great Britain. During part of this time, I was also employed as a consultant to the State Department's Bureau of International Narcotics Matters (INM) to write a report on U.S. and international efforts against drug-related money laundering activities.[5] Between 1986 and 1990, I conducted dozens of additional interviews in some of the same countries, as well as in Colombia, Mexico, and Spain. A small number of interviews were also conducted by phone. I interviewed resident DEA agents in all eighteen foreign countries visited and local law enforcement officials in most of them, supplementing my standard set of questions with others intended to elicit impressions and insights. In a few countries, I was permitted to sit in on agent conferences, observe interrogations, interview informants, and participate in surveillances of drug traffickers. I viewed my objective as finding out whatever was necessary to better understand the evolution, nature, and challenges of international law enforcement.

The interviews—most of which were conducted on a not-for-attribu-

---

5. A revised version of that report was later published as "Unlaundering Dirty Money Abroad: U.S. Foreign Policy and Financial Secrecy Jurisdictions," *University of Miami Inter-American Law Review* 18 (1986), 33–82.

tion basis—provided me with otherwise unavailable information and insights about the international and extraterritorial efforts of U.S. law enforcement officials. I learned how DEA agents had devised means of circumventing the civil law restrictions on undercover operations and the use and recruitment of informants in Europe and Latin America, how they had dealt with the obstacles presented by the virtually omnipresent police corruption in Latin America, and more generally how they compensated for the loss of their sovereign police powers on foreign territory. I learned how Justice Department officials had sought to improve their capacity to obtain evidence from abroad—in particular, financial documents from foreign financial secrecy jurisdictions—in a form admissible in American judicial proceedings. In the process, I also learned much about the nature of criminal justice and criminal investigation in foreign countries, as well as the ways in which foreign criminal justice systems had changed in response to American requests, pressures, and examples. And I gained a sense of how and why the internationalization of U.S. law enforcement had proceeded so quickly since the late 1960s.

My broader objectives, however, required that I examine not just the modern era of international law enforcement but also its historical parallels and antecedents. The international activities of the DEA, I came to realize, were part and parcel not just of U.S. international drug control diplomacy or of the domestic "war on drugs" but also of historical processes that can be traced back to Great Britain's diplomatic and naval campaigns against piracy and slavery, to the international secret police networks maintained by Metternich and the interior ministries of Russian czars and French emperors, and to the nineteenth-century efforts of U.S. customs and police agents to stem smuggling and banditry across the Canadian and Mexican borders. I initially intended these historical inquiries to serve primarily as contexts and correctives for my analysis of contemporary international law enforcement; to identify, as best as possible, the origins and evolution of international law enforcement, and to guard against the tendency to view contemporary developments as entirely new and unprecedented. But these inquiries eventually assumed a life and intellectual standing of their own, yielding a far deeper and more fundamental understanding of the nature and potential of international law enforcement endeavors, and their relationship to both political changes in the international system and technological innovations, than would have been possible had I examined only the contemporary era of international law enforcement. The results of these inquiries can be found in the more historical portions of the chapters that follow and in a forthcoming companion volume to this book tentatively entitled "Criminalization and Crime Control in International Society."

To Whom It May Concern: Questions and Audiences

This book is very much a hybrid designed to interest scholars and practitioners in many fields. Some distinguished colleagues have suggested that I address this book primarily to one audience, be it international relations, bureaucratic politics, criminal justice, international law, or some other well-defined scholarly discipline with its own favored questions, theories, and categories. I have chosen to pursue another tack: to identify and describe a heretofore unexamined domain of governmental activity, to ask a set of questions about the nature and challenges of that domain, and to offer a number of answers and hypotheses in response to those questions. In pursuing this tack, I have rifled through the scholarly literatures of diverse disciplines in search of models, analogies, and insights that might help me explain the internationalization of criminal law enforcement. I have assumed that this subject is sufficiently interesting and important in and of itself that you, the reader, have engaged this book primarily because you want to learn about this subject. But I suspect there is much in the analysis that follows to spark your thinking about subjects quite removed from this one.

This book resembles other studies of bureaucracies in that it analyzes the behavior of a particular set of agencies and officials, the tasks they perform, the challenges they confront, and the reasons they succeed or fail. It is exceptional, however, in analyzing these issues in an international rather than a domestic setting. This book resembles other studies, published principally in law journals, in its examination of issues related to extradition and mutual legal assistance. It differs from most, however, insofar as it analyzes these issues in historical perspective, focuses less on the legal issues and more on the behavior and perspectives of U.S. officials engaged in these areas, and relies on information derived from interviews with the officials themselves. This book resembles others in the field of comparative policing and criminal justice in that it compares the approaches and behavior of law enforcement officials in different countries. But it goes a step beyond these studies in its analysis of the interactions among systems and the ways in which criminal investigative norms and methods are influenced by those of other states.

This book also resembles many studies of U.S. foreign policy in its focus on how and why U.S. officials have pursued particular objectives abroad. It differs, however, in at least three respects: it examines an assortment of agencies and actors that have not previously been studied in the context of U.S. foreign policy; it focuses on the conduct of relatively low-level government officials, rather than high-level decision makers and bureaucrats; and it examines in relatively close and comparative detail the ways in which U.S. officials pursue their objectives on foreign territories. Implicit in my analysis is the assumption that much of what remains both interesting and unexplained about international relations can best be explained by multilayered analyses that integrate close examinations of domestic interests, processes, and norms with detailed analyses of international interactions.

Because this book is designed to interest scholars and practitioners in many fields, and because it addresses a set of questions that have not previously been addressed, readers may find some terms and concepts unfamiliar. I urge you, however, not to close your mind to them. Many readers, including some from the discipline of international relations, may wonder why I have resuscitated from the international relations literature of the early 1970s nearly forgotten concepts such as "transgovernmental relations" and "transnational organizations." I have done so not to pay homage to the passing fads of a discipline but rather because these concepts are peculiarly valuable for explaining much of what constitutes international law enforcement. Similarly, the notion of "harmonization" is much in vogue these days as economic and financial markets and systems become increasingly interdependent, and as governments attempt to coordinate their regulatory efforts. But I employ the notion—and define it as I do—principally because it is so valuable in describing and explaining a powerful current and objective in the evolution of international law enforcement. Many law enforcement agents, and some students of criminal justice and bureaucracy, will appreciate without further explanation what I mean by the "immobilization" of criminals. But it is also important that students of U.S. foreign policy recognize this as an increasingly important objective of foreign policy, and understand that it presents the U.S. government with challenges that are familiar in some respects and unique in others.

This book is relatively thick both in description and in analysis. Let me explain why. First, it offers not a new twist on a familiar subject but rather an introduction and series of twists on an entirely new subject (insofar as it has not heretofore been described or analyzed in any depth whatsoever). Second, it is designed, as I noted above, to interest not one scholarly or professional audience but many. I prefer that some readers skip and skim through the portions that interest them less, rather than leave those with a strong interest in the subject at hand frustrated. Third, the dominant cast of all the chapters but one (Chapter Five) is historical and evolutionary. This reflects my desire to develop the themes of continuity and change in the internationalization of U.S. law enforcement. And it is driven by my sense that any general propositions about the nature of international criminal law enforcement should meet the standards of historical scrutiny.

In choosing what to include and exclude, I had three objectives in mind: to offer a comprehensive examination of U.S. international law enforcement activities, to focus more intensively on dimensions that have not been analyzed elsewhere, and to provide new perspectives on subjects that have been examined by others. One reason why four of the six chapters that follow focus on police is because most of what has been written on U.S. international law enforcement is preoccupied with judicial decisions and law enforcement treaties. Chapter Two, which examines the internationalization of U.S. criminal law enforcement from 1789 to 1939, is included in part as a corrective to the tendency to see international criminal law enforcement as an entirely contemporary phenomenon. Chapter Three, which describes and analyzes the international activities of most federal law enforcement agencies since World War II, scopes out a domain of U.S. criminal justice and foreign policy that has not previously been identified as a distinct domain. Chapters Four and Five, which examine the operations of the DEA in Europe and Latin America, respectively, focus on the U.S. federal police agency that has been most intimately and extensively involved in international activities.

Where Chapters Two through Five describe and analyze a domain of U.S. foreign policy and criminal justice previously ignored by scholars, Chapters Six and Seven cut through familiar subjects in new ways. The collection of evidence and fugitives from abroad has been addressed in dozens of law review articles. What distinguishes Chapter Six from that literature is its focus on the negotiation of legal assistance treaties, my reliance on interviews with the Justice Department officials involved in the negotiations, and the relationships drawn between this domain of international law enforcement and others. What distinguishes Chapter Seven from other analyses of U.S. efforts to obtain fugitives from abroad is the historical nature of the analysis. Remarkably, no book-length history of the subject has been written since John Bassett Moore's classic treatise of 1891. Chapter Seven represents a modest first step toward filling that void.

Any claim to comprehensiveness demands an explanation of significant lacunae. Three related subjects are treated far too briefly in this book. The first is the role of U.S. law enforcement agencies in dealing with the transnational dimensions of espionage, terrorism, high-tech smuggling, and other criminal violations of national security laws. The second involves the complex and abundant relationships between U.S. intelligence agencies and law enforcement agencies. And the third concerns the law enforcement activities of the U.S. military investigative branches. The two first subjects—particularly the second—would have been extremely difficult to research and write about given the high degree of secrecy surrounding them. As for the third, my principal excuse is lack of time and resources. I am confident that few of the central themes in this book would be undermined or challenged by greater awareness of these subjects, but each raises important issues that I look forward to having others pursue.

Let me also explain what this book is not. First, it does not engage, at least directly, the long-standing debates among realists, neorealists, pluralists, liberals, and others in the academic discipline of international relations. I am quite satisfied to provide grist for the mill of each in the pages that follow. The realist model of the state as a unitary actor jibes nicely with reality when we focus our attention on the state as creator of laws—that is, as criminalizer. But alternative paradigms will find much support in my emphasis on the transgovernmental dimension of international law enforcement activities, in my references to the turf struggles among federal agencies, and in my discussion of the constraints on U.S. international law enforcement activities imposed by Congress and the judiciary. Realists can well point to the single-minded pursuit of U.S. law enforcement objectives abroad and to the relatively common reliance on coercive and unilateral measures by U.S. law enforcement agencies. But others can stress the high degree of consensus and mutual interest among states on many criminal justice matters, or point to the moralistic causes and consequences of injecting criminal justice objectives and concerns into U.S. foreign policy.

This book does, however, contribute to the debate over the impact of modernization on foreign policy and international politics. The technologically driven proliferation of transnational and transgovernmental interactions is changing the substance and processes of foreign policy as well as the meaning of power in international politics. Contemporary scholars are not the first to appreciate the consequences. "It has become a platitude," Ramsay Muir observed in 1932, "to say that the whole world is now interdependent." More systematic analysis of the consequences of modernization began in the late 1960s. Edward Morse, writing in 1970, observed that three sets of conditions had developed:

> First, the ideal and classical distinctions between foreign and domestic affairs have broken down, even though the myths associated with sovereignty and the state have not. Second, the distinction between "high policies" (those associated with security and the continued existence of the state) and "low policies" (those pertaining to the wealth and welfare of the citizens) has become less important as low policies have assumed an increasingly large role in any society. Third, although there have been significant developments in the instrumentalities of political control, the actual ability to control events either internal or external to modernized societies—even those that are Great Powers—has decreased with the growth of interdependence, and is likely to decrease further.[6]

Each of these observations is confirmed in the chapters that follow— although my analysis does indicate that there are some domains in which the ability of states to control particular events has increased.

Modernization also transformed the ways in which states pursued their objectives abroad. The postwar American "empire," Samuel Huntington pointed out, "was an empire of functions, not territory, . . . characterized not by the *acquisition* of new territory but by their *penetration*."[7] Wolfram Hanreider elaborated: "Access rather than ac-

6. Edward L. Morse, "The Transformation of Foreign Policies: Modernization, Interdependence, and Externalization," *World Politics* 22 (1970), 371–392.

7. Samuel Huntington, "Transnational Organizations in World Politics," *World Politics* 25 (1973), 343–344.

quisition, presence rather than rule, penetration rather than possession have become the important issues."[8] The power of states increasingly consists of their capacity to employ both municipal and international institutions and mechanisms to control transnational interactions. Where powerful states once relied on armies and navies to accomplish their objectives abroad, now police and other security officials play an increasingly important role. Spies and intelligence agencies provide an element of continuity with the past, but even they find themselves drawn into more frequent and multidimensional relationships with municipal agencies and issues.

Second, although this book addresses the question "Why have U.S. law enforcement agencies extended their efforts abroad?" that is not its sole or even principal objective. The question is not one that lends itself to broad theoretical generalizations or systematic evaluation of alternative hypotheses. The answers to the question are simply too many and too varied. One can point to the impact of technological developments, to expanding notions of jurisdiction, to municipal developments such as the creation of criminal investigative branches and the nationalization of crime control, to evolving attitudes regarding the degree to which Americans should assist foreign states in the enforcement of criminal laws, to rising levels of consensus and comity among governments in criminal justice matters, to changes in the domestic market for illicit imports, and much else. Most important, the answers to the question are so diverse because the criminal laws that U.S. agents seek to enforce both municipally and internationally are so diverse.

The criminal law identifies particular activities and labels them criminal. But all that criminal activities have in common is that they are the subject of criminal laws. Consider the variety of activities that are the subject of many U.S. international law enforcement actions: cocaine importing, insider trading, unsanctioned migration, espionage, terrorism, export of sophisticated technology to unapproved states, failure to declare purchases abroad worth more than $400, and failure to report that one has taken $10,000 or more in cash into or out of the country. Some of these activities have been treated as criminal for centuries, others not until quite recently. Just as governments employ administrative regulations to regulate domestic, transnational, and occasionally

8. Wolfram F. Hanreider, "Dissolving International Politics: Reflections on the Nation-State," *American Political Science Review* 72 (1978), 1276–1287.

extraterritorial interactions, so they employ criminal laws to bolster their regulatory efforts in a wide array of domains: trade, finance, migration, national security, the environment, public health, and much else. New criminal laws are enacted every year. Some are violated routinely, others barely at all. No single thesis comes close to explaining the internationalization of U.S. criminal law enforcement, for the same reason that no single thesis can persuasively explain the criminalization of some activities and not others.

Third, this book offers little in the way of policy prescriptions or normative judgments on U.S. involvement in international law enforcement matters. I did not perceive my task as one of telling government officials how to perform their tasks more effectively (although a number of DEA agents have told me that Chapters Four and Five should be assigned in their agency's training courses). Nor did I perceive a need or a responsibility to cast personal judgment upon the rightness and wrongness of U.S. police actions in foreign countries. More than enough commentators have already done so in the law journals and op-ed pages. I instead saw my responsibility as one of providing insights into the attitudes and methods of those who engage in international law enforcement activities.

One final prefatory note is warranted. I began this research enterprise with a strong dose of skepticism regarding the objectives, efficacy, and correctness of U.S. drug control policies. My research experience effectively confirmed my intellectual and ethical reservations. Even as I came to like and admire many drug enforcement agents and other officials, I also came to see both their efforts and the laws and policies they enforced as fundamentally misguided—for reasons that I have elaborated upon elsewhere.[9] Readers of this book, however, will find only scant references to these reservations. This study represents my effort to analyze the internationalization of U.S. criminal law enforcement as a historical, legal, and governmental process. I offer neither policy prescriptions nor normative judgments, but simply my best efforts at objective and scholarly analysis.

9. See the following articles by Ethan A. Nadelmann: "Drug Prohibition in the United States: Costs, Consequences, and Alternatives," *Science* 245 (Sept. 1, 1989), 939–947; "U.S. Drug Policy: A Bad Export," *Foreign Policy* 70 (1988), 1–39; and "The Case for Legalization," *Public Interest* 92 (1988), 3–31.

Acknowledgments

Any manuscript that begins as a Ph.D. dissertation, grows and divides into two books, and takes ten years to complete inevitably acquires an abundance of debts. I want therefore just to name the few dozens who have given the most in terms of their time, assistance, and support. I first must thank the many friends who read various chapters of the dissertation, offered their comments, and generously tolerated my obsessive bantering on this subject—in particular, John DiIulio, Aaron Friedberg, Jane Katz, Yuen Foong Khong, James Lindsay, Stephen Roof, and Nicholas Ziegler, as well as Vincent Auger, Manuel José Cepeda, Steven Cobrin, Jean-Marc Coicaud, Michael Daumer, Gregory Gause, Gustavo Gorriti, Jill Irvine, Mark Kleiman, Philip Kraft, Juan Lindau, Lloyd Lowy, Tony Malavenda, Arie Ofri, Peter Reynolds, Gabriel Schoenfeld, Michael Tiorano, Javier Trevino, and Matthew Zavitkovsky; my students David Medina, Adam Sexton, and Rhys Williams; my parents, Ludwig and Judith Nadelmann; my brothers, Jeremy and Daniel; and my sister, Deborah.

My dissertation advisors, Stanley Hoffmann, Philip Heymann, and Mark Moore, each played important roles in challenging and stimulating my thinking about various dimensions of this subject. I am most grateful to them not just for their advice but for their guidance and encouragement as well. I also must thank Robert Keohane, James Q. Wilson, Gary Marx, Peter Reuter, and especially Jorge Dominguez for their scholarly advice and comments on portions of the dissertation. Among those who have read various drafts of the manuscript since, I am particularly indebted to David Bayley, John DiIulio, Jameson Doig, Michael Doyle, Cyrille Fijnaut, Aaron Friedberg, Fred Greenstein, Peggy Hoover, Gary

Marx, Walter Murphy, Uwe Reinhardt, Mark Richard, and Sandy Thatcher, and I want to thank Michael Abbell, Christopher Blakesley, Heinrich Boge, Thomas Cash, Forrest Colburn, John Cusack, Wolfgang Danspeckgruber, Daniel Deudney, Albin Eser, Herbert Fuchs, Albrecht Funk, John Harris, Bob Hoogenboom, David Johnson, Yuen Foong Khong, Réne Lévy, John Langbein, Richard Martin, John Murphy, Richard Owens, Sebastian Scheerer, Richard Ullman, and Bruce Zagaris for their comments and advice on various chapters. Among the many able students who have worked as my research assistants, I am particularly indebted to Kristina Scott for her research and translations of German materials, Christine Zandvliet for her research and translations of Dutch materials, and David Jefferds, John Hickey, and Martin De-Santos for their overall commitment and resourcefulness. My thanks as well to my superb secretary, Sandy Paroly. I am grateful most of all to Donna Sherman, my partner in life from the time this project was conceived until its conclusion, and to our wonderful daughter, Lila.

A graduate student could hope for no finer place to write a dissertation than the Center for International Affairs at Harvard University. It provided a wonderful workplace and base of operations, as well as funding in the form of a NOMOS Fellowship and a John M. Olin Fellowship in International Security. My thanks in particular to Samuel Huntington, Chester Haskell, Michael Tiorano, Barbara Mitchell, and Janice Rand. I completed the manuscript as an assistant professor at the Woodrow Wilson School of Public and International Affairs and the Department of Politics at Princeton University. This too provided an excellent environment for research and writing, the benefits of association with Princeton's Center for International Studies and its Center for Domestic and Comparative Policy Studies, the dedicated and resourceful efforts of the Office of Interlibrary Services at Princeton's Firestone Library, as well as funding by the University Committee on Research in the Humanities and Social Sciences. My thanks in particular to Donald Stokes, Henry Bienen, James Trussell, Ingrid Reed, and Michael Stoner.

Other institutions also provided valuable financial support. A graduate student fellowship in international relations from the National Science Foundation provided funding during the genesis of this study. During the 1984–85 academic year, a graduate research fellowship (#84-IJ-CX-0065) from the National Institute of Justice provided further funding. Travel grants in 1985 from Harvard's Center for European Studies, the Program in European Society and Western Security, and the

Committee on Latin American and Iberian Studies enabled me to conduct the initial interviews in Europe and Latin America. An invitation from the United States Information Agency in March 1986 to speak at a conference hosted by the University of the Andes in Bogotá, Colombia, provided a quick research opportunity, as did invitations in March 1990 by the Centro de Estudios de Política Exterior in Madrid, Spain, and in October 1992 by the Dutch Police and Society Foundation in Amsterdam. Grants from the National Institute of Justice and the Deutsch Forschungsgemeinschaft proved essential in funding a June 1988 conference on international cooperation in law enforcement matters convened by Harvard Law School's Center for Criminal Justice, the Max-Planck-Instituts für ausländisches und internationales Strafrecht, and the Goethe Institute of Boston.

I am also grateful to the many U.S. government officials who assisted me in one way or another during the research phase of this dissertation. Some of the research was carried out while I was simultaneously preparing a report on drug-related international money laundering for the State Department's Bureau of International Narcotics Matters (INM). I must thank Jon Wiant, who opened the doors to the State Department; Robert Retka, who showed me the ropes; Mark Steinitz and Geoffrey Levitt, who provided me with their rich insights and became friends; and all of the people in INM for their hospitality during the months I worked out of their offices.

I interviewed more than three hundred individuals as part of the research. Some provided assistance and advice over and above the time and patience required to answer my questions. The most important and numerous of my interviews were with sixty-odd special agents and other officials of the Drug Enforcement Administration. I am indebted to Frank Monastero, Patrick Tarr, and Abe Azzam for opening the doors to their agency, and, for their help, assistance, and/or advice, to Bobby Nieves, Lee Rice, Jim Bramble, Richard Mangan, and Morton Goren in Washington; Gene Castillo and Jeff Hall in Latin America; and Bill Wolf, Greg Passic, Jerry Franciosa, and Dave Herrera in Europe. Other government officials who went out of their way to assist me included William Corcoran, John Harris, Alvin Lodish, Richard Owens, and Mark Richard in the Justice Department; Dick Stiener, Martin White, and Mary Jo Grotenrath, at the U.S. National Central Bureau of Interpol; Floyd Clarke and Ernest Porter, at the Federal Bureau of Investigation; Robert Liebscher, at the U.S. Marshals Service; the late

Seymour Bolten, at the Treasury Department; Lois Allder, at the Office of the Legal Adviser in the Department of State; and Eric Sterling, on the staff of the House Subcommittee on Crime. To all of them I express my gratitude.

Earlier versions of portions of this book have appeared in various journals. Portions of Chapter Five appeared in "The DEA in Latin America: Dealing with Institutionalized Corruption," *Journal of Interamerican Studies and World Affairs* 29 (Winter 1987–88), 1–40. Portions of Chapter Six appeared in "Negotiations in Criminal Law Assistance Treaties," *American Journal of Comparative Law* 33 (Summer 1985), 467–504. Much of Chapter Seven appeared in the *New York University Journal of International Law and Politics* 25 (1993). And small sections of a few of the chapters appeared in "The Role of the United States in the International Enforcement of Criminal Law," *Harvard International Law Journal* 31 (Winter 1990), 37–76.

Abbreviations

ACI	Administration of Criminal Investigation (Belgium)
ACND	Central Narcotics Department (Austria)
AFOSI	U.S. Air Force Office of Special Investigations, 1948–
AID	Agency for International Development
ATF	U.S. Bureau of Alcohol, Tobacco, and Firearms
BDAC	U.S. Bureau of Drug Abuse Control, 1965–1968
BKA	Bundeskriminalamt (German Federal Police)
BNDD	U.S. Bureau of Narcotics and Dangerous Drugs, 1968–1973
BSC	British Security Coordination
CA	country attaché
CCC	Customs Cooperation Council, 1953–
CCE	Continuing Criminal Enterprise Act, 1970
CENTAC	DEA's Central Tactical Unit program, 1973–1981
CFTC	Commodity Futures Trading Commission (U.S.), 1974–
CIA	U.S. Central Intelligence Agency, 1947–
CID	U.S. Army Criminal Investigative Division, 1918–
CNO	Central Narcotics Office (France)
CPA	U.S. Civil Police Administration, 1955–1962
CRI	Criminal Intelligence Service (Netherlands)
CTR	Currency Transaction Report
DEA	U.S. Drug Enforcement Administration, 1973–
EPIC	DEA's El Paso Intelligence Center
EXIS	ATF's Explosives Incident System
FBI	U.S. Federal Bureau of Investigation, 1909–
FBN	U.S. Federal Bureau of Narcotics, 1930–1968

FDA	U.S. Food and Drug Administration, 1927–
FIST	Fugitive Investigative Strike Team, U.S. Marshals Service, 1981–
HEW	U.S. Department of Health, Education, and Welfare
IACP	International Association of Chiefs of Police, 1893–
ICPC	International Criminal Police Commission, 1923–
IMAC	Swiss Federal Act on International Mutual Assistance in Criminal Matters, 1981
IMF	International Monetary Fund
INM	Bureau of International Narcotics Matters, U.S. State Department, 1978–1993
INS	U.S. Immigration and Naturalization Service
IOSCO	International Organization of Securities Commission
IRA	Irish Republican Army
IRS	U.S. Internal Revenue Service
ITAR	U.S. International Traffic in Arms program, BATF
LEGAT	FBI legal attaché
LKA	criminal investigative units in German states
L/LEI	U.S. Office of Law Enforcement and Intelligence, Office of the Legal Adviser, Department of State, 1979–
MLAT	mutual legal assistance treaty
MOU	memorandum of understanding
NACDL	National Association of Criminal Defense Lawyers (U.S.)
NADDIS	DEA's Narcotics and Dangerous Drug Information System
NATO	North Atlantic Treaty Organization, 1949–
NCB	National Central Bureau (Interpol)
NIS	U.S. Naval Investigative Service, 1966–
NYPD	New York Police Department
OCAM	Organization Communale Africaine et Malgache
ODALE	U.S. Office of Drug Abuse Law Enforcement, 1972–1973
OECD	Organization of Economic Cooperation and Development
OIA	U.S. Office of International Affairs, Criminal Division, Justice Department, 1979–
OLIA	Office of Liaison and International Affairs, FBI, 1987–
ONI	U.S. Office of Naval Intelligence, 1882–
ONNI	U.S. Office of National Narcotics Intelligence, 1972–1973
OPS	U.S. Office of Public Safety, 1962–1974
OSS	U.S. Office of Strategic Services, 1942–1945
PIP	Peruvian Investigative Police

PIS	U.S. Postal Inspection Service
RAC	resident-agent-in-charge
RICO	Racketeer Influenced and Corrupt Organizations Act, 1970
SA	special agent
SAC	special-agent-in-charge
SANU	Special Action Narcotics Unit (Colombia)
SCA	Servizio Centrale Antidroga (Italy)
SEC	U.S. Securities and Exchange Commission, 1934–
SEO	Special Enforcement Operation, DEA, 1981–
SIS	U.S. Special Intelligence Service, 1940–1945
SIU	Special Investigation Unit
SOG	Special Operations Group, U.S. Marshals Service, 1971–
TDY	temporary duty
TIAS	*Treaties and Other International Acts Series* (issued singly in pamphlets by the U.S. Department of State)
UMOPAR	Rural Mobile Patrol Unit (Bolivia), 1983–
USMS	U.S. Marshals Service, 1969–
USNCB	U.S. National Central Bureau (Interpol), 1962–
ZEPO	Central Police Office (Switzerland)

Chapter One

Introduction

The Internationalization of U.S. Criminal Law Enforcement

The internationalization of U.S. law enforcement cannot be explained entirely or even primarily in terms of the need to respond to a proliferation of transnational criminal activities. Rather, the principal impetuses underlying many of the more significant developments in the history of U.S. international criminal law enforcement were provided by federal statutes criminalizing activities that had not previously been regarded as criminal. Most contemporary efforts, for instance, are concerned with the enforcement of criminal laws that did not exist a century or even a few decades ago—not just drug prohibition laws, but also criminal laws directed at insider trading, money laundering, computer fraud, and the smuggling of sophisticated weaponry and other technology to blacklisted countries. The United States' imposition of immigration controls on Chinese migrants in the late nineteenth century and most other foreigners a few decades later similarly created a need for a substantial law enforcement effort. And the proliferation of federal statutes during the 1980s explicitly extending U.S. jurisdiction to terrorist and other violent acts against U.S. citizens abroad provided the legal basis for a substantial internationalization of the FBI's investigations. Conversely, the rendition of fugitive slaves constituted a central concern of U.S. international law enforcement efforts before the Civil War, and efforts to suppress the illicit traffic in alcoholic beverages preoccupied U.S. officials involved in international law enforcement matters between 1920 and 1933. Both ended with the abolition of the laws they were intended to enforce.

Given the initial impulses provided by Congressional and other legislative criminalizations, subsequent developments can be explained by a variety of factors. The United States' assumption of global economic and security responsibilities following World War II brought with it a host of international criminal law enforcement responsibilities ranging from the policing of hundreds of thousands of U.S. military personnel abroad to the creation of police training programs in dozens of less developed nations. Many increases in international law enforcement activity were motivated by perceived increases, both real and unreal, in particular types of transnational criminal activity. The explosion in transnational drug trafficking beginning in the 1960s, for instance, generated an international law enforcement response of unprecedented dimensions. The increase in transnational violations of U.S. securities laws that inevitably accompanied the dramatic internationalization of the securities markets during the 1980s similarly invited a response by the Justice Department and the Securities and Exchange Commission. Other international criminal law enforcement initiatives were motivated principally by domestic political considerations, such as when the Nixon administration extended its "war on drugs" to foreign countries during the early 1970s, and when the Reagan and Bush administrations did likewise during the 1980s. Additional incentives were provided by the proliferation of Congressional hearings addressing transnational drug trafficking and other criminal activities. The expansion of international criminal law enforcement capabilities in and of itself generated increasing activity and invited new laws. And in many cases, the principal motivations for developing a law enforcement agency's international capabilities could be traced to interagency rivalries and the desires of agency chiefs to claim more jurisdiction and responsibilities for their agencies.

The internationalization of U.S. law enforcement has involved an increasing number of federal agencies, activities, and resources. The Office of International Affairs (OIA) in the Justice Department's Criminal Division, and the Office of Law Enforcement and Intelligence (L/LEI) in the State Department's Legal Adviser's Office, both created in 1979, have assumed leading roles in coordinating extradition and other mutual legal assistance relations with foreign governments. In 1985, the Securities and Exchange Commission created its own special office devoted to handling international enforcement matters. And in 1987, the Justice Department initiated a policy of stationing its own attorneys abroad. Growing numbers of U.S. prosecutors now communicate with their foreign counterparts and travel abroad seeking cooperation and evidence in criminal cases. American judges confront an increasing number of cases in which evidence and witnesses must be obtained from abroad. And U.S. law enforcement agencies—most notably the Drug Enforcement Administration (DEA) but also the Federal Bureau of Investigation (FBI), the Internal Revenue Service (IRS), the Immigration and Naturalization Service (INS), the Secret Service, the U.S. Customs Service, the U.S. Marshals Service, the criminal investigative branches of the military services, and even state and city police departments—have dramatically increased their international responsibilities and activities. (See Appendix A.) Some of these activities have been assisted by the U.S. military and the intelligence agencies, and backed by the diplomatic efforts of the State Department, high-level Justice Department officials, and the White House. They also have come under increasingly frequent and intensive Congressional scrutiny as federal legislators have stepped up dramatically their legislative and rhetorical responses to transnational drug trafficking and other transnational criminal activity.

A few indications of the pace of the expansion can be found in the personnel statistics. Between 1967 and 1991, the number of U.S. drug enforcement agents stationed abroad rose from about 12 in eight foreign cities to about 300 in more than seventy foreign locations. (See Appendix B.) Between 1979 and 1990, the number of attorneys in the Criminal Division's Office of International Affairs rose from 4 to 40. During the same period, the U.S. national central bureau of Interpol, based in the Justice Department, increased its staff from 6 to 110, its budget from $125,000 to $6,000,000, and the number of law enforcement agencies represented from 1 to 16. The number of foreign police agencies with representatives in the United States also increased during this time, from no more than two or three to more than a dozen, and growing numbers of foreign law enforcement officials could be found in the United States on police business.

Other indications can be found in the caseload statistics. Between the early 1970s and 1990, for instance, the number of extradition requests to and from the United States each year increased from approximately 50 to 500. The number of requests for evidence and other forms of judicial assistance similarly increased, from less than 100 a year to well over 1,000. And the number of warrants for fugitives believed to be abroad rose from a few hundred to many thousands. Between 1976 and 1986, the annual caseload of the U.S. Interpol office rose from about 4,000 to 43,863, and the volume of message traffic from 14,365 to 101,859. These dramatic increases, I must stress, reflected a burgeoning of *both* transnational criminal activity *and* the capacity and desire of U.S. government agencies to handle international criminal law enforcement matters.

The Challenges of International Enforcement

The principal objective of most criminal law enforcement efforts, both domestic and international, is to "immobilize" criminals. Immobilization involves identifying individuals who engage in criminal activity, finding and arresting them, gathering the evidence necessary to indict and convict them, and finally imprisoning them; it also can, and increasingly does, include the identification, seizure, and forfeiture of the criminal's assets. For certain types of crimes, immobilization also requires seizing the criminal's contraband, be it stolen goods, drugs, weapons, counterfeit currency, computers, or anything else a criminal seeks to sell or buy illegally. As one DEA agent put it: "The bottom line is to get the dope off the street and put the cat in jail." Presumably, the more effective governments are at immobilizing criminals, the more successful they will be at deterring crime, disrupting criminal organizations, and diminishing the total level of criminal activity.

To successfully immobilize criminals, criminal justice systems typically require three things: information, evidence, and the body (i.e., the criminal). It is generally true that the more dispersed these things are, and the less they are to be found within the physical jurisdiction of the investigating government, the greater are the obstacles to successful law enforcement efforts. Law enforcement efforts within a single jurisdiction must contend with bureaucratic frictions, such as those within and among criminal justice agencies, and with legal frictions, such as those between citizens' civil liberties and the investigatory requirements of law enforcement agents. Additional frictions can arise among different jurisdictions even within one country; one need only consider the turf squabbles and other frictions that occasionally color the interactions of the FBI and other federal law enforcement agencies with local police agencies and with one another, or those that impede close cooperation between criminal justice officers of different states.

International law enforcement efforts must contend not just with the types of domestic frictions described above but also with those that stem from the need for sovereign states to interact. Whether one takes the perspective of the police officer, the prosecutor, the diplomat, or the theoretician of international politics, the fundamental "problem" of international law enforcement is the sovereign—that is, exclusive—power of governments within their own borders and virtually nowhere else. Stated otherwise, the effective jurisdiction of a state's law enforcement agents extends no further than the territory of that state (and the vessels and embassies that fly its flag). In practice, this means that although U.S. law may authorize American police to arrest and question people abroad, foreign laws do not bolster this authority; indeed, they often forbid any law enforcement activities by foreign agents. The same is true of the American prosecutor, whose subpoenas and other demands, if delivered abroad, are not backed by the police power of the state in which they are delivered. A state can claim extraterritorial effect for its criminal laws, but it is hard-pressed to directly enforce those laws beyond its borders. The sovereign power of states generally forecloses unilateral police action by one state in the territory of another. It requires that most international law enforcement efforts be in some sense bilateral, cooperative ventures. And it means that the popular image of the Interpol agent as a police officer with international arrest powers is entirely fictional.

The basic fact of state sovereignty is not the only obstacle to international law enforcement efforts. Sovereign states are distinguished not only by the territories they occupy but also by distinctive political, social, economic, and legal systems and cultures. No two are identical; the differences generate both opportunities for transnational criminals and frictions for international law enforcers. For the former, foreign territories and alien systems offer safe havens, lucrative smuggling opportunities, and legal shields and thickets to disguise their criminal enterprises. The latter, by contrast, typically find their police powers strictly circumscribed and their international efforts complicated by alien political and legal systems and inadequate transnational infrastructures. The challenge they confront is to nullify the advantages that criminals derive from operating across borders and to reduce, circumvent, or transcend the frictions that hamper international law enforcement.

The political frictions that complicate international law enforcement efforts are not substantially different in kind from the frictions that hamper other domains of international relations. Governments that are politically hostile tend to provide only the most limited forms of assistance in criminal justice matters, and may even applaud and abet criminal acts committed abroad, particularly if the act is in some respect political. Among closely allied states, conflicting political interests and viewpoints, often involving powerful domestic constituencies, may impede cooperation in law enforcement matters. And even in the absence of significant bilateral frictions, a state's pursuit of particular international law enforcement objectives is often constrained by the fact that criminal justice objectives are rarely alone, much less predominant, on its foreign policy agenda. No government has unlimited political capital available to seek all its objectives. Often the pursuit of one undermines the furtherance of another. Objectives tend to be rank-ordered, and different components of a government vie to give precedence to accomplishment of their specific objectives. This bureaucratic jockeying is a familiar dynamic of the foreign-policy-making process in most governments—one in which high-level criminal justice officials in the United States and other nations are increasingly involved and influential but hardly triumphant.

The frictions that do differ in kind from other domains of international relations are largely a consequence of asymmetries among criminal justice systems. The most basic of these involve differences in what states choose to criminalize. Most governments are reluctant to assist others in the enforcement of criminal laws that are not reciprocal. U.S. officials today, for instance, are handicapped in their efforts to investigate the extraterritorial dimensions of tax and securities law violations by the fact that many of these violations are not regarded as criminal by

other states. The same was true of international drug enforcement effo.
in decades past, of efforts by the United States and a few other states to
enforce their prohibitions on the traffic in alcoholic beverages during the
1920s, and of Great Britain's efforts to suppress the international traffic
in African slaves during the early decades of the nineteenth century. In a
similar vein, authoritarian states are typically frustrated in their efforts
to obtain assistance from nonauthoritarian regimes in enforcing criminal
laws against nonviolent political activity; and law enforcement officials
in theocratic states bemoan the lack of foreign assistance when it comes
to the prosecution of heretical activities that are criminalized within their
own nations but not elsewhere. Frictions result when states seek assistance but are rebuffed, when states employ unilateral law enforcement
measures that infringe upon the sovereign prerogatives of other states,
and when powerful states pressure weaker ones to conform.

Far more common, and often just as frustrating as the criminal law
asymmetries, are the procedural, cultural, and institutional asymmetries
that hamper law enforcement cooperation even among governments that
share the same criminal laws and sincerely want to assist one another.
U.S. law enforcement agents trying to operate abroad, for instance, are
continually confounded by different methods of criminal investigation,
alien bureaucracies, and unfamiliar cultural norms. Many drug enforcement techniques regarded as essential in the United States—including
undercover operations, electronic surveillance by means other than
telephone taps, and various methods of recruiting informants—have
been forbidden or severely circumscribed elsewhere. Plea bargaining
may be proscribed, police-prosecutor relations may differ markedly,
interrogation practices may seem alien, and standards of propriety may
not compare. U.S. prosecutors seeking evidence and fugitives from
abroad must contend with unfamiliar procedures and different laws,
some reflecting basic differences between the common law system of the
United States and the civil law systems that dominate in much of the
non-Anglophone world, others reflecting little more than national idio-
syncracies. The frictions generated by these asymmetries create a drag
on international law enforcement efforts; at the same time, efforts to
circumvent and overcome these frictions, such as by acting unilaterally
and by pressuring foreign states to accommodate their procedures and
institutions to U.S. law enforcement needs, create frictions in their own
right.

The Nature of International Enforcement

Governments and their law enforcement agencies have responded to these obstacles in a variety of ways, depending upon the degree to which their domestic societies are open or closed, the extent of the powers and resources accorded the police, the nature of the laws they are obliged to enforce, and the power of the criminals they confront. Most rely to some extent on unilateral measures both internally and externally. Governments keep track of foreigners within their borders; they mount police operations against those involved in the sale and purchase of goods exported and imported illegally; and they compile records of domestic transactions with an eye toward identifying those that are illicit. A few states, notably the United States, have also devised means of enforcing their laws extraterritorially by means of domestic legal processes, such as subpoenas issued to local branches and personnel of multinational corporations, and backed by court-ordered sanctions, requiring them to provide documents located abroad. Beyond a state's borders, its law enforcement agents retain some capacity for action on the high seas, where no nation is sovereign. Law enforcement officials working near their nations' borders have been known to cross into neighboring territories in "hot pursuit" of transnational bandits. Those based abroad may undertake unilateral law enforcement tasks in the context of joint investigations conducted in tandem with local police officials; or they may conduct their own investigations unilaterally, employing whatever discretion is required and operating in much the same fashion, and with just as few police powers, as private detectives. More dramatic measures, such as the unilateral abduction or murder of fugitives abroad, are not unknown; they are, however, relatively rare, more often conducted by agents of intelligence and security agencies than by criminal justice officials, and not always readily characterized as international law enforcement measures.

Abundant obstacles deter states from employing unilateral law enforcement measures beyond their borders. Most significant are the lack of sovereign powers and the illegality of such actions under both international law and the laws of the affected state. Also significant are the logistical difficulties, the desire to avoid generating tensions in foreign relations, the fear that one's unilateral actions will invite comparable initiatives by foreign agencies within one's own borders, and the general preference of most governments for cooperative measures over those likely to require or generate conflict. Unilateral extraterritorial measures are typically resorted to out of frustration with the inability or unwillingness of a foreign state to provide assistance, and with two objectives in mind: to obtain the information, evidence, or people required in a specific investigation; and, if the demanding state is sufficiently powerful, to pressure the uncooperative foreign state to be more forthcoming in the future.

It is not surprising that, given the severe limits on unilateral extraterritorial law enforcement activities, international law enforcement arrangements tend to be bilateral and generally cooperative. These are often episodic in nature, particularly where two states share relatively few law enforcement problems in common, or when police agencies with relatively little experience in international law enforcement matters become involved in an investigation requiring them to look beyond their borders. More frequent interactions, however, lead to patterns of relations that may point out recurring sources of conflict arising from political differences as well as tensions between different law enforcement systems, which in turn create pressures for more formal accommodations and the establishment of guidelines for future interactions. The results may include the stationing of police liaisons in one another's embassies, the creation of bilateral working groups of law enforcement officials, the negotiation of extradition and other legal assistance treaties, and the enactment and revision of domestic legislation to facilitate international cooperation against transnational crime. The net intention and effect of these arrangements, apart from the symbolic purposes occasionally served by them, is to facilitate the work of the police and prosecutors who pursue the routine law enforcement tasks involved in immobilizing transnational criminals.

Some areas of international law enforcement have invited not just bilateral but multilateral, and even global, arrangements, prompted in good part by the inadequacy of unilateral and bilateral law enforcement measures in the face of certain types of transnational criminal activity. These cannot compare with bilateral approaches in accommodating the mutual preferences and peculiarities of two different law enforcement systems; they are obliged instead to settle for the typically low level of accommodation required to win the adherence of a diversity of states. As a result, the symbolic incentives and functions of multilateral arrangements are generally greater than those of bilateral treaties. But multilateral arrangements also offer numerous advantages, not the least of which is that they may obviate the need to negotiate individual bilateral arrangements with large numbers of foreign governments. They can prove especially useful in facilitating law enforcement interactions between governments that are politically hostile, or that share relatively few law enforcement concerns in common; the communications facilities of Interpol, for instance, have proven of particular value in facilitating correspondence among police agencies in the less-developed world as well as among them and the police agencies in Europe and the United States with which they have relatively little contact. Some multilateral arrangements are designed to meet the particular law enforcement needs of multinational political alliances, such as CoCom, the postwar regime established by members of NATO and Japan to restrict the flow of sophisticated technology to Warsaw Pact countries. Others may reflect the common legal systems of countries linked by geographical proximity, similar political systems, and/or political alliances: the members of the Council of Europe, for instance, or the Soviet bloc states from the 1950s to 1989, or the majority of Latin American countries.

All multilateral law enforcement arrangements—be they regional police conferences, international police organizations such as Interpol, or the dozens of multilateral law enforcement conventions addressing either particular types of transnational activity or cooperative mechanisms such as extradition—are intended to help law enforcement agencies reduce, transcend, or circumvent the frictions generated by conflicting sovereignties, political tensions, and differences among law enforcement systems. They seek to attain consensus on the substance of each nation's criminal laws, to create commitments to cooperate, and to establish the guidelines and frameworks required to regularize and facilitate international cooperation among law enforcement systems. On a more fundamental level, these arrangements are motivated by the desire to make law enforcement systems more like one another, the guiding assumption being that like systems are better able to communicate and collaborate than unlike systems. The entire evolutionary process can well be described as one of *harmonization*, in which the notion incorporates three sorts of processes: that of *regularization* of relations among law enforcement officials of different states, that of *accommodation* among systems that retain their essential differences, and that of *homogenization* of systems toward a common norm.

Success and Failure

Why do some international law enforcement efforts succeed and others fail? The answers are many, but in the chapters that follow I advance two general propositions: that success or failure in particularly difficult cases is strongly influenced by the willingness of U.S. law enforcement officials to challenge the sovereign prerogatives of foreign states; and that success or failure over the long term depends upon the capacity of U.S. law enforcement officials to overcome the political and criminal justice obstacles to effective cooperation between the United States and foreign states. In other words, I contend that success in the first instance depends upon the willingness of U.S. officials to create, or risk generating, frictions with other states, and that success in the latter instance depends upon the capacity to reduce frictions by harmonizing criminal justice systems.

The principal criteria of success or failure in both instances are neither rates of transnational criminal activity committed or deterred nor proportions of smuggled goods seized, but rather whether transnational criminals are immobilized. The former criteria are both notoriously difficult to evaluate as well as influenced by many factors other than the quality and quantity of U.S. international criminal law enforcement efforts. One need only consider the dramatic range of estimates regarding the amount of heroin or the number of illegal immigrants that enter the United States each year; or the way in which law enforcement officials annually recite, without any evidence whatsoever, the mantra of seizing 10 percent of all drugs smuggled into the United States; or the varied factors that influence the type and amount of illicit drugs exported to the United States, and consumed therein, from one year to the next; or the sheer impossibility of establishing the number and magnitude of violations of U.S. securities, tax, and money laundering laws each year. Defining success or failure in terms of whether or not criminals are immobilized may seem a relatively trite indicator—not unlike "body counts" in counterinsurgency warfare—but it does represent both the actual objective of most international criminal law enforcement efforts and the most clearly defined and measurable one.

The Americanization of Foreign Systems

The internationalization of U.S. law enforcement during the twentieth century has shaped the evolution of criminal justice systems in dozens of other countries. No other government has pursued its international law enforcement agenda in as aggressive and penetrative a manner or devoted so much effort to promoting its own criminal justice norms to others. Foreign states have responded to the U.S. initiatives by signing extradition and other law enforcement treaties, by hosting U.S. law enforcement agents within their borders, and most significant, by adopting U.S. approaches to criminal law and policing. Beginning with the adoption of the United States' prohibitionist approach to drug control during the first decades of the twentieth century, foreign governments have followed in U.S. footsteps, adopting U.S.-style investigative techniques, creating specialized drug enforcement agencies, stationing law enforcement representatives abroad, and enacting conspiracy statutes, asset forfeiture laws, and checks and bans on drug-related money laundering. Since the 1970s, pressures to cooperate in U.S. drug trafficking investigations were largely responsible for instigating changes in the laws of Switzerland, the Bahamas, and other financial secrecy jurisdictions to authorize greater assistance to U.S. and other law enforcement authorities. And even apart from the area of drug control, the influence of the United States was readily apparent during the first decades of the twentieth century in shaping foreign and international approaches to white slavery, during the Cold War era with respect to export controls on weapons and sophisticated technology, and since the mid-1980s with respect to the regulation of securities markets, in particular the criminalization of insider trading. The result has been something of an "Americanization" of criminal justice systems throughout much of the world.

This argument obviously limits the extent to which generalizations about the nature of international criminal law enforcement can be derived from an examination of U.S. behavior. The ability and willingness of the United States to pursue its international criminal law enforcement agenda as aggressively as it has is relatively unique in the annals of international criminal law enforcement. Great Britain's global campaign against the slave traffic during the nineteenth century represents perhaps the only clear precedent. Similarly, the fact that the United States has dealt with the frictions between its own criminal justice norms and those of other states principally by inducing other states to change their norms and accommodate their systems to U.S. requirements, rather than vice versa, presents something of a special case. Nonetheless, there is much about the challenges U.S. officials have encountered in trying to immobilize transnational criminals, and the ways they have responded, that is typical of most states. The fact that U.S. law enforcement officials have on occasion acted more aggressively and unilaterally than officials of other states in obtaining information, evidence, and criminals from abroad does not mean U.S. officials have not struggled with the same types of issues and frictions encountered by others.

Objectives and Structure of This Book

The chapters that follow seek to elaborate on these themes in developing further the main objectives of this book. My principal objectives, pursued in each of the chapters, are to describe and explain the activities and issues that lie at the intersection of U.S. criminal justice and foreign policy. Chapters Two and Three examine the internationalization of U.S. policing, and particularly criminal investigation, from the origins of the nation's history until the early 1990s. The history of U.S. international criminal law enforcement efforts is one in which themes of both change and continuity are readily apparent. On the one hand, the complexity and scale of contemporary international criminal investigations have little in common with the ad hoc international police endeavors of a century ago. And one need only compare the concerns of nineteenth-century law enforcers with transnational bandits, filibusters, runaway slaves, and illegal slavers to the twentieth-century concerns with illicit drug smugglers, high-tech bandits, insider traders, and money launderers to understand how dramatically the substantive focus of U.S. international criminal law enforcement efforts have changed. On the other hand, the basic concerns with controlling the nation's borders, suppressing smuggling, and renditing criminal fugitives have remained constant. And the basic challenges presented by the need to deal with foreign sovereigns, conflicting political interests, and alien criminal law enforcement systems have persisted.

Chapters Four and Five analyze the efforts of the DEA to immobilize drug traffickers in Europe and Latin America. Chapter Four examines how DEA agents have dealt with the frictions generated by Europe's civil law traditions and general resistance to DEA-style investigative methods, and how European approaches to drug enforcement have gradually become "Americanized." Chapter Five examines the nature of drug-related corruption in Latin America and the efforts of DEA agents to immobilize drug traffickers notwithstanding that corruption. The next two chapters examine the efforts of U.S. officials, particularly those in the Justice Department and the State Department's Legal Adviser's Office, to obtain evidence and fugitives from abroad. Chapter Six focuses on the negotiation of mutual legal assistance treaties to facilitate the collection of evidence from foreign jurisdictions in a form admissable in U.S. courts. Chapter Seven analyzes both the evolution of U.S. extradition treaties and practice as well as the evolution of less formal means of recovering criminal fugitives from foreign territories.

Chapters Four and Five, the two DEA chapters, provide a link between the two chapters that precede them and the two that follow. Like Chapters Two and Three, the DEA chapters focus on the international activities of U.S. *police* officials and the nature of transgovernmental police work. But like Chapters Six and Seven, they examine in some detail how U.S. law enforcement officials have dealt with the challenges that arise in trying to extract information, evidence, and people from foreign jurisdictions. The latter four chapters contribute to my subsidiary objectives, which are to explain why some international law enforcement efforts prove more successful than others, to argue that the U.S. "war on drugs" has provided the crucial impetuses for many of the most substantial developments in the internationalization of U.S. criminal law enforcement since the late 1960s, and to provide evidence in support of the thesis that criminal justice systems throughout much of the world are evolving toward a more harmonious network of relationships strongly influenced by U.S. pressures, models, and examples.

The Internationalization of U.S. Law Enforcement, 1789–1939

Origins and American Insularity

The emergence of the United States to the forefront of international law enforcement is a relatively recent phenomenon. It dates back, at best, to the close of World War II, when the U.S. government belatedly assumed a global role in a great variety of areas, of which law enforcement was one of the less significant. As for the worldwide presence of U.S. drug enforcement agents, that unprecedented—and still unparalleled—development dates only to the early 1970s. Before the 1940s, and especially before World War I, the notion of transnational cooperation between police was far more familiar to Europeans than to Americans. Yet it is also true that the origins of U.S. involvement in international law enforcement matters can be traced back to the first decades of the American republic.

The insularity of American law enforcement from developments outside its borders was generally consistent with the overall American n toward foreign affairs until well into the twentieth century. ed by two oceans from all but two countries, and possessed of a vely huge territory and population, the American preoccupation n itself was not entirely unwarranted. From the police officer's point view, more than enough criminals remained at large somewhere within the United States to devote any resources to tracking down the relatively few who had fled to foreign lands. And given the scanty resources of the few federal law enforcement agencies, state and local police had their hands full merely trying to work with one another.

The United States' lag behind Europe in becoming more involved in the international dimensions of law enforcement also reflected different needs born of different political geographies. American fugitives on the run might flee no farther than across a state border. European fugitives fleeing an equivalent distance, on the other hand, would find themselves across a national border. For American police seeking assistance, the request would involve them in interstate but *intra*national dealings, as opposed to the international relations of their European counterparts. If an American fugitive did flee abroad, an American police officer giving chase was typically obliged to book passage on a steamer for far-off shores. European police, by contrast, needed to do little more than hop on a train or, after the turn of the century, get into a car. Only in the case of Canada, Mexico, and the few other foreign territories on the North American continent were American police not obliged to travel by sea vessel.

The federal political system in the United States posed some of the same advantages to criminals, and disadvantages to police cooperation, that national borders posed to European police. Unlike Europe, where before World War II centralized national police agencies were the norm in many countries, U.S. law enforcement was heavily dominated by state and municipal police agencies. Federal law enforcement agencies were slow to evolve, their funding and jurisdiction strictly limited by Congress and an American people wary of centralized police power. With the regulatory power of the federal government constitutionally limited to "interstate commerce," the growth of federal law enforcement agencies proceeded apace with the increase in national commerce and the judicial expansion of the notion of "interstate commerce."

So long as centralized federal law enforcement remained limited in the United States, most criminal investigations involving two or more states required the cooperation of police authorities powerless beyond their own borders. Federal authorities could transcend the jealousies and prerogatives of state sovereignty, constituting in effect a suprastate police force, but city and state officials possessed no such privileges. Even where officials from two different states proved willing to cooperate, their efforts were often hampered by the same sorts of political, legal, and institutional differences that have complicated international law enforcement efforts. Until the first decades of the twentieth century, centralized mechanisms for the collection and exchange of intelligence were nonexistent or at best skimpy. The basic problem of police officials not treating crimes committed in other jurisdictions with the same seriousness or concern as crimes committed within their own borders was omnipresent. Differences in criminal laws and procedures complicated cooperative efforts even where the will to cooperate existed. And more savvy and powerful fugitives often found havens from prosecution by cultivating relationships with local authorities in states where they had committed no crimes. With virtually no outside governmental scrutiny of any state's administration of its criminal justice system, highly irregular arrangements between criminals and law enforcement authorities were all too easy. Between the middle of the nineteenth century and the beginning of the twentieth, private detective agencies often represented the only effective option for those in need of competent criminal investigators capable of operating across and beyond state and national borders. Their clients included not just private interests but also state and local governments, the federal government, and foreign governments.

The lag in American involvement in international law enforcement could thus be explained in part by the fragmentation of American law enforcement. On the one hand, fugitives fleeing the arm of the law could find almost as reliable a refuge across a state border, and especially in distant American states, as they could in foreign countries. On the other hand, the absence of any powerful centralized law enforcement agency meant that the resources necessary for participation in international efforts were not readily available. A final consideration, which had little to do with the fragmentation of U.S. law enforcement, was the relative lag in the development of criminal investigative capabilities by American police forces. Nearly bereft of the professionalism that characterized many European police agencies, American police were more than likely to treat the departure of a criminal for foreign lands as the end of the case. With little interest in receiving foreign assistance, they can hardly have been expected to render much assistance in response to foreign requests.[1]

The principal exceptions to this insular disposition involved the border regions of the United States. Even today, with the rapid globalization of transnational crime and international law enforcement, the U.S. borders with Mexico and Canada remain the locus of most international law enforcement concerns and activities. The challenges confronted by law enforcement officials along the borders, and the tasks performed by them, include those associated with policing generally as well as many that are unique to border regions. It is not just that one can crawl, walk, run, drive, or even ride a horse, bicycle, or train across the United States' land borders with Mexico and Canada—all of which greatly ease the task of escaping, smuggling, migrating, or fomenting a revolution—but also that the frontier region is the only place where international law enforcement is often synonymous with local law enforcement. Nowhere else must local officials be so concerned about the state of law and order in a foreign country; nowhere else do state and local law enforcement officials play such a prominent role in international law enforcement matters, routinely liaising with foreign officials and crossing national boundaries; and nowhere else does one find such a diversity and concentration of federal law enforcement agencies.

Evolution and Change in U.S. Involvement

In tracing the origins and evolution of U.S. involvement in international law enforcement, we thus find that U.S. law enforcement authorities, particularly those along the land borders and in the major East Coast cities, were drawn into international law enforcement efforts by concerns not unlike those of the Europeans. Governments throughout the world were obliged to deal with the problems of transnational banditry, particularly in less-populated and less-developed frontier regions; the United States was no different, confronting outlaws first along the borders with Canada and Spanish Florida, and then with Mexico— although, unlike the Europeans, U.S. authorities also faced the maraud-

1. See Raymond B. Fosdick, *American Police Systems* (New York: Century Co., 1921), for a discussion of the sorry state of American law enforcement in the early twentieth century.

ing activities of Indian warriors. Like other governments, the United States occasionally attempted to recover fugitives who had fled abroad. But unlike most European states during the first half of the nineteenth century, it sought not just the return of criminal fugitives and military deserters, but escaped slaves as well. There were the two problems posed at sea by piracy and the illicit slave trade, both of which receded as the nineteenth century passed its midpoint. There was the need to protect the lives and interests of Americans abroad. Whenever the United States was at war, or otherwise troubled by foreign political intrigues and agitators, police agents were called upon to undertake the types of tasks that professional intelligence agencies and secret services would perform in later decades. And there was the need, which rarely required foreign travel, to respond to foreign requests to extradite fugitives from foreign justice, to keep tabs on political dissidents and agitators havened in the United States, and to enforce the U.S. neutrality laws by suppressing gun running and the plots of filibusters.

Finally, there was the very substantial concern with smuggling, not so much of forbidden goods as of goods on which customs duties were supposed to be paid. Since customs duties provided the majority of the federal government's revenues until the institution of the income tax in 1913 (excepting the years during and immediately following the Civil War, when an income tax was imposed to pay for war expenses), high priority was given to ensuring their payment. Customs agents, unlike other law enforcement agents, were primarily interested not in apprehending felons but in maximizing the collection of revenue. They therefore represented a sound economic investment in the eyes of legislators charged with appropriating funds. It is not surprising that the first significant U.S. involvement in international law enforcement arose with the delegation of Treasury agents and informants to investigate smuggling and other efforts to circumvent the revenue laws.

Although the historical analysis that follows focuses on the internationalization of police activities, it also demonstrates the porous boundaries of what may be defined as international law enforcement. On the one hand, U.S. law enforcement agents were occasionally called upon to perform chores that had little or nothing to do with the enforcement of U.S. criminal laws; their peculiar talents and skills rendered them particularly well suited for conducting espionage and counterespionage tasks for a government that had yet to develop a specialized agency for such purposes. On the other hand, police agents were neither the only nor even the principal agents of U.S. international law enforcement activities until well into the twentieth century. The U.S. Army and Navy performed law enforcement functions ranging from the suppression of piracy and slave trading to the tracking down of transnational bandits and revolutionaries and the suppression of Indian raids and revolts; the enactment of the Posse Comitatus Act in 1877 severely restricted but did not entirely end the military's involvement in domestic and international law enforcement matters. Much of the work of international law enforcement in foreign countries, including the collection of information, evidence, and fugitives, was performed by consular officials operating out of U.S. embassies. Government agencies often hired special agents to carry out the sorts of tasks that today would be performed by federal law enforcement agents. The most challenging transnational criminal investigations were routinely undertaken by private detective agencies. Fugitives in foreign lands were as likely to be pursued and apprehended by the employees of such agencies, or by freelance bounty hunters, as by officials of the U.S. government. Law enforcement raids across the Mexican border were as likely to include vigilante parties and undeputized posses as U.S. military units and officially sanctioned posses. And both government and private police agencies routinely relied upon the services of informants, including U.S. civilians, foreign nationals, and even Indian scouts, to facilitate their international activities.

No one theme can sufficiently explain the evolution of U.S. involvement in international law enforcement. Some of the most vigorous international law enforcement efforts before World War I were directly linked to the broader national security concerns of a relatively new and expanding nation contending with persistent challenges to its internal and external sovereignty from foreign states, irredentist and revolutionary movements, and aboriginal nations resisting their own dislocation and destruction. Most of these were resolved by the 1920s, although the potential for renewed political violence along the U.S.-Mexican border certainly remains. Similarly, the involvement of the U.S. military and other substantial contingents of personnel to deal with these and other transnational violations of American law seems a thing of the past— until one considers the 1983 amendment to the Posse Comitatus Act to allow the military once again to play a role in civilian law enforcement; the increased involvement of the military and National Guard units during the late 1980s in policing the border with Mexico and interdicting illicit drug shipments; and the 1989 military invasion of Panama to, among other things, arrest a foreign dictator who had been indicted on criminal charges in a U.S. court.

Other ebbs and flows in the internationalization of U.S. law enforcement reflected changing domestic political concerns, criminal laws, and police priorities within the United States. The efforts devoted to apprehending fugitive slaves who had fled across the border were little more than the international manifestations of domestic law enforcement concerns that ended with the Civil War. The same was true of the quite substantial energies devoted to curtailing the illicit import of alcohol into the United States during Prohibition. And the need to track down and immobilize transnational outlaws who robbed banks and trains, rustled cattle and generally wreaked havoc along the border with Mexico during the second half of the nineteenth century was merely the international dimension of a much broader domestic law enforcement effort directed at suppressing outlawry throughout the sparse territories and states of the West. As domestic laws and internal political and social conditions changed, thereby legalizing, eliminating, or undermining particular types of criminality, the need to contend with the transnational violations of these laws was likewise eliminated. Conversely, as criminal justice institutions came to play an increasingly important role in the domestic regulation of psychoactive drugs, so the need to investigate and suppress transnational violations of U.S. drug laws fundamentally altered the character, objectives, and scope of U.S. involvement in international law enforcement matters.

Certain aspects of international law enforcement, however, have remained relatively constant. The federal government's reliance on customs officials to investigate frauds against the customs laws dates back to the origins of the nation, as does its reliance on special agents with expertise in criminal investigation for espionage and counterespionage tasks. The peculiar day-to-day requirements of law enforcement officials alongside the border, particularly those in towns and cities a stone's throw from "twin" towns and cities in Canada or Mexico, have also changed relatively little. And even as the targets of most international law enforcement efforts have shifted from the fugitive slaves, Indians, and Mexican and American outlaws of the nineteenth century to the drug traffickers of recent decades, the basic mechanisms of rendition—extradition, deportation, and various less formal measures—have not fundamentally changed.

Apart from the changing substantive focus of U.S. international law enforcement efforts, the most significant procedural transformation since the nineteenth century has been the virtual monopolization of international law enforcement activities in the hands of government law enforcement agencies, primarily at the federal level. As federal police agencies proliferated and advanced dramatically in terms of personnel, resources, and jurisdiction during the twentieth century, they developed the capacity to more than fill the void that had existed during the previous century. And as the federal government sought to regularize its relations, both friendly and hostile, with foreign governments, its willingness to allow private citizens and even state and local governments to take international law enforcement matters into their own hands waned.

Treasury, Customs, Immigration, and Smuggling

Created in 1789, the U.S. Customs Service faced its first major challenge in 1807–8, when Congress passed the Embargo Act to protest British seizures of American vessels and sailors. The situation proved particularly acute along the Canadian border with New York and Vermont, where traders continued their trade despite its redefined status. Unable to cope with the tremendous volume of smuggling across the border, customs collector Jabez Penniman wrote to Treasury Secretary Gallatin requesting that he seek greater assistance from President Jefferson. Jefferson responded by authorizing the purchase of revenue cutters and the hiring of additional customs officers and by sending federal troops to police the border.[2] Their efforts, however, proved largely futile, as the smuggling continued even throughout the War of 1812 with Great Britain. Two years into the war, the British governor-general in Canada reported to the Foreign Office: "Two-thirds of the army in Canada are at this moment eating beef provided by American contractors, drawn principally from the States of Vermont and New York."[3] In retrospect, the Customs Service's experience with trying to enforce the Embargo Act was just the first of many futile efforts to enforce laws banning the flow of goods across U.S. borders.

Even today, but especially during its earlier years, most Customs

2. Don Whitehead, *Border Guard: The Story of the United States Customs Service* (New York: McGraw-Hill Book Co., 1963), 33–44.
3. Cited in ibid., 44.

efforts were directed not toward keeping goods out of the country but rather toward collecting a duty on their import. Early on, secretaries of the treasury and their customs collectors recognized the advantage of securing cooperation and information from abroad, whence most smuggling ventures were planned. One approach was to persuade foreign governments to cooperate against smuggling. In a letter of April 4, 1844, Treasury Secretary John Spencer urged Secretary of State John C. Calhoun to impress upon the Canadians the benefits and obligations of mutual cooperation in this area:

> The attention of this Department having been especially directed to the extensive system of smuggling heretofore existing on the Canadian Frontier, it has been suggested that among the most effective means of checking illicit traffic, would be an arrangement with the Governor of Canada, by which it would become the reciprocal duty of the officers of the Revenue on either side of the line to furnish immediate information of any known intentions to engage in unlawful trade. It is not doubted that the Canadian authorities would be ready to unite cordially with the Government of the United States in the measure proposed which, while it guarded the revenue on either side, would be calculated to promote friendly feelings between revenue officers of the respective governments, and to prevent the recurrence of incidents of an unpleasant character, such as recently took place in the seizure of the Canadian Steamboats, the Admiral and the America.[4]

The second approach involved sending or stationing agents outside the country's borders. These agents operated both overtly—liaising with foreign authorities—and covertly, even to the extent of keeping their identities secret from local officials. The employment of such agents both within and without the country represented the first systematic use of undercover techniques for law enforcement purposes by American authorities. During the first half of the nineteenth century, a number of

4. Quoted in U.S. Customs Service, *A History of Enforcement in the United States Customs Service, 1789–1875* (Washington, D.C.: Treasury Department, 1986), chap. 4, pp. 29–30; the unnamed author of the report is Michael N. Ingrisano Jr., former acting director of the Information Services Division, U.S. Customs Service. (Hereafter cited as *History of Customs Enforcement*, with chapter and page separated by a colon, as 4:29.)

these agents were assigned along the frontier with Canada. Evidence of the employment of one such agent, a N. Goodsell, was provided in a confidential letter from Treasury Secretary Ingram to the Collector at Genesee, New York, in 1829:

> Mr. N. Goodsell, who was employed by the late collector at Genesee, with the approbation of this Department as an Inspector of Customs, was confidentially charged by our late Secretary of the Treasury with the special duty of visiting the neighbouring parts of the British possessions for the purpose of discovering attempts which were understood to be on foot for introducing foreign merchandise into the U. States in violation of the revenue laws. . . . In consequence he has again been charged with the same confidential service; and will receive his instructions from, and make his reports directly to, this Department.[5]

Less than a year earlier, the customs collectors from the New York cities of Sacket Harbor, Genesee, and Oswego had met and discussed the possibility of stationing, not just sending, an undercover operative abroad. In a report on the meeting to Treasury Secretary Richard Rush, one of the attendees wrote:

> Among other things we agreed in the opinion that a suitable character ought to be employed in the City of Montreal to obtain information and to impart the name to the different collectors and for this purpose agreed to address your department. . . . By placing a suitable man at Montreal, and to render the arrangement more effectual, place another at Little York, whose sole employment should be to ascertain the names of all suspicious characters, the arrival and departures and destinations of Boats, the property on board, the Consignees of Cargoes and every aspect of information which in any degree can afford a clue to trace and detect the operators of smuggling and to impart the information weekly to each of the Colls which may be done from Montreal to Niagara by means of the mail and Steam Boat could in my estimation (considering the expense) be the most effectual means to enable us to enforce the laws.[6]

5. "Confidential" letter from Treasury Secretary Ingram to a collector, July 11, 1829, quoted in ibid., 4:8.

6. Ibid., 4:6.

No evidence has been uncovered indicating whether such a character was appointed. Further evidence that the practice continued, however, was provided in a letter from Treasury Secretary Chase to the customs collector at Lewiston, New York, in 1862:

> I have received your letter of the 26th ulto and hereby approve your nomination of Eben B. Shears at a compensation of $3 per day and William Wadsworth at $1.50 per day as Aids to the Revenue [a euphemism for secret agents], commencing July 1 to be nominally located at Lewiston but to reside in Canada, and travel from point to point as the interest of the revenue may require.[7]

Few sections of the United States proved more amenable to smuggling ventures than the region around Puget Sound, which developed rapidly during the latter half of the nineteenth century. Customs officials could expect relatively little assistance from either Canadian officials or American settlers along the border, neither of whom perceived much of an interest in enforcing U.S. tariffs on rum, sugar, wool, opium, and other goods as well as the new immigration laws directed at the Chinese.[8] Frustrated by the particular porousness of the border in that corner of the country, customs officials supplemented their more reactive border inspection and patrol functions with a variety of more proactive efforts. During the 1880s, Customs employed undercover female inspectors on passenger steamers to detect petty smugglers; it also rewarded Canadian informers by sharing cash derived from the sale of confiscated goods.[9] One particularly resourceful collector of customs, Herbert F. Beecher, hired private detectives to infiltrate smuggling rings in Canada and collect information about planned shipments.[10] He was more successful than most in immobilizing major smugglers and seizing their illicit shipments of opium and other goods, but most smugglers remained unfazed.

With the opening of the West, customs inspectors were needed to supervise the collection of revenue along the border with Mexico—and

7. Ibid., 4:18.
8. Roland L. De Lorme, "The United States Bureau of Customs and Smuggling on Puget Sound, 1851–1913," *Prologue* 5 (1973), 76–88.
9. Ibid., 81–82.
10. Ibid., 86.

special agents to detect revenue evaders. As early as 1845, immediately following Congress' vote to annex the independent republic of Texas, one John A. Parker was nominated as a "travelling agent for the Government to Texas or to Mexico."[11] A decade later, with the development of trade between the west and east coasts of the United States via the Isthmus of Panama, customs agents were assigned to special duty in the foreign transit point. In this case, their appointment was legislated by Congress. In "An Act to Extend the Warehousing System by Establishing Public Bonded Warehouses, and for Other Purposes," passed in March 1854, the treasury secretary was authorized

> to appoint special sworn agents as inspectors of the customs, to reside in said foreign territory when such goods may be landed or embarked, with power to superintend the landing and shipping of all goods passing coastwise between the ports of the United States on the Pacific and Atlantic, and whose duty it shall be, under such regulations and instructions as the Secretary of the Treasury may prescribe, to guard against the perpetration of any frauds upon the revenue.[12]

Confirmation that such an agent was in fact posted to Panama is in the Official Register of the United States for 1873, where a William Dill, customs agent in the Isthmus of Panama, is noted among the list of government employees.

In collecting information on smuggling, the Treasury Department and its Customs Service were not left solely to their own devices. U.S. embassies abroad, staffed at that time largely by members of the State Department, were charged with collecting whatever intelligence might be of use to their government. On occasion, the Customs Service was the beneficiary of such information. On March 6, 1805, for instance, Treasury Secretary Albert Gallatin forwarded to two customs collectors a confidential letter that contained an extract from a letter received from the U.S. Consul in Bordeaux, France:

> By the enclosed extract of a letter from the American Consul at Bordeaux, dated December 20, 1804, you will observe that the

11. *History of Customs Enforcement*, 4:10.
12. Act of Mar. 28, 1854, quoted in ibid., 3:9.

masters of certain vessels trading between that place and your port and whose names are annexed to the extract, are suspected of being guilty of infractions of the Revenue laws. As this information, however, has been recd from the Consul under injunctions of secrecy you will be pleased to consider it as communicated in confidence by me to you.[13]

The military branches, most notably the Navy, also offered information based on encounters and observations made at sea. Before the Civil War, a good portion of such information dealt with the illicit slave trade. On one occasion in 1799, Treasury Secretary Oliver Wolcott wrote to the collector in Boston, Benjamin Lincoln, about information he had received from the Navy:

Captain [Stephen] Decatur of the Navy has given information that during his late cruise near Cuba he met with the Brig "Dolphin" of Boston, William White, Master, with 140 to 150 slaves for sale procured on the coast of Africa.

I request you to take the requisite measures to enforce the Law against the persons who have been concerned in this traffic.[14]

Unlike Canada, or Mexico for that matter, Europe presented greater obstacles to the collection of intelligence by U.S. customs agents for the simple reason that it was so far away. Investigations took longer, given the need to cross the Atlantic. Travel expenses were higher, communications were slower, and the opportunities to regularize relations with foreign counterparts were fewer. In 1848, Treasury Secretary Robert Walker sent two agents to England to learn how the British were using bonded warehouses, which were about to be instituted in the United States.[15] Beginning in 1870, when Congress for the first time gave the treasury secretary specific authority to appoint special agents exclusively for customs business, confirmation of the presence of Treasury agents can be found in the Official Register of the United States.[16] The first such agent was Frederick Augustus Starring, a graduate of Harvard and a major-general in the Civil War, listed as a special Treasury agent

13. Quoted in ibid., 3:17.
14. Quoted in ibid.
15. Telephone interview with Michael Ingrisano, June 20, 1986.
16. *History of Customs Enforcement*, 5:2.

stationed in Europe from 1869 to 1883. His successors, according to the Official Registers of 1883 and 1885, were George Tichenor and Amos Tingle, the latter of whom later became chief of the Special Agent Section of the Customs Service. By the turn of the century, Treasury agents were stationed in five European cities—Paris, London, Berlin, Cologne, and Saint Gall—with their headquarters in the French capital under the supervision of agent Major Williams.[17] Their efforts were supplemented by visits from U.S.-based agents working on specific cases of sufficient import to warrant transatlantic travel.

The Treasury agents in Europe, as well as those who traveled abroad on shorter visits, performed a variety of tasks. They investigated plots to smuggle both licit and illicit goods into the United States, they found ways to determine the actual value of imported goods that were undervalued by those declaring them,[18] they investigated corruption among the customs inspectors, and they generally sought to uncover all other varieties of fraud on the U.S. Treasury. In 1908, William H. Theobald, a Treasury agent who had shuttled back and forth between New York and Europe for a number of years, recounted some of his exploits and those of fellow agents in his memoirs.[19] Many of the cases on which he and other Treasury agents worked involved smugglers of diamonds and jewelry, no doubt because the unpaid duties on these were substantial enough to justify the expenses for his European jaunts.[20] Some of these criminals were no more than wealthy individuals seeking to evade paying all or part of the duty on purchases for themselves. Others, however, were sophisticated international criminals who trafficked in diamonds and other jewels. Some of these had the resources to hire their own private detectives to follow and intimidate government agents and potential witnesses alike.

Theobald and other agents relied in their investigations on informants and contacts among local police, the jewelry merchants, and their

17. William H. Theobald, *Defrauding the Government* (New York: Myrtle Publishing Co., 1908), 353.

18. According to one account, "in 1879 the special agents force struggled to establish the true market value of fine kid gloves from France and proved that velvets imported from Germany were being systematically undervalued" (see Miriam Ottenberg, *The Federal Investigators* [Englewood Cliffs, N.J.: Prentice-Hall, 1962], 291).

19. Theobald, *Defrauding the Government*.

20. Andrew Tully, *Treasury Agent: The Inside Story* (New York: Simon & Schuster, 1958), 118–126.

employees. They spied on suspicious Americans making large purchases at stores such as Tiffany in Paris.[21] In one case, they even succeeded in persuading a clerk in a jewelry shop to display a smuggler's purchases in the show window so they could be photographed as evidence.[22] Often the ultimate success of a case depended upon their ability to persuade witnesses to come to the United States and testify, because U.S. prosecutors could not compel foreigners to come to the United States for such purposes. In one case involving a notorious diamond smuggler, the prosecution in the United States was successful only because the Treasury agent had persuaded a jeweler in Holland and an abandoned mistress in England to come to the United States to testify.[23]

In 1937, the Treasury Department sent Al Scharff, an experienced agent who had worked along the Mexican border for twenty years, to Paris "to assist the Treasury attache in organizing a system to combat the flow of narcotic drugs from the Far East through Europe to the United States."[24] Regarded with suspicion by the French Sûreté, Scharff turned first to a Swede in charge of the Wells Fargo Express police in Paris to make the necessary introductions; when that proved unsuccessful, U.S. Ambassador William Bullitt provided the required political leverage to open doors. With forty-six men in key European cities, Scharff was able to investigate drug smuggling throughout the continent.[25] Informers and stool pigeons were hired. Sam Schwartz, an expert smuggler and undercover operative with vast knowledge of the international narcotics traffic, was brought to Europe from Shanghai and paid $1,000 a month to assist the Treasury agents in developing cases.[26] And Scharff personally liaised with drug enforcement chiefs around the continent, including the Gestapo's narcotics chief.[27]

The westward expansion of the United States during the nineteenth century substantially expanded the duties of the customs agency. In 1886, "mounted inspectors," later known as customs patrol inspectors, were posted along the Mexican border to deter and intercept the

21. Ibid., 231.
22. Ibid., 327.
23. See the chapters on the "Lasar Diamond Case" in ibid.
24. Garland Roark, *The Coin of Contraband* (Garden City, N.Y.: Doubleday & Co., 1964), 336.
25. Ibid., 343.
26. Ibid., 342.
27. Ibid., 344.

extensive smuggling ventures. The size of the force remained relatively modest for forty years, until Prohibition prompted both the creation of a second inspector force along the northern border and an overall increase in the number of inspectors from 111 in 1925 to 723 in 1930.[28] Most of the inspectors' efforts naturally focused on interdicting the smuggling of goods and animals—particularly cattle around the turn of the century, on which a stiff protective tariff had been imposed—into the United States, but they were also obliged to keep an eye on the outward flow of particular items, notably guns being exported to Mexican revolutionaries and government forces. Following the enactment of the Chinese Exclusion Act in 1882, they were also charged with curtailing the smuggling of Chinese into the United States via Mexico and Canada—a responsibility that overlapped substantially with the morally charged campaign to suppress the "white slave trade" in Chinese women and girls to American houses of prostitution.[29] This duty was partially taken over in 1904 by the Immigration Service, which hired a renowned customs inspector, Jefferson Milton, as its first "Chinese Inspector."[30] Following the enactment of far broader and more restrictive immigration legislation in the early 1920s, an Immigration Border Patrol was created in 1924 to stem the flow of Mexicans and other aliens into the United States.[31]

Any account of the Treasury Department's efforts to investigate and deter smuggling is complicated by the many bureaucratic shufflings and reorganizations in the department's history, the frequently changing titles of its agents, and the fact that so many law enforcement agencies have been under its umbrella.[32] Not all of the Treasury agents stationed

28. Arthur Millspaugh, *Crime Control by the National Government* (Washington, D.C.: The Brookings Institution, 1937), 68.

29. Carl E. Prince and Mollie Keller, *The U.S. Customs Service: A Bicentennial History* (Washington, D.C.: Government Printing Office, 1989), 171–194. See also the account of a scandal involving illicit Chinese migration that shook Nogales in 1901, in George E. Paulsen, "The Yellow Peril at Nogales: The Ordeal of Collector William M. Hoey," *Arizona and the West* 13 (1971), 113–128.

30. J. Evetts Haley, *Jeff Milton: A Good Man with a Gun* (Norman: University of Oklahoma Press, 1948), 340–355.

31. See John Myers Myers, *The Border Wardens* (Englewood Cliffs, N.J.: Prentice-Hall, 1971). See also the celebratory account by Mary Kidder Rak, *Border Patrol* (Boston: Houghton Mifflin, 1938), and the memoir of a Border Patrol agent, Clifford Alan Perkins, *Border Patrol: With the U.S. Immigration Service on the Mexican Boundary, 1910–1954* (El Paso: Texas Western Press, 1978).

32. See Laurence F. Schmeckebier, *The Customs Service: Its History, Activities, and*

abroad reported solely to the Customs Service, and not all customs representatives abroad could be described as special agents. That being said, the network of Treasury representatives and agents stationed abroad by the 1930s could well be described as a nascent transnational police organization. Dozens of agents could be found in Europe, as well as many more in cities from Shanghai to Mexico City. Some focused on drug trafficking, others on assorted frauds, but all were charged principally with investigating and curtailing smuggling and other violations of U.S. revenue laws.

Many of the successes of the Treasury and border control agents depended upon their ability to cultivate good relations with local officials, to operate covertly, and to develop effective informant networks. Although they frequently obtained assistance from foreign police agencies, they did not always restrict their activities to those countenanced by the formal rules of international diplomacy. Nowhere was this more so than along the border with Mexico. In many ways, these agents were the forefathers of the activist approach to international law enforcement employed in recent decades by the U.S. Drug Enforcement Administration.

Suppression of the African Slave Trade

Between independence and the Civil War, the issue of slavery periodically dominated American politics, played no small part in the foreign relations of the United States, and generated an abundance of activity in the realm of international law enforcement. The "Act to Prohibit the Importation of Slaves Into Any Port or Place Within the Jurisdiction of the United States" was signed by President Thomas Jefferson in March 1807 and went into force in 1808. The law was amended and reinforced thereafter, most notably by an 1820 act that equated the illicit slave trade with piracy and authorized the death penalty for violators. From 1808 until the abolition of slavery in 1863, however, the laws prohibiting the slave trade were enforced with less vigor than almost any others passed by Congress. The initial act was not accompanied by the author-

---

Organization (Washington, D.C.: The Brookings Institution, 1924); Tully, *Treasury Agent*; and Millspaugh, *Crime Control by the National Government*.

ization of any funds or mechanisms for its enforcement. The law was repeatedly denounced by Southern politicians, including John C. Calhoun, who announced his regret that the term "piracy" had ever been applied to the slave trade. It was consistently violated by entrepreneurs all along the eastern and southern seaboard. New York City was described by *The Times* of London in 1846 as the "greatest slave-trading mart in the world," where ships were outfitted and deals negotiated to obtain black Africans from western Africa and deliver them to markets in Brazil, Cuba, and the United States.[33] As for the occasional naval officers, U.S. marshals, and others who attempted to enforce the laws seriously, they risked condemnation by superior officials as well as the likely prospect of seeing those they arrested set free by sympathetic judges and juries.[34]

Nonetheless, there were periodic efforts to enforce the prohibition on the African slave trade. The Navy patrolled the Caribbean fairly vigorously in an effort to curtail the slave traffic from Cuba to the United States. A particular target of their efforts, however, was Captain Aury, a "buccaneer governor" whose piratical attacks on slave-trading vessels both violated the law and threatened established slave-trading interests in the United States.[35] In 1820 four naval vessels were sent to patrol the west coast of Africa, where they collaborated with the Royal Navy and succeeded in capturing a number of slavers, but were withdrawn in 1823. Following the signing of the Webster-Ashburton Treaty in 1842, another naval squadron comprised of four vessels was delegated to the African coast, where it remained until the Civil War. The U.S. naval commanders who captained the small African fleet were typically committed to their mission but handicapped by their reliance on sailing vessels rather than steamers, by the 1,000-mile distance between their base at the Cape Verde Islands and the African shores from which most slaving ventures departed, and by the lack of political, logistical, and moral support at home.[36] The persistent refusal by Congress to permit

33. Quoted in Robert Ralph Davis Jr., "James Buchanan and the Suppression of the Slave Trade, 1858–1861," *Pennsylvania History* 33 (1966), 446–459.

34. Warren S. Howard, *American Slavers and the Federal Law, 1837–1862* (Berkeley and Los Angeles: University of California Press, 1963); Paul Finkelman, ed., *The African Slave Trade and American Courts* (New York: Garland Publishing, 1988).

35. W. E. B. Du Bois, *The Suppression of the African Slave Trade to the United States of America, 1638–1870* (New York: Longmans, Green & Co., 1896), 113–114.

36. W. E. F. Ward, *The Royal Navy and the Slavers* (London: Allen & Unwin, 1969), 149–161.

the Royal Navy to search suspected slavers flying the American flag placed severe limits on Britain's ability to enforce other nations' laws vicariously. U.S. naval commanders compensated by developing joint cruising arrangements with the Royal Navy's African squadron, but the small number of U.S. vessels (which never exceeded six) precluded any sustained collaborations.[37]

U.S. officials made occasional efforts to recruit informants on the slave trade, but there is little indication that these ever amounted to much. U.S. agents in Africa provided some useful information, one item of which, however, was that the slave traders "were enabled by a regular system to gain intelligence of any cruizer being on the coast."[38] The most substantial crackdown on the African slave trade did not occur until the late 1850s, when the Buchanan administration supplemented the African squadron and sent four steamers to patrol the Cuban coast.[39] The result was a dramatic increase in the number of slavers apprehended. Secretary of the Interior Jacob Thompson also took the unusual step of sending an undercover agent, Benjamin Slocumb, throughout the South to obtain information on incoming slavers and their distribution systems.[40] These belated efforts, successful as they were, underscored how much might have been accomplished if the U.S. government had committed itself to suppressing the transatlantic slave trade earlier and more vigorously. In 1861, the American squadron was withdrawn from the African coast following the outbreak of the Civil War. The slave trade picked up briefly thereafter but was brought to a fairly swift end during the course of the war.

Fugitive Slaves and Foreign Territories

The institution of slavery depended upon the capacity of slave owners to deter their slaves from escaping and to recover and punish them when they did. Slave owners who lived in close proximity to free states, and to

37. Ibid. See also Christopher Lloyd, *The Navy and the Slave Trade* (New York: Longmans, Green, 1949), 176–183; and the memoir by a U.S. naval officer who was captain of a vessel in the African Squadron in 1850–51, Andrew H. Foote, *Africa and the American Flag* (New York: D. Appleton & Co., 1854).

38. Du Bois, *Suppression of the African Slave Trade*, 126.

39. Davis, "James Buchanan and the Suppression of the Slave Trade."

40. Howard, *American Slavers and the Federal Law*, 147–154.

foreign jurisdictions in which slavery was prohibited, clearly had greater cause for concern than those ensconced in the Deep South. They viewed the territorial expansion of the United States by purchase and conquest as beneficial both because it opened up new lands to slavery and because it provided buffers between slave jurisdictions in the United States and foreign refuges for fleeing slaves. When their slaves did escape to free states and foreign jurisdictions, they sought to recover them through both formal and informal procedures. The frustrations of slave owners in attempting to recover their escaped slaves from free states were addressed in a series of federal Fugitive Slave Acts. Similar frustrations stemming from the flight of slaves to foreign jurisdictions resulted in U.S. efforts to negotiate treaties requiring the rendition of fugitive slaves. Indeed, the many efforts devoted to recovering fugitive slaves from nearby British possessions, Florida, and Mexico generated more diplomatic activity and political controversy than all other international law enforcement activities by U.S. citizens and officials prior to the Civil War.

Florida

International disputes over runaway slaves predated the independence of the American colonies. English requests to Spanish authorities in Florida for the recovery of escaped slaves date back at least to 1688.[41] Although the Spaniards were not averse to slavery—and indeed continued to uphold the institution in Cuba until after the American Civil War—they perceived the flight of slaves to Florida as both harmful to their enemy, the English, and beneficial in strengthening their own colony.[42] In 1731, the Council for the Indies in Madrid decided to reverse its previous policy of either returning escaped slaves to the British or providing compensation; thereafter, escaped slaves were assured their freedom. A settlement known as Gracia Real de Santa Teresa de Mose was established for their benefit in 1739 near Saint Augustine, and a fort, Fort Mose, constructed for their protection. Proactive efforts to entice British slaves to Florida were also made. According to one historian, "Negro sergeants, with secret *rendezvous* in Carolina, were sent into that colony

41. "Dispatches of Spanish Officials Bearing on the Free Negro Settlement of Gracia Real De Santa Teresa de Mose, Florida," *Journal of Negro History* 9 (1924), 145.
42. Kenneth Wiggins Porter, "Negroes and the East Florida Annexation Plot, 1811–1813," *Journal of Negro History* 30 (1945), 11.

to instigate desertions from the plantations and, if possible, insurrec tion."[43] The result was a constant trickle of runaway slaves into Florida, which only slowed with the ceding of the territory to Britain under the Treaty of Paris of 1763.

The flow of runaway slaves to Florida picked up again in 1775, when the British rulers of Florida began encouraging slaves to flee their rebel masters, and continued after 1783, when the territory reverted to Spanish possession. Pleas from disgruntled Carolinan and Georgian slave owners led to small steps by the federal government to stem the problem of runaways. In 1788, Secretary of State John Jay sought assurances from the government in Madrid that slaves fleeing to Florida would be returned; the Spanish, themselves concerned with the flight of a number of murderers from Florida to the United States, replied favorably, but no agreement was formalized.[44] In 1791, an agreement was signed by James Seagrove, a commissioner of the United States, with the governor of East Florida, but there is no record that it was ever executed.[45] Throughout the remainder of the decade, U.S. officials, notably the governor of Georgia, and Spanish officials in Florida continued to complain about the mutual lack of cooperation in surrendering both free and slave fugitives, but initiatives to conclude an extradition agreement similar to that included in the Jay Treaty proved inconclusive.[46]

Complaints by American slave owners also led to the negotiation of treaties with the Creek Indians in 1790 and 1796 in which the Creeks agreed to deliver all runaway black slaves in their territory, including those in Florida.[47] The provision was rejected, however, by one faction of the Creek Confederacy, the Seminoles, who had acquired many black slaves of their own during the previous decades and had thoroughly integrated them into their societies under conditions approximating equality. By 1804, the Seminoles had largely seceded from the Creek Confederacy, alienated in good part by the split over the treatment of the black runaways. The escaped slaves, or freedmen, among them soon came to play a central role in the Seminoles' struggles against the Americans, first on behalf of the Spaniards' efforts to resist annexationist

43. Ibid.
44. John Bassett Moore, *A Treatise on Extradition and Interstate Rendition* (Boston: Boston Book Co., 1891), 84.
45. Ibid., 85–86.
46. Ibid., 87–89.
47. Joseph A. Opala, *A Brief History of the Seminole Freedman* (Austin: University of Texas, African and Afro-American Studies and Research Center, 1980), 2.

plots by the United States, and thereafter on behalf of the Seminoles' efforts to resist dispossession from their homes.[48]

"The persistent desire of the United States to possess the Floridas between 1801 and 1819," K. C. Babcock wrote in 1906, "amounted almost to a disease, corrupting the moral sense of each succeeding administration."[49] Apart from the conviction of manifest destiny and the compulsion to suppress the Indians who insisted on keeping their land and their independence, the strong desire to curtail the problem of fugitive slaves ranked high among the incentives of American annexationists. "The people of Georgia," Eugene Southall wrote in 1934, "were greatly excited at seeing those who had once been slaves in South Carolina and Georgia now living quietly and happily in Florida. . . . The subject of fugitive slaves in Florida was constantly on the calendar of the Georgia Legislature."[50] Following the failure of a plot sponsored by President Madison to annex East Florida in 1811–13, troops were sent to Florida. The first Seminole war began in late 1817 when the chief of the Mikasuki Seminoles, Kenhagee, rejected a demand by the head of the U.S. expeditionary force to allow his troops to enter the Seminole territory in search of fugitive slaves; it ended a year later with Andrew Jackson's conquest of the peninsula. Some of the Seminole blacks fled to Andros Island in the Bahamas, others fled to Guanabacoa on the northern coast of Cuba, and the remainder stayed with the Seminole Indians, playing a leading role in the second Seminole war from 1835 to 1842 and therafter being removed with them to Indian territory in what is now eastern Oklahoma; in 1850, many of the Seminole blacks relocated once again, to Mexico.[51]

Canada

The principal foreign haven for American slaves, however, was Canada. By 1842, an estimated 12,000 former slaves had found freedom north of the border.[52] Although the welcome was generally not as warm as that

48. J. Leitch Wright Jr., *Creeks and Seminoles* (Lincoln: University of Nebraska Press, 1986).

49. Kendrick Charles Babcock, *Rise of American Nationality* (1906), xiii, cited in Porter, "Negroes and the East Florida Plot," 9.

50. Eugene Portlette Southall, "Negroes in Florida Prior to the Civil War," *Journal of Negro History* 19 (1934), 81, 83.

51. Opala, *Seminole Freedman*, 8.

52. Roman J. Zorn, "Criminal Extradition Menaces the Canadian Haven for Fugitive Slaves, 1841–1861," *Canadian Historical Review* 38 (1957), 285.

extended by the Seminoles,[53] the British and Canadian authorities were deeply reluctant to deliver fugitive slaves back to the United States. The issue had first emerged in U.S.-British relations following the conclusion of the American War of Independence, and then again following the War of 1812, after both of which the U.S. government sought first the return of slaves who had fled to or been seized by the British and (when the British steadfastly refused to deliver those to whom freedom had been promised) compensation for their lost property. Indeed, the most common and vigorous protests voiced against Jay's treaty during the Congressional debate over ratification concerned his failure to obtain compensation for the slaves who had fallen into the hands of the British.[54] The matter was finally brought to a close in 1826, when the British government reluctantly agreed to pay $1,204,960.

More threatening to American slave owners was the continuing lure of freedom in Canada, as well as other British possessions, such as the Bahamas, for slaves brave enough or desperate enough to venture the trip. Southern Congressmen pressured successive administrations to negotiate a treaty with the British to ensure recovery of fugitive slaves, and in 1828 the House of Representatives adopted a resolution requesting the President to open negotiations with the British on the subject.[55] The British, however, steadfastly refused to "depart from the principle recognized by the British courts that every man is free who reaches British soil."[56] Disagreements over the issue were largely responsible for the inability of the two governments to conclude an extradition treaty during the 1820s and 1830s. The only other alternatives were the abduction of slaves from Canada by slave owners and their agents, which was legal under U.S. law but illegal under Canadian law, and the initiation of extradition requests alleging that the fugitive slaves had committed criminal offenses before or pursuant to their flight. Evidence that the former technique was resorted to with some frequency appeared

53. Jason H. Silverman, *Unwelcome Guests: Canada West's Response to American Fugitive Slaves, 1800–1865* (New York City: Associated Faculty Press, 1985); Jason H. Silverman, "The American Fugitive Slave in Canada: Myths and Realities," *Southern Studies* 19 (1980), 215–227.

54. Arnett G. Lindsay, "Diplomatic Relations Between the United States and Great Britain Bearing on the Return of Negro Slaves, 1783–1828," *Journal of Negro History* 5 (1920), 391–419; and "Interesting Notes on Great Britain and Canada with Respect to the Negro," *Journal of Negro History* 13 (1928), 185–192.

55. Moore, *Treatise on Extradition* (supra n. 44), 90–92.

56. Zorn, "Criminal Extradition Menaces the Canadian Haven," 284.

in an open letter from black residents of Canada to British officials in 1828 in which the they sought a land grant to establish a settlement that would "be the means of preventing the system of kidnapping which is now carried on through his Majesty's provinces by the Georgia and Virginia kidnappers from the southern states of America."[57] The petitioners described both the recent case of James Smith, who had been abducted and taken across the Niagara River but then escaped, as well as a less-fortunate fugitive who had been successfully abducted "by Kentucky or Virginia kidnappers" the previous year. A more notorious case occurred two years later, when a slave owner from Kentucky tracked a former slave by the name of Andrew to the Canadian home of a Charles Baby on the Detroit River. When Mr. Baby adamantly refused to sell the fugitive slave back to his former master, the latter hired some men in Detroit to apprehend his former slave; their effort ended unsuccessfully, however, when Andrew and Mr. Baby fought off the kidnappers.[58] Yet another abduction, this one successful, was recorded in 1836, when a slave catcher seized two fugitive slaves in Saint Catharines.[59]

The second alternative, extradition, was provided in February 1833 when the Parliament of Upper Canada passed an act authorizing the extradition of fugitive criminals. Four requests were submitted under that law, three of them from Kentucky. The first, that same year, was for a Thornton Blackburn, a slave who had fled to Canada from Detroit after being rescued by a mob that had blocked his forced return to Kentucky under the American fugitive slave law.[60] His extradition was refused on the grounds that he had committed no crime in making his escape. The second request was for a Solomon Moseby, who had taken his master's horse in making his escape to Canada, selling the animal before departing the United States.[61] Canadian officials approved his extradition, but he was freed when a mob accosted the guards attempting to transport him back across the Niagara River.[62] Although two men died in the attack on the guards, Mosely lived out the rest of his life in

57. "Documents," *Journal of Negro History* 15 (1930), 115–116.
58. William Renwick Riddell, "The Slave in Canada," *Journal of Negro History* 5 (1920), 342–343.
59. Silverman, *Unwelcome Guests*, 36.
60. Riddell, "Slave in Canada," 345–347.
61. Ibid., 347–350.
62. Janet Carnochan, "A Slave Rescue in Niagara Sixty Years Ago," *Niagara Historical Society* 2 (1897), 7–17.

freedom in England and Canada. The third request involved another slave, James Happy, who also had stolen his master's horse in making his escape but, unlike Mosely, had arranged before crossing into Canada for the horse to be returned to its owner.[63] The request was not forwarded by the governor of Kentucky until 1837; unlike the previous two cases, it was extensively considered by Canadian and British authorities, including the attorney general, the Executive Council, and the lieutenant governor of Upper Canada, as well as the secretary of state of the British colonies, British Foreign Secretary Lord Palmerston, and the law officers of the Crown. Although the moral issue of returning a freedman to slavery was noted and debated throughout the deliberations, the final denial of the extradition request was based primarily upon Happy's obvious lack of felonious intent with respect to the taking of the horse. The law officers' decision, which was intended to provide guidance in future cases, stated that "no distinction should . . . be made between the demand for Slaves or for Freemen," but the strict legal requirements they placed upon the extradition request, including both a strict dual criminality standard and the requirement that any extradition request be supported by evidence taken in Canada, was perceived as favoring the interests of the fugitive slave.[64]

The fourth extradition request, in 1841, was the only one that resulted in the return of a slave to his American owner.[65] In making his escape, the slave, Nelson Hacket, had taken not only his master's fastest horse but also a fine beaver overcoat, a gold watch, and a comfortable saddle. His owner, a widely respected businessman in Arkansas, tracked him to the Negro settlement at Chatham in Upper Canada, where he beat him severely and then took him into custody with the assistance of the local county sheriff. The Provisional Executive Council responded favorably to the extradition request from the Arkansas governor, in good part because Hacket had not confined himself to taking no more than he needed to escape. One historian observed that the new Canadian governor-general, Sir Charles Bagot, "was not unmoved by the thought of what Hackett's fate would be if he were surrendered. But he had been

63. Riddell, "Slave in Canada," 350–354; and Silverman, *Unwelcome Guests*, 38–42.
64. Riddell, "Slave in Canada," 350–354; Silverman, *Unwelcome Guests*, 38–42.
65. Roman J. Zorn, "An Arkansas Fugitive Slave Incident and Its International Repercussions," *Arkansas Historical Quarterly* 16 (1957), 139–149; Zorn, "Criminal Extradition Menaces the Canadian Haven," 284–288.

explicitly instructed when appointed to concentrate upon restoring good relations with the United States."[66] Cognizant of the differences between Hacket's case and that involving James Happy, as well as wary of having Canada perceived as "an asylum for the worst characters provided only that they had been slaves before arriving here," Bagot authorized the fugitive slave's surrender to the Arkansas authorities.[67]

Hacket's surrender generated widespread comment and activity among abolitionists in Canada, Britain, and the United States. It occurred, interestingly enough, just shortly after the conclusion of another fugitive slave case in the Bahamas, where the U.S. consul had requested the extradition of several slaves who had seized the American ship *Creole*, killing two men in the process, and forced the crew to sail to Nassau. With no extradition law comparable to Canada's in place, the local authorities rejected the request on both legal and humanitarian grounds and were supported overwhelmingly by political and legal authorities in Britain.[68]

During roughly the same time, negotiations between the United States and Britain over an extradition treaty—which had commenced in 1839 following the State Department's rejection of a British request for the extradition of several criminals who had fled across the Canadian border into Vermont—were merged into the broader negotiations between Lord Ashburton and Secretary of State Daniel Webster intended to remedy a broad array of tensions in relations between the two nations. U.S. incentives to conclude the treaty heightened in 1841, when a British court in the Bahamas refused to extradite to the United States the men who had seized the *Creole*.[69] Article 10 of the Webster-Ashburton Treaty signed the following year renewed the bilateral extradition relationship that had been initiated by the Jay Treaty of 1794 and expired in 1807; it made no mention, however, of the specific issue of fugitive slaves. The treaty negotiators were both concerned lest the irreconcilable differences between the two governments over the slavery issue sabotage the entire treaty. "For the first time," Alexander Murray wrote, "the British ministers had to defend their policy [toward American fugitive slaves]

66. Alexander L. Murray, "The Extradition of Fugitive Slaves from Canada: A Reevaluation," *Canadian Historical Review* 43 (1962), 303.

67. Ibid., 304.

68. Ibid.

69. Howard Jones, "The Peculiar Institution and National Honor: The Case of the *Creole* Slave Revolt," *Civil War History* 21 (1975), 28–50.

against the morally indignant attacks of the abolitionists while trying to avoid embarrassing discussions with a pro-slavery American government."[70] Colonial officials were instructed to interpret Article 10 as narrowly as possible in responding to requests for the extradition of fugitive slaves.[71] In the first case to arise under the treaty—a U.S. request for the extradition of seven slaves who had escaped from Florida to Nassau, killing at least one individual in the process—the governor of the Bahamas relied on legal technicalities in refusing to deliver the fugitives.[72] The British government thereafter adhered rigidly to its narrow interpretation of the extradition clause in the face of vocal American protests and diplomatic pressures. Between 1847 and 1861, at least five occasions arose in which British and Canadian officials either refused to surrender a fugitive slave or severely punished junior officials who did.[73] The last of these, involving a fugitive named John Anderson who had killed his owner in escaping, generated enormous controversy on both sides of the Atlantic in 1860 when the provincial Court of Queen's Bench approved his surrender. Anderson was ultimately freed, however, when the Canadian Court of Common Pleas ruled that the magistrate's warrant had been technically defective.[74]

Mexico

The development of the fugitive slave issue with respect to Mexico combined virtually all of the features described with respect to Florida and Canada: frequent diplomatic overtures as well as repeated attempts to negotiate extradition treaties; private and state-sponsored expeditions across the border to recover runaway slaves; efforts by foreign citizens and officials to lure slaves across the border; steadfast refusal by the foreign government to return escaped slaves; discreet complicity by foreign officials near the border in the American initiatives to recover slaves; differences of opinion within the refuge nation regarding the desirability of inviting thousands of fugitive slaves into their territory; as

70. Murray, "Extradition of Fugitive Slaves from Canada," 312.
71. Zorn, "Criminal Extradition Menaces the Canadian Haven," 291.
72. Ibid.
73. Murray, "Extradition of Fugitive Slaves from Canada," 313–314.
74. Fred Landon, "The Anderson Fugitive Slave Case," *Journal of Negro History* 7 (1922), 233–242; Riddell, "Slave in Canada," 355–358; Zorn, "Criminal Extradition Menaces the Canadian Haven," 292–294. See also the extensive examination of the case in P. Brode, *The Odyssey of John Anderson* (Toronto: University of Toronto Press, 1989).

well as abundant links between the issue of fugitive slaves and annexationist plots, filibustering expeditions, conflicts with Indian tribes, and the variety of transnational criminal activities engaged in by free whites. The net results of all these developments between 1800 and 1862 were the escape of thousands of American slaves to Mexico and the recovery of only a small fraction of them by those who claimed ownership.[75]

Conflicts over the fugitive slave issue began immediately following the Louisiana Purchase in 1803, when the United States replaced France as Spain's neighbor on the Texas border. Within a year, tensions had arisen—not unlike those along the Florida border—over the flight of slaves from Louisiana to Mexico, reportedly at the encouragement of Spaniards.[76] Mexico's independence in 1821, her prohibition of the slave trade in 1824, and her abolition of slavery in 1829 ensured that the flight of fugitive slaves into Mexico would continue to generate bilateral tensions so long as slavery persisted in the United States.[77] Influenced in no small part by the British, many Mexicans perceived the prohibition of slavery not just as a humanitarian imperative but also as a weapon that could be useful in checking the growing influence of North Americans in Texas, many of whom had arrived with their slaves.[78] Competing pressures, however, led to the exemption of Texas from the abolition decree. In 1825, Secretary of State Henry Clay instructed the U.S. minister to Mexico to include in the proposed Treaty of Amity, Commerce, and Navigation with Mexico a provision for the "regular apprehension and surrender . . . of any fugitive slaves."[79] Although the treaty negotiators did insert such a clause, opposition to its inclusion by the Mexican Chamber of Deputies played an important role in delaying the ratification of a treaty until 1832 and resulted in the removal of the provision from the treaty.[80]

The number of slaves in Texas rose rapidly during the Texas republic's

75. The following account, unless otherwise noted, is largely from Rosalie Schwartz, *Across the Rio to Freedom: U.S. Negroes in Mexico*, Southwestern Studies Monograph No. 44 (El Paso: Texas Western Press, 1975).

76. Ibid., 5.

77. Lester G. Bugbee, "Slavery in Early Texas," *Political Science Quarterly* 13 (1898), 389–412, 648–668.

78. Alleine Howren, "Causes and Origin of the Decree of April 6, 1830," *Southwestern Historical Quarterly* 16 (1912–13), 387–390.

79. Schwartz, *Across the Rio to Freedom*, 9.

80. U.S.-Mexican extradition negotiations between 1826 and 1861 are briefly discussed in Moore, *Treatise on Extradition* (supra n. 44), 95–97.

period of independence between 1836 and 1845; so too did the number who sought refuge south of the Rio Grande, including two belonging to the president of Texas, Sam Houston. Slave owners advertised in newspapers for the return of their slaves, offering lucrative rewards, and hired agents to collect their escapees south of the border. Two Texas Rangers sent to Matamoros for this purpose, however, were arrested by Mexican officials on their arrival and sent home empty-handed.[81] Following the annexation of Texas by the United States and the conclusion of the war with Mexico that followed, slave owners in the new state continued their efforts to recover their lost slaves from Mexican territory. Pleas to Washington to negotiate an extradition treaty or otherwise secure favorable action by the Mexican government generated diplomatic activity, but all proposals were adamantly rejected by the Mexicans. They expressed their willingness to sign a treaty for the extradition of criminals alone, but the U.S. negotiator declined, "thinking a Treaty, which did not extend to all the subjects of extradition, unjust to Texas."[82] The Mexican viewpoint on the issue of fugitive slaves was firmly enshrined in Mexican law in 1857, when an article protecting fugitive Negro slaves from extradition was included in the new Mexican constitution.

Texan slave owners responded to the persistent Mexican intransigence on the issue by taking matters into their own hands and by attempting to reach accommodations with the variety of officials, generals, freebooters, and rebels operating south of the border. Particularly worrisome to the slave owners was the arrival in 1849–50 of the Seminole Indian chief Wild Cat in northern Mexico with a band of hundreds of Indian and Negro Seminoles.[83] Their presence, it was feared, would incite thousands of slaves throughout Texas to flee. Mobilized by the perceived threat, Texan slave owners created an association to provide rewards for the capture of fugitive slaves, offering greater amounts for those recovered from well south of the border.[84] They also persuaded the Texas governor, Peter Bell, to appoint a notorious filibuster and experienced "Negro-thief," Warren Adams, to recover as many slaves as possible from Mexico. Among his successes was the capture of John

81. Ronnie C. Tyler, "Fugitive Slaves in Mexico," *Journal of Negro History* 57 (1972), 2.
82. Schwartz, *Across the Rio to Freedom*, 50.
83. Kenneth W. Porter, "The Seminole in Mexico, 1850–1861," *Hispanic American Historical Review* 31 (1951), 1–36; Tyler, "Fugitive Slaves in Mexico," 5; Opala, *Seminole Freedman* (supra n. 47), 15.
84. Tyler, "Fugitive Slaves in Mexico," 5.

Horse, the acknowledged leader of the black Seminoles near Santa Rosa.[85]

When the head of one Mexican insurgency in 1851–53, Jose Carvajal, promised assistance to Texas slave owners in recovering their fugitives, many Texans supported his unsuccessful efforts to transform the northeastern Mexican state of Tamaulipas into the Sierra Madre Republic. In 1855, Texas slave owners contacted Mexican military officials in the Mexican states of Nuevo León and Coahuila to seek their assistance in slowing the flight of slaves across the border. Later that year, the governor of Texas, E. M. Pease, sent a company of Texas Rangers under the command of James Callahan across the border with the ostensible objective of suppressing the Lipan Indians who had been raiding American settlements. Abundant evidence suggested, however, that Callahan's additional—indeed, many suspected his principal—motive was the recovery of fugitive slaves.[86] The Texan expedition was repelled, however, by Indians as well as the Mexican military officials who the Texans had hoped would welcome them. With the Mexicans' rejection of yet another U.S. overture for extradition negotiations in 1857, the state of Texas enacted an "Act to Encourage the Reclamation of Slaves, Escaping Beyond the Limits of the Slave Territories of the United States," which provided that those returning runaway slaves to their owners would be rewarded from the state treasury.[87]

The American victory in the war with Mexico had not entirely sated the appetites of some American filibusters and others for Mexican territory. Some, such as Sam Houston, took advantage of the fugitive slave issue to muster support among slave owners for additional annexations. Others went so far as to demand the annexation of Cuba and the renewal of the Atlantic slave trade if Congress failed to provide Texas with the authority to negotiate an extradition treaty with Mexico. The outbreak of the Civil War in the United States, however, finally promised relief to Mexico from the demands of Texan slave owners and their advocates in the U.S. government. An extradition treaty that prohibited

85. Porter, "The Seminole in Mexico," 8. *Webster's Ninth New Collegiate Dictionary* defines "freebooter" as a pirate or plunderer, and "filibuster" as "an irregular military adventurer," specifically "an American engaged in fomenting insurrections in Latin America in the mid-nineteenth century." It is in those senses that the two terms are used in this book.

86. Ernest C. Shearer, "The Callahan Expedition," *Southwestern Historical Quarterly* 54 (1950–51), 438; Tyler, "Fugitive Slaves in Mexico," 8–9.

87. Tyler, "Fugitive Slaves in Mexico," 9–10.

the return of fugitive slaves was signed in 1861 and went into force the following year.[88] Confederate officials, however, continued to represent the interests of the slave owners. In late 1861, a Confederate captain led some fifty volunteers into Coahuila in pursuit of a fugitive slave.[89] A secret agreement between Texas slave owners and the new governor of Tamaulipas, Albino Lopez, providing for the exchange of fugitive slaves for Mexican peons who had fled north, momentarily raised the hopes of Texans, but efforts to conclude a formal agreement were doomed by the Mexican constitution. With the conclusion of the Civil War in 1865, this substantial irritant in U.S.-Mexican relations was finally eliminated.

Like the Canadians and British to the north, the Mexicans had mostly stood their ground in the face of aggressive U.S. efforts to reclaim fugitive slaves, choosing instead to forgo the advantages of appeasing the United States and regularizing bilateral law enforcement relations. Refusing either to countenance uninvited expeditions into its territory or to accede to the extradition of fugitive slaves, Mexico had provided at least as safe a haven for the enslaved blacks of the United States fleeing south as Canada had done for those heading north. Where the Canadians and British had often resorted to legalistic technicalities in rejecting American requests for the return of fugitive slaves, the Mexican response had been both more nationalistic and more moralistic—not least because American efforts to recover their slaves south of the border were so much bolder and more blatant. Moreover, the aggressiveness of the U.S. efforts reflected not just the very different tenor of the two neighborly relationships but also the fact that the Mexican haven, unlike the Canadian one, bordered on a slave state. Then as now, the different norms south of the border generated all sorts of transnational activities of particular concern to those living on the northern frontier.

The Case of the "Amistad"

The clash between slave owner efforts to recover their slaves from foreign jurisdictions, and federal efforts to suppress the extraterritorial dimensions of the slave trade, came to a head in the case of the schooner *Amistad*. In 1839, a number of black Africans on board a slaver en route from one Cuban port to another escaped from their chains, killed

---

88. The treaty is reproduced in Moore, *Treatise on Extradition* (supra n. 44), 1118–1121.
89. Tyler, "Fugitive Slaves in Mexico," 11.

the captain and mate, and took control of the schooner. Some weeks later, the *Amistad* was seized by a U.S. naval vessel off the coast of Montauk, Long Island, and the Africans were imprisoned. The Spanish government demanded the return of the Africans, who were variously described as the personal property of the Spaniards who had purchased them and as criminal fugitives. The case landed in the courts, where it ultimately climbed to the U.S. Supreme Court.[90] In an opinion delivered by Justice Joseph Story and supported by all but one justice, the Court set the Africans free.[91] The Africans could not be legally described as slaves, the Court ruled, because they had been kidnapped in Africa and imported into a Spanish colony in violation of the laws of Spain. Both the events leading up to the ruling, and the decision itself, generated substantial tensions between the governments of the United States and Spain, attracted strong interest from the British, and became a cause célèbre among both abolitionists and supporters of slavery in the United States and abroad.[92] Although the Supreme Court's decision provided little precedent for other blacks born into slavery, it represented a powerful declaration of the rights of black Africans to resist enslavement.

Earliest Law Enforcement Agencies

From the nation's origins until the Civil War, federal law enforcement in the United States was monopolized by three law enforcement agencies.[93] The Customs Service, as we have seen, was quick to rely on undercover agents and to send its operatives abroad. The second agency, whose origins also dated to colonial days, was the Postal Inspection Service. The person known as the forefather of contemporary postal inspectors was Benjamin Franklin, who, upon being appointed postmaster at Philadelphia in 1737, set out to inspect and improve the postal service. When Franklin was appointed postmaster general in 1775 by the Conti-

90. See the five documents relating to the case, including the lower court decision and the arguments by John Quincy Adams and Roger S. Baldwin before the Supreme Court, in Finkelman, ed., *African Slave Trade and American Courts* (supra n. 34), 145–408.

91. See *U.S. v. Amistad*, 15 Peters 518 (1841).

92. See the fine account of the episode in Howard Jones, *Mutiny on the Amistad* (New York: Oxford University Press, 1987).

93. See David R. Johnson, *American Law Enforcement: A History* (Arlington Heights, Ill.: Forum Press, 1981), 73–88.

nental Congress, he in turn appointed William Goddard "Surveyor of the Post." His agents, known first as "Goddard's Surveyors" and after 1800 as special agents, assumed responsibility for investigating theft of the mails.[94] In 1830 an Office of Instructions and Rail Depredations was created within the Post Office Department to organize its investigative functions. Its agents operated both openly and undercover; unlike comparable agents in most other countries, they had arrest powers.[95]

Plagued initially by charges of corruption and political involvement, the Inspection Service gained in effectiveness and prominence under the tenure of David Parker, who served as chief special agent for the United States Post Office from 1876 to 1883. Such was Parker's reputation that German postal authorities, who lacked any investigative service, turned to him for assistance in an investigation of employee theft of registered letters between Hamburg and Berlin.[96] A few decades later, another highly regarded agent, Bill Kenyon, was charged with setting up a secure postal sysem in South America to stem the theft of parcel post; in 1919, the same agent was sent to Spain, where he successfully investigated a series of thefts of funds sent by American tourists by registered mail to New York.[97] Despite these occasional contacts with foreign lands, however, the postal inspectors focused their efforts within the United States, and like the Secret Service they were often called upon to perform investigative and other law enforcement tasks having little to do with the mails—such as tracking down safecrackers, transporting gold bullion for the federal government, and protecting foreign dignitaries. The author of one celebratory account of the agency described their activities:

> They've been protecting the mails under one title or another since long before the nation was born. They hunted highwaymen on the lonely post roads of colonial times, rode west with the covered wagons, launched the "Pony Express," balked the nineteenth century brand of confidence men, warred on the "Black Hand" band of extortionists, fought it out with Prohibition era gangsters

94. On the origins of the Postal Service's special agents, see Millspaugh, *Crime Control* (supra n. 28), 62–64; Elinore Denniston, *America's Silent Investigators* (New York: Dodd, Mead & Co., 1964), 19–76; and E. J. Kahn, *Fraud* (New York: Harper & Row, 1954), 5–7.

95. See Wayne E. Fuller, *The American Mail: Enlarger of the Common Life* (Chicago: University of Chicago Press, 1972).

96. Denniston, *America's Silent Investigators*, 73–74.

97. Ibid., 95–96.

raiding post offices and mail trains, and now unravel mail frauds as complex as the mind of man can devise.[98]

The U.S. Marshals Service, authorized by the Judiciary Act of 1789 to support the federal courts, was the closest thing to a general law enforcement agency before the development of the FBI. Although it fell under the direct control of the federal judges and district attorneys, Congress too assigned it a variety of responsibilities. The result was that the U.S. marshals became, as one historian has noted, the "handymen" of a number of government agencies in the first part of the nineteenth century.[99] Among their international chores was the collection and delivery of fugitives between the United States and other countries. Marshals also assisted U.S. consular courts in China, Japan, Siam, and the Ottoman Empire, the governments of which had acknowledged the extraterritorial jurisdiction of the United States and other foreign governments over their citizens. These marshals, wrote the historian for the U.S. Marshals Service, "were essentially the same as the marshals in the United States and its territories. They served the process of the consular courts, arrested those accused of crimes, kept custody of its prisoners, and executed the orders of the courts."[100]

With the Customs Service and the Postal Inspection Service largely relegated to specific tasks, and the U.S. marshals subject to the demands of a great variety of bosses, no law enforcement agency was in a position to develop sustained contacts with foreign law enforcement agencies to handle a variety of criminal matters. Indeed, Congress had repeatedly made clear that nothing resembling a generic national police agency be created. Such an organization, it was feared, would be the first step on the road to European-style police states. The cost of such fears, however, was the great advantage given to criminals by the lack of either domestic or international law enforcement coordination. Into this void stepped

98. Ottenberg, *Federal Investigators* (supra n. 18), 309–310.

99. Larry D. Ball, *The United States Marshals of New Mexico and Arizona Territories, 1846–1912* (Albuquerque: University of New Mexico Press, 1978), 4. For an overview of the evolution of the U.S. marshals, see chapter 1 of Ball's book or Rita W. Cooley, "The Office of United States Marshal," *Western Political Quarterly* 12 (1959), 123–140. Profiles of the first sixteen U.S. marshals are assembled in Frederick S. Calhoun, "The First Generation of United States Marshals," *The Pentacle* 5 (Summer 1985), 26–35 (part 1), and 6 (Winter 1986), 28–33 (part 2). (*The Pentacle* is the periodical of the U.S. Marshals Service.)

100. Frederick S. Calhoun, *The Lawmen: United States Marshals and Their Deputies, 1789–1989* (Washington, D.C.: Smithsonian Institution Press, 1990), 175–176.

private detective agencies (of which the Pinkerton Detective Agency became the largest and most famous) and a new federal police agency, the Secret Service.

One of the Pinkerton Agency's principal clients between 1870 and 1892 was the federal government of the United States. Before 1870, the U.S. Attorney General's Office had prohibited any funds allocated for federal court and law enforcement expenses from being used to pay detectives.[101] With the formation of the Justice Department in 1870, Congress recognized the need to allocate some funds for the detection and prosecution of violations of federal law. Popular sentiment prevented the establishment at that time of a law enforcement agency within the new department, so the attorney generals sought out alternative sources of investigators. The Pinkerton Agency provided many of these until 1892, when Congress, in the aftermath of its investigation of the Pinkertons' role in suppressing the Homestead strike, prohibited the hiring of private detectives to enforce federal law.[102] The Attorney General's Office, which had supervisory powers over the U.S. marshals given them by Congress in 1861, also made frequent use of the marshals. On occasion, they appointed their own "special detectives" or "special agents," sometimes designating them "general deputy marshals." And with increasing frequency they and other government agencies in need of investigative services called upon the Secret Service housed in the Treasury Department.[103]

The Secret Service was established in 1865 with the sole purpose of preventing and investigating cases of counterfeiting. Congress had not appropriated any money for that task until 1861. During the Civil War, the Union government relied on private investigators, such as the Pinkertons, to pursue such cases. But as the war drew to an end, Treasury Secretary Hugh McCulloch suggested the establishment of a specialized agency, and President Lincoln concurred. The first chief of the Secret Service was William P. Wood, who had established his reputation as a skilled criminal investigator during the Civil War, first tracking down contractors who were defrauding the government, then developing an expertise in counterfeiting cases.[104] The agency quickly established a

101. Homer Cummings and Carl McFarland, *Federal Justice: Chapters in the History of Justice and the Federal Executive* (New York: Macmillan Co., 1937), 371.

102. Ibid., 373; James D. Horan, *The Pinkertons: The Detective Dynasty That Made History* (New York: Crown Publishers, 1967), 350–358.

103. Cummings and McFarland, *Federal Justice*, 371.

104. Michael Dorman, *The Secret Service Story* (New York: Delacorte Press, 1967), 4–7.

good reputation for criminal investigation and soon found itself called upon to perform similar services for other branches of the government.

During its first three decades, the Secret Service established connections with European and other foreign law enforcement agencies. More so than with most crimes, governments tended to recognize the benefits of reciprocity in cooperating against counterfeiters of one another's currencies. The Secret Service thus focused on detecting criminal efforts to counterfeit not only U.S. currency but foreign currency as well. One notable investigation, in 1909, uncovered a scheme based in a small Kentucky town to flood Mexico with counterfeit 100 peso notes on the Banco Nacional de Mexico. Another counterfeit currency investigation, described by the Secret Service chief in 1910 as "the most important victory for the Government since the breaking up of the Lancaster-Philadelphia gang of counterfeiters in 1898," led to the arrests of leading members of the Italian "Black Hand."[105]

However, it was in political intelligence operations, not in counterfeiting cases, that the Secret Service extended itself farthest beyond American borders. During the 1880s the Secret Service cooperated with the newly created "Special Branch" of Scotland Yard's Criminal Investigative Division (CID) against Irish terrorists seeking independence for their country.[106] In 1898, with a dynamic new chief and the war with Spain rapidly approaching, the Secret Service was obliged to undertake espionage and counterespionage operations both within the United States and abroad. In one case, Secret Service agents operating undercover in Montreal successfully exposed the somewhat incompetent espionage efforts of the naval attaché of the Spanish legation, Lieutenant Ramon Carranza.[107] In a more dramatic operation, a Secret Service operative posing as a Mexican millionaire collected valuable information in Spain on the enemy's naval preparations.[108]

With the war over, the Secret Service returned to its more traditional law enforcement tasks. In mid-1902, the chief of the agency, John Wilkie, was asked to travel incognito to Europe to investigate a lace-smuggling case involving well-connected importers.[109] In another smug-

---

105. John E. Wilkie, *Annual Report of the Chief of the Secret Service Division for the Fiscal Year Ended June 30, 1910* (Washington, D.C.: Government Printing Office, 1910), 7.

106. Thomas A. Reppetto, *The Blue Parade* (New York: Free Press, 1978), 31.

107. Don Wilkie, as told to Mark Lee Luther, *American Secret Service Agent* (New York: Frederick A. Stokes Co., 1934), 16–23.

108. Ibid., 23–25.

109. Ibid., 27.

gling case involving complicity by a corrupt customs official, the Secret Service chief ventured to London and Lyons, where he successfully investigated the matter and persuaded the necessary witnesses to come to the United States to give testimony.[110] Although there were Treasury agents delegated to customs business in foreign locations, the Secret Service was far more likely to be called upon by other government departments when criminal investigative services at home or abroad were required. Until 1908, when Congress forbade the Justice Department to borrow any Secret Service operatives from Treasury (reportedly because the agents' investigations had led to the indictment and conviction of some of their members[111]), the Secret Service reigned as the leading federal law enforcement agency. And even thereafter it continued to assist other agencies in investigating violations of U.S. drug laws, neutrality laws, and so on.[112]

The Justice Department, established in 1870, was not authorized to create its own specialized law enforcement agency until 1908.[113] Thereafter, a disproportionate amount of responsibility continued to fall on the shoulders of the prosecutors. This state of affairs was described in the leading history of federal law enforcement's early days, co-authored in 1937 by the attorney general at the time, Homer Cummings:

> Prosecuting attorneys in the states and the district attorneys of the United States also came to be regarded as responsible for the detection of offenses against both civil and criminal law and for the collection of evidence to support proceedings in the courts— duties very seldom specified in the statutes. They came to exercise the functions of an "investigator" concurrently with the sheriff or police, as well as the function of a "magistrate" in determining who should be brought to trial, the function of a "solicitor" in preparing cases for trial, and that of an "advocate" in trying them

110. Ibid., 185–186.
111. Cummings and McFarland, *Federal Justice*, 375–378.
112. The "effective cooperation between Secret-Service operatives and Treasury special agents in customs investigations, . . . particularly in the suppression of the smuggling of and traffic in smoking opium," is noted in John E. Wilkie, *Annual Report, Chief of the Secret Service Division, Fiscal Year Ended June 30, 1912* (Washington, D.C.: Government Printing Office, 1912), 8. Cooperation "in the investigation and suppression of revolutionary movements in this country in violation of the neutrality laws" is noted in ibid., *Fiscal Year Ended June 30, 1909*, 8.
113. See Albert Langeluttig, *The Department of Justice of the United States* (Baltimore: Johns Hopkins University Press, 1927).

and in arguing appeals. "This uniting of a general responsibility for enforcement of law and duty of criminal investigation with the function of carrying on prosecutions," reported the National Commission on Law Enforcement in 1931, "was appropriate enough in a simple colonial society of the eighteenth century."[114]

During its first decades, the Justice Department depended upon investigators borrowed from other agencies as well as upon a number of special agents whose status remained ambiguous. When Congress deprived the Justice Department of its principal source of investigators in 1908, the subsequent reaction from the executive branch obliged them to provide a substitute. In the face of increasing pressure and pleas from President Theodore Roosevelt, Attorney General Charles Bonaparte, and the district attorneys to allow the creation of a federal detective service, Congress relented and voted in 1908 to appropriate funds specifically for special agents in the Justice Department. The following year, Bonaparte's successor, Attorney General George C. Wickersham, christened the now officially sanctioned department of detectives (comprised initially of former Secret Service agents) the "Bureau of Investigation"[115] (the word "Federal" was added in 1935). Its jurisdiction included a hodgepodge of crimes, including bribery, antitrust and banking violations, customs, post office and internal revenue frauds, violations of the neutrality, peonage and bucket-shop laws, white slave cases, crimes on the high seas, murders on government reservations, and so on. Within a few years, the demands of reporting on Mexican revolutionary activity and enforcing the neutrality laws along the southwestern frontier would provide the Bureau with both a rationale for substantial growth and an opportunity to prove its worth. Yet until 1934, despite the wide variety of criminals they were expected to encounter, the Justice Department agents were not authorized to carry arms, serve warrants and subpoenas, or make seizures and arrests.[116] Their role during that first generation was viewed as purely investigative.

In 1916, one of the first books glorifying the work of the Bureau, *Uncle Sam, Detective,* appeared.[117] Although the author chose to create

114. Cummings and McFarland, *Federal Justice*, 367.

115. On the origins of the FBI, see ibid., 375–380; Harry and Bonaro Overstreet, *The FBI in Our Open Society* (New York: W. W. Norton, 1969), chap. 2; and Millspaugh, *Crime Control by the National Government* (supra n. 28), 73–78.

116. Cummings and McFarland, *Federal Justice*, 381.

117. William Atherton Dupuy, *Uncle Sam, Detective* (New York: McKinlay, Stone & Mackenzie, 1916).

a fictional composite of an agent, whom he named Billy Gard, as the main protagonist, each of the stories was founded on an actual investigation that Bureau agents had related to the author. It is interesting that three of the twelve stories found Special Agent Billy Gard abroad and actively engaged in undercover operations. In one he posed as a retired manufacturer on vacation in Kingston, Jamaica, while he investigated "a huge conspiracy for the smuggling of opium and Chinamen into the States." In another case, involving the illegal shipment of arms to Mexico during its revolution, Billy Gard stowed away aboard a ship while pursuing a Russian arms merchant and quite unexpectedly found himself first in the port of Odessa and then in Hamburg. And in yet another adventure, the special agent pursued a wilely fugitive wanted for customs fraud, first to Montreal and then to London and Paris. In Paris, he secured the cooperation of the local police, persuaded them to introduce an undercover agent into his surveillance operation, and then had her place a listening device (then known as a dictagraph) in the apartment where he correctly suspected the fugitive was hiding.

It is worth noting that the accounts of Bureau agent Billy Gard's activities differed little from those of the Secret Service and Treasury agents who traveled overseas. Agents from all three agencies operated relatively freely overseas, working undercover, developing informants, securing cooperation from the local police, and conducting their own surveillance when necessary. When necessary, they dabbled in political intelligence and operations as well. Al Scharff, who began his lengthy law enforcement career with the Bureau of Investigation in 1917 before transferring to the customs agency, was initially hired to locate and destroy a German wireless station on the coast of Sonora, Mexico.[118] Somewhat more surprising is that the focus of the Bureau agents and to a lesser extent the Secret Service agents, not just the Treasury agents, was on smuggling and enforcement of customs laws. The principal reason is that much of transnational crime is smuggling in one form or another. It also reflects the fact that foreign law enforcement agencies are reluctant, certainly in practice and often in principle, to devote resources to enforcing the customs laws of other governments. Customs violations are not the types of crimes that tend to inspire moral indignation. Often the specific laws violated have no parallels in the country whose assistance is sought. Indeed, the country may even derive financial

118. Roark, *Coin of Contraband* (supra n. 24), 16–42.

benefits from being the source of goods legally purchased but illegally smuggled into another country. Consequently, requests for foreign police assistance in enforcing one's customs laws are unlikely to be given the same priority that requests involving more serious crimes receive. If a government wants such matters investigated abroad, it is best to send its own agents to do so.

A final consideration has to do with the nature of the assistance American agents abroad requested from local police. Locating fugitives who have committed serious crimes is a service local police often are both willing and able to offer. The same is true of other aspects of an investigation initiated after a serious crime has been committed. For instance, foreign police have few inhibitions about offering assistance in identifying fingerprints, documents, weapons, and other evidentiary items that can help in identifying or prosecuting a criminal. However, when foreign police are asked to devote time and personnel to the *investigation* of an ongoing series of crimes or of a criminal organization, problems often arise, particularly if no crimes have been committed in their country. One of the principal developments in the evolution of international law enforcement in the past century has been the increasing willingness of foreign police to cooperate in the investigation of an ever-broadening array of crimes, including many that would not be prosecuted if committed in their own country. Enforcement of other government's customs laws, however, remains far more the exception than the rule. Only when the laws concern goods that are banned or strictly controlled in both countries is cooperation likely.

Throughout the nineteenth century and into the twentieth, the investigative dimension of international cooperation remained relatively undeveloped. In good part, this reflected no more than the fact that there were few serious crimes one could commit *from* a foreign country. Other than smuggling, primarily to evade revenue laws, and cross-border forays to commit common crimes, there were only so many crimes that could be perpetrated from abroad. This changed over the twentieth century primarily as a consequence of two developments. International consensuses calling for cooperation against transnational trafficking in goods such as drugs developed. And advances in telecommunications facilitated the commission of crimes in which the perpetrator had no need personally to cross an international border. Police increasingly needed to ask their counterparts abroad for assistance in investigating drug traffickers, money launderers, and financial charlatans. This in turn required that police work more closely with fellow investigators in foreign countries. The evolution of the transnational police community in recent decades is largely a consequence of these developments.

Law Enforcement for Hire

In 1845, a former member of the New York City police force, Gil Hays, opened "an office for the arrest of burglars and the prevention of pickpockets," which he called the "Independent Police."[119] During the next few years, former police officers in Saint Louis, Baltimore, and Philadelphia established similar agencies. In the mid-1850s, a number of investigators with no previous experience in policing also founded agencies. Calling themselves "private policemen," "preventive police," or "counterfeit police," these entrepreneurs engaged in a variety of investigative and law-related tasks, both honorable and unsavory.[120] The most famous of them was a Scottish immigrant to the United States, Allan Pinkerton. After proving himself as an amateur detective in Dundee, Illinois, he was hired as a special agent by the U.S. Post Office to investigate mail thefts. At about the same time, during the late 1840s, the newly organized Chicago Police Department hired him as its first and only detective—or "plain clothes man," as the specialization was called at first.[121] When shortly thereafter the railroad companies appealed to him to devote his skills to investigating the growing number of train robberies, Allan Pinkerton decided the time had come to open his own private detective agency.

Apart from his detective activities, Pinkerton continued to engage in another covert venture connected with an entirely different sort of railroad—the "underground railway," by which slaves were transported to freedom from their southern bondage.[122] As civil war approached, Allan Pinkerton was called upon by the federal government to organize an intelligence agency that would both spy in the South and engage in counterespionage in the North.[123] Utilizing many of the skills that are so

119. David R. Johnson, *Policing the Urban Underworld* (Philadelphia: Temple University Press, 1979), 60.
120. Ibid.
121. Richard Wilmer Rowan, *The Pinkertons: A Detective Dynasty* (Boston: Little, Brown & Co., 1931), 25.
122. Ibid., 23–24.
123. Ibid., 123–125.

easily transferred from criminal to political investigation, Pinkerton and some of his men went to work for the federal government, while the remainder kept the office running throughout the war.

Following the war, the Pinkerton agency expanded throughout the United States and around the world. Both within the United States and abroad, the agency enhanced its value and effectiveness by virtue of its ability to liaison with and between law enforcement agencies that were unable or unwilling to communicate with one another.[124] Pinkerton's sons, particularly William Pinkerton, also assumed leading roles in American police circles. They spoke out forcefully in favor of more professional police forces, adoption of modern investigative techniques, and more efficient interstate cooperation. They also were elected to high positions in American police associations, notably the International Association of Chiefs of Police.[125]

One of the Pinkertons' first multinational cases blossomed when they were hired by the Bank of England to track down the counterfeiters of its notes. In what was perhaps the most widespread criminal investigation of its time, half a dozen Pinkerton agents went to London, a few others joined the New York police in arresting one of the perpetrators as he disembarked in that city, and another agent tracked down the last of the fugitives in Havana.[126] In all aspects of the investigation outside the United Kingdom, it was the Pinkerton agency that played the lead role. Around the same time, the agency, and in particular Allan Pinkerton's son William, began its investigation of a brilliant thief named Adam Worth, who was to resist the clutches of both private and public detective agencies for virtually his entire career.[127] Traveling around Europe in pursuit of these and other international criminals, William Pinkerton developed the contacts and friendships with foreign police agencies that were to serve his agency in good stead in subsequent investigations.[128] Other agents were sent to Latin America, such as when Charles Siringo

124. James D. Horan, "The Pinkerton Detective Agency," in Allan Pinkerton, *Thirty Years a Detective* (1884; reprint, Montclair, N.J.: Patterson Smith Publishing Co., 1975), vi.

125. Frank Morn, *"The Eye that Never Sleeps": A History of the Pinkerton National Detective Agency* (Bloomington: Indiana University Press, 1982), 110–127.

126. Rowan, *The Pinkertons*, 281–289. The story is told from the perspective of one fugitive in George Bidwell, *Bidwell's Travels from Wall Street to London Prison* (Hartford, Conn.: Bidwell Publishing Co., 1897).

127. James D. Horan and Howard Swiggett, *The Pinkerton Story* (New York: G. P. Putnam's Sons, 1951), 161–200.

128. Horan, *The Pinkertons* (supra n. 102), 280–320.

was dispatched to Mexico City to locate a Wells Fargo robber who had stolen $10,000 during a train wreck in Colorado.[129] One historian of the detective agency described the evolution of the Pinkerton agency's international activities:

> In the late 1870s the operations of the Pinkertons became world-wide when they began hunting some of the most colorful, ingenious, and little-known international criminals of the Victorian Age who robbed express cars, banks, and brokerage houses of millions of dollars. The Bank of England and investment and jewelry firms in France and Belgium were among the criminals' victims. Here the Pinkertons filled the role of a paid national police force that cooperated with the principal police organizations of Europe. Letters from criminal divisions of Scotland Yard, the Sûreté, Turkish, and Cuban police, and our State Department showed they were sharing their knowledge of these colorful rogues in an informal, international pool of police information. The Pinkertons appeared to be a crude but effective Victorian Age Interpol.[130]

By the 1890s, Pinkerton's sons had opened branches in Europe.[131] So well known had the name "Pinkerton" become by then that many Europeans thought it was the title of the American criminal police.[132] But the agency's successes had also inspired a proliferation of competitors, including most notably a Saint Louis–based agency created by Thomas Furlong, who like Pinkerton had acquired his experience first as a spy for the Union Army and then headed the Missouri Pacific Railway's police, and the Burns National (later International) Detective Agency, created in 1909 by a former Secret Service agent, William J. Burns, whose fame and political contacts ultimately yielded him the directorship of the U.S. Bureau of Investigation from 1921 to 1924.[133] Burns's agency rapidly emerged as the Pinkertons' principal competitor, begin-

129. Ben E. Pingenot, *Siringo* (College Station: Texas A&M University Press, 1989), 17.
130. Horan, *The Pinkertons*, 254–255.
131. Horan, "Pinkerton Detective Agency," xviii.
132. Jürgen Thorwald, *The Century of the Detective*, trans. Richard and Clara Winston (New York: Harcourt, Brace & World, 1965), 91.
133. Thomas Furlong, *Fifty Years a Detective* (Saint Louis: C. E. Barnett, 1912); William R. Hunt, *Front-Page Detective: William J. Burns and the Detective Profession, 1880–1930* (Bowling Green, Ohio: Bowling Green State University Popular Press, 1990).

ning with its early success in winning away the more established agency's biggest single client, the American Banking Association, at a time when the Pinkerton agency had fallen into some disrepute, and eventually expanding its presence throughout the United States and abroad. It attracted substantial attention in 1920 when a Burns agent pursued a suspected bomber who had killed twenty-nine people on Wall Street all the way to Eastern Europe.[134]

The rising demand for the services of the private detective agencies arose from many corners.[135] Most prominent among these were America's industrialists, who hired the detective agencies to spy on labor organizers, compile blacklists of suspected agitators, disrupt efforts at unionization, and otherwise police their factories and other properties— all of which eventually proved harmful to the popular reputations so carefully cultivated by the leading private detective agencies. The agencies' clients, however, were far more diverse, sharing only in their capacity to pay the fees required. Major banks and other commercial institutions turned to the detective agencies to investigate significant frauds and thefts; foreign governments paid them to collect information on political émigrés and other perceived threats; and federal, state, and local governments in the United States turned to them wherever the services of government police agents were either lacking or under suspicion. All sorts of clients as well paid them to dig up dirt on political opponents, business competitors, prying journalists, and unfaithful spouses. Sometimes the detectives were hired only after police agencies had failed to provide satisfaction; on other occasions they complemented or substituted for public detective forces that had insufficient resources, sophistication, or incentive to conduct a difficult investigation for a wealthy client on their own. But most commonly they were called upon to perform the sorts of discreet detecting tasks that only private agencies could and would provide.

With their expenses paid, the Pinkertons and other private detectives did not shy away from traveling virtually anywhere in the world on behalf of an investigation or in pursuit of a fugitive. In his 1931 history of the agency, Richard Rowan described the challenges that confronted a detective, private or otherwise, on a global manhunt:

> Nowadays a fleeing rascal can hardly find a desert island which is not blanketed by governmental understandings. But before 1890,

134. Morn, "Eye That Never Sleeps," 181.
135. See Hunt, Front-Page Detective.

securing the person of a fugitive who had landed on foreign soil depended upon the luck and resolution of the pursuing detective, and the possible complaisance of local authorities. When the unbeatable Frank Froest of Scotland Yard cornered Jabez Balfour in the Argentine, he had no treaties to depend upon, and so got the notorious swindler aboard a car attached to a locomotive, which traveled at full speed to Buenos Aires, where, despite efforts to stop him, he managed to put Balfour on a ship bound for England. And Pinkerton agents, even though wanting government sanction, brought evil-doers from Asia, Africa and the South East Isles, with often an equally informal decisiveness.[136]

In 1886, the U.S. Supreme Court abetted such informal efforts when it held in *Ker v. Illinois* that a fugitive kidnapped from abroad could not claim any violation of the Constitution, laws, or treaties of the United States.[137] The incident leading to the decision arose when a Pinkerton agent, Henry Julian, was hired by the federal government to collect a larcenist, Frederick Ker, who had fled to Peru.[138] Although Julian possessed the necessary extradition papers—the two governments having negotiated an extradition treaty a decade earlier—he found there was no official to receive his extradition warrant because of a recent Chilean military occupation of Lima. Rather than return home empty-handed, Julian kidnapped the fugitive and, with the assistance of Chilean forces, forcibly placed him on a U.S. vessel headed back to the United States.[139] The Supreme Court not only affirmed the validity of such abductions but also suggested that in gaining custody of a fugitive almost any illegality abroad was permissible. Indeed, one implication for law enforcement authorities was that, even where an extradition treaty existed, it might be preferable to obtain custody of the fugitive informally because prosecution would not be limited by the terms of the treaty to the crimes for which he would have been formally extradited.

Even when Pinkerton agents were successful in locating fugitives abroad, they did not always succeed in bringing them home alive.

136. Rowan, *The Pinkertons*, 285.
137. 119 U.S. 436 (1886).
138. See Charles Fairman "*Ker v. Illinois* Revisited," *American Journal of International Law* 47 (1953), 678–686.
139. The background to the *Ker* case is in ibid. See also Michael Cardozo, "When Extradition Fails, Is Abduction the Solution?" *American Journal of International Law* 55 (1961), 127, for a discussion of this subject before more recent case law.

Between 1901 and 1907, the State Department was the recipient of protests by the Bolivian government about a number of murders and bank robberies committed by fugitive American outlaws. The perpetrators proved to be none other than Robert LeRoy Parker and Harry Longbaugh, otherwise known as Butch Cassidy and "the Sundance Kid," who had gained a certain notoriety during Cassidy's leadership of an outlaw gang known as the "Wild Bunch." The Pinkerton agency had pursued them within the United States at the behest of the American Bankers' Association, but the bankers had refused to continue footing the bill when the duo fled abroad. The State Department called on the Pinkerton agency, which sent detective Frank Dimaio to find the infamous duo in the jungles of Bolivia.[140] To the best knowledge of historians and moviegoers alike, find them he did—accompanied by a substantial detachment of the Bolivian military that brought their escapades to a violent end in 1907.[141]

In extending their operations overseas, Pinkerton and other private detective agencies had two advantages the federal agents lacked. They were already experienced in undertaking criminal investigations without the benefit of state authority, since even in their domestic investigations they were not entitled to carry any police badge. And as private rather than government investigators, they were far less likely than U.S. federal agents to be perceived as challenges to a foreign government's sovereign powers. Police around the world offered them their cooperation not out of any sense of international comity but because the Pinkerton agents were seen as fellow professionals pursuing the same ends. In the nascent transnational police subculture of the late nineteenth and early twentieth century, the Pinkertons provided the initial transatlantic link.

Border Troubles

Until just about the end of the nineteenth century, the notion of the "frontier" carried many meanings for Americans. It referred initially to the lands outside the jurisdiction of the United States, claimed by various

140. Horan, *The Pinkertons*, 383–387; Horan, "Pinkerton Detective Agency," xviii.
141. The fate of the two outlaws has never been definitively established. See Malcolm W. Browne, "On Trail of Two Outlaws, Team Finds Skeletons," *New York Times*, Jan. 17, 1992, A12.

European powers and inhabited by assorted Indian nations, that eventually would be purchased, seized, or otherwise acquired by the United States. Even following acquisition, the same territories retained the appellation "frontier," one that Americans defined as the absence of settled inhabitation by European immigrants to North America and their descendants. As the territorial reaches of the United States extended to the Pacific, Americans increasingly identified as their frontiers the U.S. borders with Canada and Mexico; for many, the notion also referred to the borderlands on either side of those geographically undistinguished political boundaries. For our purposes, the last of these definitions is the relevant one, although it is important to recall that the origins of U.S. involvement in transfrontier policing included Georgia's border with Spanish Florida, Louisiana's border with first a Mexican-owned Texas and then an independent Texas, as well as other borders that have since faded into memory.

In the United States as in Europe, the most abundant transnational law enforcement contacts have always been with one's neighbors— except in those relatively unusual cases (absent in the case of North America) when hostile states have proscribed and effectively suppressed most cross-border activities. Most of the responsibility for regulating transnational interactions has fallen to law enforcement officials in the immediate vicinity of the borders. Obliged to deal with smuggling and illicit migration, as well as the movement of criminals across borders either to commit crimes or to flee apprehension, law enforcement officials in border locales have typically tried to develop working relationships with their counterparts across the border; on many occasions too, albeit more frequently in the nineteenth century than in the twentieth, they have taken matters into their own hands, motivated as often as not by frustration with the lack of cooperation from officials across the border.

In the case of cities along the northern border of the United States, Canadian and American police tended to work out cooperative relationships, particularly after the tensions of the late 1700s and early 1800s had passed. As much as possible, one avoided complicating the relationship by involving the central government. Some formalities might be required in extradition proceedings, but typically both sides maintained a strong interest in keeping their relations informal. By contrast, law enforcement relations across the Mexican border have been far more haphazard. Mexican resentment over the seizure of their territory by

American force in the 1840s ebbed slowly and bitterly. Political relations between the two central governments have soured often and sometimes nastily, with concomitant disruptions in the law enforcement arena. The ineffectiveness and corruption of Mexican law enforcement agencies have frustrated American police officials and occasionally stirred them to take unilateral action. At the same time, if only because of their close proximity, law enforcement officials along the southern border, not unlike those to the north, have found ways to work together effectively. Far removed from their nation's capitals, they have cultivated informal links contingent upon ignoring considerations of sovereignty and international law. Even more so than with most transnational law enforcement relationships, the personal dimension has been central to the success or failure of U.S.-Mexican law enforcement efforts.

International law enforcement activities along the frontiers of the United States have consistently proven more abundant, more complex, and more politically significant than any others. The border has represented the point across which ordinary domestic law enforcement activities—the recovery of fugitive criminals and escaped slaves, the suppression of outlaw gangs and Indian marauders, the tracking down of cattle rustlers and train robbers, and even the order maintenance functions of urban and rural law enforcement officers in border towns—become internationalized. At the same time, it has represented the dividing line between two sovereign jurisdictions with distinct economic regulations, law enforcement systems, and political interests, constituencies, and upheavals. Criminals who have crossed this line have sometimes done so with indifference to its jurisdictional consequences; more often, however, they have regarded the easily crossed border as an advantage, one that has offered lucrative profits to smugglers, safe havens to bandits, fugitives, and freebooters, and economic opportunities to illegal migrants. Law enforcement officials, by contrast, have typically perceived the border as a serious impediment to their tasks. The border has symbolized the limits of their police powers, a line across which they have no control and are typically dependent on foreign authorities, and one they have crossed only at the risk of being arrested by foreign law enforcement officers and angering central governments on both sides of the border.

The first efforts to investigate and deter smuggling across the border with Canada have already been noted. U.S. customs officials alongside the northern and southwestern borders focused their efforts both on nonsmuggling customs frauds and on the smuggling of both licit and illicit goods: diamonds, watches, textiles, opium, booze, Chinese "coolies," garlic, and just about anything else that could be transported. Some of these smuggling activities, particularly across the Mexican border in the decades after the U.S.-Mexican War of 1846–48 and the 1853 Gadsden Purchase of southern Arizona, involved no more than the continuation of commercial relations that had been established before the relocation of the border; most, however, were stimulated by the desire to earn the more substantial profits associated with illicit commerce. The early efforts to collect fugitive slaves from their foreign havens have also been discussed. The pages that follow therefore focus on the other concerns and activities of U.S. law enforcement authorities alongside the border with Mexico between the Civil War and World War I. This was a period during which most of the concerns of contemporary law enforcement agencies were in evidence, as well as some that are no longer problematic and others that may well reemerge in the future.

The border during this time was also a place where the entire array of law enforcement and investigative authorities could be found: the U.S. military, including the cavalry, the intelligence divisions, National Guard units under federal control, and the special agents of the War Department; the State Department's consular officials in Mexican cities near the border, as well as the department's special agents; the assorted federal law enforcement agencies, including customs officials, U.S. marshals, the Secret Service, the Bureau of Investigation, the Postal Inspection Service, the U.S. attorneys, and immigration officials; the Ranger units and National Guards of the border states; the local sheriffs and police officials of counties, cities, and towns alongside the border; and the nongovernmental private detective agencies, undeputized posses and vigilante bands, and unorganized private citizens. This multitude of law enforcers combined, competed, and conflicted with one another, as well as with the array of federal, state, local, and private Mexican law enforcement authorities who operated across the border.

The single most important determinant of the ebbs and flows of law enforcement activity along the U.S.-Mexican border was the degree of political stability within Mexico. "The true function of the Rio Grande," two historians of the border have observed, "was to identify a region rather than to delineate a border. . . . So closely was south Texas linked to northern Mexico that a political upheaval in one was bound to have a major impact on the other."[142] The central years of the Porfirio Díaz regime in Mexico, beginning roughly in the early 1880s, when he consolidated his power, and ending a few years before his ouster in 1911, were years of relative tranquility along the border. Those before and after, during which fiercely contending forces vied for power both in Mexico City and the northern Mexican states, were far more tumultuous times for American law enforcers at the frontier.

The principal law enforcement concerns from the 1860s to the 1880s were smuggling and cattle rustling, both of which had evolved into very substantial organized criminal activities.[143] Raiding on both sides of the border by Indians—some of them native to the region, others recently transplanted to government reservations—was also of particular concern, as was cross-border raiding by assorted outlaw gangs, vigilantes, military soldiers and deserters, and hopeful filibusters and revolutionaries. Law and order on both sides of the border were generally sporadic, with political upheaval common in Mexico, the tensions of Reconstruction apparent in the southwest, and vast areas of territory with few people and almost no police protection on either frontier. Even where officials on either side of the border were willing to cooperate, such as in delivering fugitives, legal objections to the extradition of nationals stood in the way.[144] Much of the task of preserving law and order throughout the middle decades of the nineteenth century fell to the U.S. Army and Mexican armed forces.[145] Both Mexican and U.S. law enforcement officials routinely complained about lack of cooperation from counterparts across the border and occasionally accused one another of complicity in cross-border criminality. "Mexican officers and soldiers make regular raids into Texas, stealing, robbing and murdering," U.S. Attorney D. J. Baldwin wrote to the attorney general in 1872.[146] The most notorious was General Juan Nepomuceno Cortina, who was

142. Don M. Coerver and Linda B. Hall, *Texas and the Mexican Revolution: A Study in State and National Border Policy, 1910–1920* (San Antonio, Tex.: Trinity University Press, 1984), 6.

143. Robert D. Gregg, *The Influence of Border Troubles on Relations Between the United States and Mexico, 1876–1910* (Baltimore: Johns Hopkins University Press, 1937), 12–13.

144. Moore, *Treatise on Extradition* (supra n. 44), 164–167. See also *Foreign Relations of the United States 1878*, 534–540, 560–567; and *1879*, 734–741. See also Chapter Seven of the present book.

145. See Francis Paul Prucha, *The Sword of the Republic: The United States Army on the Frontier, 1783–1846* (New York: Macmillan Co., 1969).

146. Calhoun, *Lawmen* (supra n. 100), 188.

indicted by a federal grand jury in Brownsville that year for "holding a saturnalia of crime, violence and rapine upon the soil of Texas" though never arrested on either side of the border.[147] But American outlaws were also prominent along the frontier, particularly a notorious gang known as the Cowboys that raided both American and Mexican towns and homes within riding distance of Tombstone, Arizona, during the late 1870s and early 1880s.[148] So serious were their depredations that President Chester Arthur ultimately issued a proclamation against the Cowboys and declared the area in a state of rebellion, thereby circumventing the prohibitions on military involvement in civilian law enforcement imposed by the 1877 Posse Comitatus Act.[149] With respect to the Indians, the charges and recriminations were fierce and reciprocal. Mexicans charged that the U.S. authorities were insufficiently concerned with preventing both "wild" Indians and those on the reservations from staging raids into Mexico. Americans responded in kind, charging that Mexican troops were not only failing to suppress the Indians but even providing them with food and equipment and purchasing their booty.[150]

Writing late in 1877, just weeks after the border troubles had prompted Congressional attention, a correspondent of the *New York Times* placed the problem in perspective:

> The Canada border was very many years ago made use of by thieves and robbers, who would steal on one side of the line and take refuge on the other. Extradition treaties and the settlement of the country has made impossible the affairs of 50 years ago, when scarcely a week passed that the farmers in New York and Vermont were not called to unite in pursuit of thieves flying to Canada. The conditions on the Rio Grande are most favorable for plundering enterprises. There is an almost desert country, sparsely populated, the greater proportion of the inhabitants being adventurers who have drifted thither from the whole world, and who do no labor of any kind. There are scattered over a vast territory, at long distance apart, the "ranches" of such men as

147. Ibid.
148. Ibid., 189–196.
149. Ball, *U.S. Marshals*, 126.
150. Gregg, *Influence of Border Troubles*; Robert M. Utley, *Frontier Regulars: The United States Army and the Indian, 1866–1891* (New York: Macmillan Co., 1973), 353–377; Clarence C. Clendenen, *Blood on the Border: The United States Army and the Mexican Irregulars* (New York: Macmillan Co., 1969), 45–115.

attempt the honest business of stock-raising. They are too far apart to unite for defense, and when a few armed robbers come upon them they can do nothing but submit to the mercy of the band, and endeavor to secure, if possible, their own lives. If the ranch robbed happens to be upon the Mexican side, which is not often, the robbers cross into Texas. More often, because the most tempting fields are upon the American side, the flight is into Mexico. The suppression of the raids and the capture and punishment of the thieves properly devolves upon the State of Texas. But the State is powerless, and partly for the reason that the fraternity of the raiders is so widespread that the processes of courts cannot be executed, nor can the criminals be convicted and punished. The situation, therefore, instead of involving two countries in hostilities, ought to unite them in earnest attempts to suppress crime and protect the honest, bona fide settlers along the border.[151]

The consolidation of power within Mexico in the hands of President Porfirio Díaz provided the opportunity to make good on the New York journalist's recommendations. The routine response of American law enforcers—be they cavalry, posses organized by U.S. marshals, or Texas Rangers—to transnational criminality before the 1880s had been to take matters into their own hands and pursue bandits into Mexico. "Suffice it to say," Robert Gregg wrote in his study of the border, "that the United States government, starting in 1836, more or less consistently for the next forty years held to the right of pursuit by United States forces of marauders fleeing into Mexico. . . . As a rule permission was asked for such crossings and when it was not forthcoming—as it never was in the explosive state of Mexican public opinion—crossings were carried out without permission."[152] These crossings were generally confined to the "Indian country" along the upper Rio Grande and the Arizona and New Mexico boundaries. But as the number and severity of both Indian and non-Indian raids from Mexico increased in 1877, political and military officials in Washington as well as along the border sought both to regularize and to extend past practices. On June 1, 1877, Secretary of War McCrary issued an order to General Sherman officially sanction-

---

151. "The Mexican Border Difficulty," New York Times, Dec. 14, 1877, 1.
152. Gregg, Influence of Border Troubles, 15.

ing the border crossings instigated by the military commander along the Texas border, General E. O. C. Ord. The result was a fierce nationalist backlash against the order in Mexico City, which was in contrast to the strikingly cooperative relationship established between General Ord and his Mexican counterpart, General Geronimo Trevino, who risked condemnation from the capital for his efforts to maintain a successful working relationship with the Americans. During the three years the order remained in effect, U.S. troops crossed the border more than a dozen times, only once came close to open hostilities with Mexican forces, and proved increasingly successful in suppressing the border banditry.

The second step the two nations took was to sign an agreement in 1882, after years of tense negotiations, authorizing the troops of either state to cross the border, albeit only in desert or unpopulated regions, "when they are in close pursuit of a band of savage Indians."[153] With the Díaz regime in firm control of Mexican territory, and desirous to both avoid conflicts with the United States and suppress threats to civil order in the northern states, the frontier region was far more peaceful by the mid-1880s than it had been for decades. Economic development, railroad construction, and substantial settlement in the frontier regions also helped to transform the uncivilized character of the frontier. The Cowboy gang's demise represented the passing of the last of the more substantial outlaw gangs operating across the border. And the frequency of Indian raids declined as many Indians were killed and others were relocated to reservations far from the border. By the mid-1880s the Comanche, Lipan, and Kickapoo bands that had raided settled populations on both sides of the border had been effectively suppressed. The last of the Indian raiders were almost all Apaches, who raided both sides of the Arizona and New Mexico borders and fought fiercely with American troops until well into the 1890s.[154] Led by Victorio and Nana during the late 1870s and early 1880s, then by Geronimo until 1886, and finally by "Kid" during the 1890s, the Apache bands, usually numbering no more than a hundred warriors, were at times pursued by as many as 2,000 cavalry and hundreds of Indian scouts.[155] Their final

---

153. Ibid., 152.
154. The struggles of the Apaches during the nineteenth century are recounted in Paul I. Wellman, *Death in the Desert: The Fifty Years' War for the Great Southwest* (New York: Macmillan Co., 1935).
155. Gregg, *Influence of Border Troubles*, 110–111.

demise ultimately owed as much to the efforts of Mexican forces as U.S. troops, both of whom pursued the Apaches within their territories and occasionally across the borders.[156]

Law enforcement activities directed at the suppression of the Indians fell largely to the cavalry. Suppression of non-Indian outlawry, however, was largely in the hands of nonmilitary state and federal agents, in part because the Posse Comitatus Act prohibited the military from playing a role absent a declared state of emergency. U.S. marshals were often leery of devoting too much energy to policing the border, in good part because the modest compensation they received for serving process did not cover the expense and trouble of tracking down outlaws;[157] it is not surprising that they were least keen about pursuing the American bandits who raided into Mexico but refrained from criminality north of the border. Among the more dedicated and courageous marshals was Crowley Dake, the U.S. marshal for Arizona from 1878 to 1882, who pursued the Cowboys throughout his tenure, ultimately proving successful when President Arthur's emergency declaration provided him with cavalry support.[158] In Texas, the Rangers, created at the outbreak of the Texas revolution in 1835, and in particular its Frontier Battalion, which operated from 1874 to 1881, assumed many of the responsibilities for tracking down Indians and assorted outlaws.[159] The marshals, like the cavalry, occasionally crossed the border in pursuit of their antagonists, both with and without permission from Mexican authorities, but their freedom of action was constrained to some extent by directives from Washington.[160] The Rangers, by contrast, had the freedom of a relatively single-minded unit with neither distant overseers nor broader foreign policy considerations to hamper them; they crossed the border often in pursuit of Indians and outlaws and acquired a reputation for shooting first and asking questions second. On occasion, they joined the cavalry and the marshals in policing both sides of the border.

156. Utley, *Frontier Regulars*, 367–409; John Gregory Bourke, *On the Border with Crook* (1891; reprint, Chicago: Rio Grande Press, 1962); James B. Gillett, *Six Years with the Texas Rangers, 1875 to 1881*, ed. M. M. Quaife (New Haven: Yale University Press, 1925). See also C. L. Sonnichsen, ed., *Geronimo and the End of the Apache Wars* (Lincoln: University of Nebraska Press, 1986), which includes interesting essays and a useful annotated bibliography on the end of the Apache wars.

157. Ball, *U.S. Marshals* (supra n. 99), 129; Calhoun, *Lawmen* (supra n. 100), 189.

158. Ball, *U.S. Marshals*, 109–133; Calhoun, *Lawmen*, 189–196.

159. Walter Prescott Webb, *The Texas Rangers: A Century of Frontier Defense* (Austin: University of Texas Press, 1935), 305–342.

160. Ball, *U.S. Marshals*, 112–114.

The American southwestern frontier has always been intimately linked to the political and economic currents of the nation to the south. The incidence and character of smuggling was as strongly influenced by Mexican regulations and the state of the economy as by U.S. regulations and economic conditions. The security of Americans north of the border often depended as much upon the state of law and order south of the border as in neighboring American locales. Similarly, political upheavals within Mexico inevitably affected those living across the frontier. Troops, rebels, violence, and bullets spilled easily over the border. Refugees, revolutionaries, filibusters and assorted other insurrectionists viewed the United States, and particularly Texas, as a natural refuge for those fleeing oppression, disorder, and armed forces and as an ideal base of operations for those *revoltosos* plotting an insurgency, revolution, or coup d'état. For all these Mexicans, the territory north of the border represented not just a relatively safe haven into which Mexican troops and agents were leery to enter but also a source of weapons, intelligence, personnel, and the political and financial support of sympathizers among both the substantial Mexican and Mexican-American communities and other Americans with political and economic interests in Mexico's governance. At the same time, not a few Mexicans viewed the United States with great hostility; they sought both revenge and reparations for the territorial seizures, capitalist exploitations, and general arrogance of the "gringos" to the north. Their activities and dispositions influenced, and were themselves shaped by, the swirls of intra-Mexican political turbulence.

The political turbulence generated betwen 1910 and 1920 by the Mexican revolution presented law enforcement authorities north of the border with a disparate set of challenges: ensuring both the territorial integrity of the United States and the security of Americans and others north of the border; enforcing the neutrality laws of the United States, which involved surveillance of Mexican activists, suppression of armed expeditions into Mexico, and curtailment of gun running; and protection of American lives and interests south of the border. In that decade, virtually every federal, state, and local agency present at the border and empowered to carry a weapon—and even some not so empowered— played a role in responding to these challenges. Conflicts among them were often severe, reflecting not merely ordinary turf squabbles but intense differences of opinion regarding which Mexican groups should be supported or suppressed, what the United States' interests in Mexico were, what restrictions should be placed on American law enforcement operations south of the border, and how to interpret and apply the neutrality and other laws of the United States. The sharpest disagreements were typically between federal authorities in Washington and state and local officials along the border, with the latter generally dismissive of Washington's broader foreign policy concerns and perceived detachment from the particular problems of the border. Relations with Mexican authorities accordingly varied, depending upon the particular interests and perspectives of the assorted U.S. agencies involved in the fray, all of which were further complicated between 1911 and 1915 by the recurring question of which Mexican forces were actually in control of Mexico City and Mexico's northern states and cities.

An additional factor shaping the various American responses to the Mexican Revolution was the radical cant and style of many of the revolutionaries. The socialist and anarchist rhetoric and writing of many of those involved in the struggle for power within Mexico struck a tone familiar to U.S. officials and citizens faced with their own revolutionary activists and organizations. It also invited concerns for American lives and interests in foreign countries not unlike those that have provided such an important impetus for the many U.S. military interventions and covert operations in Central America and the Caribbean throughout the twentieth century. When Mexican miners in the American-run mining town of Cananea, Mexico, began a violent strike in June 1906, in which a few American foremen were killed, the reaction of U.S. law enforcement authorities suggested elements both of the response to union strikes within the United States and the response to threats to U.S. economic interests abroad; indeed, the reaction may have been shaped by the fact that the organizers of the strike included not only the radical Mexican Liberal Party but also labor agitators and socialists from the United States, notably the Western Federation of Miners.

The first to respond to calls for help from company officials and the resident American consul was Captain Rynning of the Arizona Rangers, who organized a posse of 270 cowboys, miners, and merchants from Bisbee, Arizona, and headed to Naco to confer with Mexican officials.[161] Rynning was a former Rough Rider in Teddy Roosevelt's unit during the

---

161. The exploits of the Arizona Rangers, as related in the local newspapers of the period, are collected in Joseph Miller, ed., *The Arizona Rangers* (New York: Hastings House, 1972). See also W. Dirk Raat, *Revoltosos: Mexico's Rebels in the United States, 1903–1923* (College Station: Texas A&M University Press, 1981), 84.

Spanish-American War of 1898 who had already broken a number of strikes in Arizona. The Arizona Rangers, created in 1901 by the Territorial Legislature of Arizona and modeled after the Texas Rangers, had worked closely with the Arizona Cattle Growers' Association and been previously employed to protect the local interests of Colonel William C. Greene, the Arizonan rancher who owned the Cananea mine.[162] Exactly what transpired at the point of crossing the border has never been conclusively determined. According to one historian's version, the assistance of the Rangers was solicited by the governor of Sonora, Rafael Izabal.[163] According to a journalist, Carl Rathbun, who wrote an article, "Keeping the Peace Along the Mexican Border" for *Harper's Weekly* later that year, the governor and Captain Rynning conferred at the border:

> Rynning told the governor that the occasion was urgent, and offered himself and his men as volunteers. Knowing the captain's military experience and the reputation of the Rangers, Yzabal at once accepted and proceeded to instruct him as to the manner in which he should proceed. In order to avoid international complications the Americans were instructed to cross the line as an unorganized mob, and as soon as they were on Mexican soil they would be sworn in as Mexican volunteers by the governor, who held the requisite military authority.
>
> This was done at once, and the Americans were lined up and duly sworn, thus becoming temporarily Mexican troops. Perhaps it was a bit irregular, but necessity is not a nice observer of red tape. The captain was appointed a colonel, and seven of the Ranger force who accompanied him were also given commissions as officers of the new troops. The matter having thus been arranged, the larger part of the force at Naco then proceeded to Cananea.[164]

The hometown newspaper, the *Phoenix Republican*, reported a somewhat different version:

162. Raat, *Revoltosos*, 89.
163. Paul J. Vanderwood, *Disorder and Progress: Bandits, Police, and Mexican Development* (Lincoln: University of Nebraska Press, 1981), 147.
164. Carl M. Rathbun, "Keeping the Peace Along the Mexican Border" (1906), reprinted in Miller, ed., *Arizona Rangers*, 1–12.

At the Mexican line Governor Yzabal of Sonora met Captain
Rynning and forbade his entrance into Mexico, pointing out that
permission could not possibly be given to an armed party of
Americans to come into his country. Captain Rynning replied
that they were not going in as a party but as individuals; that they
were going on a peaceful mission to Cananea to protect and
rescue Americans in peril and they were going on that train.
Governor Yzabal made the best of the situation and went along.
He afterwards lost his job when it was represented to President
Diaz that he had permitted Captain Rynning to cross the line.[165]

As events transpired, the Cananea strike was ultimately suppressed
not by Rynning's posse but by a unit of the Mexican Rurales under the
direction of Colonel Emilio Kosterlitzky, a particularly effective commander known as the "Mad Russian," who patrolled the Mexican state
of Sonora.[166] Despite the embarrassment and offense to the Mexicans
created by the presence of the American posse, conflict was avoided as a
result of the close relationship that had already evolved between Kosterlitzky and the Arizona Rangers. The principal cost of the entire episode
was to the aging Porfirio Díaz regime, which was obliged to respond to
charges that Mexican sovereignty had been violated by the U.S. intervention.[167] More significant is that the incident at Cananea foreshadowed
many of the international dimensions of the brewing Mexican revolution.

The details of the Mexican revolution south of the border and of the
activities of the *revoltosos* north of the border need not concern us here.
Suffice it to say that the two were frequently and intimately linked and
that law enforcement authorities within the United States were obliged
to pay close attention to revolutionary activities on both sides of the
border. The principal national security concern was that the violence
and armed combatants of the Mexican revolution not spill over into
American territory. This had been a minor concern during the late
1870s, when Díaz's troops had crossed into Texas in pursuit of rebel
troops led by General Escobedo, the former war minister of the Lerdo
government that Díaz had ousted; and again in 1880, when Mexican

165. Miller, *Arizona Rangers*, 124–125.
166. See Vanderwood, *Disorder and Progress*, for a fine discussion of the Rurales and
Mexican banditry.
167. Ibid., 148–149.

troops in pursuit of suspected deserters fired shots across the border.[168] The greater intensity of the conflict near the border during the revolutionary period after 1910, however, generated far greater concerns. In April 1911, a rebel attack on the border town of Agua Prieta, in Sonora, resulted in two deaths and eleven injuries in the neighboring American town of Douglas, Arizona, and an attack on Ciudad Juárez the same month killed six and wounded fifteen in El Paso, Texas.[169] In March 1913, battles in Nogales, Sonora, inevitably crossed the street into Nogales, Arizona; in late 1914, Naco, Arizona, suffered dozens of casualties during a siege of Naco, Sonora.[170] Local authorities in El Paso could not help but keep their attentions on Ciudad Juárez, which changed hands seven times during the decade. The possibility of spillover into U.S. territory similarly preoccupied Mexican combatants, with many highly cautious of transgressing the border and quick to warn American officials of forthcoming hostilities, while a few deliberately invited such incidents to provoke American intervention. Efforts both by Mexican combatants and by U.S. authorities to avoid inflicting casualties within the United States were hampered by the fact that the revolution had become something of a spectator sport on the American side of the border, with military actions in border towns drawing large crowds.[171]

The responses of U.S. authorities included mobilizations of U.S. troops, the Ranger and National Guard units of the border states, local police, and civilian posses under the command of border sheriffs. Thousands of federal troops were massed along the border, as both a warning and a deterrent to Mexican crossings and in case threats to American lives and interests in Mexico required intervention; and President Taft agreed to federal financing of the Texas Rangers, which had been on the verge of being disbanded until the Mexican revolution broke out. But despite periodic scares of cross-border violence at El Paso, Brownsville, and other points, as well as repeated calls by the governor of Texas and other local officials for U.S. military intervention across the border, Presidents Taft and Wilson studiously avoided sending federal troops into Mexico absent deliberate attacks on American citizens.

168. Gregg, *Influence of Border Troubles* (supra n. 143), 59, 98.

169. Coerver and Hall, *Texas and the Mexican Revolution* (supra n. 142), 24–27.

170. Linda B. Hall and Don M. Coerver, *Revolution on the Border: The United States and Mexico, 1910–1920* (Albuquerque: University of New Mexico Press, 1988), 32–33.

171. Coerver and Hall, *Texas and the Mexican Revolution*, 24–26; Hall and Coerver, *Revolution on the Border*, 31.

As the Mexican revolution wore on, various factions increasingly looked at the United States not just as a haven but as an enemy. The first manifestation of this was a campaign of violence during 1915 and 1916 conducted by Mexicans and Mexican-Americans against Anglos north of the border. Known as the Plan of San Diego, the campaign derived its name from a document drawn up in the small southern Texas town of San Diego calling for a Mexican-American rebellion, the slaying of all Anglo males over the age of sixteen, and creation of an independent republic in the southwest.[172] The campaign drew its sustenance from the brewing anti-American and anti-Anglo sentiment that had simmered for decades on both sides of the border; it was discreetly organized and financed, however, by Venustiano Carranza, leader of the dominant faction in the Mexican revolution during the latter part of the decade, who attempted to manipulate the violence to pressure the Wilson administration to recognize his government. Although most of the dozens of raids carried out in U.S. territory under the banner of the Plan were initiated from Mexican territory, President Wilson resolutely refused to authorize any border crossings, even in hot pursuit. American interventions were limited to the covert intelligence missions of the Justice Department's special agents and a number of Japanese-Mexican informants, who confirmed reports that Carranza had supported the raids and that representatives of the German government had provided funding, hoping to provoke the Wilson administration into a distracting war with Mexico.[173] The raids generated much hysteria and fear among non-Mexicans north of the border, but only a few dozen casualties. The cavalry restricted their police actions to the U.S. side of the border. The principal victims of the Plan were the hundreds of Mexican Americans lynched and executed by the Texas Rangers and local vigilantes and the thousands forced to hide or flee across the border to safety.

The incident that finally prompted President Wilson to order a military expedition across the border was sponsored not by Carranza but by his bitter opponent, Pancho Villa, who had turned against the United

172. See James A. Sandos, "The Plan of San Diego: War and Diplomacy on the Texas Border, 1915–1916," *Arizona and the West* 14 (1972), 5–24; Charles C. Cumberland, "Border Raids in the Lower Rio Grande Valley, 1915," *Southwestern Historical Quarterly* 57 (1954), 285–311; and Charles H. Harris III and Louis R. Sadler, "The Plan of San Diego and the Mexican–United States War Crisis of 1916: A Reexamination," *Hispanic American Historical Review* 58 (1978), 381–408, reprinted in Charles H. Harris III and Louis R. Sadler, *The Border and the Revolution* (Las Cruces: New Mexico State University, 1988), 71–100.

173. Sandos, "Plan of San Diego," 19–24.

States with bitterness following Wilson's recognition of the Carranza regime in October 1915.[174] Villa's forces began their campaign against Americans with a massacre of American mining employees en route to Santa Ysabel, Chihuahua, in January 1916; on March 9, they attacked Columbus, New Mexico, killing seventeen Americans and burning and looting the town before being chased out by U.S. Army troops, who managed to killed dozens of the *villistas*. Wilson thereupon ordered General John "Black Jack" Pershing to lead a "punitive expedition" into Mexico in pursuit of Pancho Villa and his forces.[175] But Pershing's forces failed to apprehend Villa, and their very presence in Mexico induced Carranza to renew the Plan of San Diego raids on U.S. border towns. A Mexican attack on Glenn Springs, Texas, and nearby towns on May 5 resulted in a further escalation of hostilities between Carranza and the United States. Both governments drew up plans to invade the other and massed their troops in anticipation of large-scale hostilities. U.S. Army troops were at last authorized to cross the border in "hot pursuit" of raiders. Proclaiming "I am clear of red tape, and I know no Rio Grande," Major George Langhorne led his troops into Mexico in pursuit of the Glenn Springs raiders, with "no pause," he noted, "for orders or State Department negotiations."[176] On May 9, President Wilson federalized the National Guards of Texas, New Mexico, and Arizona; on June 18, he extended the order to all National Guard units in the United States. Neither government, however, was eager for war, with Wilson wary of the potential need for U.S. troops in Europe and Carranza concerned lest a military conflict with the United States result in his downfall.[177] By July, the crisis had passed and Carranza had ordered a halt to the Plan of San Diego raids. Pershing continued to pursue Villa and even secretly commissioned two Japanese-Mexican agents to assassinate Villa with poison tablets, but both overt and covert efforts failed

174. See Clarence C. Clendenen, *The United States and Pancho Villa: A Study in Unconventional Diplomacy* (Ithaca, N.Y.: Cornell University Press, 1961).

175. Frank E. Vandiver, *Black Jack: The Life and Times of John J. Pershing* (College Station: Texas A&M University Press, 1977), 2:595–668; Clendenen, *Blood on the Border* (supra n. 150), 248–284. The argument that Pershing's expedition was designed to serve broader foreign policy objectives of the Wilson administration is advanced in Michael L. Tate, "Pershing's Punitive Expedition: Pursuer of Bandits or Presidential Panacea?" *The Americas* 32 (1975–76), 46–71.

176. Coerver and Hall, *Texas and the Mexican Revolution* (supra n. 142), 100. See Ronnie C. Tyler, "The Little Punitive Expedition in the Big Bend," *Southwestern Historical Quarterly* 78 (1975), 271–291.

177. Coerver and Hall, *Texas and the Mexican Revolution*, 105.

to do away with the Mexican rebel.[178] In early 1917, with Villa's forces still at large in Mexico but no longer operational near the border, Pershing's units were withdrawn from Mexico.

The series of Mexican raids and military responses by the United States during 1916 were significant in a number of respects. Pershing's punitive expedition represented one of the largest, as well as one of the last, employments of U.S. military force to track down criminal fugitives who had fled abroad. Like the cross-border cavalry raids against Indians in earlier decades—but unlike the posse Captain Rynning led to Cananea, or the assorted military expeditions to Central America and the Caribbean during the early decades of the twentieth century, both of which were directed primarily at the protection of American interests abroad—Pershing's expedition had as its primary objective enforcement of U.S. laws. But it also represented the last significant deployment of either police or military force across a land border of the United States on behalf of national security objectives. The border did not quiet entirely until the mid-1920s; U.S. military units continued to cross the border in pursuit of raiders, and in June 1919 they intervened in Juárez when an attack on that city by a band of *villistas* resulted in casualties north of the border from stray bullets. The cross-border attack by the military units, which were comprised largely of black infantrymen and backed by a deadly artillery barrage not previously employed along the border, dealt a devastating and fatal blow to Villa's forces and ambitions.[179] The U.S. troops were all back in the United States within two days, however. There was neither the need nor the desire to replicate Pershing's expedition.

The Neutrality Network

Even as the Army and assorted posses responded to the more large-scale threats of disorder generated by the Mexican revolution, federal and state law enforcement agents were busily engaged investigating violations of U.S. neutrality laws. Nineteenth-century American history was

178. Charles H. Harris III and Louis R. Sadler, "Termination with Extreme Prejudice: The United States Versus Pancho Villa," in Harris and Sadler, *The Border and the Revolution*, 7–23.
179. Clendenen, *The U.S. and Pancho Villa*, 305–313.

rich with plots by both American filibusters and foreign revolutionaries to launch foreign military expeditions from U.S. soil. Neutrality laws dating back to 1794 forbade such activities, but the actual enforcement of the laws varied greatly, depending upon popular attitudes, the state of relations between the United States and the targeted nation, and the varied motives of whatever administration occupied the White House. The Latin American wars of independence against Spain during the first decades of the nineteenth century attracted much support within the United States. In 1837, approximately 1,000 Canadian revolutionaries known as the "Patriots" launched a military expedition from northern New York in an effort to spark a war for independence against Britain; it was quickly suppressed, however, by British troops and Canadian militia with the assistance of U.S. marshals.[180] During the 1850s, American filibusters plotted takeovers of Cuba, Mexico, Nicaragua, Ecuador, Guatemala, El Salvador, Costa Rica, Peru, and Honduras.[181] The most notorious of these, William Walker, succeeded in conquering Nicaragua and ruling it for a year. In 1866 and again in 1870, Irish Fenians invaded Canada from U.S. territory, seeking thereby to pressure Britain to free Ireland, but they too were quickly routed by Canadian troops north of the border and U.S. troops and marshals in New York and Vermont. By the end of the nineteenth century, filibusterism and most other violations of U.S. neutrality laws consisted primarily of gun running from the United States and the plotting of foreign revolutionaries and coup makers on U.S. soil. Such activities reached their height during the Mexican revolution.

The rise of opposition to the Díaz regime in Mexico after 1905 provided the occasion for the first significant neutrality law enforcement efforts since the first years of Díaz's reign. In March 1907, the Mexican ambassador to the United States, Enrique Creel, informed Secretary of State Elihu Root of the machinations of the Mexican Liberal Party and its leader, Ricardo Flores Magón, within the United States and requested that the U.S. government take action to enforce its neutrality laws. Root, who wanted to maintain the close relationship that had developed

180. Albert B. Corey, *The Crisis of 1830–1842 in Canadian-American Relations* (New Haven: Yale University Press, 1941); Wilson Porter Shortridge, "The Canadian-American Frontier During the Rebellion of 1837–1838," *Canadian Historical Review* 7 (1926), 13–26.
181. Charles H. Brown, *Agents of Manifest Destiny: The Lives and Times of the Filibusters* (Chapel Hill: University of North Carolina Press, 1980); Calhoun, *Lawmen* (supra n. 100), 67–72.

between the United States and the Díaz regime, asked Attorney General Charles Bonaparte to take the appropriate actions. Following an armed attack by *magonistas* from Del Rio, Texas, into Mexico in June 1908, the local U.S. attorney, customs collector, U.S. marshal, cavalry commander, and the U.S. consul stationed at Ciudad Porfirio Díaz, investigated the incident and recommended "that a special secret service be established to keep in touch with Mexican revolutionary movements and border conditions."[182]

The network of agents that developed thereafter to enforce the neutrality laws outlasted both the suppression of the *magonista* movement and the fall of the Díaz regime. It ultimately included agents representing every federal law enforcement agency: U.S. Customs, the Immigration Service, the Marshals Service, the Secret Service, the Postal Inspection Service, the State Department, the Army's Intelligence Division, and the newly created Bureau of Investigation, which assumed a leading role in investigating neutrality law violations.[183] Some of the arrangements were somewhat irregular. For instance, the ambitious and well-informed U.S. consul in Ciudad Porfirio Díaz, Luther T. Ellsworth, was appointed a "special representative" of the Justice Department in November 1909 to supervise the neutrality work.[184] The prohibition on lending Secret Service agents to other law enforcement agencies was circumvented by lending a top agent, Joe Priest, to the State Department and then placing him under Justice Department supervision. Texas law enforcement officials occasionally helped enforce the federal neutrality laws—albeit with much reserve, given the substantial support enjoyed by the *magonistas* and subsequent revolutionary groups among the local Mexican-American population. Far more significantly, the U.S. neutrality network worked closely with agents of the Mexican government, including not just resident consuls and Secret Service agents but also employees of the American private detective agencies hired by the Mexican government.

Given the abundant twists and turns of the Mexican revolution and U.S.-Mexican relations, it is not surprising that the process of enforcing

182. Dorothy Pierson Kerig, *Luther T. Ellsworth: U.S. Consul on the Border During the Mexican Revolution*, Southwestern Studies Monograph No. 47 (El Paso: Texas Western Press, 1975), 15–16.

183. Charles H. Harris III and Louis R. Sadler, "United States Government Archives and the Mexican Revolution," *New World: A Journal of Latin American Studies* 1 (1986), 108–116, reprinted in Harris and Sadler, *The Border and the Revolution*, 133–141.

184. Kerig, *Ellsworth*, 25.

the neutrality laws was both complex and laden with intrigue.[185] Informants and agents often worked for two or three agencies at once, including some that were at loggerheads with one another. Private investigators—in particular, those of the Furlong Detective Agency employed by the Díaz regime and the Thiel Detective Agency hired by the Madero regime—played a central role, tracking down and even arresting *revoltosos* and others targeted by their Mexican employers.[186] State and federal officials often clashed with one another and among themselves over differing interpretations of the neutrality laws and varying perceptions of which side to support in the Mexican revolution. And Mexican agents were afforded wide latitude in investigating the various revolutionary groups, often conducting the principal investigations and only calling upon the local U.S. authorities to make the necessary arrests. Hundreds of Mexican agents and informants could be found in El Paso and other centers of revolutionary intrigue, surveilling and infiltrating the antigovernment plotters and gun smuggling rings. At one point, in mid-1912, Mexican agents were even authorized to search passengers on streetcars leaving El Paso for Juárez across the border, but the practice was discontinued after a public outcry against the notion of foreign agents searching American citizens on U.S. territory.[187] Their substantial presence, frequent indiscretions, and occasional bunglings of joint investigations also angered some U.S. authorities, but the Americans' dependence upon the Mexican agents for intelligence and personnel ensured their continued presence.[188]

Notwithstanding the plethora of U.S. agents, Mexican secret service men, private detectives, and assorted double agents often working at cross-purposes with one another, the neutrality laws of the United States were enforced with some vigor. *Revoltosos* were followed, harassed, and arrested by agents of both governments; prosecuted in U.S. courts; deported or extradited to Mexico; and occasionally kidnapped in the United States and secretly brought across the border.[189] The results

185. See Mark T. Gilderhus, *Diplomacy and Revolution: U.S.–Mexican Relations Under Wilson and Carranza* (Tucson: University of Arizona Press, 1977).

186. Furlong, *Fifty Years a Detective* (supra n. 133), 137–148.

187. Charles H. Harris III and Louis R. Sadler, "The 'Underside' of the Mexican Revolution: El Paso, 1912," *The Americas: A Quarterly Review of Inter-American Cultural History* 39 (1982), 69–83, reprinted in Harris and Sadler, *The Border and the Revolution*, 53–70.

188. Kerig, *Ellsworth*, 50.

189. Raat, *Revoltosos* (supra n. 161), esp. 124–148.

included the arrest and conviction of Flores Magón and the effective suppression of the *magonista* movement.[190] Efforts against the next leading *revoltoso*, Francisco Madero, were complicated, however, by the substantial financial, legal, and political support engendered by the politically moderate Mexican activist and by his careful efforts to avoid any appearance of violating the neutrality laws.[191] After a federal warrant for Madero's arrest was issued in February 1911, the Texas governor, Oscar Colquitt, offered his assistance in arresting Madero and facilitating the efforts of Díaz's agents, but federal agents were much less eager to aid in repressing Madero's movement.

With the fall of the Díaz regime and Madero's accession to the presidency, federal, state, and local law enforcement agents in the United States worked with Madero's agents to suppress challenges to his regime. The first challenge, by General Bernardo Reyes, a prominent military and political figure in the Díaz regime, received powerful support from leading members of the Mexican-American community and Governor Colquitt, but it was quickly suppressed in the latter half of 1911 when a federal grand jury indicted Reyes and his supporters and U.S. law enforcement authorities followed up by confiscating the arms, ammunition, and horses that the *reyistas* had assembled to mount their counter-revolution.[192] Efforts during the following year by a former ally of Madero, Pascual Orozco, to organize a rebellion against the Mexican regime from U.S. territory were significantly undermined by the success of U.S. and Mexican government agents in stemming the flow of weapons across the border.[193] Following the fall of the Madero regime in 1913, U.S. authorities refrained from aiding the short-lived regime of Victoriano Huerta and played an important role in suppressing the revolutionary movements activated by Huerta and Pascual Orozco (and partially financed and supplied by the German government) after Huerta's overthrow in 1914. Agents of the Bureau of Investigation infiltrated, surveilled, and otherwise collected intelligence on their activities. U.S. attorneys and marshals along the border were directed by the Justice

190. Ibid., 149–168.

191. Coerver and Hall, *Texas and the Mexican Revolution* (supra n. 142), 17–20.

192. Charles H. Harris III and Louis R. Sadler, "The 1911 Reyes Conspiracy: The Texas Side," *Southwestern Historical Quarterly* 82 (1980), 325–348, reprinted in Harris and Sadler, *The Border and the Revolution*, 27–50; Vic Niemeyer, "Frustrated Invasion: The Revolutionary Attempt of General Bernardo Reyes from San Antonio in 1911," *Southwestern Historical Quarterly* 67 (1963), 213–225.

193. Harris and Sadler, "The 'Underside' of the Mexican Revolution," 53–67.

Department to watch for violations of the neutrality laws.[194] By late 1915, both Huerta and Orozco had been indicted and detained by federal authorities. Orozco died violently shortly thereafter, when he escaped from confinement but was chased down and killed by a posse of federal, state, and local authorities; Huerta died in custody in January 1916 from medical complications following an operation. During the following years, U.S. authorities continued with their efforts to curtail gun running by both supporters and opponents of the Carranza regime in Mexico City, but the principal impact of their efforts to enforce the neutrality laws was the undermining of violent opposition to the Carranza government.

By 1915, U.S. military and police forces in the Southwest were concerned with yet another threat: the efforts of the German government to cultivate ties first with Huerta and other revolutionaries and thereafter with the Carranza regime. The Germans sought to create whatever troubles they could along the southwestern border, to distract U.S. attention and military forces from the conflict in Europe, and to win the Mexican government's assistance in their war with the United States. The neutrality network that had developed in response to the Mexican revolution rapidly shifted its focus to the tasks of espionage and counterespionage against German activities in Mexico and north of the border. Intelligence agents of the Army, Navy, and State Department combined with the law enforcement agents of the Treasury Department and the Bureau of Investigation as well as British intelligence agents. Charged with maintaining the economic blacklist against German firms and fronts and with collecting political and military intelligence, the U.S. agents clashed frequently among themselves over turf and tactics but ultimately succeeded in countering and even penetrating many of the Germans' efforts at espionage and other political intrigue in Mexico.[195]

The Transnational Relations of City Police

So long as the federal police agencies remained underdeveloped, most overseas investigations of noncustoms criminal matters fell to municipal

---

194. Coerver and Hall, *Texas and the Mexican Revolution*, 112.

195. Friedrich Katz, *The Secret War in Mexico* (Chicago: University of Chicago Press, 1981), 433–441; Charles H. Harris III and Louis R. Sadler, "The Witzke Affair: German Intrigue on the Mexican Border, 1917–1918," *Military Review* 59 (1979), 36–50, reprinted in Harris and Sadler, *The Border and the Revolution*, 115–129.

police agencies. Most murderers, thiefs, rapists, and other common criminals violated not federal but state and municipal laws. From the middle of the nineteenth century until the first decades of the twentieth, the detective divisions of municipal police departments were likely to be as large and as sophisticated as anything the federal government had to offer. Its principal competitors and collaborators were the private detective agencies, which were themselves often composed of former police officials. Even as early as the first half of the nineteenth century a number of chief constables in leading American cities had acquired impressive reputations based upon their knowledge of the criminal world and their detecting skills. This was especially the case with New York's finest. During much of the first half of the nineteenth century, Jacob Hays, the High Constable of New York City, was consulted frequently by European police officials.[196] In 1818, he personally pursued a counterfeiting investigation to Canada, where he located "the principal manufactory" of the criminals.[197] And in 1851, New York City's police force was sufficiently well regarded that the British government invited it, along with other leading European police departments, to send representatives to the Great Exhibition in London.[198] The first public detective branches were created in Boston in 1846, then New York in 1857, Philadelphia in 1859, and Chicago in 1861.[199] Most were quickly struck by corruption scandals and disbanded temporarily, but the rising need for their services inevitably led to their reestablishment.[200] Not until 1880, however, when an uneducated but clever Irishman, Thomas Byrnes, was appointed police chief, was New York's detective division pulled together into something of an effective force. Combining old-fashioned methods with the development of photo identification files, Byrnes saw his detective force as the equal of the French Sûreté and Scotland Yard.[201] His tenure lasted sixteen years, until he was forced from his position by Teddy

196. Gerald Astor, *The New York Cops: An Informal History* (New York: Charles Scribner's Sons, 1971), 14.

197. Johnson, *Policing the Urban Underworld* (supra n. 119), 48.

198. Phillip Thurmond Smith, *Policing Victorian London: Political Policing, Order, and the London Metropolitan Police* (Westport, Conn.: Greenwood Press, 1985), 89–93.

199. Johnson, *Policing the Urban Underworld*, 65.

200. Craig D. Uchida, "The Development of the American Police: An Historical Overview," in Roger G. Dunham and Geoffrey P. Alpert, eds., *Critical Issues in Policing: Contemporary Readings* (Prospect Heights, Ill.: Waveland Press, 1989), 14–30.

201. Thorwald, *Century of the Detective* (supra n. 132), 95–98.

Roosevelt, then the activist chief police commissioner in New York. Although much of Byrne's historical reputation has focused on his heavy-handed methods against criminals and his accommodating approach to vice control,[202] he brought his detective force into the mainstream of international police interactions. His department assembled an extensive rogues' gallery, including pictures of European as well as American criminals, and exchanged information on criminals and fugitives with European police departments.[203] Indeed, as police chief of what was fast becoming the world's most cosmopolitan city, Byrnes had little choice but to keep tabs on itinerant criminals throughout the Americas and abroad.

By the beginning of the twentieth century, municipal police departments, not just in New York but also throughout much of the United States, were undergoing the same process of professionalization that had occurred decades earlier in Europe.[204] Much of the initial impetus was provided by the increasing professionalism of criminals in the areas of counterfeiting, burglary, fraud, and fencing.[205] Motivated also by European influences, but even more so by a wave of police corruption investigations around the country, police reform movements were contributing to an increasing sophistication in American criminal investigations.[206] One aspect of these developments was the increasing police consciousness of the need to interact with foreign counterparts. First, however, police departments needed to resolve the problems of interstate cooperation and develop some sense of a national police community. The first significant efforts in this regard were sponsored in 1871 by the commissioners and chief of the Saint Louis police. They organized a National Police Convention attended by more than one hundred delegates from twenty-one states and the District of Columbia. Criminal

202. Reppetto, The Blue Parade (supra n. 106), 52–68.

203. Thomas Byrnes, Rogue's Gallery (1887; reprint, Secaucus, N.J.: Castle, 1988).

204. Robert Fogelson, Big-City Police (Cambridge, Mass.: Harvard University Press, 1977), 93–166; Johnson, American Law Enforcement (supra n. 93), 105–122; Samuel Walker, A Critical History of Police Reform: The Emergence of Professionalism (Lexington, Mass.: Lexington Books, 1977), 33–106.

205. Larry K. Hartsfield, The American Response to Professional Crime, 1870–1917 (Westport, Conn.: Greenwood Press, 1985); Johnson, Policing the Urban Underworld, 12–67.

206. See Reppetto, The Blue Parade; and Gene E. Carte and Elaine H. Carte, Police Reform in the United States: The Era of August Vollmer (Berkeley and Los Angeles: University of California Press, 1977), for a thorough discussion of these developments.

investigative techniques were discussed, criminal justice issues such as prostitution debated, and calls for greater cooperation and communication proclaimed.[207] Efforts thereafter to institutionalize police cooperation and form an association faltered, however, and no further steps were taken for more than two decades. In 1893, the National (later International) Association of Chiefs of Police was created and shortly thereafter began holding annual conferences. Three years later, a group of law enforcement officials from around the nation met in Chicago to discuss ways of improving interstate coordination in criminal investigations.[208] As American police officers gradually grew accustomed to looking beyond their municipal and state borders, the notion of dealing with foreign counterparts began to seem somewhat more realistic.

A principal factor contributing to American participation in the developing international police community was the dissemination of European developments in police science. For instance, during the 1890s, police experts around the world studied and promoted the new anthropometric method of criminal identification created by, and named after, Alphonse Bertillon.[209] The Chicago police department adopted the *bertillonage* system in 1890, and other American police departments followed suit after the Frenchman's book was translated into English in 1896.[210] Likewise, the fingerprint method was gradually gaining notice. In 1903 the International Association of Chiefs of Police (IACP) appointed a committee of three to examine the new methodology. One of the members, W. G. Baldwin of Baldwin Railroad Detectives, toured European police departments in 1904 and returned with favorable reports.[211] Another member, William Pinkerton, went to England the next year and "declared that Scotland Yard had reduced criminal investigation to a matter of bookkeeping."[212] At the 1905 World's Fair in Saint Louis, the IACP sponsored a display of the various systems of criminal identification in use around the world. Scotland Yard was

207. Walker, *Critical History of Police Reform*, 47.
208. Thorwald, *Century of the Detective* (supra n. 132), 93.
209. IACP, *Proceedings: 27th Convention* (Detroit, June 7–10, 1920), 83. See Henri Couchon, "Alphonse Bertillon: Criminalistics," in Philip John Stead, *Pioneers in Policing* (Montclair, N.J.: Patterson Smith, 1977), 121–147.
210. R. W. M'Claughry and John Bonfield, "Police Protection at the World's Fair," *North American Review* 156 (1893), 711–713.
211. Morn, *"The Eye That Never Sleeps"* (supra n. 125), 126.
212. Ibid.

persuaded to send a representative to demonstrate the "Henry Finger Print Method," which had been published five years earlier.[213] The IACP had also established a National Bureau of Criminal Identification to serve as a central repository of Bertillon cards of major criminals from around the country.[214] In the 1920s, this bureau was given over to the Justice Department. Eventually, its files and those from the federal penitentiary in Leavenworth were combined under the supervision of the FBI.

As with many techniques, fingerprinting took time to be accepted and used by American police, who were accustomed to more-familiar methods and who had already gone through the laborious process of being converted to the Bertillon method. In New York shortly after the turn of the century, the newly appointed police commissioner, William McAdoo, was eager that his department keep up with developments in Europe. Accordingly, in 1904 he sent a detective sergeant, Joseph A. Faurot, to London to learn what Scotland Yard was doing in the area of fingerprinting. Two years later, Faurot was able to prove the merits of the new identification technique to American skeptics. Back on foot patrol, he happened to arrest an Englishman who was lurking suspiciously in the Waldorf Astoria Hotel. Uncertain of his true identity, Faurot sent the suspect's fingerprints to Scotland Yard. The reply two weeks later confirmed that the Englishman was a professional hotel thief and fugitive from British justice.[215] Given prominent play in the New York newspapers, the incident helped persuade American police departments to develop fingerprint files on criminals. It also suggested the potentials of greater cooperation with foreign police departments.

At the 1905 annual convention of the IACP, Major Richard Sylvester, chief of the Washington, D.C., police and president of the association, delivered his annual report and address. The portion addressing international aspects of law enforcement, although excessively optimistic, reflected the sense of growing cooperation between police agencies around the world as well as within the United States:

> The International Association continues to grow in numbers and influence. . . . Police co-operation is more prompt and thorough

213. IACP, *Twelfth Annual Session*, May 22–25, 1905 (Washington, D.C.: IACP, 1905).
214. Ibid., 68–70.
215. Thorwald, *Century of the Detective* (supra n. 132), 98–99.

throughout the world than ever before. There was a time when responses from authorities abroad were only obtained after the aid of the State Department had been invoked and procured, but such confidence has been established within a short time between the police authorities of our own and other lands that the delays, interferences and suspicions which once prevailed have generally disappeared. The interchange of domestic and foreign descriptive circulars has largely increased. We find the finger print of England and the finger print of United States filed within the police cabinets of the principal cities of these two great countries. The photographs and measurements of the criminals of Paris may be found in the galleries of the department in Washington, and vice versa. Our own cities have established an intercourse which operates as a preventive of crime, and which in the great majority of cases surely weaves a web about the criminal who is to be detected. The head of one police department enjoys personal as well as official acquaintance with that of another. The most recent applicances and modern methods of practice have been adopted. These are but a few of the advantages which have accrued through the maintenance of your association.[216]

Despite Sylvester's plaudits, the membership of the IACP was then, as now, composed almost entirely of American and a few Canadian police chiefs. Each year, invitations were sent to chiefs of police from around the world, and each year the great majority expressed their regrets at not being able to attend. Following World War I, which severely disrupted ties with European police departments, the establishment of Interpol undermined much of the need abroad for the U.S.-based association. But within the United States it continued to serve a valuable purpose by enhancing links between municipal police departments, advancing their professionalization, furthering a sense of police community and professional association, and heightening awareness of the international dimensions of law enforcement.

Although the sense that Americans could learn something from Europe in the area of policing had first emerged in the mid-nineteenth century, it was not until the first two decades of this century that serious study of the police systems across the Atlantic began. A number of the

216. IACP, *Twelfth Annual Session*, 16–17.

"studies" by police chiefs were little more than excuses for subsidized vacations to Europe, but many were seriously motivated by concern for the credibility and effectiveness of American police departments. One impetus was the desire to learn about new criminal investigative techniques—for instance, Faurot's fingerprinting expedition. Another impetus, prompted by the 1894 Lenox investigation into police corruption in New York, and similar investigations in other cities during the following decade, was the desire to learn why the European police agencies had been relatively successful in resisting corruption. Bureaucratic reorganization was one of the principal solutions being advocated in the United States. Accordingly, these studies focused on the organization of foreign police systems.

In 1902, Avery Andrews, a former police commissioner of New York appointed by Mayor Seth Low to recommend a scheme of reorganization for the New York Police Department (NYPD), visited Europe to study their police systems; his findings were published the next year in *The Cosmopolitan*.[217] Six years later, William McAdoo, no longer police commissioner of New York but still interested in police matters, studied the London police system and published his conclusions in *The Century Magazine*.[218] Perhaps the most comprehensive and influential study of Europe's police by an American was that of Raymond Fosdick, a young scholar who had spent a few years as a city investigator of corruption.[219] Funded by the police reform movement,[220] he spent the two years before the outbreak of the world war in Europe investigating police systems throughout the continent.[221] Some years later, in a similar study of municipal police departments in major American cities, Fosdick contrasted his findings in Europe with what he found to be the rather embarrassing situation in many American cities.[222] By this time, the study of European police administration by incoming police commissioners had become virtually a prerequisite for the job. As police historian Thomas Reppetto wrote concerning the appointment of Theodore Roosevelt's protégé, Arthur Woods, as New York's police commis-

217. See Avery D. Andrews, "The Police Systems of Europe," *The Cosmopolitan*, Mar. 1903, 495–504.

218. William McAdoo, "The London Police from a New York Point of View," *The Century Magazine*, Sept. 1909, 649–670.

219. Reppetto, *The Blue Parade* (supra n. 106), 77.

220. Fogelson, *Big-City Police* (supra n. 204), 62.

221. Raymond B. Fosdick, *European Police Systems* (New York: Century Co., 1916).

222. Fosdick, *American Police Systems* (supra n. 1).

sioner in 1914: "Though not exactly an administrative expert, he had made the ritual study of European police and moved in circles where the new science was being developed."[223] Yet another study was undertaken in 1926 by Sheldon Glueck, a graduate student at Harvard who later became one of the nation's leading criminologists. Commissioned by now former Commissioner Woods, who had retained his interest in comparative police studies, Glueck's report provided a succinct update of Fosdick's findings and recommendations.[224] Also significant was the convening of a National Conference on Criminal Law and Criminology at Northwestern University in 1909, one result of which was the establishment of a committee to translate the leading books of European criminology into English.[225]

Travel abroad by municipal police agents on criminal investigations appears to have been a relatively unusual occurrence. The principal exceptions involved the collection of fugitives from abroad, such as when two Saint Louis police officers traveled to New Zealand in 1885 to collect a much-desired fugitive.[226] The same appears to have been the case with respect to visits to the United States by foreign police officers— although cities such as New York certainly received a fair number of official and unofficial visits.[227] The principal opportunities for American and foreign police to interact arose at the world's fairs. In 1893, the Chicago Police Department prepared for the Exposition by collecting Bertillon cards from large city police departments throughout the United States, Canada, Mexico, and Europe and by inviting each department to send two members to the Exposition to surveil the crowds and exchange information and techniques with one another.[228]

Perhaps the most famous instance of an American detective pursuing an investigation overseas occurred in 1909. Rising concern in New York

223. Reppetto, The Blue Parade, 158. Woods did his study in 1907 following his appointment as head of the detective bureau.

224. The report was not published until 1974. See Sheldon Glueck, Continental Police Practice in the Formative Years (Springfield, Ill.: Charles C. Thomas, 1974).

225. Hartsfield, American Response to Professional Crime (supra n. 205), 184.

226. Furlong, Fifty Years a Detective (supra n. 133), 13.

227. The visit of a French police official, M. Casselari, is recounted in the memoir of the policeman Michael Fiaschetti (as told to Prosper Buranelli), The Man They Couldn't Escape: The Adventures of Detective Fiaschetti of the Italian Squad (London: Selwyn & Blount, 1928), 147–156 (also published under the title You Gotta Be Rough [Garden City, N.Y.: Doubleday, Doran, 1930]).

228. M'Claughry and Bonfield, "Police Protection at the World's Fair" (supra n. 210), 712–715.

over the spread of the notorious "Black Hand," as the Mafia was then called, had induced Commissioner of Police Theodore Bingham to set up a "Secret Service" specifically to deal with the Italian-born criminals. Bingham appointed as its chief Joe Petrosino, the highest-ranking Italian-American in the city's police force and already head of the department's Italian Squad. A legendary figure in Italy, where he was called the "Italian Sherlock Holmes," Petrosino was sent to Sicily.[229] His tasks were to determine which criminals had left Italy for the United States, to obtain copies of the penal certificates needed to deport members of the Black Hand from the United States, and to establish a network of agents capable of supplying the New York police authorities with similar information in the future. Petrosino began his mission in Rome, where he met with the Italian interior minister and obtained from him letters to the prefects in Sicily, Calabria, and Naples ordering them to assist the New York police agent in his investigation. Once in Sicily, Petrosino liaised with the local police and kept the U.S. consul in Palermo, William Henry Bishop, informed of his work. However, Petrosino operated primarily on his own, keeping secret his plan to set up a secret information network. He quickly obtained and forwarded to Bingham the records of several criminals, assuring him that more would follow soon. His mission came to a disastrous end when he was murdered in Palermo by unknown assailants; the local Mafia chieftan, Don Vito Cascio Ferro, claimed credit, but the available evidence suggested otherwise. Bishop attempted to undertake a thorough investigation of the assassination but was hindered both by the obstructionist efforts of Sicilian authorities and by a series of death threats, which restricted his movements.

In an attempt to salvage something of Petrosino's efforts, Bingham sent two additional detectives to Italy, including Petrosino's lieutenant on the Italian Squad, Anthony Vachris, and an Italian-speaking detective sergeant, John Crowley.[230] The two spent several months in Italy, where they succeeded in persuading the authorities in Rome—who preferred that the American detectives not travel to Sicily—to provide them with the penal certificates and photographs of hundreds of Italian ex-convicts

229. The following account is based largely upon Thomas Monroe Pitkin and Francesco Cordasco, *The Black Hand: A Chapter in Ethnic Crime* (Totowa, N.J.: Littlefield, Adams & Co., 1977); Arrigo Petacco, *Joe Petrosino*, trans. Charles Lam Markmann (New York: Macmillan Co., 1974; originally published in Italian in 1972); and George E. Pozzetta, "Another Look at the Petrosino Affair," *Italian Americana* 1 (1974), 81–92.

230. Pitkin and Cordasco, *Black Hand*, 121–137.

and to forward hundreds more thereafter. Optimistic expectations that their mission would succeed in ridding New York of hundreds of Black Hand members, however, were quickly dashed by the corrupt politics of New York. Acting at the apparent behest of Tammany Hall, Mayor George McClellan reportedly ordered that the fruits of Vachris's and Crowley's labors not be harvested. Although the city's secret service, with some help from the Italian Squad, shortly thereafter concluded a major drive against a prominent gang of Black Hand counterfeiters and extortionists, the NYPD's unusual initiative to strike a major blow against the mafiosi was effectively defused. Not until 1914, when the reform administration of Mayor John Purroy Mutchel appointed Arthur Woods as police commissioner, did the Black Hand once again need to fear the city's police enforcers.

In 1920, one of Petrosino's successors as chief of the Italian Squad, Michael Fiaschetti, embarked on a similar trip to Italy.[231] The purpose of the trip was to locate two fugitives accused of murder, to investigate the whereabouts of a backlog of other criminals who the police suspected had fled to Italy, and to identify the murderer of Petrosino. Working undercover in Rome and Naples, as well as in cooperation with the Italian police, Fiaschetti was able to penetrate the Camorra and accomplish most of his objectives. Two years later, in 1922, he was obliged to return to give testimony in the trial of one of the fugitives, who was being tried in Italy because as an Italian citizen he could not be extradited. With Mussolini's Fascists now in power, the threat from the Camorra was substantially diminished. The fugitive was convicted, and Fiaschetti was decorated by the Italian government for his work in the case.

Beyond the foreign exploits of Petrosino and Fiaschetti, the NYPD possessed one other claim to fame in the early annals of international law enforcement. Throughout the 1920s and into the 1930s, it attracted the beneficence of a wealthy businessman and police buff, Baron Collier,[232] whose particular interest was furthering the international coordi-

231. The following account is derived from the detective's autobiography; see Fiaschetti, *The Man They Couldn't Escape*, 253–284. See also Pitkin and Cordasco, *The Black Hand*, 214–215.

232. The story of Collier and the police is related more fully in Harry Söderman, *Policeman's Lot* (New York: Funk & Wagnalls, 1956), 270–271; and in Trevor Meldal-Johnsen and Vaughn Young, *The Interpol Connection: An Inquiry into the International Criminal Police Organization* (New York: Dial Press, 1979), 39–41.

nation of police efforts against crime.[233] Aided by the chief inspector of the police department and given the honorary title of Special Deputy Police Commissioner in Charge of Foreign Relations, Collier pursued his objective in a variety of forums. One of these was a group not unlike the IACP, founded in 1921, called the International Police Conference. Paying all of the expenses of its occasional conferences, Collier was able to attract police from around the world. To them he promoted the notion of a new organization, the International World Police, which would in his view supplement the efforts of the International Criminal Police Commission (ICPC, the organization later known as Interpol). He argued that his organization was necessary because neither the ICPC nor the Division of Identification in the Justice Department (formerly the IACP'S National Bureau of Identification) served as a clearinghouse for international police matters involving nonfederal police agencies. Most European police chiefs, however, felt that the ICPC was already sufficient to handle such matters. By the mid-1930s, all that remained of his grand scheme was an office on the first floor of the NYPD headquarters on Center Street with "International World Police" written on the door.[234]

Perhaps the only reason Collier's idea was given serious consideration by American police was that they considered the ICPC largely irrelevant to their needs at that time. Throughout the 1920s and 1930s, American police at both the federal and the municipal level were courted by the ICPC. The organizer of the first meeting, in 1923, invited the Washington, Chicago, and New York police departments to send delegates, but only the latter sent a representative.[235] During the following years, invitations were also sent to the Justice Department, and the United States was asked to become a full-fledged member of the organization. The federal government expressed little interest, however, responding that it had limited jurisdiction over many of the crimes that concerned the ICPC and that the United States would derive little benefit from becoming a member.[236] On occasion, the U.S. embassy in whatever country was hosting the ICPC conference would send its own delegate. In 1936, for instance, the vice-consul at the U.S. embassy in Belgrade

233. Baron Collier, "International World Police," *Journal of Criminal Law and Criminology*, Sept.–Oct. 1932.
234. Soderman, *Policeman's Lot*, 270–271.
235. Meldal-Johnsen and Young, *Interpol Connection*, 41.
236. Ibid., 44.

attended. In his report, he concluded that it "brought forth nothing that is not already known to the American police."[237] On the other hand, he argued, the ICPC helped to foster among the "chiefs of the various criminal police of the world"

> an esprit de corps in the commission and, at the same time, [enabled] them to discuss in a friendly but business like manner methods which may eventually be developed into a simple and uniform international system for combatting and controlling crime.[238]

In 1937, J. Edgar Hoover sent his assistant director, W. H. Drane Lester, as a delegate to the annual meeting being held in London. Lester's report to Hoover concluded that, although the United States would not benefit from membership as much as the Europeans, the opportunity to meet foreign counterparts and obtain information on criminals warranted joining the organization.[239] The following year, Hoover recommended to Congress that the United States become a member of the ICPC. Although the organization had already fallen under the domination of the Nazis, Congress agreed.

By the 1930s, significant transformations in the relationship between municipal police departments in the United States and both federal and foreign police agencies were already apparent. Federal police agencies had continued to gain in resources and jurisdiction, first as a result of federal enforcement of the Volstead Act, and thereafter as part and parcel of the Roosevelt administration's efforts to enhance federal involvement in most domains of governmental activity, including crime control. The rising profile of J. Edgar Hoover's FBI—with its reputation for professionalism in policing and its director's penchant for public relations—stood in stark contrast to the fading profile of big city police departments, many of which had been harshly criticized in 1931 by a national crime commission created by President Hoover and chaired by former Attorney General Wickersham.[240] On the other hand, many

237. Ibid., 48.
238. Ibid.
239. Ibid., 49–51.
240. See U.S. National Commission on Law Observance and Enforcement, *Lawlessness in Law Enforcement*, vol. 11; and Walker, *Critical History of Police Reform* (supra n. 204), 125–166.

police departments had sufficiently modernized their methods that some European police officials saw merit in studying their successes. In 1933, the chief constable of Glasgow, Percy Sillitoe, attended the IACP convention in Chicago, where he met with J. Edgar Hoover, and then set out to inspect police systems in Chicago, New York, Los Angeles, Berkeley, and Portland.[241] Impressed in particular with the NYPD's pioneering use of radio patrol cars, he brought one back to Great Britain and introduced it to British policing.

The FBN on the International Scene

The use of federal law enforcement agents to enforce federal narcotics laws dates back to before the twentieth century. Beginning in 1890, Congress levied increasingly heavy duties and restrictions on imported opium,[242] which were enforced primarily by Treasury agents assisting the Customs Service and occasionally by other agencies as well. Following two international conferences condemning the international narcotics traffic, Congress completely outlawed the over-the-counter sale of opiates and cocaine with the passage of the Harrison Narcotic Act in 1914. Drafted as a revenue law, its enforcement was delegated to a Narcotics Section in the Miscellaneous Division of the Bureau of Internal Revenue in the Treasury Department. During the 1920s, the gradually expanding narcotics enforcement unit bounced around the Treasury Department under the supervision of the Prohibition Unit. In 1930, with the death knells of Prohibition growing louder by the month, enforcement of the narcotics and alcohol laws was separated. The Bureau of Prohibition was shifted to the Justice Department, and a Federal Bureau of Narcotics (FBN) was created within the Treasury Department. There the latter remained until a major reorganization of the drug enforcement bureaucracy in 1968.

For the first thirty-two years of the FBN's existence, the agency was presided over by Commissioner Harry J. Anslinger.[243] As a Foreign

241. Sir Percy Sillitoe, *Cloak Without Dagger* (New York: Abelard-Schuman, 1955), 110; A. W. Cockerill, *Sir Percy Sillitoe* (London: W. H. Allen, 1975), 114–125. Sillitoe later served as director-general of MI5 from 1946 to 1953.

242. Millspaugh, *Crime Control* (supra n. 28), 79–80.

243. See John C. McWilliams, *The Protectors: Harry J. Anslinger and the Federal Bureau of Narcotics, 1930–1962* (Newark: University of Delaware Press, 1989).

Service officer during the 1920s, Anslinger had been assigned to the Bahamas, where he focused his efforts on stopping the smuggling of liquor into the United States. After he succeeded in persuading the British to establish landing certificates that would keep a record of all ship movements, the Treasury Department asked that Anslinger be detailed temporarily to its Prohibition Unit.[244] There he soon was appointed chief of the unit's Foreign Control Section, which had agents stationed in about ten foreign countries, before being elevated to assistant commissioner of Prohibition in 1929.[245] His successful investigation of a number of liquor smuggling cases, and his leading role in negotiating a smuggling information agreement among eighteen nations, contributed to his next promotion as head of the Prohibition Bureau's Narcotics Division.[246] When that division was legislated into a separate agency a few months later, Anslinger was appointed commissioner of narcotics. Given his background and perception of the problem, it is not surprising that Anslinger began his tenure by stressing the international dimension of the narcotics traffic. As the present Drug Enforcement Administration (DEA) noted in a history of its organization:

> Henceforth, Commissioner Anslinger announced in an order to his field forces, the federal narcotics effort would be concentrated on the sources of supply. The law that created the FBN authorized the commissioner to enforce the Harrison Act and to administer the regulatory requirements of the Narcotic Drugs Import and Export Act. . . . It also gave him authority to assign certain FBN officers at ports of entry. The main enforcement problem in his view was outside the United States, and in the years to come he would spend much of his time overseas. Meanwhile, in the absence of any adequate international instruments of control, he reached personal agreements with the heads of twenty counterpart agencies in foreign countries to exchange intelligence. As a result of the new international effort, seizures took a quantum leap

244. David F. Musto, *The American Disease: Origins of Narcotic Control* (New Haven: Yale University Press, 1973), 211.

245. The Foreign Control Division is discussed briefly in Laurence F. Schmeckebier, *The Bureau of Prohibition: Its History, Activities, and Organization* (Washington, D.C.: The Brookings Institution, 1929), 26–27, 156.

246. Douglas Clark Kinder, "Bureaucratic Cold Warrior: Harry J. Anslinger and Illicit Narcotics Traffic," *Pacific Historical Review* 50 (1981), 172–173.

from 3,440 ounces of morphine in 1929 to 26,492 ounces in 1930.[247]

On the domestic front, Anslinger concentrated his energies on lobbying for stiffer and broader penalties for drug trafficking, building up his agency and protecting it from bureaucratic opponents, and going after the Mafia. Overseas, Anslinger became a leading figure in the international conferences and agencies concerned with narcotics, as well as the leading American diplomat on drug enforcement issues.[248] He also played a pioneering role in coordinating the collection and dissemination of intelligence on international drug trafficking. In 1931, Alan Block and John McWilliams have written, Anslinger "organized a secret panel of narcotics law enforcement officers from Canada, Great Britain, Germany, Switzerland, and France that functioned as a mini-Interpol, exchanging information on the movements of alleged international dope dealers. This 'Committee of One Hundred' functioned until 1939, when war in Europe disrupted global affairs."[249]

Anslinger had few inhibitions about sending his agents abroad on investigations, although they were required to seek his approval before going. Customs agents also continued to devote some of their time and resources to the drug traffic. Therein lay the roots of the bureaucratic tangles and occasionally cooperative ventures that have marked relations between the two agencies ever since. Mexico, then as now, presented perhaps the greatest challenge to U.S. drug control efforts because it was a drug supplier, transit country, and neighbor all wrapped in one. William O. Walker, in his history of inter-American drug control before World War II, notes:

Based upon its record in the early 1930s, the government in Mexico City appeared willing to act with the United States to

247. "A Chronicle of Federal Drug Law Enforcement" (editorial), *Drug Enforcement* 7 (Dec. 1980), 26.
248. See Douglas Clark Kinder and William O. Walker III, "Stable Force in a Storm: Harry J. Anslinger and United States Narcotic Foreign Policy, 1930–1962," *Journal of American History* 72 (1986), 908–927, and three books co-authored by Harry Anslinger: with William F. Tompkins, *The Traffic in Narcotics* (New York: Funk & Wagnalls, 1953); with Will Oursler, *The Murderers* (New York: Farrar, Straus & Co., 1961); and with J. Dennis Gregory, *The Protectors* (New York: Farrar, Straus & Co., 1964).
249. Alan A. Block and John C. McWilliams, "On the Origins of American Counterintelligence: Building a Clandestine Network," *Journal of Policy History* 1 (1989), 357.

stop smuggling. In 1930 the two countries concluded an informal agreement for the exchange of information on drugs. The following year officials sent a special agent to coordinate antidrug activity with Consul William Blocker in the Juarez–El Paso region. Mexico next requested that agents of both countries be permitted unrestricted border crossings there pursuant to their duties. The State Department and Bureau of Narcotics turned down the request, although United States agents would continue to cross into Mexico with Anslinger's express approval. By mid-1932 all the Mexicans had achieved was another informal arrangement for the exchange of information.[250]

Throughout the 1930s, a combination of drug enforcement agents, Treasury agents, customs officials from border stations, and U.S. consular officials continued to collect information on the smuggling of drugs across the border. Their work often was undertaken discreetly, even covertly, with the Mexican government being kept in the dark about many of the Americans' antismuggling activities. Indeed, even the consular officials were not always notifed of the agents' comings and goings.[251] Among the most active of the Treasury agents was the assisting supervisory customs agent at San Antonio, Texas—the previously mentioned Al Scharff—who cultivated close relations with Mexican officials and with the U.S. ambassador to Mexico, Josephus Daniels, but whose aggressive style alienated State Department officials wary of criminal controversies.[252] Scharff ran undercover operatives in Mexico, conducted his own investigations across the border, and played a significant role in Mexico's first major opium eradication campaign in 1938.[253]

Throughout the late 1930s and early 1940s, a major role in drug control diplomacy was played by H. S. Creighton, first in his capacity as the chief customs agent in San Antonio, Texas, and later as the Treasury Department's special representative in Mexico City. A passage from William Walker's history, dealing with talks in early 1941 between the Treasury agent and the Mexican official in charge of drug policy, is

250. William O. Walker III, *Drug Control in the Americas* (Albuquerque: University of New Mexico Press, 1981), 81.
251. Ibid., 82.
252. Roark, *Coin of Contraband* (supra n. 24); Walker, *Drug Control in the Americas*, 119.
253. Roark, *Coin of Contraband*, esp. 328–332, 356–359, 397.

indicative of the manner in which law enforcement operations were conducted:

> During the talks Creighton sought formal approval from the Avila Camacho administration for the continued presence of United States drug agents in Mexico. All prior agreements had been informal. Creighton's translator William K. Ailshie, vice consul at Mexico City, favored formalization because of the uneven record of drug control in Mexico. "The Federal Narcotics Service in Mexico City," he said, "does not have facilities to prevent the cultivation of poppy and marijuana plants throughout the Republic or the manufacture of opium derivatives, not to mention the illegal introduction of narcotics into Mexico, chiefly from Japan." The Mexicans soon agreed to formalization, but sought an official request from Washington. Herbert S. Bursley of the State Department attached a handwritten note to the report on the talks. It read: "I think it unfortunate that this question was aired. The situation regarding our people going to Mexico was OK." The United States therefore deemed a formal accord unwise, and Mexico did not insist upon one. Washington's reluctance did not greatly offend the Mexicans, for the government named Dr. Zaragoza Cuellar Garcia, new chief of the narcotics service, as correspondent with the United States for the exchange of narcotic information. His selection reinforced the informal arrangements first made in the 1930s.
>
> Throughout the year the United States continued the practice of sending agents into Mexico to investigate smuggling and other drug-related activities. Three special agents arrived at the height of anti-narcotic efforts in the fall. Discretion was in order. As [State Department official] George Morlock commented: "I said . . . that I thought Treasury should be very careful not to overrun Mexico with its agents."[254]

The most telling dimension to Walker's account of U.S. drug control diplomacy and enforcement in Mexico and Latin America during this period is the parallels it suggests with events a half-century later. Although the scale of operations has increased somewhat, as have the

254. Walker, *Drug Control in the Americas*, 164.

formalities associated with them, much remains the same: the problems of high- and low-level corruption, the economic incentives to engage in drug production and trafficking, the impossibility of adequately policing the border, the special role played by law enforcement agents stationed along the border, and the touchiness of both foreign governments and the U.S. embassy concerning the operations of freewheeling U.S. drug enforcement agents south of the border. Mexico's role has always been a special one, given the long land border and the magnitude of its illicit drug production, but in most other respects its situation has been mirrored elsewhere in Latin America.

During the 1930s, most opiates illegally consumed in the United States were smuggled from China.[255] In Shanghai, a Treasury agent named M. R. Nicholson kept tabs on smuggling of all sorts. John Pal, a former official of the Chinese Maritime Customs who stayed in Shanghai to make his fortune, referred to the agent in his memoirs. Recounting the story of some criminal escapade, Pal concluded by noting that one of the participants

> was shortly after this rounded up by U.S. Federal agent Nicholson as an escaped convict from the United States, wanted for a felony. Little "Nicky," one of the United States Treasury's smartest operators in the Far East, stood but 5 ft. 2 in. high and was therefore no muscleman in his job. All the same he brought Nemesis to bear upon numerous currency forgers and narcotic agents in the course of his stay. His was the tip which broke up a gang operating out of Shanghai around 1937–8 described by Harry Anslinger . . . in his *Saturday Evening Post* memoirs . . . and involving several deaths.[256]

255. See William O. Walker III, *Opium and Foreign Policy: The Anglo-American Search for Order in Asia, 1912–1954* (Chapel Hill: University of North Carolina Press, 1991); and Terry M. Parssinen and Kathryn S. Meyer, *Profit and Power: A History of International Narcotic Trafficking from the Eighteenth Century to the Present* (forthcoming).

256. John Pal, *Shanghai Saga* (London: Jarrolds, 1963), 161–162. The first part of Pal's book is a vivid description of the challenges facing a customs agent in cosmopolitan Shanghai. Nicholson's reports to Washington provide much of the source material for an excellent article on the opium traffic from China by Jonathan Marshall, "Opium and the Politics of Gangsterism in Nationalist China, 1927–1945," *Bulletin of Concerned Asia Scholars* 8 (July–September 1976), 19–48. Nicholson is also mentioned in Block and McWilliams, "On the Origins of American Counterintelligence," 358; and in Roark, *Coin of Contraband*, 330.

In Europe during the first years of Anslinger's tenure, narcotics matters were handled by the Treasury agents stationed in the major cities and by occasional trips by FBN agents. In 1936, it was decided to station three FBN agents in Europe. Francis X. Dilucia was based in Rome and focused on the heroin traffic out of Italy in which deported American mafiosi played a role. Charley Dyar and Quentin Violet both operated out of Paris, with the former specializing in northern Europe and the latter handling matters in the Balkans.[257] These three agents roved around Europe. "Jacks of all trades," in the words of one of their successors, "they did undercover, . . . they would energize and pull together different investigations, . . . and they would be the link in international cooperation, which was pretty good in any case."[258] Three years later, with war breaking out in Europe, they departed. A decade later, however, a new contingent of FBN agents would follow in their footsteps.

Conclusion

The internationalization of American law enforcement during the first 150 years of the nation's existence was in many respects quite modest, compared with either the European experience or the American experience to follow. It was not, however, insignificant. Along the land borders, particularly the border with Mexico, a striking array of private and public law enforcement officials, as well as a conspicuous number of foreign agents, investigated violations of both U.S. and foreign laws. And even apart from the land borders, evidence of U.S. involvement in international law enforcement endeavors could be found. Treasury agents investigated smuggling as part of their dual mandate to enhance federal revenue collection at the border and to keep out prohibited goods, animals, and people. Private detectives, notably those of the Pinkerton Agency, were commissioned not only by private individuals, corporations, and foreign governments but also by a federal government with few criminal investigative resources of its own to track down fugitives who had fled abroad and to investigate transnational criminal

257. Telephone interview with Jack Cusack, former regional director of the FBN in Europe, May 22, 1986.
258. Ibid.

activities. As municipal police departments developed their detective branches and investigative capabilities, they became part of an evolving transnational police community with a common interest in keeping track of known criminals and assisting one another in serious law enforcement matters. Along the borders, federal, state, and local police dealt with smugglers, bandits, and all sorts of other criminals who found advantage in operating on both sides of a border. And the assorted federal law enforcement agencies each engaged in international ventures related to their particular jurisdictions: the Secret Service to track down counterfeiters, the Federal Bureau of Narcotics to investigate drug smugglers, the Bureau of Investigation to search out white slave traders, con men, and assorted violators of the neutrality laws, the Border Patrol to stem illicit migration into the United States, and the U.S. marshals to assist the courts in arresting and transporting fugitives.

In comparing the internationalization of American law enforcement to the parallel process in Europe during the same period, three differences stand out. The first and most obvious was the relative detachment from the more intensive international interactions on the continent, in particular the international police conferences and the first decades of Interpol. Apart from the leading private detective agencies, and a few of the more innovative and forward-thinking public police agencies such as the NYPD, the U.S. Secret Service, and after 1930 the Federal Bureau of Narcotics, most American police officials devoted little thought to interactions beyond American borders. The second difference was the virtual absence of any extraterritorial law enforcement efforts against political émigrés. U.S. officials confronted little in the way of nationalist movements (although both the Mexican and the American Indian resistance to the territorial expansion of the United States might be categorized as such), and their concerns with anarchists, socialists, and other revolutionaries were almost entirely confined to the home front. Moreover, unlike Britain, the United States was the target of relatively few foreign pressures regarding the many political émigrés who sought refuge within its borders. Most foreign governments regarded the distant American continent as the most innocuous of havens for its enemies; indeed, the most persistent plaints—apart from those emanating from Mexico—arose from the British, who feared transnational Fenian activism. The third difference was most apparent along the Mexican border, where U.S. officials confronted transnational criminality of a sort long since absent within Europe and where they responded with an informality and disregard for neighborly sovereignty no longer permissible across the Atlantic. In late nineteenth-century Europe, no border stretched as far as that between Mexico and the United States, no frontier region retained a comparable openness and wildness, and no transnational tribes akin to the Comanches, Lipans, Kickapoos, or Apaches remained. By comparison, the roving gypsy bands that so concerned European police officials looked relatively tame.

A student of contemporary international law enforcement would observe that although the scope and magnitude of U.S. involvement in international law enforcement have expanded greatly, the fundamental obstacles, dilemmas, and nature of that involvement have not changed all that much. The very nature of the enterprise requires that law enforcement agents of one nation either depend on the resources of their foreign counterparts or else act unilaterally with a large measure of discretion. Like private detectives, they are largely deprived of the sovereign powers that normally accrue to the police agents of a state. They must rely on their own skills at cultivating personal relationships with foreign police, developing informant networks, and running under-cover operations across or outside U.S. borders, and only occasionally on the diplomatic leverage of their government. They are rarely wel-comed by the State Department's representatives abroad, and often viewed warily by local government officials, including many law enforce-ment agents. All this was true during the early years of U.S. involvement in international law enforcement, and all of it remains true today. The accretion of dozens of extradition and other law enforcement treaties, of internal agency guidelines for operating overseas, and of sophisticated telecommunications links among national police agencies have added new dimensions to the internationalization of law enforcement, but the basics of criminal investigation across and beyond national borders have remained more or less the same.

We examine the past, of course, not only because it helps to explain why the present is the way it is, but also because it suggests the possible way of the future. By 1939, the American involvement in international law enforcement was far less dependent upon navies and armies, posses and vigilante gangs, private police and bounty hunters, and even New York's finest, than ever before. Federal police agencies had assumed most of the tasks previously undertaken by this multitude of law enforcers, while those that could not readily be assumed proved no longer neces-sary. The American involvement in international law enforcement, like that of so many other nations, had been demilitarized, professionalized, and "policizied." This evolution was a function of changes in the nature of transnational criminality, of technological progessions in transnational intercourse, and of the increasingly high levels of international civil order, most notably on the high seas and along the United States' borders. But apart from its technological dimensions, the evolution was not an irreversible one. Even as the demands on law enforcers to suppress illicit slaving and recover fugitive slaves seemed unlikely to return, no comparable assurances could be offered regarding either the stability of the Mexican border or the passing of transnational criminal organizations susceptible only to the might of military forces. Changing markets and morals, and new laws and security interests, would transform the character of international law enforcement in ways both new and familiar.

Chapter Three

The Internationalization of U.S. Law Enforcement, 1940–1992

Expansion of International Efforts

That the scope of U.S. international law enforcement activities has expanded significantly since the close of World War II should come as little surprise. Indeed, the magnitude of that expansion pales beside the growth of other U.S. government activities abroad, ranging from intelligence, military, and economic ventures to diplomacy and foreign aid programs. All of these arose in good part from two developments: (1) the U.S. government's decision not to return to a policy of relative isolationism, as it had following World War I, but rather to assume leading roles in the struggle against communism and the invigoration of the capitalist world; and (2) the proliferation of transnational nongovernmental activities—financial, industrial, legal, environmental, and otherwise—in which the U.S. government perceived a political or regulatory interest.

Even absent this new internationalist perspective, however, two other developments would have obliged U.S. law enforcement officials to expand their international efforts. The more readily anticipated was the increase in transnational criminal activity that inevitably accompanied the dramatic growth in the volume of legitimate transnational intercourse. As transnational securities transactions, banking exchanges, commercial ventures, and credit card charges all increased dramatically, so too did the number of frauds associated with them. One need only assume that the criminal proportion of overall transnational economic activity has remained constant to conclude that the overall magnitude of transnational criminal activity must have increased dramatically. Less readily anticipated, from the perspectives of the 1940s and 1950s, was the remarkable growth in the illicit traffic in cannabis, cocaine, and heroin. Related to all these developments, moreover, was a persistent expansion in the reach of both the substantive criminal law and the claims of extraterritorial jurisdiction to cover an ever broader array of undesirable activities. Much of this was driven, as before, by domestic politics, but much of it was also initiated and driven—to a far greater extent than ever before—by the advocacy efforts of federal law enforcement officials.

The leadership role of the United States in the struggle against communism resulted in four significant developments in the domain of international law enforcement. First, police were needed to provide for law and order among the hundreds of thousands of U.S. military personnel stationed around the world, as well as between them and the host country populations. The criminal investigative dimension of this need was filled by the Army's Criminal Investigative Division (CID), the Naval Investigative Service (NIS), and the Air Force's Office of Special Investigations (AFOSI)—each of which has more agents stationed overseas than the Drug Enforcement Administration, which is the civilian agency with by far the greatest global presence. Second, a police training dimension was added to U.S. foreign assistance programs, motivated in part by the perceived need to bolster anticommunist governments and suppress communist insurgencies. Third, U.S. law enforcement agencies were charged with investigating violations of new laws prohibiting the export of weapons and sophisticated technology to pro-Soviet and other unfriendly governments. And fourth, espionage activities directed against the United States needed to be investigated, not just by the intelligence agencies but—because criminal prosecution of spies is the

principal counterespionage weapon employed by democratic governments—by law enforcement agents as well.

Apart from the national security incentives, the most important factor
contributing to the internationalization of both crime and law enforcement was the growing ease of transnational interactions as a consequence of developments in technology. Increasingly rapid and accessible
jet travel permitted both criminals and police to travel easily and quickly
almost anywhere in the world. Advances in telecommunications allowed
criminals to conspire and commit crimes transnationally even as the
same advances facilitated transnational exchange of information and
coordination of joint investigations among law enforcement agents.
Computers with international hookups presented new opportunities for
criminals, both in defrauding legitimate actors and in setting up their
own operations, but they also provided police with more efficient means
of keeping track of transnational criminals, exchanging intelligence with
foreign counterparts, and creating data bases on criminals and criminal
activities. In all these respects, crime and law enforcement have been
internationalized by technological developments in much the same way
as other types of transnational commerce and governmental regulation.

Almost as significant were new laws that created new types of transnational crime. Some did so by criminalizing conduct that had not
previously been criminalized. The Export Control Act of 1949 and
subsequent legislation enhancing that act extended the reach of the
criminal law to transnational activities that previously had been legal.[1]
The crime of transnational money laundering did not exist until 1970 at
the earliest, when Congress made it illegal to take $5,000 or more in or
out of the United States without reporting that fact, and it attained
independent standing only in 1986, when Congress criminalized the act
of money laundering.[2] By 1990, enforcement of criminal laws directed
at money laundering had become a major preoccupation of U.S. international law enforcement efforts. Other laws extended the reach of U.S.
criminal jurisdiction abroad, such as by criminalizing terrorist and other
offenses and conspiracies against U.S. citizens and interests that previously had fallen outside the purview of American courts.

Many of these developments followed naturally from the nationaliza-

1. Gernot Stenger, "The Development of American Export Control Legislation After
World War II," *Wisconsin International Law Journal* 6 (1987), 1–42.
2. Ethan A. Nadelmann, "Unlaundering Dirty Money Abroad: U.S. Foreign Policy and
Financial Secrecy Jurisdictions," *Inter-American Law Review* 18 (1986), 33–82.

tion of crime and crime control within the United States. The emergence of crime as a national issue, and of crime control as a federal responsibility, are best dated to 1964, when Senator Barry Goldwater focused attention on rising crime rates during his presidential campaign, and President Lyndon Johnson reluctantly responded by placing crime control on the federal agenda.[3] Both the nationalization of the crime issue and the federalization of crime control had received their first substantial impetuses during the 1930s, when the administration of Franklin Delano Roosevelt included crime control among the array of issues on his New Deal agenda.[4] Congressional interest in racketeering provided additional impetuses in following decades.[5] But by the 1960s, the inhibitions on federal intrusions into what had traditionally been perceived as domains of state jurisdiction had faded substantially. The Johnson administration laid the initial groundwork, after which the Nixon administration entered office committed to an aggressive federal involvement in crime control and a dramatic escalation in the "war on drugs."[6] The Ford and Carter administrations brought a diminution in the rhetoric as well as revelations of legal and illegal excesses by federal police agencies. But the Reagan and Bush administrations revived the crime issue and sponsored dramatic increases both in the reach of federal criminal laws and in the resources of federal criminal justice agencies. Despite modest reservations by its more liberal members, Congress endorsed most of these initiatives and occasionally supplemented them of its own accord.

The internationalization of crime and crime control represented extensions of these developments. Having declared a "war on drugs," the Nixon administration focused substantial attention and resources on the foreign sources of the heroin, cocaine, and most of the marijuana consumed in the United States. Indeed, the international dimension was attractive both because it offered a rare domain of criminal justice activity where the federal government could predominate over state and local agencies and because it provided an inviting political target for

3. Gerald Caplan, "Reflections on the Nationalization of Crime, 1964–1968," *Law and the Social Order* (Arizona State University Law Journal), 1973, 583–635.

4. See *Proceedings of the Attorney General's Conference on Crime*, Washington, D.C., Dec. 10–13, 1934, and the articles collected under the title, "Extending Federal Powers over Crime," in *Law and Contemporary Problems* 1 (1934), 399–508.

5. Craig M. Bradley, "Racketeering and the Federalization of Crime," *American Criminal Law Review* 22 (1984), 213–266.

6. Edward Jay Epstein, *Agency of Fear: Opiates and Political Power in America* (New York: G. P. Putnam's Sons, 1977).

those who preferred not to focus too much attention on the domestic causes for increasing illicit drug use. Similar motivations could be discerned in the international extensions of the antidrug campaign during the 1980s. The rapid growth of the federal law enforcement agencies—in particular, the Bureau of Narcotics and Dangerous Drugs and the DEA—also provided the institutional bases required to sustain a substantial international presence. As these agencies expanded their activities but found their investigations frustrated by both criminal ingenuity and restrictions on their investigative powers and capacities, they proposed and lobbied for new criminal legislation to improve their powers of detection and to increase the variety of legal stumbling blocks on which criminals and their accomplices might trip. The results were laws requiring information about financial transactions to be divulged, criminalizing involvement in the laundering of illicitly derived revenues, authorizing the forfeiture of assets associated with criminal activity, and otherwise seeking to complicate and uncover criminal endeavors.

For all of the U.S. law enforcement agencies, these developments have meant increases in interactions with foreign police, international travel, international investigations, and, for many of the agencies, foreign offices. Some U.S. police agents—notably those of the DEA and the military's criminal investigative units—have become intimately involved in the more operational aspects of criminal investigation abroad, typically in collaboration with foreign police officials. They have recruited and run informants, conducted physical and electronic surveillance, employed undercover operations, supervised controlled deliveries of illicit drugs and other illegal commodities, and so on. Many federal law enforcement agencies now station representatives overseas, and all are increasingly involved in developing and cultivating closer links with foreign counterparts. The internationalization of law enforcement, I should stress, has been very much a two-way street, even if most of the traffic still carry U.S. badges.

Three Models of Transnational Policing

Most international criminal law enforcement activities are aptly characterized as "transgovernmental relations"—a notion advanced by Robert Keohane and Joseph Nye Jr. to refer to "sets of direct interactions among sub-units of different governments that are not controlled or closely guided by the policies of the cabinets or chief executives of those governments."[7] High-level officials generally pay scant attention to the international activities of law enforcement agents or prosecutors—except when those activities assume political significance, attract media attention or otherwise threaten to disrupt other dimensions of a state's foreign relations. Criminal justice officials generally view international politics as a hindrance and seek to avoid involving high-level officials except when their intervention is required to gain leverage in transgovernmental interactions. In these respects, the police and prosecutors involved in international law enforcement, most of whom work for the Justice Department, have much in common with the lower-level officials in the Departments of Agriculture, Commerce, Energy, Labor, Transportation, and the Treasury charged with handling international matters. They all work for government agencies responsible primarily for domestic matters; they all are engaged in frequent interactions with foreign counterparts employed by comparable agencies; and they all seek to establish working relationships with those counterparts based upon shared expertise and divorced to some extent from considerations of high politics. International agreements negotiated at this level typically seek to depoliticize relations in a particular issue area, to set mutually acceptable standards for cooperation, and to establish channels for communication unburdened by the tensions generated by differing political and legal systems.

Three models are particularly useful in understanding the nature of transnational policing: the private detective, the liaison, and the transnational organization. The first sheds light on the more operational aspects of extraterritorial police activity. The second explains what most agents stationed abroad do; and the last applies most aptly to the military's criminal investigative units, the police advisory programs, and the DEA. The work that private detectives perform has much in common with the investigative work of publicly employed police investigators. The principal difference is that the former are obliged to pursue their vocation without benefit of any of the arrest and other powers conferred by a police shield. U.S. law enforcement agents abroad are in much the same position—with two caveats. On the one hand, the fact that they

7. Robert Keohane and Joseph Nye Jr., "Transgovernmental Relations and International Organizations," *World Politics* 27 (1974), 43.

represent and are employed by a foreign sovereign power often presents complications that to do not hamper private detectives. These may include not just local laws specifically proscribing foreign police agents from engaging in certain activities, but also the nationalist sensitivities and antagonisms that many police officials experience when confronted with foreign, and particularly U.S., police agents on their own turf. On the other hand, U.S. law enforcement agents benefit from both the spirit of international comity that often accompanies bilateral and multilateral law enforcement efforts and from the diplomatic pressures that their embassies and their government can exert when more congenial efforts fail to produce satisfaction.

Those caveats aside, the model of the private detective offers abundant clues to the nature of the U.S. law enforcement agent's tasks abroad, over and above those associated with the lack of sovereign police powers. Like the private detective, the police agent relies both on his own powers of investigation and on his contacts within government and without. His concerns are largely pragmatic ones, focused on the task at hand and relatively unconcerned with the broader ramifications or consequences of his activities. He is not particularly interested in changing local law enforcement systems, since his principal preoccupation is accomplishing the specific task requested by his client. Portions of his work—in particular, the rougher and more invasive forms of acquiring information—straddle the edge of what is legal under local law. Faced with the somewhat contradictory demands that he perform the functions of a police officer without having the powers normally associated with those functions, he relies on discretion in both senses of the word: he is circumspect yet flexible, cautiously undertaking whatever is within "the effective limits" of his power.[8]

The second model is that of the liaison, in the dual role of formal representative and informal "fixer." Like the assorted representatives of the many non–law enforcement agencies that increasingly crowd U.S. embassies, few of whom engage in detective-like activities, U.S. law enforcement agents stationed abroad are expected to act both as official representatives of their agencies and as "fixers" for the assorted requests and problems that come their way. U.S. agents abroad often find their days crowded with fielding inquiries from U.S.-based agents, transmit-

---

8. "Effective limits" should be distinguished from the narrower notion of legal limits. The term is taken from Kenneth Culp Davis, *Discretionary Justice* (Urbana: University of Illinois Press, 1971), 4.

ting requests for information and other assistance between local police agencies and U.S.-based law enforcement agencies, serving as hosts for fellow agents flown in on specific investigations, arranging reservations and programs for visiting politicians and high-level officials, dealing with the media, giving speeches, and attending assorted social functions.

The most comprehensive model—in that it sheds light not only on the nature of the agent's tasks but also on the objectives of his agency and the ramifications of its activities—is that of the transnational organization. Samuel Huntington distinguished the "transnational organization" from "international organizations" and defined it as "a relatively large, hierarchically organized, centrally directed bureaucracy [that] performs a set of relatively limited, specialized, and, in some sense, technical functions . . . across one or more international boundaries and, insofar as it is possible, in relative disregard of those boundaries."[9] His formulation highlighted the important similarities between governmental agencies such as the Central Intelligence Agency (CIA), the Army, and (although Huntington did not note it) the DEA, on the one hand, and nongovernmental organizations such as IBM, the Catholic Church, and the Pinkerton Detective Agency, on the other. Indeed, in some respects, the international activities of the DEA, and the obstacles encountered by it, are atypical of most government agencies and far more typical of multinational corporations. Like multinational corporations, the DEA's offices abroad become to some extent a part of the society they enter and must adapt their operations to local laws and customs. But as powerfully connected outsiders with substantial resources of their own, they are also occasionally able to effect changes in local laws and oblige adaptations in local customs to suit their needs. And like businessmen everywhere, DEA agents and their foreign counterparts are part of a transnational subculture based on common functions and objectives. What making a profit is to businessmen regardless of their nationality, so catching the criminal is to cops all over the world.

Huntington's formulation is peculiarly useful for our purposes, and for reasons not explicitly stated in his analysis. In pointing out the important similarities between governmental and nongovernmental transnational organizations, he laid his finger on one of the more important innovations of modern states in responding to the challenge

9. Samuel Huntington, "Transnational Organizations in World Politics," *World Politics* 25 (1973), 333.

of an increasingly complex and multidimensional interdependent world. On the one hand, the badge and gun of the police officer, and the criminal laws he or she enforces, continue to represent the ultimate symbols of a government's sovereignty. Governments understandably place a high priority on maintaining a monopoly over these symbols. Even the most compliant of governments is unwilling to tolerate the exercise of a foreign government's police powers within its territory; concessions to the right of police from neighboring states to enter one's territory in "hot pursuit" of fleeing criminals remain, for instance, very much the exception. The presence of foreign police may be accepted, but virtually never the legal authority that underpins them in their own country. On the other hand, the experience of the DEA demonstrates that it is possible for a state agency—and not just any state agency, but one specifically charged with performing the most sovereign of a state's functions—to operate and accomplish its objectives extraterritorially despite the limitations imposed by the sovereign prerogatives of foreign states. The key to the DEA's success lies in its adoption—albeit more by chance than by calculation—of the organizational model and operating principles associated with nongovernmental transnational organizations. "Only organizations that are disinterested in sovereignty," Huntington observed, "can transcend it."[10]

The Public Safety Program and Its Successors: Training Foreign Police

The U.S. experience with extending police assistance to foreign governments dates back to the first decades of the century, when U.S. Marines occupied Caribbean and Central American nations to promote internal security and U.S. interests.[11] Before departing, the occupation authorities did their utmost to ensure that native military and police forces were properly trained and disposed to maintain stability and safeguard U.S. interests. In Cuba, the first country to receive U.S. police assistance, the U.S. Marines created, trained, and equipped a constabulary following

10. Ibid., 368.
11. See Whitney T. Perkins, *Constraint of Empire: The United States and Caribbean Interventions* (Westport, Conn.: Greenwood Press, 1981).

the 1898 occupation, and retired New York City police officers helped organize the Havana police system.[12] The U.S. War Department established additional constabularies in Haiti in 1915, the Dominican Republic in 1916, and Panama in 1918, and the State Department arranged a private contract whereby a former U.S. officer in the Philippine Constabulary was hired to organize the Nicaragua Constabulary.[13] Governments other than the United States did likewise, albeit not quite on the same scale in Latin America and the Caribbean. During the mid- and late 1930s, the State Department and U.S. law enforcement and intelligence officials, as well as the British Secret Service and the German Gestapo, assisted Latin American police in their anticommunist efforts.[14] And during the 1940s the task of directing the reorganization of the Iranian national police force fell to a former superintendent of the New Jersey State Police, H. Norman Schwarzkopf.[15]

Following World War II, the U.S. experience with training new police forces in occupied countries, such as Japan and Germany, as well as in Greece and Turkey, set the stage for the expansion of police training to other parts of the world. Initially, the promotion of police and paramilitary training fell to the CIA, the Pentagon, and the Civil Police Administration (CPA) (a branch of the Agency for International Development's predecessor, the International Cooperation Administration). Created in 1955, the CPA was headed by Byron Engle, a former police officer from Kansas City who had played a leading role in restructuring the Japanese police during the postwar occupation and then joined the CIA in 1950 to train foreign police and intelligence agencies. Engle built a force of eighty police advisors, whom he stationed around the world. Training was provided in-country, at the Inter-American Police Academy in the Panama Canal Zone, and in the United States, with the International Association of Chiefs of Police playing a role in placing foreign police officials in police departments around the United States as well as at FBI headquarters.[16] The agency focused its efforts on developing the more technical capabilities of foreign police forces in such matters as admin-

12. Martha K. Huggins, "U.S.-Supported State Terror: A History of Police Training in Latin America," *Crime and Social Justice* 27/28 (1987), 149–171.

13. Ibid., 151.

14. Ibid., 152–153.

15. Roger Cohen and Claudio Gatti, *In the Eye of the Storm: The Life of General H. Norman Schwarzkopf* (New York: Farrar, Straus & Giroux, 1991), 47–56.

16. Huggins, "U.S.-Supported State Terror," 160.

istration, record keeping, and traffic control. This was viewed as an indirect means of enhancing crime control capabilities, promoting political stability, and ensuring the conditions necessary for economic growth. It also provided a cover for many of the CIA's operatives and activities related to more political dimensions of policing.[17]

The Office of Public Safety (OPS) was created by the Kennedy administration in 1962 with the intention of centralizing all police assistance to foreign countries.[18] Housed within the Agency for International Development (AID) and headed by Byron Engle, the OPS represented an expansion of the CPA's scope and mission. During its twelve-year existence, it provided aid to police agencies in approximately fifty Third World nations, spending more than $300 million on training, weaponry, and telecommunications and other equipment.[19] Hundreds of active and retired American police officers were sent to these countries, where they trained tens of thousands of police officials in administration, riot and traffic control, interrogation, surveillance, intelligence, and assorted other tasks. Thousands of mid- and high-level police officials from those countries came to Washington to study at the OPS-run International Police Academy, which had replaced the Panama-based police school. Because Great Britain and France had undertaken similar responsibilities in their former colonies, the OPS's efforts focused on other areas, primarily Latin America but also Southeast Asia, South Korea, and Ethiopia, Liberia, and Zaire.[20] The two largest recipients of OPS assistance were South Vietnam and Thailand. In Latin America the most substantial recipient was Brazil. In fiscal year 1968, the program attained its peak strength, with a budget of $55.1 million and a total of 458 advisors in thirty-four countries.[21]

17. Thomas Lobe, *United States National Security Policy and Aid to the Thailand Police* (Denver: Graduate School of International Studies, University of Denver, 1977), 4; Thomas Lobe, "U.S. Police Assistance for the Third World" (Ph.D. diss., University of Michigan, 1975); Huggins, "U.S.-Supported State Terror."

18. U. Alexis Johnson, "The Role of Police Forces in a Changing World," *Department of State Bulletin*, Sept. 13, 1971, 280–283.

19. For an official U.S. government perspective on the OPS, see the Congressional testimony of AID administrator John Hannah in *Foreign Assistance and Related Agencies Appropriations for 1974: Hearings Before the Subcommittee on Foreign Operations and Related Agencies of the House Committee on Appropriations*, 93d Cong., 1st Sess., Part 2, 181–194 (1973).

20. Ernest Lefever, "U.S. Public Safety Assistance: An Assessment" (1973), cited in Lobe, *U.S. National Security Policy and Aid to the Thailand Police*, 6.

21. Alan K. Yu, "U.S. Assistance for Foreign Police Forces," (Washington, D.C.: Congressional Research Service, 1989), 5.

Like all U.S. programs to train foreign police, the OPS confronted numerous dilemmas. The first was the problem of providing training to police in countries whose socioeconomic systems, political cultures, and law enforcement institutions varied dramatically from those in the United States.[22] There was value in teaching foreign police specific techniques, ranging from traffic and riot control to surveillance methods and administrative measures, that could be easily transferred or adapted to foreign environments. But the capacity of American police officers to apply what they had learned in the cities and suburbs of American cities to far-reaching police reform in less-developed countries was another matter. As one OPS advisor put it:

> Cement police just weren't able to advise rice paddy cops. For instance, a whole bunch of OPS advisors originated out of Walnut Creek, California, one of San Francisco's bedroom cities. When they were suppressing crime in Walnut Creek, that meant shoplifting, traffic violations, family squabbles, petty stealing, throwing beer bottles out of speeding cars, and some Friday night mooning. Are their experiences going to help poor countries?[23]

A second problem, well described by Martha Cottam and Otwin Marenin, was the tension between the two competing models of effective policing promoted by OPS officials:

> State Department officials and OPS advisors tended to argue for a civil police force subject to law, public demands, and legally instituted political authority. Civil, democratic police forces are visible, dispersed, and accessible; their members live among the people and conduct their work in the open. They use arms and force sparingly and concentrate on maintaining order, controlling crime, and providing services.
>
> In contrast, U.S. officials working for secret and military agencies tended to argue for a paramilitary, intelligence-oriented counterinsurgency police force. Such forces tend to be concen-

22. Otwin Marenin, "United States' Aid to African Police Forces: The Experience and Impact of the Public Safety Assistance Programme," *African Affairs* 85 (1986), 509–544; Thomas Lobe, "The Rise and Demise of the Office of Public Safety," *Armed Forces and Society* 9 (1983), 187–213.

23. Cited in Lobe, *U.S. National Security Policy and Aid to the Thailand Police*, 10.

trated for easy command; they are armed, secretly or openly repressive, concerned with gathering intelligence, and subject to direct political control.[24]

Despite efforts to reconcile these two models, Cottam and Marenin observed, the paramilitary one ultimately prevailed.

A third problem was the OPS's real and perceived association with political policing in foreign countries. Much of the impetus for establishing the OPS as a separate entity had derived from the Kennedy administration's strong interest in counterinsurgency. The creation of Special Force units and more general counterinsurgency training within the military was one response. The OPS was another, reflecting the recognition that counterinsurgency efforts in many countries were conducted primarily by the police, rather than the military. Although often scorned by CIA agents abroad as just police trainers, OPS advisors in many countries developed close relationships with the CIA, provided occasional cover for intelligence operations, and pursued similar goals. Their success in accomplishing their more immediate political objectives depended in good part upon their ability to develop close relationships with local police. Wherever the host government was unpopular and/or repressive, the OPS's association with the police, who epitomized the regime's power and methods, proved harmful to their public image in both the United States and the host country.

A fourth problem, which would ultimately play a significant role in the demise of the OPS, was that of police torture.[25] Although the stated OPS policy was adamantly against such methods, although such practices were explicitly condemned in classes at the International Police Academy, and although many OPS advisors personally abhorred the use of torture, the OPS could not avoid being associated with such methods. Field telephones provided with OPS funding ended up being used to administer electric shocks during interrogations. Some OPS advisors acknowledged the impossibility of "teaching" foreign police not to resort to such methods, and some even condoned them. Reports periodically emerged of Americans thought to be OPS advisors being present at, and even conducting, interrogations involving physical torture. The bottom

24. Martha Cottam and Otwin Marenin, "Predicting the Past: Reagan Administration Assistance to Police Forces in Central America," *Justice Quarterly* 6 (1989), 598–599.
25. The information in this and the following paragraph is from A. J. Langguth, *Hidden Terrors* (New York: Pantheon Books, 1978).

line, however, was that many police agencies that had received training from OPS advisors regarded the torture of suspects as an efficient and legitimate means of interrogation. In some cases, moreover, police agencies that had not previously resorted to torture on a systematic basis began to do so at the same time that OPS officials arrived to advise them. Even where not directly implicated, the OPS was found guilty by association.

By the early 1970s, Congressional critics of the OPS were beginning to question whether the agency's political liabilities outweighed the benefits in foreign police efficiency. Senator James Abourezk in particular focused public attention on the agency's abuses and associations with police torture in the Third World. Disclosures that the CIA's Operation Phoenix in Vietnam, funded in part by OPS, had tortured and killed thousands of suspected Vietcong members, many of whom had been incarcerated in the notorious "tiger cages" at Con Son prison, proved especially damaging.[26] With no powerful constituency willing to expend political capital in its support, the OPS was gradually phased out, closing its doors in 1974. At the same time, the use of foreign assistance funds to provide overseas training, advice, or financial support for foreign police, prison, or other internal security forces was legally prohibited by Congress, although an exemption was inserted to preserve drug enforcement training programs.[27] The final blow to the OPS was delivered by the Greek movie director Costa Gavras in his 1973 movie, State of Siege. Based on the true story of the 1970 kidnapping and execution of an OPS advisor, Dan Mitrione, by the Tupamaro guerrilla organization in Uruguay, the movie dramatized and distorted the OPS advisor's involvement in political policing and torture.[28] Combining ugly truths with abundant rumors, Gavras's powerful movie contributed to the growing sentiment in Congress that the United States should avoid being tainted by too close an association with the instruments of repression in Latin America.[29]

26. See the unpublished memorandum by the Congressional Arms Control and Foreign Policy Caucus, "Police Aid to Central America: Yesterday's Lessons, Today's Choices" (1986), 4.

27. See Section 660 of the Foreign Assistance Act of 1961 (P.L. 87-195), as amended on Dec. 30, 1974.

28. See Langguth, Hidden Terrors.

29. The Public Safety Program has been the subject of extensive critical analysis by leftist research organizations, which have compiled reliable information on the abuses and irregularities that attended its efforts. See Michael T. Klare and Cynthia Aronson, Supplying Repression: U.S. Support for Authoritarian Regimes Abroad (Washington, D.C.: Institute for Policy Studies,

In 1971, a staff member of the Senate Foreign Relations Committee, Pat Holt, reported on the OPS program in one Central American country. His account provides a useful summary of the activities and dilemmas of the OPS program:

> From its beginning in 1957 through fiscal year 1971, the AID public safety program has accounted for $3,787,000 or a little more than one per cent of the total post–World War II aid to Guatemala. There are currently in Guatemala six public safety advisors.
>
> The public safety program in Guatemala has had an unusually high component of equipment. The police force in Guatemala City has been completely supplied with radio patrol cars and a radio communications net has been installed. Funds have also been provided for a National Police Academy, which is yet to be built. Other than this, the program has been mainly devoted to training—on-the-job in Guatemala, in the International Police Academy in Washington, in the Canal Zone, and in third countries (mainly Puerto Rico and Colombia).
>
> The program has obviously had an impact on the Guatemalan police—after all, the blue patrol cars are highly visible. The lesson plans for the training courses taught in Guatemala by the public safety advisors say all the right things about how to control mobs with minimum force, to respect the rights of suspects under interrogation, etc.
>
> But the police in Guatemala continue to be held in low public esteem. (I upset a university rector by arriving with a police escort—insisted on by the Embassy to insure I was not kidnapped. The rector said that the mere presence of police in the vicinity, even though the policeman was only waiting for me, made him nervous. And not without reason. A few days later, a professor of economics was kidnapped by government agents. On another day, I went to a university in a taxi by myself, and

1977; rev. ed. 1981); Center for Research on Criminal Justice, *The Iron Fist and the Velvet Glove: An Analysis of the U.S. Police* (Berkeley, Calif.: Center for Research on Criminal Justice, 1975), 87–102; Mike Klare, "Over There: Policing the Empire," in National Action/ Research on the Military-Industrial Complex (NARMIC), *Police on the Homefront* (Philadelphia: NARMIC, 1971), 104–118; and Michael McClintock, *The American Connection*, vol. 2: *State Terror and Popular Resistance in Guatemala* (London: Zed Books, 1985).

everything was perfectly peaceful.) The police are widely admitted to be corrupt (and with a take home pay of $82 a month, who is to cast the stone?) and are commonly held to be brutal.

The argument in favor of the public safety program in Guatemala is that if we don't teach the cops to be good, who will? The argument against is that after 14 years, on all the evidence, the teaching hasn't been absorbed. Furthermore, the U.S. is politically identified with police terrorism.

Related to all this is the fact that the Guatemalan police operate without any effective political or judicial restraints, and how they use the equipment and techniques which are given them through the public safety program is quite beyond U.S. control. They receive their political direction from very hard-line right-wingers who have been itching for a confrontation with students. The judiciary is intimidated—not by the police, but by the guerrillas who regularly secure the release of their comrades by threatening judges. This is one reason why the corpses of alleged guerrillas are being found on roadsides instead of the bodies of live guerrillas being produced in court.

AID public safety advisors are not supposed to participate in police operations. Yet they have accompanied Guatemalan police on anti-hippie patrols. (A reportedly good grade of marijuana grows wild in parts of Guatemala, a fact which has brought on a modest influx of long-haired North American youth and which can be expected to bring more as the word spreads.) They have also worked with Guatemalan police in polygraph operations.

On balance, it seems that AID public safety has cost the United States more in political terms than it has gained in improved Guatemalan police efficiency.[30]

Despite the demise of the OPS in 1974, many of its activities persisted under different agency umbrellas, where the advisors often found new employment. Some activities were simply transferred to other divisions of the AID. In 1973, Congress authorized the Law Enforcement Assistance Administration, established in 1968 to assist in state and local law enforcement development, to provide technical assistance to foreign

30. *Guatemala and the Dominican Republic: A Staff Memorandum Prepared for the Use of the Subcommittee on Western Hemisphere Affairs of the Senate Committee on Foreign Relations,* 92d Cong., 1st Sess. (1971).

governments in the areas of drug enforcement, skyjacking, and terrorism.[31] More foreign police were invited to attend training sessions at the FBI Academy in Quantico, Virginia. The State Department's international drug control program, which had grown rapidly during the early 1970s, provided a global umbrella for any activities that could be linked to drug enforcement. Quite a number of Public Safety advisors found positions with the State Department's narcotics assistance units in the major drug-producing countries.[32]

The principal successor to the OPS program was the federal drug enforcement agency, which was undergoing a dramatic international expansion (and bureaucratic reorganization) at the same time that the OPS was winding down its activities. As the number of U.S. drug enforcement agents stationed abroad rose from about 24 in 1969 to more than 200 in 1975, a number of OPS officers merely switched organizations. With their foreign experience and extensive contacts among local police forces, they were ideally placed to facilitate the drug enforcement agency's rapid international expansion. Although their mandate was now restricted to drug matters, they no longer operated under the restraints imposed by the OPS program. Indeed, they were expected to become directly involved in local drug enforcement investigations to a greater extent than they had in their capacity as OPS advisors. During the same six-year period, the number of foreign police officials trained by the DEA (but paid for by the State Department's narcotics assistance program) in both U.S. and in-country schools rose from zero to more than 2,000 a year before declining somewhat in the latter half of the 1970s.[33] Substantial numbers also received training from the U.S. Customs Service. Where once U.S. police assistance had focused on developing police capabilities in general and counterinsurgency capabilities in particular, it now focused almost entirely on drug enforcement agencies and tasks. A foreign police agency interested in

31. See Section 515(c) of the Crime Control Act of 1973, cited by an LEAA official in *Departments of State, Justice, Commerce, the Judiciary, and Related Agencies Appropriations for 1975: Hearings Before a Subcommittee of the House Committee on Appropriations*, 93d Cong., 2d Sess., Part 1 (1974).

32. See Comptroller General of the United States, *Stopping U.S. Assistance to Foreign Police and Prisons*, General Accounting Office Report to the Congress, Feb. 19, 1976, 20–27.

33. See *Departments of State, Justice, Commerce, the Judiciary, and Related Agencies Appropriations for 1977: Hearings Before a Subcommittee of the House Committee on Appropriations*, 94th Cong., 2d Sess., Part 4 (1976), 1073.

obtaining U.S. training and funds for equipment had little chance of success if it could not establish some connection with drug enforcement.

Beginning in 1983, the Reagan administration began urging Congress to permit the renewal of OPS-type training programs. In testimony before a Congressional subcommittee investigating torture, the assistant secretary of state for human rights and humanitarian affairs, Elliott Abrams, called for changes in Section 660, the 1974 amendment to the Foreign Assistance Act that had banned foreign police assistance. As had OPS advocates one and two decades previously, he argued:

> There are still a large number of police forces in the world where they simply don't understand that they can effectively do their work without indiscriminate violence and brutality. Perhaps if they learned a little bit more about modern professional police tactics, they would be more effective and more compassionate.[34]

Increasingly concerned about the activities of right-wing and left-wing death squads in Central America, Congress responded to the administration's appeals by authorizing a number of partial waivers to Section 660.[35] The first, in late 1983, authorized the creation of the Anti-Terrorism Assistance Program, coordinated by the State Department's Office of Counterterrorism Programs, to train foreign police (albeit only in the United States) in protecting aviation and other transportation systems, strategic installations, and VIPs from terrorist attacks, in managing bombs and explosives, and in responding to hostage and other crisis situations;[36] the budget for this program rose from $2.5 million in its first year to $10 million in fiscal year 1990. A second waiver, in 1984, authorized the International Criminal Investigative Training Assistance Program (ICITAP) as part of the State Department's Administration of Justice Program directed at instituting judicial reform projects in Latin America and the Caribbean.[37] In August 1985, two additional waivers were enacted: one to allow the Defense Department to provide military

34. Congressional testimony of Elliott Abrams, May 16, 1984, cited in an article critical of renewed police training by Holly Burkhalter and Alita Paine, "Our Overseas Cops," *The Nation*, Sept. 14, 1985, 197.

35. The information in this paragraph is from Yu, "U.S. Assistance for Foreign Police Forces"(supra n. 21).

36. Foreign Assistance Act of 1961, Part II, Chapter 8, Sections 571–576, codified at Section 572 of the act.

37. Ibid., Section 534.

training to national police programs in Costa Rica and a number of Eastern Caribbean nations, most of which claim no standing military forces;[38] and another, stimulated by the June 1985 guerrilla attack on an outdoor café in San Salvador that killed four off-duty U.S. Marines and nine others, to provide emergency police assistance to El Salvador and Honduras.[39]

The assistance to El Salvador, which also included a specific allotment to train a special police unit to investigate human rights cases, quickly drew most of the attention from human rights organizations, Congressional critics, and the media.[40] Many of the responsibilities previously undertaken by the OPS were assumed by the FBI. A selected group of Salvadoran police recruits were invited to attend an intensive criminal investigative training program by the FBI in Puerto Rico. Upon returning to El Salvador, they were assigned to investigate human rights abuses, including the June 1985 attack on the café.[41] The FBI also trained a police unit to provide protection for judges and witnesses in politically sensitive trials.[42] By 1989, the cumulative efforts of the FBI, the AID, the U.S. military, and the State Department had resulted in the creation of an El Salvador Commission on Investigations specifically to investigate politically motivated and other serious crimes, and a well-trained Special Investigative Unit (SIU) and forensic laboratory to conduct the investigations. A report on the Salvadoran investigative unit by the U.S. General Accounting Office in mid-1990 concluded that it had succeeded, despite substantial political interference, in "building a reputation as an impar-

38. Ibid., Section 660(c).

39. Ibid., Section 660(d).

40. Lindsey Gruson, "Salvador Divided over Aid to Police," *New York Times*, Oct. 22, 1987, A11. A fine historical and critical analysis of U.S. police assistance to El Salvador, which also addresses most of the broader issues raised by the OPS and the successor programs, is Stephanie Nichols Simonds, "United States Aid to Central American Police—A Policy Analysis: The Case of El Salvador, 1957–1988" (senior thesis, Princeton University, 1988). See also the report by Jim Lobe, Anne Manuel, and David Holliday, "Police Aid and Political Will: U.S. Policy in El Salvador and Honduras, 1962–1987" (Washington, D.C.: Washington Office on Latin America, Nov. 1987).

41. James LeMoyne, "Duarte Meets FBI on Raid Inquiry," *New York Times*, June 27, 1985.

42. These and other developments in U.S. police and judicial assistance to Latin America are discussed in a brief report by the Bureau of Public Affairs, U.S. State Department, *Hemispheric Cooperation in the Administration of Justice*, Special Report No. 145, Apr. 1986; and in an unpublished memorandum by the Congressional Arms Control and Foreign Policy Caucus, "Police Aid to Central America," which argued against a renewal of police training until *after* the "rule of law" has been established in Central America.

tial, professional, investigative unit"—albeit one that devoted less attention to human rights cases than was initally intended.[43]

Whether the police training programs in place by the early 1990s
evolve into a program comparable to the OPS will depend as much upon
the political climate as upon their capacity to avoid the pitfalls that
contributed to the demise of the OPS. The OPS failed in part because it
never successfully separated itself from the brutal techniques used by the
foreign police with which its advisors were associated. In this respect,
the emphasis placed in the mid-1980s on training foreign police to
investigate human rights abuses and right-wing death squads provided
somewhat of an antidote to memories of the OPS's bad associations.
Equally important, however, was the significant change in the American
political climate regarding foreign policy. In the early 1970s, the growing
criticism of the OPS program reflected the strong desire to cleanse
American hands of any identification with oppression overseas—one
that contributed to the popular sentiment for withdrawing from Southeast Asia, to the emergence of human rights as a substantive foreign
policy concern, and even to such low-profile measures as the 1974
"Mansfield Amendment" restricting DEA involvement in foreign police
operations. Ultimately, a few too many reports of OPS advisors attending brutal interrogations obscured the fact that the vast majority of OPS
advisors had avoided such situations and often opposed the use of
torture. But the few accurate reports of such OPS improprieties, combined with a high degree of sensitivity to foreign misperceptions of the
OPS, were sufficient in the political climate of the early 1970s to seal the
agency's fate. During the 1980s, by contrast, the Reagan administration
proved itself far more willing, and politically able, to dirty its hands
abroad in support of U.S. foreign policy objectives regardless of the
appearance created by such activities.

One of the paradoxes of foreign police training programs such as the
OPS or the FBI's initiatives is that they are highly susceptible to public
criticism precisely because they are the least secretive of such undertakings. Both the CIA and the U.S. military, for instance, have been involved
in training foreign counterterrorist units in Central America. As the
New York Times correspondent in El Salvador noted in mid-1985, these
activities are far more suspect than the FBI's Central American efforts:

43. U.S. General Accounting Office, *Foreign Aid: Efforts to Improve the Judicial System
in El Salvador*, GAO/NSIAD-90-81, May 1990.

American military advisors have also trained a special police antiterrorist team to be used in urban areas, according to a spokesman for the United States Embassy here. The spokesman said the training was legal because the antiterrorist unit, although drawn from the ranks of the police forces, had been placed under the direct command of the Chief of Staff of the army and was therefore a military unit, rather than a police unit.

The distinction appears somewhat dubious, since army officers command all police units here and since each police force also has battalions that are indistinguishable from regular army units and in fact are deployed in sweeps against rebel forces as part of army operations.

A great deal of confusion appears to surround the new American-trained antiterrorist unit. Both Salvadoran and American officials have refused to specify who belongs to the unit, how they were selected, how they were trained and where the unit is stationed.

. . . It is believed that the unit was used to break up a strike by public hospital workers three weeks ago. Although the unit is supposedly under the control of the army Chief of Staff, [President] Duarte said it was actually commanded in the operation by Col. Lopez Nuila, who is in charge of all police forces.

In their first foray during the hospital strike, the antiterrorist specialists mistakenly killed four plainclothes policemen who had infiltrated inside the hospital. They also tied up most of the strikers and left them lying on the floor. . . .

Mr. Duarte said today that he would create special antiterrorist units in all three police forces. One of the units was sworn in today at the Treasury police, a partially reorganized force that was once notorious for torturing and killing civilians.

The new commander of the Treasury police, Col. Rinaldo Golcher, said in an interview last year that he had stopped the killing by disbanding the unit's intelligence squad. He said at that time that the Treasury police would be used only for guarding the borders to stop smugglers. Today, however, Colonel Golcher said the unit was an essential part of the struggle against Marxist terrorists.[44]

44. LeMoyne, "Duarte Meets FBI on Raid Inquiry."

The basic dilemma of U.S. police assistance programs is to some extent a subset of the broader dilemma of incorporating human rights objectives into the conduct of U.S. foreign policy. The U.S. government has repeatedly demonstrated its influence in persuading foreign governments to pursue particular criminal investigations or to release particular individuals from prison. But it has proved much less effective in changing the ways foreign political and police systems conduct their affairs, apart from a few exceptions where it has intervened directly or expended substantial political and financial resources. It was thus hardly surprising that by the late 1980s many of the Central American police officials accused of torturing and killing political dissidents and participating in death squad activities were alumni of the U.S. training programs.[45] By and large, U.S. officials have had little choice but to work with and within existing foreign systems in pursuing objectives that involve internal changes in those systems. The dilemma they now face is the same one their predecessors faced in the 1950s and 1960s: whether the benefits to be gained from training foreign police justify the political and moral costs of "dirtying their hands" in the process.

The Military Investigative Divisions: Policing U.S. Soldiers Abroad

During the American Revolution, the War of 1812, and the Civil War, a provost corps, or military police, was created to maintain order among the American troops and then disbanded at the war's end. Given the development of civilian law enforcement at those times, it is not surprising that these military police forces did not include anything resembling a detective division. Only in late 1918, as the U.S. military faced the prospect of occupying large portions of Europe for a few years, did the need for such a force become apparent. Formally established shortly after the Armistice, the Army's Criminal Investigative Division (CID) in Europe soon totaled 67 officers and 767 agents. Within a few years, however, the occupation had ended, the Army had demobilized, and the CID was virtually disbanded. Two decades later, the CID once again expanded dramatically to meet the military policing needs of World War

45. Cottam and Marenin, "Predicting the Past" (supra n. 24), 607–616.

II. With the end of that war, however, the CID remained in place to police the U.S. troops left in allied and defeated nations alike. By the late 1980s, more than 1,000 special agents of the CID were stationed around the world to handle criminal matters involving U.S. troops.[46] Their jurisdiction covered the gamut of conceivable crimes, including murder and rape, illicit trafficking in arms, drugs, and stolen goods, terrorist activities, espionage, counterfeiting, and frauds of every sort.

By and large, the greater the U.S. military presence in a country, the more active the CID's involvement. In Vietnam, for instance, hundreds of CID agents worked a tremendous variety of criminal cases. The principal responsibility for investigating drug trafficking to and by U.S. soldiers, for instance, fell to them, although the civilian drug enforcement agency also had agents stationed there. The military police were largely responsible for cracking down on drug use by soldiers and on small-scale dealing. CID agents, however, investigated the more serious trafficking, some of it involving deals between American soldiers and powerful Vietnamese criminals. They ran undercover operations, conducted electronic surveillance, ran informants, made drug purchases, and so on. Some even were killed in the process.

The CID also has retained an important role in law enforcement in Germany and Japan, in part because of the special relationships that developed with local law enforcement agencies during the postwar occupation. When civilian U.S. drug enforcement agents began opening offices around Germany in the early 1970s, the biggest problem they encountered, in the view of one of the agents, was a turf conflict with the resident CID agents, known as Detachment A, who maintained close and long-standing relations with the German police. The turf problem arose in part from the fact that the CID agents were not confining their investigations to cases with a strong connection to the U.S. military presence but were also conducting joint operations with the local police against civilian criminals and even occasional unilateral operations. They also, recalled one DEA agent with some envy, were

> doing everything that DEA did and more. . . . They were very good. They did undercover work, including some deep undercover, . . . which DEA almost never does. . . . They had more

46. Miriam Ottenberg, *The Federal Investigators* (Englewood Cliffs, N.J.: Prentice-Hall, 1982), 48–94; Joel L. Leson, "The Fight Against Drugs in Europe," *Narc Officer* 7 (Mar. 1991), 39.

> money than DEA and more authority than DEA agents, . . . for
> instance to pay large sums of money to informants. They never
> wore uniforms and rarely reported to anyone or showed up on
> base. . . . They had safe houses around Germany and ran their
> informants out of them. . . . And they travelled all around Europe,
> to Lebanon and so on.

Eventually, the DEA's regional director in Europe, Jack Cusack, and the
CID's provost-general worked out an agreement that partially resolved
the turf conflict. In the early 1980s, however, when the DEA started
closing some of the offices it had opened a decade earlier, the CID once
again stepped in to fill the void.

The criminal investigative branches of the Navy and the Air Force have
conducted themselves overseas in much the same fashion as the Army's
CID. Like the FBI but unlike the Army's CID, the Naval Investigative
Service (NIS) and the Air Force Office of Special Investigation (AFOSI)
have handled not just criminal matters but counterespionage tasks as
well. (In the Army the military intelligence division is responsible for
counterintelligence tasks.) Until 1966, the Navy's criminal investigative
needs were handled by the Office of Naval Intelligence (ONI). Created
in 1882, the ONI expanded during wartime to handle security threats to
naval installations and espionage in general.[47] Not until after World War
II did the ONI take on responsibility for investigating crimes involving
naval personnel. A bureaucratic reorganization in 1966 shifted that
responsibility to a newly created agency, the NIS. Most of its agents,
unlike those of the CID and the AFOSI, have been civilians, stationed
not only within the United States and in U.S. bases abroad but also on
U.S. aircraft carriers.[48]

The youngest of the military's criminal investigative divisions, the Air
Force Office of Special Investigation dates its origins to 1948, when a
Congressional investigation into procurement fraud led to the creation
of a centralized criminal investigative division under the inspector general.[49] Its first two directors were recruited from the FBI, and the agency

---

47. See the two books by Jeffery M. Dorwart: *The Office of Naval Intelligence: The Birth
of America's First Intelligence Agency, 1865–1918* (Annapolis: Naval Institute Press, 1979),
and *Conflict of Duty: The U.S. Navy's Intelligence Dilemma, 1919–1945* (Annapolis: Naval
Institute Press, 1983).

48. Blair M. Gluba, "Law Enforcement at Sea," *Police Chief* 55 (Nov. 1988), 85–86.

49. The story of the AFOSI's origins is told in two brief unpublished (and updated) papers
provided to me by the official AFOSI historian, Edward C. Mishler, in 1987. One was written

initially modeled itself after that agency.[50] As its responsibilities evolved, slightly less than half of its efforts were devoted to varied criminal investigations against Air Force personnel and property, with the other half split between fraud investigations and counterintelligence activities directed at espionage, sabotage, and terrorism. Like the CID, both the NIS and the AFOSI operate worldwide, although most extensively in countries, such as the Philippines, that have hosted large Navy and Air Force bases. All three military detective agencies have developed close relationships with local police forces in host countries and with civilian U.S. law enforcement agencies—notably the DEA and Customs vis-à-vis drug trafficking, and the FBI and the CIA on terrorism and espionage—although relations have also been strained by turf struggles, personality conflicts, and nationalist sensitivities. Their agents have operated abroad in much the same style as U.S. drug enforcement agents, developing their own cases, conducting undercover operations and electronic surveillance, and recruiting and paying informants. However, unlike their civilian counterparts, who have no sovereign police powers when they are outside the United States, the military detectives have benefited from their sovereign authority at least within the confines of U.S. military bases.

The announcement of awards presented each year by the International Narcotic Enforcement Officers Association provides a revealing glimpse into the more successful overseas exploits of CID, AFOSI, and NIS agents.[51] In 1990, three of the seven Army covert drug agents based in Germany were recognized for their work with different state police agencies and the German customs unit. One was praised as "a fully operational member" of a German state drug enforcement unit, and another was described as "one of two [CID] agents to be sworn as a police officer by the German government in recognition of his activity in covert operations and testimony in foreign courts." The U.S. agents investigated not only drug trafficking but also terrorist activities, counterfeiting, and transnational arms smuggling. The new deputy com-

by his predecessor, Captain Kurt K. Kunze, and entitled "The Genesis of AFOSI." The other, with no author noted, is entitled "Brief History of the Air Force Office of Special Investigations."

50. "U.S. Air Force Office of Special Investigations," and Celeste Morga, "Exclusive Interview with Brigadier General Francis R. Dillon, Commander OSI," in *Narc Officer* 4 (Nov. 1988), 13, 15, 22, 23, 25.

51. "INEOA Names 1990 Award Recipients," *Narc Officer* 6 (Sept. 1990), 60–63.

mander for operations of the AFOSI's largest detachment—at Ramstein Air Base in Germany—was praised for having revitalized a "lethargic drug suppression team." In fifteen months he supervised the drug enforcement unit's production of more than 180 convictions in German and U.S. military courts-martial, directed "the first-ever undercover drug operation at a sensitive NATO command and control center," and coordinated joint operations with the CID involving the sharing of information, informants, funds, and undercover personnel. Another AFOSI agent, stationed in the Philippines, was recognized for the success of numerous ventures with Japanese police and the Philippines drug enforcement agency, one of which involved a subordinate AFOSI agent posing undercover as a member of the Yakuza. He also was credited for his involvement, together with NIS agents, in assisting the Philippines police in their marijuana eradication campaign. Two CID agents based in Panama were also recognized for their work—one as coordinator, the other as undercover operative—in infiltrating and collecting evidence on a cocaine smuggling ring involving Colombians, Panamanians, and U.S. military personnel.

Among all the U.S. law enforcement agencies, only the military agencies appeared poised for a significant contraction in their international presence and activities during the 1990s. The principal reason was the planned withdrawal of U.S. military forces from overseas posts as the Cold War ended, as the two large U.S. bases in the Philippines readied for closure in the wake of volcanic activity and a diplomatic impasse, and as public and Congressional sentiment in the United States appeared to favor a reduction in the military's budget. The relatively brief attention devoted here to the military's international law enforcement activities should be seen as a reflection both of the little that has been published about their activities and of my own decision to focus my research resources on the international activities of the civilian agencies—not as an indication of their relative significance in the annals of transnational policing. In contrast to all the civilian U.S. law enforcement agencies, the military agencies can rightfully claim to have mounted the most substantial presence abroad, to have investigated the greatest number of crimes, and to have worked most intimately with foreign law enforcement agencies. Much of the analysis that follows is equally applicable to the military agencies, but a more substantial analysis of their international activities is certainly warranted.

The FBN Abroad:
Anslinger's "Briefcase Agents"

In its overseas capacity, the U.S. Drug Enforcement Administration plays a unique role in international politics. As a transnational organization, it is a hybrid of a national police agency and an international law enforcement organization. It represents the interests of one nation and its agents abroad are responsible to the ambassador, yet it has a mandate and a mission effectively authorized by international conventions and the United Nations. Like most agencies with representatives in U.S. embassies abroad, its principal role is one of liaison. But unlike virtually all other agencies except the CIA and the military's investigative divisions, its agents are "operational" in most of the countries where they are stationed—they cultivate and pay informants, conduct undercover operations, and become directly involved in the activities of their local counterparts. The DEA's principal objective, broadly stated, is to stem the flow of drugs to the United States, yet it has devoted considerable efforts to assisting foreign law enforcement agencies in countering drug trafficking that has little or no impact on the United States.

To pick up where I left off at the end of the previous chapter, the flow of narcotics from Europe and Asia to the United States came to a virtual halt during World War II as smuggling routes were dramatically disrupted by military hostilities. Iran, Mexico, and India replaced China, Yugoslavia, and Italy as the principal sources of illicit opiates, albeit on a much smaller scale.[52] Moreover, with the occupation of Japan and the territories it had previously occupied in Asia by British, Dutch, and U.S. troops, the government opium-smoking monopolies that had existed were liquidated by the returning colonial powers at the urging of U.S. officials.[53] This move temporarily prolonged the disruption of supplies initiated by the war. Working out of Japan, five FBN agents attached to General Douglas MacArthur's staff worked to dismantle the monopolies

52. FBN, *Traffic in Opium and Other Dangerous Drugs for the Year Ended December 31, 1943* (Washington, D.C.: Government Printing Office, 1944), 18–21.
53. See the report on the November 1943 conference convened in Washington to decide the future of opium policy in ibid., 1–3; Alfred R. Lindesmith, *The Addict and the Law* (Bloomington: Indiana University Press, 1965), 199–221; Arnold H. Taylor, *American Diplomacy and the Narcotics Traffic, 1900–1939: A Study in International Humanitarian Reform* (Durham, N.C.: Duke University Press, 1969), 279–280; and William O. Walker III, *Opium and Foreign Policy: The Anglo-American Search for Order in Asia, 1912–1954* (Chapel Hill: University of North Carolina Press, 1991), 153–158.

in Japan, Korea, and other Asian nations,[54] and another FBN agent was sent to occupied Germany to assist in reestablishing the drug control system.[55] There and elsewhere, their efforts were supplemented and aided by the criminal investigative branches attached to U.S. military forces around the world.

As affairs in Europe gradually settled down in the aftermath of the war, FBN Commissioner Harry Anslinger considered stationing his agents abroad once again.[56] In 1948, district supervisor Garland Williams was sent to Europe on a four-month exploratory survey trip. The following year, another district supervisor (and former agent of the Office of Strategic Services), George White, conducted a similar tour, albeit with a more operational dimension. In France, Italy, Germany, Turkey, Iran, and elsewhere, Williams and White made contact with local police, followed up leads developed in the United States, and conducted law enforcement operations in cooperation with local counterparts. In July 1950, a third agent, Charles Siragusa, who had worked under Williams and White in New York in the early 1940s and also served in the OSS, was sent to Europe for three months to pursue assorted leads. After visiting Istanbul, Beirut, and Athens, Siragusa rendezvoused in Rome with another agent, Benedict Pocoroba, who had been working on a specific case involving a deported American gangster, and with Henry Manfredi, an Army CID agent stationed in Trieste but with responsibility for Italy. Working with Italian and Yugoslavian police, the three succeeded in arresting a number of drug traffickers. After a winter visit to Washington, Siragusa returned to Europe for another brief tour, accompanied by agents Joe Amato and Martin Pera. Working both together and separately—with Amato covering Germany, Pera covering Turkey, and Siragusa covering Italy—the agents traveled widely, developing informants, making contacts with local police, conducting undercover operations, pursuing leads developed by agents in the United States, and so on.

54. "A Chronicle of Federal Drug Law Enforcement" (editorial), *Drug Enforcement* 7 (Dec. 1980), 37.

55. FBN, *Traffic in Opium and Other Dangerous Drugs for the Year Ended December 31, 1945* (Washington, D.C.: Government Printing Office, 1946), 4.

56. The following paragraphs are based on Charles Siragusa (as told to Robert Wiedrich), *The Trail of the Poppy* (Englewood Cliffs, N.J.: Prentice-Hall, 1966); Andrew Tully, *Treasury Agent: The Inside Story* (New York: Simon & Schuster, 1958), 104–111; Frederic Sondern Jr., *Brotherhood of Evil: The Mafia* (New York: Farrar, Straus & Cudahy, 1959), 123–166; and interviews with John Cusack, Oct. 23, 1984, and May 22, 1986.

By September 1951, Anslinger had obtained the consent of both the State Department and the Italian government to open a permanent FBN branch office in Rome. Siragusa, having served briefly as chief investigator for the Senate Rackets Committee in the interim, thus began his eight-year stint as chief of FBN operations in Europe. A few months later, he was joined by Jack Cusack, an experienced agent who would later rise to the highest levels of the DEA. In late 1952, agent Paul Knight joined them in Rome. Two years later, he opened a second FBN office—in Beirut. The three agents, joined from time to time by agents from the United States on temporary assignment in Europe, covered all of the continent as well as the Middle East. Eight years later, as Siragusa returned to the United States, the FBN's presence in Europe had barely expanded—to six agents all told.

Throughout the 1950s, FBN agents continued to operate elsewhere as well, albeit without the benefit of resident offices. They also worked together and competitively with the small number of U.S. customs agents stationed in foreign cities from Antwerp to Japan.[57] As before the war, drug trafficking activities in Mexico and Canada were dealt with by agents stationed along the borders who crossed over to conduct operations with Mexican and Canadian police and occasionally to operate and collect intelligence covertly on their own.[58] Where a case needed to be pursued or investigated overseas, Anslinger sent either the agent already working on the case or delegated one of his senior agents. George White, for instance, upon whom Anslinger relied to conduct many of the more difficult and sensitive foreign operations, worked not just in Europe but also Mexico, Canada, India, Iran, Iraq, Turkey, Ecuador, Peru, and Cuba.[59] Because the FBN agents already stationed in Europe were among the best, as well as experienced in operating outside U.S. borders, they also were charged with conducting investigations elsewhere.

In 1960, the FBN began the first of its two waves of expansion. With Jack Cusack now in charge of European operations, agent Andrew Tartaglino was delegated to open a Paris office, and Sal Vizzini began operations in Istanbul. In 1961, Anthony Pohl opened an office in

57. See Don Whitehead, *Border Guard: The Story of the United States Customs Service* (New York: McGraw-Hill, 1963).

58. Tully, *Treasury Agent*, 183–187.

59. Derek Agnew, *Undercover Agent—Narcotics* (London: Souvenir Press, 1959), 112–124.

Marseilles and Cusack participated in a global survey mission by the Treasury Department to consider where other Treasury agents should be stationed. In late 1962 and early 1963, FBN agents set up shop in Bangkok, Mexico City, and Monterrey, with the office in the former handling all of Asia and that in the Mexican capital handling all of Latin America. During the next few years, other offices were opened in Hong Kong, Singapore, Korea, and Manila. Fortunately for historians of this subject, the overseas exploits of these agents have been recounted in the autobiographies of FBN agents Siragusa and Vizzini[60] and in the celebratory accounts of FBN operations by such writers as Frederic Sondern, Derek Agnew, and Alvin Moscow.[61] To be sure, one must read these books with a certain amount of skepticism, given the literary license taken by all of the authors and their tendency to focus on incidents that reflected best on the agency. And Siragusa and Vizzini were rather unique characters, selected for their positions because they were especially adept at the skills required of an overseas narcotics agent. Yet amid all the bravado and semi-fictional dialogue, one can discern basic features of the FBN's activities abroad.

During the early years of the FBN overseas, Siragusa and the agents who reported to him operated with relatively few legal or organizational guidelines. This posed both advantages and disadvantages. On the one hand, U.S. embassies were unaccustomed to housing and assuming responsibility for gun-toting law enforcement agents who might end up shooting someone. Similarly, foreign governments often had legal and political objections to foreign law enforcement authorities operating within their borders. And foreign police could be quite sensitive about foreign counterparts presuming to tell them how to go about their business. Yet because the FBN presence abroad represented a rather new phenomenon, its agents also benefited from a lack of restrictions. With so few agents abroad, the FBN had little need to develop the detailed manuals that officially establish the constraints on DEA activities abroad today. U.S. law presented few restraints on the FBN's foreign activities. And most foreign governments had yet to establish any policies determining what such agents could or could not do. By and large, the FBN

    60. Siragusa, *Trail of the Poppy*; Sal Vizzini (with Oscar Fraley and Marshall Smith), *Vizzini: The Secret Lives of America's Most Successful Undercover Agent* (New York: Arbor House, 1972).
    61. Sondern, *Brotherhood of Evil*; Alvin Moscow, *The Merchants of Heroin* (New York: Dial Press, 1968); Agnew, *Undercover Agent*.

agents were obliged, and allowed, to work out their own methods of operating abroad.

During his eight years in Europe, Siragusa worked in twenty-nine countries.[62] Although based in Rome, his office was, in his own words, "mostly headquartered in my briefcase"[63]—or, as John Cusack put it, they were "briefcase agents."[64] Constantly on the go, they maintained contact with high-level police officials throughout Europe and the Middle East, developed informants, pressured local police and their governments to do more against drug trafficking, conducted operations both unilaterally and in league with local police, pursued leads from U.S.-based investigations, and generally performed whatever services they were called upon to provide. Siragusa, describing an undercover operation in Turkey, noted some of the features and limitations of their operations:

> In 1955 there were still only three of us assigned to Europe and the Middle East. We . . . functioned somewhat as roving ambassadors of the Federal Bureau of Narcotics. For the most part we kept in touch with a few good informers we had in Turkey by long-distance telephone, cable and the mails. As often as possible, one of us flew to Turkey to make personal contacts. We were spread thin.[65]

Even in the early 1960s, with offices in only four or five cities, the agents continued to travel extensively. Vizzini, although stationed in Istanbul, conducted investigations in Italy, France, Lebanon, Thailand, and elsewhere. As the number of offices proliferated, the need to constantly be on the road declined. Agents still continued to travel, however, not only to coordinate activities with U.S. drug agents in other countries but also to conduct the undercover aspects of investigations in other countries.

One feature of international police work that both Siragusa and Vizzini stressed in their memoirs was the receptiveness of foreign police to working together with the FBN. This, they noted, was in contrast to the attitudes of higher-level political officials. American drug agents

62. Siragusa, *Trail of the Poppy*, 169, 219.
63. Ibid., 4.
64. Interview with John Cusack, Oct. 23, 1984.
65. Siragusa, *Trail of the Poppy*, 144.

tapped into the transnational police subculture that had been developing for nearly a century. When this proved to be insufficient to overcome hostile or suspicious sentiments among political officials, FBN agents took advantage of American diplomatic power. As Siragusa noted:

> The police overseas almost always worked willingly with us. It was their superiors in the government who were sometimes unhappy that we had entered their countries. Most of the time, though, I found that a casual mention of the possibility of shutting off our foreign-aid programs, dropped in the proper quarters, brought grudging permission for our operations almost immediately.[66]

During the 1950s and 1960s, Interpol was especially valuable to FBN activities in Europe in a number of ways. Hoover had withdrawn the FBI from Interpol in 1950 when the Czechoslovakian government used the Interpol network to circulate wanted notices for political refugees.[67] Soon thereafter, the Treasury Department's law enforcement agencies—the FBN, the Secret Service, and Customs—stepped into the empty American shoes at Interpol. In 1951, Malachi Harney, assistant commissioner of the FBN, attended Interpol's annual meeting in Lisbon as an "unofficial observer" and served on the subcommittee on drugs.[68] Siragusa became a regular participant at the annual General Assembly meetings, which were attended by other Treasury representatives as well. Annual dues were also paid. In 1954, the assistant secretary of the treasury in charge of enforcement wrote: "To obtain and assure access to information from European police officials and an extra degree of collaboration and assistance by them to American Treasury agents carrying on Treasury business in Europe, it has been considered advisable to make certain payments to Interpol at a stipulated rate."[69] Siragusa, in his memoirs, commented on the value of Interpol in cutting through transgovernmental red tape. Refused permission at the Turkish-Syrian border to cross into the Arab country on an investigation, Siragusa pulled strings to persuade the border guard:

66. Ibid., 212.
67. Trevor Meldal-Johnsen and Vaughn Young, *The Interpol Connection: An Inquiry into the International Criminal Police Organization* (New York: Dial Press, 1979), 96.
68. Ibid., 98.
69. Quoted in ibid., 100.

I asked that he telephone the Syrian Chief of Police in Damascus. I told him that I was an American policeman on very important business. I hinted to the guard that he might be in serious trouble if he did not follow my instructions. He came through for me. So did the phone call. With a top priority, I was soon talking to the chief in Damascus from a line in the border shack. It only took a reminder to the chief that we had met the year before at an Interpol meeting to get clearance. I promised to explain all when I saw him in Damascus.[70]

Beyond the information and contacts, the FBN derived another benefit from its association with Interpol. With the notion of foreign law enforcement agents, especially operationally oriented ones, stationed in one's country still somewhat unfamiliar, both the U.S. government and foreign governments preferred that their status remain somewhat ambiguous. Vizzini, for instance, was officially designated an Interpol representative when he opened the FBN office in the American consulate in Istanbul.[71] The FBN also derived some benefits from the Interpol title in that it helped obscure the fact that its agents were those of a foreign government whose principal objective was the stemming of crime affecting the United States. Said Myles Ambrose, a U.S. official who was involved with international law enforcement matters on and off from the 1950s to the 1970s:

> Operational agents from the Bureau of Narcotics abroad could claim and did claim to be Interpol agents to give their work a veneer of legitimacy. We didn't give a goddamn about Interpol early on. We wanted Interpol to legitimize our police operations overseas as we were the only country in the world that sends cops abroad operationally.[72]

Even without the Interpol network, the sense of comradery among police of different nations often has succeeded in inducing cooperation between governments with severe political differences. FBN agents often found themselves in the role of intermediaries encouraging police chiefs

70. Siragusa, *Trail of the Poppy*, 31.
71. Vizzini, *Vizzini: Secret Lives*, 98.
72. Quoted in Meldal-Johnsen and Young, *The Interpol Connection*, 101–102.

from hostile countries to work together.[73] In one major heroin case, Siragusa was able to persuade police from Turkey, Greece, and Syria to put aside their political differences long enough to cooperate in a joint investigation. In another, Siragusa and Army CID agent Henry Manfredi traveled to Belgrade and secured the assistance of Tito's police.[74] Of course, relations between police of politically hostile governments are not always so successful, but when they are it is a reflection of the strength of the transnational police subculture—the sense among policemen that they are united by a common task that has nothing to do with politics.

Another feature of the FBN's early activities overseas, which is no longer so prominent as it was then, was the assistance given to criminal investigations having nothing to do with drugs. Even today, DEA agents who come across information of use to other law enforcement agencies will in most cases pass it on. But by and large, they tend not to become involved in other agencies' investigations unless there is a drug angle to them. Siragusa's and Vizzini's memoirs, however, make frequent mention of performing tasks for fellow U.S. agencies, including the intelligence agencies. The area that most distracted the FBN agents in the early 1950s was the illicit diversion of strategic materials to the Soviet bloc. A few passages from Siragusa's book suggest both the extent of his involvement in this area and the nature of cooperation with other agencies, both American and European:

> We encountered some great operators in those days as my small staff in Rome devoted a full fifty percent of its time to the problem. Every piece of information obtained about the commercial cheats was passed on to a network of European cops we trusted. Among them was a police officer in Antwerp with whom I had worked on several narcotics cases. His beat was the waterfront, and for several years he furnished me with copies of the manifests of Soviet bloc ships that called in the Belgian seaport.[75]

After describing a joint operation with the Swiss police to expose the Romanian commercial attaché, Siragusa recalled how the FBN's involvement in this area came to an end:

73. Siragusa, *Trail of the Poppy*, 3–32.
74. Ibid., 90.
75. Ibid., 137.

My agents and I had several other skirmishes with Soviet spies before the American Government woke up and assigned an excellent United States Air Force officer, Col. Edward Brown, to head a group charged with making sure that laws related to this illicit trade were properly enforced. Colonel Brown did a splendid job including the establishment of economic defense programs in American embassies throughout Western Europe.

One of the last pieces of work I did for our Intelligence people began with a conversation with a U.S. naval attaché in Rome. He told me it was important that the West obtain samples of fuel oil used by Russian vessels. On my next flight to Lebanon on narcotics business, I enlisted the aid of a Lebanese customs official. He had previously been of great help in breaking up a dope-smuggling operation. A few days later he delivered to my hotel room a quantity of oil obtained surreptitiously from a Russian freighter docked in Beirut.[76]

Vizzini's memoirs are even more revealing regarding interagency cooperation abroad. At one point he notes: "It wasn't unusual for an undercover man from one federal agency to be loaned out to another on a special assignment. I had already done stints for Customs, the C.I.A. and the Justice Department, as well as Secret Service."[77] In one counterfeiting case, which grew out of a lead developed by one of Vizzini's informants in Bangkok, the FBN agent performed the undercover work while the Secret Service agent who had flown in from Honolulu acted as the "covering agent." The two agents also received assistance from the State Department's security officer at the embassy, whose responsibilities were to some degree related to those of the law enforcement agents.[78] In another case, Vizzini went undercover for the CIA in Beirut in an operation designed to destroy a cache of arms being delivered to a Soviet-backed group.[79] In Thailand, Vizzini turned to a U.S. intelligence agency when he needed demolitions to blow up a heroin lab in the Golden Triangle.[80] And in Istanbul, Vizzini and the Turkish narcotics squad he had trained were called upon by the chief of police to work

76. Ibid., 141–142.
77. Vizzini, *Vizzini: Secret Lives*, 255.
78. Ibid., 253–269.
79. Ibid., 175–193.
80. Ibid., 246.

cases ranging from rape to bank robbery.[81] Although the notion of interagency cooperation took hold during the 1980s with the proliferation of multiagency task forces, today's overseas DEA agent is less likely to become directly involved in other agencies' cases to the extent that Vizzini and Siragusa did. The jurisdictional lines have been drawn more sharply since then, and other agencies have developed their overseas capacities.

Another aspect of overseas drug enforcement that has declined since the 1960s is the involvement of U.S. agents in "firefights" (gun battles) with drug traffickers. Vizzini's memoirs in particular, but also Siragusa's, are full of accounts of the agents being shot at, shooting others, and generally being directly involved in the more violent aspects of foreign law enforcement. Without the formal power of arrest in any country outside the United States, and often with no formal authorization to carry a weapon, FBN agents frequently found themselves in very undiplomatic situations. Although direct involvement in law enforcement operations was not officially required and in fact was often forbidden, FBN agents had numerous incentives to become so involved. This was particularly the case outside Europe. Whether in Turkey, Mexico, Pakistan, Afghanistan, Thailand, or any of a dozen other countries, a raid on a drug trafficker's hideout or lab was fraught with danger, as it is today.

FBN agents often perceived a strong need to participate in potentially dangerous operations. To a certain extent, it seemed only fair that American agents assume some of the risk when they were asking local authorities to conduct dangerous law enforcement operations on their behalf. The presence of the FBN agents also ensured that the local law enforcement agents did what they had been asked to do, and increased the chances that they would do it right. Often, an element of machismo was also involved. Vizzini, for instance, recalled that when he went to Istanbul the officer in charge of the narcotics squad "never fully accepted me until we had our first shoot-out with opium smugglers in the interior."[82] Sometimes, of course, one ended up in a dangerous situation without looking for it or expecting it—and this still happens frequently today. A simple interview or surveillance, for instance, has the potential to take a violent turn. But what has changed to some degree, in part

81. Ibid., 204–209.
82. Ibid., 209.

because of Congressionally mandated restrictions on U.S. agent involvement in foreign law enforcement operations, is the frequency of scenarios in which U.S. drug enforcement agents are the first through the door of a drug trafficker's hideout with guns ablaze.

From the perspective of the U.S. government, the prospect of agents becoming involved in firefights and killing or being killed was upsetting for a couple of reasons. Concern for the lives of the agents was of course one consideration. But of no less concern was the potential public reaction in a foreign country to its citizens, no matter how criminal they might be, being killed by American police. FBN agents were thus placed in an awkward position. On the one hand, they were drawn into potentially dangerous operations by both the unofficial requisites of the job and the expectations of the local police with whom they worked. On the other hand, political figures and high-level legal authorities tended to be both ignorant of the actual nature of FBN operations within their country and sensitive to apparent infringements on national sovereignty, particularly those seized upon by the media. State Department officials tended to be highly cognizant of the same sorts of considerations because it was they who would be obliged to offer explanations in the event that FBN agents landed in a diplomatically awkward situation. From time to time, local authorities and FBN agents conspired to avoid diplomatic imbroglios after FBN agents had killed drug traffickers by having the locals claim that they had fired the fatal shots.[83] And, as with intelligence operations, one never knows of the assorted criminals who disappeared without anyone in the government or media asking what had happened.

The BNDD and the DEA:
The Modern Era of International Drug Enforcement

Despite occasional proposals to merge the Federal Bureau of Narcotics with the FBI, which were always rejected by J. Edgar Hoover, the FBN remained an independent law enforcement agency within the Treasury

83. In his memoirs, Vizzini relates one such offer from the Turkish police, which he refused (*Vizzini: Secret Lives*, 211). A similar story, involving Mexican police, is recounted in a book by a former deputy director of the BNDD, John Finlator, *The Drugged Nation: A "Narc's" Story* (New York: Simon & Schuster, 1973), 141.

Department for almost four decades. Then, in the space of five years, the federal drug enforcement bureaucracy underwent two major reorganizations. The first occurred in 1968, when the FBN, which had been wracked by a series of corruption scandals involving its New York office, was transferred from the Treasury Department to the Justice Department. There it was merged with the Bureau of Drug Abuse Control (BDAC), which had been created in 1966 to regulate barbiturates, amphetamines, hallucinogens, and counterfeit drugs. Housed in the Food and Drug Administration (FDA) within the Department of Health, Education, and Welfare (HEW), the BDAC had come into frequent conflict with the Treasury Department's drug agency. With the consolidation of the two agencies under the Justice Department roof, the Bureau of Narcotics and Dangerous Drugs (BNDD) came into being.[84]

Five years later, a second reorganization sought to resolve the increasingly fierce turf battles between the BNDD, Customs' drug section, and two other drug enforcement agencies that had been formed in the interim: the Office of National Narcotics Intelligence (ONNI) and the Office of Drug Abuse Law Enforcement (ODALE). The proposed solution was the merger of all drug enforcement and intelligence in one organization within the Justice Department—the Drug Enforcement Administration.[85] An angry U.S. Customs agency saw 500 of its agents transferred to the DEA (although almost half soon resigned, with many returning to Customs)[86] and its overseas presence substantially curtailed. Among the thirty or so overseas Customs agents, a number merely switched hats, either merging with the resident BNDD office or opening a new DEA office.

In 1967, the last full year of the FBN's existence, the budget of the

---

84. The brief history of the BDAC and its conflicts with the FBN is in Finlator, *Drugged Nation*, 22–55.

85. "Reorganization Plan #2," as the merger was known, has been the subject of substantial analysis. One study, undertaken "to examine why reorganizations fail more often than they succeed," is Patricia Rachal's *Federal Narcotics Enforcement: Reorganization and Reform* (Boston: Auburn House, 1982). A second study, aimed at examining the difficulties in pursuing an international drug control policy, is Mark H. Moore's "Reorganization Plan #2 Reviewed: Problems in Implementing a Strategy to Reduce the Supply of Drugs to Illicit Markets in the United States," *Public Policy* 26 (1978), 229–262. A third study, with a far more novel approach, is Epstein's *Agency of Fear* (supra n. 6). Epstein draws a close link between Watergate and the reorganization, arguing that Nixon intended the DEA to be used as a clandestine political police force. His thesis is challenged by Rachal, *Federal Narcotics Enforcement*, 67–70.

86. Rachal, *Federal Narcotics Enforcement*, 136.

Treasury Department's drug agency was approximately $3 million. Roughly a dozen of its 300 agents were stationed in eight locations outside the United States. Six years and two bureaucratic reorganizations later, in the last full year of BNDD operations, the drug agency boasted a budget of $74 million and 1,446 total agents, of whom 124 were abroad in 47 offices in 33 countries. By 1976, just before a minor contraction in its size, the DEA's budget was just short of $200 million. Some 228 of its 2,117 agents were stationed overseas, in 68 offices in 43 countries. In less than a decade, a small overseas complement of American narcotics agents had grown into the first global law enforcement agency with operational capabilities. (See Appendix B.)

The drug enforcement agents, like the few dozens of overseas FBI and Customs agents, liaised with their counterparts overseas and collected intelligence of value to domestic investigations. But unlike the FBI and customs agents, they continued to participate in joint operations with local police, conducted undercover operations, and were generally more operationally oriented. In a few capitals, DEA agents restricted their activities to liaison with local officials, although an agent might be brought in from other countries or the United States if a fresh face was needed for an undercover operation.[87] As an intelligence network on international drug trafficking, the DEA was likewise unparalleled. Where once Interpol had been universally relied on for intelligence on transnational criminals and the transmission of requests to foreign law enforcement agencies, the DEA now was quicker and more effective at the same task where narcotics cases were concerned.

The dramatic expansion of the U.S. drug enforcement presence abroad was motivated in large part by the Nixon administration's declaration of a "war against drugs" and its desire to involve foreign governments in its campaign. The "Nixon doctrine," which called for foreign governments to assume responsibility for the national security tasks previously undertaken by U.S. forces, was extended to the drug war. But unlike the effort to "Vietnamize" the war in Southeast Asia, the political and diplomatic campaign to internationalize the war against drugs combined an expansion of the global presence of U.S. agents with efforts to develop the vicarious drug enforcement capabilities of foreign police agencies (see Chapters Four and Five). The U.S. drug enforcement agents sta-

---

87. References to the DEA hereinafter should be interpreted as referring to the post-FBN era of U.S. drug enforcement, not as distinct from the BNDD.

tioned overseas thus fulfilled a symbolic role, providing a visible manifestation of the U.S. government's commitment to *international* drug enforcement and its willingness to assist foreign police agencies. Their presence in U.S. embassies served as a constant reminder both to foreign governments and to U.S. ambassadors that drug enforcement was now a high-level foreign policy objective of the President and the Congress.

On a more practical level, the proliferation of overseas agents contributed to the central objective of the agency: immobilizing drug traffickers. The logic of stationing 100 or 200 agents overseas was much the same as the logic that motivated Anslinger to send Siragusa, Vizzini, and their cohorts abroad. Immobilizing drug traffickers meant obtaining the information necessary to identify and catch them, obtaining the evidence necessary to convict them, and of course apprehending the traffickers themselves. Because most illicit drugs originated from abroad, most of the information, evidence, and traffickers could be found there as well. Without agents stationed overseas, U.S.-based agents would either have to collect them on their own or rely on foreign police. The first option would require that agents travel long distances to countries where they might not know the language, the terrain, or anybody at all. The latter was problematic in that foreign police were unlikely to give a request from abroad high priority. If the request were for something relatively simple, such as a criminal record or an identification of a document or fingerprint, Interpol channels might suffice, so long as time was not important. But if something more complicated were required, such as a surveillance, interview, or undercover operation, it was highly unlikely that a foreign police agency would be either willing or able to comply. Having U.S. drug agents on the scene could therefore be highly advantageous. The agents would treat as a priority a request that local police might dismiss or delay in responding to. If the U.S. agents were unable to handle the matter personally, they at least would be in a far superior position to persuade the local police to comply. And if U.S.-based agents themselves needed to come over, overseas agents could serve as guides and liaisons with local officials.

The drug agents sent abroad were also expected to devote substantial efforts to building up and training foreign drug enforcement units to the point that they could function independent of U.S. assistance. This was true not just in Latin America, where many criminal investigative units were not specialized and were little concerned with narcotics, but also in Europe, where drugs were likewise a relatively small concern. The overseas drug agent was given the task of carving out drug enforcement units from local police forces and training them in the investigative techniques employed by the agency in the United States. In the 1970s, as already noted, the number of foreign police trained annually first by BNDD and then by the DEA jumped from zero to almost 2,000, thereby stepping at least partially into the vacated shoes of the Office of Public Safety. Unlike the OPS, the drug enforcement agency also provided specialized training for police agents from Europe and other countries with more sophisticated police forces.

Although a number of the original overseas FBN agents had attained high positions within the BNDD by the early 1970s, the opening of a new BNDD office overseas was still not an established process. One agent who opened the offices in Frankfurt and Munich recalled, "We went there stone cold. There was no game plan." Nonetheless, the BNDD agents who headed overseas to open the new offices were not stepping into entirely virgin territory. More often than not, other U.S. drug agents stationed in either the United States or in another foreign post had been there before and could help make the necessary introductions. In some cases, the agent delegated to open the office had previously been there himself on a temporary duty assignment.

Nor was the BNDD agent necessarily the first or the only American law enforcement agent in town. In the early 1970s, the FBI had some forty LEGATs (short for legal attachés) stationed in twenty foreign cities who maintained liaison relations with police agencies in dozens of countries. Customs also had a number of its attachés abroad, who handled both drug matters and a variety of others. If American military bases were nearby, agents of the criminal investigative divisions were sure to be around. And the Public Safety Program sponsored by the Agency for International Development (AID) still had a substantial number of its police advisors around the world engaged in training local police. Any of these agents was a potential source of contacts and introductions for the new drug agent. And even if left to his own devices, the drug agent could make his own introductions directly, via the embassy security officials, through Interpol channels, or any number of other ways.

In dozens of cases, BNDD agents newly arrived in a foreign city found that their greatest problems were not in making contacts with local police but in resolving turf conflicts with other U.S. agents resident in the country. The experience of the BNDD agent, described above, who

arrived in Germany only to find that the local Army CID drug enforcement unit, Detachment A, was already well connected with local police
and not about to share its contacts, was not atypical. Depending upon
the country, the CID and other military investigative agencies had more
agents, were better funded, operated under fewer restraints, and already
had years of experience in conducting drug investigations in Europe. But
the agency with which the BNDD had the most frequent turf problems
was U.S. Customs, which had long retained some jurisdiction over
international drug trafficking.[88] The conflict was exacerbated in March
1972, when Customs jurisdiction over drug cases was temporarily
expanded, allowing them to expand their international presence from
16 to 29 agents.[89] Although Customs' principal contacts were with
foreign customs agencies, turf struggles were both inevitable and bitter.
In July 1973, the conflict was resolved in the BNDD's favor when the
lion's share of jurisdiction over drug cases was given to the BNDD's
successor, the Drug Enforcement Administration.

For foreign police agencies trying to develop working relationships
with the American police, the intra-American turf struggles quickly
became a source of anger and frustration. In France, for instance, where
both Customs and the FBN had stationed agents for many years, a
French police official expressed his frustration to American reporters in
1972:

> There is one thing about the American anti-drug effort that we of
> the French police cannot understand. . . . Why is it that the two
> American agencies fighting drugs here [BNDD and Customs] are
> always fighting each other? We can't understand this. Here in
> France, we work smoothly with our people in customs. But the
> U.S. customs and the U.S. BNDD here are just about not speaking
> to each other. We don't think that this helps the battle against
> drugs.[90]

The turf struggle with other U.S. agencies presented one not insur-
mountable problem for the BNDD as it expanded rapidly abroad.

---

88. See Rachal, *Federal Narcotics Enforcement* (supra n. 85), which deals at length with
the BNDD-Customs turf conflicts.

89. Andrew Tully, *The Secret War Against Dope* (New York: Coward, McCann &
Geoghegan, 1973), 29.

90. Gilbert Raguideau, quoted in *The Heroin Trail* (New York: Holt, Rinehart & Winston,
1973), 98 (previously a series of articles published in *Newsday*, Feb. 1 to Mar. 4, 1973).

Another obstacle was the uncertainty of local officials regarding what the U.S. agents should and should not be permitted to do. Some police resented the intrusion of BNDD agents, with their different techniques and priorities and their tendency to act as if they were still on U.S. soil. In most cases, a personable and competent agent, as most of the BNDD agents were, could overcome such resistance over time, appealing to the same value system that bound police throughout the world. Somewhat tougher were the higher-level officials in foreign governments, who demonstrated a greater sensitivity to any apparent infringements on national sovereignty. From time to time, the fact that U.S. drug enforcement agents were operating out of the American embassy would emerge in media exposés intended to embarrass the government and/or the United States. In the vast majority of cases, however, the agents were not required to leave the country; they merely adopted a lower profile until the storm had passed.

One problem that the BNDD agents confronted as they went overseas was largely of their own making. They had been delegated overseas not just to make cases and handle the foreign dimensions of cases originating in the United States but also to act as drug enforcement diplomats and advocates. They were expected to push for structural changes in drug enforcement wherever they were stationed, to lobby for tougher laws, to train local police in drug enforcement techniques, to sensitize local officials to U.S. concerns in this area, and so on. But, as one scholar serving a brief stint in the upper echelons of the DEA in 1974 observed:

> The agents from BNDD did not fully understand their roles as "policy planners" and "institution builders." They were trained to make criminal cases. Their natural inclination was reinforced by a formal evaluation system that placed heavy emphasis on case production. Thus, rather than play staff roles in the development and training of effective police forces, or effective liaison roles in making specific cases, the agents often tried to operate on their own, making cases in Morocco as they did in New York City. When language or political barriers frustrated individual case-making activities, the agent lapsed into homesickness.[91]

If the passage of time has not exactly eliminated these problems, it has at least ameliorated them. Turf struggles may be a perpetual irritation

91. Moore, "Reorganization Plan #2 Reviewed" (supra n. 85), 238–239.

wherever two agencies are charged with overlapping tasks; they clearly have not disappeared from the domain of U.S. drug enforcement. But the consolidation in 1973 of almost all drug enforcement responsibilities in the DEA, combined with the passage of time since then, has rendered the turf struggles a relatively small irritant in U.S. drug enforcement activities abroad. So too most DEA agents overseas now have a keener sense of the different nature of their responsibilities abroad, although the basic preoccupation with "making cases" has not changed. Indeed, many of the institution-building chores expected of them during the 1970s have now proven sufficiently successful that the DEA agents can once again focus their efforts on immobilizing traffickers.

The single most important factor determining how DEA agents operate overseas and how successful they are is largely resistant to change; it is the personality and capability of each agent stationed abroad. The numbers of agents have remained sufficiently few, and their situations sufficiently particularistic, that the individual agent's basic characteristics continue to play a major role in defining his or her function. Some are never able to adapt to the different demands of being an overseas agent. Some adapt to the extent of being able to pursue investigations in the foreign country. Others never adjust to the loss of their police powers that is the inevitable handicap of being an overseas agent. Some respond to the demands of diplomacy and foreign lobbying with striking ease. Others are unable to acquire a feel for the local culture and ways of doing things. If a foreign office is large enough, the agents may be able to accommodate themselves to the particular abilities and preferences of each agent by assigning each the tasks that come most naturally to him or her. In an office of one or two agents, however, no such option exists. By and large, most DEA agents stationed overseas prove highly adaptable to the local environment and the constraints and demands imposed upon them—at least that was my impression based upon interviews with DEA agents in eighteen foreign countries.

The likelihood that overseas agents will possess the particular skills and dispositions required abroad is increased by the tendency for most agents to serve in foreign posts more than once. In recent years, the DEA has discouraged its agents from remaining overseas for too long, fearing they might "go native." Stories are told of agents who stayed overseas for a decade and were no longer able to adjust once they returned to the United States. The present rule, which is only rarely waived, is that no agent remains abroad for more than six years. Quite often, however, an agent is brought home for a few years and then stationed overseas again, both because he possesses or has acquired the necessary skills, language and otherwise, and because he requests the transfer overseas. Only rarely, however, is an agent sent to a city where he had been previously posted.

One pattern in agent assignments that emerged during the 1970s and 1980s was the informal division of overseas agents into two groups: those who have served in Latin America, and those who have served in Europe and Asia. Within each group, an agent will typically serve in one country or two over a six-year period, return to the United States for two to six years, and then be sent abroad again. There are now at least a few dozen agents who have served in half a dozen different cities in Latin America or in a similar number of posts throughout Europe, Asia, and the Middle East—with one to two intervening assignments in the United States. It is highly unusual, however, for an agent to have served in both Latin America and a foreign post (other than Spain) in another continent; at least a few Hispanic American agents attributed this de facto policy to a subtle sense of racism in the higher echelons of the agency.

At a very minimum, the DEA agent stationed abroad has a liaison role. This involves developing and maintaining contacts with foreign government officials who are in a position to aid or hinder the agent in his task. Most of the officials are in the police agencies; others are in the customs agency, the military, the justice and interior ministries, or other agencies with related interests. The extensiveness of the agent's contacts will depend upon a number of factors, including the size and sophistication of the foreign government, the state of the government's relations with the United States, the degree of control exercised by the government over the DEA's operations, the priority given the drug issue by the U.S. embassy, the degree of latitude and support given the DEA by the U.S. ambassador, and, perhaps most important, the needs and resourcefulness of the agent. In some countries, the DEA's contacts are mostly with lower-level officials, and those with officials in the higher reaches of government are sporadic and largely formal. This is typically the case in many European countries. Elsewhere, the DEA agent may have instant access to officials at the highest level and may have developed professional and social relationships with top police officials, generals, cabinet-level ministers, and their top aides. In a few countries, most notably in Latin America but also in countries whose governments are not on good terms with the United States, the DEA agent's access may exceed that of both the ambassador and the CIA.

An important determinant of the level of a DEA agent's contacts is his position in the hierarchy of the specific office. The top DEA agent in a foreign country, known as the country attaché (CA), is usually responsible for most high-level contacts.[92] In countries where the DEA also has offices outside the capital, such as in Guayaquil, Guadalajara, Milan, or Marseilles, high-level local liaison is handled by the head of the office, known as the resident-agent-in-charge (RAC). The likelihood that lower-ranking agents, known both inside and outside the United States as special agents (SAs), will engage in high-level contacts depends in good part upon the size of the office and the country. The smaller either is, the greater the possibility that a special agent will also interact with high-level officials. In the smaller countries, located mostly although not entirely in the Caribbean and Central America, the country attaché's contacts will likely range from lower-level detectives to top police officials and cabinet-rank ministers and their deputies. In a large foreign country with a significant DEA presence, especially outside Europe, the country attaché's contacts will probably extend to the same high levels of government, but many of the lower-level contacts will be left to the other agents in the office. These high-level contacts assume much greater significance in much of Latin America, the Caribbean, and Asia, where law enforcement, politics, and corruption are far more intimately connected than is true in most of Europe and the United States today (see Chapter Five).

Within any foreign country, the country attaché is in charge of all DEA activities ranging from liaison to training to criminal investigations. The one exception, at least until the DEA was placed under the umbrella of the FBI in 1981, was the Central Tactical Unit program (CENTAC). Designed to target major drug trafficking organizations whose activities crossed multiple state and national borders, CENTAC investigations were coordinated not by any one special-agent-in-charge (SAC) or country attaché but by a special section in DEA headquarters. Over its eight-year life span, CENTAC conducted approximately two dozen investigations, almost all of which involved foreign countries. CENTAC's three heads all had served abroad as FBN agents in the 1950s and 1960s—first Anthony Pohl, the agent who opened the Marseilles office

---

92. The head of a *domestic* DEA office is referred to as the special-agent-in-charge (SAC).

in 1961, then Martin Pera, who had worked with Siragusa in Europe in the 1950s and supervised FBN operations in Europe from the Rome office during the early 1960s, and finally Dennis Dayle, who had covered the Middle East in the mid-1960s from the FBN office in Beirut.[93] The CENTAC agents included many of the DEA's best, drawn from headquarters as well as the field offices, as well as agents from the IRS, Customs, other federal, state, and city police agencies, and foreign police agents. Despite persistent opposition from the DEA's regional directors, many of whom bitterly resented the infringements on their authority by the centrally directed units, CENTAC thrived.[94] Using less than 3 percent of the DEA's resources, it accounted for more than 12 percent of the agency's arrests of high-level violators.[95]

CENTAC's dissolution in 1981 coincided with a significant reorganization in the internal structure of the DEA. Until that year, all DEA offices and operations had been supervised by regional offices. Until 1971, and then again from 1976 to 1981, there were three such offices overseas, in Paris, Bangkok, and Mexico City. During the intervening years, three additional DEA locations were expanded into regional offices, in Manila, Caracas, and Karachi. In 1981, the DEA eliminated the organizational plan in which all overseas offices reported to one of three overseas regional offices in favor of a centralized FBI-type organizational structure stressing functional rather than geographic lines of authority. Instead of reporting to regional offices, the foreign offices, as well as the domestic offices, all reported to a heroin, cocaine, or marijuana desk based at headquarters, depending upon the type of investigation. To some extent, the reorganization represented a vindication of CENTAC's centralized direction, with its lack of geographical limits on operations. The CENTAC concept was partially retained as well, with the CENTAC units now renamed "Special Enforcement

93. James Mills, *The Underground Empire: Where Crime and Governments Embrace* (Garden City, N.Y.: Doubleday, 1986), 66–70, 117–122.

94. CENTAC's bureaucratic struggles are discussed in James Q. Wilson, *The Investigators: Managing FBI and Narcotics Agents* (New York: Basic Books, 1978), 148–152; U.S. General Accounting Office (GAO), *The Drug Enforcement Administration's CENTAC Program—An Effective Approach to Investigating Major Traffickers That Needs to Be Expanded* (1980); and Mills, *Underground Empire*, 118–129.

95. The calculation, based on the years 1976–78, is in the GAO report on CENTAC (supra n. 94). The exploits of three CENTAC investigations were the subject of a best-selling book by James Mills, *The Underground Empire: Where Crime and Governments Embrace* (1986), which vividly describes the activities and dilemmas of the CENTAC agents.

Operations" (SEOs). Like CENTAC, the SEOs have tried to deemphasize the organizational preoccupation with maximizing the numbers of arrests and seizures and have focused instead on complex, long-term conspiracy investigations aimed at destroying major drug trafficking organizations. In part because they have been more numerous, the SEOs do not appear to have accomplished the dramatic successes attributed to CENTAC.

The FBI Abroad: LEGATs and International Criminal Investigations

Throughout much of the world, the one law enforcement agency most identified with the U.S. government is the Federal Bureau of Investigation. As the lead criminal investigative agency in the United States, this is hardly surprising, although the public image cultivated by J. Edgar Hoover, the FBI's longtime director, must be credited as well. On the other hand, since the early 1970s, the FBI's overseas presence has paled beside that of the drug enforcement agencies. In 1990, its overseas agents, known as legal attachés (LEGATs), numbered only 40 in 16 countries, up from 31 in 13 countries in 1985 but down from 41 in 20 countries in 1973. (See Appendix D.) In certain respects, the FBI's foreign offices have changed relatively little since the 1950s. It has remained among the least operational of all U.S. law enforcement agencies overseas. "We've always billed ourselves as a liaison organization," one LEGAT emphasized to me; "that's part of our international reputation." On the other hand, the FBI has, like most other U.S. police agencies, significantly enhanced its international presence since the mid-1980s. FBI agents travel abroad with increasing frequency to conduct international investigations, lead training programs, lend their expertise in forensic and other investigative techniques, and attend international law enforcement conferences. Since January 1987, all of the FBI's international activities have been coordinated by an Office of Liaison and International Affairs (OLIA).

When J. Edgar Hoover was appointed director of the Bureau of Investigation in 1924, he focused his efforts on professionalizing the agency, the reputation of which had recently reached its nadir. The prospect of agents such as Billy Gard globe-trotting to foreign lands to enforce U.S. laws could hardly have appealed to the new director, concerned as he was with maintaining a tight rein on his agents. The few agents who did travel outside the country were usually stationed in American cities along the borders with Canada and Mexico. In 1939, one of these, the special agent in charge in El Paso, became the first to be stationed abroad, when he was delegated to Mexico for intelligence purposes.[96]

The heyday of the FBI's international program paralleled the history of the CIA's predecessor, the Office of Strategic Services (OSS). In June 1940, President Franklin Roosevelt assigned all intelligence responsibilities for the western hemisphere to the FBI. Shortly thereafter, Hoover created a Special Intelligence Service (SIS) to undertake the major task of countering Axis activities in South and Central America. Within a few years, 360 agents were stationed throughout the region, particularly in Mexico, Argentina, and Brazil. Some operated undercover, others served openly as legal attachés in U.S. embassies and liaison officers with foreign police forces. Hoover and his agents worked closely with the British Security Coordination (BSC), the U.S.-based British intelligence agency directed by the "Man Called Intrepid," William Stephenson.[97] South American officials working covertly for the Nazis were exposed, as were the pro-Nazi activities of the large German communities throughout the continent. In Bolivia, SIS agents foiled a planned coup d'état by pro-Axis forces. In Chile, the U.S. agents contributed to the government's shift away from its initial support for Germany. Elsewhere, the agents used their influence with friendly governments to have pro-Axis elements jailed or deported. Local police were cultivated with money and invitations to the National Police Academy in Washington. Throughout the war, a network of FBI-trained police that would continue to aid the FBI's more mundane law enforcement efforts in peacetime was built up.

Toward the end of the war, Hoover vied with the OSS to have the SIS

96. Sanford J. Ungar, *FBI* (Boston: Little, Brown, 1975), 226.
97. The FBI's activities in Latin America are discussed in Stanley E. Hilton, *Hitler's Secret War in South America, 1939–1945* (Baton Rouge: Louisiana State University Press, 1981), 196–229; Leslie B. Rout Jr. and John F. Bratzel, *The Shadow War: German Espionage and American Counterespionage in Latin America During World War II* (Frederick, Md.: University Publications, 1986); and Silvia Galvis and Alberto Donadio, *Colombia Nazi* (Bogotá: Planeta, 1986), esp. 39–54. See also the brief discussions of the SIS in Ungar, *FBI*, 225, and in Richard Gil Powers, *Secrecy and Power: The Life of J. Edgar Hoover* (New York: Free Press, 1987), 251–253, 545.

serve as the nucleus of the postwar intelligence system. When he failed, many of the SIS agents based in Latin America went to work for the new CIA. A few remained where they had been stationed, in Latin America, London, and Ottawa, becoming the first of what would soon develop into a modest international network of LEGATs. Some were assigned to new locations where the OSS rather than the SIS had handled wartime intelligence activities. And a number were delegated, at General Douglas MacArthur's request, to assist the American occupation forces in Japan. Unlike the SIS agents, the LEGATs were charged not just with counter-espionage responsibilities but with investigating criminal matters as well. They also were ordered to refrain from engaging in the types of operational activities undertaken by the SIS during the war and by U.S. drug enforcement agents thereafter. Within a few years, the LEGATs became widely recognized as the official U.S. police liaisons to foreign governments and police agencies.

LEGATs are expected to handle all international matters that fall within the FBI's jurisdiction. This includes counterintelligence, criminal investigation (much of it involving white-collar crime and organized crime) and counterterrorism (which can involve both counterintelligence and criminal investigative tasks and contacts). With respect to the first, most of the LEGATs' contacts are with foreign intelligence agencies, of which there are typically two—one engaged in domestic intelligence, the other specializing in foreign matters. Because the FBI is responsible for counterintelligence in the United States and the CIA has jurisdiction over similar matters overseas, substantial overlap occurs between the two agencies. This is partially resolved by the FBI's focusing on the aspects of counterintelligence that have some link with domestic cases. In the counterterrorism area, the LEGAT usually needs to liaise with both of the local intelligence agencies as well as with the criminal investigative agencies and the CIA—a task that requires a fair degree of diplomatic skill, given the often fierce turf squabbles between the two intelligence agencies in each country as well as between them and the police agencies. Almost every LEGAT, for instance, can recall instances of being provided with information by a foreign intelligence agency only on condition that the LEGAT not share it with the other intelligence agency in the country.

In the criminal area, the LEGAT, like the U.S.-based FBI agent, oversees a hodgepodge of matters. He typically refrains from investigating criminal matters personally, confining his involvement to one of liaison between American and local law enforcement agencies and prosecutors. His role is that of a facilitator of requests to and from the United States for information, evidence, interrogations, searches, arrests, and extraditions. The requests may be transmitted in a variety of ways: informally by phone, wire, letter, or personal visit, or formally via Interpol, letters rogatory, or the procedures laid out in the few mutual legal assistance treaties to which the United States is a party. Although the LEGAT need not be involved in, or even know of, many of the requests, a resourceful agent can play a crucial role in cutting through red tape and hastening a response. He is likely to know personally a variety of local police officials, including the national police director, in whichever countries fall under his jurisdiction. He can use his informal contacts with local authorities to gain information or to prod them to respond quickly to a request from the United States. Where information is required in the form of evidence admissable in U.S. courts, U.S. prosecutors may request by letter rogatory or pursuant to a treaty that the LEGAT be permitted to conduct an interview, or attend an interrogation, or collect documents. The more extensive a LEGAT's connections with foreign law enforcement officials, the more effective the LEGAT is likely to be and, as one FBI agent put it, "the more business he is likely to generate." "In the Legats perhaps more than anywhere else in the FBI," Sanford Ungar wrote, "the special agent is a combination of investigator, bureaucrat, diplomat, gumshoe, gossip, and public relations man."[98]

Throughout the 1950s and 1960s, the LEGAT program was limited to approximately ten foreign offices, with each responsible for liaison with many other countries as well. Early in the Nixon administration, the program grew when Hoover persuaded the President of the advantages of expanding the LEGAT network, primarily for intelligence purposes. He reportedly argued that his agents could provide better intelligence than the CIA was producing, and that the growing number of Vietnam draft resisters, deserters, and black extremist fugitives overseas, as well as the increasing volume of terrorism, hijacking, drug trafficking, and other transnational criminal cases, required an expanded international presence.[99] Within a few years, the number of overseas offices had doubled—despite persistent opposition by the FBI's chief of intelligence, William Sullivan, who argued that the CIA could handle

98. Ungar, *FBI*, 224.
99. Ibid., 241–242.

most of the intelligence tasks and that the State Department could handle the criminal liaison functions.[100] In his view, Ottawa and Mexico City were the only foreign cities where LEGATs were required because of the large volume of criminals and spies crossing the borders. And even with respect to Mexico City, Sullivan opposed Hoover's instructions to the Mexico City LEGAT office authorizing its agents, unlike those in all other countries apart from Canada, to be operational.

Sullivan's objections were difficult to refute in the early 1970s when even the LEGATs themselves wondered what they were supposed to be doing in places like La Paz and Singapore. Some agents within the FBI also questioned the dedication of the agents abroad, cynically referring to what they called the "LEGAT shuffle." As one agent put it, "LEGATs have the reputation of never doing any work and giving everyone the runaround. As soon as they get overseas, they think they work for the State Department, and all they do is go to cocktail parties and play golf."[101] On the other hand, the LEGAT network has repeatedly proven its value in numerous international criminal investigations. Perhaps the most vivid description of what a dedicated LEGAT can accomplish is provided in *Labyrinth*, a book by Taylor Branch and Eugene M. Propper about the U.S. investigation of the 1976 Washington, D.C., murder of Orlando Letelier, the Chilean foreign minister during the Allende regime. Robert Scherrer, the LEGAT in Buenos Aires with responsibility for liaison in Chile as well, played a crucial role in the investigation, conducting a variety of tasks ranging from record searches to tactical advice on evidence-gathering to prying information out of the chiefs of the Chilean intelligence and police agencies. During his six-year stint in Argentina, Scherrer undertook a great variety of responsibilities, some of them at his own initiative. During the mid-1970s, he worked with the U.S. ambassador in Paraguay to dissuade the Paraguayan president, General Stroessner, from offering a haven to international fugitives, such as Robert Vesco and Meyer Lansky.[102] Within Argentina, he was able to make use of his contacts among the police to find out the fate of suspected leftists who had been "disappeared"; among those he assisted was Rabbi Morton Rosenthal, an American rabbi who specialized in

100. See William C. Sullivan, *The Bureau: My Thirty Years in Hoover's FBI* (New York: W. W. Norton, 1979), 39–41, 199–201, 241–242, 272–273.

101. Quoted in Taylor Branch and Eugene M. Propper, *Labyrinth* (New York: Viking Press, 1982), 328–329.

102. Ibid., 401.

locating Jewish citizens seized by rightist regimes in the southern part of the continent.[103]

Until Hoover's death in 1972, LEGATs were charged with handling all international dimensions of U.S. investigations. U.S.-based agents were not permitted to pursue their investigations overseas, no matter how important or complicated the case. Exceptions were made for FBI agents stationed in border cities, but even they were constrained by strict guidelines that limited the amount of time they could spend in Canada or Mexico.[104] A special exception was made in 1965, when sixteen agents were sent to the Dominican Republic in the wake of the military intervention to conduct security checks on potential members of the provisional government and collect intelligence on political developments.[105] The agency's restriction on foreign travel was predicated in part upon the assumption that LEGATs could handle any foreign matters that might arise. In fact, many cases arose in which it became clear that LEGATs, no matter how well they knew their country, could not substitute for a U.S.-based agent who had spent months investigating a particular case.

The case that ultimately prompted the FBI to change its policy on agents traveling overseas involved an international securities fraud investigation initiated by the New York City Police Department (which also broke with tradition in sending an agent overseas). In late 1972 the FBI's acting director, L. Patrick Gray, agreed to permit agent Richard Tamarro to accompany New York City detective Joseph Coffey on a trip to Germany, Luxembourg, and Austria to pursue their investigation.[106] By 1978, the policy against foreign travel had been relaxed enough that FBI agents investigating the Letelier killing were permitted to accompany a U.S. prosecutor on his trips to Venezuela and Chile despite the presence of LEGATs in those countries. Although the FBI still prefers to rely on its LEGATs to handle foreign matters, and it remains wary of sending lower-level agents overseas lest they create diplomatic imbroglios, foreign travel by FBI agents has become far less of an exceptional undertak-

103. Ibid., 400.

104. Ungar, *FBI* (supra n. 96), 226.

105. Athan G. Theoharis and John Stuart Cox, *The Boss: J. Edgar Hoover and the Great American Inquisition* (Philadelphia: Temple University Press, 1988), 396; W. Mark Felt and Ralph de Toledano, *The FBI Pyramid from the Inside* (New York: G. P. Putnam's Sons, 1979), 82–85.

106. Richard Hammer, *The Vatican Connection* (New York: Holt, Rinehart & Winston, 1982), 148, 272–277.

ing. By the late 1980s, a LEGAT in Paris recalled, he could expect to see a U.S.-based FBI agent passing through his office either on an investigation or en route to a conference about once a week. (Agents from other U.S. law enforcement agencies might also drop by, particularly if their agency lacked a representative in the embassy, but the LEGAT could often send them down the hall to the State Department's Regional Security Officer.) And even though most FBI agents must still secure approval from FBI headquarters to travel abroad, those stationed near the Canadian and Mexican borders routinely liaise with law enforcement authorities, crossing into foreign territory frequently and with no need to secure prior approval from headquarters. The same is true, albeit to a slightly lesser degree, of the agents stationed in Miami and Puerto Rico who cover the Caribbean islands.

The incentives and pressures on the FBI to shed most of its inhibitions regarding international involvements arose from a variety of sources. In 1982, the FBI was made the parent agency of the DEA and given joint jurisdiction over drug cases involving organized crime. The DEA's international drug enforcement activities were little affected by this development except in three locations: Italy, Canada, and to a lesser extent Switzerland. Largely because drug trafficking investigations in those countries tend to have some connection with "traditional" organized crime—that is, the Mafia—the FBI and the DEA agreed that the parent agency would retain its own lead in domestically initiated drug cases. In the early 1980s, FBI and DEA agents, working with the New York Police Department and federal prosecutors, began investigating a new generation of Sicilian mafiosi who had become involved in trafficking heroin to the United States. In what became known as the "Pizza Connection Case," FBI and DEA agents as well as Italian police engaged in a wide-ranging investigation that took them to Italy, Spain, Switzerland, Brazil, Canada, and the United States.[107] A U.S.-Italian Working Group on Organized Crime was created early in the investigation to promote closer cooperation and resolve disputes. FBI agents shed some of their traditional reluctance to operate more aggressively overseas; Italian police were drawn into surveillances in the United States. In early 1987, the case was successfully concluded in U.S. and Italian courts with

107. See Ralph Blumenthal, *Last Days of the Sicilians* (New York: Times Books, 1988); and Claire Sterling, *Octopus: The Long Reach of the International Sicilian Mafia* (New York: W. W. Norton, 1990).

the conviction of most of those involved in the drug trafficking operation.

Another incentive for the FBI to become more active overseas arose during the 1980s in response to the rising number of terrorist incidents and politically motivated murders involving American citizens. Until well into the 1970s, the FBI played a very limited role in investigating terrorist incidents abroad, even those directed at American citizens, because no federal laws were violated by such acts. In 1978, its extraterritorial activities, and the extraterritorial reach of U.S. law, expanded with the investigation of the death of Congressman Leo J. Ryan and a U.S. embassy official in Jonestown, Guyana, the subsequent prosecution of Larry Layton, and the federal court's assertion of jurisdiction over the crime.[108] In 1983, FBI forensics specialists were sent to Beirut to investigate the April bombing of the U.S. embassy and the October bombing of a U.S. marine facility.

The principal impetus for an expanded FBI role in investigating international terrorist incidents was provided by Congress, which in 1984 and 1986 enacted legislation that greatly broadened the United States' extraterritorial jurisdiction over terrorist acts.[109] Coordinating its efforts with the CIA and the State Department's Counterterrorism Office, as well as with foreign police agencies, FBI agents participated in investigations of more than fifty terrorist incidents outside U.S. borders between 1985 and the middle of 1989, including the repeated abductions of American citizens in Lebanon.[110] FBI agents traveled frequently to El

108. D. F. Martell, "FBI's Expanding Role in International Terrorism Investigations," *FBI Law Enforcement Bulletin* 56 (Oct. 1987), 28–32. See also *U.S. v. Layton*, 509 F.Supp. 212 (N.D. Cal. 1981), appeal dismissed, 645 F.2d 681 (9th Cir. 1981), cert. denied, 452 U.S. 972 (1981); and *The Assassination of Representative Leo J. Ryan and the Jonestown, Guyana Tragedy: Report of a Staff Investigative Group to the House Committee on Foreign Affairs*, 96th Cong., 1st Sess. (1979).

109. The Comprehensive Crime Control Act of 1984, for instance, included a new law, 18 U.S.C. 1203, which implements the International Convention Against the Taking of Hostages. The statute provides for U.S. federal jurisdiction over any hostage taken overseas in which the victim or the perpetrator is an American citizen, in which the United States is the target of the hostage-taker's demands, or in which the offender is found within the United States. The Omnibus Diplomatic Security and Antiterrorism Act of 1986, 18 U.S.C. 2331, broadened the extraterritorial jurisdiction of the United States to include any terrorist act in which an American citizen is killed or seriously injured.

110. See *Extraterritorial Jurisdiction over Terrorist Acts Abroad: Hearings Before the Subcommittee on Crime of the House Committee on the Judiciary*, 101st Cong., 1st Sess. (May–July, 1989), 5 (testimony of Oliver B. Revell), which refers to investigations of twenty-two incidents. See also *FBI Authority to Seize Suspects Abroad: Hearing Before the Subcommittee on Civil and Constitutional Rights of the House Committee on the Judiciary*, 101st

Salvador during the 1980s, for instance, where they trained local police and investigated the killings of Americans both by leftist guerrillas and by the government's security forces.[111] When four U.S. marines and nine others were killed in a San Salvador café in June 1985, FBI agents even met with the Salvadoran President, José Napoleón Duarte, to seek his assistance. A few months later, FBI Director William Webster announced that he had sent "two crack teams" of FBI agents to assist in the investigation of the hijacking of the Italian cruise ship *Achille Lauro*, in particular to gather forensic information on board the ship.[112] Agents also were sent to investigate the June 1985 hijackings of TWA Flight 847 while en route from Athens to Rome and of Royal Jordanian Airlines (Alia) Flight 402 in Beirut (which carried three American passengers), the November 1985 hijacking of Egypt Air Flight 648, the April 1986 bombing of TWA Flight 840, and the September 1986 bombing of Pan Am Flight 73 in Karachi.[113] The investigation of the Alia hijacking proved more successful than most when one of the hijackers, a Lebanese named Fawaz Younis, was lured out of his Lebanese haven in a sting operation code-named "Operation Goldenrod" and arrested in international waters off the Cypriot coast in September 1987.[114]

During the latter part of the 1980s, FBI agents joined with agents of the military's law enforcement agencies in investigating bombings at U.S. military bases in Spain, Italy, Greece, and the Philippines, as well as the assassinations of U.S. military personnel in Athens in June 1988 and Manila in April 1989 by the "17 November" organization and the Philippine New People's Army, respectively; they combined with Italian police in investigating the Japanese Red Army's attack on the U.S. embassy in Rome in June 1987; they participated in the investigation of the August 1988 airplane crash in Pakistan that killed President Mohammad Zia ul-Huq, many top Pakistani military officials, and the U.S. ambassador, Arnold Raphel (although only after Congressional criticism

Cong., 1st Sess. (Nov. 8, 1989), 48 (statement of Oliver B. Revell), which refers to "at least 50 separate investigations."

111. LeMoyne, "Duarte Meets F.B.I. on Raid Inquiry" (supra n. 41).

112. Peter T. Kilborn, "F.B.I. Chief: A U.S. Trial Far Off," *New York Times*, Oct. 13, 1985, 26; "FBI Sends Agents to Italy to Monitor Case," *Boston Globe*, Oct. 13, 1985, 28.

113. Martell, "FBI's Expanding Role" (supra n. 108), 30.

114. See G. Gregory Schuetz, "Apprehending Terrorists Overseas Under United States and International Law: A Case Study of the Fawaz Younis Arrest," *Harvard International Law Journal* 29 (1988), 499–531.

of the initial State Department decision to bar the FBI agents from Pakistan cleared the way ten months later);[115] and they investigated the May 1989 assassination of two Mormon missionaries in Bolivia by a group known as the "Fuerzos Armadas de Liberación Zarate Willco," which a year earlier had attempted to bomb the motorcade of Secretary of State George Shultz during a visit to La Paz. Throughout the decade, agents also investigated leads regarding the abduction of seventeen Americans in Lebanon during the 1980s. The most intensive international investigation by the FBI during the decade, however, involved the terrorist explosion of Pan Am Flight 103 over Lockerbie, Scotland, in December 1988. Dozens of FBI agents, including LEGATs as well as forensic experts and other agents based in the United States, combined with English, Scottish and German police in tracking down leads in over forty countries from Sweden and Malta to the Far East.[116]

By early 1987, the need to provide some coordination of the FBI's growing number of international activities had resulted in the creation of an Office of Liaison and International Affairs (OLIA) at FBI headquarters. By 1990, the OLIA's responsibilities included supervision of the rising number of LEGAT offices, the two agents stationed at the U.S. Interpol office, the three agents based at Interpol headquarters in Lyons (including the chief of Interpol's antiterrorism unit), and the stream of agents from headquarters and the field offices on TDY (temporary duty) assignments abroad. OLIA also was charged with supervising the growing number of foreign police representatives based in the United States, as well as most visits by foreign police officials. The tendency of many high-level foreign police officials to visit FBI headquarters when they come to the United States—be it to pursue an investigation, attend a conference, seek medical care, or visit a child at an American school—has helped ease the growing internationalization of the FBI's activities. Additional opportunities to develop close relationships with foreign law enforcement officials have emerged at the FBI's National Academy in Quantico, where 50–100 of the 800 students participating in the school's eleven-week command-level training program in recent years are from

115. Robert Pear, "FBI Allowed to Investigate Crash That Killed Zia," *New York Times*, June 25, 1989, 13; *Extraterritorial Jurisdiction over Terrorist Acts Abroad: Hearings* (supra n. 110).

116. Steven Emerson and Brian Duffy, *The Fall of Pan Am 103: Inside the Lockerbie Investigation* (New York: G. P. Putnam's Sons, 1990).

abroad; some efforts are made to maintain contact with its foreign alumni. Top-level FBI officials and the LEGATs in Europe have also attended, albeit officially with observer status, the periodic sessions of TREVI—the collaborative arrangement among European interior ministers and top law enforcement officials designed to improve cooperation against terrorism, drug trafficking, organized crime, and other threats to public security. Particularly influential in many of these foreign initiatives was Oliver "Buck" Revell, a top FBI official throughout the 1980s who served as a high-level advocate for internationalizing the FBI's outlook and operations.

The U.S. Customs Service: Dealing with High-Tech Smugglers, Money Launderers, and Contrabandistas

The one agency whose jurisdiction has most naturally encompassed transnational crime is the U.S. Customs Service. For much of the century, its overseas presence exceeded that of any other civilian law enforcement agency, until the Bureau of Narcotics and Dangerous Drugs (BNDD) surpassed it during the late 1960s. From 1930 to 1973, Customs vied first with the Federal Bureau of Narcotics and thereafter with the BNDD for greater jurisdiction over international drug trafficking cases, but the turf struggle was ultimately resolved to Customs' detriment when a major bureaucratic reorganization in 1973 led to the merger of its drug enforcement departments with the BNDD into the newly created Drug Enforcement Administration (DEA).[117] Thereafter, most of the overseas Customs agents transferred to the DEA; the remainder were either recalled or limited their investigations to what was left of Customs' overseas jurisdiction. The Customs Service retained some jurisdiction over drug cases by virtue of its border authority, but the follow-up investigation of leads resulting from seizures was delegated to the DEA. Periodic memoranda of understanding between the heads of Customs and the DEA were necessary thereafter to resolve lingering tensions between the two agencies.[118] Customs eventually acknowledged the

117. The best discussion of these developments is Rachal, *Federal Narcotics Enforcement* (supra n. 85).

118. One such memorandum of understanding, dated Dec. 11, 1975, is reproduced in *The*

DEA's lead in drug matters and, for the remainder of the decade, confined its few remaining overseas offices to enforcement of anti-dumping statutes and non-drug-related smuggling. By 1979, its presence abroad had been reduced to eight foreign offices.

With an eye constantly open to new overseas opportunities, however, the Customs Service was able in the early 1980s to take advantage of two developments to expand its jurisdiction and presence overseas. The first was the increasing concern over the smuggling of sophisticated technology to Soviet-bloc countries as well as to others, including close allies of the United States, who had been refused an export license for either security or competitive commercial reasons. The Customs Service had overseen this area since the beginning of the Cold War, but new opportunities emerged with the passage of the 1979 Export Administration Act, the Carter administration's growing interest in this issue following the Soviet invasion of Afghanistan, and the high priority subsequently given the issue by the Reagan administration. In late 1981, Customs launched Operation Exodus, a more systematic effort to investigate and curtail high-tech smuggling. At first, its agents were criticized for their lack of expertise in investigating and deterring this form of smuggling.[119] Within a few years, however, they had acquired a much more sophisticated knowledge of the illicit commerce, the principal criminals, and their methods—all of which differ substantially from the drug traffic. Although the FBI, the Bureau of Alcohol, Tobacco, and Firearms (ATF), the Commerce Department, and the intelligence agencies all retain some slice of jurisdiction in this area—one consequence of which was the fierce turf struggles during the early 1980s with the Commerce Department's Export Enforcement Office, which opened offices in Vienna, Bern, and Stockholm during the 1980s[120]—the Customs Service has remained the lead agency in most regards.[121] By the late 1980s, high-tech smuggling had emerged as the top priority of virtually all Customs attachés overseas, whose numbers have been gradually growing to pre-1973 levels.

Mexican Connection: Hearings Before the Subcommittee to Investigate Juvenile Delinquency of the Senate Committee on the Judiciary, 95th Cong., 2d Sess. (1978), 157–161.

119. August Bequai, *Technocrimes* (Lexington, Mass.: Lexington Books, 1987), 92–93.

120. U.S. Department of Commerce, Bureau of Export Administration, *Annual Report, FY 1989* (Washington, D.C.: Government Printing Office, 1990).

121. The principal account of Customs' efforts to stem the flow of high technology, and its turf struggles, is Linda Melvern, David Hebditch, and Nick Anning, *Techno-Bandits* (Boston: Houghton Mifflin, 1984).

The second development, the potential of which Customs was initially slow to recognize, was the enactment of the Bank Secrecy Act in 1970. The legislation was prompted by growing concern over the use of foreign financial secrecy jurisdictions to launder illegally earned money, and by the emerging realization that tracing the paper trail of laundered money could implicate the high-level drug traffickers and other criminals who received most of the profits.[122] One provision of the act, which required that individuals taking more than $5,000 in or out of the country file a Currency Transaction Report (CTR), provided Customs with a reentry into the area of narcotics investigation as well as other areas of criminal investigation. In the first interagency task force to focus on money laundering—Operation Greenback, in Miami—customs agents once again began to travel overseas in drug-related cases, although their focus was now on the movement of money rather than drugs. In late 1983, after overcoming DEA resistance, Customs opened an office in the Panama City embassy—its first in Latin America (excluding Mexico) since it lost its jurisdiction over drug cases a decade earlier. Although that office resembled others overseas in that its first priority was high-tech smuggling out of the Colón Free Trade Zone, its second priority was investigating drug-related money laundering through Panama's infamous banks.[123] Its efforts thereafter to expand its presence in Latin America were stymied, however, by resistance from the DEA. An attempt in 1986 to station an agent in Bogotá on more than a TDY basis failed, and no additional offices were opened in South America until 1990, when permission was granted to station an agent in Montevideo, one of the few Latin American capitals without a resident DEA agent. That office, however, represented U.S. Customs' twentieth foreign office—a far cry from the diminished presence of a decade before. (See Appendix A.) Also significant was the negotiation of an interagency agreement under which 1,000 customs agents were designated to investigate drug smuggling and money laundering—an accomplishment that the new commissioner of customs, Carol Hallett, described as her greatest achievement.[124]

122. See Chapter Six for a more thorough analysis of U.S. efforts to deal with international money laundering.

123. *U.S. Narcotics Control Programs Overseas, an Assessment: Report of a Staff Study Mission to Southeast Asia, South America, Central America, and the Caribbean, August 1984 to January 1985, to the House Committee on Foreign Affairs,* 99th Cong., 1st Sess. (1985), 33.

124. Robert D. Hershey Jr., "In the Customs Service, an Open Door at the Top," *New York Times,* Aug. 18, 1990, 9.

Apart from high-tech smuggling and money laundering, Customs' attachés have continued to investigate violations of antidumping laws, commercial fraud, arms and pornography smuggling, and other contraband activities. In one major investigation during the mid-1980s, known as "Operation Retread," customs agents conducted a worldwide investigation into the illicit diversion of U.S. military equipment to proscribed governments.[125] Their attachés have tended to be slightly more "operational" than the LEGATs in that they become directly involved in investigations, but with one or two exceptions (such as Germany) they have exercised greater restraint in their activities than most overseas DEA agents. Only toward the late 1980s did the Customs Service start shedding its inhibitions against acting more operationally overseas. In one case, Customs collaborated with British authorities in an investigation of a front company for the Iraqi government's arms-procurement network that involved undercover negotiations by a customs agent as well as a controlled delivery of detonator components.[126] But customs attachés still interact primarily with foreign customs agencies, which in most cases (Great Britain is an exception) lack the police powers and sophistication of the U.S. agency.

Customs' principal obstacle abroad—one that it shares with the Immigration and Naturalization Service—is that many of the violations of U.S. laws that concern it are not violations of local laws, or are violations only in egregious cases. Only toward the end of the 1980s, for instance, did a number of governments begin to criminalize money laundering. Similarly, most non-NATO countries demonstrated relatively little interest in regulating high-tech exports, and even the NATO members differed on important details of the export controls. And with regard to many other forms of contraband, often foreign governments do not prohibit the export of goods that cannot be imported legally into the United States. All of this contrasts with the laws that the DEA and the Secret Service are charged with enforcing, which are in effect throughout the world and backed by global conventions. Customs has tried to compensate for this disadvantage by vigorously developing bilateral relationships with dozens of foreign customs agencies—not least by offering a broad array of training and other assistance programs—and by playing a leading role in the Customs Cooperation Council (CCC)

125. See *Federal Licensing Procedures for Arms Exports: Hearing Before the Senate Committee on Governmental Affairs*, 100th Cong., 1st Sess. (1987), 48–49, 103–139.

126. *U.S. Customs, Update 1990*, 16–17.

and the assorted regional customs conferences.[127] Its efforts to cultivate a transnational community of customs officials akin to that which bonds drug enforcement agents across borders have yielded dividends, but the diversity of its mandate ensures that it will never attain the level of consensus that underlies U.S. efforts to suppress drug trafficking and counterfeiting.

The Secret Service:
Contending with Counterfeiters

With more than half of all counterfeit U.S. dollars produced and circulated overseas, where they are found in roughly fifty countries each year, the Secret Service has been obliged to operate internationally since its origins.[128] The emergence of the U.S. dollar as a sort of international currency following World War II increased this need. The Secret Service has maintained an agent in Europe since 1947, when three Secret Service agents were sent to France to investigate a criminal ring engaged in counterfeiting U.S. dollars. Working undercover and in cooperation with the Sûreté, the agents succeeded in identifying and apprehending the counterfeiters.[129] With the problem of counterfeiting U.S. dollars widespread in Europe in the years after the war, an agent was assigned to operate out of the U.S. embassy in Paris and maintain contact with European law enforcement agencies. The one office sufficed until 1985 when an apparent rise in international activity in counterfeit dollars prompted an expansion of the Secret Service's international presence. With the Paris office overwhelmed by requests for assistance from Italian police, a second foreign office was opened in Milan in 1985 and then relocated to Rome in 1988. By the end of the 1980s, two agents had also been stationed in Bonn and London, from where they reported to the Paris office. Liaison with Asia was handled out of the Honolulu office and, beginning in 1987, a resident office in Bangkok; by the end of the decade, a Secret Service agent could also be found on a virtually constant TDY basis in the Philippines. Latin America and the Caribbean were

127. Ibid., 28–30.
128. In 1989, approximately $100 million in counterfeit U.S. currency was seized within the United States, and approximately $120 million abroad.
129. Michael Dorman, *The Secret Service Story* (New York: Delacorte Press, 1967), 74–79.

covered until 1986 by the San Juan, Puerto Rico, office; thereafter an international squad in the Miami office assumed responsibility for Latin America, Jamaica, and the Bahamas, with San Juan retaining responsibility for the remainder of the Caribbean islands. The principal focus of first the San Juan office and then the Miami office throughout the 1980s was Colombia, which has long been regarded as one of the principal sources of counterfeit dollars; plans to station an agent in Bogotá were seriously considered during the 1980s but ultimately abandoned in good part because of security considerations. Mexico, which in contrast to other areas of transnational crime has been the source of relatively little counterfeit currency, is covered by Secret Service offices stationed in U.S. cities near the border. Agents stationed in cities near the northern border handle liaison with the Canadians, whose counterfeit currency laboratory based in Ottawa works closely with the Secret Service's lab in Washington. Within the Honolulu, Miami, and San Juan offices, individual Secret Service agents are each charged with responsibility for liaising with foreign officials in particular countries.

Unlike many U.S. law enforcement agencies abroad, the Secret Service has not had to contend with the common problem of disinterest on the part of foreign law enforcement agencies. Because most counterfeit dollars are produced and circulated in foreign countries, most police agencies recognize the counterfeiting of U.S. dollars as not merely a violation of local laws but also a threat to domestic interests. The tendency of most counterfeiters to diversify into counterfeiting other currencies as well as passports and other official documents has also abetted the coincidence of interests between the Secret Service and their foreign counterparts. Virtually no non-U.S. counterfeit currency, however, is believed to be produced within the United States; as a result, few foreign police ever need to come to the United States on a counterfeiting investigation, and the involvement of Secret Service agents in investigations of foreign currency counterfeiting is largely limited to investigations abroad involving co-production of counterfeit dollars and foreign currencies.

The general disposition of Secret Service agents abroad is to maintain a low profile but to "be prepared," as one agent put it, "to be able to make themselves available to do whatever local agents need them to do." The most common task required of the overseas agents is to assist in the identification of counterfeit dollars, a process that generally involves checking a suspected note against the "circularized note" files at headquarters.[130] The array of activities performed by Secret Service agents stationed overseas, as well as by those sent on TDY visits, is quite as diverse as that of DEA agents. Secret Service agents have cooperated closely in foreign investigations, providing intelligence on suspected counterfeiters and their techniques, assisting in the recruitment, evaluation, and payment of informants,[131] performing undercover roles, testifying in court, providing affidavits, keeping tabs on retail paper producers, and offering technical and professional advice to foreign police agencies. The level of assistance provided by foreign police has varied, of course, depending upon the existence of counterfeit specialists within foreign police agencies, their level of competence, and their governments' willingness to extend assistance. An agent based in Europe during the early 1980s recalled that the German Bundeskriminalamt, Scotland Yard, and the French, Swiss, and Dutch police agencies each had fine counterfeit squads; the Belgian and Italian police agencies were generally less sophisticated, although both possessed a few highly qualified counterfeit experts. The same agent also recalled that in at least one case he had worked closely with the Hungarian police agency—an indication that counterfeiting, even more so than drug trafficking, is the sort of criminal activity that inspires law enforcement agencies to transcend political differences.

The Secret Service expects to expand its international presence in the future, albeit not dramatically. Although counterfeiting of U.S. dollars appears to have increased steadily over the years, it has remained, as one agent put it, "a nickel and dime business. . . . The Mafia knows the Feds are involved, they know the tracking [through the circularized note files] is superb, and they know there's not big money involved. . . . They're more drawn to forged bonds, which can be very big money," but which typically does not fall within the Secret Service's jurisdiction unless government bonds are involved. Another agent lamented the change in

130. All counterfeit dollars are "circularized"—a process that involves analyzing a note to identify its distinctive features, determining whether it is part of a previously identified counterfeit series, establishing a new file if it is not, and collating all available information about the movement of all notes within a particular counterfeit series. By the end of the 1980s, between 2,500 and 3,000 new notes were being identified each year. The United States is the only government that circularizes its own currency. The counterfeit division at Interpol headquarters provides this service for a number of national currencies.

131. The Secret Service's budget for informants pales in comparison with that of the DEA. Informants routinely are paid several hundred or several thousand dollars. A five-figure payment, according to one agent interviewed in 1990, "happens once in a decade."

the character of the counterfeiters: "They used to be skilled printers looking for a challenge or down on their luck; now there's many more drug traffickers involved, looking to rip off one another," and getting caught when they try to buy drugs from an undercover agent with counterfeit currency. The 1985 movie about a Secret Service investigation of counterfeiters, *To Live and Die in L.A.*, is also held accountable for inspiring many novices to try their hand at counterfeiting. "Up to 40 percent of counterfeiters," one agent claimed, "say they got the idea from the movie." By and large, counterfeiting is seen as a "dumb crime" offering criminals relatively low rates of return despite the high risks involved in putting the currency into circulation.

The rather prominent international profile of the Secret Service has stemmed from more than its international assistance in investigating counterfeit dollar cases. Apart from its responsibility in this area, as well as its jurisdiction over check forgery and various frauds against the government, which consume a relatively small proportion of international duties, the Secret Service has covered the globe on behalf of its other chief responsibility—protecting U.S. officials and other notable persons on their trips abroad. This task has involved extensive liaison with foreign officials but little in the way of criminal investigation apart from the collection and dissemination of intelligence on potential threats to their charges. The prominent role of counterfeiting investigation in the evolution of international policing may also account for some of the Secret Service's high profile internationally, one symbolized by the appointment of a Secret Service agent, Richard Stiener, as chief of the U.S. Interpol office in 1979, and by the 1985 election of the head of the Secret Service, John Simpson, to a four-year appointment as president of Interpol.

The U.S. Marshals Service: Apprehending Fugitives, Protecting Witnesses

The federal agency that has undergone the most dramatic expansion in overseas activities is the U.S. Marshals Service (USMS). In November 1979, the attorney general transferred some of the responsibility for apprehending federal fugitives from the FBI to the Marshals Service; this authority was augmented in August 1988, much to the annoyance of the

FBI.[132] The agency responded by setting up an international branch to coordinate the apprehension and recovery of fugitives who had fled abroad. Much of the marshals' international work involves no more than escorting fugitives who already have been captured by foreign police agencies back to the United States. But during the 1980s, the marshals began to play a more direct role in locating fugitives abroad, assisting foreign police in their apprehension, and devising sting operations to lure fugitives to the United States or into the hands of cooperative authorities overseas. In a major Florida-based Fugitive Investigative Strike Team (FIST) effort in 1985 to capture fugitives, U.S. marshals operated throughout the Caribbean, working with local police on the islands to return fugitives to U.S. territory.[133] In early 1985, a special unit of marshals joined an international team of investigators including Israelis and West Germans to determine the location of the Nazi war criminal, Josef Mengele. Their investigation ended apparently success- fully with forensic and documentation experts confirming the Nazi doctor's death in Brazil.[134]

The most challenging of the marshals' work has involved international undercover operations, called "ruses" by the marshals, that target white- collar fugitives—including such famous swindlers as Robert Vesco, Marc Rich, and Takis Veliotis.[135] A small number of marshals, trained in the intricacies and fashions of international high finance, today operate globally, trying to trick the high-flying fugitives into making the deal that will allow U.S. authorities or the police of a friendly government to seize them. In one scheme, which ultimately faltered, the plan involved persuading the fugitive to board a helicopter thinking that he was being taken to a yacht when in fact the intended destination was a U.S. aircraft carrier patrolling the Mediterranean near Libya. In another case, involv- ing an investigation of a former CIA agent, Edwin Wilson—who had become a major supplier of plastic explosives and other lethal equipment to the Qadaffi regime in Libya—an undercover U.S. marshal and an informant duped Wilson into leaving his Libyan haven to attend a

132. See *Departments of Commerce, Justice, and State, the Judiciary, and Related Agencies Appropriations for 1990: Hearings Before a Subcommittee of the House Committee on Appropriations*, 101st Cong., 1st Sess., Part 2 (1989), 1814–1816.

133. *The Pentacle 5* (Summer 1985), 3–5.

134. Ibid., 17.

135. A. Craig Copetas, "White-Collar Manhunt," *New York Times Magazine*, June 8, 1986, 45.

meeting in the Dominican Republic, where police authorities had already agreed to seize him and put him on a plane to the United States.[136] A few months later, the prosecutor in the Wilson case, accompanied by the operational chief of the marshals, Howard Safir, and two other marshals, flew to Beirut in hopes of apprehending one of Wilson's accomplices, Frank Terpil. Arrangements had been made with the Phalangists to have the local police make the arrest. When the Lebanese police failed to seize the American fugitive, the prosecutor and the marshals began their own stakeout on the streets of Beirut, which ultimately proved unsuccessful.[137] And in yet another case, U.S. marshals played a leading role in persuading Honduran officials to put a notorious drug trafficker, Juan Matta Ballesteros, on a plane to the Dominican Republic, from which he was quickly transferred to the United States.

Apart from their involvement in collecting and delivering fugitives, the U.S. Marshals Service has shared its expertise in other matters with foreign law enforcement agencies. During the 1980s, police officials in a number of countries confronting threats by organized crime and terrorist groups became aware of the Marshal Service's Witness Protection Program; representatives from Canada, Britain, Australia, Italy, and Germany came to the United States to learn about the program, and in a few cases the U.S. program was even used to assist foreign criminal justice authorities in protecting vulnerable witnesses. By late 1989, both Australia and Germany were actively considering the creation of similar programs at the national level. In the area of court security, the Marshals Service has both assisted foreign criminal justice systems, such as El Salvador and Grenada following the U.S. invasion in 1983, and studied the court security systems of foreign countries, notably France and Italy, which have been obliged to protect their judicial officials and courtrooms from Arab terrorists and powerful organized crime gangs.[138] The Marshals Service's Special Operations Group (SOG), created in 1971 to respond to such emergency situations as civil disturbances, terrorist incidents, and the more difficult courtroom security and fugitive apprehension tasks, has trained foreign police in counterterrorist methods and played a role in coordinating the transport of particularly notorious fugitives to the United States; the two most prominent examples during the 1980s were the first drug traffickers extradited by Colombia in 1985,

136. Peter Maas, *Manhunt* (New York: Random House, 1986), 238, 255, 266–267.
137. Ibid., 286–287.
138. Howard Safir, "International Court Security," *The Pentacle* 7 (Summer 1987), 23–28.

and Panamanian dictator General Manuel Noriega, following the U.S. invasion of Panama in late 1989.

Unlike the DEA, Customs, and the FBI, with their numerous foreign representatives abroad, the Marshals Service has not been able to rely on representatives stationed abroad; the one exception is the U.S. marshal stationed at Interpol headquarters in France, who occasionally is called upon to handle fugitive investigations in Europe. By the late 1980s, two marshals were stationed in the Alien Fugitive Enforcement Unit at the U.S. national central bureau of Interpol, through which pass most international requests both to and from the United States for the apprehension of fugitives. Marshals also have cultivated contacts with the growing number of foreign police representatives stationed in the United States.[139] The international branch at the Marshals Service's headquarters has attempted to compensate for its lack of an international presence by taking advantage of the diverse contacts, and opportunities to establish contacts, available to the agency. It has relied on its various training programs, the occasional visits by foreign police to the United States, and the growing number of international police conferences to develop the sorts of personal contacts with foreign police that so often prove crucial to successful international investigations. Particularly useful has been the International Association of Chiefs of Police (IACP), a U.S.-based police association that undertook significant efforts during the 1980s to internationalize its membership. Much of the Marshals Service's success in developing its international contacts and reputation can be attributed to its chief of operations for much of the 1980s, Howard Safir, whose personal contacts with foreign police officials may well have exceeded those of any other U.S. law enforcement agent. Having developed an awareness of the importance of personal relationships with foreign law enforcement authorities during his service with the DEA, Safir traveled abroad frequently to pursue investigations, attend conferences, and participate in periodic meetings, such as the Italian-American Working Group on Organized Crime, and became prominently involved with the IACP, serving as the only U.S. vice-chairman of the IACP's Advisory Committee for International Policy.

139. As of 1990, the United States was host to police liaison officials from Australia, Canada, France, Germany, India, Israel, Japan, Korea, and the United Kingdom. Most were stationed in their governments' embassies in Washington, D.C., but a few were based in Los Angeles, Miami, and New York City.

The Bureau of Alcohol, Tobacco, and Firearms: Cracking Down

Foreign demands to crack down on the smuggling of firearms and explosives out of the United States during the early 1970s required the Bureau of Alcohol, Tobacco, and Firearms (ATF) to adopt a more international perspective. Although this issue fell primarily within the jurisdiction of the Customs Service and the FBI, ATF was called upon by both foreign police agencies and Congress because of its greater expertise in regulating domestic sales of weapons. The first to request its assistance was the Mexican government, which had enacted a tough gun control law in 1968 that generated a lucrative black market for imported firearms; it was particularly concerned about the flow of weapons into the hands of domestic insurgencies.[140] Additional requests followed from the British government, whose concerns focused—as they had for more than a century—on weapons acquisitions in the United States by and for the Irish Republican Army (IRA). ATF responded by creating a program it called ITAR (International Traffic in Arms) to concentrate on identifying and apprehending those involved in arms dealing destined for foreign markets. Although most of its energies were devoted to gun running across the Mexican border—a subject that attracted Congressional interest in 1977[141]—it also collaborated with foreign police in investigations of weapons-smuggling to the United Kingdom, Jamaica, Haiti, Canada, Japan, Lebanon, Colombia, Nicaragua, and Rhodesia.[142]

During the 1980s, Mexico remained a target of concern even as the number of ITAR investigations proliferated. Many of the requests from abroad involved no more than help in tracing seized weapons—the most notable of which involved the Italian government's request for assistance in tracing the Browning semi-automatic pistol seized from Mehmet Ali Agca, the Turk accused of shooting Pope John Paul II. In 1987, ATF responded to a Jamaican police request for assistance in tracing eight handguns; the subsequent investigation played a role in uncovering the

140. See the extensive discussion of ATF's relationship with Mexican officials during the mid-1970s in *Illicit Traffic in Weapons and Drugs Across the United States–Mexican Border: Hearing Before the Permanent Subcommittee on Investigations of the Senate Committee on Government Operations*, 95th Cong., 1st Sess. (1977), 55–87 (testimony of ATF Director Rex Davis).

141. Ibid.

142. See annual reports of the ATF for fiscal years 1974 (p. 12), 1975 (p. 8), 1976 (pp. 6–7), and 1978 (pp. 11–13).

extensive criminal activities of organized criminal groups called "Jamaican posses" in the United States.[143] By the late 1980s, ATF's international investigations were increasingly focused on gun running to Brazil, Colombia, the Dominican Republic, and the Philippines.[144] As during the 1970s, many of these involved gun running to antigovernment groups in foreign countries, but an increasing share of its international investigations, as well as most of the firearms reported to it from abroad for tracing, involved drug trafficking cases.

The Bureau of Alcohol, Tobacco, and Firearms has played a similar role in its efforts to curtail the illicit traffic in explosives. In the late 1970s and early 1980s, its agents participated in the investigation of former CIA agent Edwin Wilson.[145] At the request of the State Department and various foreign governments, ATF agents have trained foreign law enforcement personnel in explosives detection and handling. Foreign investigators have benefited from ATF's computerized data base known as EXIS (the Explosives Incident System), which includes information on common devices, components, trends, targets, and methods of operation in explosions—although a separate data base on foreign explosives incidents (known as I-EXIS) was created only in 1986. In 1987, ATF established liaison with bomb data centers in Canada, Germany, Australia, and Israel to exchange information on explosives incidents in those countries.[146] The agency has also attempted to introduce an element of standardization to the reporting of explosives incidents abroad by developing a format that can be circulated through Interpol channels.

Despite the expanding array of contacts with foreign law enforcement officials, as well as closer collaboration on international terrorism investigations with the FBI, the CIA, and the State Department's Counterterrorism Office, ATF had yet to assume a strong international presence by the end of the 1980s. The 258 firearms smuggling investigations completed by ATF during 1988 represented a substantial increase over its caseload a decade earlier but a small fraction of what

143. Wayne King, "A Bureau That Battled Bootleggers Is Tough Target for Budget-Cutters," *New York Times*, Feb. 1, 1988, A26.

144. *Treasury, Postal Service, and General Government Appropriations for Fiscal Year 1990: Hearings Before the Subcommittee on the Treasury, Postal Service, and General Government Appropriations, House Committee on Appropriations*, 100th Cong., 1st Sess., Part 1 (1989), 542–543, 751.

145. See Maas, *Manhunt* (supra n. 136).

146. *Treasury, Postal Service, and General Government Appropriations for Fiscal Year 1990*, 552.

other federal agencies were involved in. Persistent requests since the mid-1970s to station an attaché in Mexico City had failed to meet with success, although by 1990 ATF had informally opened an office in Bogotá.[147] International travel by agents had increased during the 1980s—most frequently to Colombia but also to Jamaica, Japan, and Mexico—as ATF became more involved in joint operations with the DEA and in its own international investigations. But operational activity by ATF agents abroad, such as engaging in undercover operations, recruiting and running informants, and accompanying foreign police on surveillances, is still rare. In the Edwin Wilson investigation, for instance, ATF agents operated undercover within the United States, but the principal reason for traveling abroad in that case, as in most others, was the need to conduct an interview.[148] Like most other federal U.S. law enforcement agencies, ATF's most frequent foreign contacts have been with law enforcement authorities in Canada and Mexico, and like the U.S. Marshals Service and other agencies with few or no foreign offices, ATF has been obliged to make the most of its participation in international gatherings and in the International Association of Chiefs of Police to establish ties with foreign counterparts. The basic reason for its relatively modest international presence has been the fact that the FBI, Customs, the DEA, and other agencies claim primary jurisdiction over most of the international dimensions of ATF's domestic jurisdiction. In 1979, for instance, the FBI had created a special squad to investigate illicit flows of weapons and money to the IRA.[149] ATF's director of enforcement summed up his agency's international role—as one of supporting the investigations of sister agencies—in Congressional testimony in March 1989. Responding to a question about ATF's involvement in counterterrorism investigations, he explained:

> For a long period of time we have supported the FBI domestically, and then in foreign law enforcement, as well as the Department of Defense and the CIA internationally in explosives and firearms. We have programs that are set up for the tracing of American arms that are recovered anywhere in the world so we can trace

147. *Connection Between Arms and Narcotics Trafficking: Hearing Before the House Committee on Foreign Affairs*, 101st Cong., 1st Sess. (1989), 11–12.

148. Maas, *Manhunt* (supra n. 136), 192.

149. James Adams, *The Financing of Terror* (New York: Simon & Schuster, 1986), 145–153.

them back to the purchaser, and sometimes provide investigative leads. We also provide explosives training on tracing for recovered explosives that may turn up in other parts of the world. We track the types of devices being used by certain groups where we can prepare a list of components and sometimes provide a signatory mark identifying the group that has committed the crime. . . .

We are very active in the terrorist area, although we function more in a support mode for our expertise on weapons and explosives rather than jurisdiction.[150]

The INS, the IRS, and the PIS

The principal law enforcement concerns of the seventeen Immigration and Naturalization Service (INS) offices abroad (see Appendix A)—most of which include at least one special agent—have been twofold: investigating and deterring efforts to smuggle illegal aliens into the United States, and ensuring that aliens with criminal records do not enter the United States. Reasoning, like the drug enforcement agency, "that it is easier and more cost efficient to intercept or prevent potential illegal aliens from entering the country before their actual arrival at our gates," the INS decided in 1985 to increase the criminal investigative responsibilities of its overseas agents.[151] The INS has increasingly concerned itself not just with violations of the immigration laws but also with any number of criminal activities in which the role of aliens has been conspicuous. Often, a violation of U.S. immigration laws, like a violation of tax laws, has provided the relatively innocuous hook with which to indict criminals guilty of far more serious crimes for which they cannot be prosecuted for one reason or another. In one case, for instance, a senior member of the Japanese organized crime group Yakuza was convicted of false statements in connection with obtaining a visa and entry into the United States.[152] The INS's most extensive foreign interactions, however, have involved Mexico and the long border separating the two countries.

150. *Treasury, Postal Service, and General Government Appropriations for Fiscal Year 1990*, 568 (testimony of Daniel Hartnett).
151. *INS Reporter*, Fall/Winter 1985–86, 13.
152. Ibid., 15.

The Postal Inspection Service (PIS), which claims to be the oldest of the federal law enforcement agencies, has stationed one agent, known as a postal inspector, at Interpol headquarters in France since 1983 and another in Wiesbaden, Germany, since 1993. Its jurisdiction includes mail fraud, mail theft, and pornography sent through the mail, as well as many of the insider trading cases.[153] In the latter area, it has worked closely with the Securities and Exchange Commission, which opened its own international enforcement section in 1985. The postal inspectors, who are given much greater latitude in their investigations than, for instance, FBI agents, are permitted to travel overseas, although the trip must first be cleared with top officials at headquarters. In fact, relatively few agents, perhaps a dozen or so, actually travel abroad each year. The reasons for doing so vary: someone may need to be interviewed; a request for evidence or an extradition may need to be accompanied by some personal diplomacy; and continuation of an undercover operation begun within the United States is always a possibility, although an infrequent one. One of the more notable international investigations by a postal inspector occurred in 1950, when an agent in Honolulu uncovered an extensive black market in U.S. postal money orders. His international investigation ultimately led to the uncovering of a number of counterfeiting rings in the Philippines and a money laundering operation involving Chinese communists working out of Hong Kong.[154] Agents are also sent overseas on occasion to liaise with foreign police, explain their agency's particular law enforcement interests, and seek assistance in accomplishing them. For instance, two postal inspectors were sent to Denmark, Sweden, and the Netherlands in the early 1980s to discuss the traffic in pornography from those countries to the United States.

The Internal Revenue Service (IRS) opened its first overseas office in 1938 in Manila, when the Philippines were still a possession of the United States, and its first foreign offices in 1939 in Paris and London.[155] It currently stations approximately the same number of representatives abroad as the FBI. Virtually all of them, however, are primarily concerned with providing tax assistance to Americans resident abroad.[156]

153. The activities of the PIS are briefly described in Arnold H. Lubasch, "Postal Inspectors' No-Frills Unit Handles Big Cases," *New York Times*, June 16, 1986, B5.

154. The story is in Ottenberg, *Federal Investigators* (supra n. 46), 318–332.

155. John C. Chommie, *The Internal Revenue Service* (New York: Praeger Publishers, 1970), 120.

156. Ibid., 117–136.

One or two have some background in criminal investigation, but it is highly unusual for an IRS representative in a U.S. embassy to become directly involved in investigating criminal violations of U.S. tax laws. The Intelligence Division, created in 1919 and renamed the Criminal Investigation Division in 1978, has never stationed agents abroad— although its agents occasionally have pursued their investigations to foreign territories.[157] Most governments are reluctant to offer assistance in a foreign government's criminal investigation of tax evaders within their borders. Only in Mexico and the Caribbean, where U.S. law enforcement agents admit to operating occasionally "as if they are in their own back yard," have IRS agents actively pursued criminal investigations. In a number of cases, IRS agents operating undercover have pursued their targets to various Caribbean tax havens, although arrests have always taken place in the United States. Nowhere has this been more true than in the Bahamas, which for many decades served as perhaps the principal tax haven and offshore money laundering center for American criminals of all sorts. In 1965, the Miami office of the IRS's Intelligence Division initiated an aggressive investigation, known as "Operation Tradewinds," into the uses of Bahamian banks to evade U.S. tax laws.[158] During the following ten years, until it was undermined by a newly appointed IRS commissioner—Donald Alexander, who strongly opposed most of the IRS's criminal investigative initiatives— IRS agents recruited informants, operated undercover, bought information from bank employees, and employed a wide array of other investigative techniques to gather information and evidence on the illicit uses of the banks.[159] The successes of that operation yielded another one, "Project Haven," which together provided the IRS with unprecedented intelligence on the means employed both by the banks and by those interested in their confidential services; the operations also provided something of a model for future investigations into Caribbean-based money laundering.

157. The history of the Intelligence Division's first fifty years is in Hank Messick, *Secret File* (New York: G. P. Putnam's Sons, 1969).

158. See Alan A. Block, *Masters of Paradise: Organized Crime and the Internal Revenue Service in the Bahamas* (New Brunswick, N.J.: Transaction Publishers, 1991).

159. The struggle between Commissioner Alexander and the Intelligence Division agents is discussed in ibid., 215–246; and in David Burnham, *A Law Unto Itself: Power, Politics, and the IRS* (New York: Random House, 1989), 103–107.

Big City and Border City Policing

Unlike the federal police agencies, whose international activities generally increased over time, the municipal police departments never institutionalized their international links. In New York, a police department policy was instituted, apparently in the 1920s, forbidding any police to travel abroad on official investigations. Not until 1972, fifty years after Fiaschetti's second trip to Italy, was this policy reversed. An NYPD detective, Joseph Coffey, conducting an electronic surveillance on an apparently low-level mafioso was surprised to find the criminal making plans to go to Munich. Given permission to continue the surveillance in Europe, Coffey liaised with the Munich police—and with the CIA, who provided the bugging devices—and ended up uncovering a criminal ring marketing hundreds of millions of dollars of stolen and forged securities. Those implicated included not only American mafiosi and an odd selection of international con men, but also high-level officials in the governments of Italy and the Vatican.[160]

Having broken the ice, a trickle of New York City police agents began to travel abroad on investigations. With most of the more sophisticated and far-reaching criminal investigations under the jurisdiction of federal agencies, the opportunities have hardly been abundant. Some have arisen in the course of joint federal-city investigations into organized crime and drug trafficking. In one case involving car-theft and other charges against the Gambino Mafia family in New York, two NYPD detectives traced a shipment of stolen cars from Port Newark, New Jersey, to Kuwait. In 1983, they traveled to the sheikdom and secured the cooperation of the national police in finding the cars.[161] Such cases, however, have hardly been typical of the police department's investigations. With fewer financial resources than the federal agencies, and with the ability to draw on the international resources of the DEA and the FBI as well as the Interpol network, the city police have typically handled most international investigations from within the boundaries of the five boroughs. Nonetheless, the fact that most criminal investigations in the United States are conducted by municipal police, combined with the fact that many criminal offenses still do not fall under federal jurisdiction, suggests that

160. The entire case, in which the FBI and a number of European law enforcement agencies ultimately became involved, is recounted in Hammer, *Vatican Connection* (supra n. 106).

161. Ronald Smothers, "Gambino Jury Following Paper Trail," *New York Times*, Nov. 24, 1985, 42.

city and state police agencies throughout the United States have become far more involved in transnational travel and communication than ever before.

The city and state police forces with the greatest experience in transnational policing are those who work near the borders with Mexico and Canada. Although posses no longer ride headlong across the border in pursuit of cattle rustlers and other criminals, the problems shared by the successors to Colonel Kosterlitzky and Captain Rynning have not changed all that much. Relations between police departments on either side of the U.S.-Canadian border tend to be very close and professional, not all that different in many cases than relations across municipal and state borders in the United States. Relations along the Mexican border are more varied, ranging from close and long-standing personal relationships that can cut through any red tape, to bitter antagonisms and suspicions stemming as often as not from corrupt and criminal behavior by the Mexican police. During the 1970s and 1980s, state and municipal police agencies near both borders—but most significantly along the Mexican border—took steps to regularize and formalize their cross-border relations, in part by creating specialized liaison units to handle cross-border matters. Indeed, not just border cities but also others within a few hours' driving distance from the border undertook similar steps. The Los Angeles Police Department, for instance, created a Foreign Prosecution Liaison Unit in 1984 when it realized that approximately 100 of its 237 murder warrants involved suspects who were Mexican nationals.[162] During the same time, but particularly after the mid-1980s, the federal law enforcement presence along the border increased dramatically, motivated primarily by the intensification of the war on drugs and secondarily by a renewed desire to crack down on illicit migration from Mexico.

In late 1976, the San Diego Police Department began an eighteen-month experiment to deal not with the customary problem of illegal immigration but with the increasing crimes directed against the *pollos*, as the migrants were called, during the nighttime crossings. Known as BARF, for Border Alien Robbery Force, the exploits and travails of its dozen-odd members were recounted by Joseph Wambaugh in *Lines and Shadows*. The BARF police worked undercover, dressing, talking, and

---

162. Daryl F. Gates and Keith E. Ross, "Foreign Prosecution Liaison Unit Helps Apprehend Suspects Across the Border," *Police Chief* 57 (Apr. 1990), 153–154.

walking like the *pollos* they had been delegated to protect. In conversations with the *pollos*, they heard numerous accounts of their being robbed, extorted, and even killed by Mexican police. Shortly after the squad began patrolling the border, they too were accosted by thieves and extortionists that turned out to be Mexican police. The results were encounters in which American and Mexican cops were drawing on one another, and in a few cases actually shooting at each other.

The San Diego Police Department, like other municipal police departments along the border, assigned a few officers to handle foreign liaison. In 1977, the principal responsibility for liaison with the Mexican police fell to two Mexican-Americans on the force named Manuel Smith and Ron Collins. In *Lines and Shadows*, Joseph Wambaugh described their duties:

> Both cops were of patrolman rank, Ron Collins having been a liaison officer longer but Manuel Smith generally thought of as the spokesman by virtue of his incredible connections south of the imaginary line. He had a cousin in the *judiciales* [the Mexican police] and another in the municipal police. Just watching him operate was a thing to behold. Manuel Smith couldn't even cross the border without having to pause and chat with the Mexican border guards, who normally only stopped cars heading south when they wanted to peddle some tickets to the police rodeo at the downtown bullring.
>
> And when he got to the headquarters of the *judiciales* it was as though Santa Claus had arrived. Tijuana cops had a thousand problems that needed solving up north. There were personal problems, relatives who needed assistance with documents, immigration problems, insurance problems, employment problems. There were professional needs, the endless information search by cops who had no access to computers. There was impounded property linked to persons who traveled south to do business, legal and otherwise. The Mexican authorities had to labor under a maddening information gap that Manuel Smith and Ron Collins could help them narrow through American sources.
>
> By the time he could even set foot inside state judicial police headquarters, Manuel Smith had a laundry list hanging out every pocket, and more to come when he got inside. An FBI agent coming to the same headquarters might cool his heels in the lobby

> for a whole afternoon, while Manuel Smith had ten *judiciales* falling all over themselves just to help him locate the son of some American cop who was last seen smoking pot laced with PCP and running naked through the Tijuana cemetery on a big frat weekender.[163]

In many respects, the liaison role played by Manuel Smith represents the most traditional, typical, and universal dimension of transnational police relations.[164] Relations among the law enforcement agents of neighboring countries, and especially among agents who are stationed close to the border, fall into a special category notable for its familiarity and informality. The friendlier the governments, and the greater the overall scale of cross-border commerce, travel, and general interaction, the more this is so. Under such conditions, mutually beneficial transnational understandings and operating procedures that are best comprehended within the context of the border environment emerge. These often may be unsanctioned by and even unknown to central government officials in the capital, but they are essential to the functioning of law enforcement where national laws and international politics retain the potential to create bureaucratic and legal nightmares. Sensitivities of national sovereignty may still get pricked from time to time, such as when agents "forget" which side of the border they are on or fall into personal or policy disputes. But by and large, cross-border law enforcement cooperation functions on a scale and level of familiarity unparalleled by more distant transnational law enforcement relationships. That is the case along the United States' borders with Canada and Mexico, and it is also true of friendly borders throughout the rest of the world. It is even true, albeit to a lesser extent, of U.S. law enforcement dealings with Bermuda and many Caribbean islands.

One other factor that accounts for the informality of relations between police on either side of a border is the jurisdictional and bureaucratic

163. Joseph Wambaugh, *Lines and Shadows* (New York: Bantam Books, 1984), 144–145.

164. For an interesting discussion by a political scientist of law enforcement relations across the U.S.-Mexican border, see Marshall Carter, "Law Enforcement and Federalism: Bordering on Trouble," *Policy Studies Journal* 7 (1979), 413–418; Marshall Carter, "Law, Order, and the Border: El Paso del Norte" (Paper presented at the annual meeting of the National Council on Geographic Education, Mexico City, Nov. 1979); and C. Richard Bath, H. Marshall Carter, and Thomas J. Price, "Dependence, Interdependence, or Detachment? Three Case Studies of International Relations Between El Paso, Texas, and Ciudad Juárez, Mexico" (Paper presented at the Third World Conference, Omaha, Nebraska, Oct. 1977).

distance between law enforcement agents in border locales and the central government. This is particularly the case in federally constituted nations such as the United States and Germany, but even in most nonfederated countries municipal and state police in border towns and cities often have little occasion or desire to deal with federal authorities other than those stationed in the vicinity. They tend to adapt to local law enforcement needs without much regard for the formalities and niceties of diplomacy and international law. From their perspective, dealing with counterparts across the border is regarded not as international relations but as police business. If investigating a case or seizing a fugitive means working the other side of the border, then one contacts one's counterparts across the border directly. If that is seen as being either unnecessary or potentially problematic, one goes it alone and "to hell with sovereignty." Unlike federal agents, who often operate in much the same fashion anyway, local agents need not worry quite so much about accounting for their cross-border operations to a national headquarters with a keener sense of correct international behavior than the local mayor or state police chief.

U.S. Involvement in Interpol: Assuming Leadership

Unlike other federal law enforcement agencies, the U.S. office of Interpol, known as the National Central Bureau (Interpol-USNCB), is not charged with the enforcement of any federal criminal laws. Its function is primarily one of facilitating communication between U.S. and foreign police agencies by providing a central office through which international messages can be both channeled and distributed. With some 20,000 federal, state, and local police agencies in the United States, foreign police are often at a loss as to whom to contact in providing and seeking information and other assistance. The same holds true of most police departments in the United States, many of which occasionally need to communicate with foreign police but have little idea how to do so efficiently if at all. As police departments have become more aware of the accessibility of the Interpol system and the identity of the National Central Bureau, the process of internationalization has begun to penetrate the provincialism of many local police forces.

The U.S. involvement in Interpol can be roughly divided into three phases. The first, from about 1950 to 1969, was more a case of noninvolvement by the United States. The FBI director, J. Edgar Hoover, generally shunned the international agency, preferred that U.S. police agencies rely on the LEGAT system to communicate internationally, and made small efforts to preclude other federal agencies from participating in Interpol. The Secret Service and the Federal Bureau of Narcotics nonetheless participated on an informal basis, and in 1958 the attorney general officially designated the Treasury Department—which oversaw both agencies—as the official U.S. representative to Interpol. The second phase began in 1969, when the USNCB, which had been officially created in 1962, was provided with an office and a staff of three. The scale of its operations throughout the 1970s remained limited, with the NCB handling an average of 300 cases a year. The most notable developments involved legal suits against Interpol by the Church of Scientology, attempted exposés of the agency's history and misdeeds, and Congressional inquiries into U.S. involvement in Interpol, none of which led to significant revelations. Their principal impact was to remind the USNCB forcefully of the need to screen all transmissions adequately to ensure that they were for legitimate criminal investigative purposes.[165]

The third phase, beginning in 1979, was ushered in with the appointment of a dynamic Secret Service agent, Richard Stiener, as chief of the USNCB. Stiener quickly resolved the controversies surrounding the NCB, reassuring those who had criticized the office that it was a valuable and nonsecretive member of the law enforcement community.[166] Stiener also embarked on an ambitious and successful campaign to increase dramatically the NCB's staff and budget, computerize its operations, involve the federal law enforcement agencies in its activities, publicize its existence and services to state police agencies, and enhance the USNCB's role and status at Interpol headquarters in France. Between 1979 and 1990, the NCB staff increased from 6 to 110, its budget rose from $125,000 to $6,000,000, and the number of law enforcement agencies represented at the NCB went from 1 to 16. Concerns that the bureau

165. See U.S. General Accounting Office, *United States Participation in Interpol, the International Criminal Police Organization*, GAO/ID-76-77, Dec. 27, 1976; and Diana Gulbinowicz, "The International Criminal Police Organization: A Case Study of Oversight of American Participation in an International Organization" (Ph.D. diss., City University of New York, 1978).

166. See Malcolm Anderson, *Policing the World: Interpol and the Politics of International Police Co-operation* (New York: Oxford University Press, 1989).

would be hampered by civil and criminal claims filed against it were allayed by President Reagan's designation of Interpol as a public international organization entitled to civil and criminal immunity under U.S. law.[167] In an international organization frequently criticized for its unwillingness to integrate advanced techonlogy, the USNCB devoted substantial efforts to computerizing its files and installing automated electronic communications systems. Its personnel gained access to most of the major computerized law enforcement records systems in the United States. And participation by state police agencies in Interpol increased significantly in response to the rising need for its services and the promotional efforts of Stiener and his staff. By 1990, most state police agencies were formally affiliated with the NCB, many had established their own Interpol liaison office, and one—the Illinois State Police—had stationed an agent in the NCB. Also significant was the full implementation of the U.S./Canadian Interface Project, a semi-automated link between U.S. and Canadian law enforcement information networks that allows police in each country to get information from other nations' networks.[168]

Not all U.S. law enforcement agencies depend on the NCB for their international communications. The FBI and the DEA, with their international networks of overseas agents, are the least dependent upon Interpol; indeed, other police agencies, both U.S. and foreign, have been known to turn to the DEA, and to a lesser extent the FBI, when Interpol channels have been too slow or unresponsive. Although both agencies do make use of Interpol's facilities, particularly in communicating with countries in which they are not represented, their representatives at the NCB tend to handle far more incoming than outgoing requests. For state and city police, on the other hand, as for police in most other countries around the world, the absence of ongoing relationships and liaison with police in other countries makes the Interpol network virtually indispensable in conducting transnational inquiries and tasks—although one survey of police chiefs in 1991 found that relatively few had ever found Interpol of assistance to their agencies.[169] The same is even more true of

167. See Executive Order No. 12,425, 48 Fed. Reg. 28,069 (1983), and the discussion in William R. Slomanson, "Civil Actions Against Interpol: A Field Compass," *Temple Law Review* 57 (1984), 553–600.
168. Department of Justice, *1990 Annual Report of the Attorney General of the United States*, 51.
169. Jerry Seper, "Police Chiefs Seek Interpol Curbs," *Washington Times*, Apr. 4, 1991, A4.

U.S. federal law enforcement agencies that station few if any representatives abroad and that can expect only limited assistance from overseas
DEA agents and FBI LEGATs. Given Interpol's near-global membership,
moreover, the NCB has often provided the only means of communicating
with police agencies whose governments are not on friendly terms with
the United States. During the 1980s, routine requests were exchanged
with Soviet-bloc states and with Qadaffi's Libya.

Between 1976 and 1986, the annual caseload of the USNCB increased
from approximately 4,000 to 43,863, and the volume of message traffic
went from 14,365 to 101,859. Collection of such statistics was abandoned thereafter, but the numbers most certainly continued to increase.
The requests range from checks on driver's licenses, auto registrations,
addresses, phone numbers, and criminal record histories, to identification of photographs, fingerprints, and documents, requests for bank
records, location and seizure of stolen property, and the arrest of
fugitives. The dramatic increases in the NCB's caseload were a function
not only of the rising demand for its services but also of its success in
promoting its value to U.S. and foreign police agencies and of its
"pivotal position in a criminal intelligence communications network"
linking the international Interpol communications system with the on-
line computerized systems of the FBI, the DEA, the INS, and the Treasury
Department.[170]

U.S. participation in Interpol has contributed to the evolution of
international law enforcement in at least three ways. In providing a link
between the police agencies of most governments that is relatively quick
and efficient, it has increased the capacity of city, state, and national law
enforcement agencies to deal with the challenges posed by transnational
crime. Interpol is primarily responsible for the increasing difficulty that
fugitives face in finding a haven where they can remain undetected. When
Interpol issues an international wanted notice, for instance, police
agencies in more than 150 countries are put on notice—in theory if not
always in practice—to arrest that person. The same is also true, albeit to
a lesser extent, of stolen property.

Second, Interpol offers an international professional association for
police. Its annual meetings in recent years have drawn delegates from
more than 100 countries. Its regional conferences similarly play a role
in bringing together police from nearby countries in a forum where they

170. Anderson, *Policing the World* (supra n. 166), 85.

are able to exchange information and opinions and establish the personal relationships that will help speed requests and cut through red tape thereafter. Interpol also acts as a channel for the dissemination of new police methods and investigative techniques. Its publication, translated into half a dozen languages, is the only police magazine circulated around the world. In many respects, Interpol is, as Secretary-General Raymond Kendall claimed, "the only existing organization which is structured to deal with the handling of international police information."[171]

The third contribution is the most recent. Interpol in recent years has become an increasingly effective means for the U.S. government to internationalize its law enforcement concerns. During the 1970s, the emphasis was placed on drug trafficking. During the 1980s, the U.S. government encouraged Interpol as an organization, and through Interpol other governments, to improve their international cooperation against terrorism and the financial aspects of drug trafficking. The first efforts to raise the issues of money laundering and forfeiture of drug-related assets were made by Customs agents in the late 1970s. During the 1980s, two Customs agents were stationed at Interpol headquarters in Saint Cloud, where they created a small financial intelligence section. By the end of the decade, Customs' efforts had been joined by the USNCB as well as upper echelons of the Treasury and Justice Departments, and foreign law enforcement agencies were increasingly receptive to pursuing similar and joint investigations. Much the same occurred with respect to counterterrorism efforts. Until the early 1980s, Interpol resisted cooperating in terrorist cases, fearing that its reputation as a strictly apolitical organization would be undermined. But significant U.S. pressures, combined with the recognition that Interpol's failure to reform in this area would relegate it to the sidelines of a crucial domain of international law enforcement, led to a change in policy. As the United States has come to play a more dominant role in the previously Europe-centered organization—the head of the U.S. Secret Service was elected Interpol president in 1985—its ability to internationalize its own law enforcement concerns and approaches has grown apace.

Even as the NCB emerged as a significant player in the internationalization of U.S. law enforcement, the charges leveled against it by the Church of Scientology and other critics persisted. These charges were

---

171. Philip Shenon, "Interpol, aka 'Strait-Laced Guys,' " *New York Times*, Oct. 5, 1985, 7.

publicized anew in early 1991, when the National Association of Chiefs of Police (not to be confused with the International Association of Chiefs of Police) sent a questionnaire regarding Interpol—and copies of a pamphlet produced by the Church of Scientology, entitled "Interpol: Private Group, Public Menace"—to directors of 14,000 U.S. police agencies throughout the United States.[172] Principal among these were accusations that the USNCB was cooperating with foreign NCBs, such as those in Panama and Mexico, directed by police officials who had been implicated in drug trafficking and other crimes. Others focused on the possibility that sensitive information could be provided to police officials in countries implicated in terrorist activities against U.S. citizens, such as Libya. The charges reflected the inevitable vulnerability of any global organization to charges of consorting with unseemly governments. But it also pointed to the frictions inherent in an international organization seeking both to maximize the speed, breadth, and intensity of police cooperation across borders and to minimize the possibility that its facilities might be taken advantage of by criminals.

Conclusion

The internationalization of U.S. law enforcement since the end of World War II cannot be explained by any one event or theory. To describe it as a response to either the internationalization of crime or the proliferation of transnational criminal activities would be only partially true, given the substantial impact of U.S. legislation in defining as crimes, both substantively and jurisdictionally, activities that were not the business of U.S. law enforcers just decades ago. Indeed, when we stretch our horizons backward to the early years of the American republic, we realize that most of what today engages U.S. international law enforcement efforts was then either inconceivable or legal. Eighteenth- and nineteenth-century law enforcers would have recognized the efforts of contemporary customs officials to collect the revenues, and of special agents to investigate transnational frauds and recover fugitives, and even

172. See Seper, "Police Chiefs Seek Interpol Curbs," and the response to the charges by the Church of Scientology in Darrell W. Mills, "A Clearer Picture of What Interpol Is and Does," *Washington Times*, Mar. 19, 1991, G2. See also unpublished commentaries available from the USNCB.

of FBI and ATF agents to enforce the neutrality laws, but they would have regarded as quite novel the contemporary efforts to restrict the transnational movements of people, money, cannabis, and derivatives of the coca and opium plants. Certainly much of the contemporary expansion can be explained by national security concerns; the more broadly we define the term, the more robust the explanation. Nonetheless, a national security thesis—even broadly construed—fails as well to capture much of what was described above, for the simple reason that so much of international law enforcement is concerned with the extraterritorial dimensions of common crimes familiar to the average citizen.

When we focus on the perspective of the United States not as creator of laws but as enforcer, one can say that all of the international efforts—with the partial exception of the police assistance programs—have been motivated by two basic objectives: the "immobilization" of criminals and the seizure of contraband. These objectives have required law enforcement agents to collect information, evidence, and criminals wherever they can be found, which increasingly has included foreign territories. The same objectives have also yielded an abundance of transgovernmental interactions ranging from discreet efforts to operate abroad unilaterally and in informal relationships with foreign police, to the institutionalization of foreign offices and liaison relationships. At the same time, U.S. police have played a central role in the evolution of a transnational police community, training tens of thousands of foreign police officials, advocating more intensive and systematic bilateral and multilateral cooperation, making its computerized data bases and other intelligence resources available to foreign investigators, and initiating new endeavors in both criminal procedures and criminal legislation.

The specifics of these efforts, however, have varied substantially from one agency to the next. Some extended their efforts abroad to investigate smuggling of one sort or another more effectively. This was especially true of Customs, the INS, ATF and the FBN, the BNDD, and the DEA. Some were drawn overseas by national security concerns: the military needed to police itself; the Office of Public Safety was designed in good part to aid anticommunist governments in maintaining public order; U.S. Customs was delegated to investigate the smuggling of high technology to hostile countries; and the FBI was directed to deal with espionage and terrorist acts against U.S. citizens and interests abroad. Most U.S. agencies were obliged to locate, apprehend, and attempt to recover fugitives from abroad. The DEA and the FBI have been particularly involved in such efforts, but no one agency as much as the U.S. Marshals Service in recent years.

The methods and styles of U.S. police operations abroad have changed in some respects but not in others. Posses no longer chase cattle rustlers over the border with Mexico, and military expeditions no longer pursue the likes of "Pancho" Villa—although the amendment to the Posse Comitatus Act and the paramilitarization of U.S. drug enforcement activities in Bolivia and Peru during the late 1980s pointed to a revival of large-scale law enforcement ventures. Respect for foreign sovereignty has climbed noticeably in the domain of international law enforcement, albeit not so much that the Bahamas' sovereignty is given the same deference as Canada's. To the extent that any trends can be discerned, two stand out. The first has been the overall increase in the scope and magnitude of U.S. police efforts abroad. The second has been the emergence of a transnational police community and subculture based upon common tasks and the common objective of "immobilizing" the criminal and powerfully shaped by the fact of U.S. involvement.

Chapter Four

The DEA in Europe:
Dealing with Foreign Systems

Drug Enforcement in Comparative and International Perspective

"To get the dope off the street and put the cat in jail." That, as one agent from the Drug Enforcement Administration concisely put it, has remained the central objective of American drug enforcement agents since the beginning. Whether based in Miami, Marseilles, or Mexico City, be it 1939, 1969, or 1989, U.S. drug enforcement agents have concentrated their energies on immobilizing drug traffickers and seizing illicit drugs within or destined for American markets. Time and place have, of course, affected the nature of the agents' challenges and tasks, and a variety of political and bureaucratic considerations have often determined where the agents are stationed and the identities of their targets, both human and psychoactive. (See Appendix C.) Yet even as the assorted directives have flowed from above, the agents have kept their sights on the agency's central objective.

My objective in this chapter is to analyze, more deeply than in the preceding chapters, the relationship between the objectives and tasks of U.S. law enforcers and the foreign environments in which they have operated. The fact of operating extraterritorially dramatically transforms the nature of the DEA agent's work, which is why the task of an agent stationed in Frankfurt has more in common with that of an agent stationed in Lima or Bangkok than one located in Detroit or Los Angeles. Within the United States, the DEA agent is lawfully authorized to arrest those who he believes have violated federal drug laws. He is often expected to coordinate his efforts with state and municipal drug enforcement agents, but it is not a legal condition of his work. By contrast, the agent abroad retains no powers of arrest, and the requirement that he coordinate his efforts with local agents is ignored only rarely and at some risk. In many foreign countries, DEA agents are forbidden to carry firearms, and in some they are legally precluded from even conducting interviews and other investigatory inquiries on their own.

The relationship between the DEA agent abroad and host police agencies is thus one of substantial dependence. If the latter close their doors to him, there is relatively little he can accomplish. On the other hand, the resourceful agent is typically successful at creating a relationship of mutual dependence based upon his own access to intelligence, funds, and expertise desired by his hosts.

All three of the models of transnational policing advanced in the previous chapter provide insights into the nature of the DEA's tasks and challenges abroad. Like the private detective, the DEA agent pursues his investigations without benefit of any sovereign powers, relying on his investigative skills, contacts, and an abundance of discretion. In his capacity as liaison and "fixer," he handles an array of mundane and extraordinary matters. When we recall the disparate activities of Siragusa, Vizzini, and the other FBN and BNDD agents sent overseas in the 1950s, 1960s, and early 1970s, both models are clearly in evidence. When we focus on the DEA's country attachés in foreign capitals, especially those who either preside over relatively large offices or are precluded by local laws from acting in a more operational capacity, the liaison model readily applies. And when we consider the work engaged in by most DEA agents stationed abroad, as well as by most of those sent abroad on TDYs and individual cases, the model of the private detective rings true.

The most comprehensive model, however, is that of a transnational organization. Like a private corporation that retains most of its operations within the United States but earns a disproportionate share of its profits from its overseas activities, the U.S. drug enforcement agency has always retained a strong international orientation despite the small proportion of its personnel stationed abroad. Among all other federal law enforcement agencies, only U.S. Customs has shared a comparable perspective. Driven by both the international nature of drug trafficking and the strong international orientation of its first chief administrator, the Federal Bureau of Narcotics, and thereafter the Bureau of Narcotics and Dangerous Drugs and the Drug Enforcement Administration, always emphasized the inherently international nature of the task delegated to them. But while the central objective of the DEA in 1990 differed in no substantial way from that of the FBN in 1930, the ways in which the contemporary agency has pursued its objectives, as well as the consequences of its activities for foreign law enforcement systems, have differed substantially from those associated with the original drug enforcement agency. If we say that the FBN's international activities are similar to those of a small corporation with modest but highly profitable sales overseas, we can fairly say that the DEA's international operations can be analogized to those of leading multinational corporations such as IBM, General Motors, and MacDonald's. By and large, smaller organizations extract what they require without changing in any substantial way the environments in which they operate. By contrast, major multinational organizations powerfully influence both the foreign environments in which they operate and the ways in which comparable institutions pursue comparable objectives. That influence stems not just from the pressures they exert but also from the models they provide, the examples they suggest, and the concessions they expect as the costs of doing business together.

When we focus on the efforts of American drug enforcement agents in Europe between the late 1960s and the late 1980s, all three models are applicable, but that of the transnational organization is the most valuable. During that time, the central objective of the agency remained constant, as did most of the limitations on its agents' actions imposed by considerations of national sovereignty. By the mid-1970s, the agency's personnel in Europe had also reached the level it would more or less maintain thereafter. As for their quarry, the people who were doing the drug trafficking changed over time, as did many of their routes, their evasive tactics, and to a certain extent the drugs in which they trafficked, but the basic contours of their activities remained much the same. What did change, however, were the criminal justice environments in which the American drug enforcement agents pursued their objectives.

These changes were of three types. One was institutional. Until well into the 1960s, relatively few European police agencies had specialized drug enforcement squads, and virtually no prosecutors specialized in drug trafficking cases. By the late 1980s, most European police agencies, be they national, state, cantonal, or municipal, claimed such units and quite a few worked closely with specialized prosecutors.

A second change was operational. When U.S. drug enforcement agents arrived in Europe, they brought with them a variety of investigative techniques—including "buy and bust" tactics and more extensive undercover operations, "controlled delivery" of illicit drug consignments, various forms of nontelephonic electronic surveillance, and offers of reduced charges or immunity from prosecution to known drug dealers to "flip" them into becoming informants—that had been practiced in the United States for decades and approved by U.S. courts during Prohibition if not before.[1] Throughout most of continental Europe, however, virtually all of these techniques were viewed, even by police officials, as unnecessary, unacceptable, and often illegal.[2] Only the internal security agencies in certain countries resorted to such techniques with any frequency, and their activities were rarely subjected to any sort of judicial oversight. Nonetheless, during the following two decades most of these investigative tactics were adopted by European drug enforcement units, albeit at strikingly different rates and to very different degrees.

A third change was legal. Even as European drug enforcement agents adopted DEA-style techniques during the 1970s and 1980s, their legality remained highly questionable. Judges, and even prosecutors, were often kept in the dark as to the exact nature of the agents' investigations, and all sorts of charades were concocted in order to obscure the true nature of many of the drug enforcement operations. By the late 1980s, however, many of the DEA-style methods had been not only adopted by the local

1. Kenneth M. Murchison, "Prohibition and the Fourth Amendment: A New Look at Some Old Cases," *Journal of Criminal Law and Criminology* 73 (1982), 471–532.
2. References to Europe hereafter refer only to the western and central European nations on the continent, all of which adhere to the civil law tradition. The common law nations of Great Britain and Ireland, as well as the previously socialist law nations of Eastern Europe, are excluded from the discussion.

police but also authorized, and hence legalized, by local courts and legislatures.

All of these changes can be viewed as part and parcel of the harmonization of drug enforcement both within Europe and in relation to the United States. But how one evaluates these changes depends in good part upon one's perspective. From the perspective of the DEA, and more generally of the U.S. government, all of these changes were of consequence less in and of themselves than for what they contributed to the accomplishment of the DEA's central objective. This is not to say that the changes occurred only as incidental by-products of the DEA's efforts, or to suggest that the urge to proselytize or the satisfaction derived from seeing one's own approaches adopted by others were entirely absent. Quite the contrary, DEA agents consciously advocated and lobbied for the reforms and felt a sense of vindication when they were adopted by their hosts. Their principal motivation, however, was to improve the capacity of the DEA, and by extension European police agencies, to immobilize drug traffickers and seize illicit drugs destined for American markets. Underlying this motivation was the realization that the DEA's success abroad depended less upon its own freedom of action in foreign territories than upon its capacity to generate effective vicarious drug enforcement capabilities within foreign police agencies.

From the Europeans' perspective, however, the changes wrought in part by the efforts of the DEA were of significant consequence in and of themselves. This was particularly true of the changes in the laws, which occurred in many countries only after substantial political, legal, and professional debate about the nature of policing and the proper reaches and methods of the state. As in the United States, but in a far more compressed period of time, judicial, legislative, and executive authorities in Europe were obliged to address difficult legal issues regarding the distinction between legitimate undercover techniques and entrapment, the degree to which undercover agents could participate in criminal activities, the credibility of informants who had been offered financial or judicial compensation for their services, the need to shield informants' identities in court, and the proper limits on electronic surveillance. But unlike their American counterparts, European judges, administrators, and legislators also had to address more basic obstacles to the "Americanization" of their drug enforcement, including a deeply felt, and historically rooted, antipathy toward the notion of *agents provocateurs* and even undercover agents generally, the absence of any clear legal authority for police undercover operations, and the powerful influence of the "legality principle," or "rule of compulsory prosecution"—all of which greatly hindered the acceptance of undercover operations and controlled deliveries as well as the ability of criminal justice agents to recruit informants from among those arrested for illicit drug dealing or any other crime.

It is fair, I believe, to speak of the "Americanization" of European drug enforcement, provided the term is understood broadly and the substantial differences within Europe are acknowledged at the outset. The notion of "Americanization" applies most accurately to the changes demanded and incited by the Americans. With respect to some, evidence of the DEA's active hand is readily apparent and openly acknowledged by the Europeans: the creation of specialized drug enforcement units in major police agencies; the initial adoption of DEA-style undercover tactics and the subsequent training of European police in a variety of DEA-style techniques; the notion of "flipping" informants; and the enactment of legislation authorizing the forfeiture of drug traffickers' assets. But the notion of "Americanization" can also be understood more passively as including changes in European drug enforcement caused not only by American pressures, incitements, and training but also those changes shaped by the experience gained in working with U.S. drug enforcement agents, by the models and examples suggested by the DEA's own history and modus operandi, and by the popularization through fiction and nonfiction media of the American approach to drug enforcement.

There is, of course, an even more passive sense in which one can speak of the "Americanization" of European drug enforcement, one that suggests only an element of chronology, not one of causality. Many of the changes in European drug enforcement may well have had nothing whatsoever to do with the influences or examples of the Americans; rather, they may have reflected the simple lack of effective alternatives for dealing with the spread of illicit drug trafficking. That those changes appeared as an "Americanization" of European drug enforcement was simply a consequence of the Americans' chronological "advantage" both in confronting a drug trafficking boom some years before the Europeans, and in having first addressed many of the same difficult legal issues raised by drug enforcement tactics decades earlier during Prohibition— an experience in alcohol control eschewed by most European nations south of Scandinavia. On the other hand, the fact that some European countries, notably Germany, Austria, and Belgium, have followed closely in the footsteps of the Americans while others, such as France and Italy, have proven more resistant, suggests that the DEA's approach to drug enforcement was not the only option for dealing with the common problem of illicit drug trafficking.

The process of "Americanization" described in this chapter can well be contrasted with the very different "Americanization" of criminal justice and other governmental domains that preceded it.[3] Many of the curbs on police powers that have so frustrated DEA agents were initially imposed by U.S. occupying forces in the aftermath of World War II. U.S. policy makers initially regarded the centralization of police and other governmental power associated with the defeated fascist regimes as an evil to be avoided in the postwar era. But the onset of the Cold War, rising concern with Soviet espionage and communist agitation, and the growing threat of terrorism all provided incentives for U.S. policy makers to reverse stride and encourage the expansion of police powers in Europe as in America. Criminal justice norms and institutions were among the first to be shaped by the "national security state" mentality that emerged in tandem with the Cold War.

The evolution of European drug enforcement since the late 1960s has also been shaped by other influences.[4] Many of the tactics and laws initially devised to investigate and suppress such terrorist groups as the Red Brigade in Italy and the Baader-Meinhof in Germany provided the initial experience, legal authority, and practical models for subsequent responses to illicit drug trafficking and organized crime.[5] National approaches to drug enforcement within Europe have also been influenced by the initiatives taken by individual countries as well as by multilateral initiatives. The German BKA (Bundeskriminalamt), for instance, has promoted itself as a model for other European police agencies and assumed a leading role in inter-European police affairs. Multilateral law enforcement conventions, as well as multilateral arrangements such as Interpol, TREVI, the Council of Europe, and the Pompidou Group have played an increasingly important role.[6] The European Court of Human

3. I am indebted to Walter Murphy for this point.
4. See Ethan A. Nadelmann, *Criminalization and Crime Control in International Society* (New York: Oxford University Press, forthcoming); and Hans-Jörg Albrecht and Anton van Kalmthout, eds., *Drug Policies in Western Europe* (Freiburg: Max-Planck-Institut, 1989).
5. See, e.g., Leonard Weinberg and William Lee Eubank, *The Rise and Fall of Italian Terrorism* (Boulder, Colo.: Westview Press, 1987), 125–133.
6. Cyrille Fijnaut, "The Internationalization of Criminal Investigation in Western Eu-

Rights has exercised some influence by virtue of its decisions in a number of cases involving the use of informants and of electronic surveillance.[7] Regional arrangements, such as those among the Scandinavian and the Benelux nations respectively, have shaped the domestic law enforcement policies of the member countries. And more generally the prospects of open borders in 1992 have created pressures for greater conformity among European criminal justice systems.[8]

My focus on the adoption of U.S.-style methods in Europe should not obscure the extent to which European police have been able to take advantage of police powers that do not exist in the United States. In many European countries (but not all), police and prosecutors can legally detain criminal suspects for much longer than is permissible in the United States; access to counsel can be more delayed and restricted; telephone taps can be more easily obtained and kept in place longer; warrantless searches can be conducted more readily; evidence gathered illegally is rarely excluded from court; residents are required to carry special identity cards; and police are legally entitled to ask anyone to show them those cards. U.S. agents in Europe have been known to covet these powers, but they have also found that the Europeans' greater authority and discretion to question, detain, and search do not compensate for the restrictions on their ability to use the types of investigative methods that are regarded as so essential by U.S. agents. It is worth observing, however, that even as European drug enforcement has been becoming increasingly "Americanized," it is also possible to point to evidence of what one might call a "Europeanization" of American law enforcement—albeit one in which the hands of the Europeans are nowhere apparent. In a series of U.S. Supreme Court decisions beginning in the 1980s and continuing into the 1990s, many of the European police powers coveted by the few DEA agents familiar with them have been legalized in the United States. The scope of warrantless searches has been expanded, the exclusionary rule narrowed, the right to counsel circumscribed, and the allowable period of detention lengthened.[9] The

rope," in C.J.C.F. Fijnaut and R. H. Hermans, eds., *Police Cooperation in Europe* (Lochem: Van den Brink, 1987), 32–56; Paul Wilkinson, "European Police Cooperation," in John Roach and Jürgen Thomaneck, eds., *Police and Public Order in Europe* (London: Croom Helm, 1985).

    7. Note, "Secret Surveillance and the European Convention on Human Rights," *Stanford Law Review* 33 (1981), 1113.

    8. Clyde Haberman, "Europeans Fear '92 Economic Unity May Benefit Mafia," *New York Times*, July 23, 1989, 1.

    9. This trend is critically analyzed in Steven Wisotsky, "Not Thinking Like a Lawyer:

cumulative consequences of developments in drug enforcement on both sides of the Atlantic since the 1970s have been a convergence toward similar and greater police powers.

The "Americanization" of European drug enforcement has also involved more than the changes in criminal investigative methods discussed in this chapter. Europeans have encountered many of the same sorts of illicit drug problems the Americans encountered, albeit more belatedly and somewhat less dramatically. They responded, as in the United States, by imposing increasingly severe criminal sanctions beginning in the late 1960s.[10] During the 1970s, the movement to decriminalize the sale of small amounts of cannabis and the possession of small amounts of "harder" drugs spread throughout much of Europe. During the 1980s, European legislatures renewed the trend toward broader and tougher sanctions, enacting stiffer penalties for illicit drug possession and distribution as well as laws designed to seize drug traffickers' assets, to identify and punish drug-related money laundering, and to better prosecute drug trafficking conspiracies.[11] More recently, rising frustration over the apparent lack of success of drug laws in stemming drug abuse, and growing concern over the spread of AIDS by illicit drug abusers, have sparked a renewal of calls for drug legalization, implementation of "harm reduction" measures, and generally greater reliance on public health approaches to the problems of illicit drug abuse.[12] Since the early 1970s, the Netherlands has developed and quietly defended its more public health-oriented policies, while Germany has taken the lead in advocating the more punitive criminal-justice-oriented approaches emanating from the United States.[13] Among the Scandinavian countries,

The Case of Drugs in the Courts," *Notre Dame Journal of Law, Ethics, and Public Policy* 5 (1991), 651–692.

10. See European Committee on Crime Problems, *Penal Aspects of Drug Abuse* (Strasbourg: Council of Europe, 1974); and Albrecht and Kalmthout, eds., *Drug Policies in Western Europe* (supra n. 4).

11. Alexander MacLeod, "Europe Plans Assault on Growing Drug Menace," *Christian Science Monitor*, Sept. 14, 1989, 1.

12. See, e.g., the interview with Hamburg Mayor Hennig Voscherau in *Spiegel*, July 17, 1989, 27–30; the interview with former German Health Minister Rita Süssmuth in *Frankfurter Allgemeine*, Nov. 7, 1988; "Burton Bollag, "To the Swiss and Dutch, Tolerance Is Anti-Drug," *New York Times*, Dec. 1, 1989, A4; and cover stories on drug legalization, in *L'Espresso*, Apr. 2, 1989, and *Cambiol* 6, October 2, 1989. See also Peter Cohen, "Building upon the Successes of Dutch Drug Policy," *International Journal on Drug Policy* 2 (1989), 22–24. More generally, see Albrecht and Kalmthout, eds., *Drug Policies in Western Europe*, 77–78 (Austria), 104–105 (Belgium), 127–128 (Denmark), 150–151 (France), 182–184 (Germany), 221–225 (Italy), 255–256 (Netherlands), 298–299 (Spain), and 373–378 (Switzerland).

13. See Sebastian Scheerer, "The New Dutch and German Drug Laws: Social and Political Conditions for Criminalization and Decriminalization," *Law and Society Review* 12 (1978),

Denmark's more lenient drug prohibition policies—in particular its toleration of the counterculture communities of Christiania and Frøstrup-Lejren—have similarly upset its neighbors.[14] Hard-liners throughout Europe were also hostile to Spain's revision of its drug laws in 1983, which introduced a Dutch-like distinction between "soft" and "hard" drugs and formalized the decriminalization of drug possession previously instituted by the courts.[15] In all these respects, one can find evidence of "Americanizing" pressures, examples, and precedents, be it in the influence of the American counterculture on European youth and culture during the 1960s and 1970s, the Europeans' adoption of methadone maintenance programs developed initially in the United States, the trend toward decriminalization of cannabis during the mid-1970s, or the more prevalent trend toward tougher and broader criminal sanctions since the 1960s. Indeed, some of the countries that have been the most outspoken in advocating "harm reduction" approaches to drug abuse and small-scale drug dealing have also been the quickest to adopt DEA-style approaches to investigating drug trafficking.

It is not surprising that evidence of any real "Europeanization" (in the active sense of the term) of American drug enforcement, or even of

---

585–606; Ineke Haen Marshall, Oscar Anjewierden, and Hans Van Atteveld, "Toward an 'Americanization' of Dutch Drug Policy?" *Justice Quarterly* 7 (1990), 391–420. Henk Jan van Vliet, "The Uneasy Decriminalization: A Perspective on Dutch Drug Policy," *Hofstra Law Review* 18 (1990), 717–750; E. D. Engelsman, "Dutch Policy on the Management of Drug-Related Problems," *British Journal of Addiction* 84 (1989), 211–218, and subsequent commentaries at pp. 989–997; David Downes, *Contrasts in Tolerance: Post-war Penal Policy in the Netherlands and England and Wales* (Oxford: Clarendon Press, 1988), 123–162; Govert F. van de Wijngaart, "A Social History of Drug Use in the Netherlands: Policy Outcomes and Implications," *Journal of Drug Issues* 18 (1988), 481–495; O. Anjewierden and J. M. A. van Atteveld, "Current Trends in Dutch Opium Legislation," in Albrecht and Kalmthout, eds., *Drug Policies in Western Europe* (supra n. 4), 235–258; A. M. van Kalmthout, "Characteristics of Drug Policy in the Netherlands," in Albrecht and Kalmthout, eds., *Drug Policies in Western Europe*, 259–291; and Frits Ruter, "The Pragmatic Dutch Approach to Drug Control: Does It Work?" reprinted in *Legalization of Illicit Drugs, Impact and Feasibility: Hearing Before the Select Senate Committee on Narcotics Abuse and Control*, 100th Cong., 2d Sess., Part 1 (1988), 517–538.

14. Flemming Balvig, "Crime and Criminal Policy in a Pragmatic Society: The Case of Denmark and Christiania, 1960–1975," *International Journal of the Sociology of Law* 10 (1982), 9–29; J. Jepsen, "Drug Policies in Denmark," in Albrecht and Kalmthout, eds., *Drug Policies in Western Europe*, 107–141, esp. 107–108.

15. See J. L. de la Cuesta, "The Present Spanish Drug Criminal Policy," and J. L. Díez-Ripollés, "Principles of a New Drug Policy in Western Europe from a Spanish Point of View," both in Albrecht and Kalmthout, eds., *Drug Policies in Western Europe*, 293–320 and 321–341.

American criminal justice generally, has been relatively scant. During the 1970s, a number of legal scholars on both sides of the Atlantic debated whether the American criminal justice system might learn something from Europe's "inquisitorial" legal system, but no apparent changes resulted. Alternative drug control policies in the United Kingdom— where doctors had retained the power to prescribe maintenance doses of heroin, injectable methadone, and other prohibited drugs for addicts— also stimulated debate, but no changes in U.S. policy.[16] Of potentially greater consequence was the rising sense among American drug policy experts toward the end of the 1980s and into the 1990s that the United States might have something to learn from European "harm reduction" policies directed at stemming the transmission of AIDS by and among illicit drug users, but even that injection of European influence had yet to penetrate official government policies in the United States.[17] All of these differences of opinion and policy both within Europe and between some European states and the United States have occasionally colored relations among drug enforcement officials, but they have had relatively little impact on the debates over the criminal investigative tactics discussed below.

Finding and Creating Foreign Partners

The cooperation which foreign governments and law enforcement agencies are willing and able to give the DEA varies dramatically from one country to the next. With governments that are more willing but less able, the DEA has sought as free a hand as possible in conducting its

16. See Edwin M. Schur, *Narcotic Addiction in Britain and America* (Bloomington: Indiana University Press, 1962); Alfred R. Lindesmith, *The Addict and the Law* (Bloomington: Indiana University Press, 1965); Horace Freeland Judson, *Heroin Addiction in Britain* (New York: Harcourt Brace Jovanovich, 1973); and Arnold S. Trebach, *The Heroin Solution* (New Haven: Yale University Press, 1982).

17. Pat O'Hare, Russell Newcombe, Alan Matthews, Ernst C. Buning, and Ernest Drucker, eds., *The Reduction of Drug Related Harm* (London: Routledge, 1991); Nick Heather, Alex Wodak, Ethan Nadelmann, and Pat O'Hare, eds., *Psychoactive Drugs and Harm Reduction: From Faith to Science* (London: Whurr Publishers, 1993). See also John Strang and Gerry V. Stimson, eds., *AIDS and Drug Misuse: The Challenge for Policy and Practice in the 1990s* (New York: Routledge, 1990); and Robert J. Battjes and Roy W. Pickens, eds., *Needle Sharing Among Intravenous Drug Abusers: National and International Perspectives* (Washington, D.C.: National Institute on Drug Abuse, 1988).

operations. With others, such as in Europe, who are more able to give assistance but less flexible in allowing the DEA a free hand, the DEA has sought greater cooperation in gathering intelligence, making seizures, and arresting and prosecuting traffickers. In both cases, however, the DEA has pursued a common subsidiary objective: the development of effective drug enforcement capabilities within local police agencies. Where such a capability already exists, the DEA has sought to augment it and increase its effectiveness by offering training, information, and other assistance. Where the capability has been lacking, the DEA has devoted its resources to creating specially trained units with whom it can work. Where such a capability has existed but is endangered, the DEA has tried to protect it from whatever political, budgetary, or other forces threatened it. Particularly in the last case, which is far more likely in less developed countries, the DEA's efforts have been supplemented by political pressures from Washington and the State Department.

The priority the DEA has placed on creating and maintaining effective drug enforcement capabilities within foreign countries stems from a number of factors. To begin with, any foreign drug enforcement force, even a relatively corrupted one, can assist the DEA in its mission— particularly if it is familiar with drug enforcement techniques. Moreover, the DEA has little choice but to depend on local law enforcement agencies for many of the functions it would carry out itself within the United States. Budgetary and personnel restrictions pose severe limits on DEA resources around the world. Two hundred agents abroad may be more than twice the total of all other civilian American law enforcement agents stationed overseas, but it is not much when a major investigation is under way. And even if the DEA had enough agents in a country, the laws of both the United States and the foreign country bar U.S. agents from conducting many of the tasks normally associated with law enforcement. For instance, no government other than the United States empowers U.S. agents to arrest people within its borders, or to conduct a search or seizure, to compel witnesses or suspects to talk to them, or to obtain the necessary search warrant. In many countries, they are not even allowed to carry a gun. Indeed, in some countries foreign prosecutors and law enforcement agents may be jailed for engaging in unauthorized activities as innocuous as questioning a resident compatriot or asking to see a hotel register.[18]

18. See, e.g., Claus Schellenberg, "The Proceedings Against Two French Customs Officials in Switzerland for Prohibited Acts in Favor of a Foreign State, Economic Intelligence Service and Violation of the Banking Law," International Business Lawyer 9 (1981), 139–140.

DEA agents abroad rely greatly on their ability to establish strong working relationships with foreign counterparts that can be isolated from political influences and accommodated to the often undiplomatic requirements of international law enforcement. These relationships, based upon both personal and professional links, are essential to cutting through red tape, bending rules and laws that can restrict an agent's flexibility, and even securing cooperation in matters on which higher levels of their respective governments do not see eye to eye. As one FBI LEGAT put it, reflecting the views of most law enforcement agents, cooperative efforts across borders tend to work "so long as issues are resolved among the agents themselves rather than decided by the policymakers. When politics get involved, things stop working." This is not to say that foreign law enforcement agents will betray their country's interests out of friendship or police comradery. But it is to say that police tend to place a higher priority than most politicians on going after criminals, and a lower priority on political considerations and sensitivities of national sovereignty. The common sentiment that a cop is a cop no matter whose badge he or she wears, and that a criminal is a criminal no matter what his or her citizenship is or where the crime was committed, serves as a kind of transgovernmental value system overriding political conflicts between governments. It provides, in many ways, the oil and glue of international law enforcement.

Transgovernmental values aside, among the most difficult challenges to effective DEA liaison and cooperation overseas has been its need to avoid the bureaucratic minefields and turf struggles of foreign law enforcement agencies. In many countries, the tensions between law enforcement agencies with overlapping drug enforcement responsibilities are at least as severe as those between the DEA and other U.S. agencies.[19] In each country, the DEA's choice of which law enforcement agency to work with is determined by a variety of factors. In many cases, the choice is taken out of its hands by an interagency agreement, a memorandum of understanding, an oral agreement, or a government fiat specifying who the DEA must notify regarding its activities and who the DEA may and may not deal with. In other cases, the DEA can deal with whomever it chooses so long as it gives prior notice to some designated office. And in still other countries, the DEA has a free hand to deal with whomever it chooses.

19. This challenge is not unique to the DEA; the FBI often encounters similar problems abroad in its dealings with local law enforcement and intelligence agencies.

When given the choice of whom to work with, the DEA considers many factors. It may take advantage of one agency's expertise in one area, such as visual or electronic surveillance, and a different agency's expertise in another area, such as intelligence, undercover operations, interrogation, searches and seizures, arrests, or internal liaison. It may rely entirely on one agency because it is better trained in all tasks, or because there are established personal and political relationships with that agency, or because it is free of corruption or at least less corrupt than the alternatives. It may make an effort to work with all agencies, even where working with one would be just as effective, in order to maintain good relations all around. And it may forgo or limit its contacts with particular agencies by agreement with other U.S. agencies, such as U.S. Customs.

In Europe, where degrees of corruption are far less of a consideration, the DEA tends to work with whichever agency proves most helpful. DEA agents generally have found the drug enforcement units of the national, state, or municipal police more useful than those of the more paramilitary police agencies supervised in whole or in part by European defense ministries. In quite a number of countries, however, the DEA's options are controlled or supervised by a special unit set up to coordinate all national and international drug enforcement activities. In France, that unit is the Central Narcotics Office (CNO) (Office Central de Répression du Trafic Illicite de Stupéfiants) within the Criminal Investigative Department (Police Judiciaire) of the National Police, which during the mid-1980s included about 100 agents.[20] If DEA agents want to deal with any of the other police units, such as the Gendarmerie, the customs agency, the Air and Frontier Police (Service Central de la Police de l'Air et des Frontières), or Paris' municipal drug unit (the Brigade des Stupéfiants et du Proxénétisme), the agents must request permission from the head of the CNO. In Italy, an interagency unit, the Servizio Centrale Antidroga (SCA), has a say in whether the DEA will work with the State Police, the paramilitary Carabinieri, or the Treasury police (the Guardia di Finanza), each of which has its own drug enforcement units.[21] During

20. For an overview of the French police (though one that devotes little attention to the issues discussed here), see Philip John Stead, *The Police of France* (New York: Macmillan, 1983), and the briefer description in J. R. Jammes, "Some Aspects of the French Police," *Police Journal* 55 (1982), 113–124.

21. A brief but solid history of the Italian police is Richard O. Collin, "The Blunt Instruments: Italy and the Police," in Roach and Thomaneck, eds., *Police and Public Order in Europe*, 185–214. A classic study of the Italian police is Robert C. Fried, *The Italian Prefects:*

the mid-1980s, the DEA office in Milan worked most closely with the Guardia di Finanza, while the Rome office relied primarily on the other two agencies, working principally with the State Police in Rome but also with the Carabinieri in Naples. The preferences were less a reflection of the three police agencies' respective specializations than of the personalities involved.

In the Netherlands, the DEA is required to coordinate its activities with the National Criminal Intelligence Service (Centrale Recherche Informatiedienst, CRI) in the Ministry of Justice. The CRI acts as a coordinating and advisory body for both domestic and international criminal investigations, but its personnel are mostly nonoperational. Most of the DEA's dealings are with the municipal police forces (Gemeentepolitie), especially those in major cities, such as Amsterdam and Rotterdam.[22] Similarly, in Switzerland, a small, nonoperational central police office (ZEPO) coordinates the DEA's work with the canton police, who are responsible for almost all law enforcement operations. In Spain, the DEA works primarily with the drug enforcement agents of the National Police, coordinating its activities with the Central Narcotics Brigade, which like the Dutch CRI is largely nonoperational, and with the twelve drug enforcement brigades distributed around the country.[23] About 20 percent of the DEA's work involves the Guardia Civil, whose drug enforcement agents are distributed similarly to the way the National Police brigades are, and about 5 percent requires the cooperation of Spain's customs agency. One of the few countries that places no restrictions on whom the DEA may work with is Belgium. There the DEA may choose between the Judiciary Police (Police Judiciaire/Gerechtelijke Politie) and the Gendarmerie (Rijkswacht), neither of which has large drug units but both of which have jurisdiction over drug law violations and certain agents who specialize in drug enforcement. In cases with an inter-European angle, the DEA will likely work with the Gendarmerie because its liaison with other European law enforcement agencies is quite good. But in cases initiated by the DEA, or involving

A *Study in Administrative Politics* (New Haven: Yale University Press, 1963), although it does not address the criminal investigative matters discussed here.

22. An interesting analysis of Dutch policing is Maurice Punch, *Policing the Inner City: A Study of Amsterdam's Warmoesstraat* (London: Macmillan & Co., 1979). The CRI also publishes an annual report in English on the activities of its Narcotics Branch.

23. The organization of the Spanish police is briefly described in Robert Hudson, "Democracy and the Spanish Police Forces Since 1975," *Police Journal* 61 (1988), 53–62.

just Belgium, the DEA agents prefer to work with the Judiciary Police, who are generally more aggressive in recruiting informants and initiating proactive investigations—so aggressive, in fact, that their efforts period- ically have resulted in public scandals not unlike those that occasionally flare up in American cities.

In West Germany, the DEA's principal partner has changed over time. When the BNDD first opened a number of offices around Germany in the early 1970s, the federal police agency (the Bundeskriminalamt, BKA), based in Wiesbaden, was largely nonoperational, similar in many ways to the CRI in Holland today. Like the Dutch service, it provided some coordination in criminal investigations, served as a central reposi- tory of criminal information, and acted as the national central bureau of Interpol. The vast majority of law enforcement investigations, includ- ing those with international dimensions, were conducted by the police forces of the individual German states (Länderpolizeien). On occasion, the BKA's few investigators might initiate a drug investigation of its own or participate in a state police investigation at the behest of the latter. Although the DEA maintained a liaison relationship with the BKA, most of its operations were done jointly with the state police agencies. During the 1970s, however, this decentralization of police power, which had originally been demanded by the occupying powers after the war, came under increasing pressure. The urgings of U.S. drug enforcement officials provided some of the impetus, but most of the incentive was provided by the dramatic increase in terrorist attacks sponsored by the Baader- Meinhof gang and the subsequent recognition of the need for better national coordination of complex criminal investigations. In 1973, new legislation gave the BKA original jurisdiction in cases involving counter- feiting, arms trafficking, and international drug trafficking.[24] Thereafter, the state police were required to clear any contacts with foreign law enforcement agencies, apart from routine cross-border communications, through the federal agency. Frustrated by the "provincialization" of the state police, the DEA cut back on its interactions with state police, closed its office in Munich in 1982, and began working much more closely with the BKA.

The BKA has grown rapidly since the 1970s, with its drug enforcement

24. See Reinhard Schweppe, *FBI und BKA* (Stuttgart: Ferdinand Enke Verlag, 1974), which argues that the BKA had been heavily influenced by the FBI and would continue to evolve in its footsteps as a consequence of the 1973 legislation. See also A. F. Carter, "The West German Bundeskriminalamt," *Police Journal* 49 (1976), 199–209.

responsibilities providing a substantial impetus for new initiatives both within Germany and abroad. By the mid-1980s, most of the Länderpolizeien had also jumped back into the drug enforcement fray. All of the Länderpolizeien created their own elite criminal investigative units (Landeskriminalamt, LKA), which are generally modeled after U.S. drug enforcement units and the BKA. The BKA typically takes the lead in most transnational and multi-Länder investigations, and it retains the power to preempt criminal investigations initiated by the LKAs. As in the United States, most drug enforcement is still performed by nonfederal police agencies, and evidence of a vigorous rivalry between the BKA and the LKAs abounds (as is also true in the United States of relations between the DEA and the FBI, on the one hand, and state and local agencies, on the other), but today most of the DEA's operations are coordinated with the federal agency, whose drug unit has emerged as the most innovative and aggressive in Europe.[25] The relationship has been a robust one, with complaints on both sides. The Germans, one DEA agent commented to me, "often fail to realize that international cooperation is a two-sided affair." Some tensions were also characteristic of any relationship between a mentor agency and its rapidly maturing protégé. But by and large, the DEA has viewed favorably the emergence of the BKA as a major force in its own right.

Although the DEA has been responsible for inspiring or instigating a number of the organizational changes in European drug enforcement forces, few agencies have been as influenced by the Americans as Austria's. As in Germany, the postwar occupiers and popular sentiment as well had resisted any return to a national police agency. Until the late 1970s, neither the Federal Police (Bundespolizei), whose units reported to the security director in the respective Länder, nor the Gendarmerie devoted virtually any personnel to drug enforcement. Following the opening of a DEA office in Vienna in 1974, an Austrian Central Narcotics Department (ACND) was established in the Federal Police headquarters. With only two agents available to cooperate with local police on drug cases, it was, in the words of one DEA agent, primarily a "paper-pushing agency responding to requests from Interpol." The first DEA attaché, Robert Waltz, is credited by Austrians with playing a central role in the development of Austria's drug enforcement capabili-

25. A fine overview of the German police is Jürgen Thomaneck, "Police and Public Order in the Federal Republic of Germany," in Roach and Thomaneck, eds., *Police and Public Order in Europe* (supra n. 6), 143–184.

ties.[26] By the early 1980s, the ACND had been transformed into the only operational police unit at the national level. Its agents were involved in most major drug investigations, although the Gendarmerie and local units of the Federal Police continued to work on drug cases as well. During the mid-1980s, resident DEA agents much preferred to work directly with the ACND and its longtime chief, Herbert Fuchs. The Federal Police units, one agent told me, "were just not that good. They're not well funded, not that imaginative, not that adaptable, and tend to do things very much by the book."

The requirement that the DEA notify or request permission from a central drug enforcement unit to work with a different agency does not mean that lines of authority are never crossed. Once resident DEA agents have established working relationships with their counterparts in local drug enforcement units, informal links tend to obscure formal lines of authority. Often local police resent interference from the central unit, not only in their dealings with the DEA but in their dealings with other foreign law enforcement agencies as well. This is especially so among police working along the border, who may have more in common with foreign counterparts across the border than with their fellow agents based at headquarters in the capital. In a number of countries, responsibility for informing the central drug enforcement unit of a cooperative investigation falls to the agency that initiated the lead. If that agency is the DEA—which often it is, given the DEA's generally superior intelligence network—the central unit is typically notified, albeit not always in advance. But if a local agency is the initiator, it may choose not to notify the central unit; the DEA tends to remain uninvolved in such decisions. Much also depends upon the individual personalities and the criminal justice cultures. In France and Austria, for instance, the lines of authority are relatively strict, in Italy a little less, in Holland even less so, and in Belgium they barely exist. In Germany, the DEA attaché described a situation not unlike that in many other countries: "Sometimes the LKAs come directly to us. They might ask us to work undercover. We tell them they're supposed to notify the BKA. But ultimately it's their responsibility."

The DEA's foreign partners also include local prosecutors, investigating magistrates, and judges, particularly those who specialize in drug

26. Herbert Fuchs, "DEA's Role in Austria" (unpublished manuscript by the director of the ACND, 1986).

cases. The extent and closeness of these relationships depends greatly on the nature of the relationship between local police and prosecutors. As in the United States, most police/prosecutor relationships are characterized by tensions involving differences in class and culture, professional perspectives, turf and tactics, but some transcend these differences and become quite intimate. DEA agents abroad tend to view their relationships with local prosecutors and other judicial officers through the same eyes as at home. They generally take their lead from the local police with whom they are working. The results are closer relationships in some countries than in others, very close relationships in particular situations, but generally cool and somewhat distant relationships in most cases.

Intelligence-Gathering and Informants

A fundamental aspect of making cases against drug traffickers is the collection of intelligence on their identities, organizations, methods, and activities. The DEA has distinguished three types of intelligence:

> The first is *tactical* intelligence which contributes directly and immediately to making a case. The collection requirements are usually defined by either the agent on the case or the intelligence analyst supporting him. . . . The second is *operational* intelligence, i.e., that which may contribute to a case against a specific violator, but does not necessarily fit into the case at the time. . . . Usually the purpose is to develop profiles of traffickers and do network analysis. The third type is *strategic* intelligence which is general information about drug sources and the external environment in which DEA operates. Strategic intelligence does not necessarily contribute to making any single case, but does influence the overall plan of operation. In general, it provides an overview of the narcotics threat and trend and of the magnitude and direction of the domestic supply. It enables U.S. policy makers to place political emphasis on foreign governments when required.[27]

27. "Drug Enforcement Administration Appropriation Summary Statement," in *Departments of State, Justice, and Commerce, the Judiciary, and Related Agencies Appropriations for 1977: Hearings Before a Subcommittee of the House Committee on Appropriations*, 94th Cong., 2d Sess., Part 4 (Department of Justice, 1976), 1065.

Intelligence on drug trafficking is gathered not only by DEA agents but also by most other U.S. law enforcement agencies, the military and intelligence agencies, and foreign law enforcement agencies. It is then processed through one or both of the DEA's two computerized intelligence support systems: the El Paso Intelligence Center (EPIC), which acts as a clearinghouse for operational and tactical drug enforcement information, and the Narcotics and Dangerous Drugs Information System (NADDIS), a "data base which consist[ed in 1976] of about 1,800,000 records on persons, businesses, ships, aircraft and certain airfields, [and] is the centralized index of all DEA investigative reports."[28] The DEA's intelligence analysts, of whom about two dozen are located overseas, assess and analyze the information, develop estimates, look for trends, and disseminate the processed intelligence to DEA offices, other U.S. law enforcement and intelligence agencies, and favored foreign drug enforcement agencies.

The DEA's capacity to collect intelligence overseas depends upon three factors: the intelligence capabilities of the local law enforcement agencies, the willingness of those agencies to share their intelligence with the DEA, and the DEA agent's freedom and ability to gather his or her own intelligence, such as by recruiting informants. Accordingly, the DEA agent seeks to maximize all three. With regard to the first, his or her efforts include encouraging local police to devote greater resources to intelligence collection and coordination, advocating the adoption of DEA-style methods for recruiting informants, and assisting the German BKA in developing its own NADDIS-type computer system. The second factor also varies greatly, depending not only upon personal and bureaucratic relationships but also, particularly in countries where corruption is more pervasive, upon the local agent's need to keep the DEA in the dark on some matters.

The DEA agents' ability to collect information on their own depends upon any number of factors, the most important of which is the agent's capacity to cultivate and recruit informants. Visual surveillance is among the simplest forms of information collection. Discreetly following a suspect or keeping an eye on an apartment is an activity in which virtually all agents engage. Somewhat more complicated, from the legal viewpoint, is questioning people who may have information—for in-

28. *Reauthorization of the Drug Enforcement Administration for Fiscal Year 1988: Hearing Before the Subcommittee on Crime of the House Committee on the Judiciary*, 100th Cong., 1st Sess. (1987), 88.

stance, talking to a relative or friend of a suspect, interviewing a possible witness to a crime, or obtaining information from hotel employees regarding their guests. But given the nature of drug trafficking, the importance of informants to drug enforcement cannot be overestimated. This is especially true in the many foreign countries where undercover operations and most types of electronic surveillance are strictly circumscribed or illegal, and where prosecutors are legally prohibited from offering immunity or a reduction in charges to criminals in return for their cooperation in an investigation. The value of informants often extends beyond the information they provide; many assist DEA activities in a more operational manner, either acting in an undercover role themselves or providing undercover DEA agents with the necessary contacts and entrees.

The DEA agent's process of recruiting informants abroad does not differ much from the process in the United States,[29] with the significant exception that the agent's capacity to coerce those involved in illicit drug dealing into becoming informants by first arresting them or threatening them with arrest is inevitably diminished by lack of arrest powers. The agent's ability to recruit informants in this fashion—which is the principal means of informant recruitment in the United States—thus depends entirely upon his or her relationship with local agents and their willingness and ability either to lend the necessary legal coercion to his efforts or engage in the same tactics themselves. Also crucial are the agent's personal abilities; some are better at recruiting informants from a particular milieu. The variety of motives that induce people to become informants is not determined by geography, although DEA agents have noticed that a higher proportion of the best informants in Europe are "walk-ins"—people who simply come into the police station or the DEA office in the U.S. embassy and volunteer to become informants. Money

29. For a more developed discussion of the recruitment and use of informants by the DEA and the FBI during the mid-1970s, see James Q. Wilson, *The Investigators*, chap. 3. The FBN's use of informants is discussed in "Informers in Federal Narcotics Prosecutions," *Columbia Journal of Law and Social Problems* 2 (1966), 47–74. See also Peter K. Manning, *The Narcs' Game: Organizational and Informational Limits on Drug Law Enforcement* (Cambridge, Mass.: M.I.T. Press, 1980), 47–49, 140–191; Mark Harrison Moore, *Buy and Bust* (Lexington, Mass.: Lexington Books, 1977), 121–185; Jay R. Williams and L. Lynn Guess, "The Informant: A Narcotics Dilemma," *Journal of Psychoactive Drugs* 13 (1981), 235–245; Michael F. Brown, "Criminal Informants: Some Observations on Use, Abuse, and Control," *Journal of Police Science and Administration* 13 (1985), 251–256; and Paul Fuqua, *Drug Abuse: Investigation and Control* (New York: McGraw-Hill, 1978), 171–179.

is usually a factor, although not necessarily the initial incentive. That may come from the fear of a participant in a drug deal who decides he wants out, the vengeance of a jilted lover, the self-interest of a business competitor or political opponent, the need for self-esteem, a sense of identity with police agents, or simply a sense of friendship with a law enforcement agent. Sometimes the motive is nothing more than a citizen's sense of obligation to report a crime he or she has witnessed. This sense of obligation, a number of DEA agents have noticed, seems more developed in parts of Europe than in much of the United States. They attribute it to the greater homogeneity of European populations, a greater respect for the law and the police, and, as one DEA agent in Holland put it, the greater tendency of people "to mind each other's business." It has also been argued that "the French system of the *correspondant honorable*—who works out of love, fear of blackmail, and for small favors—is not as fully developed in the United States."[30]

The law enforcement agent's relationship with a criminal informant is often a complex one replete with legal and ethical ambiguities. Agents have been known to supply seized drugs to their addict informants, to ignore their informants' continued involvement in criminal activities, and to intervene with other law enforcement authorities who had arrested their informants.[31] The relationship can be one marked by strong mutual dependencies. Agents rely on their informants for information and introductions, without which they are unable to do their jobs, and informants are dependent upon the agents not only for money and protection from the law but also, on occasion, for protection against other criminals who have discovered they are stool pigeons. More often than not, most aspects of the agent's relationship with an informant are not supervised closely, if at all, by superior officers, prosecutors, or judges. Although certain procedures are usually required when an informant is initially recruited—for instance, filling out an official form and meeting with a superior officer—the nature of the relationship is determined largely by the personal discretion of the drug agent and the personality of the informant.

In recruiting informants, DEA agents seek out anyone who may be in

30. Gary Marx, "Thoughts on a Neglected Category of Social Movement Participant: The Agent Provocateur and the Informant," *American Journal of Sociology* 80 (1974), 419.

31. For a vivid description of all these aspects of the agent-informant relationship, see Robert Daley, *Prince of the City* (London: Granada Publishing, 1979), 227–230, 237–238, 244–249.

a position to provide or discover useful information. Contacts are developed and potential informants sought out at all levels of society, ranging from the barrios and urban slums to the diplomatic receptions and elite social clubs. At one level, the agent must, in the words of one who was stationed in Latin America, "establish a working relationship with the scumbag community." Both inside and outside that community, the agent must make contacts with anyone in a position to see or overhear activity related to drug trafficking. Typical sources include bouncers, bartenders, prostitutes, hotel doormen, hotel clerks, and other hotel employees. At the airports, the DEA agent looks to recruit informants among the pilots, baggage handlers, stewardesses, security people, and other employees. Bank employees, taxi drivers, waitresses, and others who come into contact with many people, especially out-of-towners, on a daily basis may also prove valuable sources of information.

The DEA's policy with respect to informants varies from country to country. In some, especially in Latin America, it closely guards the identities of its informants, even from local counterparts. In others, it is obliged to share those identities with local police, and it does so. Likewise, the DEA's freedom to recruit informants varies substantially from one country to another.[32] In countries with financial secrecy laws, the DEA must be concerned with violating the law if it recruits informants from among bank employees. Recruiting informants among government officials can also be tricky, particularly in countries where corruption is rampant. Most DEA informants, however, are private citizens, and a substantial proportion have some relationship with ongoing criminal activity.

The extent to which the DEA shares its informants with local law enforcement agencies, and vice versa, depends upon a number of factors. When informants are recruited by the local agency, they may be shared with, or given to, the DEA because the American agency has funds to pay informants whereas most foreign law enforcement agencies, even in Europe, have relatively little or no money for such purposes. Indeed, the DEA's reputation in that regard is often a strong incentive for potential informants to seek out the DEA overseas, although the agency tends to

32. In Singapore, for instance, the DEA reportedly was prohibited from recruiting any citizens as informants. See *U.S. Narcotics Control Programs Overseas, An Assessment: Report of a Staff Study Mission to Southeast Asia, South America, Central America, and the Caribbean, August 1984 to January 1985, House Foreign Affairs Committee*, 99th Cong., 1st Sess. (1985), 9.

pay only in cases that have a clear connection to the American drug market. By 1990, the DEA· and other U.S. law enforcement agencies were authorized by law to pay informants up to $250,000 a case if their assistance resulted in the seizure from a drug dealer of cash and other assets worth more than $1 million.[33] Throughout virtually all of Latin America, police themselves are paid so little that the idea of paying informants for information is often perceived as somewhat bizarre. In Europe, the traditional reluctance to pay informants is waning as greater priority is given to drug enforcement and as asset-forfeiture laws, often modeled after those passed in the United States, are implemented. At the same time, agencies that have long been accustomed to paying informants have tended to increase the size of their payments at a pace more than sufficient to cover the effects of inflation. Where once European police agents who sought to recruit informants were obliged to dig into their own pockets, now they are increasingly able to turn to their agencies for the money. In Europe, the most generous are the Germans. During the 1970s, payments of a few hundred dollars were common.[34] By the late 1980s, both the BKA and the Landespolizei in the wealthier states were able to pay their most valuable informants up to $100,000. The Dutch and the British also pay informants, but only after the drugs have been seized.[35] The Danes have no specific budget for paying informants, but they will compensate informants out of their general operating funds; the highest payments authorized as of 1990 amounted to between $1,000 and $1,500. The Spanish typically pay the equivalent of a few hundred dollars, although one exceptionally valuable informant in the late 1980s was paid $20,000—half by the Spanish police, half by the DEA. The French police have long maintained a discreet policy of paying informants, one that became public only in 1986.[36] Most pay-

33. Arnold H. Lubasch, "Drug Trial Shows the Rich Rewards of Informing," *New York Times*, Nov. 4, 1990, 47.

34. According to a 1977 BKA report, information leading to the confiscation of cannabis was valued at 45 DM per kilogram, with bonuses paid for special efforts. In one case, an undercover informant was paid 700 DM for a tip that led to the arrest of five Italian drug traffickers and confiscation of 13 kilos of marijuana. In another case, an informant received 1,700 DM for a tip that led to the arrest of four Turkish traffickers and the seizure of 26 kilos of cannabis. See "Dem Verbrechen an die Wurzel," *Spiegel*, May 5, 1977, 62–73.

35. Both the Dutch and the Irish police were reported to have access to funds to pay informants in James Leo Walsh, "Research Note: Cops and 'Stool Pigeons'—Professional Striving and Discretionary Justice in European Police Work," *Law and Society Review* 6 (1972), 299. The same has long been true in England. See John Coatman, *Police* (New York: Oxford University Press, 1959), 134.

36. Edwy Plenel, "Le ministre de la sécurité augmente la rémunération des informateurs," *Le Monde*, May 21, 1986, 12.

ments were quite modest, although a few informants during the 1980s received more than 100,000 francs for information on terrorist attacks and assassinations, and French police reportedly spent 500,000 francs for information on the terrorist bombing of the Goldenberg restaurant in 1982.[37] DEA agents in France during the same period reported that the French customs agency was able to pay drug-related informants more than the police were. Payment simply for information, or for the cultivation of informants, remains highly atypical in Europe. Many law enforcement agencies will also share their informants with the DEA as a matter of course whenever it believes that the DEA may be interested in the information for sale. Likewise, the DEA will often share its informants with local law enforcement agencies, particularly if the information provided bears on investigations within the country. As the money available to pay informants has increased all around, so too have the conflicts over their "ownership" both between European police agencies in the same country and between them and the DEA.

Although most DEA informants overseas are shared with local agencies, the DEA does shield the identities of some. Informants may approach the DEA because they do not trust the local law enforcement agency; they may think the local agency lacks either the interest or the resources to use the information they want to give, trade, or sell, or they may worry that the information will be accidentally revealed, thereby exposing the informant's identity. Even in Germany, with its highly professional police, one DEA agent complained: "The BKA doesn't understand the 'third agency rule'—that you're supposed to check with the provider of information before giving it to a third agency." There is also a chance that a corrupt law enforcement agent will resell the information to those willing to pay for it, or will otherwise use the information to his or her own advantage and the informant's detriment. Finally, an informant who wishes to sell information relating to government corruption in drug enforcement may not know who, if anyone, can be trusted with the information. In all these cases, the DEA's relatively clean reputation makes it an attractive purchaser of information. Unlike virtually all other foreign law enforcement agencies, moreover, the DEA can offer informants a well-established witness protection program and other resources to safeguard those whose lives are endangered.[38] A number of foreign informants initially recruited by foreign

37. Ibid.
38. See *Federal Witness Security Program and Protection of Foreign Nationals: Hearing Before the Government Information, Justice, and Agriculture Subcommittee of the House Committee on Government Operations*, 101st Cong., 2d Sess. (1990).

law enforcement agencies have ended up in this program; the most famous of these was Tomasso Buscetta, the highest-ranking member of the Sicilian Mafia ever to break the code of *omerta*, whose information and testimony played a central role in the mid-1980s "Pizza Connection" case against Mafia drug trafficking and money laundering.[39]

That most high-level drug informants around the world are recruited and paid by the DEA is not all that surprising given the agency's global presence. Among all national drug enforcement agencies, it has the largest budget, the greatest number of agents, the most sophisticated equipment, the most extensive files, and the political power of the United States government behind it. Wherever the DEA is represented, local drug enforcement agencies depend heavily upon its international network of agents and informants for the leads and other information needed to make cases within their borders. By the mid-1970s, the DEA had come to be regarded, by both foreign police and criminals, as a sort of operational Interpol with vast resources at its disposal. "If we want to know who lives in Kuala Lumpur, Bondstreet, No. X, on the third floor," former BKA Director Horst Herold stated in an interview, "we just ask the DEA Paris office and we get the information in a few hours."[40] Although the popular image of the DEA is surely overblown, it serves as both a deterrent to drug traffickers and as a drawing card for foreign law enforcement agencies and potential informants. And the fact that the DEA can provide or withhold abundant information provides perhaps the greatest incentive for foreign drug enforcement units to cooperate with DEA investigations.

European drug enforcement agents are no different from their American counterparts in being heavily dependent upon informants; they are, as one German police chief put it, "as indispensable as radio-patrol cars, guns, and the officers themselves."[41] Aside from their relatively limited budgets for paying informants and their comparatively provincial intelligence systems, European prosecutors and drug enforcement agents have been sorely handicapped by their legal inability to make the sorts

39. See Ralph Blumenthal, *Last Days of the Sicilians* (New York: Pocket Books, 1988); and Shana Alexander, *The Pizza Connection* (New York: Weidenfeld & Nicolson, 1988).

40. *Frankfurter Rundschau*, Oct. 12, 1979, 3, quoted by Sebastian Scheerer, "Drogen und Strafrecht" ("Drugs and Criminal Law"), in Jan van Dijk et al., eds., *Criminal Law in Action: An Overview of Current Issues in Western Societies* (Arnhem: Gouda Quint, 1986), 199–213.

41. "Drugs: Dicker Manny," *Spiegel*, July 7, 1981, 68–70, quoting the veteran chief of the Hamburg Criminal Investigation Department (Kripo-Chef) Hans Zühlsdorf.

of deals with informants that play such a central role in U.S. drug enforcement, by the ambiguous legal status of informants, and by strict limitations on the use of informants as undercover operatives. These obstacles have slowly been overcome by changes in European laws, judicial decisions, and police practices, but even today much of what is deemed acceptable and legal in U.S. drug enforcement remains not permissible in Europe.

The most valuable informants tend to be those who are directly involved in illicit drug dealing. In the United States, a common recruitment tactic, known as "flipping" an informant, involves arresting, or threatening to arrest, a person for his or her involvement in drug trafficking or other crimes and then offering that person a deal in return for cooperation in making cases against other traffickers, ideally those operating at a higher level of criminal activity. The nature of the deal depends in part upon when it is struck. It may involve not proceeding with the arrest, or arranging to have the charges reduced or dropped, or getting the sentence reduced. Once the arrest is processed, the cooperation of a prosecutor, and often a judge, may be necessary to approve a deal. Unlike the typical "plea bargain," in which a prosecutor and defense attorney agree to have the defendant plead guilty to a lesser charge in return for forgoing the right to a trial, the deal between the drug agent or prosecutor and the prospective informant involves greater consideration by both sides. An informant who makes such a deal is said to be "working off a beef." Informants may be given their freedom, or a promise of freedom, and be paid for whatever information and assistance they provide.

Although informants are valuable for the information they possess at the time they are flipped or otherwise recruited, their greatest value often stems from the services they provide after that point. Criminals who get immunity from prosecution in return for testimony against fellow conspirators and other criminals are among the more passive types of informants. Far more essential to drug and other proactive criminal investigations are informants who retain their freedom and continue to interact with others engaged in crime. Such informants may be left in place after recruitment so they can help build a case against already known criminals. Or they may become employees of sorts of the law enforcement agency, either retaining their real identity or assuming aliases and operating entirely in an undercover capacity. The use of informants in these ways raises some of the same issues that arise when law enforcement agents themselves operate undercover.

Outside the United States, the DEA agent's ability to flip informants is limited by the simple fact that the agent lacks the power to arrest anyone. But the DEA agent, as well as local police and prosecutors, has also been handicapped by the questionable legality of the flipping process in many civil law countries.[42] The principal obstacle has been the "legality principle," which requires that the police arrest and the prosecutors prosecute anyone known to have committed a crime. Also known as "the rule of compulsory prosecution," this restraint on police and prosecutorial discretion greatly hampered the introduction of DEA-style informant recruitment methods, especially in Germany,[43] Austria, and Italy.[44] But even in Belgium,[45]

42. The flipping process is relatively common in most common law countries. In Britain, informants are known as "grasses." Much has been written about the informants, referred to as "supergrasses," who operate undercover and provide the most valuable intelligence to the police. See Steven C. Greer, "Supergrasses and the Legal System in Britain and Northern Ireland," *Law Quarterly Review* 102 (1986), 198–249, and Paddy Hillyard and Janie Percy-Smith, "Converting Terrorists: The Use of Supergrasses in Northern Ireland," *Journal of Law and Society* 11 (1984), 335–355. The British police must obtain the grant of immunity for a "supergrass" from the director of public prosecutions. The use of "supergrasses" and the quality of their information has been the subject of substantial criticism. See, e.g., David Seymour, "What Good Have Supergrasses Done for Anyone but Themselves?" *LAG Bulletin*, Dec. 1982, 7–9; and Etienne Bloch, "The Struggle Against Terrorism in France and Northern Ireland: A French Jurist's Perspective" (Paper for the International Security Studies Program, Woodrow Wilson International Center for Scholars, Washington, D.C., January, 1987).

43. The German practice is discussed in Hans-Heinrich Jeschek, "The Discretionary Powers of the Prosecuting Attorney in West Germany," *American Journal of Comparative Law* 18 (1970), 508–517; Glenn Schram, "The Obligation to Prosecute in West Germany," *American Journal of Comparative Law* 17 (1969), 627–632; Mirjan R. Damaška, "The Reality of Prosecutorial Discretion: Comments on a German Monograph," *American Journal of Comparative Law* 29 (1981), 119–138; John H. Langbein, "Controlling Prosecutorial Discretion in Germany," *University of Chicago Law Review* 41 (1974), 439–467; and Joachim Herrmann, "The Rule of Compulsory Prosecution and the Sagente of Prosecutorial Discretion in Germany," *University of Chicago Law Review* 41 (1974), 468–505, reprinted with comments in Kenneth Culp Davis, ed., *Discretionary Justice in Europe and America* (Chicago: University of Illinois Press, 1976), 16–74.

44. The Italian attitude with respect to prosecutorial discretion is discussed in Guido Neppi Modono, "The Italian Versus the American Response to the Mafia: A Comparison Between Two Juridical Cultures" (Paper presented at the Center for European Studies, Harvard University, Apr. 27, 1987). See Lawrence J. Fassler, "The Italian Penal Procedure Code: An Adversarial System of Criminal Procedure in Continental Europe," *Columbia Journal of Transnational Law* 29 (1991), 245–278, for an analysis of revisions to the penal code in 1988–89.

45. A brief introduction to Belgian criminal procedure can be found in Marc Chatel, "Human Rights and Belgian Criminal Procedure at Pre-trial and Trial Level," in J. A. Andrews,

France,[46] the Netherlands,[47] and Denmark,[48] where the alternative "opportunity principle" (or "expediency principle") permitted the prosecutor to take the public interest into account in deciding whether to prosecute, "the ethic of compulsory prosecution nonetheless persist[ed],"[49] thereby hindering the flexibility of prosecutors and police to make deals with potential informants.[50]

Human Rights in Criminal Procedure: A Comparative Study (The Hague: Martinus Nijhoff, 1982), 188–201.

46. The French practice is well described in Edward A. Tomlinson, "Nonadversarial Justice: The French Experience," 42 *Maryland Law Review* 42 (1983), 131–195, esp. 146–147. A good description that devotes greater attention to the role of the police is Stead, *The Police of France*, 144–157. See also A. E. Anton, "L'instruction criminelle," *American Journal of Comparative Law* 9 (1960), 441–457; George W. Pugh, "Administration of Criminal Justice in France: An Introductory Analysis," *Louisiana Law Review* 23 (1962), 1–28; and Robert Vouin, "The Role of the Prosecutor in French Criminal Trials," *American Journal of Comparative Law* 18 (1970), 483–497.

47. The Dutch practice is described in Arthur Rosett, "Trial and Discretion in Dutch Criminal Justice," *UCLA Law Review* 19 (1972), 353–390; L. H. Leigh and J. E. Hall Williams, *The Management of the Prosecution Process in Denmark, Sweden, and the Netherlands* (Warwickshire: James Hall, 1981), 41–71; and A. C. 't Hart, "Criminal Law Policy in the Netherlands," in van Dijk et al., eds., *Criminal Law in Action* (supra n. 40), 73–99.

48. See Leigh and Williams, *Management of the Prosecution Process*, 9–23; and Ole Krarup, "The Free Town of Christiania and the Role of the Courts," *International Journal of the Sociology of Law* 10 (1982), 31–47.

49. Abraham Goldstein and Martin Marcus, "The Myth of Judicial Supervision in Three 'Inquisitorial' Systems: France, Italy, and Germany," *Yale Law Journal* 87 (1977), 240–283, quote from 269.

50. During the late 1970s and early 1980s, a number of legal scholars debated whether European prosecutors were as constrained in their exercise of discretion as the principle of compulsory prosecution suggested. The impetus for the debate was concern over the growth and abuse of the plea bargaining system in the United States, and curiosity as to whether certain aspects of Europe's "inquisitorial" system contained lessons for the American common law system. Although the debate proved somewhat inconclusive, it did stimulate greater inquiry into the actual functioning of Europe's criminal justice systems. In a controversial article entitled "The Myth of Judicial Supervision in Three 'Inquisitorial' Systems: France, Italy, and Germany," two scholars from Yale, Abraham Goldstein and Martin Marcus, argued that European criminal procedures were not dramatically different from American processes. Contrary to conventional wisdom, they argued, European judges did not exercise much greater control over criminal investigations and prosecutions; European police and prosecutors did exercise substantial discretion in their investigations and charging; and European prosecutors and defendants often participated in negotiations analogous to plea bargaining. Some critics, such as John Langbein and Lloyd Weinreb, charged that the pair had carried their analogizing too far. Neither set of scholars, however, investigated the extent to which prosecutors were parties, both explicitly and discreetly, to bargains with criminal suspects for information. Each acknowledged that such deals occurred, but they did not pursue the matter in detail. See Goldstein and Marcus, "Myth of Judicial Supervision"; John Langbein and Lloyd Weinreb, "Continental Criminal Procedure: 'Myth' and Reality," *Yale Law Journal* 87 (1978), 1549–

That being said, one of the most significant changes in European drug enforcement since the early 1970s has been the easing of the "legality principle" in drug-related cases. Where once police shied away from efforts to flip drug dealers, and prosecutors studiously avoided any suggestion that they make deals with drug traffickers, today police and prosecutors in most European countries openly acknowledge their involvement in such practices. What began as a discreet police tactic employed first by DEA agents working closely with local agents, and then by local agents operating without the clear sanction of the law, has evolved into a relatively common law enforcement practice explicitly authorized by European prosecutors, courts, and legislatures. In some European countries, the initial impulses in this direction were motivated by the need to extract information about terrorist groups from members who had been arrested by the police. But in quite a number of countries, the evolution was one in which the hand of the DEA—as proponent, example, tutor, and lobbyist—was also readily apparent.

Although the legality principle is supposed to constrain both prosecutors and police, its strictures have always applied more strictly to the former than to the latter. European prosecutors, however, tend to be more powerful vis-à-vis the police than is the case in the United States and Great Britain; in many countries, the hierarchical nature of this relationship is set out explicitly in codes of criminal procedure. As a consequence, the ability of European police to negotiate and make deals with criminal suspects for their cooperation has depended greatly upon the nature of police-prosecutor relations, both legal and personal. This has been true both in Germany, where the prosecutor is bound by the *Legalitätsprinzip*, and in France and the Netherlands, where the prosecutor's discretion is much greater.[51] In Europe, the point at which a

---

1569; and the rebuttal by Goldstein and Marcus, "Comment on 'Continental Criminal Procedure,' " *Yale Law Journal* 87 (1978), 1570. See also the assessment of this debate in Mark G. Gertz, "The Dynamics of Plea Bargaining in Three Countries," *Criminal Justice Review* 15 (1990), 48–63; and Dennis P. McLaughlin, "Dealing with Dealing: Plea Bargaining in the Federal Republic of Germany," in Gale A. Mattox and John H. Vaughan Jr., eds., *Germany Through American Eyes* (Boulder, Colo.: Westview Press, 1989), 129–143.

51. In Germany, the public prosecutor's leading role in directing criminal investigations is mandated by the Code of Criminal Procedure, notably paragraph 161, which requires the police to assist the prosecutor in conducting his investigation and to make available to him any relevant information. In France, in the words of Tomlinson ("Nonadversarial Justice: The French Experience" [supra n. 46], 146–147), "Prosecutorial supervision of the police is quite intensive by American standards. The Code of Criminal Procedure places the police's investigatory activity under the direction of the local prosecutor; and in actual practice, the French prosecutor works more closely with the police than does his American counterpart, particularly

prosecutor's involvement is legally required tends to come earlier than in the United States. In most European countries, as in the United States, the police may not conduct an electronic surveillance or search a residence without authorization from a prosecutor, investigating magistrate, or judge. But unlike their American counterparts, police in most European countries require a prosecutor's approval to conduct an undercover operation, pay an informant, and take a variety of other investigative steps. In some countries, prosecutors are required to be present at the interrogation of suspects once there is a reasonable suspicion that the suspect is guilty, although the question of when a suspect is sufficiently suspicious so that the police must stop interrogating is in practice left up to the police to decide.[52]

Police in every country, however, tend to avoid involving prosecutors in investigations until it is absolutely necessary. They also can be quite resourceful in devising ways to circumvent the requirements for prosecutorial supervision, and hence the strictures of the legality principle as well.[53] Informants may be compensated from sources other than a prosecutorial supervised fund. A search can be made without a warrant whenever police can reasonably claim that the police were looking for a weapon. The moment of arrest, when the prosecutor's powers relative to the police suddenly multiply, can be delayed by the police in any number of ways—for instance, "if a suspect can be made to feel that the heat is on," a DEA agent in France said, "he may try to cut a deal" before

during the early stages of an investigation. In addition, the Code requires the police to inform the prosecutor promptly of any offenses known to them and to forward to him the dossier they prepare during the course of their investigation. Members of the prosecutor's office normally arrive at the scene of a serious offense soon after the police." Relations between police and prosecutors in the Netherlands are analyzed in Leigh and Williams, *Management of the Prosecution Process*, 45–71; and in L. H. C. Hulsman, "The Dutch Criminal Justice System from a Comparative Legal Perspective," in D. C. Fokkema et al., eds., *Introduction to Dutch Law for Foreign Lawyers* (The Netherlands: Kluwer-Deventer, 1978), 300–313. The powers of Dutch prosecutors are contrasted with those of British prosecutors in Leigh and Williams, *Management of the Prosecution Process* (supra n. 47), and in Downes, *Contrasts in Tolerance* (supra n. 13), 13–18.

52. K. W. Lidstone and T. L. Early, "Questioning Freedom: Detention for Questioning in France, Scotland, and England," *International and Comparative Law Quarterly* 31 (1982), 488, 492.

53. David K. Linnan, "Police Discretion in a Continental European Administrative State: The Police of Baden-Württemberg in the Federal Republic of Germany," *Law and Contemporary Problems* 47 (1984), 200–203; Gunther Artz, "Responses to the Growth of Crime in the United States and West Germany: A Comparison of Changes in Criminal Law and Societal Attitudes," *Cornell International Law Journal* 12 (1979), 49, 54–55.

being arrested. To the extent the agent is bluffing, it is worth observing, he is not in violation of the legality principle. Quite often, prosecutors and judges are aware of the greater discretion exercised by the police; indeed, they often rely on the police to "screen" cases and work out their own informal arrangements with informants.[54] Especially in drug investigations and others in which there is no victim to file a complaint, police and prosecutors often have an implicit understanding that any deals with criminal informants will be worked out informally without involving the prosecutor's office. In countries in which prosecutors exercise a strong hand in supervising investigations, this may require a conscious effort on the part of the prosecutor not to examine or question too closely some otherwise unexplainable aspects of the police's investigation. Some prosecutors are concerned about this abdication of power to the police; in Germany, for instance, prosecutors and legal scholars have expressed great concern at the "police-izisation" of criminal procedure generated by the proliferation of proactive drug trafficking investigations in which police have naturally seized the initative, but their efforts to curtail this development have been frustrated by the slow pace of legal evolution in this area.[55]

Once a drug dealer has been arrested and taken to the police station, the drug enforcement agent's ability to "flip" the dealer depends upon when a prosecutor must be informed. In this respect, most European drug enforcement agents have an advantage over U.S.-based agents. In France, which is typical in this regard of many European countries, police may question suspects for twenty-four hours—and up to seventy-two hours in drug and terrorist cases—before bringing them before a prosecutor. Once a prosecutor is introduced into the picture, however, the agent's ability to flip the dealer diminishes greatly. At that point, about all that can be offered in return for cooperation is a chance at a reduced sentence. European police also have less flexibility than American police in protecting an informant who has been arrested by another officer.

54. The argument that the police play a major role in alleviating the pressures on prosecutors created by the legality principle is advanced in Damaška, "The Reality of Prosecutorial Discretion" (supra n. 43), 123–124.

55. Michael Füllkrug, "Neue Formen der Kriminalitätsbekämpfung und ihre Auswirkungen auf das Verhältnis von Staatsanwaltschaft und Polizei" ("New Forms of Crime Fighting and the Consequences for the Relationship Between the Public Prosecutor and the Police"), *Zeitschrift für Rechtspolitik* 17 (1984), 193–195.

The challenge for the European drug enforcement agent is thus to identify drug traffickers, persuade them that there is sufficient evidence to arrest, then flip them, and finally protect them as best the agent can, given that no assistance can be expected from the prosecutor's office. With all these constraints, it is no wonder that few European drug enforcement agents are able to build up the networks of informants that are the pride and necessity of the better American drug enforcement agents. DEA agents in Europe regard the German, Austrian, and Swiss police as increasingly aggressive and sophisticated in flipping informants, the Dutch a little less so, and the Italians and French as not particularly interested in adapting the DEA's methods.

Nonetheless, as public and law enforcement concerns over illicit drug trafficking rose during the 1980s, so too did the pressures to allow criminal justice officials greater latitude and power in investigating and prosecuting traffickers. And as police responded to the new challenge, and to the influence of the DEA, by informally developing their capacity to recruit informants, pressures built to legalize and regulate what the police were already doing anyway and to allow the prosecutors and the courts the authority to reduce or drop charges, or reduce sentences, in return for cooperation. In 1982, German law was revised and the courts were explicitly provided with the discretion to reward drug trafficker defendants with a reduced sentence, or even no punishment at all, in return for their cooperation in a successful investigation.[56] In Italy, similar laws were enacted in 1978, 1980, and 1982 to induce repentant (*pentiti*) terrorists to cooperate with counterterrorist investigations, but efforts to offer repentant drug dealers comparable inducements have met with greater resistance.[57] In Belgium and Germany, drug laws were revised at the urging of drug enforcement officials to allow defendants who cooperated to be granted immunity from prosecution for misdemeanors and a milder sentence for felonies. Unlike their American counterparts, however, prosecutors in both countries have generally shied away from making the most of these revisions, perhaps because

56. Section 31 of the Narcotics Law (*Betäubungsmittelgesetz*). See Hans-Jörg Albrecht, "Criminal Law and Drug Control: A Look at Western Europe," *International Journal of Comparative and Applied Criminal Justice* 10 (1986), 17, 37.

57. Weinberg and Eubank, *Rise and Fall of Italian Terrorism* (supra n. 5), 127–130. The Italian legislation (Law No. 304 of May 29, 1982) is briefly discussed in *Terrorism and Security: The Italian Experience*, 98th Cong., 2d Sess. (1984), S. Rpt. 246.

they retain an inkling of the civil law's historic antipathy toward such deal-making.[58] Nonetheless, in Germany the provision was extended in 1989 to those involved in terrorist acts. In most European countries, moreover, including a number that have not enacted any legislation regarding those who turn state's evidence, prosecutors can request that judges take into account a defendant's cooperation in deciding on the sentence.[59] Although judges are not obliged to accept prosecutors' recommendations, they typically are taken into account.

More difficult to legislate have been guidelines for the recruitment and management of informants by police.[60] As the use of informants has expanded significantly, the courts and criminal justice authorities have struggled with the difficulties of providing explicit legal authority and effective regulation.[61] In Germany, the legal basis for the authority of the police to use informants remains the subject of debate among criminal justice officials and scholars.[62] Periodic rulings by the German Supreme Court, the Bundesgerichtshof, have been perceived as vague and open to varied interpretations by law enforcement officials. Internal guidelines regulating the use of informants, as well as undercover operations, have been slow to develop.[63] Even within high-level police circles during the

58. E. Boutmans, "The Situation in Belgium," and Hans-Jörg Albrecht, "Drug Policy in the Federal Republic of Germany," both chapters in Albrecht and Kalmthout, eds., *Drug Policies in Western Europe* (supra n. 4), 89–105 and 175–194, esp. 95–96 and 184.

59. Jürgen Meyer, *Betäubungsmittelstrafrecht in Westeuropa: Eine rechtsvergleichende Untersuchung im Auftrag des Bundeskriminalamts* (Freiburg im Br.: Max-Planck-Instituts für Ausländisches und Internationales Strafrecht, 1987), 809–810.

60. The use of informants in undercover operations, which has presented the most difficult legal and policy issues, is discussed in the following section.

61. See "Abgetönte Scheibe, Verstellte Stimme: Hamburgs Innensenator Alfons Pawelczyk (SPD) über die V-Leute der Polizei" ("Tinted Glass, Disguised Voice: Hamburg's Senator for Internal Affairs Alfons Pawelczyk on Undercover Police Agents") *Spiegel*, May 3, 1982; Harald Körner, "Die Bekämpfung der organisierten Rauschgiftkriminalität durch V-Leute" (The Fight Against Organized Drug Criminality by Undercover Agents") in *Taschenbuch für Kriminalisten* 35 (1985), 29–113.

62. See, e.g., the discussion in Hans Ellinger, "Aktuelle Fragen des Betäubungsmittel-rechts—Eine Tagung der Deutschen Richterakademie" ("Current Questions Regarding the Narcotics Law: A Conference of the German Judges' Academy"), in *Monatsschrift für Kriminologie und Strafrechtsreform* 67 (1984), 271–276; and Peter Marqua, "Rechtliche Grauzone? Ein Hearing der Grünen zur V-Mann-Problematik—zwischen faktischen Zwängen und juristischer Bewertung" ("Gray Legal Area? A Hearing of the Greens on Informants— Between Actual Restraints and Legal Assessment"), in *Deutsche Richterzeitung*, no. 4, (1985), 153.

63. The frustration of BKA drug enforcement officials with the slow pace of legal evolution to accommodate more effective investigative techniques is reflected in a four-part series on drug enforcement in *General Anzeiger*, Sept. 20–23, 1989.

late 1970s, discussion was muted and largely limited to exchanging experiences and debating the appropriateness of past actions;[64] only in 1982 did Hamburg become the first German state to establish guidelines for police working with informants.[65] These issues are gradually being resolved, albeit at varying paces and in different ways in the various German states. The Dutch reportedly have modernized their system for managing informants along DEA lines, identifying informants by numbers, appointing special agents to manage particular informants, and maintaining blacklists of undesirable informants. Other European countries have tended to lag behind the Dutch and the Germans in addressing these issues.

Most European courts have also struggled—as in the United States—over the degree to which the identity of informants, undercover agents, and other witnesses can be shielded in court. By the end of the 1980s, no consensus could be discerned, with some states absolutely prohibiting the introduction into court of information provided anonymously, others permitting it with relatively few restrictions, and a number debating the extent to which police officials could be allowed to report (as hearsay) what they had learned from their anonymous informants. In France, a police officer is not required to divulge the name of an informant in court. Switzerland and Italy are quite strict about prohibiting the introduction of such evidence provided by anonymous informants.[66] In the Netherlands, the use of anonymous witnesses attracted substantial controversy during the 1980s, with two advisory panels appointed by the Dutch judiciary association and the government concluding that evidence provided anonymously should not be excluded so long as the interests of the defendant were taken into account.[67] In Germany, the Bundesgerichtshof first addressed the question in 1952 and struggled with it repeatedly thereafter without coming to any final resolution. The trend during the 1980s favored permitting police to testify to information provided by an anonymous informant.[68] Only in

64. "Dem Verbrechen an die Wurzel" ("Attacking the Roots of Crime"), *Spiegel*, May 5, 1977, 62–73.

65. "Abgetönte Scheibe, Verstellte Stimme" (supra n. 61).

66. See A. Manna and E. Barone Ricciardelli, "The Limitations and Formalities of Criminal Law Provisions Concerning Narcotics: Considerations on Legislation in Italy," and H. Schultz, "Drugs and Drug Policies in Switzerland," both in Albrecht and Kalmthout, eds., *Drug Policies in Western Europe* (supra n. 4), 195–234 and 361–381, esp. 247, 366.

67. See Anjewierden and Atteveld, "Current Trends in Dutch Opium Legislation," (supra n. 13), 247–248, which refers to both reports.

68. Klaus Lüderssen, ed., *V-Leute: Die Falle im Rechtsstaat* (Frankfurt: Suhrkamp, 1985),

1991 was the issue largely resolved by federal legislation requiring informants to reveal their faces but allowing them to withhold other information about their identities if necessary for their personal security. In Denmark, a 1986 revision of the drug laws, stimulated in part by a controversial Supreme Court decision in late 1983, restricted the prosecution's use of anonymous informants; judges were authorized to exclude all nonrelevant individuals as well as the defendant from the courtroom and to swear the defense attorney not to reveal the informant's identity, but defendants retained their right to read the informant's testimony.[69] In both Denmark and Germany, as in the United States, restrictions on the ability of prosecutors to shield the identities of their informants in court have provided some of the stimulus for creating witness protection programs.

From the perspective of DEA agents working in Europe, the evolution in police practices, judicial rulings, and legislative enactments has proven helpful both directly and vicariously. What began as a discreet effort by European police agents to accommodate and adapt the DEA's methods of cultivating and running informants had evolved in much of Europe by the late 1980s into a legally sanctioned system of informant recruitment and maintenance that in many respects shared more in common with the American system than it did with the European system of the 1960s. Nonetheless, DEA agents have continued to find the legal inhibitions on flipping drug dealers, and the ambiguity of their informants' legal status, a source of substantial frustration in collecting intelligence and making cases. Making deals with drug dealers in return for their cooperation, and inducing criminals to testify against others in return for immunity from prosecution, still strike many Europeans as somewhat bizarre and risky means of attacking crime; indeed, these methods continue to be criticized in the United States, particularly after revelations about informants who implicated innocent individuals.[70] The process of recruiting

---

502–507, 514–516; Körner, "Die Bekämpfung" (supra n. 61), 73–106; Albrecht, "Drug Policy in the Federal Republic of Germany" (supra n. 58).

69. Sysette Vinding Kruse, "Drug Criminality from a Legal Point of View," in Per Stangeland, ed., *Drugs and Drug Control, Scandinavian Studies in Criminology,* vol. 8 (Oslo: Norwegian University Press, 1987), 34–52; J. Jepsen, "Drug Policies in Denmark" (supra n. 14), 115–116. See the Supreme Court decision of Dec. 2, 1983 (Ugeskrift for Retsvaesen 1984, 81 H) and Section 848(2) of the Code of Procedure, as formulated by Act No. 321 of June 4, 1986 ("Prohibition Against Anonymous Informants").

70. See, e.g., Mark Curriden, "No Honor Among Thieves," *ABA Journal* 75 (1989), 52–56.

informants in Europe will no doubt continue to follow in American footsteps, albeit gradually and in haphazard fashion.

Undercover Operations

Aside from the low priority given to drug enforcement by most foreign governments until recently, the greatest challenge facing U.S. drug enforcement agents as they expanded their international operations during the late 1960s and 1970s was the widespread and deeply felt resistance to using undercover investigative methods. From the beginning of the postwar era until the late 1960s, and in many countries until well into the 1980s, most Europeans, including many police, viewed the use of undercover tactics by law enforcement agents as anathema. The very notion instantly conjured up images of the despised *agent provocateur* employed by governments in previous decades and centuries to discredit dissident political groups.[71] So great was the antipathy toward this tactic that the use of infiltrators not to provoke but solely to gather information was also cast into disrepute. To the greatest extent possible, Europeans preferred that police not disguise their identity in investigating crime. Resistance to police reliance on informants and other nonpolice agents to conduct undercover tasks was felt only slightly less strongly.

One reaction of European legal systems to their bitter experience with *agents provocateurs* was their preference for a strict interpretation of the legality principle and their rejection of a legal notion that has become central to proactive law enforcement in the United States, that "[a]cts which would be criminal when done by a private citizen are justifiable and not criminal when done by a government agent in the reasonable exercise of law enforcement power."[72] In much of Europe, police could

71. See Paul Chevigny, *Cops and Rebels: A Study of Provocation* (New York: Pantheon Books, 1972), esp. chap. 10; and Walter Otto Weyrauch, "Gestapo Informants: Facts and Theory of Undercover Operations," *Columbia Journal of Transnational Law* 24 (1986), 553–596. Perhaps the finest description of the *agent provocateur* is Joseph Conrad, *The Secret Agent* (New York: Knopf, 1992).

72. Robert I. Blecker, "Beyond Undercover in America: Serpico to Abscam," *New York Law School Law Review* 28 (1984), 823, 855. The best overall discussion of undercover operations is Gary T. Marx, *Undercover: Police Surveillance in America* (Berkeley and Los Angeles: University of California Press, 1988). See also the essays collected in Gerald M. Caplan, ed., *ABSCAM Ethics: Moral Issues and Deception in Law Enforcement* (Cambridge, Mass.: Ballinger, 1983).

not even go through the motions of a criminal act. Undercover agents could not pretend to take or offer a bribe in order to catch a corrupt politician or public official; they could not play the role of a fence and purchase stolen goods in order to gather evidence against thieves; and they could not assume the guise of a drug trafficker interested in purchasing drugs. If agents performed any of these "crimes," they were as guilty as any criminal performing the same act for real. The same restrictions also applied, albeit not always as strictly, to informants and others acting at the behest of law enforcement agents.

Beyond the traditional association with *agents provocateurs,* the DEA also was obliged to overcome two other misperceptions. The first was the tendency of most Europeans to regard all undercover operations as an unacceptable form of entrapment. The second was the popular image of all undercover operations as "deep cover" operations—those in which an agent becomes deeply enmeshed in a criminal organization or milieu and is obliged to play the role of a criminal virtually twenty-four hours a day for months at a time.[73] The reality of most undercover operations, at least those engaged in by DEA agents, is something quite different. The DEA, like most other U.S. law enforcement agencies, occasionally runs deep cover undercover operations. The vast majority of undercover operations involving DEA agents, however, are part-time affairs in which the agent is able to return to office or home after meeting someone in an undercover capacity. Few DEA operations require an agent to remain undercover for more than a few days at a time.

Despite European antipathies and restrictions, throughout the 1950s and 1960s American drug enforcement agents employed by both the FBN and the Army's Criminal Investigative Division routinely operated undercover and ran undercover informants.[74] Relying on personal contacts and an abundance of extralegal discretion to skirt the legal prohibitions on their U.S.-style tactics, the few FBN agents stationed in Europe pursued their cases without trying too hard to change the local systems.

With the expansion of the U.S. drug enforcement presence in Europe during the early 1970s, however, the U.S. agents began actively encour-

73. A fine example of this type of operation is recounted in Joseph Pistone with Richard Woodley, *Donnie Brasco: My Undercover Life in the Mafia* (New York: New American Library, 1987).
74. See the memoirs of Charles Siragusa (*The Trail of the Poppy* [Englewood Cliffs, N.J.: Prentice-Hall, 1966]); and of Sal Vizzini (*Vizzini: The Secret Lives of America's Most Successful Undercover Agent* [New York: Arbor House, 1972]).

aging their European counterparts to integrate undercover techniques into their own drug enforcement investigations. They were motivated not just by the proven effectiveness of undercover operations but also by their agency's institutional bias in favor of the technique. Electronic surveillance was also important, but many European police agencies already had developed their expertise in this area independent of U.S. influences. DEA efforts initially focused on familiarizing European police with undercover tactics.[75] As they developed a constituency for undercover operations among the police, the DEA agents extended their advocacy efforts to higher levels of European law enforcement systems. They briefed prosecutors, judges, and legislators regarding their investigative techniques and the changes in the law necessary to accommodate them. In particular, they sought to persuade high-level European law enforcement officials either that undercover operations did not clash with local laws or that local laws should be changed or reinterpreted to sanction such tactics.

Throughout much of Europe in the early 1970s, the straightforward "buy and bust" tactic so fundamental to drug enforcement in the United States was regarded as either illegal or at best of questionable legality and rarely employed. An undercover agent who purchased drugs was, according to the dominant legalist interpretation, as guilty of violating the law as the illicit drug dealer from whom they were purchased. DEA agents working in Europe responded to this constraint by developing circuitous tactics on their own and by co-opting local police and prosecutors in their efforts. One approach involved a slight modification of the "buy and bust" technique, in which an undercover agent would set up an illicit transaction but not actually complete the purchase. For instance, agents might arrange with a trafficker to purchase some drugs, meet with the trafficker to inspect the drugs, and then either back out of the deal or excuse themselves for a moment—at which point the local police would introduce themselves and make the arrest. One problem with this approach was that it made it difficult to charge traffickers with anything more than possession because the agent, who was obliged to remain anonymous, could not offer evidence regarding the planned sale. In some countries, this limitation was partially remedied by creating a

---

75. Examples of DEA training lessons are provided by Mortimer D. Moriarty, "Undercover Negotiating: Dealing for Your Life," *Police Chief* 57 (Nov. 1990), 44–47; and Gary E. Wade, "Undercover Negotiating: Flashroll Management," *Police Chief* 57 (Nov. 1990), 48–49.

legal presumption that possession of a sufficiently large amount of drugs assumed the intent to sell them.

The receptivity of European prosecutors and judges to participating in these charades varied not just among countries but also among districts and even personalities. In Denmark, where undercover operations had been legally sanctioned but employed relatively infrequently for decades, DEA agents encountered little resistance—although the 1986 revision of the drug laws imposed greater judicial control over such tactics and prohibited the use of nonpolice agents and informants as undercover operatives.[76] In Italy, much depends upon the personal views of the investigating magistrate. Those who want to cooperate, one DEA agent observed, "usually know an agent or informant has played a part, and they let it go if they can, but you can't slap the judge in the face with the facts." In some countries, most notably the Netherlands, Germany, and (somewhat later) Spain, certain prosecutors became specialists in drug trafficking cases and quickly learned to accommodate the DEA's methods. This in effect required keeping two sets of files on a case. The unofficial one, which was not necessarily compiled in any formal sense, would describe the investigation exactly as it had taken place. The official one, to be delivered to the judge, would present the charade according to which an unidentified participant in the transaction—the undercover agent or informant—"failed to appear" or "escaped."[77] An arrest warrant might even be issued for that participant, although the name would likely be the alias used by the undercover agent or informant. If, however, the arrested trafficker were able to identify the undercover agent or informant by his or her real name, serious difficulties could result. On occasion, the police have been obliged to issue an arrest warrant for an undercover informant whose cover has been blown, although not without first warning the informant to leave the country.[78] When the accurately identified undercover operative is a law enforcement agent, it is highly unlikely that the informant will be charged. But on the rare occasions when an undercover agent is identi-

76. Section 754 (a-d) of the Code of Procedure, as formulated by Act No. 319 of June 4, 1986, discussed briefly in Jepsen, "Drug Policies in Denmark" (supra n. 14), 114–115.

77. Boutmans, "The Situation in Belgium" (supra n. 58), 95, briefly refers to a number of court cases in which this ruse was employed: C. A. Antwerp, Dec. 2, 1977, *Rechtkundig Weekblad*, 1978–79, 875; *Corr Tongeren*, Nov. 9, 1977, and July 13, 1977, *Limburgs Rechtsleven*, 1978, 47, and 1979, 215.

78. There are a few cases in which informants whose covers have been blown have been obliged to spend years in virtual exile from their countries.

fied, courts are prone to dismiss the case as in clear violation of the prohibition against *agent provocateur* operations.

This charade continues to be integral to undercover drug investigations in a few countries, notably France, but it became far less of a necessity during the 1980s. The first to do away with it were the Germans, who adopted DEA models of investigation more quickly, and with fewer inhibitions, than any other Europeans. During the early 1970s, DEA agents stationed in Germany actively lobbied for the acceptance and use of undercover techniques. At first they conducted most undercover operations themselves, and virtually acted as informants for the German police. With relations among German police and prosecutors generally closer then than they are now, DEA agents also proved successful in persuading the latter of the merits of undercover techniques. As their resistance dwindled, the DEA agents, often in league with local police, gave presentations on undercover operations to judges. By the mid-1970s, some of the judges had not only gotten to know the U.S. agents but also come to view the fact that they were involved in a case as an indication that it should be taken more seriously. DEA agents also testified in German courts, which was a departure from the usual agency policy of maintaining as low profile a presence as possible. Since their testimony could prove helpful in protecting the identities of German police informants, German police were all the more grateful for DEA involvement.

The DEA's undercover tactics were quickly adopted by the BKA and by the LKA in Bavaria and Hesse. During the 1980s, resistance in other parts of Germany dwindled as the tactics became increasingly familiar and as drug enforcement assumed greater importance in German policing. By the late 1980s, few German drug enforcement units depended any longer on DEA agents to perform undercover tasks. The few exceptions were mostly investigations requiring an American undercover role, or an agent capable of posing as an Italian or Latin American, as a number of the Italian-American and Hispanic-American agents could.

From the late 1960s to the late 1980s, prosecutors, courts, and legislators struggled to respond to the undercover initiatives of the police.[79] The Bundesgerichtshof ruled on the undercover issue numerous times without ever clarifying either the legal basis for undercover operations or the boundaries of permissible activity by an agent.[80] Debate over

79. See Lüderssen, *V-Leute* (supra n. 68); and Körner, "Die Bekämpfung" (supra n. 61).
80. The rulings of the Bundesgerichtshof include BGH 10.6.1975, BGH 15.4.1980, BGH

appropriate guidelines for undercover activities by police and informants was also a central issue of discussion at the periodic conferences of the interior and justice ministers of the German states.[81] In the fall of 1986, the ministers agreed to two sets of guidelines, one regulating the use of informants, the other regulating the employment of undercover police agents. But their lack of consensus was reflected in their appeal to the Ministries of Justice and the Interior to clarify the legal status of undercover agents and to create the legal basis for employing them. Only in 1991 were most of the legal issues resolved by federal legislation formally legalizing undercover operations but requiring that they be approved by a prosecutor and employed only when less-intrusive tactics appeared not feasible.[82]

In Austria, a similar process occurred, albeit on a much smaller scale and more belatedly than in Germany. Throughout the mid-1970s, the Austrian police relied on the DEA to perform all undercover tasks. In 1977, a new activist chief of Austria's Central Narcotics Department, Herbert Fuchs, encouraged the resident DEA agents to train Austrian police in U.S. drug enforcement techniques. Shortly thereafter, the chief judge of the Salzburg region was persuaded to reinterpret the prohibition on undercover tactics in drug investigations. By creating a legal presumption that a person caught in possession of a large amount of drugs was intending to sell them, the contrary presumption that the sale had been "provoked" by the undercover agent was negated. During the 1980s, more substantial legal support for undercover operations was provided by a "legal interpretation" contained in a parliamentary report and by a number of supreme court decisions.[83] Until well into the 1980s,

---

21.10.1980, BGH 6.2.1981, and BGH 23.5.1984. See the discussions in Körner, "Die Bekämpfung" (supra n. 61); Arthur Kreuzer, "Wenn der Spitzel lockt: Die Karlsruher Richter billigen fragewürdige Praktiken der Polizei" ("When the Informant Entraps: Judges of Karlsruhe Approve Questionable Police Practices"), *Zeit*, Jan. 29, 1982, 53; and in Albrecht, "Drug Policy in the Federal Republic of Germany" (supra n. 58), 184–185.

81. See Klaus Rogall, "Strafprozessuale Grundlagen und Legislative Probleme des Einsatzes Verdeckter Ermittler im Strafverfahren" ("Criminal Trial Elements and Legislative Problems of Using Undercover Agents in Criminal Proceedings"), *Juristen Zeitung* 42 (1987), 847–853.

82. See Section 110 of the 1991 Organized Crime Act.

83. See the discussion in Manfred Burgstaller, "Drogenstrafrecht in Oesterreich," in Jan van Dijk et al., eds., *Criminal Law in Action* (supra n. 40), 187, 189, 190. Burgstaller notes that the 1980 amendment has been challenged in the legal literature as conflicting with Section 25 of the Austrian Penal Code, which generally prohibits the police from committing a crime for the purpose of gathering information or implicating a criminal. For critical analyses of the legalization of undercover operations, see A. Pilgrim, "Die Kosten der Kriminalisierung des

however, police and prosecutors generally continued to write up their reports as they had before the change in the law—that is, omitting any explicit mention of the undercover agent or informant. Only toward the end of the decade did the reluctance to be explicit about the use of undercover tactics gradually fade.

The Austrian situation regarding undercover operations is typical of much of the rest of Europe as well. In most countries, it remains a matter of controversy, but the general movement is in favor of increased use of the tactic; the European Commission for Human Rights bolstered this trend in 1986 when it declared that the use of undercover agents could be reconciled with Articles 6 and 8 of the European Human Rights Convention.[84] In Switzerland, where police agents trained by the DEA and the BKA have utilized undercover techniques in drug and counterfeiting cases, both the 1975 drug law and a 1986 judicial opinion by the Federal Tribunal have supported their use.[85] Drug enforcement agents in Spain do work undercover but typically must rely on the types of charades described above.

In Italy, Spain, and France, there is still substantial resistance to employing law enforcement agents in undercover capacities. The resistance, it should be noted, stems not only from the reluctance of prosecutors and judges to approve the use of such tactics but also from the unfamiliarity of the police with employing them. Exceptions do, however, exist. For instance, one DEA agent spoke of working closely during the late 1970s with an agent of Corsican origins on the Parisian police force who excelled at posing as a drug trafficker. Another agent, based in Spain, observed that it was relatively unusual for Spanish police to engage in undercover operations but that a number of agents of the National Police drug branch based in Madrid were very good and aggressive at working undercover.

Drogenkonsums" ("The Costs of Criminalizing Drug Consumption"), in R. Mader and H. Strotzka, eds., *Drogenpolitik zwischen Therapie und Strafe* ("Drug Policy Between Therapy and Punishment") (Vienna, 1980), 117–148, discussed in J. Fehérváry, "Drug Policy in Austria," in Albrecht and Kalmthout, eds., *Drug Policies in Western Europe* (supra n. 4), 67–68. I have also relied upon information provided in a correspondence from Mag. Herbert Fuchs, Apr. 20, 1990.

84. Rogall, "Strafprozessuale Grundlagen" (supra n. 81).

85. See the brief discussion in Schultz, "Drugs and Drug Policies in Switzerland" (supra n. 66), which refers to Section 23(2) of the 1975 Drug Law and the Federal Tribunal decision reported at BGE 112 (1986) 1a, 21, c. 3 and 4, which held that undercover operations were legal even in cantons that had not explicitly authorized their use.

By and large, however, police in southern Europe specializing in drug trafficking investigations do not view undercover operations as integral to their job. The fact that the courts remain reluctant—despite the lobbying efforts of the DEA—to permit any extended forms of undercover operations no doubt contributes to this view. In both France and Italy, for instance, an undercover agent cannot actually purchase drugs but can only do a "knock-off"—that is, order the drugs and then seize them without paying. The principal difference between the Italian practice and the French and Spanish practice is that whereas the former are similarly leery of using informants in undercover roles, the latter have shown no such reserve.

In Belgium, U.S. drug enforcement agents of both the BNDD and the Army's Criminal Investigative Division began encouraging local police to recruit informants and work undercover during the late 1960s. Their efforts contributed to the creation of a special criminal intelligence unit, the Administration of Criminal Investigation (ACI) in the Ministry of Justice in 1971, which in turn prompted the Gendarmerie to establish their own criminal intelligence unit two years later. The ACI unit quickly integrated DEA-style tactics into their investigations but encountered resistance from prosecutors. Top Gendarmerie officials meanwhile resisted pressures by the DEA and the chief of the Gendarmerie drug unit, Captain François, to incorporate similar tactics into their investigations. Their resistance dwindled following a 1974 drug enforcement conference in which the U.S. ambassador praised François as a model law enforcement officer, and then increased when corruption in the drug enforcement unit, and a scandal involving Francois and an informant, were exposed to public view.[86]

During roughly the same time, the ACI was also shaken by a series of scandals. As a result, both drug enforcement units were dissolved and undercover work was gradually integrated into the regular criminal investigation branches of the Gendarmerie and the Police Judiciaire. As in Germany, the courts have struggled with defining the legal authority and limits of undercover operations, with the trend toward acknowledging the legitimacy of the basic technique.[87] During the 1980s, Police

---

86. Cyrille Fijnaut, *De Zaak François* ("The François Case") (Antwerp: Kluwer, 1983).

87. See esp. the June 1984 decision by the Tribunal Correctionnel, 24th Chamber of the State Court of Brussels, which acknowledged the legality of undercover operations and controlled deliveries, discussed in Körner, "Die Bekämpfung" (supra n. 61), 39. See also Boutmans, "The Situation in Belgium" (supra n. 58), 93–94, which notes a series of cases in which Belgian courts have struggled with the appropriate limits on undercover operations.

Judiciaire agents were more likely than agents of the Gendarmerie to work undercover, but their efforts similarly resulted in scandal when three top police officials in the drug enforcement brigade in Brussels were suspended by the minister of justice in 1990 for excesses related to the employment of undercover operations and informants.

In the Netherlands, the impetus for employing undercover operations was provided by the dramatic growth of the Chinese-dominated heroin trade in Amsterdam in the early 1970s. Totally unprepared for this development, the Dutch police turned to the DEA for assistance. DEA agents and their informants began working undercover, setting up drug busts and co-opting Dutch police into the legal charades required to square DEA methods with Dutch law. Some local police reacted uneasily. "One detective in the Drugs Squad," Maurice Punch noted in his analysis of Dutch policing, "was said to have had 'sleepless nights and sweaty palms' about the 'dicey' reports he had to write to cover certain operations and was relieved when he was transferred because in Dutch law the DEA men were as guilty as anyone else involved in a deal."[88] On occasion, Dutch courts responded to these developments by dismissing cases in which the evidence had been gathered by undercover agents and informants and in which the police refused to reveal the identity of their informants.[89]

By the late 1970s, however, Dutch police officials were increasingly interested in integrating undercover operations into their own investigations. The willingness of the courts to grant a degree of legitimacy to undercover operations eased the process.[90] Particularly notable was the 1979 *Tallon* case, involving a DEA undercover investigation that had begun in the United States and culminated in arrests on Dutch territory, in which a court acknowledged that not all undercover tactics constituted entrapment. During the mid-1980s, the police chief of Amsterdam, Kees Sietsma, investigated the possibility of formally integrating undercover operations into Dutch criminal investigations, in part by participating in a Canadian undercover training program, and decided in favor. He was opposed, however, by the police chief of Rotterdam.[91] Two

88. Maurice Punch, *Conduct Unbecoming: The Social Construction of Police Deviance and Control* (New York: Tavistock Publications, 1985), 46.

89. Ibid.

90. See Anjewierden and Atteveld, "Current Trends in Dutch Opium Legislation" (supra n. 13), 245–246, which refers to two supreme court decisions: HR Nov. 1, 1983, NJ 1984, 586; and HR Jan. 1984, NJ 1984, 405.

91. "Undercover Agents: gevaar en verleiding groter dan resultaten," *Elseviers Magazine*,

commissions set up to propose changes in the drug laws also debated whether and how undercover techniques should be employed.[92] In 1985, the Ministry of Justice formally authorized their use, and the Amsterdam police force quickly established its own undercover unit. Virtually all undercover operations were initially employed in drug trafficking investigations. By 1990, however, almost half involved other sorts of crimes.

During the 1980s, public controversy over undercover operations and foreign drug enforcement operations focused not on the DEA but on German drug enforcement efforts. In one case, German police were publicly embarrassed when Dutch television reporters posing as drug traffickers tricked German drug enforcement agents into conducting a unilateral law enforcement operation in Dutch territory and filmed them in the act. In other cases, tensions flared when German drug enforcement agents conducted undercover operations in the Netherlands, or used informants and private detectives to lure drug traffickers across the border, without notifying CRI officials in advance—although in a number of cases, local Dutch authorities consented to the operations but did not inform the CRI (the Dutch National Criminal Intelligence Service).

There is little question that European attitudes toward undercover operations have evolved greatly since the 1970s. At the one extreme are the BKA and some of the Landespolizei, who have followed increasingly in the DEA's footsteps. At the other extreme are the southern Europeans, who employ police agents in undercover operations relatively infrequently and who are still obliged to rely on charades to circumvent the legal restrictions. Between the two extremes, one can discern a number of common attitudes regarding use of the tactic.

As in the United States, European courts have struggled with where to draw the line between legitimate undercover techniques and those that qualify as entrapment; most continue to interpret entrapment far more broadly than do American courts. Even where undercover agents are able to purchase drugs legally, most countries still require that the seller be arrested at that time. The notion of an undercover agent making a series of undercover buys to establish one's credibility, to expand one's

May 11, 1985; Carel Brendel and Theo Gerritse, "De undercover-agenten van commissaris Sietsma," *Vrij Nederland*, May 11, 1985, 1.

92. See the discussion in "Politie, openbaar ministerie and bewijsverkrijging" ("Police, Public Prosecutors, and Obtaining Criminal Evidence"), *Handelingen der Nederlands Juristen-Vereninging* 112 (1982), 5–66.

contacts, and to work one's way up the hierarchy of a drug trafficking organization, has yet to be accepted widely in Europe.

One also finds persistent resistance to the straightforward "buy and bust" tactic so commonly employed by American drug enforcement agents. The notion, derived from the historical experience with *agents provocateurs*, that a police agent should not "provoke" a crime remains quite powerful. An agent may properly be introduced into a situation in which a drug transaction is going to take place anyway, but he or she may not create the situation. More penetrative techniques, such as deep undercover operations, are exceptionally rare, and no European police agencies have yet followed the DEA's lead in employing "reverse undercover," or "sell-and-bust," operations.[93] One also finds a common disposition that undercover techniques should only be used as a last resort, when more traditional and less intrusive tactics have failed or offer no promise of success, and that they should be employed only in investigations of relatively serious offenses. With some exceptions, informants are generally freer than law enforcement agents to stretch some of the guidelines defining appropriate behavior in the service of the law. Many European drug enforcement units continue to rely heavily on DEA agents and the informants recruited by them to perform undercover tasks in major investigations; they also welcome the "flashrolls" provided by the American agency, which can amount to as much as $5 million. And in most countries undercover agents are still used only or primarily in drug investigations. The general trend, however, is in the direction of expanded use of undercover operations throughout Europe. In short, the integration of undercover operations into European drug enforcement has progressed dramatically over the last two decades, but it has yet to approximate the extensive and aggressive use of undercover operations by U.S. drug enforcement agents.

Controlled Deliveries

The technique of controlled delivery, in which drug enforcement agents "let the drugs walk"—that is, allow a consignment of illicit drugs they

93. These operations are discussed by Captain Timothy A. Raezer, "Needed Weapons in the Army's War on Drugs: Electronic Surveillance and Informants," *Military Law Review* 116 (1987), 1–65.

have detected "to go forward under [their] control and surveillance . . . in order to secure evidence against the organizers of such illicit drug traffic"—is regarded by many drug enforcement agents as a particularly valuable tactic,[94] one that has been employed for decades.[95] During the 1970s, DEA agents and cooperative European agents continually found their efforts to investigate drug trafficking organizations hampered by the legality principle's requirement that the agents seize illicit drugs immediately upon identifying their location or coming into contact with them, and by customs regulations requiring that all imported goods be declared and cleared through customs. The result was that many investigations ended with the seizure of the drug consignment, or at best with the arrest of the "mules," or drug couriers, who often knew little about the organizations for which they worked. As with the evolution of undercover operations, DEA and European agents responded to the legal prohibition of a valuable investigative technique first by discreetly employing it anyway, then by persuading and pressuring prosecutors to sanction it, and ultimately by inducing judges and legislators to legalize it. Because so many controlled deliveries cross national borders, the control and legal status of this investigative technique have been addressed not just within the confines of individual European states but by the Council of Europe and various international associations and conferences of drug enforcement agents as well. Particularly influential was the inclusion in the United Nations Convention Against Illicit Traffic in Narcotic Drugs and Psychotropic Substances (1988) of provisions encouraging the use of controlled deliveries.[96]

In relying on controlled deliveries to investigate drug trafficking organizations, DEA agents first co-opted those local agents willing to bend the law for legitimate investigative goals. Prosecutors were kept in the dark, as were other law enforcement agents, particularly customs officials, who might not be inclined to cooperate with the drug agents;

94. P. D. Cutting, "The Technique of Controlled Delivery as a Weapon in Dealing with Illicit Traffic in Narcotic Drugs and Psychotropic Substances," *Bulletin on Narcotics* 35 (Oct.–Dec. 1983), 15–22.

95. The annual report of the FBN in 1931 discusses an investigation of an opium shipment from Istanbul destined for the United States via Amsterdam and Hamburg in which Dutch officials agreed to allow the opium to pass through its port so that the drug traffickers could be identified and arrested in Hamburg. See U.S. Treasury Department, *Traffic in Opium and Other Dangerous Drugs for the Year Ended December 31, 1931* (Washington, D.C.: Government Printing Office, 1932), 43.

96. See Art. 11 of the U.N. Convention.

the likelihood that customs officials would find the drugs crossing the border without a tip from the drug agents was slight. The same held true for foreign law enforcement and customs agents, who might seize the drugs either because they felt bound by the legality principle or customs regulations or because they wanted the credit for the seizure. Whoever was not essential to conducting the controlled delivery was simply not informed. According to the recollections of DEA agents who had worked in France and Italy, for instance, police would allow the drugs "to walk" if they had found out about the drug delivery from an informant or by monitoring an illegal wiretap. But if the tap had been legally authorized by a prosecutor, who would have access to the transcripts of any recorded conversations, the police would carry out their official duties and arrest the drug courier. Although prosecutors were highly unlikely actually to prosecute drug agents for conducting unauthorized controlled deliveries, the agents generally refrained from defying the prosecutors' authority.

Since the mid-1980s, however, prosecutors in almost every European country have begun to play at least some role in authorizing, supervising, or informally shielding controlled deliveries. This has involved first circumventing, then bending and ultimately redefining the legality principle to accommodate controlled deliveries. Initially prosecutors agreed to ignore or wink at the legal charades engaged in for their benefit by the police. It has since progressed to the point where prosecutors can legally authorize a controlled delivery, impose certain constraints on its conduct, and demand certain assurances from the police. They may require the police to guarantee that they will not lose the drugs once they walk; they may insist upon an assurance that the courier will be prosecuted in the destination country; they may prefer that the courier be flipped before proceeding with the controlled delivery; and they may prefer that the drugs be discreetly seized and that only a small portion of the drugs, combined with some innocuous white powder, be substituted for the original package in the controlled delivery. From the perspective of the police, the importance of the prosecutors' growing role stems less from their oversight functions than from their ability to authorize, and in effect legalize, an essential investigative technique. Controlled deliveries are now regarded as legal throughout most of Europe even if their changed status has yet to be codified in the assorted codes of criminal procedure.

Responsibility for reinterpreting the legality principle to allow controlled deliveries has fallen not just to the prosecutors and the courts but also to legislators, interior and justice ministers, and international working groups. The courts have responded by relaxing customs regulations and the requirements of the legality principle to allow broader use of controlled deliveries. Legislators under increasing pressure during the 1980s to enact tougher drug legislation have enacted laws explicitly authorizing the investigative technique. In Austria, efforts by DEA and local drug enforcement agents to employ controlled deliveries along the notorious "Balkan connection" raised the same sorts of legal disputes that had hampered the introduction of undercover operations.[97] When those were resolved favorably by the Austrian supreme court, debate focused on customs regulations requiring that all goods imported into Austria be declared and cleared; a 1985 amendment to the customs laws removed this obstacle and further allowed for the reexport of illicit drug shipments provided they remained under surveillance.[98] The practice is much the same in France, where controlled deliveries from Spain to the Netherlands are not unusual; magistrates will authorize a controlled delivery but insist that the police arrest the couriers and seize the drugs if they think there is a chance they will lose track of either. In Denmark, controlled deliveries have been regarded as entirely legal; Dutch and Danish police cooperate frequently, particularly on shipments passing through Denmark en route to Sweden. In Germany, the interior and justice ministers of the Länder appointed working groups to devise national guidelines for conducting controlled deliveries. In 1983 and 1986, for instance, the Northern Working Group on the Suppression of Drug Trafficking, which includes police representatives from the Netherlands and the Scandinavian countries, the German border control and customs agencies, and Hannover, Bremen, Hamburg, Berlin, and Kiel, conducted controlled delivery exercises—code-named Baltica 83 and Baltica 86—to test the capacity of the police to transfer surveillance across national borders.[99] Elsewhere, legal formalities continue to pose substantial problems. In Spain, for instance, a South American informant employed by the DEA on a controlled delivery from Bolivia to Spain in 1988 was arrested by Spanish customs because the DEA and

97. The disputes, which focused on Section 25 of the Austrian Code of Criminal Procedure, are briefly discussed in Fehérváry, "Drug Policy in Austria" (supra n. 83), 68.

98. The information is in correspondence from ACND chief Herbert Fuchs to the author, Apr. 20, 1990. See Art. 121 of the 1955 Austrian Customs Law as amended on May 10, 1985.

99. W. Tabarelli, "Baltica 86, an International Exercise on Controlled Deliveries," in Fijnaut and Hermans, Police Cooperation in Europe (supra n. 6), 79–84.

Spanish police had failed to notify the proper customs authorities; two years later, the unfortunate informant remained incarcerated in a Spanish jail. Throughout much of Europe, however, pressures to better coordinate controlled deliveries—generated in part by the elimination of border checks in 1992—are certain to lead to greater harmonization of the laws and guidelines regulating uses of the technique.

Wiretapping

Among the various investigative techniques best suited to drug trafficking investigations, wiretapping was the one with which most European police agencies were most familiar when American drug enforcement agents began fanning out through Europe in the 1960s and 1970s. Indeed, many relied on electronic surveillance with substantially greater frequency than was the case in the United States. As in the United States, however, the investigative technique generated substantial political and legal controversy. Some forms of electronic surveillance, such as pen registers (which reveal only the telephone number that one has dialed), are relatively less invasive as such techniques go. Wiretaps on telephones, and listening devices ("bugs") in people's homes, offices, and cars, are far more intrusive. Most governments authorize but strictly control the use of such devices by law enforcement authorities.[100] The principal exception is Belgium, which absolutely forbids their use, although information obtained abroad from a legal wiretap is admissible in Belgian courts.[101] Others routinely rely on them in conducting criminal investigations. In a few countries, the police make frequent use of illegal wiretaps. The broad exception to all restrictions on electronic surveillance is national security. In much of Europe, wiretapping by the intelligence agencies is subject to even less vigorous scrutiny and oversight than it is in the United States, although occasional media exposés, most notably in Germany and Britain, have generated intense debate about the use of such techniques and how they should be regulated.[102]

100. Council of Europe, Legal Documentation and Research Division, *Telephone Tapping and the Recording of Telecommunications in Some Council of Europe Member States,* Legislative Dossier No. 2 (Strasbourg, 1982).

101. Cass. May 24, 1983, Rechtskundig Weekblad 1984-9-84, 1701, cited in Boutmans, "The Situation in Belgium" (supra n. 58), 97.

102. See Note, "Secret Surveillance and the European Convention on Human Rights" (supra n. 7).

During the 1980s, wiretapping practices also came under scrutiny by the European Commission of Human Rights and the European Court of Human Rights.[103]

The country with the most ambiguous legal attitude toward wiretapping is France, in which an estimated 70,000 wiretaps were reportedly employed each year as of the late 1980s.[104] Wiretapping was not considered a punishable offense until 1970, when the French Parliament amended the privacy provisions of the penal code to make overhearing or intercepting private telephone conversations a *délit* (minor crime).[105] On the other hand, the practice has never been explicitly authorized by the French legislature, and the courts have yet to arrive at a consistent approach. The Criminal Court of the Seine in Paris, in a series of decisions dating back to the 1950s, consistently admitted wiretap evidence, even for minor crimes such as illegal bookmaking.[106] Appellate courts, conversely, rejected wiretapping as unreliable or "indelicate."[107] In the 1980 *Tournet* case, the Court of Cassation for the first time upheld the use of a wiretap, provided it had been authorized by the *juge d'instruction* (examining magistrate) in the course of a judicial investigation following the *inculpe* (formal accusation of a suspect).[108]

Even as the courts have debated the legality of wiretaps, the French police routinely have used wiretaps for purposes of gathering intelligence on criminal matters. As one student of the French system noted in the early 1980s:

> It is widely acknowledged in France that the police always have done a good deal of illegal wiretapping and have used the

103. See the *Malone Case*, E.C.H.R., Series A, No. 82, and the *Klass Case*, E.C.H.R., Series A, No. 28, 2 E.H.R.R. 214, discussed in John Andrews, "Telephone Tapping in the United Kingdom," *European Law Review* 10 (1985), 68–70; and in Istvan Pogany, "Telephone Tapping and the European Convention on Human Rights," *New Law Journal* 134 (1984), 175–177, 290, 300.

104. Meyer, *Betäubungsmittelstrafrecht in Westeuropa* (supra n. 59), 808.

105. The discussion of wiretapping in France is drawn largely from Walter Pakter, "Exclusionary Rules in France, Germany, and Italy," *Hastings International and Comparative Law Review* 9 (1985), 1; and Tomlinson, "The French Experience" (supra n. 46).

106. Pakter, "Exclusionary Rules," 37.

107. Ibid.

108. In 1985, the same court narrowed the discretion of the *juge d'instruction* somewhat, holding that he could only authorize a wiretap on probable cause justifying opening an investigation for a specific infraction, and that the tap must be under his control, without any artifice or compromise of the suspect's rights. See ibid., 38.

information they obtain as leads for the subsequent acquisition of the same information in a legal fashion. The *procès verbal* [*written* report] presented in the court reflects only the second operation and is thus in proper legal form. The courts generally have shown little interest in probing into the sources for the second, apparently legal police operation. Their concern is primarily to preserve the legal formalities and not to regulate police behavior. The latter concern is collateral to a particular defendant's guilt or innocence, and the French courts have always been hostile to collateral issues because they deflect the official inquiry from its central task.[109]

As one DEA agent described the process, although the surveillance transcripts cannot be used as evidence, the information acquired from them is used, for instance, to obtain a legal search warrant from the *juge d'instruction*. In the formal request for the warrant, the source of the information is referred to as a confidential informant. Although more often than not the *juge d'instruction* knows better, he usually refrains from pressing for the informant's true identity. As for the DEA, any information garnered from an illegal French wire can also be used to obtain a warrant from an American judge. For instance, if a conversation intercepted by an illegal wiretap in Paris makes reference to a stash of drugs in an apartment in New York City, the DEA can obtain a legal warrant based upon that information (provided the DEA did not ask the French police to intercept an American's conversations). The rationale for this sanctioning of illegal police behavior abroad is that the U.S. courts have interpreted the exclusionary rule as primarily intended to deter illegal conduct by U.S. law enforcement agents within the United States and against U.S. citizens overseas.[110]

By the late 1980s, the wiretapping practices of the French police were

109. Tomlinson, "The French Experience," 177–178.

110. In 1990, the U.S. Supreme Court resolved a number of the lower court disputes over the applicability of the Fourth Amendment to the extraterritorial actions of U.S. law enforcement agents when it held that U.S. agents need not obtain a warrant from either a U.S. judge or a foreign judge to conduct a search directed against a foreign national in a foreign country. See *U.S. v. Verdugo-Urquidez*, 110 S.Ct. 1056, *International Legal Materials* 29 (1990), 441. The issue is discussed in Andreas F. Lowenfeld, "U.S. Law Enforcement Abroad: The Constitution and International Law," *American Journal of International Law* 83 (1989), 880–893; continued at *American Journal of International Law* 84 (1990), 444–493. The specific case is discussed in a note on the case by Ruth Wedgwood, *American Journal of International Law* 84 (1990), 747–755.

coming under increasing attack from both domestic and European critics.[111] In 1982, a study commission on wiretapping chaired by French Supreme Court Justice Robert Schmelck criticized the police practice of employing wiretaps without the authorization of *juges d'instruction* and before the formal initiation of a judicial inquiry. Its recommendations for placing all control of wiretaps in the hands of the judiciary, however, were largely ignored. In late 1988, a report issued by the European Commission of Human Rights criticized not just the police practices but also the failure of the French penal code to provide sufficient guarantees against arbitrary judgments involving wiretaps, which it regarded as violative of Article 8 of the European Convention on Human Rights. One year later, the French Supreme Court echoed the European Commission's conclusions in a decision involving a drug trafficking case.[112] The court ruled that the common police practice of installing a wiretap without a warrant from a *juge d'instruction*, and then "regularizing" the tap thereafter by obtaining post facto approval from a magistrate or *juge d'instruction*, violated both the European Convention of Human Rights and the French code of penal procedure. Whether this decision will in fact curtail the long-standing reliance of the French police on unauthorized wiretaps, however, remains to be seen. In 1991, the French government partially addressed the issue with new legislation authorizing nonjudicial "preventive" wiretapping in terrorism, organized crime, economic espionage, and national security investigations in which the police request had been countersigned by a responsible cabinet minister; the new law established a special commission to provide oversight over all such wiretaps.

In postwar Germany, wiretapping in criminal investigations was permitted on a fairly restricted basis after 1949. The first federal legislation formally authorizing the legal use of wiretapping by law enforcement and intelligence agencies was passed in 1968, the same year in which the U.S. Congress first enacted a federal wiretapping statute.[113] Since that

111. The following analysis is derived from Edwy Plenel, "Un arrêt de la Cour de cassation: Les écoutes téléphoniques non autorisées par un juge sont illégales" ("A Ruling of the Supreme Court of Justice: Wiretapping Not Authorized by a Judge Is Illegal"), *Le Monde*, Mar. 21, 1990, 14.

112. *Epoux Huvig contre France*, requête no. 11105/84 (Dec. 14, 1988), Judgment of November 24, 1989.

113. The U.S. wiretapping legislation, known as Title III of the Omnibus Crime Control and Safe Streets Act, is codified at 18 U.S.C. 2510–2520 (1970). The United States did not enact legislation covering wiretapping by the intelligence agencies until the Foreign Intelligence Surveillance Act of 1978, codified at 50 U.S.C. 1801–1811. The 1968 German law authorizing

time, the use of wiretapping by police has become a relatively routine matter. During the late 1970s, approximately 500 a year were granted. By comparison, in the United States the total numbers granted each year were only 100 to 200 more.[114] James Carr, a U.S. magistrate who investigated Germany's wiretapping procedures during the late 1970s, found that in at least three respects German procedures allowed a greater degree of intrusiveness than did the provisions of Title III in the United States: wiretaps in Germany were subject to less judicial supervision; they could be installed for three months, as opposed to one month in the United States; and there were no restrictions, like the American "minimization requirement," to limit the agents from taping conversations having nothing to do with the investigation at hand.[115] In a speech to the International Narcotics Enforcement Officers Association in 1988, the head of the BKA's drug enforcement branch, Jürgen Jeschke, discussed electronic surveillance in Germany:

> There are hardly any investigations today in which not at least one or even several telephone taps are put in place. It is not merely the high evidential value which plays a role. Telephone taps are to an increasing extent used as a tactical means, for example in addition to or during the surveillances and for the preparation of tactical measures. Contrary to the U.S., the legal threshold for telephone taps is lower in my country. They have to be ordered by a judge in principle, provided that certain requirements are fulfilled, but in very urgent cases a telephone tap may be ordered at short notice by the Public Prosecutor—limited to a period of three days, however. New transmission systems currently present big practical problems to us as far as the monitor-

---

the wiretapping was divided into two parts: the "G-10 Law" covering wiretapping by federal and state intelligence and internal security authorities; and Section 100a–101 of the Code of Criminal Procedure providing for police wiretapping. See the excellent discussions in James G. Carr, "Wiretapping in West Germany," *American Journal of Comparative Law* 29 (1981), 607–645; and Thomas Weigend, "Using the Results of Audio-Surveillance as Penal Evidence in the Federal Republic of Germany," *Stanford Journal of International Law* 24 (1987), 21–53.

114. See Carr, "Wiretapping in West Germany," 607–608, for the specific numbers, which count only law enforcement, not intelligence, wiretaps.

115. Ibid., 644. For an interesting discussion comparing German and British approaches to wiretapping, see Note, "Secret Surveillance and the European Convention on Human Rights" (supra n. 7), 1113.

ing of telecommunications facilities is concerned. We have, for example, not yet found a way of tapping telefax machines.[116]

Elsewhere in Europe, police reliance on wiretaps is at least as common as it is in Germany and the United States. In Italy, where many more cases are developed by wiretaps than from informants or undercover operations, one FBI attaché noted that the police have "much broader wiretap authority. . . . They can just call the magistrate and get an oral OK. It's very informal and quick . . . compared to the U.S."[117] Much the same is true in Spain, where wiretapping was initally authorized by the 1980 "Antiterrorist Act." In Austria, Switzerland, Denmark, and the Netherlands, wiretaps are similarly considered relatively routine.[118] In Denmark, the number of court orders authorizing wiretaps increased from 30 in 1975 to about 330 in 1982 and to 700 in 1985, some 95 percent of which involved drug trafficking investigations.[119] In the Netherlands, a Justice Ministry official estimated in 1985 that between 100 and 200 wiretaps were installed each year, most of them in drug trafficking cases. In 1991, an Amsterdam police official pointed out that the principal limitation on wiretaps was financial and that only so many lines could be tapped at any one time—that number had increased from four to fifteen in 1983, and was set to double again by 1992. He estimated the total number of wiretapping cases in Amsterdam that year at about 250, of which about 80 percent involved drug trafficking investigations. As in the United States, a police request for permission to have a wiretap installed must be joined by a prosecutor and approved by a judge, but as is also the case in the United States, judges rarely if ever deny such requests. Similarly, evidence obtained by an unauthorized wiretap must be excluded from court.[120] The extent to which police

116. Jürgen Jeschke, "Drug Crime and Drug Enforcement in the Federal Republic of Germany," *Narc Officer* 4 (Dec. 1988), 33–35.

117. The legal status of wiretapping in Italy is discussed briefly in Pakter, "Exclusionary Rules" (supra n. 105), 48–50. Wiretaps can be authorized by a prosecutor or an investigating judge; see Arts. 226 and 339 of Italy's Code of Criminal Procedure.

118. Wiretapping in Austria is authorized by Article 10 of the Austrian Constitution and regulated by Arts. 149(a), 149(b), and 414. In Switzerland, it is controlled by Arts. 66 and 72 of the Federal Criminal Procedure Act as well as by the law of the cantons.

119. Jepsen, "Drug Policies in Denmark" (supra n. 14), 109. Wiretapping is authorized by Art. 72 of the Danish Constitution and regulated by Art. 787 of the Administration of Justice Act.

120. The Dutch wiretapping law can be found in articles 125g–h of the Code of Criminal Procedure. It is discussed in N. Keijzer and J. H. A. Steenbrink, "The Results of Electronic Eavesdropping as Evidence in Criminal Procedures," in P. H. M. Gerver, E. H. Hondius, and

resort to illegal wiretaps to gather criminal intelligence obviously varies from country to country. Given the relative ease with which legal wiretaps can be obtained, the principal reason to install an unauthorized tap is the absence of sufficient evidence to persuade a court to authorize a legal tap.

Most European countries have differed significantly from the United States in their treatment of forms of electronic surveillance other than telephone wiretaps. In much of Europe, it is the Postal Ministry that attaches the wiretap, typically by adding a secret extension line between a central post office telephone exchange and the police listening post.[121] The police tend not to get involved in the installation process, which may explain in part the reluctance of many states to legalize the placement of listening devices in homes and offices and the practice of wiring an undercover agent or informant for sound to gather incriminating information. By the late 1980s, both these practices were becoming increasingly common in Europe, although courts have remained reluctant to admit as evidence the information gained by such means. In Germany, for instance, undercover agents and informants may wear body wires for their own protection, but the information recorded cannot be used as evidence. Indeed, the entire practice of consensual wiretapping, in which only one party to a conversation knows that it is being recorded, has proven far more controversial in most European countries than in the United States, where it is the most frequently employed electronic surveillance technique and need not even be judicially approved.[122] By the late 1980s, however, European police investigators were pushing hard to legalize and integrate most of the electronic surveillance techniques employed in the United States, including not just body wires and "bugs" in vehicles and residences but also video cameras

---

G. J. W. Steenhoff, eds., *Netherlands Reports to the Twelfth International Congress of Comparative Law, Sydney-Melbourne 1986* (The Hague: T. M. C. Asser Instituut, 1987), 309–316.

121. Carr, "Wiretapping in West Germany" (supra n. 113), 631.

122. The federal wiretapping statute passed by Congress in 1968 explicitly authorized consensual wiretapping; see 18 U.S.C. 2511(2)(c). The constitutionality of warrantless consent surveillance was upheld by the Supreme Court in *U.S. v. White*, 401 U.S. 745 (1971). See the discussion in James G. Carr, *The Law of Electronic Surveillance*, 2nd ed. (New York: Clark, Boardman, 1985), 3–55ff. It is interesting that although evidence obtained from an improperly executed wiretap cannot be excluded from a German trial, evidence gained from a consensual recording is inadmissible in court. The basis for this application of an exclusionary rule stems from the German constitutional right to the "free development of one's personality." See Craig M. Bradley, "The Exclusionary Rule in Germany," *Harvard Law Review* 96 (1983), 1032.

and parabolic microphones. As in the United States, police agencies were also working with private companies to develop new technologies to intercept communications by telefax, cellular phones, and other emerging means of telecommunication. All of these developments were in evidence, for instance, in the Netherlands, which only a decade earlier had shown relatively little enthusiasm for following down this path.

Given the persistent reluctance of many European police agencies—particularly in southern Europe—to engage in undercover operations, electronic surveillance has remained important to the investigation of drug trafficking even as growing numbers of drug traffickers have learned to exercise greater discretion in their use of telecommunications. Local police often oblige the DEA and other civilian and military law enforcement agencies by installing wiretaps requested by them and permitting their agents to jointly monitor the taps or read the transcripts.[123] The DEA, and the FBI, which traditionally has resorted to wiretapping more often and undercover operations less often than the U.S. drug enforcement agency, have permitted foreign police agents to do the same in the United States.[124] In the "Pizza Connection" investigation of Mafia drug trafficking and money laundering during the mid-1980s, U.S. and foreign law enforcement agents tapped phones in the United States, Brazil, Switzerland, Sicily, and Mexico.[125] Although that investigation was unusual in terms of its scope and notoriety, it reflected the trend toward increased cooperation among police agencies in conducting electronic surveillance. The same trend could also be discerned in the Council of Europe's consideration and adoption of a 1985 recommendation to facilitate inter-European cooperation in the interception of telecommunications.[126]

123. The use of electronic surveillance by the U.S. Army's Criminal Investigative Division (CID), virtually all of which is conducted overseas, is discussed in M. Wesley Clark, "Electronic Surveillance and Related Investigative Techniques," *Military Law Review* 128 (1990), 155–224.

124. Indeed, foreign agents are sometimes essential to decipher local dialects. Few European police, for instance, are able to understand the dialects of Caribbean and American blacks. Israeli, African, and Sicilian police have likewise assisted with wiretaps on their compatriots in the United States.

125. Alexander, *Pizza Connection* (supra n. 39), 154.

126. See Council of Europe, *Letters Rogatory for the Interception of Telecommunications (Recommendation No. R(85) 10 Adopted by the Committee of Ministers of the Council of Europe on 28 June 1985)* (Strasbourg, 1986).

Conclusion

The central paradox of international law enforcement is the need for law enforcement agents to perform outside their nation's borders a function that relies primarily on the sovereign powers of the state. Aside from simple liaison functions, much of what is expected of a DEA agent working abroad does not mesh neatly with the requirements of U.S., foreign, and international law. DEA agents accordingly rely on the exercise of substantial discretion in carrying out some of their tasks unilaterally or in informal cooperation with foreign counterparts. This was especially true before the late 1960s, when the few FBN agents overseas cultivated personal relationships with foreign police, took advantage of Interpol to obscure their national identity, and focused on the traditional tasks of criminal investigation. But with the expansion of the BNDD's international presence during the late 1960s and early 1970s, and the institutionalization of the DEA's global presence thereafter, U.S. drug enforcement agents devoted greater efforts to persuading foreign police to develop their own drug enforcement capabilities and to model them after the DEA's model. The "Americanization" of foreign drug enforcement came to be seen as a useful means of sharing the burden of international drug enforcement, improving the capacity of foreign criminal justice systems to assist U.S.-based investigations, and easing the DEA's ability to carry out its own investigative functions abroad. Stated otherwise, the transnational law enforcement organization recognized that the key to its success abroad lay not in expanding its own freedom of operation in foreign territories but in developing vicarious capabilities within and among foreign police agencies.

   In developing their drug enforcement capabilities, most European criminal justice systems have been motivated less by the DEA than by their own need to respond to significant increases in domestic illicit drug trafficking. Indeed, it is reasonable to assume that even in the absence of an agency such as the DEA, European police would have developed their own drug enforcement capabilities and adopted many of the proactive investigative techniques identified with the DEA once the limitations of their customary methods of criminal investigation became apparent. But there can also be little doubt that the DEA has played a central role in hastening and shaping the evolution of European drug enforcement. The U.S. agency provided a substantial impetus for the initial creation of specialized drug enforcement units within European police agencies; it has provided much of the intelligence on local involvement in transnational drug trafficking needed to stimulate local concern and enable local police to target local drug traffickers; it has served as an advocate for the integration of undercover operations, controlled deliveries, and new means of recruiting informants into European drug enforcement; and it has provided a role model and mentor for European drug enforcement units. Not since the European powers trained colonial police forces has one nation's police agency exerted such a powerful international influence.

The integration of DEA-style methods into European drug enforcement has required metamorphoses not just in the modus operandi of European police but in the laws regulating their behavior as well. Changes in the laws of criminal procedure can be seen as responses both to changing public demands on the police and to changing police practices. Courts, legislators, and the authors of internal police guidelines tend to respond to perceived police excesses by restricting the power and discretion of the police, and to perceived inadequacies by expanding their power and discretion. In the latter case, the pressures often arise from the need to legalize and regulate what the police have already begun to do "extralegally" or illegally. The evolution of European drug enforcement since the early 1970s has been characterized by exactly this process. Where once most bargaining between European police and informants was both informal and illegal, today prosecutors in many countries can legally offer drug dealers who have been arrested the possibility of reduced charges or even immunity in return for their cooperation. Where once European police agents relied on their informants or DEA agents to perform undercover tasks illegally, today European drug enforcement agents are increasingly able to conduct legal undercover operations themselves. Where once police were obliged to reach into their own pockets to pay informants small amounts of money, today many police agencies in Europe can legally pay their best informants many thousands of dollars. And where once all sorts of charades were necessary to keep prosecutors and judges in the dark about the exact nature of drug trafficking investigations, today many of the techniques drug enforcement agents rely on are both legal and supervised by prosecutors. To be sure, no European criminal justice system has legalized all of the drug enforcement tactics that are legal in the United States, and many Europeans still cling to their traditional views of the legality principle and the ban on *agents provocateurs*, but the trend in most of Europe seems to favor continuing in American foot-steps. European drug enforcement, and in certain respects European criminal procedure as well, are becoming increasingly "Americanized."

Throughout this chapter, I have portrayed this evolution as both a process and a consequence. From the perspective of U.S. drug enforcement agents, the "Americanization" of European drug enforcement has represented not an end in itself but rather a means of improving their own capacity to immobilize drug traffickers. Even as DEA agents have spoken with pride of the changes in European drug enforcement stimulated by their efforts and examples, they also have observed that the changes are of significance only insofar as they represented vicarious extensions of the DEA's own objectives and capabilities. Europeans, however, have viewed those same transformations as significant consequences in their own right. Harmonization, from their perspective, has involved not just regularization of relations with the U.S. drug enforcement agency but also accommodation and adaptation to American methods.

Chapter Five

The DEA in Latin America: Dealing with Institutionalized Corruption

The Most Troublesome Problem

Among the many obstacles that hamper U.S. drug enforcement objectives abroad, drug-related corruption of foreign government officials ranks as the most troublesome. It is present in virtually every country. Witness the testimony of DEA administrator John Lawn, as he is questioned by Senator John Kerry during hearings before a Senate subcommittee in July 1988:

> SENATOR JOHN KERRY: What do you think will happen to an honest law enforcement person who wants to do the job when the government is corrupt and it can simply transfer and fire him, move him out, put him on the night shift. What does it mean?
> DEA ADMINISTRATOR JOHN LAWN: It means, sir, that there is a serious problem with corruption in every single country.
> If I could take a moment, sir, to read something.

SENATOR KERRY: Sure.

MR. LAWN: This is an end of the tour report, one of our personnel leaving a country. His summary was this. "Police corruption is endemic in this country. The government pays extremely low salaries. Yet, it is not uncommon for police to drive luxury cars and own more than one multimillion dollar residence. Corruption is not limited to the police and is, in fact, widespread throughout the government. Furthermore, it is a way of life in that it has been going on for hundreds of years. Police bid for transfers to lucrative posts on the borders such as—where the winning bid may be as high as x number of dollars just to get the job so that the individuals will be in a position to accept corruption."

I read that report at a meeting of country attachés representing 14 [Latin American] countries. I said would you, in hearing that commentary, tell me which country that described. All 14 country attachés told me it described accurately their particular country.[1]

In many of the less developed nations in Asia, Africa, Latin America, and the Caribbean, such institutionalized corruption is pervasive. Not just police officers and customs officials, but also judges, generals, cabinet ministers, and even presidents and prime ministers are implicated. Corruption in most of these countries is nothing new, although the temptations posed by the illicit drug traffic are unprecedented. Nor are U.S. officials unaccustomed to dealing with foreign corruption. Their experience dates back to the origins of American foreign relations. But the need to rely on foreign criminal justice systems to accomplish U.S. foreign policy objectives has posed challenges that are in some respects unique.

The central objective of the DEA in Latin America and the Caribbean, as in every other part of the world, is not to weed out corruption or reform foreign police agencies but to immobilize drug traffickers. In pursuing this objective south of the United States, DEA agents have encountered all of the same obstacles that have hampered their efforts in

1. Congressional testimony of DEA administrator John C. Lawn, in *Drugs, Law Enforcement, and Foreign Policy, the Cartel, Haiti, and Central America: Hearings Before the Subcommittee on Terrorism, Narcotics, and International Operations of the Senate Committee on Foreign Relations*, 100th Cong., 2d Sess., Part 4 (July 12, 1988), p. 124.

Europe: the legal and policy restrictions on flipping informants, conducting undercover operations, and conducting controlled deliveries of
drugs; the institutional limitations of local police agencies with skimpy
budgets and inadequate resources, irritating frictions with competing
agencies, few if any specialized drug enforcement agents, and little if
any money to pay informants; the occasional professional and nationalist resistance to working with the better paid and more sophisticated
police agents of the United States; and, of course, the basic lack of
sovereign police powers in foreign territories. As in Europe, many of
these obstacles have dwindled substantially since the late 1960s, although
the progress in Latin America and the Caribbean pales beside that in
much of Europe. But the one problem that has posed the greatest
obstacles, and required DEA agents to make the most of their diplomatic
skills, personal charms, and association with the U.S. government, has
been that of corruption. The nature of that problem, and the means by
which DEA agents have dealt with it, are the subject of this chapter.

From the perspective of interstate relations, epitomized by dealings
between the U.S. ambassador and high-level officials in the host government, diplomatic efforts aimed at reducing corruption can be particularly frustrating because they involve a form of transgovernmental
penetration that traditional diplomacy is ill-suited to accomplish. In
many respects, reforming drug-related corruption in foreign governments poses problems that are little different from those involved in
trying to reduce human rights abuses. The U.S. government must contend with different criminal justice traditions and modi operandi, conflicting political interests, and insufficient power at the top of government to challenge vested interests at lower levels. In some cases, foreign
heads of government would like to oblige U.S. demands but lack the
capacity to do so. For instance, just as the civilian presidents of El
Salvador and Guatemala typically lack the political power to punish
senior military officials responsible for severe human rights abuses, so
the presidents of Peru, Colombia, and Bolivia are not powerful enough
to order the prosecution of every official known to have been corrupted
by drug traffickers. Alternatively, foreign heads of government may have
sufficient power to accommodate U.S. demands but lack the desire to do
so. This apparently was the case during the 1980s with both the top-to-
bottom corruption that permeated the military establishments in Panama and Paraguay and with the human rights abuses perpetrated by
military dictatorships in Latin America and elsewhere throughout the

century. Then again, the apparent power of a Stroessner, a Noriega, or a Pinochet certainly depended at least in part upon their willingness to tolerate behavior condemned by external observers. To the extent that was the case, U.S. pressures on those dictators to reform their corrupt agencies were no more likely to succeed than pressures on well-intentioned civilian leaders whose lack of power was more evident to outsiders.

Where U.S. efforts to deal with foreign drug-related corruption differ from those targeted at human rights abuses is in the existence of an agency—a transnational organization—specifically tasked to address that problem. The DEA, with its agents stationed in most Latin American countries, has offered a hands-on complement to the diplomatic efforts of State Department representatives and other high-level officials. DEA agents, with their greater access to and influence over the actual workings of foreign government agencies, are often in a stronger position to effect, at least to some degree, changes in government behavior. There is virtually no counterpart in the human rights area, or in almost any other area of international relations, with the possible exception of the CIA, and perhaps the U.S. military in a few countries. Because DEA agents work together with foreign police agencies, they are in a position to provide some degree of oversight and direction. Their influence is limited, however, because they lack any sovereign powers and are obliged to rely on foreign police as their vicarious surrogates. What influence they are able to exert derives from their connection to the U.S. government, their ability to reward and threaten local police in various ways, and their own powers of diplomacy and persuasion.

Even where DEA-backed efforts to reform corrupt agencies are successful, the reforms are seldom institutionalized in any meaningful way. Elite investigative units and anticorruption squads eventually are corrupted. Young and idealistic agents eventually mature into older, more cynical agents with more substantial material concerns. And legislative and media oversight of corrupt agencies can be maintained only for so long. When we analyze corruption from the perspective of international law enforcement, the notion of harmonization advanced in the preceding and following chapters loses much of its explanatory power. Given the extraordinary difficulties of institutionalizing anticorruption reforms, neither homogenization nor accommodation of criminal justice systems makes much sense. Only the notion of regularization—understood in its more personal as distinct from institutional sense—offers any analytical value. The keys to circumventing the obstacles of drug-related corruption ultimately boil down to personal relationships and political pressures.

Perspectives on Drug-Related Corruption

Drug-related corruption of governments in Latin America and the Caribbean can be viewed from a number of perspectives. First, it clearly is a consequence of the creation and failure of the global drug prohibition regime.[2] If the international markets for marijuana, cocaine, and heroin had never been criminalized, the need and opportunities for government officials to be corrupted by drug trafficking organizations would have been far less, akin perhaps to the corruption attendant to government regulation of the coffee markets in Latin American countries. Alternatively, if the global drug prohibition regime had proven successful in preventing the emergence of a tremendous consumer demand for those substances, drug corruption similarly would have been relatively insignificant. Drug-related corruption can thus be seen as a consequence of the tensions between the two demands emanating from the United States: the U.S. government's demand that Latin American and Caribbean governments criminalize the drug markets and enforce the laws aimed at their suppression; and the demand of American consumers for the psychoactive substances produced and exported by those countries. In the absence of either demand, drug-related corruption would be a fraction of what it is today.

Second, drug-related corruption can be seen as a necessary and perhaps inevitable corollary to the economic opportunities presented to Latin American and Caribbean countries by the illicit drug traffic. The foreign demand for illicit drugs has represented a principal source of foreign exchange and a significant proportion of the gross national product for many of them, as well as an important source of employment for hundreds of thousands of mostly poor people in Bolivia, Peru, and Colombia and tens of thousands in Mexico, Jamaica, Belize, and elsewhere. The notion of turning their backs on the substantial opportunities presented by the illicit traffic has made no more sense to them than

2. See Ethan A. Nadelmann, "Global Prohibition Regimes: The Evolution of Norms in International Society," *International Organization* 44 (1990), 479–526.

ignoring large discoveries of oil or gold would have. Indeed, given the relative paucity of legitimate sources of wealth and employment, the antidrug laws have been largely incapable of deterring people from taking advantage of the only significant economic opportunity available to them. From this perspective, drug-related corruption can be seen as the inevitable consequence of trying to repress a highly dynamic and economically significant market.

Corruption is typically associated with the impoverishment of countries, as government officials siphon off disproportionate shares of the public treasury and complicate the worthwhile endeavors of local and foreign enterprises. Drug-related corruption, however, presents exactly the opposite situation, since the lucrative economic opportunities created by wealthy foreign markets would be much less available if the drug laws were strictly enforced. This form of corruption thus offers support for the "revisionist" school of political scientists who argued during the 1970s that corruption could have beneficial consequences in developing polities.[3] But whereas the revisionists stressed the political benefits of corruption, the benefits of drug-related corruption have been almost entirely economic while the political consequences have been largely disastrous.[4] Viewed from this perspective, drug-related corruption is the most effective means available for reconciling the economic needs of developing countries with the international legal obligations imposed by the more powerful developed countries.

Third, drug-related corruption can be seen as merely an extension and expansion of preexisting corruption throughout much of Latin America and the Caribbean. Bribery of police, customs officials, and other government regulators to waive their enforcement of minor laws is the norm in many countries. So is the expectation that many politicians and high-level officials will seek to enrich themselves while in office. Viewed from this perspective, the bribes paid by drug traffickers to government officials are little different from the bribes paid by otherwise legitimate businesses to evade taxes, duties, and a variety of burdensome government regulations. But it is also possible in many countries to

3. These arguments are summarized and analyzed in Gabriel Ben-Dor, "Corruption, Institutionalization, and Political Development," *Comparative Political Studies* 7 (1974), 63–83.

4. See Ethan A. Nadelmann, "U.S. Drug Policy: A Bad Export," *Foreign Policy* 70 (1988), 83–108; and "Víctimas involuntarias: Consecuencias de las políticas de prohibición de drogas," *Debate Agrario* 7 (1989), 127–164.

avoid arrest and prosecution for major crimes, up to and including murder, by bribing and if need be threatening police, prosecutors, and judges. Victims of crime, moreover, often must pay the police and prosecutors to conduct their criminal investigations. In such environments, drug traffickers typically find it relatively easy to pay rather than be prosecuted for their crimes.

Fourth, the relatively high levels of drug-related corruption in Latin America and the Caribbean can be seen as a function of "overcriminalization."[5] Antony Simpson noted two of the consequences in his study of police corruption:

> The first consequence is an increase in that proportion of the population engaged in behavior which has been defined as criminal. This leads to a greater likelihood of confrontation between the police and the public which in turn produces a hostile environment for the individual officer. His role in society is made more difficult, and he is likely to become disillusioned and cynical as he is obliged to enforce laws which a large proportion of the population (including, possibly, the officer himself) considers to be neither just nor reasonable.
>
> A second consequence of the existence of an "overcriminalized" body of law is the likelihood of illegal institutions arising to meet demands which are not legitimized by the society. Faced with these popular but unlawful institutions, police may come to redefine their role from enforcers of the law to *regulators* of illegal markets. They certainly will be tempted to share the illicit and usually substantial profits from the activities they regulate.[6]

The opportunity for vice control agents to become corrupted is also increased by the fact that the criminal activity is not one that creates victims with an interest in complaining to the authorities. When a police officer accepts a bribe or even extorts a payment from a drug trafficker, there usually is no one to complain that the law has not been enforced as a consequence. Furthermore, the strong dependence of drug enforce-

5. See Sanford Kadish, "The Crisis of Overcriminalization," *Annals of the American Academy of Political and Social Science* 374 (1967), 157–170.

6. Antony E. Simpson, *The Literature of Police Corruption* (New York: John Jay Press, 1977), 94. These arguments are also developed in Bruce L. Benson, "An Institutional Explanation for Corruption of Criminal Justice Officials," *Cato Journal* 8 (1988), 139–163.

ment agents on informants, undercover operations, and other deceptive techniques presents uniquely corrupting opportunities, what Peter Manning and Lawrence Redlinger have called the "invitational edges of corruption."[7] Or, as one DEA agent put it to me, "Anyone involved in vice enforcement for too long becomes part of the subculture . . . and eventually evolves into a corrupt animal."

Fifth, the uniqueness of drug-related corruption in Latin America and the Caribbean must also be acknowledged. No other criminal activity comes close in terms of its magnitude, its lucrativeness, its capacity to corrupt the previously uncorruptible, its political consequences, and its impact on international relations. The bribes paid by drug traffickers are much greater, both in an absolute sense and in proportion to government salaries, than those paid by any other type of criminal. Moreover, unlike the sizable bribes paid by foreign corporations, which are available only to a select group of high-level officials, drug traffickers' bribes are available to all who can place themselves in the right place at the right time. They are most available, however, to employees of the criminal justice system from the lowly police officer and prison guard to the judge and cabinet minister. Such is the magnitude of the drug traffic in many countries that not just individuals but entire agencies have been corrupted.

The drug-related corruption also derives its specialness from the tremendous power of some of the drug trafficking organizations. As one DEA agent well acquainted with drug corruption in Latin America reflected, "Almost everyone has their price, and the drug trafficker can usually pay it." Most criminals corrupt government officials with money and other valuables. Drug traffickers typically do the same, but they also have been effective in corrupting with threats as well as money. Often, both inducements are used. Officials are warned to accept the money "or else." The choice, as some traffickers have put, is to take the *plata o plomo*—the silver or the lead (bullet). This power has been the ultimate corrupter of government institutions, because even the most honest officials are hard-pressed to resist such pressures. At the same time, the increasing brazenness of the drug traffickers in intimidating government

7. Peter K. Manning and Lawrence John Redlinger, "Invitational Edges of Corruption: Some Consequences of Narcotic Law Enforcement," in Paul E. Rock, ed., *Drugs and Politics* (New Brunswick, N.J.: Transaction Books, 1977). See also Gary T. Marx, *Undercover: Police Surveillance in America* (Berkeley and Los Angeles: University of California Press, 1988).

officials has represented the principal instigator of government action to suppress the drug traffic.

Sixth, drug-related corruption in Latin America and the Caribbean can be viewed as an obstacle to the international drug enforcement efforts of the U.S. government. There would, of course, still be a substantial flow of illicit drugs from and through the region even if government corruption in Latin America and the Caribbean were comparable to that found in the United States and Western Europe. The economics of the market, the characteristics of the commodity, and the nature of the activity all ensure this. But the intensity and pervasiveness of drug-related corruption in Latin America has certainly played an important role in undermining U.S. efforts to immobilize drug traffickers.

Different forms and degrees of corruption obviously present different problems and different opportunities to be circumvented or reformed. Much of what is presented below is characteristic of other drug-producing and transit regions outside Latin America and the Caribbean, including the Golden Crescent in southwestern Asia, the Golden Triangle in southeastern Asia, most of Africa, and even parts of the Mediterranean region. The only difference is that the cocaine boom since the late 1970s has had a proportionately greater impact on some Latin American and Caribbean countries than any other form of drug trafficking elsewhere.

It is worth noting that corruption in Latin America, despite its breadth and depth, has been the subject of strikingly little analysis by scholars (although journalists have produced an increasingly impressive body of work). The same is true of police corruption in all of the less developed world (except India). When Arnold Heidenheimer assembled fifty of the leading writings on political corruption into one volume in 1970, not a single one was devoted solely or even primarily to either corruption in Latin America or police corruption in the less-developed world.[8] A subsequent edition, published in 1989, included two articles on political corruption in Latin America, but the bibliography to the volume listed fewer publications on Latin America than on any other multinational continent, and virtually nothing still on police corruption in less-developed nations.[9] When Antony Simpson published an excellent and

8. Arnold J. Heidenheimer, ed., *Political Corruption: Readings in Comparative Analysis* (New York: Holt, Rinehart & Winston, 1970).
9. Arnold J. Heidenheimer, Michael Johnston, and Victor T. LeVine, eds., *Political Corruption: A Handbook* (New Brunswick, N.J.: Transaction Publishers, 1989).

exhaustive bibliographical review of the literature on police corruption in 1977, there was virtually nothing that could be included on the less-developed world except for the work of David Bayley and a few others on India.[10] What follows is in part an effort to develop the link between these two bodies of literature.[11]

Virtually all studies of government corruption and anticorruption efforts view their subject within the context of a self-contained unit, be it a city, a country, or a multinational region. Outsiders are not deemed to have an interest in such matters, and in fact they rarely exercise any influence even when they are affected. Many factors no doubt account for the irrelevance of outsiders, ranging from their sense that corrupt ways are an accepted mode of interaction with the local government, to a feeling of helplessness about any outsider being able to effect any changes, to an assessment that attempting to remedy the corruption is not worth the effort, to a belief that local corruption is not any outsider's business and that outside interference would be neither warranted nor welcome. There are, of course, a few exceptions. One, which does not fall totally within the outsider/insider distinction, is the investigation of local corruption in the United States by federal authorities, especially the FBI.[12] The other is the burst of attention and Congressional action that greeted reports of bribes by American multinational companies to foreign officials in the late 1970s.[13] Even in that case, however, the

10. Simpson, *Literature of Police Corruption*, 94. On India, see David H. Bayley, *The Police and Political Development in India* (Princeton: Princeton University Press, 1969). The chapter on corruption is reprinted in Lawrence Sherman, ed., *Police Corruption: A Sociological Perspective* (Garden City, N.Y.: Anchor Books, 1974). It is worth noting that I have found nothing to suggest that more extensive materials on this subject can be found in any language other than English.

11. One of the few scholars to devote attention to both police corruption and political corruption in developing polities, albeit the American one, was V. O. Key Jr. in his *Techniques of Political Graft in the United States* (Chicago: University of Chicago Libraries, 1936), and "Police Graft," *American Journal of Sociology* 40 (1935), 624.

12. Charles F. C. Ruff, "Federal Prosecution of Local Corruption: A Case Study in the Making of Law Enforcement Policy," *Georgetown Law Journal* 65 (1977), 1171–1228, excerpted in Heidenheimer, Johnston, and LeVine, eds., *Political Corruption* (supra n. 9), 627–637.

13. W. Michael Reisman, *Folded Lies: Bribery, Crusades, and Reforms* (New York: Free Press, 1979); Neil H. Jacoby, Peter Nehemkis, and Richard Eells, *Bribery and Extortion in World Business: A Study of Corporate Political Payments Abroad* (New York: Macmillan Co., 1977); Yerachmiel Kugel and Gladys X. Gruenberg, *International Payoffs: Dilemma for Business* (Lexington, Mass.: Lexington Press, 1977); Victor T. LeVine, "Transnational Aspects of Political Corruption," in Heidenheimer, Johnston, and LeVine, eds., *Political Corruption*,

reaction was prompted not by outrage at corruption in foreign governments but by the purportedly unethical practices of American businessmen. One might imagine that a third exception would involve efforts by
the United States, multinational banks, and international organizations
such as the World Bank and the International Monetary Fund (IMF) to
pressure indebted governments to reduce the corruption that siphons off
so much of foreign loans and aid.[14] Yet to my knowledge none of these
exceptions has received more than a smattering of scholarly attention.

Government corruption, and in particular police corruption, are not
easily amenable to precise definition.[15] For instance, lawyers and political
scientists differ in their understanding of the term. The former tend to
begin by looking at the letter of the law. Corruption, from their perspective, is government conduct that violates a legal obligation. Political
scientists, on the other hand, are more concerned with examining the
phenomenon in its political or societal context. It is the *norms*, not the
law, that determine whether conduct is corrupt. Corruption, from this
perspective, "is behavior of public officials which deviates from accepted
norms in order to serve private ends."[16] In Latin America, where the
divergence between *the law* and *accepted norms* is often strikingly broad,
defining corruption is a particularly ambiguous task. As Alan Riding
has written, with specific reference to Mexico:

> The problem starts with the very word "corruption," which
> inserts the custom into a moral context that many Mexicans do
> not recognize: for them, economic crimes do not carry the same
> weight as human or spiritual offenses. What the Protestant ethic
> might consider corruption emerged as a practical way of bridging
> the gap between idealistic legislation and the management of day-
> to-day living. Rigid laws have always been adopted, but they were
> promulgated in an environment where they could not be applied.
> Corruption was therefore an aberration of the law, but not of
> society. And in a traditional Mexico, it provided a parallel system
> of operating rules. If corruption has become a political problem

685–700; and Michael Rosenthal, "An American Attempt to Control International Corruption," in Heidenheimer, Johnston, and LeVine, eds., *Political Corruption*, 701–715.

14. This problem is discussed in James S. Henry, "Where the Money Went," *New Republic*,
Apr. 14, 1986, 20–23.

15. See Heidenheimer, Johnston, and LeVine, eds., *Political Corruption*, 3–66, 165–172.

16. Samuel P. Huntington, *Political Order in Changing Societies* (New Haven: Yale University Press, 1968), 59.

today, it is because Mexico's new "Westernized" middle classes now measure it with alien yardsticks. But even they focus only on government corruption, unwilling to look for its deeper roots in society itself.[17]

A second reason why corruption in many Latin American countries has become such a political problem and resists definition is that external forces, not just domestic political forces, are vitally and indignantly interested in it. The fundamental reason for this external interest, which emanates principally from the United States, is that corruption is widely perceived as being principally responsible for the failure of states to curtail the flow of drugs to the United States. In examining drug corruption in Latin America, one's analysis is thus further complicated by the clash between two standards of ethical governmental behavior—that of the local government and that of the U.S. government. This clash is not entirely unfamiliar. During the 1960s and early 1970s, it created disputes among the political scientists who debated the significance of corruption in their analyses of political development in less-developed countries.[18] Shortly thereafter, the same clash generated substantial controversy and even foreign policy repercussions when payments by U.S.-based multinational companies to foreign politicians were exposed in the American media and Congress responded with the Foreign Corrupt Practices Act. But whereas many Americans viewed the multinationals' bribes with a fair degree of indifference, readily accepting the notion that other nations employed different standards, few were prepared to view drug-related corruption in the same light. Drug trafficker payoffs to police tended to be considered not in the context of meager government salaries but as government corruption, pure and simple. As a consequence, the label of "corruption" was attached to economic transactions that were viewed by many Latin Americans and Caribbeans as normative rather than corrupt behavior. It was not that the notion of corruption did not exist in these countries, just that it was interpreted according to different standards.

Of course, much of the corruption that baffles U.S. drug enforcement policies in Latin America can hardly be described by any other label.

17. Alan Riding, *Distant Neighbors: A Portrait of the Mexicans* (New York: Alfred A. Knopf, 1985), 113.
18. See the articles collected in Heidenheimer, ed., *Political Corruption* (supra n. 8), and Heidenheimer, Johnston, and LeVine, eds., *Political Corruption* (supra n. 9).

There is, for instance, a clear distinction in the eyes of both North and South Americans between a clerk who accepts a "tip" to expedite the processing of some routine government function and a police officer or judge who takes a substantial bribe in return for throwing out a case against a major drug trafficker. In the latter case, few would question that the official is corrupt. Since most drug enforcement corruption is relatively clear-cut, defining it poses less of a problem than defining corruption in general. Government corruption will therefore be defined here as complicity by a government official in criminal activity in return for some benefit, typically a material one. This definition is equally applicable to both North and South American contexts. What varies, however, is the extensiveness and pervasiveness of the corruption in the southern context.

To be sure, the United States has had its own fair share of corruption at all levels of government. From the White House to the municipal police officer, corruption has rarely been absent from the administration of criminal justice and government in general in the United States. In New York, for instance, the cycle of police corruption, investigatory commission, reform, and corruption once again has run its course every twenty years for the last hundred years.[19] During the late 1960s, an investigation into corruption among the FBN agents in New York City led to the discharge of more than fifty agents and the indictment of more than a dozen for selling drugs and taking bribes.[20] During the 1980s, virtually every federal police agency saw at least a few of its agents prosecuted on charges of drug-related corruption.[21] Yet by comparison with many municipal police departments, the federal police agencies

19. See Commission to Investigate Allegations of Police Corruption and the City's Anti-Corruption Procedures, Commission Report, published as The Knapp Commission Report on Police Corruption (New York: George Braziller, 1973), 5. Corruption in the New York City Police Department is also the subject of Peter Maas, Serpico (New York: Bantam Books, 1973), and Leonard Shecter with William Philips, On the Pad (New York: G. P. Putnam's Sons, 1973). Corruption can infect not just police agencies but also all aspects of the criminal justice system. See Robert Daley, Prince of the City (New York: Granada, 1978); and Todd S. Purdum, "Drugs Seen as an Increasing Threat to Police Integrity," New York Times, Nov. 12, 1988, 29.

20. John Finlator, The Drugged Nation: A "Narc's" Story (New York: Simon & Schuster, 1973), 65–67.

21. Richard L. Berke, "Corruption in Drug Agency Called Crippler of Inquiries and Morale," New York Times, Dec. 17, 1989, A1. A year-long investigation into corruption in the U.S. Customs Service, for instance, resulted in sixteen criminal prosecutions of customs inspectors in a dozen cities. See "Customs Inquiry Finds Drug Bribes," New York Times, June 18, 1987, A18.

have proven relatively free of corruption. New York City has not been alone, nor even the worst, in terms of corruption in its criminal justice system—witness the exposés of police corruption in Miami, Los Angeles, and even rural Georgia during the mid-1980s.[22] Throughout the United States, police, prosecutors, judges, and other government officials in the criminal justice systems and other branches of government have repeatedly demonstrated their susceptibility to corrupting influences.[23] The police have proven most vulnerable in their enforcement of the vice laws, in particular the drug laws.[24] In many cities, drug corruption has emerged as the pinnacle of police corruption, enriching law enforcement agents more than any other vice activity and inviting the most heinous forms of criminal complicity. Even more damaging to the nation, however, was the corruption at all levels of government that contributed greatly to the savings and loan crisis in the United States during the 1980s. Latin Americans who respond defensively to U.S.-fingerpointing at corruption in the southern hemisphere have accurately observed that corruption to the north often appears less pervasive because it is more "white collar," better insinuated into the political establishment, better obscured by the legal establishment, and not so vulnerable to the prying oversight of outsiders.

Yet despite the abundance of corruption in the United States, four checks prevent it from descending to the levels of corruption found in much of Latin America. The first is the potential of the media and investigatory commissions to expose the corruption periodically, to cleanse the police departments, and to institute reforms that impede the renewal of corrupt practices. Typically, this occurs in Latin America only with a radical change in the form of government, such as a military takeover. In most countries, the media are cowed from probing too deeply, or the civilian authorities are too weak to impose fundamental reforms despite revelations in the media. Where brave journalists occa-

22. The corruption of Southern sheriffs by drug traffickers is described in Fred Grimm, "Moonshiners' Network in Dixie Adapts Easily to Cocaine Trading," *Miami Herald*, Dec. 11, 1985, 8A. The corruption of the Miami Police Department is described in Paul Eddy, Hugo Sabogal, and Sara Walden, *The Cocaine Wars* (New York: W. W. Norton & Co., 1988). Corruption in New York City is described in Crystal Nix, "Drug Influx a Strain on the Beat," *New York Times*, Sept. 26, 1986, B1.

23. See Philip Shenon, "Enemy Within: Drug Money is Corrupting the Enforcers," *New York Times*, Apr. 11, 1988, A1; John Dillin, "Drug War Takes Its Toll on Integrity of U.S. Law Enforcers," *Christian Science Monitor*, May 31, 1990, 1.

24. John Dombrink, "The Touchables: Vice and Police Corruption in the 1980s," *Law and Contemporary Problems* 51 (1988), 201–232.

sionally have banded together to investigate and expose corruption in high places, they often have seen their presses destroyed, their newspapers censored, and their lives threatened.[25] Even when civilian leaders are able to discharge corrupt officials, they have little chance of deterring their replacements from taking advantage of the same opportunities that enriched their predecessors.

The second check is the role played by the federal government. Even despite the crimes of the Watergate period and the occasional scandals in the federal government and law enforcement agencies, the U.S. government has maintained a higher standard of integrity than most municipal and state governments. Both in presenting criminals with a powerful and largely incorruptible opponent, and in investigating corrupt activities by state and municipal authorities, its prosecutors and law enforcement agencies have strengthened the norms and power of legitimate government and the legal system. In much of Latin America, on the other hand, national government agencies have often been little more than magnified versions of corrupted municipal governments. The same is true of many, if not most, national police agencies.

The third, related check is the relative independence of the federal judiciary from political influence, intimidation, and bribery. From the mid-1930s to the mid-1980s, few federal judges were prosecuted for corruption, only one was impeached, and only one was killed by criminals.[26] These numbers increased during the late 1980s but still totaled barely 1 percent of the federal judiciary. Constant investigations and prosecutions of high-level officials in each administration have demonstrated that few if any Americans remain above the criminal law for long. In much of Latin America, on the other hand, judges are

25. Journalists writing about drug trafficking and drug-related corruption in Mexico and Colombia have been especially in danger. See "Dying by the Sword in Mexico," *Newsweek*, July 28, 1986, 15, which focuses on the murder of Ernesto Flores, the publisher of *El Popular* in the border town of Matamoros, after he published numerous reports of drug trafficking and government corruption. In Panama, the opposition newspaper, *La Prensa*, was the target of violence and censorship for its critical reporting of corruption in the Noriega regime. The same was true during the 1980s of *ABC Color* in Paraguay. During the mid-1970s, the most vigorous reporter of government corruption in Colombia was *Alternativa*, a magazine published by a number of young journalists who braved various intimidations and challenged the more traditional forces in the government and the media. In Peru, Gustavo Gorriti, a courageous investigative reporter for the leading news magazine, *Caretas*, reported extensively on drug-related corruption in police agencies, the military, and political circles during the mid-1980s.

26. A somewhat different perspective on the American judiciary is Charles R. Ashman, *The Finest Judges Money Can Buy* (Los Angeles: Nash Publishing, 1973), but even that book focuses primarily on the corruption of state, as opposed to federal, judges.

ordered and threatened by powerful officials and private individuals to pervert the law. In Colombia, the drug traffickers so intimidated the Supreme Court during the 1980s that the justices twisted the law in an effort to absolve themselves of any responsibility over cases involving the extradition of drug traffickers. Elsewhere, judges dare not find against a powerful government official accused of corruption or other crimes. The cowing of the judiciary in Latin America thus eliminates a crucial check on government corruption. At the same time, it undermines the cases the police do make and reduces whatever incentive they may have to resist being corrupted.

A fourth check, if it can be called that, is that most law enforcement agents in the United States are paid a livable salary so that, at least in theory, their economic survival is not dependent upon accepting bribes. Most judges, especially at the federal level, may make significantly less than they would as lawyers in private practice, but they too are able to maintain a respectable standard of living. This is clearly not the case in most of Latin America, where salaries are insufficient to permit economic survival and where the acceptance of bribes is tacitly understood to be an essential economic perquisite of a law enforcement agent's job.[27] Most judges are also poorly paid, which reflects not just the tradition of low government salaries but also the fact that lower court positions are held in lesser esteem and filled by relatively young and inexperienced lawyers (as is the tradition in most civil law countries).[28] The relatively low pay of criminal justice officials, combined with the opportunities presented to them by virtue of their positions, seems to be the single most important reason for the high level of corruption in Latin American criminal justice systems.

Mordida Typologies: Drug Corruption in Latin America

That corruption varies in kind, degree, and effect goes without saying. The challenge for scholars is to impose some order on this subject

27. Mary Williams Walsh, "Many Mexican Police Supplement Low Pay with 'Tips' and 'Fines,'" Wall Street Journal, Nov. 21, 1986, 1.

28. John Henry Merryman, The Civil Law Tradition, 2nd ed. (Stanford, Calif.: Stanford University Press, 1985), 34–38.

without distorting the complicated reality. Students of police corruption have been particularly imaginative in this respect, generating typologies that focus on different aspects of corruption. The Knapp Commission, which investigated police corruption in New York City in 1971, categorized corrupt police officers into two groups: the "grass-eaters" and the "meat-eaters." The former took bribes only when the opportunity arose; the latter actively sought out opportunities.[29] They and others also distinguished between "clean" and "dirty" graft, the latter being tied to illicit activities generally considered more odious, such as drug trafficking.[30] One of the leading scholars in this area, Lawrence Sherman, has also constructed a "typology of corrupt police departments." Focusing on three features, "the *pervasiveness* of corruption, its *organization*, and the *source* of bribes," Sherman distinguished between the least corrupt departments, which he designated "Rotten Apples and Rotten Pockets," those with "Pervasive Unorganized Corruption," and those with "Pervasive Organized Corruption."[31] What follows are my own adaptations of these typologies, one for individual corruption, one for organizational corruption, and one for moral corruption, each of which can be laid out along a continuum from least to most corrupt. Although the typologies apply to all law enforcement corruption in Latin America, I have constructed them with drug corruption particularly in mind. *Mordida*, it should be noted, is the Mexican term for a payoff. Translated literally, it means "a bite."

The typology of individual corruption distinguishes corrupt officials by their degree of complicity in criminal activity. The least corrupt is best described as a *passive cooperator*, the moderately corrupt is typically a *facilitator*, and the most corrupt is the *initiator*. At one end of this continuum is the honest police officer who cooperates only because his or her family has been threatened. At the other end is the drug dealing police chief, general, or dictator. The compensation which each receives for corrupt activity may vary both in frequency and in amount. He or she may receive a retainer or be paid only when an occasion arises. The amount may be as little as a few dollars or as much as hundreds of thousands of dollars. Although there tends to be a correlation between the size of the bribe and the official's rank, there is no substitute for

29. *Knapp Commission Report*, 65.
30. "Narcotics and the Police in New York," in ibid., 91–115, reprinted in Sherman, ed., *Police Corruption* (supra n. 10), 129–152.
31. Introduction to Sherman, ed., *Police Corruption*, 6–12.

being in the right place at the right time to extract the maximum possible bribe. Not a few lowly officials have put away the equivalent of a lifetime's savings for neglecting their official duties for just a moment. At the same time, many drug traffickers have supplemented and even replaced their bribe offers with threats to harm the official and his family if he fails to cooperate. In Colombia, for instance, where threats and murders are frequently used to eliminate official meddling, bribes are reportedly lower than in other countries, where drug traffickers and officials treat one another in a more civilized manner.

Passive cooperators are typically those who are paid to look the other way. Rather than being paid to do something, they are paid to do nothing. Passive cooperators may either be offered a bribe or demand (i.e., extort) one. Law enforcement agents can become passive cooperators in a number of ways: they can stumble across information or a transaction and be offered or demand a bribe merely for not acting as their official capacity requires; they can be offered or demand a bribe in advance to not investigate a case; they can be offered or demand a retainer from a known drug trafficker for not interfering in the dealer's business; or they can simply be intimidated by threats to refrain from interfering in drug trafficking. This last form of corruption, although it is the least assailable from an ethical perspective, is the most threatening to a society and government because it represents a shift in the balance of power between criminal elements and the legitimate government in favor of the former. This is particularly so when the intimidated officials occupy high levels of the government.

The *facilitator's* participation in drug trafficking can assume many forms. Perhaps the most common is the sale of information: the time and place of police raids; the identity of informants; the fact that the trafficker is under surveillance; the radio frequencies used by police to communicate with one another; and any other information that can help the drug trafficker avoid seizure of his drugs and his own apprehension, arrest, and/or prosecution. Other facilitators may become far more involved with drug traffickers, sometimes to the extent of actually becoming their partners. They may provide transportation; they may assist with security, either in person or by providing uniforms and equipment; and they may offer protection from interference by other law enforcement agents, both honest and corrupt. The relationships between facilitators and drug traffickers can vary greatly depending on their relative power, the degree to which either is beholden to the other, and the existence of any nonfinancial components to the relationship. For instance, facilitators may be willing to aid a drug trafficker so long as they are not caught red-handed or caught by an agent or agency more powerful than the facilitators or their agencies. If that event occurs, the facilitator may disavow any knowledge of the trafficker and the illegal activities.

Initiators are often the most elusive of drug traffickers because they are able to disguise and shield their activities by virtue of their position. Many initiators become involved by selling what they seize from drug traffickers. For instance, an agent may arrest a trafficker with 5 kilograms of cocaine, keep 2 kilograms to resell, and deliver the remainder to the authorities. Another agent may keep all 5 kilograms and silence the ripped-off trafficker by threatening or killing him or her. Two other types of initiators are both connected to high levels of the government. One type (who lies outside the bounds of this typology) is the diplomat or other official (or the official's friend or relative) who acts as a courier, taking advantage of diplomatic immunity or special status to minimize or avoid searches at the border. The other type is the high-level military or police official who controls all drug trafficking in the district and receives a large share of the profits. Those who control and share less of the profits fall more readily into the category of facilitators.

A second typology that is useful in examining corruption from a comparative perspective distinguishes the organizational networks of corrupt officials by size, sophistication and hierarchical structure. At one end of this continuum is corruption that may be deemed *sporadic*. In the middle are two forms of what may be termed *systemic corruption*. And at the other end is what may be called *institutionalized corruption*.

Sporadic corruption is characterized by the absence of a broad pattern of corruption. It involves individuals or small groups of officials who take bribes but who do not share either their payoffs or knowledge of their activities with others in the government. Although sporadic corruption may occur in countries where the more organized forms of corruption also exist, it is more likely to occur in societies in which corruption is not viewed as a natural feature of government and law enforcement.

There are two types of systemic corruption, which conform to Sherman's "pervasive unorganized" and "pervasive organized" corruption. The first is typified by a society in which corruption is pervasive but poorly organized. In such a society, corruption may be rampant, but one cannot safely assume that everyone is corrupt. Although most police and judges may accept bribes, those who are honest can perform their duties without being harassed by others within the government. Given the right connections and/or enough money, drug traffickers who encounter such officials can eventually circumvent them by relying on other corrupt officials to set things right. The second type of systemic corruption is characterized by hierarchical payoff systems in which lower-level officials turn over most of what they collect in bribes to their superiors, who in turn must give most of their share to their superiors. Money may also flow in the reverse direction because most large-scale traffickers will cut their deals directly with the high-level officials. Those officials then direct their underlings to ignore or aid the drug trafficker's activities. The wiser and more generous high-level officials will distribute some of their intake down the ladder to keep their underlings both happy and loyal. Lower-level officials who engage in sporadic corruption despite the existence of this type of systemic corruption must beware because their "freelancing" may be regarded by their superiors as impermissible skimming of their own profits.

Individual countries may each have a number of such "payoff cones" within their borders. Often, one such cone will exist in each subdivision of the country, such as a province, police district or military district. Problems arise when two cones overlap or share the same district. In such cases, the head military officer and the head police commander, for instance, may compete for traffickers' payoffs and seek to undermine the deals the other makes with traffickers.

When all "payoff cones" fall within the umbrella of a centralized national "payoff cone," or when only one "payoff cone" exists for the entire country, the nation may be said to have *institutionalized* corruption. In such a system, the president or other effective authority in the country controls virtually all corrupt arrangements of any magnitude, particularly within the military and the police. This control typically includes knowledge of such transactions, veto power over them, and perhaps a direct or indirect cut in them. The official may personally arrange deals with drug traffickers, delegate that responsibility to a trusted assistant, or give approval to arrangements worked out independently by high-level officers. Although this official may not personally take a cut of each bribe, he or she will aim to distribute the opportunities for earning corrupt dollars as a form of patronage. The official may also exercise substantial influence over the judicial system, ensuring that its decisions do not endanger or expose his or her arrangements. When the payoff cone is dependent largely on drug-related money, the regime may fairly be characterized as a "formal narcocracy."[32]

The Pinnacle of Corruption

Classifying countries according to the above typology is a tricky process. Countries tend to shift from one category to another over time as regimes and political systems change and as crackdowns on drug trafficking alter payoff patterns. Different cities and regions within the same country may fall into different categories. And in some cities and regions, two categories may coexist simultaneously. Moreover, it is often impossible for an outsider to discern the true nature of a corrupt system because so much of the evidence is kept secret by those who participate in it.

At the same time, both typologies are useful in that they allow one to understand better the variations and gradations in both individual and organized corruption. Institutionalized corruption, for instance, is most likely to be found wherever an antidemocratic strongman has consolidated his position and is able to remain in power for more than a few years—consider Paraguay under General Alfredo Stroessner, Panama under General Manuel Antonio Noriega, Nicaragua under General Anastasio Somoza, Haiti under the Duvaliers, the Dominican Republic under Rafael Leónidas Trujillo, Cuba during Fulgencio Batista, and a host of others.[33] Although each was obliged to worry about challenges from below, and none was entirely free to eliminate potential rivals or threats, each exercised dominant control over all payoff cones of significance in his country for at least part of his reign. Individual colonels and generals may have established their own cones in the districts under their supervision, but all fell under the umbrella of the dictator's national cone.

Although each of these dictators accumulated much of their fortunes

32. The notion of formal and informal narcocracies is developed in Anthony Henman, "Cocaine Futures," in Anthony Henman, Roger Lewis, and Tim Malyon, *Big Deal: The Politics of the Illicit Drugs Business* (London: Pluto Press, 1985), 118–189.

33. See Laurence Whitehead, "On Presidential Graft: The Latin American Evidence," in Michael Clarke, ed., *Corruption: Causes, Consequences, and Control* (London: Frances Pinter, 1983).

by taking a share of legitimate activities and simply stealing from their national treasuries, almost all certainly profited from involvement in illegitimate transnational commerce, most notably drug trafficking. During the 1950s, Fulgencio Batista established close ties with such American mobsters as Meyer Lansky and the Mafia boss in Tampa, Santo Trafficante.[34] In return for cash payments to the Cuban dictator, the American criminals were provided with lucrative casino concessions as well as substantial freedom in the conduct of their other criminal activities. With Batista's ouster in January 1959, the Mafia sought a new gambling haven in the Caribbean and approached Haiti. According to one account:

> François ("Papa Doc") Duvalier entertained Joseph Stassi, a member of the Carlo Gambino family of Cosa Nostra, at the Presidential Palace. Later, a gambling concession was issued to Vito Filippone, a Bonnano family man. In 1964 and 1965, Cosa Nostra men pushed two series of Haitian lottery tickets in this country.[35]

While in the Dominican Republic,

> [Rafael Trujillo] bought machine guns and other small arms from Joseph ("Bayonne Joe") Zicarelli, a Capo in the Bonanno family, after the U.S. had shut him off from military aid. Later, Zicarelli arranged for the assassination of Andres Requena, an anti-Trujillo exile living in New York, and for the kidnapping and delivery to Santo Domingo of Jésus de Galindez, another political enemy of the dictator.[36]

In the case of Somoza, one trafficker middleman reportedly negotiated personally with the president in the late 1960s for unencumbered use of three Nicaraguan airports and several Pacific ports for his clients. Thereafter, he told one source:

34. Lansky's relationship with Batista and other Cuban leaders is discussed in Dennis Eisenberg, Uri Dan, and Eli Landau, *Meyer Lansky: Mogul of the Mob* (New York: Paddington Press, 1979).

35. Ralph Salerno and John S. Tompkins, *The Crime Confederation* (Garden City, N.Y.: Doubleday, 1969), 386–387.

36. Ibid., 388.

My own dealings with the Somoza government amounted to giving them a total of more than $13.5 million over a period of about ten years. All was paid in cash to Anastasio or [his brother] Luis, or other family members. Now and then I would give money to one or more of the generals in his government in order to keep them happy, because you never can tell in a country like Nicaragua; you have to make sure that everyone is taken care of. The President also had many cousins. They all needed assistance from time to time, and three of them manned the airports in the highlands. We made our deals man to man, I always paid in cash, and it was always understood that Somoza's relatives would receive appropriate payoffs commensurate with their positions within the government.[37]

Among all Latin American countries, Stroessner's Paraguay stood out for the blatant involvement of its officials in the contraband trade, including drug trafficking. With the exception of one incident in the early 1970s, when the Nixon administration vigorously insisted on the extradition of an infamous drug trafficker, Auguste Ricord, the Paraguayan leader and his cronies managed their illicit transnational enterprises with little foreign interference.[38] One account, typical of many of the reports that have emerged from Paraguay over the years, described the situation in 1971:

Since the early sixties the contraband traffic has replaced the public sector as the major source of finance for the purchase of equipment by the Paraguayan armed forces. Arms for the armoured divisions, which were previously paid for by siphoning funds from the state alcohol monopoly (APAL), are now financed out of the profits from the traffic in contraband cigarettes, which is controlled by the chief of the *Caballarria*—General Andrés Rodríguez. Traffic in scotch whiskey has likewise replaced funds from the state water board (CORPOSANA) in the case of Stroessner's own crack *Regimiento Escolta*. And the traffic in heroin has replaced the customs department as the major financial support

37. Andrew Starrhill Vallejo, quoted in Wayne Greehaw, *Flying High: Inside Big-Time Drug Smuggling* (New York: Dodd, Mead & Co., 1984), 43–44.
38. For a full account of the Ricord episode, see Evert Clark and Nicholas Horrock, *Contrabandista!* (New York: Praeger, 1973), 177–231.

for the counter-insurgency Regimiento group—R114—whose chief, General Patricio Colmán, is one of the organizers of the heroin smuggling. General Rodríguez handles re-export by air with old DC-4's belonging to the government, and also his own private fleet of Cessnas. River borne contraband is handled by Rear-Admiral Hugo González.[39]

The severance of the French and Latin American heroin connections the following year temporarily took Paraguay out of the drug trade. Within a few years, however, the developing cocaine boom had opened up new opportunities. In January 1985, another flap in U.S. relations with Paraguay arose when President Stroessner refused to destroy a large shipment of ether and other chemicals, which had been imported into Paraguay to process cocaine. Information soon emerged that General Andrés Rodríguez—a former backer of Ricord and reportedly the second most powerful person in the country—was deeply involved in the transaction.[40] By the mid-1980s, with Stroessner aging, the precise balance of power between the president and his generals and colonels, and the intricacies of the payoff relationships, could no longer be assumed to favor Stroessner. When he was ousted in a coup led by General Rodríguez in 1988, it appeared that that the payoff system was sufficiently well institutionalized that it would survive his passing.[41]

In the case of Panama, claims of official involvement in drug trafficking date back at least to the early 1970s. Top officials, including Joaquim Him Gonzales, a well-connected figure in Panama who held the position of chief of air traffic control and deputy inspector general of civil aviation, and Moises Torrijos, the brother of President Omar Torrijos Herrera, who also served as Panama's ambassador to Spain, were both indicted by U.S. prosecutors on drug trafficking charges.[42] Suspicions

39. *Latin America Newsletter*, Nov. 19, 1971, cited in Whitehead, "On Presidential Graft," 153. The official involvement in the contraband trade is also described in Paul H. Lewis, *Paraguay Under Stroessner* (Chapel Hill: University of North Carolina Press, 1980), 135–137; Catherine Lamour and Michel R. Lamberti, *The International Connection: Opium from Growers to Pushers*, trans. Peter and Betty Ross (New York: Pantheon Books, 1974), 52–53; Jack Anderson, "Drug Traffic in Paraguay," *Washington Post*, May 24, 1972, B15.

40. "The Guaraní Connection," *Latin America Regional Reports Southern Cone*, Aug. 2, 1985.

41. Tina Rosenberg, "Smuggler's Paradise," *New Republic*, June 8, 1987, 14–16.

42. Lamour and Lamberti, *International Connection*, 53–56; Evert and Horrock, *Contrabandista!* 193–203.

also centered on Foreign Minister Juan Tack, on Manuel Antonio Noriega, then the chief of the military's intelligence unit, G-2, and even on President Torrijos personally—although a special investigation by the Senate Intelligence Committee, discussed in a closed-door session of the U.S. Senate, revealed no conclusive evidence that Omar Torrijos was involved in or otherwise sanctioning official involvement in drug trafficking.[43] In all of these cases, official Panamanian involvement in the drug traffic was played up by U.S. opponents of the Panama Canal Treaty, most notably Senator Robert Dole.[44]

With the death of General Torrijos in 1981 and the emergence of Noriega as Panama's de facto ruler, the 15,000-person Panama Defense Force evolved into "a kind of Mafia that makes millions from kickbacks and drug dealing."[45] American drug enforcement agents had suspected Noriega of involvement in drug trafficking since his days as chief of intelligence under Torrijos. Indeed, in 1972 Noriega's name had been included on a list of major traffickers drawn up by a special unit within the Bureau of Narcotics and Dangerous Drugs, made up largely of former CIA agents, that considered assassinating leading drug traffickers around the world, although reportedly the plan was vetoed by top BNDD officials.[46] General Torrijos was personally informed of Noriega's involvement in drug trafficking by the head of the BNDD, John Ingersoll, but no action was taken by the Panamanian leader. More than a decade later, little had changed. In 1985, new information emerged linking Noriega with a major Peruvian drug trafficker, Reynaldo Rodríguez López. In June 1986, the investigative reporter, Seymour Hersh, provided an extensive exposé of Noriega's, and the Panamanian military's,

43. See the account by the former U.S. ambassador to Panama, William J. Jorden, *Panama Odyssey* (Austin: University of Texas Press, 1984), 523–524. See also *New York Times*, Feb. 17, 1978, 2; and Feb. 22, 1978, 1.

44. Jorden, *Panama Odyssey*.

45. James LeMoyne, "Elements in Ouster of Panama Chief: Beheading and a Power Duel," *New York Times*, Oct. 2, 1985, A12.

46. The plan to set up an assassination unit within the DEA was investigated in 1975 by a special team appointed by the attorney general. The final report, named for its principal author, was "The DeFeo Report." Although classified, information about the report and the report itself were leaked to journalists. See Richard Wieland, "Secret Report Reveals Panama Death Plot," in *Freedom*, June 1978 (published by the Church of Scientology). E. J. Epstein also refers to the assassination plans, although without naming Noriega as a target, in *Agency of Fear: Opiates and Political Power in America* (New York: G. P. Putnam's Sons, 1977), 141–146. See also Seymour M. Hersh, "U.S. Aides in '72 Weighed Killing Officer Who Now Leads Panama," *New York Times*, June 13, 1986, A1.

involvement in drug and arms trafficking and money laundering activities.[47] Two years later, he was indicted on drug trafficking charges in a U.S. court, and in late 1989 he was arrested by U.S. agents in Panama City following the U.S. military invasion mounted to oust him from power.

In each of these cases, a dictator with firm control over the country's military forces was able to exercise a strong influence over most large-scale corruption within the country. Payoffs were extracted from legitimate foreign and local businesses; government contracts were awarded to one's family and friends and oneself; and special arrangements were negotiated with transnational criminals. That such leaders typically developed close relationships with American mafiosi, Colombian drug traffickers, and other transnational criminals was no doubt a reflection of their common methods, common mind-sets, and kindred spirits recognizing common interests. As Stanislav Andreski pointed out in his analysis of Latin American and Caribbean "kleptocracy," the "levying of tribute by the pretorians . . . is simple and exactly analogous to that used by the Mafia in Sicily or by Al Capone in Chicago, the only difference being that here the gangsters are recognized as the official government."[48] Sharing both a gangster mentality and an overriding interest in acquiring illegitimate revenue, dictators and transnational criminals have represented a natural match.

Corruption All Around

Most Latin American and Caribbean governments tend to be characterized by systemic but disorganized corruption. Indeed, one of the basic characteristics of civilian regimes in the region is the presence of disorganized corruption, although military regimes in which no one general is dominant also may fit this description. Within each country, corruption in certain localities may fit into either the sporadic or the payoff cone model. Relations between corrupt officials vary from close cooper-

47. Seymour M. Hersh, "Panama Strongman Said to Trade in Drugs, Arms, and Illicit Money," New York Times, June 12, 1986, A1.
48. Stanislav Andreski, Parasitism and Subversion: The Case of Latin America (New York: Pantheon Books, 1966), 66.

ation in profiting from drug traffickers to intense infighting to attract the drug traffickers' bribes and business. Perhaps nowhere are relations so complex as in Mexico. Throughout the 1970s and 1980s, federal, state, and local police alternately competed and cooperated with one another and with assorted prosecutors, judges, military units, political officials, and agents of the security services in extracting bribes from drug traffickers, actively participating in drug trafficking operations, and cracking down on drug trafficking. Even though top-level officials in Mexico City reportedly exercised substantial influence over career, policy, and operational decisions with implications for drug enforcement and drug-related corruption, substantial power was exercised more or less independently by regional commanders and political bosses.

To the extent that Mexican corruption can be described as unique, that is largely a reflection of Mexico's greater size and its proximity to the United States.[49] Otherwise, the above description is equally valid for most other Latin American and Caribbean countries, provided adjustments are made for scale. To be sure, every country has its small share of mostly or entirely honest government officials. The growth of the international drug traffic, however, has reduced that share by increasing the size of the temptations to unprecedented levels and by supplementing the temptations with threats. Especially in the more impoverished countries, the lure of drug dollars has virtually overwhelmed preexisting resistance to corruption. In the Bahamas, for instance, numerous high-level officials, including Prime Minister Lynden Pindling and a number of his cabinet ministers, were accused during the 1980s of accepting bribes from a variety of American and Colombian drug traffickers, including the notorious Colombian drug trafficker, Carlos Lehder.[50] Elsewhere in the Caribbean, top officials in Haiti,[51] Trinidad and To-

49. The evolution of drug-related corruption in Mexico from 1960 to 1990 is described well by Peter A. Lupsha, "Drug Lords and Narco-Corruption: The Players Change but the Game Continues," *Crime, Law, and Social Change* 16 (1991), 41–58.

50. See the excellent six-part series on drug trafficking and corruption in the Bahamas by Carl Hiaasen and Jim McGee, "A Nation for Sale," *Miami Herald*, Sept. 23–28, 1984; and Joel Brinkley, "Drugs and Corruption Color Vote in Bahamas," *New York Times*, June 14, 1987, A1.

51. In Haiti, suspicions centered on Ernest Bennett, father-in-law of former President Jean-Claude Duvalier, who reportedly became known as the "Godfather" because of his role in assisting Colombian drug traffickers using Haiti as a transshipment point. See Don Bohning, "Duvalier Father-in-Law Linked to Colombian Cocaine Traffic," *Miami Herald*, June 13, 1986, 1A.

bago,[52] the Turks and Caicos islands,[53] and the British Virgin Islands[54] were all implicated during the mid-1980s in illegal dealings with drug traffickers.

In many of these countries, corruption had either been relatively absent or at low levels commensurate with the economic activity on the islands. When American and Colombian drug traffickers were drawn to the islands by the need to transport their drugs and launder their funds, however, the nature of corruption on the islands was dramatically altered. Some government officials suddenly were provided with the opportunity to become wealthy beyond their wildest dreams. But at the same time, outsiders such as the DEA developed an interest in how they had acquired their new, and often conspicuous, fortunes. By the late 1980s, none of the island nations had figured out how to deal with the tensions between the drug traffickers' temptations and the DEA's unfortunate interest in the recipients of those temptations.

Virtually no government in Latin America and the Caribbean has been untouched by the lure of drug dollars. The important variations between countries are in the extent to which government was corrupted before the advent of drug dollars, and in the degree to which drug-related corruption has changed the nature and scale of overall corruption. Government in Bolivia, for instance, has long been notoriously corrupt, but the lure of cocaine dollars virtually eliminated whatever limits had previously existed. The apex, or nadir, was reached when a cocaine trafficking junta led by a General Luis García Meza seized control of the government in 1980 and maintained itself in power for a year and a half. Although U.S. pressures eventually forced the regime from power, and although the subsequent civilian leaders, Hernan Siles Zuazo and Víctor

52. In April 1984, Prime Minister George Chambers appointed a Commission of Enquiry to investigate drug-related corruption. Its report, released in January 1987 by Chambers's successor, Prime Minister A. N. R. Robinson, implicated two of Chambers's cabinet ministers, two magistrates, and fifty-three police officers, including senior officials and hotel operators, with drug trafficking in Trinidad and Tobago. See *Latin American Monitor—Caribbean*, Mar. 1987, 393; and *Caribbean Insight*, Mar. 1987, 13.

53. In March 1985, Chief Minister Norman Saunders, Minister of Commerce and Development Stafford Missick, and another legislator were arrested in a DEA undercover operation in Miami after accepting bribes to provide safe transit for cocaine shipments. See Liz Balmaseda, "Drug Net Snares Island Ministers," *Miami Herald*, Mar. 6, 1985, 1A; and Jon Nordheimer, "U.S. Arrests Atlantic Islands' Leader in Drug Plot," *New York Times*, Mar. 6, 1985, A1.

54. New elections were called after revelations that Chief Minister Cyril Romney held a majority share in a company under investigation by British police and the DEA for suspected money laundering. See *Latin American Monitor—Caribbean*, Sept. 1986, 329.

Paz Estenssoro, were regarded as relatively honest, drug-related corruption has continued to permeate the military, the criminal justice system, the legislature, and reportedly even the cabinet. The transition from García Meza's regime to the relatively impotent civilian regimes that followed thus represented no more than a switch from a formal narcocracy to an informal narcocracy. Neither the economy's dependence on the cocaine trade nor the debilitating consequences of the pervasive drug-related corruption changed in any significant way.

In Colombia, where traditions of official rectitude are somewhat stronger, drug traffickers nonetheless succeeded during the 1970s and 1980s in corrupting all levels of government, including a significant share of the legislature and cabinet-level ministers. In 1978, for instance, President Alfonso Lopez Michelsen was told by top U.S. drug enforcement officials that some thirty high-level officials, including two cabinet ministers and five federal judges, had been corrupted by drug traffickers.[55] No action was taken, however, by the Colombian leader. Even the Colombian military, which has remained a powerful and relatively corruption-free organization, could not resist the inducements offered by the drug traffickers. In 1978, martial law was declared in the Guajira peninsula, where most Colombian marijuana is grown, and the military took over drug enforcement responsibilities from the national police. Two years later, the military was removed after drug traffickers had succeeded in corrupting most high-level military officials in the region.[56] During the 1980s, the drug traffickers grew even more powerful, investing in the legitimate economy, buying protection from all branches and levels of government, and bribing, intimidating, and killing those who challenged them.

Peru's situation is of a similar magnitude but slightly different character than Colombia's. Its military also has remained largely indifferent to drug trafficking, fearing its corrupting effects and preferring to concentrate their energies on combatting the two leftist insurgencies: Sendero Luminoso (Shining Path) and the Túpac Amaru Revolutionary Movement. During the mid-1980s, its customs agency was regarded as

55. The U.S. delegation included the DEA administrator Peter Bensinger and the chief drug officials in the White House and State Department, Peter Bourne and Mathea Falco. Interview with Peter Bourne, November 1, 1984. This incident was also the subject of a CBS "60 Minutes" story entitled "The Cocaine Memorandum," April 2, 1978.

56. Peter Lupsha, "Drug Trafficking: Mexico and Colombia in Comparative Perspective," *Journal of International Affairs* 35 (1981), 95–115.

entirely corrupt and the other law enforcement agencies—the Peruvian Investigative Police (PIP) and the Guardia Civil—as mostly so. The same was true of the various intelligence agencies.[57] The judiciary has remained underpaid, overworked, virtually inoperative, and riddled with corruption.[58] In late 1985, the new president, Alan García Perez, launched a "moralization" campaign against the extensive corruption that had been uncovered throughout the government.[59] Suspicious connections between a major drug trafficker, Reynaldo Rodríguez López, and top officials in the interior ministry were investigated. Dozens of police generals suspected of collusion with the drug traffickers were dismissed, as were many others of lower rank,[60] but many of those dismissed simply went to work full-time for the traffickers. By the time García left office in 1990, the names and faces of the corrupt officials benefiting from the traffickers' largesse had changed, but not the essential patterns of corruption.

Although Bolivia, Colombia, and Peru have been the leading producers of illicit cocaine for the international market, the corruption attendant to the traffic has reached to high and low levels of virtually every government in the region. The extent of specifically drug-related corruption depends primarily on the availability of opportunities, which is in turn dependent on the impact of law enforcement efforts in other countries and the routes preferred by the traffickers. For instance, the Colombian government's periodic crackdowns on the drug trade since mid-1984 have diverted substantial portions of the traffic to neighboring countries such as Brazil,[61] Venezuela,[62]

57. Corruption in the Peruvian police is noted in James Mills, *The Underground Empire: Where Crime and Governments Embrace* (Garden City, N.Y.: Doubleday, 1986), 879.

58. That was the conclusion of an extensive investigation by the West German Friedrich Naumann Foundation. "Report condemns Peru's Judiciary," *Latin America Weekly Report*, Feb. 22, 1985, 6.

59. See Jeffrey L. Klaiber, "Reform Politics in Peru: Alan Garcia's Crusade Against Corruption," *Corruption and Reform* 2 (1987), 149–168.

60. Alan Riding, "Peru Joins Attack on Cocaine Trade," *New York Times*, Sept. 1, 1985, A1. See the exposé, "Las amistades de don Reynaldo," *Caretas* (Peru), Aug. 12, 1985, 12–20; and "Caso Gigante," *Caretas*, July 30, 1985, 40–46.

61. See the following three articles by Alan Riding: "Brazil Tries to Stop Spread of Cocaine Trafficking," *New York Times*, Mar. 14, 1985, A6; "Brazil Acting to Halt New Trafficking in Cocaine," *New York Times*, June 7, 1987, 19; and "Brazil Now a Vital Crossroad for Latin Cocaine Traffickers," *New York Times*, Aug. 28, 1988, 1. See also James Brooke, "Brazil's Amazon Basin Becomes Cocaine Highway," *New York Times*, Apr. 14, 1991, 14.

62. Merrill Collett, "Venezuela Gaining Notoriety as Pipeline for Illegal Drugs," *Miami*

Panama,[63] and Ecuador,[64] creating new opportunities for their law enforcement and other officials. As the European market for cocaine has grown, Uruguay and Argentina have become increasingly important transit countries for Bolivian and Peruvian cocaine shipped east—with the northern Argentine province of Salta gaining special notoriety in recent years.[65] Similarly, Central American police and military officials have occasionally seized opportunities to provide transit services, such as airstrips and docking locations, for the drug traffickers.[66] Some have also offered their countries as refuges to assorted traffickers willing to pay their hosts handsomely. Even as the national and ethnic identities of the traffickers changed from the Corsican and Italian heroin traffickers of the 1960s to the Colombian, Peruvian, and North American cocaine and marijuana dealers of the 1970s and 1980s, the patterns remained the same.

In Ecuador, which is fortuitously situated between Peru and Colombia, DEA agents described the corruption as pervasive from top to bottom during the mid-1980s. According to one agent who had been stationed there for more than five years:

> The whole country is a dog and pony show. . . . If you have money, you don't spend time in jail. You buy the cops, or the judges, the evidence disappears . . . you escape from jail. . . . The leading trafficker in Ecuador . . . has tons of relatives, not one of whom has ever spent more than a week in jail. . . . The chief of the prison is always being thrown in jail for letting criminals

Herald, Dec. 21, 1986, 34A; Alan Riding, "Cocaine Finds a New Route in Venezuela," *New York Times*, June 18, 1987, A15; Alan Riding, "Colombian Drugs and Rebels Upset Venezuela," *New York Times*, Jan. 20, 1988, A9.

63. *Drugs, Law Enforcement, and Foreign Policy—Panama: Hearings Before the Subcommittee on Terrorism, Narcotics, and International Operations of the Senate Committee on Foreign Relations,* 100th Cong., 2d Sess., Part 2, Feb. 8–11, 1988.

64. Richard L. Berke, "Drug Cartels, Squeezed, Are Turning to Ecuador," *New York Times*, Mar. 25, 1990, A22.

65. Shirley Christian, "Drug Traffic Rises Sharply in Argentina," *New York Times*, Apr. 28, 1988, A5.

66. Drug-related activities in Honduras are discussed in Wilson Ring, "U.S. Looks at Honduras as Drug Transfer Point," *Washington Post*, Dec. 7, 1987, A27; James LeMoyne, "Military Officers in Honduras Are Linked to the Drug Trade," *New York Times*, Feb. 12, 1988, A1; Mark B. Rosenberg, "Narcos and Politicos: The Politics of Drug Trafficking in Honduras," *Journal of Interamerican Studies and World Affairs* 30 (Summer–Fall 1988), 143–166; and Mort Rosenblum, "Hidden Agendas," *Vanity Fair* 53 (Mar. 1990), 102–106, 114–120.

> escape; then he becomes the head again. . . . And traffickers "escape" from jail with all their furniture.

Such descriptions of drug-related corruption were repeated to me in one form or another by DEA agents who had served in most Latin American and Caribbean countries. For every country there were stories of customs and drug enforcement agencies corrupted from top to bottom, of ludicrously porous prisons, of prosecutors and judges taking bribes and even actively seeking them out, of legislators, regional governors, and cabinet ministers linked to powerful drug traffickers, and of military officers providing protection to drug traffickers. There were exceptions, of course—occasional honest officials, relatively uncorrupted police agencies and military branches, upstanding cabinet ministers, and so on. But overall the atmosphere of corruption pervades most governments throughout the region.

The most corruption-free governments—those fitting the model of sporadic corruption—emerge during the years immediately following the ouster of a democratic regime by a military coup d'état.[67] Both Chile immediately following Allende, and Argentina following the ouster of Isabel Perón, fit into this category. A number of factors probably account for this. Coup leaders typically justify their actions by promising to eliminate the rampant corruption of the previous regime.[68] This is not to say that coups are primarily motivated by revulsion at civilian corruption, just that the military does have a stake in minimizing corruption to gain popular support and legitimize itself. A second factor, which also accounts for the greater preponderance of corruption among police services than within the military, is the professionalism of the military services. Trained in prestigious military academies, and inculcated with

67. The term "corruption-free" refers only to the absence of the type of corruption discussed in this chapter—that is, complicity in criminal activity in return for a material benefit. The lawless killing of civilians suspected of leftist activities by Latin American militaries after they overthrow a civilian government constitutes a very different form of corruption, one that typically is at its worst immediately following a coup d'état. The latter form of corruption is analyzed in Arnold A. Rogow and Harold D. Lasswell, *Power, Corruption, and Rectitude* (Englewood Cliffs, N.J.: Prentice-Hall, 1963).

68. Eric Nordlinger, in *Soldiers in Politics: Military Coups and Governments* (Englewood Cliffs, N.J.: Prentice-Hall, 1977), 85–88, 92–93, notes that charges of corruption are intrinsic to the political rhetoric of coups but that the corruption itself is not a strong motivating factor for the coup. Rather, the corruption helps to set the stage for the coup by reducing the respect of the military and the public for the civilian regime and by undermining the regime's legitimacy.

notions of honor and order, military officers are often predisposed against engaging in corrupt activities, particularly the more shady varieties such as drug trafficking. A third factor is that most new regimes, including democratic ones, enter power with a relatively clean reputation, which lingers for a while. Typically, the initial period of rule is marked by a sense of idealism and fervor for good government, which creates a hostile environment for corrupt activities. Equally important, the new power holders and those who wish to secure favors from them have yet to make contact, establish trust in one another, and get down to business.

Despite the sense of professionalism instilled in the academies, military regimes are little better than their democratic counterparts in resisting the temptations that corrupt those who hold power. The longer they remain in power, the more this is so. And when their power persists to the point of becoming institutionalized, their corruption can exceed that of the most corrupt democratic regimes. Without a free press or relatively independent judiciary, there is almost no check on corruption, no matter how blatant, outside the internal politics of the regime itself. To an outside observer, the corruption in a democratic regime may appear greater because it is more broadly distributed given the nature of the regime. But the depth and virulence of the corruption in an aging military regime are difficult to replicate even in the most decadent of democracies. More than three decades of Stroessner's rule in Paraguay attested to this. Argentina shortly before the return of civilian rule also was marked by a dramatic upswing in corruption from the earlier years when the military had concentrated its energies on repressing the left and their suspected allies. In Chile, one of Pinochet's first gestures to the United States following his seizure of power was the delivery of a number of drug traffickers, including Chilean citizens, to the U.S. government. Ten years later, one of the two national police agencies, the Investigaciones, was regarded as perhaps the leading drug trafficking organization in the country.

The Relative Immorality of Drug-Related Corruption

In addition to the typology/continua of individual and organizational corruption, a third typology/continuum is useful in analyzing the nature of corruption, particularly with regard to drug trafficking. That is the typology/continuum of moral corruption.[69] What makes it both interesting and difficult to examine is that in many ways it bears little relationship to the other two typology/continua. In other words, the corrupt *initiator* and the *institutionalized* system of corruption are not necessarily the most immoral. Rather, the best indicator of the "corruption" or immorality of a corrupt individual or system is not the extent of participation in corrupt deeds but the nature of the activity in which the corrupt individual or system acquiesces or participates. The more heinous the crime, the more immoral is the corruption that aids it. Evaluating the moral corruption of crimes and corrupt deeds is, however, a highly subjective process in which assessments vary greatly depending on the religious, cultural, ideological, and other values of an individual community or society at any one time.

Of all the apolitical crimes, with the possible exception of white-collar crimes such as insider trading, vice crimes are the most prone to widely varying moral judgments. Unlike most other acts that fall within the purview of the criminal law, vice crimes do not involve the government in punishing individuals for the harm they cause to one another or the state. Instead, they are activities involving only consenting parties that are criminalized by the government to reflect its, and often the majority's, sense of moral disapproval. To a certain extent, the criminalization of such acts also stems from a belief in human nature's susceptibility to the temptations of vice, and from the fear that such acts would proliferate if they were not illegal. Enforcing such laws becomes problematic not only because there often are no complaining parties to notify the police of the act's occurrence, but also because the consensus that underlies most criminal laws tends to dissipate in the absence of a victim. The greater the disparity between the severity of laws governing vice crimes and the tolerance or indifference of those charged with enforcing vice laws, the greater the likelihood of corruption.

Of all the vice crimes, drug trafficking has probably attracted the most varied moral judgments in Latin America and the Caribbean in recent decades. The harshest judgments are usually reflected in the criminal laws. Popular attitudes in most countries tend not to be as severe, and significant minorities in many are highly skeptical of the laws against

69. This theme is addressed in four articles by John G. Peters and Susan Welch, Michael Johnston, Kenneth M. Gibbons, and Laurence Whitehead reproduced in Heidenheimer, Johnston, and LeVine, eds., *Political Corruption* (supra n. 9), 719–800.

drugs and drug trafficking. Thus, although drug trafficking is often treated in both the penal law and political rhetoric as the equivalent of crimes such as murder and kidnapping, there are countless criminals and government officials whose ethical codes would allow them to profit from the former but not the latter. In the words of one DEA agent, most Latin American police "don't look at the trafficker as just a crook. Rather, they see him as a businessman who happens to deal in drugs, with certain contacts, interests and protectors." They deal with him accordingly, and the DEA agent often has little choice but to deal with the trafficker's counterparts within the constraints of that context. The widespread sense in Latin America that drug trafficking is qualitatively and morally almost indistinguishable from trafficking in other forms of contraband plays an important role in undermining American efforts to generate the moral outrage that might facilitate cooperation.

The location of drug enforcement corruption in the typology/continuum of moral corruption is thus a highly subjective matter. The consensus emerges only with respect to the subsidiary crimes and corruptions that often accompany corruption in drug enforcement. Killing in and of itself is not necessarily seen as all that reprehensible because violence is often the sole means of protection and contract enforcement in an illicit market. The murder of innocent people and honest officials, however, does not fall within the gray area of moral judgments. Typically, it is only when drug traffickers and the officials whom they corrupt sink to that level of behavior that the public and the government perceive a need to crack down on drug trafficking and corruption.

Clearly each society is characterized by certain expectations regarding what types and degrees of corruption in law enforcement are tolerable. Such expectations are shaped by traditional modes of interaction between a government and its citizens, by changes in regimes and the values they stress, and by fluctuations in the economy. At the same time, when one examines the course of corruption in drug enforcement in Latin America from the 1970s to the 1980s, one can discern a tendency for it to increase along each of the three continua described above. In some countries, the tendency characterizes the entire nation; elsewhere, it is true only of certain regions or cities. Each society, however, seems to have a breaking point at which its tolerance for corruption ceases. The breaking point may be occasioned by a particularly outlandish act, such as the killing of Colombia's justice minister in April 1984, or by total capitulation to corruption, which characterized the Bolivian regime of General Luis García Meza in 1980–81, or by the findings of a commission of inquiry like that which investigated Bahamian involvement in drug trafficking in 1983–84, or by a combination of media exposés and a change in regime, such as occurred in Peru in 1985 with the election of Alan García to the presidency. Following the breaking point, corruption subsides as the most egregious violators are dismissed and as others who are corrupt wait for the wave of moral fervor to recede. But so long as the drugs retain both their illegal status and their foreign markets, the renewal of the cycle of escalating corruption is inevitable.

The DEA's Unique Challenge: Dealing with Foreign Corruption

How have DEA agents dealt with the obstacles posed by drug-related corruption in Latin America and the Caribbean? The following analysis differs from virtually all other studies of corruption and reform in two respects. First, it focuses on the role played by an outsider, one that lacks any sovereign powers, in trying to influence the nature and impact of government corruption. Second, it is primarily concerned with how corrupt agencies are induced to perform their designated tasks despite that corruption, not with how they are reformed. The question addressed below is thus one involving a hitherto unstudied aspect of foreign policy behavior: When Government A seeks cooperation from Government B in pursuing Policy Objective A' but is hindered by corruption in Government B, what are the options available to it? More specifically, when the U.S. government seeks cooperation from Latin American and Caribbean governments in apprehending, arresting, prosecuting, and punishing drug traffickers, but is hindered by corruption in those governments, what are the options available to it? Even more specifically, how does the DEA pursue its objective of immobilizing drug traffickers abroad despite pervasive corruption in foreign governments?

The DEA's capacity to deal with foreign corruption in any country is influenced most strongly by the type of organizational corruption characteristic of that country. Even in countries in which drug-related corruption is integrated into institutionalized corruption, however, DEA agents have options beyond packing their bags and leaving. The diplomatic leverage of the U.S. government, combined with the international consensus of sorts among governments that drug trafficking is both illegal and evil, ensure that no government can blatantly turn its back on U.S. requests for cooperation without incurring some costs. Even where a government has thoroughly succumbed to the influences of drug traffickers, skilled agents can still rely on their own diplomatic skills and appeals to the transnational value system of police. And no matter how deeply rooted the corruption, the fact remains that almost no one is totally corrupt. Even those who have virtually no moral limits on their corruption still will lack on occasion the opportunities to be corrupted. It may be because they have failed to make the necessary contact, or because the spotlight is on them when the opportunity arises. Whatever the case, it means that at times they may have no option left but to cooperate with the DEA agent.

In most Latin American countries, the DEA agent encounters drug-related corruption at every level of government, from the street cop and airport customs official, to the police chief, the military general, and the cabinet minister. The breadth of the corruption tends to reflect two factors. The first is the number of government agencies involved in drug enforcement. The fewer the agencies, the less dispersed the corruption, since there is little need or incentive for drug traffickers to bribe officials whose jurisdiction does not include them. The second is the pervasiveness of drug trafficking in the country. The more pervasive it is, the greater the opportunity for officials who have nothing to do with drug enforcement to profit by becoming corrupt facilitators and initiators. Thus, in Mexico, Bolivia, Colombia, Peru, Belize, Jamaica, Ecuador, the Bahamas, much of the Caribbean, and most of Central America, drug-related corruption has infected many levels and departments of government from top to bottom. Elsewhere, particularly in countries that have played a relatively minor transit role, the opportunities to profit from drug-related corruption often have been limited to top government officials and those involved in law enforcement.

Customs officials in most countries have generally been regarded as the most corruptible, perhaps because of their long experience in "regulating" all forms of contraband smuggling. The military, which has stayed out of drug enforcement activities in most Latin American countries, has had the greatest success in preserving a reputation for clean hands in this area, although there are conspicuous exceptions. In Mexico, for instance, military officers and police officials have competed for the largesse of drug traffickers. In Colombia, the military was unable to resist the corrupting influences of the drug traffickers when it briefly assumed principal responsibility for marijuana eradication in the Guajira in 1979–80. According to some reports, the general in charge of the effort retired shortly after the military was withdrawn, having become a wealthy man during his months in the Guajira. Indeed, the fear of drug traffickers' corrupting powers has been a major consideration of both military and civilian chiefs in choosing to keep the military out of drug enforcement. Military officers also have found that opportunities to profit from the drug trade exist even when the military is not charged with drug enforcement responsibilities. Among the police services, the agencies and units specializing in drug enforcement have tended to acquire the most notorious reputations for corruption. The exceptions are a number of elite units with which DEA has worked very closely— about which more below. Drug-related corruption also tends to be more pervasive in outlying areas as opposed to the capitals. Far from the prying eyes of superiors and DEA agents, police and military *comandantes* typically feel far more at ease working out their profitable relationships with drug traffickers. Not surprisingly, many regard a transfer to headquarters in the capital as a serious financial setback.

Finding Someone You Can Trust

In most Latin American countries, DEA agents have a great degree of freedom—much more so than in most of Europe—in choosing which agencies and agents they will work with.[70] This provides some degree of flexibility in their efforts to circumvent corruption, although the degree of corruption is not the only factor the DEA considers in choosing with whom to work. Often DEA agents prefer to work with a corrupt agency or agent instead of an honest one because of significant differences in their abilities. As one DEA agent who had worked throughout much of Latin America said of the Mexican Federal Police: "Sure the *Federales* are corrupt, but when a *Federale* is doing his job, there's no better cop anywhere." In Bolivia, the U.S. embassy pressured the Siles Zuazo

70. A conspicuous exception during the mid-1980s was Panama, where the resident DEA and Customs agents were required to clear virtually everything they did through a high-level official who reported directly to General Noriega.

government to appoint as head of the government's Narcotics Coordination Committee someone they knew to be corrupt because the alternative was an honest but ineffective official. The corrupt appointee, on the other hand, was a smart, ambitious politician who could get things done—even if he would accept and even solicit bribes in some cases. The U.S. embassy hoped that it could work around his corruption while it used him to get the antidrug programs under way. Then, once the programs had become somewhat institutionalized, the embassy would get him fired and replaced by a more honest official—at least that was the plan.

In international law enforcement efforts, there is little substitute for the cultivation of good personal and working relationships based on trust, even with those who are corrupt. With scarce personnel and resources in any country outside the United States, the DEA country team abroad has little choice but to rely on local agents for most investigative tasks. When the agent with whom the DEA agent works is always on the lookout for corrupt sources of money, the DEA agent has little choice but to appeal to one of an agent's three basic instincts: friendship, the pride and professionalism of a fellow police officer, and fear. Although all three, and particularly the first two, are often linked, the first seems to be the most important.

Most DEA agents in Latin America seek to develop special relationships with a few local agents. These relationships are characterized by different forms of trust. Of these agents, a DEA agent might say: "I'd trust him with my life," or "He's one hundred percent honest," or "I know he'll always be straight with me," or "He's a great cop," or "I tell him about everything we're doing here." Many DEA agents consider the development of these relationships the most essential aspect to effective functioning abroad, especially in a corrupt environment. There are a number of reasons for this: the legal, political, and practical constraints on unilateral DEA actions abroad; the discretionary nature of law enforcement, which makes it impossible to operate effectively "by the book"; the vulnerability of the agent to violence or otherwise being set up; the need for a free flow of information; and the need to recognize the variety of obstacles that might render DEA efforts against certain traffickers futile. To some extent, there is also a requisite element of mutuality to such relationships based on both friendship and professional courtesy. As one agent stationed in the Caribbean said: "It's just like in the U.S. If the guy finds out you're holding back information from him, he'll stop helping. He'll 'do' you, tell you to go through formal channels. Then you may as well forget about it. So you try to be up front and sincere."

The fact that a DEA agent trusts a local agent does not necessarily indicate that he never accepts a bribe. But it does tend to mean that the DEA agent can trust him totally on whatever matters they work on together. Indeed, given the corrupt environment and low pay of most police in Latin America, DEA agents typically assume that almost all police—with the exception of a few well-paid, honest high-level officials and an occasional person of exceptional principle in the lower ranks—will find illicit sources of money somehow. What the agents count on, however, is that to the extent the local agent is corrupt, he or she will not let it undermine their relationship. These local agents won't take bribes in a case they are working on with a DEA agent. If the local agent is being paid by a particular trafficker, he or she will find a way to let the DEA agent know there is no point in wasting time pursuing that target. And regardless of whom local agents may be taking money from, they will not let the DEA agent get hurt.

In the rare cases where a DEA agent cultivates a relationship with a local agent who is both intelligent and honest, he often must make special efforts to maintain the relationship. One effort is financial, in the form of supplements to the local agent's salary. Another is more political and requires that the DEA agent develop a good sense for the internal politics of the domestic law enforcement agency. With some agencies, DEA agents can use their influence to lobby for promotions, salary raises, and other perquisites, such as trips to the United States to testify in a case or to attend a DEA training session. In more corrupt organizations, however, too-favorable comments from the DEA can represent, as one DEA agent put it, a "kiss of death" for the local agent because they indicate that the agent is not playing by the de facto rules of his agency. Such an agent can find himself transferred to an exceptionally undesirable position. One DEA agent described the situation in Peru, which is not atypical, as follows:

> Sure there are honest cops, not at the top but among the majors and colonels. But they get screened. One major who had made some big drug cases was sent for two years to a post on the Peruvian border with Brazil—a horrible jungle area. When he

came back to Lima, he wasn't doing narcotics anymore. And he'll probably never get promoted again.

Depending upon the influence of the DEA and the American embassy with the local government, the DEA can offer some protection to those who help them, in effect shielding them from their superiors. But in the long run, the DEA and cooperative agents must hope for a change in the regime or the organization if they are to outlast the superiors they have antagonized.

Since there are so few police whom DEA agents can trust entirely, and since many law enforcement operations involve at least a few agents, the DEA has little choice but to work with corrupt agencies and agents. This is particularly so when agencies do not have overlapping or competing jurisdictions. The modes of operation that DEA agents develop under such conditions vary dramatically, depending upon the degrees of organizational and individual corruption, the susceptibility of the government to pressures from both traffickers and the United States, and the freedom and willingness of agents to increase the extent of their operational activities. Much also may depend upon the relationship between the DEA office in the embassy and the ambassador, whose willingness to back the resident DEA agents when they get into trouble, and to use his or her influence on behalf of DEA objectives, can be crucial to the success of DEA activities.

One of the most successful measures employed by the DEA has been the creation of elite drug enforcement units composed of local police. Resident DEA agents have taken an active hand in creating these units, often training them, handpicking their chiefs and overseeing their hiring, and generally working closely with them in all aspects of their operations. Some of these units have been independent agencies, others part of an established police agency. In some cases, they have been funded in good part by the DEA and the State Department, with all of their training and much of their nonlethal equipment provided at U.S. expense. Because these units typically have represented a threat to established institutions and interests, both the DEA and the U.S. ambassador often have been obliged to use their influence to guard against interference by corrupt officials and others.

During the mid-1980s, the elite units generally fell into two categories: the paramilitary units known as Mobile Rural Patrol Units (UMOPAR) in both Peru and Bolivia, and as Special Action Narcotics Units (SANU) in Colombia (although the formal names tended to change every few years) that were primarily involved in raiding and destroying coca bushes and refineries in the outlying areas; and the elite criminal investigative divisions, usually within the national police agencies, with whom the DEA worked drug cases. In Colombia and, to a lesser extent, Bolivia, the investigative units maintained relatively good reputations for staying mostly clean of drug-related corruption. In Bolivia, the unit was closely supervised by the DEA and sheltered from those seeking to undermine it by the political influence of the ambassador. In Colombia, the unit had the first pick of new police recruits, and its agents were rotated to other units after a while to avoid their developing overly close relations with traffickers. In Argentina, the DEA began to carve out a small narcotics unit in the customs agency. And in other countries, the DEA carved out less-formal groups or divisions, often headed by an intermediate-rank official whom the DEA agents respected for his or her honesty and ability.

The ability of the DEA to maintain such units both free of corruption and operationally effective depends upon the political will of the United States and the host government, as well as upon key personalities within and above those units. The DEA's experience with the creation of Denactie in Ecuador provides a warning. There the DEA office succeeded in having a trusted friend of one its agents, a European-born Ecuadoran, appointed as head of the new agency. After a brief run of success, however, the agency was unable to resist the political pressures that arose when it arrested two traffickers who turned out to be the children of two high-level officials, including one of the most powerful generals in the country. After refusing a bribe and then being threatened, the agency chief resigned. Thereafter, Denactie proved unable to resist not only corrupting influences but also political pressures from higher-ups and a competing drug enforcement division in the national police.

Somewhat different problems plagued the Bolivian UMOPAR unit, known as the Leopards. The first serious problem was apparently unrelated to the drug traffic. Shortly after the 300-member strike force was created, funded, and trained by the United States, U.S. officials were deeply embarrassed when the unit led a coup against the Siles Zuazo government, kidnapping the president in the process.[71] After the U.S. ambassador intervened, the coup was defeated with little violence and

71. Marlise Simons, "Bolivian Plot Embarrasses the U.S.," *New York Times*, July 17, 1984.

UMOPAR's commanders were replaced. A second problem that arose in both Bolivia and Peru stemmed from the military's resentment about the emergence of an independent paramilitary force consisting of police officers. In Bolivia, the military seized a foreign gift of expensive guns intended for the Leopards and confined the unit to its barracks by declaring the Chaparé, where much of the coca is grown, a military zone.[72] In Peru, military operations against the Maoist Shining Path guerrilla movement led to the suspension of antidrug operations in the coca-growing region around Tingo María.[73] Although both UMOPAR units survived and continued to operate, the antagonisms and jealousies of the military and other police units persisted.

A third problem was the underfunding of the elite units by local governments. The DEA and the State Department's Narcotics Assistance Units were unwilling to assume the entire burden for funding the drug enforcement units, believing that foreign governments should share the responsibility. The governments, however, proved far from generous in funding these units. Bolivia's UMOPAR troops, for instance, went for months without receiving their salaries, money for rations, medical supplies, and other essentials.[74] In Ecuador, agents in the Denactie unit were better paid than most other Ecuadoran police but otherwise provided with virtually no money for weapons, transportation, gasoline, or almost anything else. Its chief was obliged to appeal to foreign weapons manufacturers and local citizens for contributions to keep his unit operating.

The general problem of lack of funding contributed to a fourth problem: the tendency for even the elite units to become corrupted as well. In virtually all of the countries where the DEA and the State Department have assisted in the creation of such units, drug-related corruption has extended to the very highest levels of government, up to and including the interior and defense ministers, top military and police officials, and their aides. No amount of diplomatic pressure and liaison has been sufficient to isolate the elite units from the corruption all around them. Ed Merwin, who served as the chief U.S. government adviser to UMOPAR in Bolivia from 1984 to 1986, described in an interview the corruption he had encountered:

72. "Caged 'Leopards' of the Drug War," *New York Times*, Sept. 12, 1984, A16.
73. Marlise Simons, "Peruvian Rebels Halt U.S. Drive Against Cocaine," *New York Times*, Aug. 13, 1984, A1.
74. David Kline, "How to Lose the Coke War," *Atlantic Monthly*, May 1987, 22–27.

Q: You had eight different commanders?

A: Eight. It was mostly because they either got too blatant about accepting bribes or, in the case of the only really good tactical field commander we had, he refused to take a bribe and he got fired by his boss, who had offered him the bribe.

Q: So the drug dealers were buying off [former director of the Narcotics Police] Colonel Guido López while you were there, as far as you know?

A: I was under that impression.

Q: How solid is the information?

A: Very solid.

Q: Can you reveal the source of it?

A: No, not really. . . . The U.S. is a very technological society and we have a lot of capabilities. That's something that the Bolivians never quite understood. Every time they talked on the telephone, we knew about it, you know.

Q: Is [the current director of the Narcotics Police] on the take?

A: I don't even know who he is right now. . . . If this one isn't, his predecessors all were.

Q: All of them?

A: To my knowledge, all of them.

Q: In what ways?

A: New cars. Send your kids to the States to go to school. One of the former Leopard commanders who was dishonest—he was bad when we got him and he got worse—I understand that he now has a really nice ranch. Has a new BMW. Wears very nice clothes. All of the national directors [of the Narcotics Police], very natty dressers. Some of them had amazingly good taste.

Q: And the rest of the enforcement structure in Bolivia . . . how corrupted was that structure?

A: I have to tell you I think that a hundred percent of the Bolivian enforcement structure was corrupted.

Q: Bought by the cocaine traffickers?

A: Yeah.[75]

Yet even given all of these problems, the elite drug enforcement units have been indispensable to the DEA's efforts to immobilize drug traffick-

---

75. Ibid., 24.

ers in Latin America. They often offer the only opportunity to accomplish anything at all. Especially with units that have an esprit de corps, DEA agents have been able to conduct fairly sophisticated operations against major drug traffickers. These operations have been most successful when their objective has been to do no more than seize a trafficker and spirit him or her out of the country as quickly as possible. More typical, however, are the successful operations that have been undermined by the capacity of the drug traffickers to corrupt others in the criminal justice system who have the power to undo what the elite units had accomplished.

The question of rotation of police in and out of drug enforcement units, and in and out of regions where drug trafficking is pervasive, is also a complicated one. On the one hand, rotation is regarded as an important check on the potential for police and other government officials to be corrupted. In Mexico, for instance, where the military was heavily involved in both drug enforcement and drug-related corruption during the mid-1980s, the de la Madrid government responded to U.S. pressures in early 1987 by deploying a unit of 5,000:

> The Mars Task Force, named after the Roman god of war, roams the Sierra Madre in 35-man units, searching for the marijuana and poppy plantings that seem to be omnipresent in the region and destroying them.
>
> Brig. Gen. Adrián Almazán Alarcón, commander of the task force, said his soldiers, volunteers from various army units, undergo a rigorous training and drug education program. They are then sent into the mountains for six months, and food and other supplies are airlifted to them every two weeks.
>
> He said the men are under orders not to go into hamlets or to socialize with the local people; even contact with their own families is discouraged. At the end of their tour of duty in the Mars Task Force, the men are returned to their former units.
>
> General Almazán added that his own assignment is temporary. He said that in a few weeks after having served six months, he and his entire staff will take on new commands elsewhere and that their replacements will also serve for six months.
>
> General Reta [regional commander of the Mexican armed forces] said the strict rotation and discipline policies are intended to prevent troops from "acquiring the habits of the populace."

Other Mexican and foreign sources were more blunt: They said the task force is so organized in hopes of reducing the potential for corruption that has crippled previous drug eradication campaigns.[76]

On the other hand, rotation presents serious problems. It makes impossible the creation of an institutional memory within the drug enforcement units. It undermines the DEA's efforts to create a trained corps of drug enforcement agents in the police force. And it requires resident DEA agents to build new relationships with local police every year. In Argentina, for instance, the resident DEA agent expressed his frustration with the annual rotation of the federal police every December. The operating assumption of the agency was that its agents were not specialists but generalists, who should be exposed to all areas of policing as they are transferred and promoted. Argentine police trained by the DEA in drug enforcement methods were no exception, so that every year the narcotics unit of the Federal Police was transferred practically en masse to other units. The DEA agents were thus obliged to form new relationships every year with a new crop of drug enforcement agents. Occasionally, they were able to request that a particularly skilled agent continue to work with them, but only at the cost of creating tensions and jealousies with other police officials.

In Peru, the DEA country attaché expressed even greater frustration with the annual rotations, known as *cambios*. Police in all of the agencies, including the top officials, were transferred every year with few exceptions. During the mid-1980s, 300 to 400 Peruvian police were being trained by the DEA each year but then being transferred to other units. In an effort to retain trained personnel to work with for a longer period, the DEA office refused in 1984 to send any Peruvian police to the much-desired training course in the United States. It also demanded that agents trained by the DEA remain in the drug enforcement units for at least two years and that the DEA choose which agents would be sent to training programs. In the DEA's view, the *cambio* had not significantly reduced the susceptibility of police to corruption. Rather, most police officials transferred to the drug unit regarded the move as an opportunity to earn more illicit revenue than they could in other units. As the DEA

76. Larry Rohter, "Mexico Battles Drugs Anew, Says War Is Far from Over," *New York Times*, June 15, 1987, A1, A10.

agents saw it, the increased risk of corruption presented by two years in the drug unit, as opposed to one, was outweighed by the benefit of being able to work with better-trained agents and particularly by the opportunity to retain the few good agents who also happened to be more honest and dedicated.

The Ins and Outs of Working Around Corruption

Instilling fear may not secure eager cooperation, but at least it will limit the degree to which joint operations are undermined. As one DEA country attaché stated regarding his approach toward corrupt officials: "I just tell them I don't care how they make their money as long as they don't screw me on drug cases. If they do, I tell them, I'll nail 'em to the wall; I'll get them arrested or kicked out of their job. And I can do it."

The capacity of DEA agents to maintain their credibility and fulfill their threats depends upon the existence of higher-ups in the government, typically in the Ministry of the Interior, to whom the agents can appeal. Although even the higher-ups are not necessarily honest, they may be more sensitive to considerations of professionalism, the "image" of the police force, and the government's international reputation. And if they are not getting paid off by the same trafficker as their underling, or getting a cut, they may have little to lose by complying with the DEA's wishes.

The DEA agent's capacity to threaten directly and to carry through on the threat also is dependent on the rank and connections of the corrupt official. The most vulnerable is obviously the lower-level agent, who can be influenced by any DEA agent. The next is the middle ranking official, on whom the country attaché can either apply direct influence or seek support from his superiors. Less vulnerable are those who occupy high-level positions. Dealing with such officials can become a far more politically sensitive matter. The DEA agent, even the country attaché, is unlikely to try to threaten or intimidate them directly. Rather, the agent or the ambassador may approach a higher-level official (assuming that one is available) to ask that something be done. Finally, there are officials, such as interior ministers and senior generals, whose power is such that they can be regarded as essentially untouchable by the United States. To these may be added the relatives and close friends of the most powerful officials. In such cases, the ambassador must often decide whether seeking the assistance of the head of government is worth the potential political backlash that may result. On occasion, a senior-level official from Washington, such as the DEA administrator, the assistant secretary of state for international narcotics matters, or the chief White House aide on drug matters, may bring up sensitive cases when he or she meets with top officials either in Washington or in the foreign country. As for the occasional country in which the president himself is suspected of being involved in drug trafficking, U.S. government officials must rely on less direct methods of expressing their dissatisfaction—such as leaks to the media.

The susceptibility of the highest-level officials to American pressure in this area is tied closely to their overall dependence on the United States and the leverage the U.S. government has and is willing to exercise. With few exceptions, the U.S. government has rarely accorded the drug control objective such priority that it has been willing to sacrifice all other objectives. This has been true not just of Mexico, where the tremendous importance of other U.S. interests is obvious, but even in relatively small countries such as Bolivia, Paraguay, and the Bahamas, whose leaders were strongly suspected of complicity with drug traffickers. Only in Bolivia was the U.S. government able and willing to exert significant pressure to have the García Meza regime deposed—and even there it required more than a year of overt and covert pressures. Nor have cabinet-level ministers been much more vulnerable to pressures from the U.S. government. U.S. ambassadors in a number of countries have found that even after presenting foreign leaders with indisputable evidence of drug-related corruption by their cabinet ministers, those ministers have remained in office. Foreign leaders have responded with expressions of curiosity, sympathy, and even anger, but rarely by dismissing their political cohorts and almost never by throwing them in jail.

When informed by U.S. officials about drug-related corruption in their governments, foreign leaders often have responded by asking to see the evidence. More often than not, the U.S. officials have declined to provide it, claiming the need to protect their sources. Consider the following incident in 1985, as reported in the *New York Times*:

> The scene was familiar, both to John Gavin, then the U.S. Ambassador to Mexico, and to the Mexican officials he was meeting, including President Miguel de la Madrid.

United States officials had put together information implicating a Mexican Government official in drug trafficking, and . . . Mr. Gavin wanted to tell Mr. de la Madrid about the case, as he had done with others before it.

But this time the case involved the son of the Defense Minister, who directs a significant part of Mexico's drug-eradication program.

Asked how the Mexican officials reacted to his information, Mr. Gavin imitated them with a shrug and a grimace of mock concern.

In that case and several others, Mr. Gavin said with frustration, "they would say to to me: 'Show me the proof. Show me the proof.' "

"But as they knew," he said, "to show the proof would be the death warrant for my sources."[77]

Another source U.S. officials have not felt comfortable revealing, for very different reasons, are the telephone, electronic, and satellite intercepts provided by the CIA and especially the National Security Agency. Indeed, that probably has constituted the principal source of U.S. information on high-level drug-related corruption in foreign governments.[78] Often it is so highly classified that even the DEA is not privy to it. Nor is information derived from such sources usable for purposes of prosecution. The availability of such information has thrust U.S. ambassadors and others in the frustrating position of knowing about drug-related corruption but not being able to provide the evidence to U.S. prosecutors or foreign leaders.

It is only in the smallest countries that the United States can fully throw its weight around, and even there its options are limited. In the Bahamas, for instance, an abundance of information indicated that a number of cabinet ministers, up to and including Prime Minister Sir Lynden O. Pindling, were receiving payoffs from drug traffickers. Direct U.S. pressures met with little response. Only when the information was

77. Joel Brinkley, "Mexico and the Narcotics Traffic: Growing Strain in U.S. Relations," *New York Times*, Oct. 20, 1986, A1.

78. See Kline, "How to Lose the Coke War." Seymour Hersh, in his exposé of Panamanian General Noriega's involvement in drug trafficking, similarly notes that much of the information U.S. government officials gave him was "gleaned from National Security Agency intercepts." See Hersh, "Panama Strongman" (supra n. 47). See also James Bamford, *The Puzzle Palace* (New York: Penguin Books, 1982), 325–336.

leaked to the U.S. media, causing an uproar in the Bahamas and providing ample ammunition for his political opponents, was Pindling pressured to appoint a commission of inquiry to investigate the corruption charges. Pindling survived the uproar, but a number of his ministers were obliged to resign.[79] Three years later, however, as charges of drug-related corruption dominated pre-election campaigning, Pindling indicated that if he won it was "very possible" that he would reappoint one of the ministers who had been obliged to resign.[80]

For DEA agents abroad, high-level corruption in foreign governments is particularly frustrating in part because it directly undermines their basic instinct of going after not just the biggest traffickers but also the people who are most in the public eye, such as celebrities and politicians. Most agents who spend no more than a few years abroad are reluctant to abandon this operating principle and to accept politically motivated constraints on their operations. This can, of course, lead to frictions with State Department officials in the embassy whose institutional and occupational predispositions make them shy away from viewing foreign officials as criminals. High-level corruption in foreign governments in effect imposes specific limits on which cases DEA agents can pursue. In many countries, for instance, they never know when an investigation will lead to the door of an official who is, for all intents and purposes, untouchable.

In some instances, corruption has been so pervasive and institutionalized that the DEA's capacity to function effectively has been almost totally undermined. In the case of the García Meza regime, the U.S. government went public with its protests and withdrew both its ambassador and the DEA presence, although undercover DEA agents continued to operate within Bolivia.[81] Agents within the DEA are divided as to the merits of such a policy. Some believe that it is always better to maintain the agency's presence in a country, no matter how widespread and high-level the corruption, because it at least represents something of a deterrent to drug traffickers and can be useful for gathering intelli-

79. See *Report of the Commission of Inquiry (Appointed to Inquire into the Illegal Use of the Bahamas for the Transshipment of Dangerous Drugs Destined for the United States of America, November 1983–December 1984)* (Bahamas, 1984); and Hiaasen and McGee, "A Nation for Sale" (supra n. 50).

80. Joel Brinkley, "Drugs and Corruption Color Vote in Bahamas," *New York Times*, June 14, 1987, 1.

81. Jonathan Kandell, "The Great Bolivian Cocaine Scam," *Penthouse* 14 (1982), 73–74, 164–170.

gence. Others feel that there is a point at which it is no longer worth the cost of maintaining the overseas office, and where the symbolic value of withdrawing the office and announcing the reason for doing so is ultimately more valuable.

The typical decision in such cases is to maintain the DEA presence provided that a minimum of cooperation is forthcoming and that high-level involvement in the drug trafficking is not too blatant. As one DEA agent who worked in Paraguay and Panama said:

> You can't dwell on drug involvement at the highest levels. There's nothing you can do about it. If you do, you'd just get depressed. What you can do is play on their weaknesses, for instance, their desire for a better international image. And you try to show them why they have an interest in helping you out.

In such situations, DEA agents abroad recognize two limits on their activities. They do not target the most powerful officials, even though agents may gather intelligence on their involvement in drug trafficking. And DEA agencies don't bother trying to get the richer and more powerful traffickers prosecuted within the country. What they can do is secure cooperation in gathering intelligence, arresting drug couriers, seizing vessels and airplanes transporting drugs, seizing shipments of ether and other chemicals used to refine coca into cocaine, collecting evidence for prosecutions in the United States, and getting a few high-level drug traffickers deported or extradited to the United States.

DEA agents who tacitly accept this arrangement are of course open to the criticism of having acquiesced in the most virulent forms of drug trafficking in return for cooperation in getting the "small fry." The criticism is most acute when trafficking in the country is dominated by a few powerful "untouchables" within and outside the government. The DEA's willingness to work with rather than against such people can be perceived as succumbing to the organizational temptation to build up the number of seizures and arrests while allowing the biggest violators to go about their business unimpeded. In fact, such a strategy can be viewed as a boon to the untouchable traffickers because it helps to eliminate competition and increase their control of the traffic at the same time that the corrupt officials are publicly lauded for what limited assistance they offer.[82] The DEA's response is typically threefold: that

82. This argument has similarities to Mark Kleiman's analysis of domestic drug enforce-

pursuing such a limited strategy is better than the alternative, that is, closing the office in the country; that given the constraints imposed by the State Department they in effect have no choice; and that they are just waiting for the time when the "untouchables" become vulnerable.

One price the State Department and, to a lesser extent, the DEA have paid in pursuing such a policy is that they must publicly endorse the drug enforcement efforts of corrupt officials both in Congress and within the countries. For instance, when the leading opposition newspaper in Panama, *La Prensa*, published a report linking General Noriega to a notorious Peruvian drug trafficker, the progovernment newspaper was able to respond the following day with a disclaimer from the resident DEA agent. Following other charges, Panama's embassy sent out copies of a letter from the DEA administrator to Noriega thanking the general for his cooperation against drug traffickers.[83] In Congressional testimony, high-level DEA officials have similarly lauded the token efforts of the Bolivian, Colombian, Peruvian, Jamaican, and other foreign governments, while mostly avoiding any direct criticism of corruption at the highest levels. They have repeatedly cited their frequent drug seizures, courier arrests, and crop destruction forays as evidence of increasing cooperation, portraying such steps in the most optimistic light possible.

At the same time, it would not be entirely accurate to accuse the DEA, and even the State Department, of pursuing a policy of accommodation in every case. In some countries, the DEA has simply acknowledged the futility of getting anything accomplished by a resident agent and closed the country office. That reportedly was the action taken in Paraguay, where the local police had to steer clear of interfering in the drug trafficking activities of the military who run the country. The opposite tack was pursued in the Bahamas for a brief period. There the two resident DEA agents, a Miami-based FBI agent, and the embassy's chargé d'affaires (who was in charge pending the arrival of a new ambassador) pursued an aggressive law enforcement policy that thoroughly antago-

---

ment, in which he argues that "under conditions of increased enforcement, those traffickers most willing and able to use violence and corruption to avoid punishment—the ones who most resemble 'organized crime'—will gain competitive advantages over their rivals." See Mark A. R. Kleiman, "Allocating Federal Drug Enforcement Resources: The Case of Marijuana" (Ph.D. diss., Harvard University, 1985).

83. Copies of the DEA administrators' letters to Noriega are reproduced in *Drugs, Law Enforcement, and Foreign Policy—Panama: Hearings Before the Subcommittee on Terrorism, Narcotics, and International Operations of the Senate Committee on Foreign Relations*, 100th Cong., 2d Sess., Part 2, (Feb. 8–11, 1988), 391–398.

nized the Pindling government. The activism in this case no doubt reflected a number of factors: the personalities of the agents, the presence of a State Department official interested in giving drug enforcement top priority, the vast influence of the United States over the Bahamas, and the fact that the Bahamas were regarded as the principal transit point for cocaine on its way from the Colombian coast to the southern part of the United States.

In the Bahamian case, however, pressures for a more conciliatory policy eventually won out. According to some reports, the DEA decided, or was told, not to reveal evidence it had obtained that strongly suggested drug payoffs had been given to Prime Minister Pindling. When the Bahamian Commission of Inquiry subpoenaed the U.S. agents who had dealt with the Bahamas, the DEA responded by sending the Miami special-agent-in-charge, who played down the tensions that had arisen. Pindling responded by agreeing to substantially increased cooperation, including an extensive U.S.-Bahamian joint interdiction effort code-named Operation BAT and the commencement of negotiations on a treaty to improve cooperation in criminal prosecutions.[84]

In countries (most typically democracies) in which extensive personnel changes occur following elections and changes in the government, the levels of corruption and the DEA's capacity to work with corrupt officials follow a cyclical pattern. The worst corruption typically emerges toward the end of a political administration, be it a civilian or military regime, when officials actively pursue any and all opportunities to enrich themselves before leaving office. One agent discussed the typical evolution of a DEA agent's relationship with a *comandante* of the Mexican Federal Judicial Police during the *sexenio*:

> When a new *Federale* arrives in town, for instance at the beginning of a new presidential term, he has a couple of incentives to cooperate with the DEA. First, he needs DEA most then. Usually his predecessor will leave nothing but an empty filing cabinet—if that. So he must rely on DEA to find out who is who and what is what. Second, he has an interest in making a statement, cracking down hard soon after his arrival to show who's in charge. Thus, during the first year or so, DEA will tend to get excellent cooperation from him.

84. Joel Brinkley, "In Fighting Drug Traffic, Attitude Wins the Aid," *New York Times*, Oct. 7, 1986, A28.

Sometime during the first year, the traffickers will try to cut deals with the commandante to buy protection. So the commandante starts receiving offers: a car, an apartment, a house, women, free dining and travel, and so on. Eventually, he decides which offers he will accept. Then he and the chosen traffickers will reach a special understanding, usually involving a retainer. The traffickers understand that if they do anything stupid, the police will have to act. But there is also an understanding that he will not pursue them too hard. He will stall and find ways to avoid cooperating with other authorities, such as the DEA, who have targeted the traffickers. There are many subtle aspects to this, but eventually the DEA agent will get the message. At that point, there is often little he can do.

During the next three years, the DEA agent will often get great cooperation in any operations not involving one of the commandante's special relationships. It is important to understand that unlike most Latin American police, a Mexican *Federale* is a great cop, when he's being a cop. They can also be pretty rough, but they know how to get the job done.

The last year or two, however, cooperation can really go down hill. Everyone is trying to make a killing before he leaves office. As the end of the term nears, the chances for any cooperation get very slim. By that point, there is almost nothing the DEA can do.

Probably seventy five percent of DEA-*Federale* relationships fit this model. The other twenty five percent don't because of bad relations. The two don't hit it off, the *Federale* is insecure, he's greedy, he's anti-U.S., any number of things.

Is this "corruption"? By U.S. standards, sure—although the U.S. has lots of corruption itself. But in Latin America, that's just the way the system works. Every cop goes along with it or he's out.[85]

One option available to the DEA agent, although it may entail risks to his relationship, involves deceiving the local agent. For instance, the DEA agent may persuade the local agent to arrest a trafficker who, unknown to the local agent, has high-level protection from someone superior to the local agent or outside his or her jurisdiction. When the

85. This is a nonverbatim quote that has been reconstructed from my notes.

heat comes down on the local agent, the DEA agent may blame the informant or create some other excuse. Obviously, the willingness of a DEA agent to utilize such techniques depends upon his or her assessment of the risks to the local agent and the quality of the relationship between the two.

Another tactic to circumvent corrupt officials to which DEA agents often resort is withholding information until the very last minute of an operation. Since most traffickers of any substance have contacts within the police who are paid to provide them with information and warnings of impending raids, the DEA is often frustrated by leaks before major operations. Throughout the 1980s, police raids aimed at arresting such major traffickers as the Bolivian Roberto Suárez Gómez and the Colombians Pablo Escobar Gaviria and Carlos Lehder Rivas arrived at their destinations only to find the houses empty and the refineries shut down. To minimize the potential for such leaks, the DEA agent often tries to withhold the identity of a target of a planned raid until the local agents involved are no longer in a position to notify the target. Typically, a trusted senior local agent will be provided with the information, since often DEA has no choice, but on occasion no one will be told until after the operation has commenced. Only when all the agents are already in the car or helicopter en route to the target will the ultimate destination be revealed to the driver or pilot.

Because most countries in Latin America have at least two agencies that play overlapping roles in drug enforcement, the DEA can often work with the one that is less corrupt. In 1984–85, for instance, the DEA office in Peru had reduced its reliance on the increasingly corrupt Peruvian Investigative Police (PIP) in favor of the somewhat less corrupt Guardia Civil, although it retained its links with a few PIP officers who had proven relatively cooperative. In Chile during the same period, drug-related corruption in the Investigaciones had become so extensive that the DEA office had refused to work with them and was relying solely on the Caribineros. Although some agencies seem to have long-standing biases for or against extensive corruption, variations do occur over time, particularly following large-scale overhauls or the appointment of new officials at the top of the agency. In a few countries, the DEA may work with one agency in one city and another agency elsewhere. For instance, in Ecuador the two agencies involved in drug enforcement, Denactie and Interpol (no relation to the international Interpol), were far from immune from corrupting influences. They also were fierce competitors, with the drug section of Interpol, the national police agency under the Minister of Interior, resentful of the upstart Denactie, which had been created in the Justice Ministry at the DEA's urging with the hope that it would become an elite police force. Each was headed by both honest and corrupt officials during the 1980s, and the DEA's working relationships varied accordingly. At one point, when corruption was within tolerable but troublesome limits in both agencies, the Quito DEA office worked only with Interpol and the Guayaquil office only with Denactie. The split reflected both personal relationships and different degrees of corruption among the local agents.

A DEA agent also can exact some leverage from the fact that most foreign law enforcement agencies are highly dependent upon the DEA for leads and other information. Such access is important for making the arrests and seizures an agency needs to justify itself bureaucratically and politically. It also is useful for less-legitimate purposes, such as maintaining some control over the illicit drug market for corrupt purposes. The DEA's intelligence, used corruptly, can provide opportunities to extort money from drug traffickers and to seize drugs that will be resold rather than turned in as evidence for prosecution. When the local DEA office ostracizes an agency that is deemed too corrupt to work with in preference for working solely with a competitor agency, the former consequently loses a valuable creator of both legitimate and illegitimate opportunities.

One factor that has particularly complicated the DEA's efforts in Latin America has been the intense competition between law enforcement agencies. This has especially been so when the DEA has chosen to work solely with one agency to the exclusion of another. In such cases, relations between the two have become quite nasty, with the more corrupt unit trying to undermine its competitor by arresting its informants and agents, spreading rumors and planting evidence implicating them in drug trafficking, and even threatening, wounding, and killing the competitor agency's informants and agents. From the DEA's perspective, such virulent competition is particularly problematic when the target is an agency with whom it has developed a good working relationship. On the other hand, the DEA has occasionally benefited from such competition when corrupt agents and traffickers under their protection have been arrested by a competitor agency.

Elsewhere, DEA agents have encountered problems where the arresting unit in a police agency has undermined the intelligence unit with which the DEA agents have been working. In both Bolivia and Argentina during the mid-1980s, for instance, the DEA developed very good relationships with select units in the national police that had the capacity to develop and undertake sustained drug investigations. These units, however, were considered primarily as intelligence units and thus lacked the authority to make arrests in drug cases. As an investigation neared completion, the unit was obliged to call in the drug enforcement unit of the national police agency to make the arrest. In both countries, the drug units demonstrated exceptional capacities for corruption. On numerous occasions, DEA agents and the police unit collaborating with them saw cases developed over many months destroyed shortly after arrest because the target had succeeded in bribing the drug unit to eliminate the evidence or otherwise undermine the case. Although the DEA tried to circumvent corruption in the narcotics units and pressured them to cooperate, its efforts met with scant success. The uncorrupted police units, moreover, typically refrained from reporting their fellow officers' corruption because of their loyalty to the national police agency.

Even where the DEA has created or identified a relatively corruption-free agency with which it can work, the ultimate objective of putting the high-level traffickers in jail for any length of time has remained elusive. Any high-level trafficker who is so careless or unfortunate as to get arrested in the first place still has multiple opportunities to gain freedom. He or she can bribe other police agencies who may have become involved, or the *fiscal* (prosecutor), or the judge, or, as a last resort, the prison warden. In the absence of overwhelming political and/or public pressure to punish the trafficker, it is a rare criminal of any means who will not be able to avoid a lengthy stay in jail. In exceptional cases, pressures emanating from the U.S. government and occasionally from the local media and politicians have managed to keep a major trafficker in prison for a longer period of time. As for the officials who are implicated in drug-related corruption and obliged to resign, they almost never spend any time at all in prison. More often than not, they are simply transferred to another district or agency. Some quietly leave office and maintain a low presence until the storm has passed.

The inability of the DEA, and the U.S. government in general, to follow through on cases after the arrest stage has represented the greatest failing of the DEA's transnational efforts to deal with drug-related corruption in Latin America. Often all DEA efforts to circumvent police corruption have come to naught as soon as higher-level judicial officials have entered the picture. As in Europe, the extent of the DEA's contact with *fiscals* usually depends on how closely *fiscals* in the country work with the police. In Mexico, for instance, where police and *fiscals* often work fairly closely, DEA agents have tended to become familiar with them. Elsewhere in Latin America, the relationship has often been far more distant and formal, in good part because of the strong class divisions that separate them. But even where local police and *fiscals* work closely together, DEA agents often are reluctant to pursue cases through the courts for another reason. As one New York City police officer said regarding the frustration of seeing criminals whom one had arrested go free a short while later: "What happens in the courts is somebody else's business—we teach that in the academy—and if cops allowed themselves to be frustrated, they'd be doing nothing in the streets."[86] Many DEA agents abroad find it difficult to alter the police mind-set in which their role is largely over once the criminal is arrested. And even where they do adapt, the options for dealing with corruption among prosecutors and judges are far more limited than they are with respect to the police.

Corruption in the higher reaches of law enforcement systems is particularly debilitating, not just because it renders futile the successful investigations and arrests of uncorrupted police officials but also because it undermines their morale and weakens whatever incentive they may have had to remain honest. When police believe that any wealthy or powerful criminal they arrest will be able to gain freedom by bribing a prosecutor or judge, the incentive to pocket the bribe personally can become both logical and irresistible. When the DEA does succeed in obliging its counterparts to resist drug-related corruption, the chief impact is often to shift the financial benefit from police agent to judge. Only in cases that generate either extensive publicity or U.S. pressure must the judge beware of crossing the DEA.

Obviously, levels of judicial corruption vary widely from country to country, from court to court, and even from year to year. In Ecuador during the mid-1980s, judges reportedly competed, and even bid, to hear drug-related cases because those presented the most lucrative opportunities. In Argentina, the judge who rejected a U.S. extradition request for the former Bolivian interior minister, Luis Arce Gómez, was

---

86. Jane Gross, "In the Trenches of a War Against Drugs," *New York Times*, Jan. 8, 1986, B4.

rumored to have received half a million dollars for his decision. Similarly, corruption of the judiciary has been rampant in Mexico, Bolivia, and Peru, although many honest judges can still be found in those countries. In Colombia, where traffickers are known to shoot before offering a bribe and where the tradition of judicial rectitude is stronger, many judges resist placement in districts where drug cases abound. So great is the drug traffickers' power to intimidate in Colombia that even the Colombian supreme court has caved in to their threats. After upholding the validity of an extradition treaty between the United States and Colombia that authorized the extradition of Colombian citizens, the supreme court saw half its members murdered in a 1985 attack by the guerrilla group M-19 that many believe was organized at the behest of the drug traffickers. During the following two years, another justice was murdered and two chief justices in succession resigned when the threats became too fierce.[87] The result was a persistent effort during the 1980s by a majority of the supreme court to abdicate any responsibility over cases involving the drug traffickers.[88]

The abundant possibilities of securing one's cooperation by corrupt means are supplemented by the significant potential that legitimate legal procedures offer. Most police in less-developed countries are even less likely than their U.S. counterparts to abide by all the procedural requirements of the law, such as obtaining a proper warrant, in carrying out their operations. In all these countries, as in the United States, high-priced and sophisticated legal counsel are available to take every advantage of technicalities and loopholes in the law to protect their client. In some countries, of course, a drug trafficker may still have to pay a judge to go by the book, but the legal route is frequently an important option for the trafficker with the means to pay his or her way through it.

Most DEA efforts abroad seek to immobilize drug traffickers by having them arrested, prosecuted, and incarcerated in Latin American prisons. But the most effective tactics have involved getting major traf-

87. Supreme Court President Fernando Uribe Restrepo resigned in March 1986 after four months in office. His successor, Nemesio Camacho Rodriguez, resigned in January 1987. See *Miami Herald*, Jan. 22, 1987, 4A.

88. In early 1987, the Colombian supreme court invalidated the extradition treaty on a technicality. When the defect was corrected, the court was no longer empowered to rule on extradition requests. In March 1987, it declared unconstitutional the state-of-siege measures enacted by the Barco government that gave the military special powers to judge civilians arrested in drug trafficking cases. See "Colombia Resurrects Extradition Treaty," *Miami Herald*, Dec. 16, 1986, 15A; and *Latin American Monitor—Andean Group*, Apr. 1987, 405.

fickers into U.S. courts by formal extradition procedures, less formal deportation orders, and informal rendition tactics. These are analyzed in detail in Chapter Seven. Suffice it to say at this point that no method of immobilization has stimulated more innovation by U.S. agents than the informal rendition of fugitives from abroad. Both drug traffickers and law enforcers know that once a drug trafficker is on a plane to the United States the possibilities of buying or intimidating one's way to freedom are nil.

Conclusion

Corruption is not the only obstacle to immobilizing major drug traffickers in Latin America and the Caribbean; indeed, some DEA agents would say that the underfinancing and poor training of police throughout Latin America constitute equally severe obstacles. Nor is corruption solely or even principally responsible for the continuing flow of illicit drugs to the United States and Europe. Even if corruption in Latin America and the Caribbean were far less severe, drug traffickers would continue to thrive just as they do in Europe and the United States. Nonetheless, drug-related corruption has substantially hindered the DEA's efforts to immobilize major drug traffickers in Latin America and the Caribbean.

With no more than a hundred agents stationed throughout all of Latin America and the Caribbean, and entirely bereft of any extraterritorial police powers, the DEA has been hard-pressed in pursuing its objective. Yet as we have seen, DEA agents have devised means of working above and around the corruption that infests criminal justice agencies throughout the region. They have pleaded, cajoled, threatened, and tricked their local counterparts into cooperating with them. Relying both on the diplomatic leverage exercised by the U.S. ambassador, and on the transnational police subculture that unites police the world over, DEA agents have succeeded in immobilizing many top traffickers who thought they had purchased their safety. Indeed, by 1990 virtually every one of the most notorious drug traffickers of the previous decade was either dead or in prison. In many cases, DEA agents have gone well beyond the privileges accorded them as representatives of a foreign police agency. Their diplomatic efforts, if their activities in the region can be called

that, have most closely resembled those of the CIA and various nongovernmental transnational organizations in their pursuit of a common
mission around the world and in their persistent but discreet disregard
of sovereign prerogatives.

The intensity and pervasiveness of drug-related corruption can be
explained in many ways: as a consequence of the creation and failure of
the global drug prohibition regime; as an extension and magnification
of preexisting patterns and traditions of governmental behavior throughout Latin America and the Caribbean; as a natural response of economically impoverished peoples and regions to an immensely lucrative
economic opportunity; as a function of "overcriminalization"; and as a
consequence of what the criminologist Donald Cressey called "multiple
moralities."[89] Unlike other obstacles that hinder U.S. international law
enforcement efforts in this region and elsewhere, the frictions generated
by drug-related corruption are likely to prove far more resilient. Governments can change their laws to better accord with U.S. preferences and
modi operandi, and foreign law enforcement agencies can adapt U.S.
approaches to criminal investigation, but there is little the U.S. government can do to undermine the temptations presented by drug trafficker
bribes and threats. Among all the obstacles to the long-term harmonization of criminal justice systems, governmental corruption represents the
most resilient.

It thus is difficult to foresee an end to the drug-related corruption that
pervades Latin American and Caribbean governments so long as the
international market for marijuana, cocaine, and heroin remain both
lucrative and illegal. In a few cases, such as Mexico in the mid-1970s,
successful drug eradication programs succeeded in destroying most of
the illicit crops for a number of years, thereby limiting the availability of
corrupting opportunities. But within a few years, the same officials
responsible for the successful programs succumbed to the temptations
proffered by the drug traffickers. Throughout virtually all of Latin
America and the Caribbean, no government has succeeded in devising a
means of institutionalizing checks against corruption. Resources are
lacking to pay government employees enough so that they will not feel
dependent upon accepting bribes to maintain a decent standard of living.
Governmental elites are often too few in number for officials to deal

89. Donald R. Cressey, "Why Managers Engage in Fraud," in *White Collar Crime: Hearings
Before the Senate Committee on the Judiciary*, 99th Cong., 2d Sess. (1986), 112–140.

with corruption by arresting one another. Legitimate economic opportunities are typically too limited to condemn with conviction those who seize the opportunity to profit from the drug traffic. And black markets are too pervasive, and often too essential to local economies, to contemplate any radical change in popular perceptions of legitimate versus illegitimate economic activity. The cumulative impact of U.S. economic assistance programs, witness protection programs, and other aid to Latin American and Caribbean criminal justice agencies pales beside the power of the incentives associated with drug-related corruption.

Most DEA agents who have spent time in Latin America and the Caribbean recognize the contextual limitations on what they can accomplish. But in many respects that does not matter, for their task is relatively straightforward: to immobilize drug traffickers. The fact that all their efforts have almost entirely failed to curtail the flow of illicit drugs to the United States pales beside the fact that they have essentially succeeded in their basic objective. The drug-related corruption that they encounter each day is regarded not as something to be reformed but as a challenge to be circumvented, circumscribed, transcended and occasionally used to their advantage. The process of dealing with it day in and day out is exceptionally frustrating. Some agents are overcome with a profound sense of cynicism, and others occasionally ponder the existentialist question of what it's all about anyway. But for most, the chase is the challenge—one in which they eventually prevail.

Chapter Six

International Evidence-Gathering

The Challenges

Obtaining evidence from abroad—in a form admissible in American judicial proceedings—is as essential to the success of criminal prosecutions as collecting intelligence and obtaining the offender. It is also the most dependent upon legal formalities and affords the least latitude for the sorts of informal measures and understandings upon which police normally rely in their international dealings. The obstacles are varied. Differences between national law enforcement systems—in particular, between the adversarial, common law system of the United States and the inquisitorial, civil law system found in much of Europe and Latin America—generate confusions, misunderstandings, and tensions that even the most cooperatively inclined of officials find difficult to circumvent. Foreign courts are unfamiliar with the constitutional safeguards and evidentiary rules of U.S. law, and U.S. courts regard foreign legal processes as equally strange. Prosecutors and judges may lack the legal authority to obtain evidence on behalf of foreign judicial proceedings. Local laws may bar foreign law enforcement authorities from engaging in even the most limited judicial tasks. Justice ministries may lack any officials charged with oversight of international requests for evidence. Long-standing laws and traditions may require elaborate procedures for the transnational collection and transmission of evidence. And, most seriously, financial and corporate secrecy laws as well as blocking statutes designed specifically to limit the availability of information to inquiring parties may impede prosecutors' efforts to secure essential documents.

The demands of American prosecutors for evidence located abroad have risen dramatically since the 1960s. The reasons are varied. Traditional transnational criminal activities such as drug trafficking, terrorism, tax evasion, and assorted frauds have proliferated. Congress has both criminalized and asserted extraterritorial jurisdiction over an ever-widening array of transnational activities and granted U.S. law enforcement agencies greater extraterritorial powers. The internationalization of the securities and commodities markets has required the Securities and Exchange Commission (SEC) and the Commodity Futures Trading Commission (CFTC) to expand the scope of their regulatory efforts overseas. And all of the federal law enforcement agencies have become far more aggressive in targeting, investigating, and prosecuting transnational activities. Where once the need to collect bank or corporate records from overseas, or to locate and interview witnesses abroad, was sufficient to deter an investigator or prosecutor from pursuing an investigation or prosecution, today law enforcement authorities have a growing number of increasingly effective mechanisms to secure such evidence.

The pace of developments in the area of international evidence-gathering is such that any analysis becomes rapidly dated. New treaties and other international agreements are being negotiated by the Justice Department, the Treasury Department, the SEC, and the CFTC each year. New legislation is being enacted by Congress in one session after another. Growing numbers of federal and even state prosecutors are looking and traveling abroad in search of evidence, and the more innovative among them are devising new and increasingly effective means of obtaining that evidence. Federal courts are deciding dozens of relevant cases annually, and generally validating the prosecutors' innovations. New offices charged with responsibility for international law enforcement are popping up throughout the federal law enforcement bureaucracy. Foreign states are similarly enacting new laws and regulations—sometimes of their own initiative, sometimes in response to U.S. examples, actions and pressures—with great import for U.S. evidence-gathering efforts. And international meetings, conventions, and organizations are introducing resolutions, promoting and adopting model legislation, and otherwise attempting to facilitate international cooperation in the transmission of evidence.

All of these efforts can be seen as part and parcel of a global campaign—inspired originally by the United States but increasingly involving multinational initiatives—to better immobilize transnational criminals by obtaining the evidence required not just to indict and convict them in courts of law but also to freeze, seize, and forfeit their assets. As with other domains of international law enforcement, the broader story is one of trying both to transcend the basic obstacles created by notions of national sovereignty and to alleviate the frictions that occur when different law enforcement systems are obliged to interact; one in which the United States has made modest accommodations to foreign legal systems, and foreign authorities have made much greater accommodations to U.S. demands; one in which cooperative efforts have mixed with more coercive inducements; and one involving not just bilateral treaties and other arrangements but also unilateral measures and multilateral undertakings. On one level, the mutual legal assistance treaty (MLAT) negotiations analyzed below can be seen as quite fascinating exercises in comparative law in which U.S. and foreign government negotiators struggled to reconcile different legal systems and thereby reduce the frictions that had impeded international evidence-gathering efforts. On another level, however, many of the MLATs must be understood in the context of the bilateral conflicts generated by U.S. efforts to obtain evidence unilaterally, efforts designed both to obtain evidence in individual investigations and prosecutions and to pressure foreign governments more generally to be more accommodating to U.S. law enforcement needs. Indeed, the principal incentive for many foreign governments to negotiate MLATs with the United States was, and remains, the desire to curtail the resort by U.S. prosecutors, police agents, and courts to unilateral, extraterritorial means of collecting evidence from abroad. (See Appendix E for a list of MLATs signed by the United States between 1973 and 1992.)

The principal targets of U.S. extraterritorial evidence-gathering efforts have been multinational banks and other corporations. The increasing power, resources, and scope of multinational corporations during the twentieth century has been perceived variously as a challenge to the sovereign powers of all states and as a development favoring the interests of more-powerful states at the expense of less-powerful states.[1] The history of international law enforcement in recent decades lends strong support to the latter view. Multinational corporations have provided, most notably for the United States, a vicarious means of extending the state's sovereign powers extraterritorially.[2] Not just American multinational corporations, but foreign ones as well, have found that their affiliates and other contacts within the United States render all their operations outside the United States susceptible to court orders and sanctions imposed by U.S. courts as well as other requirements of U.S. law. Foreign companies have found themselves subject to American antitrust laws and export control laws; foreign banks have been ordered to hand over to U.S. criminal justice authorities financial documents stored in branches outside the United States, often in the face of financial secrecy laws and blocking statutes to the contrary. These extraterritorial extensions of jurisdiction have not been available to most states; the United States' capacity to make the most of these options has reflected not just the fact that almost all major multinational firms maintain affiliates and other contacts in the United States, but also the fact that those contacts are sufficiently important that foreign firms are willing to tolerate the extraterritorial assertions of the United States as a necessary cost of doing business. The broader point, however, is that even as the proliferation of transnational interactions has challenged the state's control of its territory, the same process has also provided opportunities for expanding its jurisdictional reach.

This chapter provides abundant evidence of the *harmonization* of criminal justice systems along lines suggested and dictated by the United States. The MLATs, with their emphasis on reconciling the needs,

1. Raymond Vernon, *Sovereignty at Bay* (New York: Basic Books, 1971).

2. This point is touched upon in Richard Cooper, "Economic Interdependence and Foreign Policy in the Seventies," *World Politics* 24 (1972), 169–170; and in Louis T. Wells Jr., "The Multinational Business Enterprise," in Robert O. Keohane and Joseph S. Nye Jr., eds., *Transnational Relations and World Politics* (Cambridge, Mass.: Harvard University Press, 1972), 111. It is consistent, moreover, with the basic thrust of Robert Gilpin's thesis that "the multinational corporation is actually a stimulant to the further extension of state power in the economic realm." See Robert Gilpin, "The Politics of Transnational Economic Relations," in ibid., 69.

procedures, and customs of different legal systems, epitomize the notion of *accommodation*. The promotion of model legislation and the enactment of legislation by many governments criminalizing activities such as insider trading and money laundering provide ample evidence of the *homogenization* of criminal norms. The proliferation of transgovernmental links among prosecutors and Justice Ministry officials of different nations, as well as the creation of governmental offices specializing in international law enforcement matters, exemplifies the *regularization* of international law enforcement. My principal objective in this chapter is to explain how U.S. law enforcement officials have accomplished this harmonization. But the analysis also advances two of the principal arguments of this book: that the U.S. "war on drugs" has provided the crucial impetuses for many of the most substantial developments in the internationalization of U.S. criminal law enforcement since the late 1960s, and that criminal justice systems throughout much of the world are evolving toward a more harmonious network of relationships strongly influenced by U.S. pressures, models, and examples.

I should, in all fairness, include a word of warning to the reader at this point. This chapter, to a greater extent than any other, addresses fairly technical issues in U.S. and foreign laws. Unlike most law review articles, it focuses its attentions on the perceptions and behavior of government officials involved in efforts to collect evidence abroad and to reduce the tensions that have hampered such efforts in the past. More attention is also devoted to the political and criminal justice contexts of these efforts. But it is impossible to explain the internationalization of evidence-gathering without reference to U.S. and foreign statutes and legal procedures. New federal statutes and legal innovations devised by prosecutors and approved by U.S. courts have significantly enhanced the capacity of prosecutors to obtain evidence from abroad. At the same time, many of the constraints that continue to complicate international evidence-gathering efforts and to hinder the admissibility in U.S. courts of the evidence that is obtained stem from the strictures imposed by the U.S. Constitution and the Federal Rules of Evidence. In short, the internationalization of law enforcement cannot be fully understood without some reference to the legal and somewhat technical issues addressed in this chapter.[3]

3. Readers interested in a *more* technical and comprehensive treatment of these issues should consult Michael Abbell and Bruno A. Ristau, *International Judicial Assistance* (Washington, D.C.: International Law Institute, 1990), vol. 3.

The analogy to interstate law enforcement cooperation within the United States and other federally constituted nations is useful for understanding both the objectives and the limitations of evidence-gathering efforts across borders. The interstate compacts and uniform acts to which most American states subscribe share much in common with the more multilateral efforts of national governments to facilitate international cooperation in criminal justice matters. Indeed, domestic uniform acts have provided models for the U.S. negotiators of international law enforcement treaties, and the treaties have been described as the natural extensions of those acts. Similarly, judicial decisions regarding the cross-border collection of evidence within the United States have provided legal analogues for addressing issues of international evidence gathering. We will see in the next chapter that the same analogies have also influenced the development of law and practice regarding the rendition of fugitives. There are, of course, substantial limitations to the federalist analogy. Absent is any supranational entity akin to the federal government. National legal systems are far more heterogeneous than the legal systems of the American states, with the partial exception of Louisiana's. And differences in languages and customs are far more pronounced in the international realm. But the fundamental objectives and challenges of collecting evidence from "foreign" jurisdictions do not differ substantially from the federal to the international system.

Letters Rogatory:
The Origins of International Evidence-Gathering

Both the MLAT negotiations and many of the other initiatives intended to facilitate the collection of evidence from abroad can be understood as responses to the inadequacy of pre-existing methods. The principal means of requesting evidence from foreign authorities even today is by "letters rogatory"—written requests from a court in one state to a foreign court requesting the provision of evidence or some other form of assistance needed in a judicial proceeding. Law enforcement officials typically resort to letters rogatory when Interpol and other international police channels are unable to produce the requested evidence, typically because a court's authority is required to obtain the evidence. Governments vary dramatically, however, in the degree to which they require that requests for law enforcement assistance be transmitted by letters rogatory. Where some are willing, for instance, to obtain documents, conduct an interview, identify an unlisted telephone number, or undertake a joint undercover operation in response to a request forwarded via Interpol or a police liaison, others require that the request be transmitted by letter rogatory. Many U.S. requests, particularly those directed to financial secrecy jurisdictions such as Switzerland, Luxembourg, Liechtenstein, and the Caribbean islands, seek bank documents; some are for corporate documents, such as shipping bills; some request that a foreign court compel a suspect or witness to provide testimony; others seek permission for a U.S. law enforcement official or defense attorney to interview a suspect or witness, accompany a local official on such a requested interview, or attend and participate in a foreign judicial proceeding. During the 1980s, the Justice Department began to use letters rogatory to request that foreign governments freeze the assets of suspected criminals.

Letters rogatory remain the principal means of obtaining evidence from abroad and can be relatively effective when dealing with foreign authorities who are familiar with both the letters rogatory process and U.S. evidentiary requirements. They have proven ill-suited, however, to the increasingly complex and voluminous needs of modern international law enforcement efforts.[4] MLATs, and the legislation typically required to implement them, were intended and designed to remedy many of the limitations of letters rogatory. Whereas letters rogatory are executed solely as a matter of comity, MLATs obligate the requested country to provide evidence and other forms of assistance. Whereas letters rogatory are typically transmitted circuitously, passing through assorted layers of justice ministries and diplomatic channels on their way from one court to another, MLAT requests bypass both U.S. courts and all diplomatic channels, thereby drastically shortening the time required to secure foreign assistance. Unlike letters rogatory, MLATs can establish a procedural framework for ensuring that the evidence obtained will be admissible in U.S. courts; they also can require that requests under the treaty, as well as the responses to those requests, be kept confidential. And, most important, MLATs (and the accompanying implementing legislation) provide a powerful means of penetrating the financial secrecy laws that have so often frustrated U.S. criminal investigators.[5]

4. Harry Leroy Jones, "International Judicial Assistance: Procedural Chaos and a Program for Reform," *Yale Law Journal* 62 (1953), 515–562, esp. 554.
5. See "Prepared Statement of Mark M. Richard," in U.S. Senate, *Mutual Legal Assis-*

In 1927, fifty years before the first MLAT negotiated by the United States, with Switzerland, went into force, a Committee of Experts for the Progressive Codification of International Law, which had been appointed by the Assembly of the League of Nations, asked member nations to consider whether it was possible "to establish by means of general convention provisions concerning the communication of judicial and extra-judicial acts in penal matters and letters rogatory in penal matters."[6] Eighteen countries responded favorably to the codification proposal; Great Britain and four other members of the Commonwealth expressed their preference for bilateral agreements rather than a general convention, and one—the United States—dissented without offering any alternative.[7] In its view, no agreement was possible in light of state jurisdiction over criminal procedure and the restraints imposed by the Sixth Amendment of the U.S. Constitution.[8] The rare foreign judicial authority persistent enough to seek evidence in the United States by means of letter rogatory was more than likely to find the request ignored or rejected. Although Congress had enacted legislation in 1855 authorizing U.S. courts to execute foreign letters rogatory, the statute was inadvertently but severely restricted thereafter by later legislation and by the reluctance of U.S. courts to facilitate foreign judicial requests.[9] Foreign requests were more likely to receive a favorable response in many state courts than in federal court.

In the aftermath of World War II, however, the new American consciousness of the global responsibilities of the United States began to penetrate the domain of international law enforcement. The process was facilitated by the increasing homogenization of state criminal procedures as the U.S. Supreme Court incorporated much of the Bill of Rights into the Fourteenth Amendment and as interstate compacts and uniform criminal codes proliferated. In 1948, Congress responded to the new

---

tance Treaty Concerning the Cayman Islands, 101st Cong., 1st Sess., Exec. Rept. No. 101-8 (1989), 95–96.

6. Jones, "International Judicial Assistance," 554.

7. Ibid., 557.

8. Ibid., 554, 557.

9. Walter B. Stahr, "Discovery Under 28 U.S.C. 1782 for Foreign and International Proceedings," Virginia Journal of International Law 30 (1990), 597–641. The 1855 legislation can be found at 10 Stat. 630 (1855). Examples of a U.S. court's belief that it was not empowered to execute a letter rogatory in a criminal case include In re Letters Rogatory from Examining Magistrate of Tribunal of Versailles, 26 F.Supp. 852 (D.Md. 1939), and In re Letters Rogatory of Republic of Colombia, 4 F.Supp. 165 (S.D.N.Y. 1933).

conditions, albeit somewhat meagerly, with legislation (thereafter referred to as Section 1782) authorizing an expansion of American judicial assistance to foreign states.[10] Many of the limitations of this legislation—including the failure to provide for compulsory process in obtaining evidence, and the requirements that the foreign proceeding be before a court and that only U.S. procedure be permitted in the taking of testimony—were ameliorated in 1964 when Congress enacted a substantially revised version of Section 1782.[11] Even so, U.S. courts continued to interpret the amendments—which had substituted the word "tribunal" for "court" in order to broaden the availability of U.S. assistance to include administrative and quasi-judicial proceedings[12]—so narrowly as to bar assistance to foreign law enforcement authorities not recognizable as "tribunals" in the eyes of the court.[13] In the absence of legal challenges by defendants, however, U.S. authorities were more often than not willing to extend foreign judicial authorities fairly broad latitude in collecting evidence in the United States.

When U.S. prosecutors and police looked abroad for evidence, they encountered many of the same types of obstacles, as well as even higher

10. Act of June 25, 1948, ch. 646, 62 Stat. 949 (codified at 28 U.S.C. Sec. 1782 (1976); amended to encompass criminal proceedings as well, in Act of May 24, 1949, ch. 139, 63 Stat. 103). See also *In re Letter Rogatory from the Justice Court, Dist. of Montreal, Canada*, 523 F.2d 562, 564–565 (6th Cir. 1975), the appendix of which contains the texts of the various historical congressional acts relating to letters rogatory from abroad. See too the discussion of these laws in Jones, "International Judicial Assistance" (supra n. 4), 541–542; and in R. Doak Bishop, "International Litigation in Texas: Obtaining Evidence in Foreign Countries," *Houston Law Review* 19 (1982), 361–426, esp. 416.

11. Brian Eric Bomstein and Julie M. Levitt, "Much Ado About 1782: A Look at Recent Problems with Discovery in the United States for Use in Foreign Litigation Under 28 U.S.C. 1782," *Inter-American Law Review* 20 (1989), 429–472; and Stahr, "Discovery Under 28 U.S.C. 1782" (supra n. 9), 604.

12. H.R. Rept. 1052, 88th Cong., 1st Sess. 9 (1963); S. Rept. 1580, 88th Cong., 2d Sess. 1, reprinted in 1964 U.S. Code Cong. & Ad. News 3782, 3788. See also Bruce I. McDaniel, "What Is Foreign Tribunal Within 28 U.S.C. Section 1782 (as amended in 1964) . . . ," *ALR Fed.* 46 (1980), 956–960; Morris H. Deutsch, "Judicial Assistance: Obtaining Evidence in the United States, Under 28 U.S.C. Section 1782, for Use in a Foreign or International Tribunal," *Boston College International and Comparative Law Review* 5 (1982), 175–193; Comment, "International Judicial Assistance," *Texas International Law Journal* 12 (1977), 106; Comment, "International Judicial Assistance," *Texas International Law Journal* 9 (1974), 108.

13. *In re Letters Rogatory Issued by the Director of Inspection of the Government of India*, 385 F.2d 1017 (2d Cir. 1967); *In re Letters of Request to Examine Witnesses from the Court of Queen's Bench for Manitoba, Canada*, 59 F.R.D. 625 (N.D. Cal. 1973), aff'd per curiam, 488 F.2d 511 (9th Cir. 1973); and, rejecting a request from Colombia, *Fonseca v. Blumenthal*, 620 F.2d 322 (2d Cir. 1980). See the discussion in "Much Ado About 1782," 437–444.

levels of sensitivity to the performance of U.S. judicial functions on foreign territory. Even more problematic were inadequacies in U.S. law regarding collection of evidence from abroad. Not until 1926, in the aftermath of the Teapot Dome scandal, did Congress pass legislation on the subject.[14] The Walsh Act provided federal courts with the authority to issue letters rogatory to foreign courts requesting them to compel U.S. citizens and domiciliaries to "appear and testify" before them, and to issue subpoenas to compel U.S. citizens or domiciliaries in foreign countries to appear in the United States as witnesses in federal criminal trials.[15] In 1936, Congress enacted legislation providing for the admissibility of foreign business records in federal criminal trials.[16] Neither of these statutes, however, was all that useful to federal prosecutors. Few foreign laws obliged their courts to employ their powers on behalf of foreign law enforcement authorities, much less to accommodate foreign judicial procedures. Foreign courts were prone to reject requests emanating from grand juries and various regulatory agencies that had no counterparts in their own countries. Some were reluctant to obtain any evidence for foreign criminal proceedings or to permit U.S. officials any leeway in collecting evidence. As in the United States, justice ministries abroad lacked any officials specifically charged with responding to letters rogatory. U.S. prosecutors seeking evidence from abroad consequently found themselves in much the same situation as American attorneys seeking evidence in private suits, obliged to hire foreign counsel to pursue their requests. Even when foreign courts were willing to provide evidence, the chances were good that it would be provided in a form inadmissible in U.S. courts. Civil law judges typically did not take kindly to altering their customary procedures to accommodate U.S. constitutional and evidentiary needs, such as the right of confrontation by defendants and the demand for verbatim transcripts of testimony. U.S. prosecutors mostly had little choice but to rely on the good will and flexibility of foreign judges. The only other alternative involved persuading individuals living abroad to come to the United States to testify in court.[17] More often than not, the mere prospect of trying to collect

---

14. See Abbell and Ristau, *International Judicial Assistance* (supra n. 3), 3:14.

15. Act of July 3, 1926, Ch. 762, Sec. 1, 44 Stat. 835 (1926). See Abbell and Ristau, *International Judicial Assistance*, 3:15, 145–147.

16. Act of June 20, 1936, Ch. 640, Sec. 2–8, 49 Stat. 1561. See Abbell and Ristau, *International Judicial Assistance*, 3:15.

17. The memoirs and biographies of U.S. law enforcement officials active in international law enforcement matters consistently refer to such suasive efforts. See Don Wilkie, as told to

evidence from a foreign state was sufficient to deter an American prosecutor from even pursuing a case in which crucial evidence could only be found abroad.

Section 1782 and its subsequent amendments did, however, represent part of a broader movement during the 1960s and 1970s to reconcile the differences between legal systems by standardizing or equating judicial procedures. These included the negotiation of three Hague conventions to which the United States became a party: the convention abolishing the requirement of legalization for foreign public documents;[18] the convention on the service abroad of judicial and extra-judicial documents in civil or commercial matters;[19] and the convention on the taking of evidence abroad in civil or commercial matters[20]—all of which, however, largely excluded criminal matters from their consideration. The movement also included the negotiation between 1976 and 1979 of approximately twenty-four "executive agreements" for international judicial assistance following the revelations that American companies (most notably the airplane manufacturers, Boeing, Lockheed, and McDonnell-Douglas) had paid bribes to foreign officials.[21] The hectic negotiation of these agreements set the stage to some degree for the negotiation of the far broader mutual legal assistance treaties. Other precedents for international cooperation against crime were being encouraged by the United States' promotion of multilateral treaties against terrorism[22] and

---

Mark Lee Luther, *American Secret Service Agent* (New York: Frederick A. Stokes Co., 1934), 202–203; Garland Roark, *The Coin of Contraband* (Garden City, N.Y.: Doubleday, 1964), 364; William H. Theobald, *Defrauding the Government* (New York: Myrtle Publishing Co., 1908), 172.

18. Done at the Hague, Oct. 5, 1961; entered into force for the U.S. Oct. 15, 1981; TIAS 10072; 527 UNTS 189.

19. Done at the Hague, Nov. 15, 1965; entered into force for the U.S. Feb. 10, 1969; 20 UST 361; TIAS 6638; 658 UNTS 163.

20. Done at the Hague, Mar. 18, 1970; entered into force for the U.S. Oct. 7, 1972; 23 UST 2555; TIAS 7444. See Sharon DeVine and Christine M. Olsen, "Taking Evidence Outside of the United States," *Boston University Law Review* 55 (1975), 368–386.

21. These treaties are listed and discussed in an article by the former director of the Justice Department's Office of Foreign Litigation, Bruno Ristau, "International Cooperation in Penal Matters: The 'Lockheed Agreements,' " in *Transnational Aspects of Criminal Procedure*, 1983 Michigan Yearbook of International Legal Studies (New York: Clark Boardman, 1983), 85–104.

22. Convention to Prevent and Punish the Acts of Terrorism Taking the Form of Crimes Against Persons and Related Extortion That Are of International Assistance (done at Washington Feb. 2, 1971; entered into force for the United States Oct. 20, 1976; 27 UST 3949; TIAS 8413). Also, Convention on the Prevention and Punishment of Crimes Against Internationally

hijacking.[23] Also important were amendments to Rule 15 of the Federal Rules of Criminal Procedure permitting federal prosecutors to take depositions from witnesses who refused or were unable to appear in court. The first amendment, in 1970, was limited to organized crime cases.[24] The second, in 1975, extended the new prosecutorial power to all federal criminal trials, thereby eliminating a substantial obstacle to federal prosecutions dependent upon evidence from abroad.[25]

Breaking the Ice the Hard Way: Treaty with Switzerland

By the late 1960s, U.S. law enforcement officials were increasingly exasperated by the widening gap between criminals' abilities to hide transactions and assets abroad and their own abilities to detect and investigate what was going on. Organized crime, it was feared, was growing ever richer and more powerful, at least in part because of the protection afforded by foreign financial secrecy jurisdictions such as Switzerland.[26] But efforts by U.S. criminal investigators to obtain evidence from these jurisdictions were blocked time and time again by the refusal of foreign banks and government officials to cooperate with American criminal investigations.

During 1967–68, officials in the State, Justice, and Treasury Departments, and the Securities and Exchange Commission, agreed to seek an accord with the Swiss. This was not the first attempt to persuade the Swiss to negotiate a mutual legal assistance treaty; previous efforts had failed in 1922, 1925, and 1938, and again in 1963.[27] The two govern-

---

Protected Persons Including Diplomatic Agents (done at New York Dec. 14, 1973; entered into force for the U.S. Feb. 20, 1977; 28 UST 1975; TIAS 8532).

23. The three antihijacking treaties, which entered into force for the U.S. between 1969 and 1973, are (1) at 20 UST 2941; TIAS 6768; 704 UNTS 219; (2) at 22 UST 1641; TIAS 7192; and (3) at 24 UST 564; TIAS 7570.

24. Pub. L. 91-452, Title VI, Sec. 601, 84 Stat. 934 (1970), 18 U.S.C. 3503.

25. See Abbell and Ristau, *International Judicial Assistance*, 3:15. See also Michael J. Burke, "*United States v. Salim*: A Harbinger for Federal Prosecutions Using Depositions Taken Abroad," *Catholic University Law Review* 39 (1990), 895–943.

26. See Nicholas Faith, *Safety in Numbers: The Mysterious World of Swiss Banking* (New York: Viking Press, 1982).

27. Lionel Frei and Stefan Treschel, "Origins and Applications of the United States–Switzerland Treaty on Mutual Assistance in Criminal Matters," *Harvard International Law Journal* 31 (1990), 77–97, esp. 78–79.

ments had also struggled since World War II over the efforts of the United States and other Allied powers to uncover Nazi assets hidden in Swiss banks, as well as the efforts of German companies, in particular a holding company associated with I. G. Farben's international operations, Interhandel, to recover its seized assets from the U.S. government.[28] By the late 1960s, however, the U.S. government was far more concerned with the Mafia's uses of Swiss banks than the Nazis' uses.

Although other financial secrecy jurisdictions were known to accommodate organized criminals, Switzerland was chosen as the first subject of negotiations for a number of reasons. First, U.S. law enforcement officials perceived Switzerland as the toughest case and believed that an agreement with Swiss authorities would provide an especially effective precedent. Second, the Swiss represented a significant problem in two respects: they had erected substantial legal barriers against supplying information to foreign investigators, and their bank and government officials, unlike those in many other bank secrecy jurisdictions, were professional and generally uncorruptible, thus narrowing the informal and illegal options otherwise often available to American investigators in other financial secrecy jurisdictions.[29] Third, the Americans perceived in the Swiss certain advantages that would facilitate an agreement. While Swiss laws strictly limited the divulsion of information to foreigners, they nonetheless allowed for broad disclosure to Swiss investigators. This differed from the laws in some other financial secrecy jurisdictions, such as Panama, which prohibited disclosure even to their own judicial officials. The Americans reasoned that if Swiss law could be changed to allow Swiss judicial authorities to collect evidence at the request of the United States, then many of the previous obstacles could be overcome. The Americans also counted on the strong sense of law and order for which the Swiss had earned a reputation. The Swiss were known to have

28. See Elliot A. Stultz, "Swiss Bank Secrecy and United States Efforts to Obtain Information from Swiss Banks," *Vanderbilt Journal of Transnational Law* 21 (1988), 63–125, esp. 81–91; see also Faith, *Safety in Numbers*, chaps. 2 and 4.

29. The Swiss were not entirely immune to illicit approaches. During the mid-1970s, French customs officials investigating exchange control violations succeeded in buying a list of French clients of the Swiss bank corporation from an informant, in violation of Swiss law. However, a similar effort in 1980 backfired when two French customs officials were arrested in Basel, prosecuted for economic espionage, and convicted. See Faith, *Safety in Numbers*, 338–342; and Claus Schellenberg, "The Proceedings Against Two French Customs Officials in Switzerland for Prohibited Acts in Favor of a Foreign State, Economic Intelligence Service, and Violation of the Banking Law," *International Business Lawyer* 9 (1981), 139–140.

been embarrassed by the publicity in the United States associating Swiss banking institutions with organized crime. At the very least, the Swiss perceived a need to appear to be cooperative with American initiatives against organized crime. Finally, the Americans were conscious of Swiss priorities in their conduct of foreign relations. As a small, prosperous, and historically neutral country, Switzerland had concentrated in its foreign affairs on staying out of trouble and making as few enemies as possible. Clearly, there were limits to which the Swiss could turn their backs on a serious American proposal.

In 1967, Fred Vincent, the assistant attorney general in charge of the Criminal Division, visited Switzerland to discuss the need for increased cooperation. The Swiss officials responded by suggesting that the two countries negotiate a mutual legal assistance treaty. Unlike the Americans, the Swiss were already party to one such treaty, the European Convention on Mutual Assistance in Criminal Matters, done at Strasbourg on April 20, 1959.[30] Although that treaty was to provide substantial guidance during the negotiations, it had not provided the Swiss with any experience in negotiating with a common law country. There was, to the best knowledge of both sides, no precedent for a mutual legal assistance treaty between a civil law state and a common law state. Pressures to begin formal negotiations increased substantially in December 1968, when the influential U.S. Attorney in Manhattan, Robert Morgenthau, harshly criticized the Swiss at a hearing of the House Committee on Banking and Currency. Negotiations began in earnest in April 1969, when Swiss and U.S. officials met in Washington to discuss organized crime, narcotics trafficking, and SEC violations, and "to define the means by which private Swiss facilities were used by Americans to further or conceal illegal activities."[31] Under continuing pressure from Congress, the Swiss government consented to extended and relatively open-ended negotiations.

Unlike most other negotiations in the criminal law area, the MLAT

30. European Treaty Series No. 30; a protocol added in 1978 is at European Treaty Series No. 99.

31. *Foreign Bank Secrecy and Bank Records: Hearings on H.R. 15073 Before the Committee on Banking and Currency, House of Representatives*, 91st Cong., 1st and 2d Sess. (1969–1970), 15 (statement of Assistant U.S. Attorney General Will Wilson). See the Treaty Between the United States of America and the Swiss Confederation on Mutual Assistance in Criminal Matters, signed May 25, 1973; 27 UST 2019; TIAS 8302 (effective Jan. 23, 1977). Both the text and a section-by-section analysis of the treaty appear in U.S. Senate Exec. F, 94th Cong., 2d Sess. (1976). See also U.S. Senate Exec. Rept. 94-29, 94th Cong., 2d Sess. (1976).

talks included relatively high-level officials on both sides, up to and including the respective ambassadors. The demands were relatively one-sided insofar as both parties expected most of the requests for evidence to emanate from the United States. It is not surprising that the internal Swiss consultative process proved to be far more involved and politically sensitive than the American, in part because articles in the Swiss press periodically heightened suspicions regarding the negotiations and American intentions. Many banking and business leaders were concerned that any compromise of Swiss financial secrecy laws would encourage investors to seek more secure havens for their funds elsewhere.[32] By late 1971, as the treaty began to take shape, the Swiss negotiators reached out to leaders in the banking and business communities whose support was deemed essential to ensure acceptance of the treaty by the Swiss cantons and ratification by the Swiss Federal Council. Banking and business leaders were invited to participate in the negotiations and to meet individually with the U.S. negotiators. Eventually, the educational and consensus-building process proved effective in assuaging the fears of the banking-business community and winning support for the treaty in the cantons and the national government.

The American objectives in the MLAT negotiations with the Swiss, and in most subsequent negotiations with other governments, were twofold. They wanted the Swiss to be more forthcoming in providing evidence requested by U.S. authorities, and they wanted to ensure that the evidence would be provided in a form that would be admissible in U.S. courts. These objectives would later be supplemented by more ambitious objectives, requiring the Swiss not merely to accommodate U.S. evidentiary demands but also to adopt the assumptions and objectives of U.S. law enforcement officials as their own. In the early 1970s, however, the American negotiators had no choice but to set their sights on the more limited objectives. Indeed, even they had only a hazy notion of where these first steps would lead two decades later.

The principal source of conflict in the negotiations was over the extent to which Americans would be allowed to pierce the veil of secrecy that shrouded Swiss bank transactions. The principal American objective required the Swiss to pierce the veil of secrecy created by Article 47 of the Swiss Banking Code and Article 273 of the Swiss Penal Code.[33] That

---

32. The opposition of the Swiss banking community to the proposed treaty is discussed in *New York Times*, Aug. 12, 1972, 29.

33. See esp. Mario Kronauer, "Information Given for Tax Purposes from Switzerland to

veil, the Swiss were quick to point out to the Americans, had been created in 1934 primarily to prevent the Nazi government from identifying and seizing the assets of Jewish depositors in Swiss banks. Indeed, some Swiss pointed out, the tradition of secrecy had originated some two centuries before, when Swiss co-religionists of persecuted minorities elsewhere had been obliged to protect their assets against the inquiries of acquisitive governments.

The veil consisted principally of two laws: Article 47 of the Swiss Banking Code (as amended in 1970), which provided that any officer or employee of a bank or any auditor or any officer or employee of the Banking Commission who violated the duty of secrecy, or anyone who induced or attempted to induce such a person to violate that duty, could be punished with up to six months imprisonment and fined up to 50,000 francs;[34] and the economic espionage provision of the Swiss Penal Code, Article 273, which made it a crime to "elicit a manufacturing or business secret in order to make it available to any foreign official agency or to a foreign organization or private enterprise" either directly or through an agent, and to make such secrets available to such foreign authorities or organizations.[35]

The two foremost concerns of the Swiss were to protect the identities of "innocent parties" (i.e., persons who appeared not to be connected in any way with the offense for which assistance was requested) and to prevent the Americans from using any evidence for tax purposes. With regard to the first concern, the Swiss practice had been to excise the names of innocent parties from documents requested by letters rogatory. This posed two problems for the Americans: it rendered the documents inadmissible in American courts (although not in Swiss courts), and it disrupted efforts to trace the transactions of criminals seeking to hide

---

Foreign Countries Especially to the United States for the Prevention of Fraud or the Like in Relation to Certain American Taxes," *Tax Law Review* 30 (1974), 47–99; Walter Meier, "Banking Secrecy in Swiss and International Taxation," *International Lawyer* 7 (1973), 16–45; and M. Magdalena Schoch, "What Is a Secret Swiss Bank Account?" in *Hearings on Foreign Bank Secrecy and Bank Records* (supra n. 31), 363–368. See also Kurt Mueller, "The Swiss Banking Secret," *International and Comparative Law Quarterly* 18 (1969), 360–377; and Note, "Secret Swiss Bank Accounts: Uses, Abuses, and Attempts at Control," *Fordham Law Review* 39 (1971), 500.

34. The article did not apply to federal and cantonal provisions concerning the duty to testify and the duty to present information to an official. See the translation of Art. 47 in Meier, "Banking Secrecy," 18.

35. Schoch, "What Is a Secret Swiss Bank Account?" 364.

their assets. The American negotiators were able to make only limited headway on this issue, conceding to the Swiss a provision by which each government reserved the right "to balance the interests of [the innocent party] . . . with the need and the importance of the criminal investigation or proceeding in the requesting State [i.e., the United States]."[36] The Swiss further reserved the right to exclude American representatives in situations (involving the execution of American requests) where banking or manufacturing secrets would be disclosed[37] and insisted on a provision in which the Americans agreed to seek a protective order limiting access to documents provided by the Swiss which disclosed the identity of innocent parties.[38] Finally, the treaty included a reserve clause permitting each state to refuse assistance to the extent that "the requested State considers that the execution of the request is likely to prejudice its sovereignty, security or similar essential interests."[39]

The second concern of the Swiss—that information provided by them not be used to prosecute tax and other fiscal offenses—remained the principal bone of contention in the last two years of the negotiations and was only resolved with a vague formulation just days before the treaty was signed. The Swiss insisted that any requests for assistance in tax matters come under the bilateral Income Tax Convention of May 24, 1951[40]—a treaty that was notably lacking in the eyes of U.S. tax and law enforcement authorities.[41] The MLAT negotiators ultimately arrived at "a compromise between the Swiss concept of specialty of use which, in effect, holds that information furnished pursuant to a request for assistance may only be used for the specific purpose for which it was furnished, and the view of the United States that properly obtained information or evidence should be usable for any purpose by the requesting State."[42] The compromise allowed the United States to use

36. See the technical analysis of the Swiss MLAT, U.S. Senate Exec. Doc. F (supra n. 31), 48.

37. See Art. 12 of the Swiss MLAT.

38. Ibid., Art. 15. An accompanying letter set forth the parties' understanding with respect to which this provision was limited by the Supreme Court's interpretations of the public trial provision of the Sixth Amendment.

39. Ibid., Art. 3.

40. Convention for the Avoidance of Double Taxation with Respect to Taxes on Income (signed at Washington May 24, 1951; entered into force Sept. 27, 1951; 2 UST 1751; TIAS 2316; 127 UNTS 227).

41. See Kronauer, "Information Given for Tax Purposes" (supra n. 33).

42. See the technical analysis of the Swiss MLAT, U.S. Senate Exec. Doc. F, 41–42.

the information in other cases so long as it notified the Swiss in advance, and so long as Swiss assistance could be given in those cases (i.e., not including cases involving fiscal offenses).[43]

Insofar as much of the impetus for the treaty negotiations had derived from the mutual concern over the advantage taken by organized crime of Swiss banking secrecy laws to hide their ill-begotten proceeds, the Swiss agreed to waive the limitations on cooperation in investigations involving organized crime figures. Indeed, the Swiss believed that the U.S. negotiators would refuse to sign any treaty that did not waive the dual criminality requirement to allow assistance in tax and other fiscal offenses involving organized crime figures.[44] The Swiss regarded the American practice—employed most famously in the prosecution of Al Capone—of prosecuting organized figures for income tax evasion when admissible evidence of more serious crimes could not be obtained as somewhat strange and distasteful.[45] They nonetheless agreed to make the furnishing of assistance obligatory in organized crime cases even where the alleged offenses neither met the dual criminality test nor were included in the Schedule. The Swiss insisted, however, on stringent criteria where assistance was requested to investigate income tax violations. Wary of American "fishing expeditions" and a flood of requests from prosecutors seeking information on the lower-echelon "runners" and "bagmen" of organized crime, the Swiss demanded that requests be limited to cases in which the evidence requested was absolutely essential to incarcerating "upper-echelon" figures for substantial periods of time. The American negotiators ultimately acceded to this formulation in the hope that the prophylactic effect of the treaty itself, combined with a few cases, would cause organized crime figures to move their funds from Switzerland.[46]

Persuading the Swiss to let down the veil of their secrecy laws represented only part of the American challenge in the negotiations. The

43. An additional compromise, designed to reconcile conflicting positions regarding the future use of a witness's testimony (in the requested state) in any later criminal proceeding (in the requesting state) against that witness, provided that such testimony was admissible only if the witness had been advised at the time of his or her appearance of his or her right under the treaty to refuse testimony on the basis of possible self-incrimination or any other privilege available in either state.

44. Frei and Treschel, "Origins and Applications of the Swiss MLAT" (supra n. 27), 83.

45. Ibid., 80. See *Capone v. U.S.*, 56 F.2d 927 (1932); John Kobler, *Capone: The Life and World of Al Capone* (New York: Fawcett Crest, 1971).

46. See Swiss MLAT, Arts. 6, 7, 8.

Americans also needed to familiarize the Swiss with American legal requirements and to create guidelines so that evidence provided by Swiss judicial officers under Swiss law would be delivered in a form that would be admissible in U.S. courts and without undue delay. Swiss law strictly forbade the performance of judicial functions by foreign officials on Swiss territory; exceptions were not even permitted for the most innocuous tasks.[47] Although U.S. law similarly prohibited foreign judicial functions on American territory,[48] the statute had not been strictly enforced. The Swiss, by contrast, had surprised a number of foreign government officials with the stringency of their application. Both French and Dutch government attorneys, for instance, had landed in jail for doing no more than deposing their own nationals located in Switzerland.[49] American law enforcement authorities were thus particularly dependent upon Swiss officials for the performance of all judicial tasks, but Swiss officials—in particular, those at the cantonal level responsible for conducting most law enforcement tasks—were unlikely to be familiar with the evidentiary and constitutional requirements of U.S. law.

The substantial differences between the nature of judicial proceedings in the two countries had been responsible for many of the misunderstandings that hindered the letters rogatory process. For instance, whereas the judge in a common law system typically plays a quite limited role in obtaining evidence, relying on the adversary process to perform this function, the civil law judge "conducts every aspect of the proceeding and questions all witnesses himself":

> All proceedings following the institution of the suit are considered as parts of the "trial," which may be conducted as a series of evidentiary hearings. The trial is not viewed as a separate, isolated event apart from the rest of the suit. In many civil-law nations,

47. According to Art. 271 of the Swiss Penal Code, "Whoever, on Swiss territory, without being authorized so to do, takes on behalf of a foreign government any action which is solely within the province of a [Swiss] government authority or a [Swiss] government official, whoever does anything to encourage such action, . . . shall be punished by imprisonment, in serious cases in the penitentiary" (Jones, "International Judicial Assistance" (supra n. 4), 520). Switzerland was not the only state with such a restriction on the taking of evidence by foreigners. Denmark, Iran, Liechtenstein, Luxembourg, Venezuela and Zambia were also among the countries that regarded such actions as an infringement of their national sovereignty. See DeVine and Olsen, "Taking Evidence Outside of the United States" (supra n. 20), 374.

48. See 18 U.S.C. 951.

49. Schellenberg, "Proceedings Against Two French Customs Officials" (supra n. 29).

witnesses are not placed under oath before they testify, and cross-examination is virtually unknown. Evidence taken by the judge automatically becomes part of the record in the case, even though no verbatim transcript of the proceedings is made. Instead, the judge summarizes the testimony, which may be subscribed by the witness later. Furthermore, many countries regard it as improper for the lawyers to talk with the witnesses before they testify.[50]

Many of the MLAT's provisions were designed to authorize the two very different systems to accommodate each other's requirements. One provision, for instance, stated that assistance could be granted in "investigations or court proceedings in respect of offenses the punishment of which falls or would fall within the jurisdiction of the judicial authorities of the requesting State or a state or canton thereof." The intention of this wording was threefold: to avoid falling prey to litigation over the inclusiveness of a narrower term, such as the "tribunal" in the modified Section 1782; to make clear to civil law judges that grand jury proceedings and investigations by regulatory agencies, notably the SEC, warranted cooperation to the same degree as requests at more-advanced stages of a criminal investigation; and to meet the general requirements of dual criminality. The Swiss regarded the phrasing as a significant concession on their part, arguing that traditional continental European concepts restricted assistance to requests emanating from judicial authorities, not administrative agencies such as the SEC.[51]

Other portions of the treaty were similarly devoted to reconciling the differences between civil law and common law procedures. Most of these were relatively uncontroversial once both sides understood the concepts underlying the other's procedural requirements. Various provisions accordingly provided for the authentication of documents, the taking of evidence under oath, the protection of constitutional privileges such as that against self-incrimination, and the presence and participation of foreign officials, defendants, and other representatives in the judicial proceeding—measures all designed to incorporate as much as

50. Bishop, "International Litigation in Texas" (supra n. 10), 363–364; see also Rudolph B. Schlesinger, *Comparative Law*, 4th ed. (Mineola, N.Y.: Foundation Press, 1980), 398. A fine description of European courts by an American writer is Sybille Bedford's *The Faces of Justice: A Traveller's Report* (New York: Simon & Schuster, 1961).

51. Frei and Treschel, "Origins and Applications of the Swiss MLAT" (supra n. 27), 80–83.

possible U.S. procedures into Swiss judicial actions taken at the behest of U.S. prosecutors. On the one hand, government prosecutors were aided in their efforts to gain relevant and admissible evidence. On the other hand, defendants' Sixth Amendment rights of confrontation were ensured, as were Swiss and American rights against self-incrimination. Special provisions provided for the retention of defendants and witnesses in custody when necessary, as well as for the safe conduct of witnesses who might be liable to prosecution in the court's jurisdiction. The Swiss refused, however, to include in the treaty a provision permitting U.S. law enforcement officials to conduct informal interviews in Switzerland.[52]

One article of the treaty addressed the problems that had arisen in the past as a result of differences in defining substantive crimes. Rigid and nonimaginative interpretations of the "dual criminality" requirement had resulted in the rejection of many letters rogatory requests on the grounds that the crime alleged in the request was not recognizable in the penal code of the requested state. U.S. authorities had encountered frequent frustrations as a consequence of the wording of many federal criminal statutes, which refer to the federal government's power over interstate commerce in order to bring an offense under federal jurisdiction. Violations of mail fraud and wire fraud statutes, for instance, are often incomprehensible to foreign judges. More than one foreign judge had been known to deny a U.S. request for judicial assistance on the grounds that it was not illegal in his country to use the telephone.[53] The negotiators sought to resolve this difficulty by attaching a "Schedule for Which Compulsory Measures Are Available" to the treaty and by requiring that judges look at the substance rather than the characterization of the crime alleged in the request. More difficult to resolve were Swiss doubts as to whether U.S. crimes such as money laundering and insider trading, neither of which were immediately recognizable in Swiss law, met the dual criminality requirement. Persistent disputes over this issue were ultimately addressed by the Swiss supreme court, Swiss legislation, and further agreements between the two governments.

The MLAT, accompanied by six exchanges of interpretive letters, was signed in 1973. An additional exchange of letters was required in late

52. Ibid., 92.
53. Lawrence Chamblee, "International Legal Assistance in Criminal Cases," in John M. Fedders, Joel Harris, Roger M. Olsen, and Bruno A. Ristau, eds., *Transnational Litigation: Practical Approaches to Conflicts and Accommodations* (Washington, D.C.: American Bar Association National Institute, 1984), 1:188.

1975 as a result of a misunderstanding regarding variations in cantonal law. Both governments ratified the treaty in 1976, which went into force in January 1977, almost a decade after the subject of negotiations had first been broached. Mobilized in part by the MLAT negotiations, in 1981 the Swiss Federal Assembly enacted a Federal Act on International Mutual Assistance in Criminal Matters (IMAC), which codified and expanded many of the provisions in the MLAT with the United States and the European Convention, offering, for instance, broader cooperation in tax fraud cases.[54]

Much to the dismay of the Justice Department, however, the Swiss debate over the implementing legislation had provided a second opportunity for banking and business interests to undermine the negotiators' concessions to the Americans. Combined with preexisting law, the IMAC provided both targets of an investigation as well as "innocent third parties" repeated opportunity to challenge Swiss compliance with U.S. requests for bank records and other confidential documents.[55] The treaty also failed to resolve fully the obstacles generated by variations in cantonal procedural law. And even where the treaty authorized Swiss courts to accommodate American evidentiary requirements, the reluctance of Swiss *juges d'instruction* to vary their customary procedures continued to present difficulties not unlike those that antedated the treaty.

U.S. prosecutors also found particularly irksome two treaty provisions of particular advantage to suspects of an investigation. One, in conjunction with Swiss domestic law, required that "[u]pon receipt of a request for assistance, the requested State shall notify . . . any person from

54. The Swiss Federal Act is briefly summarized in Lionel Frei, "International Mutual Assistance in Criminal Matters: The Swiss Federal Act," *Commonwealth Law Bulletin* 8 (1982), 794. The Swiss IMAC, which entered into force Jan. 1, 1983, was preceded by an Austrian IMAC and followed by a German IMAC. The Austrian Federal Law of Dec. 4, 1979, "Concerning Extradition and Mutual Assistance in Criminal Matters," is translated and analyzed in Edith Palmer, *The Austrian Law on Extradition and Mutual Assistance in Criminal Matters* (Washington, D.C.: Library of Congress Law Library, 1983). The German IMAC, enacted Dec. 23, 1982, can be found in English translation in *International Legal Materials* 22 (1983), 945–982.

55. A subject could file an objection with the Swiss Justice Department and then appeal a negative ruling first to the Swiss Federal Tribunal, then to the Consultative Commission specially created by the Swiss implementing legislation, and finally to the Swiss Federal Council, the composition of which resembles that of the American cabinet. An "innocent third party" was likewise entitled to pursue the same procedure.

whom a statement or testimony or documents, records, or articles of evidence are sought;"[56] the consequence was to forewarn suspects of the fact that they were under investigation (at an earlier stage of the investigation than was required under the Federal Rules of Criminal Procedure), thereby allowing them greater opportunity to shift their funds and otherwise obscure the evidentiary trail. The other troublesome provision required that a request for assistance include not only "the subject matter and nature of the investigation or proceeding" but also "*a description of the essential acts alleged or sought to be ascertained*";[57] the result was to notify the suspect of the prosecution's theory at a relatively early stage in the investigation—in the United States, the defendant often does not discover that theory until the indictment—and to "stick" the prosecution with a potentially untested theory vulnerable to attack and questioning in the Swiss courts.[58]

The most significant sources of tension, however, arose as a result of U.S. frustrations in attempting to obtain evidence in insider trading and tax fraud investigations, and Swiss anger at the Americans' resort to unilateral measures involving U.S. court orders compelling suspects and Swiss banks to provide evidence in violation of Swiss secrecy laws.[59] The rapid internationalization of the securities markets during the late 1970s required a comparable internationalization of the SEC's regulatory efforts. The agency's initiatives, however, engendered tensions with a number of governments that were unwilling to cooperate because their

56. Swiss MLAT, Art. 36(a).

57. Ibid., Art. 29(1)(a).

58. Many of these obstacles became apparent when U.S. prosecutors sought to obtain evidence in the *Interconex* case, one of the most significant investigations requiring Swiss assistance shortly after the MLAT went into force. See *U.S. v. Carver*, Crim. No. 81-00342 (D.C. 1981), aff'd sub nom. *U.S. v. Lemire*, 720 F.2d 1327 (D.C. Cir. 1983). "Interconex" was the name of one of the parties. The *Interconex* case is analyzed in Richard S. Shine, "Transnational Litigation in Criminal Matters: A Case Study of the *Interconex* Prosecution," in Fedders et al., *Transnational Litigation* (supra n. 53), 533. See also the testimony of D. Lowell Jensen, former assistant attorney general in charge of the Criminal Division, in *Crime and Secrecy: The Use of Offshore Banks and Companies, Hearings Before the Permanent Subcommittee on Investigations of the Senate Committee on Governmental Affairs*, 98th Cong., 1st Sess., S. Hrg. 98-151 (1983), 3–14, 210–233. Although the U.S. prosecutors regarded the issues in the *Interconex* case as not particularly complex, they were unable to obtain an indictment until just a few days before the running of the statute of limitations.

59. Lionel Frei, "Overcoming Bank Secrecy: Assistance in Tax Matters in Switzerland on Behalf of Foreign Criminal Authorities," *New York Law School International and Comparative Law Review* 9 (1988), 107–129.

laws did not treat insider trading and other violations of U.S. securities laws as criminal activities.[60] Pressures between the United States and Switzerland mounted in 1981 when the Swiss Federal Tribunal rejected a request from the SEC (via the Justice Department) for assistance in an investigation of insider trading involving the Kuwait Petroleum Corporation's takeover of Sante Fe International Corporation, asserting that the failure to meet the requirement of dual criminality precluded assistance.[61] Subsequent negotiations led to the signing of a Memorandum of Understanding (MOU) to facilitate the SEC's access to information relevant to investigations of violations of American insider trading laws.[62] The MOU included two provisions: an "exchange of opinions" in which the parties agreed that insider trading would under certain conditions constitute fraud, disclosure of business secrets, or other crimes that would pass the test of dual criminality and warrant compulsory assistance; and a description of a proposed private agreement,

60. See John M. Fedders, Frederick B. Wade, Michael D. Mann, and Matthew Beizer, "Waiver by Conduct: A Possible Response to the Internationalization of the Securities Markets," *Journal of Comparative Business and Capital Market Law* 6 (1984), 1–54, and "Response to Fedders' 'Waiver by Conduct,' " *Journal of Comparative Business and Capital Market Law* 6 (1984), 307–354; John J. Ryan IV, "International Enforcement of Insider Trading: The Grand Jury Process, Court Compulsion, and the United States–Switzerland Treaty on Mutual Assistance in Criminal Matters," *American Criminal Law Review* 26 (1988), 247; and Michael D. Mann and Joseph G. Mari, "Developments in International Securities Law Enforcement" (Paper, International Securities Markets, Practicing Law Institute, March 1990).

61. *SEC v. Certain Unknown Purchasers of the Common Stock of and Call Options for the Common Stock of Sante Fe International Corporation,* 81 Civ. 6553 (WC) (S.D.N.Y. Oct. 26, 1981). The opinion of the Swiss Federal Tribunal in the Santa Fe case has been translated into English and summarized in *International Legal Materials* 22 (1983), 785.

62. See Memorandum of Understanding, Aug. 31, 1982, United States–Switzerland, reprinted in *International Legal Materials* 22 (1983), 1. See also the discussion (and text) of the 1982 memorandum in Peter C. Honegger Jr., "Demystification of the Swiss Banking Secrecy and Illumination of the United States–Swiss Memorandum of Understanding," *North Carolina Journal of International Law and Comparative Regulation* 9 (1983), 1–49; Recent Developments, "International Agreements: United States–Switzerland Investigation of Insider Trading Through Swiss Banks," *Harvard International Law Journal* 23 (1983), 437–443; Lionel Frei, "The Service of Process and the Taking of Evidence on Behalf of U.S. Proceedings: The Problem of Granting Assistance," *Wirtschaft und Recht* 35:2/3 (1983), 196–210; JoAnn M. Navickas, "Swiss Banks and Insider Trading in the United States," *International Tax and Business Lawyer* 2 (1984), 159–191; and Beth A. Rushford, "The Effect of Swiss Bank Secrecy on the Enforcement of Insider Trading Regulations and the Memorandum of Understanding Between the United States and Switzerland," *Boston College International and Comparative Law Review* 7 (1984), 541–570. See also Ellen R. Levin, "The Conflict Between United States Securities Laws on Insider Trading and Swiss Bank Secrecy Laws," *Northwestern Journal of International Law and Business* 7 (1985), 318–350.

known as Convention XVI, among members of the Swiss Bankers' Association designed to facilitate cooperation with the SEC in cases involving tender offers or other acquisitions even when the SEC was unable to meet the dual criminality test.[63] The MOU had the intended impact of improving cooperation in U.S. investigations of securities violations. Continuing frustrations, however, inspired the SEC's enforcement division to propose the notion of "waiver by conduct," according to which investors who utilized a foreign bank or brokerage firm to buy or sell securities in a U.S. market would thereby waive their right to keep their identity secret from the SEC and to withhold their foreign bank accounts and trading secrets.[64] In the face of heated opposition, including a reported warning by the Swiss government to the SEC "to abandon the proposal or risk jeopardizing U.S.-Swiss agreements on law enforcement," the SEC ultimately abandoned the proposal.[65] In late 1987, however, the Swiss Parliament did oblige the SEC when it voted, after years of debate, to criminalize insider trading, thereby allowing U.S. authorities to obtain assistance under the MLAT.[66] No longer were Swiss authorities obliged to determine whether a particular charge of insider trading in the United States would have constituted a violation of Swiss law as well.

Perhaps no U.S. action during the 1980s so angered the Swiss as the Justice Department's efforts to penetrate Switzerland's secrecy laws unilaterally by issuing subpoenas *duces tecum* to the U.S.-based branches and subsidiaries of foreign corporations. (The use of these tactics is discussed in greater depth below in the context of the U.S. negotiations with the Cayman Islands.) Two cases in particular generated serious tensions. The first arose

63. See the brief discussion of the memorandum of understanding in the prepared statement by John Fedders, director of the SEC's Division of Enforcement, to the Senate Permanent Subcommittee on Investigations, in *Crime and Secrecy: Hearings* (supra n. 58), 326–327.

64. Fedders et al., "Waiver by Conduct."

65. Ingersoll, "SEC Proposal to Override Foreign Laws on Bank Secrecy Draws Wide Criticism," *Wall Street Journal*, Feb. 11, 1985, 13; "Response to Fedders' 'Waiver by Conduct.' "

66. A fine history of U.S.-Swiss relations regarding the bank secrecy issue (which includes a discussion and copy of the 1987 memorandum as well as the text of the insider trading law) is Stultz, "Swiss Bank Secrecy and United States Efforts" (supra n. 28), 63. The domestic Swiss opposition to the law, which described it as "a foreign body in the Swiss legal system," is discussed in Pierre de Charmant, "Switzerland," *International Lawyer* 21 (1987), 1212–1219. The evolution of the Swiss insider trading law is discussed in Peter Schibli, "Insider Trading: A New Criminal Bill in Switzerland Called 'Lex Americana,' " *International Enforcement Law Reporter* 3 (1987), 234–240. The law is described in H. R. Steiner, "Switzerland," *International Business Lawyer* 17 (1989), 138–142.

338   International Evidence-Gathering

in an SEC investigation of insider trading involving a tender offer by the Canadian corporation, Seagrams, for all the outstanding shares of St. Joe Minerals Corporation.[67] When a Swiss bank, Banca Della Svizzera Italiana, refused to disclose a customer's identity in response to a discovery motion by the SEC delivered to the bank's New York office, arguing that to do so would subject it to civil and criminal liability in Switzerland, the SEC obtained a court order compelling the bank to disclose the requested information.[68] Even before the court order was issued, however, the bank capitulated, having obtained a waiver of the Swiss secrecy provision from its customers. The second, and far more serious, case involved the largest tax evasion case in American history. In an attempt to compel a highly successful commodities trader named Mark Rich and his associates to deliver documents to the United States, U.S. prosecutors had subpoenas issued to Marc Rich and the U.S. subsidiary of his Swiss-based company.[69] The two-year struggle that ensued between 1982 and 1984 became a principal source of tension in the two countries' relations, with the Swiss deeply resentful of the Justice Department's "heavy-handed tactics" and wary lest precedents be set for future evidence-gathering efforts.[70] By contrast, the Americans saw little reason not to make use of whatever evidence-gathering mechanisms they possessed, given the scale and profit-ability of Marc Rich's criminal activities. The case was finally settled in late 1984 when the Swiss-based corporation bearing Marc Rich's name paid $200 million in fines, including $21 million in contempt-of-court fines that had accumulated at the rate of $50,000 a day for failing to comply with the subpoena. The Swiss refused, however, to extradite Marc Rich and his principal associate, who had fled to Switzerland to avoid arrest by U.S. authorities.

One outgrowth of the Marc Rich conflict was the negotiation of a second MOU between the two governments, signed in 1987. In a concession to the Swiss, the agreement stipulated that every effort would be made to use the

67. See Andreas F. Lowenfeld, "Bank Secrecy and Insider Trading: The Banca della Svizzera Italiana Case," *Review of Securities Regulation* 15 (1982), 942–945.

68. *SEC v. Banca Della Svizzera Italiana*, 92 F.R.D. 111 (S.D.N.Y. 1981).

69. *In re Grand Jury Subpoena Directed to Marc Rich & Co., A.G.*, 707 F.2d 663 (2d Cir.), cert. denied, 463 U.S. 1215 (1983); *In re Grand Jury Subpoena Duces Tecum*, 731 F.2d 1032 (2d Cir.); *In re Marc Rich & Co., A.G.*, 736 F.2d 864 (2d Cir. 1984), 739 F.2d 834 (2d Cir. 1984).

70. Ingo Walter, *Secret Money: The Shadowy World of Tax Evasion, Capital Flight, and Fraud* (London: Allen & Unwin, 1985), 53–58; Sarah M. Barish, "International Paper Chase: Federal Grand Jury Subpoena Duces Tecum in Conflict with Swiss Nondisclosure Law," *Brooklyn Journal of International Law* 11 (1985), 149–169.

MLAT before resorting to unilateral measures, that the appropriate authorities would consult with one another in order to avoid or minimize jurisdictional conflicts, and that efforts would be made to prevent any unnecessary disclosure of the judicial assistance provided. In return, the Swiss promised to streamline the implementation process, the length of which had occasioned substantial American frustration, and to maximize their assistance in investigations of drug traffickers, money launderers, and other sorts of organized criminals.[71]

The principal Swiss frustration with U.S. assistance concerned the freezing and forfeiting of assets, which had been authorized in the Swiss legislation implementing the MLAT. Swiss officials were generally disappointed during the 1980s at the lack of reciprocity in this area. They noted that although Switzerland had frozen assets in response to U.S. requests, U.S. officials had failed to reciprocate, apparently because they lacked the authority to do so with the same dispatch that Swiss officials possess.[72] They also complained that whereas they had seized and forfeited criminal proceeds to the victims of crimes outside Switzerland,[73] the United States had failed to reciprocate. The Anti-Drug Abuse Act of 1986 sought to address some of these concerns by incorporating provisions authorizing the U.S. government to seize and forfeit the proceeds (or substitute assets) of drug traffickers charged with violating foreign drug laws and to share any forfeited proceeds with governments that assisted in the seizure or forfeiture.[74] In August 1989, the Justice Department accordingly announced that it would give $1 million each to Switzerland and Canada for their help in the investigation and prosecution of the Panama-based Banco de Occidente.[75]

By the end of the 1980s, many of the kinks in the treaty and the obstacles created by the implementing legislation had been successfully corrected or circumvented. The MOUs and new Swiss legislation were partially responsible, as were rulings by the Swiss Federal Tribunal and U.S. federal courts rejecting most challenges to the MLAT and international judicial assistance generally.[76] The growing cooperation of the Swiss banking community,

71. Somewhat to the dismay of the Justice Department, the provisions of the MLAT providing for expanded assistance in organized crime investigations had proven too restrictive to accommodate most U.S. requests.

72. Frei and Treschel, "Origins and Applications of the Swiss MLAT" (supra n. 27), 90–91.

73. See, e.g., "Government Obtains Bribe Money from Swiss Bank Accounts," *International Enforcement Law Reporter* 5 (1989), 287–288.

74. 18 U.S.C. 981(a)(1)(B) and 981(i) (1986).

75. Michael Isikoff, "U.S. to Pay 2 Nations $1 Million for Drug-Case Aid," *Washington Post*, Aug. 15, 1989, A14; *International Enforcement Law Reporter* 5 (1989), 283–285.

76. U.S. federal courts have rejected most challenges to the Swiss MLAT on the grounds

reflected in its adoption in October 1987 of stricter rules with respect to receiving foreign funds, provided an important complement to the government's actions.[77] Also important, however, was the growing familiarity of both Swiss and U.S. judicial authorities with the treaty's provisions and procedures. By 1983, six years after the MLAT entered into force, the Justice Department had made 202 requests under the treaty and the Swiss 65.[78] By 1990, the two central authorities were processing an estimated 100 requests a year, including a rising number involving the seizure and forfeiture of illegally derived funds deposited in Swiss banks. The Federal Tribunal's decisions, moreover, were a result of the willingness of officials in the Swiss Justice Department to faithfully pursue U.S. requests that had been challenged in Swiss courts throughout the lengthy appeals process.

The importance of Swiss assistance to U.S. criminal investigations was already apparent by the early 1980s. In January 1983, Justice Department officials estimated that the evidence obtained under the MLAT had contributed to 145 federal and state convictions, including those of the notorious Italian financier Michele Sindona, for fraud in connection with the collapse of the Franklin National Bank, and of an organized crime figure, Anthony Giacolone, for a $3 million embezzlement of Citibank.[79] By the end of the 1980s, the Swiss government's cooperation in international efforts to identify and freeze the assets of fallen dictators such as the Philippines' Ferdinand Marcos,[80] Haiti's Jean-Claude Duvalier,[81] Paraguay's Alfredo

---

that the treaty provides no standing to private parties. See *U.S. v. Johnpoll,* 739 F.2d 702 (2d Cir.), cert. denied, 469 U.S. 1075 (1984); *U.S. v. Davis,* 767 F.2d 1025 (2d Cir. 1985); and, rejecting a challenge to a freeze of assets by the Swiss government pursuant to an MLAT request, *Barr v. U.S. Department of Justice,* 819 F.2d 25 (2d Cir. 1987). In a series of Swiss judicial decisions involving challenges by third parties to U.S. requests for documents, the Federal Tribunal ruled that their identities could be disclosed if they were in any way connected with the subject of the investigation. The court also was liberal in its interpretation of the dual criminality requirement. See Frei and Treschel, "Origins and Applications of the Swiss MLAT" (supra n. 27), 84–88.

77. See the reports by Peter Schibli in *International Enforcement Law Reporter* 3 (1987), 154–58, and (1988), 148–150.

78. James I. K. Knapp, "Mutual Legal Assistance Treaties as a Way to Pierce Bank Secrecy," *Case Western Reserve Journal of International Law* 20 (1988), 405, 414.

79. Ibid., 414.

80. Pieter J. Hoets and Sara G. Zwart, "Swiss Bank Secrecy and the Marcos Affair," *New York Law School International and Comparative Law Review* 9 (1988), 75–105; Peter Norman, "Hasty Swiss Freeze on Marcos Millions Raises Questions on Banking Secrecy," *Wall Street Journal,* Apr. 4, 1986, 25; Olivier Dunant, "Switzerland," *International Lawyer* 22 (1988), 854, 856–860; the periodic reports in *International Enforcement Law Reporter,* 2:370, 3:79–81, 4:69–70, 5:366–367, 431–432, 463 (1986–89).

81. Clemens Kochinke, "Judicial Assistance Requests: The Duvalier and Marcos Cases, Two Approaches Toward Switzerland," *International Enforcement Law Reporter* 2 (1986), 370.

Stroessner, Romania's Nicolae Ceaușescu, and Panama's Manuel Noriega;[82] its substantial assistance in the Iran Contra investigation;[83] and its willingness to provide documents in the various investigations of Wall Street shenanigans,[84] and export control violations involving the Soviet Union[85] and North Korea,[86] stood in stark contrast to its response to similar efforts in earlier years.[87] Also significant was the Swiss Parliament's vote in late 1989 to criminalize money laundering, in effect criminalizing a wide variety of banking functions that had previously been regarded as virtually part and parcel of a banker's profession in a financial secrecy jurisdiction.[88] By all accounts, the Swiss have emerged as among the world's leaders in matters of international law enforcement.

Lessons, Spin-offs, and the Second Generation of MLATs

The negotiation of the Swiss treaty provided valuable experience in anticipating future pitfalls and objectives in other treaty negotiations. Also, the treaty went into effect as demands for international judicial

82. "Ex-Despots Can't Bank on the Swiss," *Los Angeles Times*, Jan. 31, 1990, A1.

83. Note, "Swiss Bank Secrecy and United States Efforts" (supra n. 28), 64–65; Philip Shenon, "Swiss Bank Records in Iran-Contra Case Are Released to U.S.," *New York Times*, Nov. 4, 1987, A1; Taylor, "Iran-Contra Counsel Walsh Is Upheld on His Authority, Access to Swiss Data," *Wall Street Journal*, Aug. 21, 1987, 38; Peter Schibli, "Swiss Supreme Court Rules Geneva Bank Accounts in the Irangate Affair Must Be Opened to U.S. Investigators," *International Enforcement Law Reporter* 3 (1987), 283–284.

84. Nathaniel Nash, "Swiss Help in Insider Case," *New York Times*, May 15, 1986, D1.

85. Bruce Zagaris and Clemens Kochinke, "Swiss Supreme Court Grants Request in the USSR Computer Case," *Taxes International* 56 (1984), 81.

86. Clemens Kochinke, "Swiss Supreme Court Defines Cooperation in Export Control Cases," *International Enforcement Law Reporter* 4 (1988), 12–13.

87. The Swiss had previously rejected, for instance, Ethiopian and Iranian requests to obtain the assets of Emperor Haile Selassi and the Shah. See John Tagliabue, "The Swiss Stop Keeping Secrets," *New York Times*, June 1, 1986, sec. 3, p. 4; but see Mark Schapiro, "Swiss Banks Still Sell Secrecy," *The Nation*, Sept. 6, 1986, 177–180. See also Paolo Bernasconi, "Swiss Bank Secrecy: Recent Developments in International Mutual Assistance in Criminal Matters," *International Enforcement Law Reporter* 5 (1989), 362–367.

88. Art. 305 of the Swiss Penal Code, as amended effective Aug. 1, 1990, makes it a crime to hinder an investigation of the origins, discovery, or confiscation of assets that an individual knows, or must assume, stem from criminal activity. See Nathalie Kohler, "Swiss Money Laundering Bill: Debates and Adoption by One of the Chambers of the Swiss Parliament," *International Enforcement Law Reporter* 5 (1989), 437–440, and the periodic reports in ibid., 5:121, 244–245; 6:96.

assistance and some coordination of U.S. international judicial respon-sibilities were increasing dramatically. The Swiss MLAT had included a provision requiring each government to establish a central authority for the processing of requests pursuant to the treaty. In 1979, Philip Heymann, the assistant attorney general in charge of the Criminal Division in the Department of Justice, created an Office of International Affairs (OIA). This office soon assumed responsibility for coordinating the Justice Department's international law enforcement concerns, han-dling extradition and judicial assistance matters and taking the lead in negotiating extradition treaties, MLATs, prisoner transfer treaties, and a variety of other law enforcement agreements.[89] By 1990, the size of the office had increased from the four attorneys present at its inception to more than forty attorneys; one attorney was stationed in Rome, addi-tional offices in Mexico City and Hong Kong had been authorized, and plans were under way to expand the OIA's presence in Europe.

At about the same time the OIA was created, an Office of Law Enforcement and Intelligence (LEI) was created within the Legal Advis-er's Office in the State Department. The two offices quickly worked out a relatively cooperative relationship, with attorneys from both partici-pating in treaty negotiations.[90] What tensions resulted were principally a reflection of the differing concerns and expertise of the respective offices. Whereas the State Department attorneys were more attuned to the political aspects of judicial assistance and treaty negotiations, as reflected by their greater involvement in more political issues such as U.S. counterterrorist policy, the OIA attorneys were strongly influenced by their prosecutorial backgrounds and their day-to-day experience in dealing with foreign judicial requests and personnel. These differences occasionally resulted in a mutual skepticism, with the State Department negotiators bemoaning OIA's insensitivity to diplomatic considerations, and the OIA lawyers doubting their counterparts' awareness of the requirements of criminal law and procedure. The OIA lawyers also chafed somewhat at the State Department's involvement in MLAT negotiations, particularly because one of the principal reasons for nego-tiating the treaties was to eliminate the time-consuming diplomatic

89. The OIA was officially designated by the attorney general as the Central Authority referred to in all MLATs. See 28 C.F.R. 0.64-1, and Justice Department Directive 81, 44 FR 18661, Mar. 29, 1979, as amended at 45 FR 6541, Jan. 29, 1980; 48 FR 54595, Dec. 6, 1983.

90. Whereas MLATs typically specify that the attorney general is the responsible authority, in the area of extradition the secretary of state has retained the principal statutory authority.

channels through which letters rogatory were required to pass. When all was said and done, however, the OIA attorneys generally welcomed the involvement of their State Department counterparts for a number of reasons: their presence at treaty negotiation sessions was an indication to the foreign counterpart that the U.S. government attached diplomatic significance to the negotiations; they provided diplomatic leverage and expertise when the negotiations become somewhat acrimonious (as in the early stages of the negotiations with the Swiss); and, as one OIA attorney recounted cynically, their involvement prevented the State Department from later disavowing any agreements negotiated by the OIA lawyers.

Several lessons were gained from the negotiation of the Swiss treaty and the ensuing attempts to utilize its provisions. The first was never again to let the negotiations become so drawn out and complex. To some extent, the negotiators' lack of experience in negotiating MLATs was a source of delay. And Switzerland's extraordinary concern with bank secrecy, its strong tradition of legality, and its prickly sense of national sovereignty created time-consuming obstacles too. When confronted with similar concerns in future MLAT negotiations, American negotiators would strive to complete the negotiations quickly and to avoid the length, complexity, and tortured clauses of the Swiss treaty. As the OIA lawyers became involved in negotiating other treaties, they soon realized that the process would be facilitated if their foreign counterparts included at least one representative with experience in criminal prosecution. Such an individual was deemed necessary to explain the concepts underlying the other nation's criminal law and procedure, to communicate the practical requirements of its criminal justice system, and to establish a relationship with the American negotiators that would aid in the treaty's implementation. Accordingly, the OIA lawyers requested of each government that such an individual be included on the negotiating team. They also included, and expected to be included on the other's team, individuals with expertise in any areas (such as drug enforcement, securities regulation, or tax administration) that might be a subject of the negotiations.

As the OIA's attorneys became more familiar with the potential and limitations of the Swiss MLAT, in particular the length of the appeals process authorized by the Swiss implementing legislation, they also realized the need to amend U.S. law to better accommodate the admissibility of evidence supplied by foreign authorities. At their behest, Congress included five provisions in the Comprehensive Crime Control Act of 1984 specifically designed to assist the foreign evidence gathering process: 18 U.S.C. 3505, which allows a foreign business record (or copy) to be admitted into evidence without requiring a deposition of the custodian of the records;[91] 18 U.S.C. 3506, which requires a national or resident of the United States who files a formal opposition in a foreign court to an official U.S. request for evidence to serve a copy of that pleading on the United States;[92] 18 U.S.C. 3507, which specifically authorizes U.S. courts to appoint a special master to attend and preside over depositions conducted abroad and to advise foreign courts on U.S. law; 18 U.S.C. 3292, which permits a court to suspend the running of the statute of limitations in cases in which the indictment has been delayed by the need to obtain foreign evidence;[93] and 18 U.S.C. 3161(h), which allows exclusions from the running of the Speedy Trial Act in cases delayed by the need to obtain evidence abroad.[94]

One positive spin-off of the Swiss treaty was that it generated substantial interest in foreign justice ministries around the world. In many countries, particularly those with tough bank secrecy laws, governments were none too eager to allow greater access to snooping American prosecutors; indeed, some, reportedly including Austria, Luxembourg and Liechtenstein, took advantage of the changes in Switzerland to promote themselves as safer financial security jurisdictions. But in others, particularly elsewhere in Europe, government prosecutors began expressing interest in the Swiss treaty with the Americans. At the same time, the attorneys in the OIA and the LEI were involved in negotiating new extradition treaties around the world to replace the increasingly

91. The constitutionality of the statute was upheld by a federal court in 1987 in response to a challenge by a defendant who contended that it violated the confrontation clause of the Sixth Amendment. See *U.S. v. Miller*, 830 F.2d 1073 (9th Cir. 1987).

92. The Swiss have objected to this statute, contending that it circumvents the treaty process and violates Swiss law by requiring an individual, the identity of whom may be the subject of a U.S. request under the MLAT, to disclose his or her identity by affirming the existence of an account or deposit. See Frei and Treschel, "Origins and Applications of the Swiss MLAT" (supra n. 27), 89–90.

93. In 1987, a federal court rejected various challenges to the statute. See *U.S. v. Miller*, 830 F.2d 1073 (9th Cir. 1987).

94. See U.S. Department of Justice, *Handbook on the Comprehensive Crime Control Act of 1984*, Chap. 12, Part K (Foreign Evidence), 176–180; and the Congressional hearing on the provisions, *Foreign Evidence Rules Amendment: Hearing on H.R. 5406 Before the Subcommittee on Criminal Justice of the House Committee on the Judiciary*, 98th Cong., 2d Sess. (1984).

outdated existing ones. At these negotiations, questions were being raised about the increasing need for judicial assistance in criminal investigations and proceedings short of extradition.

The incentives for entering into MLAT negotiations with foreign governments varied substantially. In the case of Turkey, the treaty was demanded as a precondition for other treaty negotiations requested by the United States. The Turkish government had been incensed by the incident and publicity leading up to the filming and distribution of the movie *Midnight Express*, which was based on the account of an American who had been imprisoned in Turkey for attempting to smuggle hashish. Its request that the U.S. government intervene to stop the distribution of the film was, quite naturally, rejected—albeit for reasons not readily comprehensible to the Turks. At the same time, in response to pressures by families of Americans held in Turkish prisons, the U.S. government suggested to the Turkish government that they negotiate a prisoner transfer treaty similar to one the United States had already negotiated with Mexico. The Turks responded indignantly not only that the Americans had failed to do anything about the film, but also that negotiation of such a treaty would only embarrass them by giving credence to the movie's portrayal of the Turkish judicial and penal systems. They suggested, instead, that such a treaty be included in a three-part treaty package including extradition and mutual legal assistance treaties as well. The Americans agreed.

The MLAT negotiations with Colombia, by contrast, arose in response to the need to prosecute Colombian drug traffickers and counterfeiters more effectively. Those with Italy emerged in response to growing concern over the role of the Italian Mafia in the heroin traffic from southwestern Asia and a number of major extradition cases involving legal ambiguities and diplomatic sensitivities, notably that of the Italian financier Michele Sindona.[95] The MLAT with the Dutch reflected both mutual concern over drug trafficking and other transnational criminal activity, as well as the desire to head off potential conflicts involving U.S. efforts to obtain bank records located in the Netherlands Antilles. Similarly, efforts to negotiate an MLAT with the German government were motivated by the abundance of international law enforcement issues involving the two states, as well as the desire to avoid conflict over

95. See *Sindona v. Grant*, 619 F.2d 167 (2d Cir. 1980), and the discussion in *New York Times*, Mar. 22, 1980, 25; see also Nick Tosches, *Power on Earth* (New York: Arbor House, 1986).

unilateral efforts by U.S. prosecutors to secure documents from Germany. And the MLAT negotiations with Morocco may well have been motivated primarily by the need for some official agreement for U.S. Attorney General William French Smith to sign when he visited the kingdom.

The MLAT negotiations with the Swiss, as well as the subsequent talks and MOUs, had provided the American negotiators with useful precedents for reconciling the requirements of the U.S. common law system with foreign civil law systems and for penetrating foreign secrecy laws. In MLAT negotiations with other governments, the U.S. negotiators sought to build on this experience by designing treaties that were simpler and more effective both in obtaining evidence and in avoiding future squabbles. They experimented with more open-ended phrases and formulations intended to broaden the availability of evidence and minimize the likelihood that courts of either nation would impede the provision of legal assistance. Model MLATs were drafted and provided to potential negotiating partners to facilitate subsequent negotiations. And each treaty negotiation was viewed as an opportunity to experiment with a potentially more effective innovation.

The MLAT negotiations with the Turks were quick and relatively simple, even though they were combined with negotiation of the extradition and prisoner transfer treaties. There was no great concern with organized crime or bank secrecy, and the negotiations focused on the technical legal problems of reconciling the two rather different legal systems. The Americans' principal concern was to avoid the tortured compromises of the Swiss treaty and to create a fresh precedent for future negotiations by negotiating quickly a MLAT that would be short, simple, and straightforward. They succeeded easily in attaining all these objectives. The treaty was signed on June 7, 1979.[96] In a dramatic contrast with the flow of requests under the Swiss MLAT, by early 1988 the Turks had made ninety-eight requests in a variety of matters ranging from serious felonies to minor offenses while the United States had forwarded only one.[97]

The MLAT negotiations with the Colombians were taken far more

96. The "Treaty with the Republic of Turkey on Extradition and Mutual Assistance in Criminal Matters" was signed in Ankara and entered into force on Jan. 1, 1981 (32 UST 3111; TIAS 9891). The prisoner transfer treaty (officially the "Treaty on the Enforcement of Penal Judgments") was signed and entered into force on the same days (32 UST 3187; TIAS 9892).

97. Knapp, "Mutual Legal Assistance Treaties" (supra n. 78), 416.

seriously by the Americans. The U.S. ambassador to Colombia, Diego Asencio, played a fairly active behind-the-scenes role in the negotiations, as did a special assistant to President Turbay, Dr. Alvaro Perez Vives. Consideration was initially given to combining the MLAT and the extradition treaty in a single document, as had been done with Turkey, but the notion was rejected because of concern over how the Colombian Congress would respond to the MLAT. It was believed that the extradition treaty would have a better chance of being approved if its consideration were not complicated by the inclusion of a novel and controversial treaty. The Colombians lacked any experience in negotiating an MLAT and were wary of agreeing to anything that might be perceived as an infringement of their national sovereignty.[98]

As in other MLAT negotiations, the U.S. negotiators sought to facilitate the flow of information and admissible evidence to the United States.[99] They also were interested, however, in enhancing the Colombians' capacity to collect whatever evidence they required to prosecute drug traffickers in their own courts. Because neither party was particularly interested in narrowing the range of cases in which evidence could be provided, the negotiating sessions focused largely on reconciling the needs of the very different legal systems. Special provisions were inserted to make evidence provided by the other government admissible in the courts of the receiving country. In a significant departure from the Swiss treaty, the requirement of "dual criminality" was eliminated and the obligation to provide assistance was extended to civil and administrative investigations and proceedings. As in the Turkish MLAT, but unlike the Swiss MLAT, law enforcement officials were authorized to release government records to the same extent that they would be available to

98. The Organization of American States had briefly considered a proposal for a multilateral MLAT, but the proposal had never gotten off the ground. However, the Colombians were not novices in the area of judicial assistance. They claimed extensive experience in the use of letters rogatory and were party to two judicial assistance agreements with the United States. One was the multilateral Inter-American Convention on Taking Evidence Abroad, signed on Jan. 13, 1975; the other was the bilateral Executive Agreement with Colombia on Mutual Assistance in the Lockheed Investigation, signed on Apr. 22, 1976; entered into force Apr. 22, 1976; 27 UST 1059, TIAS 8244; extended by TIAS 9809 in the Textron Investigation and by TIAS 9860 in the Bethlehem Steel Investigation.

99. The treaty, accompanied by the Presidential message transmitting it to the Senate, is reproduced in U.S. Senate Treaty Doc. 97-11, 97th Cong., 1st Sess. (1981). Much of the following analysis of the treaty is taken from U.S. Senate Exec. Rept. 97-35, 97th Cong., 1st Sess. (1981), which includes a summary of the major provisions as well as a section-by-section analysis.

domestic authorities, with some limitations. Likewise, officials were formally authorized to grant foreign requests for searches and seizures, provided the request met the evidentiary standard of the requested state.

Among the more significant innovations of the Colombian MLAT was a provision designed to overcome domestic legal restrictions on disclosures by tax authorities. Its purpose was less to open up foreign bank accounts to U.S. investigations than to resolve some doubts, and perhaps bureaucratic resentments, on the part of the IRS. Under Title 26 U.S.C. 6103(k)(4), the IRS was authorized to disclose information in its possession to foreign authorities under any "convention relating to the exchange of tax information" subject "to the terms and conditions of such convention." However, since the Tax Reform Act of 1976 had imposed stringent standards on the disclosure of information, many officials at the IRS had adopted what many Justice Department officials regarded as an exceptionally restrictive view of the tax disclosure provision. In the case of the Colombian treaty, the "IRS had [expressed] some doubts whether it could make such disclosures under general mutual assistance treaties, in which another government official, the Attorney General, serves as the Central Authority designated to transmit the requested information to the foreign country."[100] The language of the treaty was accordingly designed to permit the IRS to disclose information to the attorney general "solely for communication to Colombian authorities." The "doubts," it would appear, arose in part from the IRS's sensitivity to the apparent infringement by the Justice Department on its jurisdictional authority.

The treaty was signed in August 1980 and ratified by the U.S. Senate in January 1982. In Colombia, however, the MLAT made little headway in the ratification process. Advocates of the extradition treaty were initially wary lest debate over the MLAT complicate the difficult task of securing approval for the extradition treaty. Shortly after the extradition treaty was ratified, President Julio Turbay Ayala was succeeded by Belisario Betancur, who initially showed little enthusiasm for promoting a treaty that jibed poorly with his nationalist rhetoric. Following the murder of Justice Minister Rodrigo Lara Bonilla by drug traffickers in April 1984, however, the Betancur government reversed course and launched a crackdown against the drug traffickers that included closer law enforcement cooperation with the United States. By that point,

100. See the technical analysis of the MLAT, U.S. Senate Exec. Rept. 97-35, 17.

however, few Colombians in either the Congress or the administration were interested in an additional struggle over the MLAT ratification process. By the end of the decade, the MLAT had become, to all intents and purposes, a dead letter in both the Colombian Congress and U.S.-Colombian relations. Indeed, in April 1988, the Justice Department official charged with overseeing most international law enforcement matters informed Congress that the Justice Department was "in no rush to see Colombia ratify our mutual legal assistance treaty," given the possibility that evidence provided to Colombia might end up in the hands of the traffickers.[101]

The attorneys in the OIA were eager to negotiate a treaty with the Dutch. The extradition treaty with the Netherlands was out of date, and as with other countries it was deemed beneficial to negotiate both treaties simultaneously. The Americans sensed that the Dutch were interested in 'getting results" and would negotiate accordingly, and they hoped that a treaty with the Dutch would provide a beneficial model for future agreements with European governments. Moreover, both the Justice Department and the IRS were eager to penetrate the financial secrecy laws of the Netherlands Antilles and to reduce or eliminate the special status of the Netherlands Antilles as an offshore banking haven. That status had been granted in 1963 to allow U.S. businesses to obtain low-interest financing so they would not suffer competitively from European access to similar funds.[102] By 1981, however, the Dutch islands had become both "the largest tax haven recipient of U.S. source income reported to the IRS" and "the tax treaty country most widely used by U.S. and foreign persons seeking to evade U.S. taxation."[103] The benefits

101. Testimony of Mark Richard, in U.S. Senate, *MLAT . . . Caymans* (supra n. 5), 69.

102. See the Protocol modifying and supplementing extension to the Netherlands Antilles of the convention for avoidance of double taxation and prevention of fiscal evasion with respect to income and certain other taxes, Apr. 29, 1948, signed at the Hague Oct. 23, 1963, entered into force Sept. 28, 1964; 15 UST 1900; TIAS 5665; 521 UNTS 377. The treaty allows American corporations to issue Eurobonds to foreign investors and to exempt from the American withholding tax the interest paid to them.

103. The negotiations and the problem are discussed at length in *Tax Evasion Through the Netherlands Antilles and Other Tax Haven Countries: Hearings Before the Commerce, Consumer, and Monetary Affairs Subcommittee of the House Committee on Government Operations*, 98th Cong., 1st Sess. (1983). See in particular the committee staff memorandum on the subject (568–572), which summarizes the American perspective and position, and the statement of the Netherlands Antilles government (798–810). Much of the following discussion is drawn from those documents. An excellent analysis of the tax haven phenomenon and the problems it presents for the United States can be found in Richard A. Gordon, *Tax Havens and Their Use by United States Taxpayers: An Overview*, a special report submitted to the

of the 1963 treaty, supplemented by the country's minimal level of taxation on financial transactions, and domestic laws requiring strict bank secrecy and permitting the use of anonymous "bearer share" corporations and financial accounts, had led the assistant secretary of the treasury for enforcement to characterize the Antilles as "one of the four countries having the most 'iron clad secrecy.' "[104]

Many of the issues that needed to be resolved were similar to those in the Colombian negotiations and were in fact resolved similarly in most cases.[105] The principal difference reflected the concern over the Netherlands Antilles, which accordingly attracted substantial interest and involvement by the IRS. Some of their concerns were similar to those noted with respect to the Colombian treaty—that is, that information provided by the IRS not be used for nontax purposes and that the Department of Justice not infringe on their jurisdictional turf. But the IRS was also involved in simultaneous efforts to renegotiate the U.S. tax convention with the Netherlands Antilles. IRS officials naturally preferred that as much authority as possible be provided for in the tax convention, under which the secretary of the treasury was designated the "competent authority." After some debate in the higher levels of the Treasury Department, however, a policy decision that supported the inclusion of tax matters in MLATs was reached. One implication of this decision was that the IRS thereby acknowledged that a foreign prosecutor was entitled to the same access as an American prosecutor in obtaining tax information for nontax-related criminal investigations under 26 U.S.C. 6103(i). The negotiators accordingly inserted a clause in the diplomatic note accompanying the MLAT to "make . . . it clear that [the] treaty is a 'convention relating to the exchange of tax information' within the meaning of 26 U.S.C. 6103(k)(4), under which the disclosure of tax information is authorized."[106] Much to the dismay of the Americans, however, the representatives of the Netherlands Antilles at the negotiations insisted on reserving the right to refuse requests for

---

commissioner of internal revenue, the assistant attorney general (Tax Division), and the assistant secretary of the treasury (Tax Policy) in Jan. 1981.

104. *Tax Evasion: Hearings* (supra n. 103), 569.

105. The treaty, accompanied by the Presidential message transmitting it to the Senate, is reproduced in U.S. Senate Treaty Doc. 97-16, 97th Cong., 1st Sess. (1981); it can also be found at TIAS 10734. Much of the following analysis of the treaty is taken from U.S. Senate Exec. Rept. 97-36, 97th Cong., 1st Sess. (1981), which includes a summary of the major provisions as well as a section-by-section analysis.

106. See the technical analysis of the Dutch MLAT, U.S. Senate Exec. Rept. 97-36, 6.

assistance in fiscal offenses until the tax convention had been renegotiated.[107] Unable to budge the negotiators from the Netherlands Antilles
on this matter, or to persuade the Dutch government to use its influence
on this issue, the Americans assented to the reservation.[108]

The renegotiation of the tax convention, it should be noted, was part
of a broader effort initiated by the Treasury Department and the Tax
Division of the Justice Department during the late 1970s to increase
international cooperation in prosecution of tax violations. Most of the
thirty-odd tax conventions to which the United States was a party were
oriented primarily toward cooperation in civil cases and only a few
allowed for disclosure in fraud investigations. To a certain extent, this
reflected the traditional mind-set of finance ministries, whose principal
concern was not criminal prosecution of tax evaders but rather assessment and collection of revenues. But as U.S. law enforcement authorities
became increasingly interested in prosecuting drug traffickers and other
organized criminals on tax evasion charges, IRS officials realized that
the tax conventions would need to be revised to authorize cooperation
in criminal prosecutions.[109]

Another issue that generated debate in both the extradition and MLAT
negotiations involved the necessity of including a "political offense"
exception in the treaties. The inclusion or exclusion of this grounds for
refusing assistance was frequently a sensitive issue in extradition and
MLAT negotiations; indeed, both the United States and many foreign
states were wary of negotiating law enforcement treaties with governments viewed as likely to use or misuse their judicial systems to punish
or harass political opponents. When obliged to negotiate such treaties
with nondemocratic governments because of broader concerns such as
drug trafficking, U.S. negotiators typically insisted on including the
"political offense" exception clause. They saw little need, however, to

107. See the statement of the Netherlands Antilles government in *Tax Evasion: Hearings*
(supra n. 103), 808.
108. The final word belonged to Congress. As part of the Deficit Reduction Act of 1984,
Congress repealed the 30 percent withholding tax on interest earned by foreigners, thereby
making it possible for American corporations to sell Eurobonds directly to foreign investors
without setting up subsidiaries in the Antilles. The effect on the economy of the Netherlands
Antilles, their minister plenipotentiary in the Washington, D.C., predicted in 1984, would be
"devastating." See Oppenheimer, "U.S. Taking Lid Off Tax Havens' Secrets," *Miami Herald*,
Oct. 8, 1984, Business Section, 1, 10.
109. Among the first to be renegotiated to include criminal provisions were those with
Cyprus (TIAS 10965), Jamaica (TIAS 10206), Australia (TIAS 10773), and New Zealand
(TIAS 10772).

include the clause in treaties with Western Europeans, particularly in MLATs. Some European negotiators, however, including the Dutch, were less convinced that the clause should be excluded; they were influenced by their own perceptions of the conflicts between civil rights activists and law enforcement officials in the American South during the 1960s, and by cases such as that involving the "Chicago 7." The American negotiators took umbrage at any suggestion that violations of U.S. laws, or prosecutions of criminal offenses, could be politically motivated or justified; they agreed, however, that insofar as extradition was deemed the most extreme form of international assistance in criminal cases, a "political offense" exception might be warranted in such treaties. They saw no need, however, for its inclusion in the MLAT. When the Dutch insisted, the Americans relented, but the negotiators agreed that "the 'political offense' grounds for refusing assistance . . . should not be invoked as readily as in extradition." They further noted their "appreciat[ion] that the United States adheres to the narrower 'British view' of political offenses, while the Netherlands adheres to the broader 'Swiss view.' "[110]

The MLAT was signed in June 1981 and went into force in September 1983.[111] By the late 1980s, the OIA was forwarding approximately twenty-five requests a year to the Dutch, approximately half of which were for information in the Antilles, and receiving about a dozen requests a year from Dutch authorities.[112]

The MLAT with Italy was notable primarily because of two novel provisions: an "international subpoena," whereby one state could request another to *compel* a person to appear and testify in the requesting state; and a provision authorizing the immobilization of assets in the requested state and their forfeiture to the requesting state. In the MLAT negotiations, the Italians agreed to virtually all of the provisions in the Americans' model treaty, including the elimination of any requirement of dual criminality.[113] Unlike the previous treaties, a provision was

110. See the technical analysis of the Dutch MLAT, U.S. Senate Exec. Rept. 97-36, 11.

111. Further analysis of the MLAT, with particular attention to the implications for the Netherlands Antilles, can be found in J. M. Saleh, "International Judicial Assistance Techniques in the Light of Modern International Need," *Tijdschrift voor Antilaans Recht-Justicia*, 1987, 110–126.

112. Knapp, "Mutual Legal Assistance Treaties" (supra n. 78), 416.

113. The treaty, accompanied by the Presidential message transmitting it to the Senate, is reproduced in U.S. Senate Treaty Doc. 98-25, 98th Cong., 2d Sess. (1984). A section-by-section analysis of the treaty appears in U.S. Senate Exec. Rept. 98-36, 98th Cong., 2d Sess. The two governments were not entirely inexperienced in the negotiation of mutual legal

included allowing the *requesting* state to "request that the application for assistance, the contents of the request and its supporting documents, and the granting of such assistance be kept confidential," thereby facilitating the use of the MLAT in grand jury investigations.[114] The first of the two major innovations provided that "[i]n emergency situations, the Requested State shall have authority to immobilize assets found in that state which are subject to forfeiture" and to order the forfeiture of those assets to the Requesting State. As with some of the forfeiture provisions in the Racketeer Influenced and Corrupt Organizations Act (RICO) and other antidrug trafficking statutes, this provision reflected the spreading belief in law enforcement circles that the most effective way to deter and punish drug traffickers was to immobilize their assets. Unlike the Swiss treaty, the proceeds were forfeited to the prosecuting country, not the seizing country.

The inclusion of the "international subpoena" provision in the treaty was regarded by many of the attorneys involved in international legal assistance as a potentially "revolutionary" development in mutual legal assistance, one that would pave the way for the same provision in a multilateral convention on mutual legal assistance.[115] Before the Italian treaty, all MLATs had required the consent of a witness requested to testify in a requesting state (whether he was in custody or not). The negotiators of the Italian treaty eliminated the requirement of consent and agreed that the requested state would compel a witness to go to the

---

assistance agreements. In 1976, they had signed a treaty to facilitate cooperation in investigating the Lockheed Aircraft Corporation matter (27 UST 3437; TIAS 8374). The MLAT, as well as the extradition treaty, is analyzed in Paolo Mengozzi, "A View from Italy on Judicial Cooperation Between Italy and the United States: The 1982 Mutual Assistance Treaty and the 1983 Extradition Treaty," *NYU Journal of International Law and Politics* 18 (1986), 813–831.

114. See Art. 8(2) of the Italian MLAT. Like the Swiss MLAT, the Italian treaty also allowed the *requested* state to require that the evidence and information provided be kept confidential, thereby making it easier for U.S. officials to provide Italy with tax information and information obtained during a grand jury investigation. The Italian treaty, like the Dutch, was also characterized as a "convention relating to the exchange of tax information" within the meaning of 26 U.S.C. 6103(k)(4). The provision of tax information to the Italian authorities remained contingent upon their request meeting the requirements of 26 U.S.C. 6103(h) and/or 6103(i). The grand jury information could be obtained pursuant to a court-ordered disclosure under Rule 6(e)(3)(C)(i), Federal Rules of Criminal Procedure. See the technical analysis of the Italian MLAT, U.S. Senate Exec. Rept. 98-36, 6.

115. The international subpoena is analyzed at length in Kenneth I. Juster, "International Legal Assistance in Criminal Law Enforcement" (Paper on file at the John F. Kennedy School of Government, Harvard University, April 1980).

requesting state so long as it had "no reasonable basis to deny the request" and insofar as "the person could be compelled to appear and testify in similar circumstances in the Requested State."

In anticipation of a skeptical Congressional response to their novel concept, the negotiators devoted a good part of the treaty analysis which they submitted to the Foreign Relations Committee to preempting potential criticisms of it.[116] They argued that the term "international subpoena" was a misnomer insofar as the state in which the subpoenaed witness resided served as an intermediary and evaluator of the request. Moreover, "since the requested country is to employ the procedures it uses in domestic cases when it compels a witness to appear and testify in the requesting country, witnesses in the United States, whose appearance and testimony in Italy is sought pursuant to the Treaty, will be able to move the court to quash the subpoena if compliance would be unreasonable or oppressive."[117] More important, they suggested, the notion was little more than an international extension of the Uniform Act to Secure the Attendance of Witnesses from Without a State in Criminal Proceedings—the intrastate compact, to which every state but one is a party, allowing each state to obtain compulsory appearance and testimony in its legal proceedings of witnesses located in other states.[118] Given the speed of modern jet transportation, the negotiators argued, the inconvenience of being ordered to go to Italy was little greater than that of being required to make a transcontinental flight to another state. Finally, they noted, persons compelled to appear in response to an international subpoena were further protected by another treaty provision, which (unlike the Uniform Act) afforded them immunity with respect to any truthful testimony given in the requesting country.[119]

The treaty with Italy was signed in November 1982 and went into force—after delays involving not the "international subpoena" but rather the forfeiture provisions—in November 1985. Within just two years, the MLAT had proven its value in facilitating both Italian and U.S. prosecutions of the Sicilian Mafia, including those implicated in the

116. See the technical analysis of the Italian MLAT, 6.

117. *Amsler v. U.S.*, 381 F.2d 37, 51 (9th Cir. 1967). Cf. Rule 17(c), Federal Rules of Criminal Procedure, U.S. Senate Exec. Rept. 98-36, 10.

118. 11 U.L.A. 1.

119. Theresa M. Catino, "Italian and American Cooperative Efforts to Reduce Heroin Trafficking: A Role Model for the United States and Drug-Supplying Foreign Nations," *Dickinson Journal of International Law* 8 (1990), 415–440.

"Pizza Connection" case in New York and the large-scale prosecution of hundreds of mafiosi in Sicily; the Italian requests, which numbered about twice as many as the U.S. requests, were largely for taking depositions and serving documents on witnesses.[120]

The sixth treaty to be signed, with the kingdom of Morocco, was the first with a nondemocratic government.[121] Both parties regarded the negotiations in part as a trial run for future negotiations on an extradition treaty. But the Moroccans' refusal to include a "political offense" clause in the MLAT reduced the Americans' interest in proceeding to the next step. As with the previous MLAT negotiations, the preliminary talks and early parts of the negotiating sessions were devoted to explaining domestic legal concepts and their consequences. Moroccan criminal law had been inherited largely from the French Napoleonic Code system and had assimilated some aspects of Islamic law as well. The Moroccan negotiators thus required much the same sorts of explanations as the Americans' previous partners in MLAT negotiations: why the Americans preferred not to rely on the traditional letters rogatory process; why arrest warrants were signed by clerks, and other requests for assistance by prosecutors, rather than by judges; what the rights of confrontation and cross-examination were and why they needed to be accommodated even in foreign judicial proceedings despite the inconveniences they entailed; why verbatim transcripts of judicial proceedings were necessary; why other parties might be required to be present at judicial proceedings; and so on.

Given the mutual concern over drug trafficking through Morocco, the treaty included an article on forfeiture that provided for "[t]he goods and assets held by any person punishable under laws relating to criminal narcotics matters . . . [to] be seized" and held until the requesting state had completed its judicial proceedings. Unlike the provision in the Italian MLAT, which specifically authorized the forfeited proceeds to be delivered to the Requesting State, the provision in the Moroccan MLAT was modeled after a practice that had developed under (but had not been specified in) the MLAT with the Swiss. It was anticipated that this provision would permit each government to seize and ultimately forfeit

---

120. Knapp, "Mutual Legal Assistance Treaties" (supra n. 78), 416–417.

121. The treaty, accompanied by the Presidential message transmitting it to the Senate, is reproduced in U.S. Senate Treaty Doc. 98-24, 98th Cong., 2d Sess. (1984). A section-by-section analysis of the treaty appears in U.S. Senate Exec. Rept. 98-35, 98th Cong., 2d Sess. (1984).

drug trafficker assets within its borders pursuant to a prosecution of the trafficker in the other state.

The principal difference between the Moroccan MLAT and others negotiated by the United States was the exclusion of any provisions for transferring witnesses or defendants in custody from one state to the other to give testimony. The Moroccan delegation claimed that their domestic law did not allow for the possibility of incarcerating an individual who had not committed a violation of Moroccan law. They also insisted that such provisions were more appropriate to an extradition or prisoner transfer treaty. Although the Americans suspected that Moroccan opposition stemmed primarily from an anticipation of bureaucratic complications in gaining assent to such a novel provision, they had little choice but to concede the provision.

More generally, the Moroccan treaty differed from the previously negotiated MLATs in terms of its relative lack of specificity. Many of the routine provisions describing the preferred procedures for gathering evidence or taking testimony so that it would be admissible in U.S. courts were either simplified or eliminated in the Moroccan treaty. Also absent were the self-executing provisions that had created a narrow exception to the hearsay rule by providing for foreign officials to certify the chain of custody of seized objects and the authenticity of government documents. The willingness of the U.S. negotiators to forgo these provisions probably reflected both their anticipation that they would make relatively little use of the treaty, as well as the apparent need to complete the negotiations quickly in anticipation of Attorney General Smith's planned visit to the kingdom. In any event, the MLAT between the two countries was signed in October 1983 during the U.S. attorney general's visit. The United States ratified it the following year, but the Moroccans had yet to do likewise as of 1993.

Extraterritoriality in the Caribbean: British Dependencies Past and Present

Even as U.S. officials were gradually succeeding in breaching the walls of secrecy surrounding Switzerland's banks, nations and dependencies throughout the Caribbean were enacting and tightening their own secrecy statutes and lenient tax laws. The Bahamas and a variety of British dependencies, notably the Cayman Islands but also including the Turks and Caicos, Anguilla, Montserrat, and the British Virgin Islands, were attracting billions in U.S. dollars from Americans and others drawn to the nearby, English-speaking islands. Panama was proving equally successful in attracting billions from Latin America and beyond. And the Netherlands Antilles remained an attractive haven as well. The financial secrecy jurisdictions offered legitimate tax havens to U.S. corporations as well as a protective shield for those trying to illegally avoid taxes or to hide and launder criminally derived funds. More often than not, requests for assistance by way of letters rogatory failed to produce satisfaction.

U.S. law enforcement officials responded to the situation in the Caribbean with a range of unilateral tactics designed both to obtain evidence in particular investigations and to pressure local governments into negotiating judicial assistance agreements. Undercover tactics were employed, bribes were paid to local government and bank officials, and subpoenas were directed to foreign banks and bankers with contacts in the United States. These led, not surprisingly, to substantial tensions between the U.S. government and those in the Caribbean. They also angered the British government, which represented many of the island dependencies, and the Canadian government, which found its sovereignty challenged by U.S. assertions of extraterritoriality directed at the Caribbean branches of Canadian banks. The unilateral tactics and other pressures did result, however, in the negotiation of MLATs and similar agreements with Canada and most of the Caribbean governments by the end of the 1980s.

The Cayman Islands

In 1976, the *Field* case, involving an official of a Cayman bank visiting the United States who received a grand jury subpoena compelling him to give testimony before a U.S. grand jury, persuaded the Cayman government to tighten its financial secrecy laws and increase the sanctions for unauthorized disclosure.[122] U.S. prosecutors, however, responded with an array of additional techniques for extracting documents from the Cayman Islands and other havens. They obtained the support of federal courts for the issuance of letters rogatory to Cayman courts.[123]

---

122. The use of the subpoena was upheld in *U.S. v. Field*, 532 F.2d 404 (5th Cir. 1976); cert. denied, 429 U.S. 940 (1976).

123. *U.S. v. Carver* (unpublished), aff'd sub nom., *U.S. v. Lemire*, 720 F.2d 1327 (D.C. Cir. 1983).

But when the Cayman courts rejected such requests, U.S. prosecutors resorted to more unilateral measures. The most controversial of these arose when a grand jury investigating tax and drug law violations issued a subpoena *duces tecum* in September 1981 to the Miami branch of the Canadian Bank of Nova Scotia for records maintained in the bank's Bahamian branch;[124] subsequent subpoenas issued in March 1983 sought additional documents in the bank's Bahamian branch as well as its branches in the Cayman Islands and Antigua.[125] When the bank refused to comply, claiming that to do so would place it in violation of the islands' bank secrecy laws, the U.S. courts levied daily fines of $25,000 on the bank. Although the *Bank of Nova Scotia* case was not the first in which U.S. attorneys had resorted to the technique thereafter identified with the case—indeed, the resort to compulsory process to compel U.S. corporations to provide documents located in their foreign branches dated back decades—it was the first in which they had responded to resistance in providing the evidence by obtaining sanctions from a court.

Unable to resolve the dispute through law enforcement channels, the Caymans' case was taken up by the British, who conduct the Caymans' foreign affairs, and by the Canadians, whose banks were those principally affected. The motivations of the British, beyond their legal obligation to represent the Caymans, included their concern for the economy of their former colony, their general objection both to U.S. assertions of extraterritoriality and to the notion of an American court presuming to "balance" U.S. interests with those of another state, and their attachment to the principle of financial confidentiality (often referred to as the *Tournier* principle).[126] The Canadians' motivations overlapped to a certain extent with those of the British; they also were upset not only by the threats to their politically influential banks but also by the unilateral nature of the American actions despite Canada's excellent record of

124. *U.S. v. Bank of Nova Scotia*, 691 F.2d 1384 (11th Cir. 1982), cert. denied, 462 U.S. 1119 (1983) (often referred to as *Bank of Nova Scotia I*).

125. *In re Grand Jury Proceedings, U.S. v. Bank of Nova Scotia*, 740 F.2d 817 (11th Cir. 1984), cert. denied, 469 U.S. 1106 (1985) (often referred to as *Bank of Nova Scotia II*).

126. The leading English case of *Tournier v. National Provincial and Union Bank* states that there is a duty of confidentiality between bankers and their customers. See the Library of Congress study by S. F. Clarke, "Bank Secrecy Jurisdictions in the English-Speaking Caribbean and Atlantic Regions," in *Crime and Secrecy: The Use of Offshore Banks and Companies, Staff Study by the Permanent Subcommittee on Investigations of the Senate Committee on Governmental Affairs*, 98th Cong., 1st Sess., S.Rpt. 98-21 (1983), 181–185.

cooperation in all other law enforcement matters. As for the Caymanians, their basic objective was to preserve, by whatever means possible, their lucrative reputation as a reliable financial secrecy jurisdiction.[127]

In an initial effort to resolve the dispute, the governments of the United States, the United Kingdom, and the Cayman Islands entered into a gentleman's agreement in October 1982 to cooperate in criminal investigations, such as of drug trafficking, where the mutuality-of-offense requirement was met.[128] The agreement, however, failed either to enhance Caymanian cooperation or to prevent U.S. prosecutors from obtaining grand jury subpoenas; indeed, no bank records had been delivered by the end of 1983.[129] One year later, the issue finally came to a head after the Cayman Grand Court twice enjoined the Bank of Nova Scotia from releasing documents held in the Caymans in response to a U.S. court order. Under pressure from the Bank of Nova Scotia, which was incurring substantial fines as a result of its failure to comply with the subpoena (a failure caused in part by the bank's negligence in locating even those documents it had been authorized by the Bahamian attorney general to deliver), the British intervened and obliged the Caymanian governor to order that the documents be disclosed.

The tensions generated by this and other disputes over extraterritoriality led to a November 1983 meeting between the American undersecretary of state, Kenneth Dam, and the British minister for foreign and commonwealth affairs, Malcolm Rifkind, one outcome of which was the establishment of a number of working groups to address particular disputes. One of these was charged specifically with the task of examining the problems created by criminal uses of the Caribbean secrecy jurisdictions. At about the same time, and in response to other international tensions generated by the flurry of *Bank of Nova Scotia* type of subpoenas obtained by prosecutors in the wake of that case, the Justice Department ordered that all subpoenas to institutions in the United

127. The perspective of the British and the Caymanians is well presented in their *amici curiae* brief to the U.S. Supreme Court in the *Bank of Nova Scotia* case, No. 84-329 (October term, 1984).

128. The letters clarifying each government's interpretation of the agreement can be found at Fedders et al., *Transnational Litigation* (supra n. 53), 737–743.

129. Disagreement over the extent and significance of the agreement was ultimately resolved by the Eleventh Circuit Court of Appeals in *Bank of Nova Scotia II*, which deemed the agreement "not a binding, enforceable agreement but rather an experimental and tentative alternative for the production of documents." See *U.S. v. Bank of Nova Scotia*, 740 F.2d 817, 829 (11th Cir. 1984).

States for records located abroad be cleared through the Office of International Affairs. The need for the order, which became known as "the Jensen memorandum" (after Associate Attorney General D. Lowell Jensen), was readily apparent.[130] It reflected the recognition that federal and other prosecutors, in their quest for evidence, would utilize whichever means seemed most effective and expedient, regardless of their broader consequences. Apart from the infrequently read U.S. Attorney's Manual, which required that prosecutors check with the Justice Department before taking any action that might have an impact on foreign relations, most prosecutors perceived few if any constraints on their resort to subpoenas to obtain evidence. As a result, OIA attorneys had been unpleasantly surprised and embarrassed on a number of occasions during 1982 and 1983 by angry phone calls from their foreign counterparts, particularly in London and Ottawa, complaining about the issuance of *Bank of Nova Scotia* subpoenas without any prior efforts to obtain the desired evidence through more conciliatory, bilateral channels. The Jensen memorandum, by requiring that all international requests be channeled through the OIA, thus allowed the Justice Department to gain greater control over the foreign policy of evidence-gathering. It provided OIA attorneys with an opportunity to inform prosecutors of more effective and less abrasive techniques for gathering evidence, some of which involved the OIA's own informal and expedited arrangements with foreign counterparts. And it allowed them as well as higher-level Justice Department officials to better manage their relations with both cooperative and less-cooperative foreign justice ministries. Although the Jensen memorandum did not apply to civil subpoenas and administrative summons issued by the SEC and other regulatory agencies, it effectively canalized through the OIA all criminal investigative requests for evidence located abroad.

Another outcome of the Dam-Rifkind meeting was the initiation of negotiations in early 1984 between U.S. and British officials on a legal assistance agreement with the Cayman Islands. Unlike the other MLATs negotiated by the United States, this one was limited, at the request of the British, to cooperation in narcotics cases and predicated on the provisions against drug trafficking in the multilateral Single Convention on Narcotic Drugs.[131] American law enforcement agencies were divided

130. The memorandum is reproduced in the appendix of Paul B. Bschorr, " 'Waiver by Conduct': Another View," *Journal of Comparative Business and Capital Market Law* 6 (1984), 307–318, esp. 313–315.

131. The Single Convention on Narcotic Drugs, 1961. Done at New York Mar. 30, 1961;

as to the advisability of negotiating a legal assistance treaty limited solely to drug investigations, but it was decided to accept the British condition. Under some pressure from the British, Caymanian officials accepted the necessity for an agreement but expressed their concern that the agreement not provide a means for U.S. law enforcement agencies, notably the IRS, to engage in "fishing expeditions."[132] The U.S. delegation was eager to minimize the amount of information that would have to be provided in support of a request for evidence; they were deeply concerned that the targets of some of the investigations involving Cayman banks, who included the more powerful Colombian drug traffickers, not be provided an opportunity to undermine U.S. investigations by means of either legal recourse or illicit intimidation and bribery. The mutual concerns were resolved by an agreement that the U.S. attorney general would personally certify that each request was for a drug-related prosecution. The second principal concern of the British and Cayman negotiators was to limit the use of subpoenas *duces tecum* by U.S. prosecutors. In what constituted their principal concession, the Americans "swallowed hard," as one Justice Department official put it, and agreed to waive their prerogative of obtaining a subpoena *duces tecum* and to confine their requests in drug related cases (but not in others) to the procedures specified in the agreement.

The agreement was signed by the British and U.S. governments on July 26, 1984, and went into effect on August 29, when the Caymanian implementing legislation took effect.[133] Unlike the MLAT with the Swiss, the Cayman agreement specified that any American request be kept confidential by both the Cayman attorney general and the provider of

entered into force Dec. 13, 1964; for the U.S. June 24, 1967; 18 UST 1407; TIAS 6298; 520 UNTS 204.

132. They were, however, willing to permit information they provided to be used to prosecute drug traffickers on Title 26 charges.

133. Exchange of Letters Between the Government of the United Kingdom of Great Britain and Northern Ireland and the Government of the United States of America Concerning the Cayman Islands and Matters Connected with, Arising from, Related to, or Resulting from Any Narcotics Activity Referred to in the Single Convention on Narcotic Drugs, 1961, as Amended by the Protocol Amending the Single Convention on Narcotic Drugs, 1972. The agreement can be found in *International Legal Materials* 24 (1985), 1110. The Caymanian implementing legislation is reproduced in ibid., 937. Because the agreement was an executive agreement rather than a full-fledged MLAT, Senate ratification was not required. Some of the events and cases noted above are also discussed in Comment, "Piercing Offshore Bank Secrecy Laws Used to Launder Illegal Narcotics Profits: The Cayman Islands Example," *Texas International Law Journal* 20 (1985), 133.

the documents; it waived the standard MLAT requirement that a request be accompanied by supporting documents, requiring only the U.S. attorney general's certificate. And the Cayman implementing legislation omitted the types of procedural hurdles that had so hampered the Swiss MLAT. For all these reasons, as well as the fact that requests could be sent only one way, many U.S. officials were reluctant to trade in the executive agreement for a full-fledged MLAT with the Caymans.

The Cayman agreement stipulated, however, that the signatories enter into MLAT negotiations before the end of 1985. On July 3, 1986, a full-fledged MLAT was signed by representatives of the U.S., British, and Cayman governments.[134] It was the first between the United States and a Caribbean financial secrecy jurisdiction, as well as the first MLAT of any kind signed by the British, who traditionally had avoided involvement in such arrangements—including the European Convention on Mutual Assistance—because of doubts that their strict rules of evidence could be accommodated to foreign judicial proceedings on their behalf.[135] From the U.S. perspective, the principal disadvantage of the MLAT (insisted upon by the British/Cayman delegation) was that the attorney general's certification could no longer substitute for the need to provide supporting documents spelling out the alleged offense. Justice Department officials had found, both in implementing the Swiss MLAT and in continuing to execute letters rogatory, that the need to provide supporting documents spelling out the alleged offense represented a substantial deterrent to U.S. prosecutors seeking evidence from abroad. Their concern was that the information provided in the request might be released—because of legal process, carelessness, corruption, or whatever—thus jeopardizing the success of the investigation and/or the source of the information. Although the U.S. delegation was disappointed about losing the novel certification provision in the Cayman agreement, they were partially reassured by the high level of trust developed in mutually

134. The treaty, accompanied by the Presidential message transmitting it to the Senate, is reproduced in U.S. Senate Treaty Doc. 100-8, 100th Cong., 1st Sess. (1988), and in *International Legal Materials* 26 (1987), 537. A section-by-section analysis of the treaty, as well as additional analysis of the treaty in response to Senate inquiries, appears in U.S. Senate Exec. Rept. 101-08, 101st Cong., 1st Sess. (1989), 8–50, 122–129, 140–145. See also Ilene Katz Kobert and Jonathan D. Yellin, "The United States Treaty with the United Kingdom Concerning the Cayman Islands and Mutual Legal Assistance in Criminal Matters: The End of Another Tax Haven," *Inter-American Law Review* 19 (1988), 663–697.

135. Michael Havers, "Legal Cooperation: A Matter of Necessity," *International Lawyer* 21 (1987), 185–193, esp. 192.

implementing the first agreement, by the inclusion of confidentiality clauses in the MLAT, and by the fact that in the future fewer requests would entail the sorts of risks involved in investigating the financial activities of Colombian drug traffickers.

The MLAT did, however, offer numerous advantages over the previous agreement. Not only was it not limited to drug-related cases, but the British and Cayman negotiators even agreed to cooperate in cases (such as insider trading and violations of the Foreign Corrupt Practices Act) in which the mutuality of offense requirement was not met. Tax offenses were explicitly excluded from the scope of the treaty, but the British agreed that evidence provided by Caymanian authorities could be used to prosecute fraud in connection with tax shelters and tax evasion or filing false statements with respect to illegally obtained income. Another advantage of the MLAT was that it included far broader types of assistance than were authorized in the executive agreement, including not just the production and authentication of documents but also the taking of testimony, serving documents, locating persons, transferring persons in custody for testimonial purposes, executing requests for searches and seizures, and assistance in freezing and forfeiting criminally obtained assets.[136]

Among the most important issues debated by the MLAT negotiators was the continued resort by U.S. prosecutors to subpoenas and other unilateral means of extraterritorially asserting U.S. jurisdiction. U.S. prosecutors had continued to employ *Bank of Nova Scotia* subpoenas in nondrug related investigations, particularly those involving tax shelter frauds, although they had tried to minimize their resort to such methods and to consult with their counterparts in the Cayman Islands before proceeding. The 1984 agreement had also not precluded an alternative technique devised by U.S. prosecutors to obtain evidence from foreign financial secrecy jurisdictions. Known as a *"Ghidoni* waiver" (after the first prominent court decision upholding its use), the technique involved obtaining a court order compelling the target of a grand jury investigation to authorize foreign banks to disclose the records sought in the subpoena.[137] Although intended to allow banks to comply with U.S.

136. U.S. Senate, *MLAT . . . Caymans* (supra n. 5), 125–128.
137. *U.S. v. Ghidoni*, 732 F.2d 814 (11th Cir. 1984), cert. denied, 469 U.S. 932 (1984) (involving a grand jury subpoena issued to the Miami branch of the Bank of Nova Scotia commanding it to produce documents located in its Cayman Islands branch). The "*Ghidoni* waiver" is critically analyzed in Harvey M. Silets and Susan W. Brenner, " 'Compelled Consent': An Oxymoron with Sinister Consequences for Citizens Who Patronize Foreign

subpoenas without violating foreign secrecy laws, the "compelled consent" technique had been rejected by the Grand Court of the Cayman Islands in 1984.[138] U.S. prosecutors, however, had largely ignored the ruling by the Cayman court, and most U.S. courts had upheld the use of the technique against constitutional challenges, notably the claim that it violated defendants' Fifth Amendment rights against self-incrimination.[139] During the MLAT negotiations, the British and Cayman delegates pressured the U.S. negotiators on this issue. The resultant compromise forbade U.S. authorities from seeking a *Bank of Nova Scotia* subpoena or *Ghidoni* waiver until after the assistance had been requested under the treaty and Cayman authorities had had ample opportunity to comply.[140] The U.S. negotiators refused, however, to apply the same conditions to the issuance of subpoenas or material person warrants for persons temporarily in the United States (i.e., the type of subpoena employed in the *Field* case) or to the issuance of administrative summons by the IRS, the SEC, or the CFTC unless the investigation concerned a "criminal offense" under the treaty.[141] They claimed that such a concession would constitute an undesirably broad restriction on each party's territorial sovereignty. Still wary of American "fishing expeditions," the Cayman and British negotiators also insisted on a provision, not included in other MLATs negotiated by the United States, requiring each request to contain "reasonable grounds" to believe both that the specific crime had been committed and that the information requested could be found in the territory of the requested state.[142] Although wary of

---

Banking Institutions," *Case Western Reserve Journal of International Law* 20 (1988), 435–508.

138. Chief Judge Summerfield stated: "On the face of it, the consent given in Ghidoni's case is consent given under compulsion and does not amount to consent for the purposes of our law." *In re an Application by ABC, Ltd. Under the Confidential Relationships (Preservation) (Amendment) Law, 1979*, Judgment of July 24, 1984, Grand Court, Cayman Islands, July 24, 1984 (Cause No. 269), discussed in Ellen C. Atwater, "Compelled Waiver of Bank Secrecy in the Cayman Islands: Solution to International Tax Evasion or Threat to Sovereignty of Nations?" *Fordham International Law Journal* 9 (1986), 680–733, esp. 703–705.

139. See *U.S. v. Ghidoni*. The *Ghidoni* waiver was upheld in *U.S. v. Davis*, 767 F.2d 1025 (2d Cir. 1985), *In re U.S. Grand Jury Proceedings (Cid)*, 767 F.2d 1131 (5th Cir. 1985), and *In re Grand Jury Subpoena*, 826 F.2d 1166 (2d Cir. 1987), but invalidated in *In re Grand Jury Proceedings (Ranauro)*, 814 F.2d 791 (1st Cir. 1987). The Supreme Court ultimately resolved the dispute in favor of the *Ghidoni* waiver in *Doe v. U.S.*, 108 S.Ct. 2341, 487 U.S. 201 (1988).

140. See Art. 17 of the Cayman MLAT.

141. See the technical analysis of the treaty in U.S. Senate, *MLAT . . . Caymans* (supra n. 5), 45–46.

142. See Art. 3(2)(c) of the Cayman MLAT.

tinkering with new language, the U.S. negotiators conceded the wording, confident that it would not prove onerous in practice.[143]

Among Caymanians, debate over the treaty and the implementing legislation was heated, as had been the case following the signing of the 1984 agreement. In an election held a few months after the agreement went into effect, the accord with the United States was a major campaign issue. Many of those in the government were ousted from office. Some observers suspected that the signing of the agreement was responsible and that the old government was perceived as having gone soft and caved in to the pressure exerted by the Americans and the British.[144] Despite the fallout from the 1984 agreement, and despite heated debate over the new MLAT, the Cayman legislature passed the necessary implementing legislation only weeks after the treaty was signed. Ratification by the U.S. Senate, however, was delayed as a result of unanticipated objections discussed below. The MLAT ultimately took effect late in 1989.

As anticipated, the executive agreement with the Caymans proved highly successful in obtaining evidence. By mid-1986, according to a British count, 39 requests had been transmitted,[145] and most had been processed quite rapidly by the Cayman authorities. By October 1, 1987, according to an American count, 51 initial requests and 40 follow-up requests had been transmitted; the evidence provided had contributed to the conviction of 95 drug traffickers, including approximately 30 for violation of the federal "drug kingpin" statute, and proven highly useful in asset forfeiture proceedings as well.[146] And by the time the MLAT entered into force, U.S. officials had used the executive agreement to transmit an estimated 200 requests. It was anticipated that the high level of assistance would continue under the MLAT.

The paramount question, in the eyes of the Caymanians and all other financial secrecy jurisdictions as well, was what impact the agreement would have on the Caymans' bank industry. Some bankers suggested that an outflow of funds to Panama and other financial secrecy jurisdictions followed the signing of the initial agreement. Others indicated that

143. See the technical analysis of the treaty in U.S. Senate, *MLAT . . . Caymans* (supra n. 5), 123.

144. Conflicting reports also suggested either that the police chief of the Caymans had been forced out of office for appearing too forthcoming with the Americans, or that he had merely retired in due course.

145. Havers, "Legal Cooperation," (supra n. 135).

146. Knapp, "Mutual Legal Assistance Treaties" (supra n. 78), 417. The "drug kingpin" statute is 18 U.S.C. 848, otherwise known as the Continuing Criminal Enterprise Statute.

the outflow has been negligible, that drug money had never constituted more than a small proportion of the funds sent to the Caymans, and that in fact the benefit to the Caymans' reputation as a result of the agreement has attracted business—just as the Swiss had claimed following the signing of their MLAT. Indeed, after the executive agreement the number of banks opening branches in the Cayman Islands continued to climb. Just days before the MLAT was signed, an article appeared in the *Miami Herald* on the Cayman banking industry. Its title: "Caymans Grow as 'Geneva of the Caribbean.' "[147]

Both the agreement and the treaty with the Caymans were expected to serve as models for future agreements with other financial secrecy jurisdictions, notably Britain's other dependencies in the Caribbean. The first to follow was the Turks and Caicos, whose banking assets were believed to be second only to the Caymans among the British financial secrecy jurisdictions in the Caribbean. The negotiators may also have been influenced by the islands' reputation for involvement in drug smuggling, a notoriety highlighted by the arrest of the Turks and Caicos Islands' chief minister and two other high-ranking officials in a DEA undercover operation in Miami in March 1985.[148] In September 1986, following an official inquiry into corruption that resulted in the dissolution of the Islands' governing Executive Council by the British governor-general, American and British negotiators signed an agreement that was virtually identical to the 1984 Cayman agreement.[149] Similar agreements were concluded and went into force the following year with Anguilla,[150] the British Virgin Islands,[151] and Montserrat.[152] By 1990, the total number of requests transmitted under all four of the agreements num-

147. James Russell, "Caymans Grow as Geneva of the Caribbean," *Miami Herald*, June 22, 1986, 1F.

148. Jon Nordheimer, "U.S. Arrests Atlantic Islands' Leader in Drug Plot," *New York Times*, Mar. 6, 1985, A1; Liz Balmaseda, "Drug Net Snares Island Ministers," *Miami Herald*, Mar. 6, 1985, A1; Mary Thornton, "Caribbean Prime Minister Arrested in Miami on Drug Charges," *Washington Post*, Mar. 6, 1985, A16. The reaction to the arrest in the Turks and Caicos was split, with many people angered by the arrest and the fact that the resident British governor had cooperated with the DEA. See Geoffrey Tomb, "Drug Arrests Divide Poverty-Stricken Turks and Caicos," *Miami Herald*, Mar. 12, 1985, 14A; Mary Thornton, "Drug Arrests Raise Islands' Tension," *Washington Post*, Mar. 11, 1985; and Joseph B. Treaster, "In Old Pirate Haunt, Daunting News of Drug Trade," *New York Times*, Mar. 13, 1985, 2.

149. Philip Shenon, "Pact Gives U.S. Access to Data in Drug Haven," *New York Times*, Sept. 19, 1986, B2.

150. Exchange of letters at Washington, Mar. 11, 1987; entered into force Mar. 27, 1987.

151. Exchange of letters at London, Apr. 14, 1987; entered into force Aug. 12, 1987.

152. Exchange of letters at Washington, May 14, 1987; entered into force June 1, 1987.

bered no more than two dozen, but British and U.S. officials were nonetheless preparing to extend the Cayman MLAI to the four dependencies in much the same fashion as they had the executive agreements.

Canada

Even as U.S. negotiators were hammering out the initial agreement with British and Caymanian officials, negotiations of comparable importance were under way with the Canadians; indeed, the Canadian MLAT was the first to address the dispute over *Bank of Nova Scotia* subpoenas.[153] It was not, however, the first time that the two governments had squared off on the issue of U.S. assertions of extraterritoriality. Canada had been among the nations most affected by U.S. efforts to extraterritorialize its laws after World War II. Conflicts over U.S. antitrust laws dated back to a 1947 investigation of Canadian paper and pulp companies, one result of which had been Ontario's first blocking statute. Further conflicts had arisen in response to U.S. antitrust charges against Canadian and other uranium producers during the early 1970s, as well as to U.S. efforts to apply its export control laws to Canadian trade with Cuba and Canadian involvement in the construction of the Siberian pipeline—all of which had led to both provincial and federal blocking statutes in Canada as well as frequent high-level negotiations and three memoranda of understanding designed to find a satisfactory compromise.[154] The rise in tensions over the *Bank of Nova Scotia* case during the early 1980s contributed to enactment of Canada's most sweeping blocking statute to date.[155] At the same time, the flood of subpoenas directed at Canadian bank branches in the Caribbean and other financial secrecy jurisdictions prompted the formation in 1983 of a U.S.-Canadian Subpoena Working Group composed of law enforcement and diplomatic officials from both

153. The treaty, accompanied by the Presidential message transmitting it to the Senate, is reproduced in U.S. Senate Treaty Doc. 100-14, 100th Cong., 2d Sess. (1988), and in *International Legal Materials* 24 (1985), 1092–1099. A section-by-section analysis of the treaty appears in U.S. Senate Exec. Rept. 101-10, 101st Cong., 1st Sess. (1989).

154. The blocking statutes and the 1969 MOU are reproduced in A. V. Lowe, *Extraterritorial Jurisdiction* (Cambridge: Grotius Publications, 1983). See also Sharon A. Williams and J.-G. Castel, *Canadian Criminal Law: International and Transnational Aspects* (Toronto: Buttersworth, 1981).

155. Catherine Botticelli, "Recent Canadian Blocking Legislation: A Vehicle to Foster Extraterritorial Discovery Cooperation Between the United States and Canada?" *Fordham International Law Journal* 10 (1987), 671–688.

nations. Among its conclusions was the recommendation that an MLAT be negotiated to formalize and facilitate the extensive law enforcement relations between the neighboring states.[156]

The MLAT negotiations were the first for Canada, as well as the first between the United States and a fellow common law state—albeit one with quite different criminal procedures. The two delegations began with the mutual understanding that the MLAT would provide for broad and wide-ranging cooperation. The principal obstacle to U.S. requests for assistance arose not from any penchant for secrecy in Canada's laws but rather from Canadian court decisions that had severely restricted the provision of assistance to U.S. prosecutors at the preindictment phase of grand jury proceedings.[157] The Canadians agreed to rectify the problem by inserting the appropriate language both in the treaty and in the implementing legislation.[158] They also agreed to waive any requirement of dual criminality, thereby authorizing assistance in U.S. investigations of money laundering and other activities that had not yet been criminalized in Canada.

The only significant disagreements over principle in the negotiations involved the *Bank of Nova Scotia* subpoenas and other U.S. assertions of extraterritorial jurisdiction, an irritation that the Canadians had come to perceive—in the words of one of the MLAT negotiators—as "a hardy perennial in U.S.-Canadian relations." The U.S. negotiators responded to the Canadians' desire for more cooperative bilateral mechanisms of

---

156. A summary of some of the Canadian views by one of the Canadian MLAT negotiators, Jonathan Fried, can be found in Serge April and Jonathan Fried, "Compelling Discovery and Disclosure in Transnational Litigation: A Canadian View," *NYU Journal of International Law and Politics* 16 (1984), 961. See also J.-G. Castel, "Compelling Disclosure by a Non-Party Litigant in Violation of Foreign Bank Secrecy Laws: Recent Developments in Canada–United States Relations," *Canadian Yearbook of International Law* 23 (1985), 261–284. For an overview of the extraterritoriality issue from the Canadian perspective, see William C. Graham, "Reflections on United States Legal Imperialism: Canadian Sovereignty in the Context of North American Economic Integration," *International Journal* 40 (1985), 478–509.

157. Canadian courts had interpreted Section 43 of Canada's Evidence Act as forbidding the use of compulsory process in behalf of foreign authorities unless the court were satisfied that the evidence produced would be used at trial and that it was not sought solely for the purpose of furthering an investigation. See in particular *Re United States of America and Executive Securities Corporation* (1977) 77 D.L.R. (3d) 157 (O.H.C.). See also the technical analysis of the treaty in U.S. Senate Exec. Rept. 101-10, 9, 34.

158. The same language also nullified the similar limitation that U.S. courts had placed on providing assistance under Section 1782 to foreign administrative agencies. See *Fonseca v. Blumenthal*, 620 F.2d 322 (2d Cir. 1980) and *In Re Letters Rogatory Issued by the Director of Inspection of the Government of India*, 305 F.2d 1016 (2d Cir. 1967).

evidence-gathering by agreeing to a "first resort" provision requiring both parties to seek assistance initially via the treaty and to consult thereafter in the event that the treaty mechanisms failed to provide the requested evidence. The formulation was to provide a model for the Cayman MLAT, which incorporated and expanded on the Canadian provision, and for the MLAT with the Bahamas. (It failed, however, to accommodate German officials, who were equally concerned about the United States' resort to subpoenas and other unilateral measures. Indeed, the relatively rapid negotiation of the Canadian MLAT, which required little more than a year, contrasted starkly with the German MLAT negotiations, which had begun during the early 1980s and then been stalled for the remainder of the decade primarily over differences regarding treaty restrictions on the United States' resort to unilateral measures.)

The remainder of the treaty provisions were relatively broad and noncontentious, reflecting both the United States' growing experience in negotiating and utilizing MLATs and the tradition of cooperative law enforcement relations between the two nations. No mention of political offenses or comparable limitations on assistance was included in the treaty. The negotiators specifically agreed that assistance *would* be granted for fiscal offenses.[159] As with most of the other MLATs apart from those with the Cayman Islands and the Bahamas, the treaty was recognized as a tax convention permitting the IRS to provide assistance. No restriction was placed on the use of information or evidence once it had become public in the requesting state. The "proceeds of crime" provision was broader and more open-ended than in previous MLATs, authorizing cooperation in "the forfeiture of the proceeds of crime, restitution to the victims of crime, and the collection of fines imposed as a sentence in a criminal prosecution." Its effect was to modify the long-standing rule of international law, articulated by Chief Justice John Marshall in the *Antelope* case, that "the courts of no country execute the penal laws of another."[160] Other concerns, such as the need to protect the identity of informants and the desire that individuals requested to appear in the requesting state be notified of outstanding warrants or other judicial orders, were addressed either with particular treaty language or with understandings formalized in the technical analysis ac-

159. See the technical analysis of the Canadian MLAT, U.S. Senate Exec. Rept. 101-10, 36.
160. 23 U.S. (10 Wheat.) 66, 123 (1825).

companying the treaty. In March 1985, President Ronald Reagan and the Canadian prime minister signed the completed MLAT in Quebec City.

Bahamas

Perhaps the most acrimonious MLAT negotiations were those with the Bahamians. As with the Cayman Islands, abundant evidence pointed to the advantage taken of the Bahamas' financial secrecy laws by drug traffickers and other criminals to launder and hide the proceeds of their activities.[161] But unlike the Caymans, the archipelago had also emerged as a major transshipment point for marijuana and cocaine in transit from Colombia to the United States. Until late 1984, the Bahamian government proved at least as uncooperative as that of the Caymans in refusing to provide assistance to American investigations;[162] the Justice Department in turn pursued a confrontational approach in its efforts to obtain information and evidence, utilizing *Bank of Nova Scotia* subpoenas and other judicial mechanisms to collect evidence, as well as a variety of informal, unilateral police measures. Periodic efforts to improve cooperation, and specifically to commence MLAT negotiations, were hampered by evidence of high-level corruption in the Bahamas, tensions over U.S. law enforcement operations in the Bahamas, and exposés of both in the U.S. Congress and media.[163] During late 1983, matters came to a head when DEA and FBI agents were declared persona non grata and when reports of high-level involvement in drug trafficking obliged Prime Minister Pindling to set up an independent Commission of Inquiry.[164]

161. *Crime and Secrecy: Staff Study* (supra n. 126), 54–62; Richard H. Blum, *Offshore Haven Banks, Trusts, and Companies: The Business of Crime in the Euromarket* (New York: Praeger, 1984), 133–146.

162. Reginald Stuart, "U.S.-Bahamian Relations Are Straining Under Drug Investigations," *New York Times*, Sept. 28, 1983, A21.

163. Law enforcement officials in both countries claimed they had broached the subject of MLAT negotiations as early as 1980 and been rebuffed by the other. The account of the director of the OIA, Philip White, is provided in his testimony to the Task Force on International Narcotics Control, in *U.S. Narcotics Interdiction Programs in the Bahamas: Hearings Before the Committee on Foreign Affairs, House of Representatives*, 98th Cong., 1st Sess. (1983), 184–193. The Bahamian perspective is provided in *Narcotics Review in the Caribbean: Hearing Before the Committee on Foreign Affairs, U.S. House of Representatives*, 100th Cong., 2d Sess. (1988), 54–56, 79–87.

164. One explosive exposé was delivered by NBC Nightly News on Sept. 5, 1983. It cited American officials who claimed that major drug traffickers, reportedly including the infamous

By late 1984, both governments had begun to reverse direction and restore their relationship. U.S. law enforcement agents were invited back, and joint drug enforcement operations were initiated. At about the same time, the Commission of Inquiry completed its report.[165] Among its recommendations were that an MLAT be negotiated and "that problems connected with the revenue laws of the United States . . . be set aside when negotiating an agreement to trace drug related funds."[166] MLAT negotiations accordingly commenced in January 1985 and were completed in mid-1987, a period during which relations between the two governments continued to wax and wane.[167] The negotiation sessions themselves were strongly influenced by the forceful and somewhat combative personalities of the two heads of delegation: Paul Adderley, a close associate of Prime Minister Pindling who served as both attorney general and foreign minister of the Bahamas during much of the negotiations; and Carol Hallett, a political appointee to the U.S. ambassadorship in the Bahamas who was later appointed commissioner of U.S. Customs by the Bush administration.[168] With both Adderley and Hallett closely attuned to, and responsible for, most other law enforcement and diplomatic issues between the two nations, the tenor and timing of the MLAT negotiations were rather more affected by external political considerations than any other MLAT negotiations.[169]

The Bahamians were also influenced initially by the Canadians. The fact that Canada had negotiated an MLAT with the United States in

---

fugitive Robert Vesco, were paying off Bahamian officials, including the prime minister. A second NBC Nightly News report, on Feb. 22, 1984, cited a DEA report in which Prime Minister Pindling was reported to have taken bribes from a Colombian trafficker.

165. Many of the commission's findings were detailed in a thorough report on corruption in the Bahamas that appeared in the *Miami Herald* in late 1984. See the six-part series entitled "A Nation for Sale," Sept. 23–28, 1984.

166. Report of the Commission of Inquiry (Appointed to Inquire into the Illegal Use of the Bahamas for the Transshipment of Dangerous Drugs Destined for the United States of America, Nov. 1983–Dec. 1984), Bahamas (Dec. 1984), 285. The commission also noted (353–356) that the United States had failed to respond to earlier proposals by Attorney General Paul Adderley to enter into negotiations.

167. The trend toward favorable relations is stressed in Joel Brinkley, "In Fighting Drug Traffic, Attitude Wins the Aid," *New York Times*, Oct. 7, 1986, A28.

168. Robert D. Hershey, "In the Customs Service, an Open Door at the Top," *New York Times*, Aug. 18, 1990, 9.

169. The treaty, accompanied by the Presidential message transmitting it to the Senate, is reproduced in U.S. Senate Treaty Doc. 100-17, 100th Cong., 2d Sess. (1988), and in *International Legal Materials* 24 (1985), 1092. A section-by-section analysis of the treaty appears in U.S. Senate Exec. Rept. 101-12, 101st Cong., 1st Sess. (1989).

which the issues of extraterritoriality and bank secrecy were addressed provided a precedent that the Bahamian government found useful in justifying its decision to commence MLAT negotiations with the United States. The text of the Canadian treaty also proved useful as the first model of a comprehensive MLAT between the United States and a common law nation concerned with financial secrecy. The Canadian government, moreover, was eager to avoid a repeat of the sorts of tensions and embarrassments generated by the *Bank of Nova Scotia* case; its diplomatic representatives accordingly let Bahamian officials know that they would favor their entering into MLAT negotiations with the United States. By the time those negotiations got seriously under way, however, the U.S. MLAT with the Cayman Islands had replaced the Canadian MLAT as the principal model for the Bahamian negotiations— although the Bahamian delegation also drew on draft uniform legislation regarding mutual legal assistance among the members of the Commonwealth.

Much discussion was devoted to the scope of offenses for which assistance would be required under the treaty. The Bahamians, like the Caymanians, insisted on excluding run-of-the-mill tax evasion investigations and refused to ensure cooperation in civil or administrative proceedings, such as those initiated by the SEC and the CFTC, but they agreed to cooperate in investigations of tax fraud as well as anything connected to drug trafficking, including tax and money laundering offenses.[170] The Bahamian delegation also resisted the extensive listing of criminal offenses for which assistance would be required that had been included in the Cayman MLAT, insisting on a briefer listing, albeit one that was worded to include most of the offenses inserted in the Cayman MLAT. As in the Canadian and Cayman negotiations, the U.S. negotiators were anxious that the treaty and implementing legislation

170. Among the more notable requests for assistance processed during the negotiations was one that involved the SEC's investigation of illicit transactions by Dennis Levine. Having failed in a previous investigation to obtain documents via Bahamian courts, the SEC successfully appealed to Attorney General Paul Adderley to issue the necessary written opinion to permit Bank Leu International to hand over the requested documents without violating the Bahamas' secrecy laws. Although the Bahamian government subsequently issued a press release limiting the precedential value of its assistance in the Levine case, its willingness to cooperate in the Levine investigation provided a further indication of the Bahamian government's changing attitude toward U.S. criminal investigations. See the defendant's account of the case in Dennis B. Levine with William Hoffer, *Inside Out: An Insider's Account of Wall Street* (New York: G. P. Putnam's Sons, 1991).

specify that cooperation be forthcoming in grand jury investigations and forfeiture proceedings;[171] the Bahamians in turn noted that a U.S. court had interpreted Section 1782 so as to preclude U.S. assistance in response to a request from the Bahamian Commission of Inquiry.[172] Both delegations agreed that the MLAT would address the concerns of the other.

The Bahamians also insisted upon additional restrictions that had been included in some previous MLATs. Whereas the Canadian MLAT stipulated that any information provided pursuant to the treaty that was publicly revealed in a court proceeding could thereafter be used with no restrictions, the Bahamians preferred to follow the Caymanian MLAT in imposing continued restrictions on the use of such information.[173] They also copied the Caymanian MLAT's anti-"fishing expedition" clause requiring that a U.S. request contain "reasonable grounds" to believe both that the specific crime had been committed and that the information requested could be found in the territory of the requested state. Concerned that U.S. requests for location of persons and service of documents not overburden the Bahamas' relatively limited law enforcement resources, the Bahamian delegation asked for and received concessions by the U.S. delegation on this score. They also insisted upon a provision derived from the Commonwealth Scheme precluding assistance in cases involving prosecution or punishment on account of a suspect's race, religion, nationality, or political opinions.[174] Their particular concern, the Bahamians noted, involved racially motivated requests.[175] With respect to the single most important issue in the view of the Bahamians—the resort by U.S. prosecutors to *Bank of Nova Scotia* subpoenas and

171. A 1978 British court decision had cast doubt on the ability of a court to execute a request from a U.S. grand jury. *Rio Tinto Zinc Corp. v. Westinghouse Electric Corp.* (1978) 1 All E.R. 434, per Lord Diplock (H.L.), discussed in the technical analysis of the treaty, U.S. Senate Exec. Rept. 101-12, 15.

172. *In the Matter of the Request for Judicial Assistance from the Supreme Court of the Commonwealth of the Bahamas*, Misc. No. 84-0113 (D.D.C., application denied June 5, 1984).

173. See Art. 8 of the MLAT.

174. See Art. 3(1)(d) of the MLAT.

175. U.S. Senate, *MLAT . . . Caymans* (supra n. 5), 138. The attitudes of the Bahamian negotiators on this score may have been reflected in an outburst by Bahamian Attorney General Adderley during the heat of the 1987 election campaign in which the U.S. government made known its preference for the opposition. U.S. officials, Adderley reportedly stated, "are too big, too white and too American to listen to us poor black fools down here in the Bahamas. . . . They're presumptuous and bloody arrogant." See Joel Brinkley, "Drugs and Corruption Color Vote in Bahamas," *New York Times*, June 14, 1987, 1.

other unilateral measures—the negotiators agreed to follow the Canadian MLAT in requiring first resort to the treaty process but permitting alternative measures where the MLAT process failed to provide satisfaction.[176] Unlike the Caymanians, however, the Bahamian delegation was not particularly concerned about the use of *Ghidoni* waivers, nor had their courts ruled on the legitimacy of the tactic under Bahamian law.

The treaty was signed by the Bahamas on June 12, 1987, just days before Prime Minister Pindling won reelection to a sixth term in a highly acrimonious campaign involving accusations of corruption hurled by the challenger and a successful manipulation of anti-U.S. sentiment by the prime minister.[177] In an unusual break from precedent, U.S. officials decided to delay their signature, preferring both to await the election returns and to get a glimpse of the proposed legislation implementing the MLAT. The Americans were concerned for a number of reasons. Bahamian law, as in most common law nations apart from the United States, regards treaties as inferior to domestic constitutions and laws unless implemented by appropriate domestic legislation. "In the eyes of a local judge," one OIA attorney indicated, the treaty would represent "little more than an interesting piece of paper" without the necessary implementing legislation. The Bahamians had reinforced this point by insisting on a provision in the MLAT requiring that "all requests . . . be executed in accordance with and subject to the limitations imposed by the laws of the Requested State." Although the legal systems of both Canada and the Cayman Islands presented similar concerns, the turbulent course of U.S.-Bahamian relations gave the Americans greater cause for concern. They feared in particular a replication of the problems occasioned by the Swiss implementing legislation a decade before. Shortly after the Bahamian government signed the MLAT, however, it reassured the U.S. delegation by providing them with a draft of the proposed implementing legislation. Although concerned about a few of the provisions contained in the draft,[178] the U.S. delegation expressed its satisfaction, and Ambassador Hallett signed the MLAT in August 1987.

Despite the hostilities generated during the campaign, the signing of the MLAT foreshadowed an impressive effort during 1988 by the Bahamian government to accommodate the U.S. drug enforcement effort; it

176. See Art. 18(2) of the MLAT.
177. Joseph B. Treaster, "Anti-U.S. Mood Was Key Bahamas Issue," *New York Times*, June 21, 1987, 3.
178. See U.S. Senate, *MLAT . . . Caymans*, 136–137.

included not just the passage of legislation implementing the MLAT in March 1988, but also additional legislation increasing mandatory minimum sentences for drug trafficking offenses, enacting asset forfeiture laws like those in the United States, and requiring mandatory drug testing of police and military personnel.[179] The government also established special drug courts, created an internal corruption unit in its police agency, began training police to form a drug enforcement unit, and extended far broader cooperation to DEA and other law enforcement agents than had previously been the case.[180] Although U.S. officials continued to express skepticism regarding the Bahamians' actual implementation of their new drug control measures, and to regard "the Bahamas as one of the toughest relationships to regularize," by the end of the 1980s the level of cooperation between the two governments stood in stark contrast to the hostile relations early in the decade.[181]

More MLATs and Problems in the U.S. Congress

Among the three remaining MLATs negotiated by the United States by 1988—with Belgium, Thailand, and Mexico—the first two encountered few legal or political obstacles.

Belgium

The MLAT with Belgium, which had not previously negotiated such a treaty with a common law state, was in most respects an updated version of the Dutch MLAT, although lacking the issues involving the Netherlands Antilles.[182] Like the Dutch MLAT negotiations, those with the

---

179. U.S. General Accounting Office, *Drug Control: Anti-Drug Efforts in the Bahamas* (March 1990), 29–35.

180. Ibid.

181. The continued skepticism is reflected in the report on the Bahamas in *Drugs, Law Enforcement, and Foreign Policy: A Report Prepared by the Subcommittee on Terrorism, Narcotics, and International Operations of the Senate Committee on Foreign Relations*, 100th Cong., 2d Sess. (Dec. 1988), S. Rrt. 100-165, 14–24.

182. The treaty, accompanied by the Presidential message transmitting it to the Senate, is reproduced in U.S. Senate Treaty Doc. 100-16, 100th Cong., 2d Sess. (1988). A section-by-section analysis of the treaty appears in U.S. Senate Exec. Rept. 101-11, 101st Cong., 1st Sess. (1989).

Belgians were linked to extradition treaty negotiations. They too were seen as "an opportunity to negotiate, in a rather short period, an MLAT with a European country that is a major commercial and financial center, and in doing so, to set the stage for MLAT negotiations with neighboring countries with legal systems quite similar to those of Belgium."[183] The MLAT included the same provisions designed to facilitate interaction between the common law and civil law judicial systems and to qualify the treaty as a tax convention under U.S. law. Like the Dutch MLAT, it also waived the requirement of dual criminality except with respect to requests requiring searches and seizures, in which case the alleged offense had to be punishable in both states by more than one year in prison.[184] But the Belgian MLAT was also tailored to accommodate broader types and levels of cooperation. Whereas the Dutch treaty required cooperation in "criminal investigations and proceedings," the Belgian MLAT referred to "all matters relating to the investigation, prosecution and suppression of offenses," thereby making clear that a much broader array of proceedings could be accommodated by the treaty. Fewer restrictions were placed on the use of information provided under the treaty and on the obligation to keep the information confidential. Broad cooperation in seizing and forfeiting the proceeds of crime and in ensuring restitution for victims was included—although the treaty omitted the clause included in other MLATs requiring assistance in the collection of fines imposed as a sentence in a criminal prosecution. The political offense exception to providing assistance was narrowed with the caveat that it should not apply to any offense not regarded as a political offense under other international agreements signed by both states. During the negotiations, the Belgian delegation assured the Americans that cooperation would be forthcoming in investigations of illicit arms shipments, sabotage, treason, and espionage involving states unfriendly to both the United States and Belgium, but that they were less certain about extending cooperation in cases such as the Iran Contra investigation.[185] The treaty was signed in January 1988 but had not yet been put into force by the end of the decade.

183. See statement of Mark Richard (supra n. 5), 205.
184. See Art. 7 of the MLAT. See Art. 6 in the Dutch MLAT, as well as the diplomatic note accompanying the treaty.
185. See the technical analysis of the MLAT, U.S. Senate Exec. Rept. 101-11, 14–15.

Thailand

The MLAT negotiations with the Thais, which followed the completion of extradition treaty negotiations, similarly proved relatively straightforward.[186] The Justice Department was eager both for a new extradition treaty and for an MLAT with Thailand in light of its prominent role in the flow of heroin (and to a lesser extent marijuana) to the United States and the important role it played as a meeting place and financial center for East Asian drug traffickers.[187] The Thais, who had recently negotiated an MLAT with the French, and who were already hosts to the largest DEA contingent outside the United States, agreed to fairly broad levels of cooperation. Their extensive experience in working with the resident DEA agents, and in responding to requests for evidence and other assistance transmitted from the United States via those agents, prepared them for negotiations with the United States. Absent from the treaty were the extended caveats regarding assistance in penetrating financial secrecy laws and restrictions on the use of unilateral measures. No requirement of dual criminality was imposed on requests for assistance, thereby permitting Thai assistance in drug conspiracy cases despite the lack of an exact counterpart in Thai law, and authorizing U.S. assistance in violations of Thai currency control laws for which dual criminality might not be found in U.S. law. The provision authorizing cooperation in the seizure and forfeiture of criminal assets was broadly worded, anticipating cooperation in restitution, the collection of fines, and the transfer of forfeited assets to the other state. An appendix to the treaty— also appended to the MLATs with the Bahamas and the Cayman Islands—included three certification forms designed by the United States to facilitate the admissibility of evidence provided by the Thais.

The few peculiarities of the Thai treaty included a provision, modeled after one in the Thai-French MLAT, requiring each state to consider a request from the other to initiate criminal proceedings in a particular case.[188] Although the provision made more sense in the context of

---

186. The treaty, accompanied by the Presidential message transmitting it to the Senate, is reproduced in U.S. Senate Treaty Doc. 100-18, 100th Cong., 2d Sess. (1988). A section-by-section analysis of the treaty appears in U.S. Senate Exec. Rept. 101-13, 101st Cong., 1st Sess. (1989).

187. See the prepared statement of Mary V. Mochary, in U.S. Senate, *MLAT . . . Caymans* (supra n. 5), 91–92.

188. See Art. 14 of the MLAT.

requests between civil law states with personal jurisdiction over their citizens' criminal activities abroad, the U.S. negotiators consented to its inclusion in the treaty because it did not impose any mandatory requirements.[189] The U.S. delegation also agreed to a unique provision specifying that any non-American served with a legal document in Thailand requiring him or her to appear in the United States would not be punished for failing to comply.[190] The Thais were concerned that Thai citizens might be compelled to travel to the United States in response to such a subpoena—a possibility that they regarded as a potential extraterritorial violation of their sovereignty. Because U.S. law typically did not provide for such sanctions, however, the U.S. negotiators raised no objection. The treaty was signed in Bangkok in March 1986 during a visit by Attorney General Meese; it entered into force on June 10, 1993. To a greater extent than in most other countries, the process of obtaining evidence and other assistance for use in the United States continued to rely heavily and quite successfully on the resident DEA offices.

Mexico

The MLAT negotiations with Mexico, like those with the Bahamas, were pursued in the context of acrimonious relations over drug trafficking, with legislative and executive officials in the United States castigating the Mexican government for its lack of cooperation in drug trafficking investigations, and Mexican officials incensed by the U.S. charges, particularly those involving alleged corruption in the Mexican government. Nonetheless, the MLAT ultimately signed by the two states resembled those negotiated with the Thais, the Canadians, and the Belgians more than it did the MLATs with the Caribbean islands.[191] No requirement of dual criminality was included, thereby allowing cooperation even in the investigation of tax offenses. Broad levels of cooperation were afforded in a variety of proceedings and with respect to the seizure and forfeiture of criminal assets. The Americans were reassured

189. The U.S. delegation also noted that the general language in most MLATs authorizing cooperation in matters not specified in the treaty rendered such a provision unnecessary.

190. See Art. 10(4) of the MLAT.

191. The treaty, accompanied by the Presidential message transmitting it to the Senate, is reproduced in U.S. Senate Treaty Doc. 100-13, 100th Cong., 2d Sess. (1988), and in *International Legal Materials* 27 (1988), 443. A section-by-section analysis of the treaty appears in U.S. Senate Exec. Rept. 101-9, 101st Cong., 1st Sess. (1989).

that Mexico's bank secrecy laws would not present serious obstacles to the provision of evidence, and that Mexican authorities would not object to the employment of *Ghidoni* waivers by U.S. prosecutors. The principal concession to Mexican sensitivity with respect to U.S. claims of extraterritorial jurisdiction was the inclusion of a provision asserting that the treaty did not create any new jurisdiction or operational authority by either state to undertake actions in the territory of the other.[192] The principal peculiarity of the treaty, albeit not one reflected in the provisions of the treaty, was the Mexicans' insistence that the taking of testimony requested by U.S. authorities could be compelled under Mexican law only if the alleged offense appeared to fall within Mexican jurisdiction. The Mexican delegation assured the U.S. negotiators that there was little chance of amending Mexican law to ameliorate this limitation. The Americans therefore consented, deriving some solace from the fact that the reach of Mexican jurisdiction far exceeded that of the United States, relying not just on the territorial and protective principles common in U.S. law but also on the nationality and passive personality notions of jurisdiction.[193] The treaty was signed and ratified by the Mexican government in December 1987. It thereby became the first MLAT with the United States to be ratified by a Latin American government.

Trouble in the U.S. Congress

The MLATS with Canada, Mexico, the Bahamas, the Cayman Islands, Belgium, and Thailand were submitted to the U.S. Senate for consideration in early 1988. State and Justice Department officials hoped and anticipated that the ratification process would involve no more than the pro forma reviews required for the previous generation of MLATs. But they quickly encountered a powerful series of obstacles from an eclectic array of critics, including Senator Jesse Helms, the American Civil Liberties Union, the criminal defense bar, and the first director of the OIA, Michael Abbell, who subsequently had become a criminal defense attorney.[194] In his statement submitted to the Foreign Relations Commit-

192. See the technical analysis of the MLAT, U.S. Senate Exec. Rept. 101-9, 12.
193. Ibid., 20–22.
194. The evolution of the MLAT ratification process, and of the debate over the treaties, is discussed in *International Enforcement Law Reporter* 3:345–351 (1987); 4:44–48, 131–136, 160–164, 197–200, 303–304, 350–352, 420–421 (1988); 5:146–148, 186–188, 258–259, 385–386 (1989). See also Bruze Zagaris, "Developments in International Judicial Assistance

tee, Abbell provided a technical critique of the MLATs from the perspective of the defense attorney, a viewpoint that had not been given much heed in previous hearings.[195] He criticized the Mexican and Thai treaties for "effectively amend[ing] the Federal Rules of Evidence . . . in an unacceptable manner; the Mexican treaty alone for failing to specifically authorize the presence of defendants and their attorneys at foreign judicial proceedings; the Canadian and Mexican treaties' omission of safe conduct provisions for those requested to appear and provide testimony under the treaties; the Belgian treaty's lack of restrictions on the use and disclosure of information and evidence provided under the treaty; and, most significant, all of the treaties for precluding their use on behalf of defendants in criminal cases."[196] It was neither fair nor consistent with the compulsory process clause of the Sixth Amendment, Abbell contended, to require defendants to continue to rely on letters rogatory when prosecutors had available the advantages of an MLAT.[197] Abbell bolstered his claims by obtaining the support of the National Association of Criminal Defense Lawyers (NACDL), the American Civil Liberties Union, and the American Bar Association.

Justice Department officials reacted angrily, and with some degree of

---

and Related Matters," *Denver Journal of International Law and Policy* 18 (1990), 339, 335–337.

195. One criticism leveled at the Justice Department in the hearings was its failure to make the treaties and the accompanying technical analyses publicly available until just shortly before the Congressional hearings. See the statement of Bruce Zagaris in U.S. Senate, *MLAT . . . Caymans* (supra n. 5).

196. See the prepared statements of Michael Abbell to the Senate Foreign Relations Committee, May 6, 1988, and June 14, 1988. The Thai and Bahamian MLATs provided that the treaties were intended solely for assistance between the criminal law enforcement authorities of the contracting states and are "not intended or designed to provide such assistance to private parties." The four other MLATs specified that the treaties "shall not give rise to a right on the part of a private party to obtain, suppress, or exclude any evidence, or to impede the execution of a request."

197. The notion of excluding private parties from access to MLATs had not been contained in the first MLATs negotiated by the United States—with Switzerland, Turkey, and the Netherlands—but had been included in the Colombian MLAT, in good part because it provided for assistance not just in criminal matters but in civil and administrative investigations and proceedings as well. The Moroccan MLAT specified that it was "established solely for mutual assistance between the law enforcement authorities of the Contracting States," and the Italian MLAT stated that it was "intended solely for mutual assistance between authorities of the Contracting States." However, neither made specific mention of private parties. Abbell argued that whereas the exclusion of private parties had been justified in the Colombian MLAT, given its inclusion of civil and administrative proceedings, it was not warranted in the six MLATs under consideration, which were restricted to assistance in criminal matters.

bitterness, to the criticisms by their former colleague, perceiving them as a thinly veiled attempt to scuttle all of the MLATs. In their testimony, they dismissed all of Abbell's criticisms. With respect to his claim that defendants be provided with access to the MLATs, Justice Department officials argued that "the treaties are frankly intended to be law enforcement tools" and further justified the exclusion of defendants on the grounds that the government, unlike defendants, bore the burden of proving guilt beyond a reasonable doubt. They asserted that the decision to preclude use of the treaties on behalf of defendants reflected the wishes not just of the U.S. negotiators but of both delegations in all of the MLAT negotiations. Indeed, the U.S. negotiators were deeply concerned that any reservations attached by the Senate in support of Abbell's claims would, at the very least, require additional and difficult treaty negotiations and, at the worst, cause the treaty partners to reject the treaties entirely.[198]

Far more troubling to the Justice Department than Abbell's criticisms, however, was the opposition of Senator Helms. Helms reiterated many of Abbell's criticisms—indeed, his staff had initiated the involvement of Abbell and other legal critics of the MLATs in the Senate ratification process—and insisted that he would oppose the Senate's ratification of the MLATs unless a reservation was attached to each specifying that nothing in the MLAT "requires or authorizes legislation or other action by the United States prohibited by the U.S. Constitution as interpreted by the United States." The reservation was identical to the Lugar-Helms reservation to the Genocide Convention that had been approved by Congress in February 1986. Senator Helms perceived the reservation as effectively creating a check on the power of the executive branch to impose its own interpretations on U.S. treaties. Justice Department officials argued that the reservation was unnecessary both because nothing in the MLATs could be construed as unconstitutional and because U.S. courts had always held that the Constitution supersedes treaties. They were deeply concerned that appending such a reservation would bolster the constitutional challenges to the MLATs raised by defendants, necessitate further clarifying negotiations with the treaty partners, invite some of the partners to append their own reservations, and generally aggravate relations with them.[199]

198. U.S. Senate, *MLAT . . . Caymans* (supra n. 5), 272–275.
199. Ibid., 265–272.

Both Senator Helms and Senator Murkowski also expressed concerns about the absence of dual criminality requirements in the MLATs—a clause that the U.S. negotiators had viewed as primarily beneficial to U.S. prosecutors given the broader scope of U.S. criminal law relative to most other treaty partners, but that also invited foreign requests for assistance in matters not regarded as criminal in the United States. Senator Murkowski, for instance, inquired during the hearing about the possibility that Canadian law enforcement authorities might seek assistance under the MLAT in criminal investigations regarding acid rain or other areas of contention between the two nations.[200] Senator Helms noted his concern that some foreign governments might use the treaties to obtain assistance in investigating capital flight from their countries.[201] He also articulated a concern typically voiced by the United States' treaty partners: that U.S. officials might be subjected to foreign "fishing expeditions" and otherwise flooded with requests. Many foreign governments, he noted, requested far more assistance from the United States under the MLATs or by letters rogatory than did U.S. officials from abroad (although he failed to note that the flow of requests with foreign financial secrecy jurisdictions was disproportionately in favor of the United States).

Senator Helms's principal motivation for opposing the MLATs, however, was apparently his general concern with drug-related corruption in the Bahamas and Mexico and his specific concern that the MLATs with those countries would be taken advantage of by corrupt officials. Having recently convened his own hearings with the specific intention of publicly castigating the Mexican government for its lack of cooperation in the American war on drugs, the senator reiterated the ample evidence of governmental corruption south of the border and in the Bahamas. The Justice and State Department officials testifying in favor of the treaty assured the senator that, despite persistent problems in law enforcement relations with the two governments, both had provided extensive cooperation in U.S. investigations, that the treaties would inevitably facilitate cooperative efforts, that U.S. officials were highly sensitive to potential misuses of the MLATs, and that any suspicious requests could be rejected. Not reassured, Senator Helms insisted that the two treaties be approved only on condition that reservations providing assurances

200. Ibid., 74–76.
201. Ibid., 174.

that no corrupt officials would be provided with assistance under the MLATs be attached.

Helms's objections met with overwhelming opposition by his colleagues on the Foreign Relations Committee. Senator John Kerry, who had assumed responsibility for marshaling the MLATs through the hearings, articulated the arguments favoring approval and rejecting the proposed reservations. He was joined by Senator Lugar, who explained why he did not favor burdening the MLATs with the same reservation appended to the Genocide Convention. Although the committee voted in favor of the treaties without appending any reservations by a vote of 17 to 2, the North Carolina legislator succeeded in preventing full Senate approval in 1988. Following an additional set of hearings in 1989, at which no critics of the treaties testified but during which Senator Helms repeated his objections, the Foreign Relations Committee once again rejected the senator's reservations and voted 17 to 2 to recommend that the Senate give its consent. Helms persisted, however, with the result that the MLATs were approved by the Senate in late 1989 with reservations reflecting the senator's objections—albeit in compromise language watered down to accommodate the concerns of the Justice and State Departments.[202] On January 2, 1990, President Bush signed the instruments of ratification for all six MLATs.

As the U.S. MLAT negotiators anticipated, their negotiating partners did not take kindly to the reservations. The Canadians expressed mild irritation but let it be known that they viewed the reservations as an American domestic matter of no concern to Canada. With the Canadian implementing legislation already in place, the MLAT entered into force on January 24, 1990. The Bahamian, Mexican, and Cayman/British delegations, however, were less prepared to write off the U.S. reservations with the Canadians' dispatch. Each proceeded to append its own reservations to the treaties containing comparable language regarding their own constitutions. With the British not particularly interested in complicating issues, the Cayman treaty entered into force on March 19, 1990. Bahamian and Mexican officials, however, who were specifically targeted by the reservations regarding corrupt officials, were incensed.

202. The reservations did not directly address any of Abbell's criticisms, in particular the issue of defendant access to the MLATs. Justice Department officials indicated, however, that they would respond to a court order requiring them to make use of an MLAT to obtain evidence sought by a defendant—as in fact had previously occurred with respect to a request by Michel Sindona for evidence under the Swiss MLAT.

Both perceived the Helms-inspired action as an ungrateful response to the fairly extensive assistance that their governments had provided to U.S. law enforcement officials. They also were not disposed to accept the assurances of the U.S. delegations that the reservations would have no impact on the actual implementation of the MLATs. After adding their own reservations to the treaties, both governments ratified the revised MLATs. The MLAT with the Bahamas entered into force on July 18, 1990, and the MLAT with Mexico on May 3, 1991.

Broader Developments:
Drugs, Money, Securities, and Taxes

As the end of the 1980s approached, U.S. Justice Department officials persisted in their efforts to negotiate MLATs with dozens of other governments. U.S. officials had signed more-limited mutual legal assistance agreements with Haiti on August 15, 1986, and with Nigeria on November 2, 1987, both of which had emerged as significant drug transit countries during the 1980s. The Nigerian agreement was followed by a full-fledged MLAT in September 1989. An MLAT with Jamaica was also completed in July 1989. These were followed by MLATs with Spain in November 1990, Argentina in December 1990, Panama in April 1991, and Uruguay in May 1991. As this book went to press in mid-1993, only the MLAT with Argentina had entered into force. (See Appendix E.) Also high on the Justice Department's priority list in the early 1990s were Germany, which had been involved in sporadic MLAT negotiations with the United States since the early 1980s; Britain, whose officials desired to resolve a wide range of concerns about U.S. extraterritorial assertions; and Hong Kong, whose financial secrecy laws had attracted a broad array of transnational criminal activities ranging from securities and tax frauds to drug-related money laundering.

Even as the rising number of MLATs were easing the collection of evidence from abroad for prosecutors, federal judges were making it easier for evidence collected in other ways to be admitted in their courts. The U.S. Constitution and the Federal Rules of Evidence, with their strong preference for live testimony in criminal trials, had long presented U.S. prosecutors with substantial obstacles in their efforts to depose witnesses abroad who would not or could not come to the United States.

Indeed, prosecutors had been forbidden to take domestic depositions in criminal cases until 1970, when Congress responded to the problem of Mafia intimidation of witnesses by authorizing government depositions in organized crime cases.[203] Five years later, the authorization was extended to all other criminal cases. And as the need to obtain evidence from abroad increased dramatically during the 1980s, judges responded both by encouraging attorneys to employ videotapes and other new technological developments to simulate live depositions and preserve testimony, and by interpreting the constitutional and evidentiary requirements less strictly.[204] In the most far-reaching of the many cases to arise during the 1980s, *United States v. Salim*, a federal judge conducting a jury trial allowed as evidence a deposition conducted in France according to French procedures at which neither the defendant nor his defense attorney was permitted to be present.[205] Upheld on appeal, the case provided a clear indication of the increasing willingness of U.S. courts to make accommodations for the difficulties involved in obtaining evidence abroad.

During the 1970s and 1980s, many U.S. courts were also required to rule on the admissibility of evidence collected abroad by U.S. and foreign police agents. The Supreme Court had held in 1957 that American citizens abroad were entitled to most of the constitutional safeguards to which they were entitled within the United States.[206] Lower courts thereafter were confronted with numerous cases in which defendants argued that evidence collected abroad by law enforcement agents was not admissible in court because it had not been obtained in accordance with U.S. constitutional requirements. Most courts held that the protec-

203. Gordon Mehler, "Use of Foreign Depositions in Federal Criminal Trials," *New York Law Journal*, Oct. 3, 1988, 2, 6.

204. See *U.S. v. Kehm*, 799 F.2d 354 (7th Cir. 1986) (admitting transcript of deposition taken in the Bahamas); *U.S. v. Johnpoll*, 739 F.2d 702 (2d Cir.), cert. denied, 469 U.S. 1075 (1984) (admitting transcript of deposition taken in Switzerland); *U.S. v. Sindona*, 636 F.2d 792 (2d Cir. 1980) cert. denied, 451 U.S. 912 (1981) (deposition taken in Italy and attended by lead defense counsel admissible); *U.S. v. Sines*, 761 F.2d 1434 (9th Cir. 1985) (admitting government deposition taken in Thailand in a heroin trafficking case); *U.S. v. King*, 552 F.2d 833 (9th Cir. 1976), cert. denied, 430 U.S. 966 (1977) (admitting government deposition taken in Japan in a heroin trafficking case); and *U.S. v. Trout*, 633 F.Supp. 150 (N.D. Cal. 1985) (granting defendant's motion to depose witnesses in Brazil in a cocaine trafficking case).

205. *U.S. v. Salim*, 664 F.Supp. 682 (1987); 855 F.2d 944 (2d Cir. 1988). See Burke, "*United States v. Salim*: A Harbinger" (supra n. 25), as well as the account by the federal prosecutor in the case: Mehler, "Use of Foreign Depositions in Federal Criminal Trials."

206. *Reid v. Covert*, 354 U.S. 1 (1957).

tions of the Fourth Amendment and the exclusionary rule applied to evidence gathered overseas by U.S. agents acting unilaterally or in a "joint venture" with foreign officials[207] but not to evidence collected by foreign police acting on their own unless their actions were such as to "shock the conscience" of the court.[208] Much of the debate accordingly focused on whether evidence collected by foreign police at the behest of U.S. officials, or based on information supplied by them, constituted a "joint venture."[209] In 1990, the Supreme Court addressed the related issue of whether the Fourth Amendment protected not just U.S. citizens but also foreign nationals from extraterritorial actions involving U.S. officials—and ruled that it did not. There was no need, Chief Justice Rehnquist wrote, for U.S. law enforcement agents to obtain a warrant to conduct a search abroad when the target was a foreign national who lacked any "substantial connection" to the United States.[210] A Supreme Court decision to the contrary, many federal law enforcement officials had feared, would have significantly hampered the increasingly aggressive U.S. international drug enforcement campaign.

By the end of the 1980s, many other governments were following in the footsteps of the United States, and some were proceeding a step ahead. A Commonwealth Scheme for Mutual Assistance in Criminal Matters had been negotiated by senior officials from twenty-nine countries in London in early 1986 and endorsed some months later at a law ministers' meeting in Harare.[211] By 1990, the Canadian government had

207. *Powell v. Zuckert*, 366 F.2d 634 (D.C. Cir. 1966).

208. *Rosado v. Civiletti*, 621 F.2d 1179 (2d Cir. 1980), cert. denied, 449 U.S. 856.

209. See the analyses from the late 1970s and early 1980s by Keith Raffel, "Searches and Seizures Abroad in the Federal Courts," *Maryland Law Review* 38 (1979), 689–732; Stephen A. Saltzburg, "The Reach of the Bill of Rights Beyond the *Terra Firma* of the United States," *Virginia Journal of International Law* 20 (1980), 741–776; Steven M. Kaplan, "The Applicability of the Exclusionary Rule in Federal Court to Evidence Seized and Confessions Obtained in Foreign Countries," *Columbia Journal of Transnational Law* 16 (1977), 495–520; Roszell Dulany Hunter IV, "The Extraterritorial Application of the Constitution: Unalienable Rights?" *Virginia Law Review* 72 (1986), 649–676; and Steven H. Theisen, "Evidence Seized in Foreign Searches: When Does the Fourth Amendment Exclusionary Rule Apply?" *William and Mary Law Review* 25 (1983), 161–187.

210. *U.S. v. Verdugo-Urquidez*, 110 S.Ct. 1056, *International Legal Materials* 29 (1990), 441. The fact that the target was already incarcerated in the United States in anticipation of his prosecution for violation of U.S. laws did not, in the view of the Court, constitute a "substantial connection." The lower court decision, which held to the contrary, can be found at 856 F.2d 1214 (9th Cir. 1988). See the analysis of the Supreme Court decision in Mark Gibney, "Policing the World: The Long Reach of U.S. Law and the Short Arm of the Constitution," *Connecticut Journal of International Law* 6 (1990), 103–126.

211. David McClean, "Mutual Assistance in Criminal Matters: The Commonwealth Initiative," *International and Comparative Law Quarterly* 37 (1988), 177–190.

signed additional MLATs with Australia, France, Mexico, the United Kingdom, and the Bahamas; entered into negotiations with the Swiss and the Dutch; and enacted its own Mutual Legal Assistance Act. The Australian government had enacted similar legislation in 1987 and was also engaged in negotiating MLATs with a growing number of countries. Britain had finally signed the European Convention on Mutual Assistance, persuaded in part by the U.S. example that legal assistance arrangements between civil law nations and its own common law system could be worked out. It had also concluded a series of bilateral agreements with the United States and other governments providing for enhanced cooperation in drug enforcement matters; and in late 1989 it had introduced the legislation required to implement its proliferating mutual legal assistance arrangements.[212] Governments of financial secrecy jurisdictions such as Switzerland, Luxembourg, Austria, and Hong Kong had also initiated their own rounds of MLAT negotiations.

Of even greater significance were developments in four areas—drug enforcement, efforts directed at money laundering, securities and commodities regulation, and tax administration—in each of which U.S. initiatives undertaken unilaterally, bilaterally and multilaterally were complemented by the domestic and multilateral initiatives of other nations. Throughout the 1980s, the most powerful impetus to advances in international law enforcement was the rising global concern over illicit drug trafficking. Few governments did not expand and stiffen their penalties for drug trafficking and related activities. During the second half of the decade, U.S. influences began to be felt in the area of asset seizure and forfeiture. Governments throughout the world adopted legislation permitting the seizure and forfeiture of drug trafficker assets;[213] regional organizations, notably in Europe, committed themselves to broader cooperation; and international organizations such as Interpol and the United Nations' drug control organs promoted model legislation and international cooperation. By far the most significant development was the negotiation of the United Nations Convention Against Illicit Traffic in Narcotic Drugs and Psychotropic Substances, which mandated extensive cooperation in all law enforcement tasks directed at interna-

---

212. William C. Gilmore, "International Action Against Drug Trafficking: Trends in United Kingdom Law and Practice," *International Lawyer* 24 (1990), 365, 391.

213. See Jürgen Meyer, *Gewinnabschopfung bei Betaubungsmitteldelikten* (Weisbaden: Bundeskriminalamt, 1989), 31–59, which contains a comparative analysis, in English, of European and U.S. laws regarding the confiscation of proceeds derived from illicit drug trafficking.

tional drug trafficking, including extradition, mutual legal assistance, and the forfeiture and seizure of assets.[214] The U.N. convention was widely seen as providing both added legitimacy and legal authority for many of the international law enforcement measures designed to investigate and prosecute drug trafficking. It entered into force in November 1990.

The heightened focus on money laundering was largely a function of the rising sensitivity among drug enforcement officials to the financial dimensions of drug trafficking. By the end of the 1980s, the notion that "going after the money" was the most effective way to immobilize drug traffickers had become the conventional wisdom among government investigators and legislators in the United States, Canada, much of Europe, and a number of other countries. It was perceived as essential both to identifying and prosecuting the higher-level drug traffickers who rarely if ever came into contact with their illicit goods, and to tracing, seizing, and forfeiting their assets.[215] At the same time, the belief spread that individuals who assisted drug traffickers in laundering the proceeds of their activities merited harsh criminal sanctions as well.

U.S. legislation directed at money laundering had begun with the enactment of the Bank Secrecy Act in 1970, although the law's requirements that banks report cash transactions of $10,000 or more and that individuals transporting $5,000 or more in cash across the border submit currency reports were not seriously enforced until the mid-1980s. In 1986, however, Congress specifically criminalized the act of laundering drug-related proceeds. On the international front, the Justice Department assured foreign governments that the extraterritorial potential of the law would be substantially restricted.[216] It encouraged foreign governments, however, to enact parallel legislation and to cooperate in U.S. investigations and prosecutions of drug-related money laundering

214. U.N. Doc. E/Conf. 82/15 Dec. 19, 1988; *International Legal Materials* 28 (1989), 493. See David P. Stewart, "Internationalizing the War on Drugs: The U.N. Convention Against Illicit Traffic in Narcotic Drugs and Psychotropic Substances," *Denver Journal of International Law and Policy* 18 (1990), 387–404.

215. Ethan A. Nadelmann, "Unlaundering Dirty Money Abroad: U.S. Foreign Policy and Financial Secrecy Jurisdictions," *University of Miami Inter-American Law Review* 18 (1986), 33–82.

216. The assurance is contained in a letter of April 16, 1987, from Deputy Attorney General James Knapp to the British embassy, discussed in Bruce Zagaris, "Justice Letter Clarifies Extraterritorial Application of Money Laundering Act," *International Enforcement Law Reporter* 3 (1987), 221–223.

by waiving bank secrecy laws in drug trafficking investigations. In an indication of the growing importance of cooperation in this area, the G-7 summits in 1988 and 1989 addressed the subjects of money laundering and asset seizure and forfeiture. A Financial Action Task Force created at the latter meeting included not just the G-7 governments of the United States, Japan, Britain, France, Canada, Italy, and West Germany, but also the governments of Australia, Austria, Belgium, Luxembourg, the Netherlands, Spain, Sweden, and Switzerland. In its first report in early 1990, the task force urged governments to ratify the U.N. convention and to enact domestic legislation broadening the definition of money laundering and requiring financial institutions to screen and maintain records of customers and their transactions. The task force was subsequently expanded to include representatives of Denmark, Finland, Greece, Hong Kong, Ireland, New Zealand, Norway, Portugal, Turkey, and the Gulf Cooperation Council. By the end of the decade, Britain, France, Spain, Switzerland, and Luxembourg had all criminalized money laundering; the European Community Commission and the Council of Europe's Pompidou Group had assumed active roles in promoting legislation and cooperation against money laundering; the Bank for International Settlements in Basel, Switzerland, had prepared a "code of conduct" for banks regarding suspicious transactions; Interpol was actively promoting model legislation criminalizing money laundering; and even the principality of Liechtenstein, which many had perceived as taking advantage of Switzerland's declining reputation for secrecy, had effected an agreement with its banks regarding suspicious transactions and committed itself to criminalizing money laundering in the near future. In a development of potentially great significance, the Council of Europe adopted a new Convention on Anti-Money Laundering and the Search, Seizure, and Confiscation of Proceeds of Crime in November 1990 and invited the governments of Canada, Australia, the United States, and Eastern Europe to join.[217] Prominent both at the forefront of these developments and behind the scenes in task force meetings and negotiations were U.S. officials.

The dramatic internationalization of the securities and commodities markets since the 1970s had created a concomitant need to internationalize the regulation of those markets. This too was an area in which U.S.

217. *International Legal Materials* 30 (1991), 148. See Jeffrey Lowell Quillen, "The International Attack on Money Laundering: European Initiatives," *Duke Journal of Comparative and International Law* 1 (1991), 213–240.

officials, particularly SEC officials, took the lead.[218] As in other domains of international law enforcement, the SEC's experience during the early 1980s with seeking evidence by means of unilateral compulsory processes such as subpoenas and administrative summons had taught its officials both the extent and the limits of such measures. At the same time, the agency's extensive experience in working with Swiss officials had provided a sense of the potential of more cooperative initiatives. Following in the footsteps of the Justice Department, the SEC created its own Office of International Affairs in its Division of Enforcement in 1985. It rapidly began to negotiate, first, memoranda of understanding with its counterparts in Britain,[219] Japan,[220] Brazil, and the Canadian provinces of Ontario, Quebec, and British Columbia,[221] and thereafter, in 1989, more formal agreements with France[222] and the

218. More complete analyses are provided in Ronald E. Bornstein and N. Elaine Dugger, "International Regulation of Insider Trading," *Columbia Business Law Review* 2 (1987), 375–417; Mann and Mari, "Developments in International Securities Law Enforcement" (supra n. 60); Edward F. Greene, Alan B. Cohen, and Linda S. Matlack, "Problems of Enforcement in the Multinational Securities Market," *University of Pennsylvania Journal of International Business Law* 9 (1987), 325–373; Harvey L. Pitt, David B. Hardison, and Karen L. Shapiro, "Problems of Enforcement in the Multinational Securities Market," *University of Pennsylvania Journal of International Business Law* 9 (1987), 375–452; Michael A. Gerstenzang, "Insider Trading and the Internationalization of the Securities Markets," *Columbia Journal of Transnational Law* 27 (1989), 409–441; Harvey L. Pitt and Karen L. Shapiro, "Securities Regulation by Enforcement: A Look Ahead at the Next Decade," *Yale Journal of Regulation* 7 (1990), 149; and Paul G. Mahoney, "Securities Regulation by Enforcement: An International Perspective," *Yale Journal of Regulation* 7 (1990), 305–320.

219. The Memorandum of Understanding on Exchange of Information Between the United States Securities and Exchange Commission and the United Kingdom Department of Trade and Industry in Matters Relating to Securities and Between the United States Commodity Futures Trading Commission and the United Kingdom Department of Trade and Industry in Matters Relating to Futures, September 23, 1986, is in *International Legal Materials* 25 (1986), 1431. See Elizabeth E. Barlow, "Enforcing Securities Regulations Through Bilateral Agreements with the United Kingdom and Japan: An Interim Measure or a Solution?" *Texas International Law Journal* 23 (1988), 251–268; and Gerald A. Polcari, "A Comparative Analysis of Insider Trading Laws: The United States, the United Kingdom, and Japan: The Current International Agreements on Securities Regulation," *Suffolk Transnational Law Journal* 13 (1990), 167–199.

220. The Memorandum of the United States Securities and Exchange Commission and the Securities Bureau of the Japanese Ministry of Finance on the Sharing of Information, May 23, 1986, is in *International Legal Materials* 25 (1986), 1429. See the discussion in Barlow, "Enforcing Securities Regulations," and in Polcari, "Comparative Analysis."

221. Mark Roppel, "Extraterritorial Application of Securities Laws Between the United States and Canada," *Gonzaga Law Review* 24 (1988–89), 391–414.

222. Robert Bordeaux-Groult, "Problems of Enforcement and Cooperation in the Multi-

Netherlands.[223] It promoted resolutions on cooperation through the International Organization of Securities Commissions (IOSCO); it secured domestic legislation in Congress specifically authorizing and facilitating cooperation with foreign agencies;[224] and it encouraged foreign governments to develop and strengthen their own securities commissions and to criminalize such activities as insider trading. By 1989, the SEC's efforts, combined with the rising sensitivity elsewhere to the need for more-intensive securities regulation, had resulted in new laws criminalizing insider trading and creating more powerful regulatory agencies throughout much of Europe as well as Canada, Japan, and Hong Kong; the Council of Europe adopting a Convention on Insider Trading;[225] and the European Community being apparently well on its way to criminalizing insider trading in all member states by 1992.[226] Similar developments, many of them promoted by the CFTC, were simultaneously under way in the regulation of commodities trading, albeit with a lower profile.[227]

By far the most difficult area in which to create a consensus on

national Securities Market: A French Perspective," *University of Pennsylvania Journal of International Business Law* 9 (1987), 453–465.

223. Mark S. Klock, "A Comparative Analysis of Recent Accords Which Facilitate Transnational SEC Investigations of Insider Trading," *Maryland Journal of International Law and Trade* 11 (1987), 243–266; Pamela Jimenez, "International Securities Enforcement Cooperation Act and Memoranda of Understanding," *Harvard International Law Journal* 31 (1990), 295–311.

224. Theodore A. Levine and W. Hardy Callcott, "The SEC and Foreign Policy: The International Securities Enforcement Cooperation Act of 1988," *Securities Regulation Law Journal* 17 (1989), 115–150. See also *Globalization of Securities Markets: Hearing Before the Subcommittee on Telecommunications and Finance of the Committee on Energy and Commerce, House of Representatives*, 100th Cong., 1st Sess. (1987); *Insider Trading: Hearings on H.R. 4945 Before the Subcommittee on Telecommunications and Finance of the Committee on Energy and Commerce, House of Representatives*, 100th Cong., 2d Sess. (1988); and *International Securities Enforcement: Hearing on H.R. 1396 Before the Subcommittee on Telecommunications and Finance of the Committee on Energy and Commerce, House of Representatives*, 101st Cong., 1st Sess. (1989).

225. The text of the convention can be found in European Treaty Series No. 130 and in *International Legal Materials* 29 (1990), 309. See John P. Lowry, "The International Approach to Insider Trading: The Council of Europe's Convention," *Journal of Business Law*, Nov. 1990, 460–468.

226. P. L. Davies, "The European Community's Directive on Insider Dealing: From Company Law to Securities Markets Regulation?" *Oxford Journal of Legal Studies* 11 (1991), 92–105.

227. Peter G. McGonagle, "Serving Subpoenas Abroad Pursuant to the Future Trading Act of 1986," *Fordham International Law Journal* 10 (1987), 710–732.

international law enforcement matters concerned the administration of tax collection and the investigation of tax evasion and fraud. Yet even in this domain, substantial progress was recorded during the 1980s.[228] Some of the advances were a result of U.S. pressures—applied both bilaterally and by means of unilateral compulsory measures to obtain evidence—on its MLAT partners to provide cooperation in investigations of drug-related tax evasion and tax shelter frauds. Other advances were a result of IRS efforts to negotiate and renegotiate its international tax conventions to expand assistance not just in the administration of taxes but in the investigation of tax offenses as well. The Caribbean Basin Initiative and other legislation by Congress provided incentives for foreign governments to broaden their cooperation in U.S. tax investigations. The most significant development of the 1980s, however, was the completion of a Convention on Mutual Administrative Assistance in Tax Matters in January 1988 by the Council of Europe and the Organization of Economic Cooperation and Development (OECD).[229] Despite substantial controversy in Europe over the convention and the European Community's efforts to harmonize its members' tax policies, the United States signed the convention (with reservations) in June 1989. Although international cooperation in the enforcement of tax laws continued to lag behind other areas of international law enforcement, with numerous governments resisting on what they claimed were matters of principle, evidence of progress was tangible and clearly visible.

Amid the multiagency rush to expand and improve their international law enforcement capabilities during the 1980s, relatively little in the way of domestic opposition had emerged within the United States. Even as bankers and stock traders abroad had fiercely opposed their governments' concessions to U.S. law enforcement authorities, American businessmen had been relatively quiescent—with the possible exception of their vocal opposition to the SEC's "waiver by conduct" proposal. Fears that overly restrictive regulation of money movements and securities transactions might chase away foreign investors had generally been

228. John Turro, "The 'War on Drugs' Is Causing U.S. to Increase Investigations of Tax Evasion Through Tax Havens," *Tax Notes International* 2 (1990), 807–811.

229. The text can be found in European Treaty Series No. 127 and in *International Legal Materials* 28 (1988), 1160–1175. The treaty is analyzed in Karen Brown, "Allowing Tax Laws to Cross Borders to Defeat International Tax Avoidance: The Convention on Mutual Administrative Assistance in Tax Matters," *Brooklyn Journal of International Law* 15 (1989), 59–108; and in "Recent Developments," *Harvard International Law Journal* 30 (1989), 514–523.

counterbalanced by confidence in the overall attractiveness of investing in Americans banks and securities. Throughout the 1980s, moreover, foreign governments had directed relatively few requests for documents held by banks within the United States.

By the end of the decade, however, concern was emerging among sectors of the U.S. business community with respect to the impact of U.S. laws and treaties on foreign flight capital invested in the United States. In many respects, the United States had long represented the principal financial secrecy jurisdiction in the world, attracting hundreds of billions of dollars in investments by foreign citizens evading their own nations' tax and exchange control laws. Unlike the United States, which placed no prohibitions on the outflow of dollars from the United States, dozens of governments, both in the less-developed world and in Europe, restricted the outflow of their currencies. Before the late 1980s, U.S. officials had provided relatively little assistance to foreign governments investigating violations of their exchange control laws, and they had not been particularly cooperative with respect to the efforts of Latin American governments and others in the less-developed world to enforce their tax laws. Various developments in the late 1980s, however, suggested shifts in U.S. policy. With the criminalization of money laundering in 1986, many of the techniques legitimate businesses abroad use to invest in the United States and avoid their own nation's controls came under suspicion because they were often indistinguishable from the techniques drug traffickers use to launder their illegally derived funds.[230] At the same time, new tax conventions, notably the one signed with Mexico, were viewed with apprehension by foreign businessmen because of broadly worded provisions authorizing cooperation in investigations of tax offenses. Moreover, U.S. courts were increasingly receptive to requests for assistance from foreign law enforcement authorities, interpreting Section 1782 less restrictively than courts in the past.[231] The result of these developments, many in the American financial community feared, would be to chase foreign flight capital to countries that offered more secure confidentiality than the United States.

230. Jeff Gerth, "U.S. Seeks Tougher Line on Flight Capital," *New York Times*, Feb. 12, 1990, D1.
231. See, e.g., *In Re Request for Assistance from Ministry of Legal Affairs of Trinidad and Tobago*, 848 F.2d 1151 (11th Cir. 1988); Deirdre Fanning, "Fishing Expedition," *Forbes*, Oct. 31, 1988, 110; and "Much Ado About 1782" (supra n. 11).

Conclusion

Until well into the 1970s, the U.S. Justice Department and American prosecutors viewed the collection of evidence from abroad as a cumbersome and often unproductive process to be pursued only in the most important cases. The letters rogatory process was both slow and uncertain to produce documents in a form admissible in American courts. Few prosecutors were familiar with the requirements of foreign legal systems. Neither the Justice Department nor any other federal department had an office with expertise in collecting evidence from abroad. U.S. courts tended to look upon both letters rogatory from abroad and the evidence provided by foreign officials with jaundiced eyes, making few concessions to the irregularities of international evidence collection. Overseas, foreign law enforcement officials had few incentives to treat letters rogatory from the United States expeditiously. Judges and magistrates in civil law countries were unlikely to make allowances to the evidentiary requirements of U.S. law. And financial and corporate secrecy laws in Switzerland, the Caribbean, and other financial secrecy jurisdictions ensured that most requests for documents would meet with unsatisfactory responses.

As the demands of international law enforcement increased rapidly during the 1970s, so did the recognition that the United States' international evidence-gathering capabilities were grossly underdeveloped and needed to be improved. The MLAT with the Swiss provided the crucial opening, and the subsequent conflicts, negotiations, and agreements presented a series of opportunities for reducing the frictions and obstacles that had impeded the effective transmission of evidence to U.S. prosecutors. In the Caribbean, U.S. law enforcement officials encountered obstacles not unlike those in Switzerland, but in an environment that allowed them somewhat greater leeway to innovate, act unilaterally, and apply greater pressures. In Italy, U.S. law enforcement officials found accommodating allies eager to break new ground in forging ever-closer law enforcement relations. And the MLAT with the Canadians presented an opportunity to regularize law enforcement relations with a close friend and neighbor that had become increasingly annoyed by the extraterritorial infringements on its jurisdiction.

Ever since the end of World War II, the U.S. government had been criticized harshly by its closest allies for its aggressive assertions of extraterritorial jurisdiction in such areas as antitrust and export controls. Many had taken the step of enacting blocking statutes expressly forbidding local compliance with extraterritorial orders emanating from the United States. These hostile reactions, however, exercised little influence on U.S. officials seeking evidence in criminal investigations involving organized crime generally and illicit drug trafficking particularly. Indeed, it was precisely the focus on these domains of transnational criminality that provided the foot in the door for U.S. efforts to change the norms of international judicial assistance. Governments might differ on issues of antitrust and export controls, but the norms of international society no longer tolerated dissent on the issue of illicit drug trafficking. Neither the principle of financial secrecy nor the economic interests of states in maintaining their status as financial secrecy jurisdictions could stand in the way of the global campaign against illicit drug trafficking. Foreign governments thus acquiesced to U.S. demands for evidence in illicit drug trafficking investigations and thereby established a precedent for providing judicial assistance in cases that have nothing to do with drugs.

Viewed from the perspective of U.S. law enforcement officials, the evolution in international evidence-gathering capabilities since the 1970s can be equated with the development of an ever more powerful and efficient vacuum cleaner. The unilateral tactics devised during the early 1980s, such as the *Bank of Nova Scotia* subpoenas and the *Ghidoni* waivers, have proven useful both in obtaining evidence in specific cases and in inducing foreign governments to sign MLATs with the United States and otherwise improve their commitment and ability to provide assistance in criminal investigations. Those tactics remain in the arsenal of U.S. prosecutors and continue to be used effectively. The growing number of MLATs have provided relatively efficient bilateral arrangements for securing evidence from abroad. Changes in U.S. law both by the Congress and by the federal courts have facilitated the admissibility of evidence collected abroad. The creation of specialized offices in the Justice Department, the State Department, and the SEC with expertise in international law enforcement matters has provided a repository of information, assistance, and contacts that is valuable to prosecutors throughout the United States. Those offices have also made possible a coherent foreign policy of evidence collection and transmission. And the creation of comparable offices in foreign justice ministries has provided U.S. officials with reliable transgovernmental partners who share their language and their objectives.

All of these developments can be described as part and parcel of the regularization of international judicial assistance between the U.S. government and a growing number of foreign governments. But it is important to recognize that what began during the 1970s as a U.S. effort to persuade foreign governments to accommodate the evidentiary needs of its judicial system evolved during the 1980s into a far broader and more ambitious effort to bring foreign laws into greater accordance with U.S. laws. Foreign states began to criminalize money laundering and insider trading and to enact domestic laws authorizing the seizure and forfeiture of assets derived from illicit drug trafficking and other criminal activities. The U.S. government was not, of course, solely responsible for these developments. Just as the Council of Europe had developed its own multilateral MLAT and other international law enforcement arrangements decades before U.S. officials opted to do likewise, so the Council of Europe, some of its member states, and other multilateral organizations began during the 1980s to pursue their own initiatives in international judicial assistance. Particularly significant were the Council of Europe's new conventions on tax assistance, insider trading, and the detection, seizure, and forfeiture of criminal assets, as well as the European Community's efforts to better supervise securities transactions. Increasingly, efforts to improve international cooperation in judicial assistance involved not just mutual accommodation but also homogenization of legal systems.

Although the number of MLATs negotiated by U.S. officials by 1990 represented barely 15 percent of the number of U.S. extradition treaties, the MLAT partners represented a substantial diversity of governments from around the world—Europe, Asia, Africa, Latin America, the Caribbean, and Canada—and were proliferating rapidly. These bilateral law enforcement tentacles were supplemented by the 1988 U.N. antidrug trafficking convention, with its abundant provisions directed at enhancing international law enforcement cooperation. The cumulative result was an ever more inclusive net of national, bilateral, and multilateral criminal justice controls designed to deter, detect, and prosecute drug trafficking conspiracies, money laundering schemes, violations of securities laws, and other transnational criminal activities.

Chapter Seven

International Rendition of Fugitives

Issues, Methods, and Scope

The ultimate objective of most criminal investigations, both domestic and international, is to "immobilize" people who have violated the laws. When U.S. law enforcement officials want to "immobilize" a criminal who has fled to another country or who is living abroad and refuses to come to the United States to face trial, they have a number of options. They can request that the government of that country formally surrender the fugitive to the United States pursuant to its extradition laws or an extradition treaty with the United States. They can request that the foreign government make the fugitive available to U.S. authorities by less formal means, such as by employing more expeditious deportation procedures or otherwise kicking him out of the country. They can ask the foreign government to prosecute the fugitive in its own courts. Or they can attempt to gain custody over the fugitive by other methods, such as abduction or trickery. U.S. officials have employed each of these

methods since early in the nation's history, and with increasing frequency since the 1970s.

This chapter, unlike the preceding chapters, focuses not only on the
extraterritorial law enforcement efforts of the U.S. government but also
on its responses to foreign government requests for assistance in law
enforcement matters. The reasons are threefold. First, because unlike
the domains of transnational police activity and evidence-gathering, in
which the U.S. government has assumed a highly proactive and even
aggressive profile, the domain of extradition is one in which the U.S.
government has been the recipient of almost as many requests as it has
sent; second, because the norm of reciprocity has loomed larger in the
history of U.S. extradition than in other areas of international law
enforcement; and third, because most of the controversies generated by
U.S. involvement in extradition cases have involved foreign requests for
the extradition of fugitives from the United States rather than vice versa.
I should stress that none of these reasons apply to types of fugitive
rendition other than formal surrender by means of extradition, but they
provide ample justification for devoting some attention to the reactive
side of U.S. involvement in international law enforcement matters.

U.S. efforts to obtain custody of fugitives from abroad are hindered
principally by consideration of the sovereignty, laws, and political reactions of foreign states. By contrast, neither Congress nor the courts have
created any significant legal obstacles to securing fugitives from abroad
akin to those that so complicate the international collection of evidence.
Nor have the restrictions on fugitive rendition imposed by international
law played a prominent role since the first decades of the nation's history.
U.S. officials generally have regarded extradition by treaty or the laws of
foreign states as the preferred means of obtaining fugitives from abroad.[1]
It has long been viewed as the accepted means of securing fugitives; it
comports with the laws of the United States, the requested state, and
international society; its procedures are detailed in written laws and
treaties; and it typically allows for both judicial evaluation and executive
oversight of all requests.

The option of extradition, however, is not always available. There may
be no treaty between the United States and the foreign government, and

1. All U.S. extradition treaties in force (in 1993) are listed by country in Appendix F.
Also see the annual editions of *Treaties in Force* published by the U.S. Department of State.
The texts of the treaties are collected in Michael Abbell and Bruno A. Ristau, *International
Judicial Assistance* (Washington, D.C.: International Law Institute, 1990), vol. 5.

even if there is a treaty, the foreign government may be reluctant, for any number of domestic and international political reasons, to honor its commitments under the treaty. The treaty may fail to cover either the particular crime or the particular fugitive sought, or it may create other obstacles to extradition or to the delivery of the fugitive on terms desired by the U.S. government. And even when a foreign government is willing and able to extradite a fugitive according to its laws or a treaty, U.S. officials may prefer to obtain custody of the fugitive by more expeditious means.

The basic dilemmas of U.S. extradition—which date back to the origins of the nation's history—reflect two limitations imposed by U.S. laws and one generated by the laws of most foreign states. The U.S. government, unlike most other governments, lacks the legal authority either to extradite anyone in the absence of an extradition treaty or to prosecute anyone for acts committed abroad that violate foreign laws but not U.S. laws. Neither of these limitations is required by the U.S. Constitution, but they do reflect legal traditions deeply embedded in American jurisprudence. The result has been to make of the United States a safe haven in which fugitives from foreign justice know they are immune from prosecution so long as the United States and the government of the country in which they committed their crimes are not bound by an extradition treaty. Most foreign governments, especially those shaped by civil law traditions, are bound by a very different limitation, one that the United States does not share. Their laws, and in some cases their constitutions, prohibit the extradition of their citizens to other states. The fact that they are able to prosecute their citizens for crimes committed abroad partially compensates for this limitation, although this compensation has often been more evident in rhetoric and principle than in practice. There is no compensation, however, for the limitations imposed by U.S. law. Much of the history of U.S. rendition of fugitives can be understood in terms of U.S. and foreign government efforts to compensate for these limitations without disavowing them.[2]

Tension between the executive and judicial branches of government is virtually inherent to the extradition process both in the United States

2. A fine discussion of the incompatibilities, both real and imagined, between European and U.S. criminal justice systems and extradition norms is in Christopher L. Blakesley and Otto Lagodny, "Finding Harmony Amidst Disagreement over Extradition, Jurisdiction, the Role of Human Rights, and Issues of Extraterritoriality Under International Criminal Law," *Vanderbilt Journal of Transnational Law* 24 (1991), 1–73.

and in most other nations. It stems primarily from the fact that the approval of both branches of government is typically required to allow the extradition of a fugitive to a foreign country and secondarily from the fact that a fugitive who is delivered to the United States eventually has an opportunity to assert certain rights before a court of law. On the one hand, extradition falls within the province of the secretary of state—even though it has been handled principally by attorneys in the Justice Department's Office of International Affairs since 1979—and has traditionally been viewed as a component of foreign relations. On the other hand, extradition, unlike other domains of international relations, is concerned with individual human beings not as representatives of a state but as residents of the United States entitled to the rights accorded by its laws and Constitution. It thus entails judicial proceedings whenever a fugitive insists on challenging the extradition order of the executive branch. It presents the possibility that the will of the executive branch may be thwarted by a court's ruling that extradition is not permitted. And it provides a forum in which individuals may demand and obtain standing to assert their rights—limited though they may be—under a treaty.

The tensions between the two branches of government are best reflected in the evolving language of U.S. extradition treaties. On the one hand, these treaties have represented enablers and facilitators of rendition, providing both the requisite legal authority for the U.S. government to satisfy foreign rendition requests, and the guidelines for carrying out the process. On the other hand, they have played an important role as limiters of the rendition process, imposing constraints on the executive's freedom both to deliver fugitives to foreign governments and to prosecute those extradited to the United States as it might wish. Those constraints have reflected not only the explicit language of the treaties and U.S. and foreign extradition laws, but also the interpretations and (it is fair to say) the misinterpretations of the language by U.S. and foreign courts as well as U.S. and foreign executive branch officials. In some cases, the ambiguity of the treaty language has lent itself to misinterpretation by subsequent interpreters. In others, however, the misinterpretations have fairly been attributed to ignorance of and indifference to the negotiators' intentions, as well as willful disregard of the evident meaning of the language.

The evolution of U.S. extradition law and treaties has been largely one of expanding the scope of rendition between the United States and foreign states. In each case of an extradition relationship between the U.S. government and a foreign government, a treaty was first required to establish the legal basis for fugitive rendition. Subsequent laws and treaties, including both supplementary revisions and new replacements, were thereafter required to correct for the limiting interpretations imposed by courts and occasional executive branch officials, to incorporate new types of criminality created by legislation in each nation, and to reflect the desires of both parties to afford one another broader cooperation than before. U.S. treaty negotiators thus sought to narrow the many conditions on which extradition could not be granted, to shift responsibility for making crucial determinations of fact from the judicial branch to the executive branch, and to draft language that would be sufficiently open-ended to accommodate foreseeable changes in each nation's laws. Particularly significant in this evolutionary process was the gradual shift from the rather explicit and formalistic notions of reciprocity that characterized U.S. extradition treaty language and practice during the nineteenth century to a more substantive and instrumental notion of reciprocity by the middle of the twentieth century.

The two trends of ever-increasing numbers of fugitives to extradite and ever more encompassing and accommodating extradition treaties did not, however, result in any substantial increase in extraditions until the 1970s. Between 1842 and 1890, the U.S. government requested the extradition of 549 fugitives, of which 206 were delivered to the United States, and foreign governments requested the extradition of 604 fugitives from the United States, of which 237 were delivered.[3] During the 1880s, the number of extradition requests by and to the U.S. government averaged about 40 a year[4]—a rate that was not exceeded until the 1970s. By the late 1970s, however, the number had risen to about 150,[5] and in 1982, it totaled 350.[6] And by the late 1980s, the U.S. government was

3. John Bassett Moore, *Treatise on Extradition and Interstate Rendition*, 2 vols. (Boston: Boston Book Co., 1891), 2:1060–1065. These and all other statistics on extradition must be viewed warily because they may include renditions to the United States other than formal extradition pursuant to a treaty. Moore's *Treatise on Extradition* contains the texts of all extradition treaties signed by the United States before 1891.

4. John Bassett Moore, *Report on Extradition* (Washington, D.C.: Government Printing Office, 1890), 167–229, cited in Abbell and Ristau, *International Judicial Assistance*, 4:11.

5. The annual totals for 1979, 1980, and 1981, broken down by country, are provided in *Extradition Reform Act of 1981: Hearings on H.R. 5227 Before the Subcommittee on Crime of the House Committee on the Judiciary*, 97th Cong., 2d Sess., Serial No. 72 (1983), 308–312.

6. David Lauter, "There's No Place to Hide: Extraditions Have Tripled, and It's Only the Beginning," *National Law Journal*, Nov. 26, 1984, 1.

receiving more than 200 requests a year and sending out more than 300.[7]

The single most important reason for the dramatic increase in the number of extraditions, as well as the even greater growth in the numbers of requests for evidence in criminal cases, was the creation of the Office of International Affairs (OIA) in the Justice Department in 1979. Established "for the purpose of centralizing and giving greater emphasis and visibility to [the Justice Department's] prosecutorial service functions in the international arena," the OIA quickly emerged as a repository of information, experience, and advice on most international law enforcement matters.[8] Although a sister Office of Law Enforcement and Intelligence (L/LEI) was created in the State Department's Legal Adviser's Office at about the same time, the attorneys in the OIA assumed principal responsibility for processing fugitive rendition requests to and from the United States. They began to renegotiate the United States' more dated extradition treaties; they provided assistance to federal prosecutors seeking the rendition of fugitives from abroad; they assumed an active role in supporting and representing foreign extradition requests to the United States; and they took over responsibility for processing all extradition requests from state prosecutors to foreign governments.[9] Federal and state prosecutors no longer had to process their requests through unfamiliar and often indifferent State Department channels, and foreign governments no longer were obliged to hire local counsel in the United States to file and press their extradition requests. And whereas the State Department's attorneys had often viewed extradition requests through the somewhat confining lenses of international law, diplomatic protocol, and traditional notions of reciprocity, the OIA attorneys, with their prosecutorial backgrounds, proved less distracted by such considerations and more focused on immobilizing fugitives by whatever means were likely to work. By the late 1980s, the OIA's existence and capabilities were widely known among law enforcement officials within and without the United States, a fact that in and of itself generated ever-increasing numbers of extradition requests.

The OIA's successes were dependent on comparable institutional

7. The U.S. Marshals Service, responsible for collecting fugitives from abroad, reported that it carried out 240 extraditions in FY 1989 and 230 in FY 1990. See the annual reports of the attorney general for 1989 (p. 39) and 1990 (p. 50).

8. Abbell and Ristau, *International Judicial Assistance*, 4:16–17.

9. Ibid.

developments abroad. The fact that similar specialized offices had already been created in many foreign justice ministries, and that others were soon to follow, provided the OIA with the essential partners it required to conduct its transgovernmental affairs. Equally significant was the development during the 1980s of Interpol's international capabilities and the U.S. National Central Bureau of Interpol in the Justice Department. Even as formal extradition procedures continued to require the attentions of courts and prosecutors, the challenges of locating and arresting fugitives fell principally on the shoulders of police officials. Interpol's facilities, and in particular its standardized system of notices, provided them with a rapid and reliable system of keeping tabs on the movements of criminal suspects. The circulation of a "red notice" provided an efficient means of informing foreign police that a fugitive should be arrested when found and provisionally detained until the formal extradition request could be forwarded—although in practice many governments, including that of the United States, have treated a "red notice" only as a notice to locate a fugitive and have refused to make an arrest until the extradition request has been received.[10] Although officials in the OIA and the U.S. Interpol office clashed during the late 1980s over who would control the processing of "red notice" requests, the system itself provided an essential channel for expedited communications among police apart from the extradition process.

The persistent enhancement of the U.S. government's capacity to extradite fugitives to and from abroad might have been expected to reduce its dependence upon other means of international rendition. In fact, quite the opposite was the case. The enhancement of the U.S. government's extradition capacity may have been persistent, but it also was slow. Treaties took time to negotiate, and the number of officials in the Departments of State and Justice with the necessary expertise to undertake the process was small. The demand for fugitive rendition, by contrast, increased at a more rapid pace, particularly following World War II, and it accelerated dramatically with the internationalization of drug enforcement in the 1970s and 1980s. U.S. law enforcement agents, prosecutors, and the Justice Department responded by developing and employing an array of tactics to apprehend fugitives from foreign territories. One result was the regularization of what had become known as irregular rendition.

10. Michael Fooner, *Interpol: Issues in World Crime and International Criminal Justice* (New York: Plenum Press, 1989), 138–147.

The Evolution of U.S. Extradition

American attitudes regarding the apprehension of fugitives who have fled abroad have evolved substantially since the nation's origins. Until well into the nineteenth century, Americans gave little thought to issues of extradition. Criminals were far more likely to flee across state borders or into less-settled regions of North America than to foreign countries, and those who did flee abroad were typically seen as good riddance. Indeed, the request and delivery of criminal fugitives from one state to another was called "extradition" until the end of the nineteenth century, when John Bassett Moore's comprehensive and authoritative *Treatise on Extradition and Interstate Rendition* drew a sharp distinction between international and intranational renditions.[11] Some attention was devoted to crimes committed at sea and by sailors at port. But the concerns with cross-border banditry and vagabondage that motivated many of the first extradition treaties in Europe were relatively insignificant in the United States. Most Americans were wary about entering into extradition treaties that would require reciprocal responsibilities, so strong were their perceptions of the United States as a haven from the oppressions of foreign governments. The principal exceptions, discussed in Chapter Two, reflected the efforts of slave owners to recover their human chattel from foreign havens by unilateral action, diplomatic undertakings, and pressures on the U.S. government to negotiate treaties with Spain, Mexico, and Great Britain. Unilateral action to obtain other types of fugitives was generally regarded as unwarranted and unwise.

Apart from an extradition provision in the Jay Treaty of 1794 with Britain,[12] which expired in 1807, no extradition agreement was signed by the U.S. government until the inclusion of an extradition provision in the Webster-Ashburton Treaty of 1842 with Britain. On rare occasions, U.S. officials asked foreign governments to hand over certain fugitives despite the absence of an extradition treaty and the inability of the U.S.

11. See Moore, *Treatise on Extradition* (supra n. 3). See also John Bassett Moore, "The Difficulties of Extradition," *Publications of the American Academy of Political Science* 1 (July 1911), reprinted in *The Collected Papers of John Bassett Moore* (New Haven: Yale University Press, 1944), 3:314–322, esp. 320.

12. Art. 27 of the Treaty of Amity, Commerce, and Navigation, United States–Great Britain, 8 Stat. 116, TS No. 105 (signed at London, Nov. 19, 1794; submitted to the Senate, June 8, 1795; resolution of advice and consent voted by Senate on condition, June 24, 1795; ratified by United States, Aug. 14, 1795; ratifications exchanged at London, Oct. 28, 1795; proclaimed on Feb. 29, 1796); TS 105, 12 Bevans 13, 8 Stat. 116, 18 Stat. 269.

government to reciprocate. On other occasions, foreign governments simply took the initiative in delivering fugitives—many of them mutineers on American ships—to the United States even in the absence of any request.[13] No more than a few dozen, however, were delivered in such a manner during the first half of the nineteenth century. The number handed over by U.S. officials to foreign governments during the same time probably amounted to no more than half a dozen, although very informal renditions by U.S. officials near the borders with Canada and other foreign territories might well have gone uncounted. One was extradited pursuant to the Jay Treaty. A few were delivered pursuant to a New York State extradition statute enacted in 1822 and subsequently ruled unconstitutional in 1872.[14] And a few others may well have been handed over by U.S. officials unfamiliar with the laws and policies that forbade any delivery of fugitives to foreign authorities. The very novelty of extradition generated substantial suspicion among Americans, and some state courts intervened by habeas corpus to negate federal court decisions authorizing the extradition of fugitives.

The most notable extradition case during this period—one that preoccupied Congress for two months in early 1799—was that of Jonathan Robbins, alias Nash, whom British authorities had charged with murder on board a British man-of-war on the high seas.[15] So powerful was the popular opposition to extraditing Robbins—who claimed, falsely, that he was an American citizen who had been impressed upon a British ship—that President John Adams's decision to deliver him to the British was subsequently viewed as a significant factor in Adams's failure to be reelected. The President's decision was opposed by both Attorney General Charles Lee and Secretary of State Timothy Pickering, who argued that the treaty did not apply to crimes committed on the high seas.[16] Others focused their criticism on the absence of any federal legislation regulating the extradition process or providing for any judicial review of the British charge. But Adams's decision was supported by John Mar-

13. Moore, *Treatise on Extradition*, 45–49.
14. The early extradition laws of U.S. states and territories are discussed in ibid., 53–78. Moore's analysis led him to conclude that no state extradition law other than that of New York was ever used to extradite a fugitive. The New York statute was ruled unconstitutional by the New York Court of Appeals in *People v. Curtis*, 50 N.Y. 321 (1872).
15. Moore, *Treatise on Extradition*, 90, 136, 550–51, 1039. See also the fine analysis of the *Robbins* case and its broader significance in Ruth Wedgwood, "The Revolutionary Martyrdom of Jonathan Robbins," *Yale Law Journal* 100 (1990), 229–368.
16. Moore, *Treatise on Extradition*, 136.

shall, a prominent congressman soon to be appointed secretary of state and thereafter Chief Justice of the Supreme Court, who argued persuasively that it was the duty of the President to fulfill the treaty obligations in the absence of any directive by Congress.[17] The controversy surrounding the case, John Bassett Moore wrote a century later, "served to retard rather than promote the progress of extradition."[18]

The formal origins of U.S. extradition can best be dated to the 1840s, when the U.S. government signed its first full-fledged extradition treaty and Congress enacted its first federal extradition statute.[19] The 1848 statute specified the procedures to follow in extradition proceedings, but it did not authorize extradition in the absence of a treaty. The new law thus codified what most U.S. officials had long assumed—that the U.S. government could not extradite anyone in the absence of a treaty specifically authorizing extradition. Combined with the strongly enshrined notion that no one could be prosecuted in U.S. courts for violations of foreign laws, it presented the U.S. government with the choice of negotiating an abundance of extradition treaties or continuing to present the United States as a haven for foreign criminals.

During the following decades, the U.S. government rapidly emerged as a world leader in the negotiation of bilateral extradition treaties. Between the enactment of the 1848 extradition law and the start of World War I, U.S. officials negotiated thirty-three extradition treaties. Only France, which by 1870 had extradition treaties in force with twenty-eight governments, as well as other sorts of extradition arrangements with dozens of others, claimed more.[20] U.S. courts, moreover, produced a jurisprudence of extradition that was cited and referred to throughout the world. "In the matter of extradition," Sir Edward Clarke wrote in his 1874 treatise, "the American law was, until 1870, better than that of any other country in the world; and the decisions of the American judges are the best existing expositions of the duty of extradition, in its relations at once to the judicial rights of nations and the general interests of the civilisation of the world."[21] Most of the issues

17. Wedgwood, "The Revolutionary Martyrdom of Jonathan Robbins," 333–353; Francis Wharton, *Digest of International Law of the United States* (Washington, D.C.: Government Printing Office, 1886), 2:803–804.

18. Moore, *Treatise on Extradition*, 1059.

19. U.S. extradition law is codified at 18 U.S.C. 3181 and 3184, enacted in 1848 and largely unchanged since then. See Moore, *Treatise on Extradition*, passim.

20. I. A. Shearer, *Extradition in International Law* (Dobbs Ferry, N.Y.: Oceana Publications, 1971), 16–19.

21. Quoted in ibid., 16.

that continue to dominate extradition negotiations today were first addressed during that time.

The initial extradition treaties negotiated by U.S. officials included a hodgepodge of governments, mostly but not entirely in Europe: France in 1843, the Hawaiian Islands in 1849, Switzerland in 1850, Prussia, Bavaria, and Hanover between 1853 and 1855, the Two Sicilies in 1855, and Austria-Hungary in 1856.[22] During the next forty years, eighteen new treaties were signed with a variety of governments in Europe and Latin America, as well as with Japan and the Ottoman Porte.[23] The last treaty signed, with Russia in 1893, generated substantial opposition within the United States among those opposed to the czar.[24] Like the extradition provision in the Webster-Ashburton Treaty, a number of these—with the Dominican Republic, the Hawaiian Islands, Haiti, the Orange Free State, Switzerland, the Two Sicilies, and Venezuela—were small sections of more comprehensive treaties. As extradition norms developed, as particular controversies required more formal and antici-patory resolutions, and as new governments replaced old, many treaties were either supplemented or replaced by entirely new treaties. Between 1900 and 1914, U.S. negotiators concluded fourteen new treaties, ten of them with governments in Latin America, as well as fifteen supple-mentary and replacement treaties.[25] During the 1920s, U.S. efforts focused on signing new treaties with eight Eastern European govern-ments.[26] Between 1932 and 1943, six new treaties were signed—with Greece, Albania, Iraq, Liechtenstein, Liberia, and Monaco—but most efforts focused on concluding nineteen supplementary treaties as well as three replacement treaties, principally to expand the list of extraditable offenses.[27] Treaty negotiations ground to a virtual halt thereafter until 1970. Only one new treaty was signed—with Israel in 1963—as well as a few supplementary and replacement treaties, with South Africa, Swe-den, Belgium, and Brazil, although the last (signed in 1961) was signifi-

22. These and all other extradition treaties signed by the U.S. government before 1890 are reproduced in Moore, *Treatise on Extradition*, 1059–1187.

23. The treaties are listed in Abbell and Ristau, *International Judicial Assistance* (supra n. 1), 4:6.

24. See the commentary of John Bassett Moore (who favored ratification of the treaty) in "The Russian Extradition Treaty," *The Forum* 15 (1893), 629–646, reprinted in *Collected Papers of John Bassett Moore* (supra n. 11), 1:256–273.

25. The treaties are listed in Abbell and Ristau, *International Judicial Assistance*, 4:7–8.

26. Ibid., 8.

27. Ibid., 9–10.

cant in that Brazil had become a notorious haven for fugitives from American justice since the abrogation of the previous treaty in 1913.[28] The pace of negotiations picked up dramatically during the 1970s, motivated both by the general need to modernize the United States' increasingly dated extradition treaties and by the particular demands generated by the dramatic internationalization of U.S. drug enforcement efforts. Between 1970 and 1990, U.S. negotiators concluded more than two dozen replacement and supplementary treaties.[29] The most significant treaty, in at least one respect, was that signed with Great Britain on December 22, 1931. Although the two governments eventually replaced that treaty with a more modern one in 1971, the 1931 treaty was retained by most of the colonies of the British Empire when they gained their independence. As a result, more than thirty of the roughly one hundred U.S. extradition treaties formally in force by the 1980s were represented by the same document.[30]

The large number of bilateral extradition treaties negotiated by the U.S. government could be explained not just by its inability to extradite anyone in the absence of a treaty but also by its reluctance to join multilateral extradition conventions. A substantial number of these had emerged by the 1980s:[31] the European Convention on Extradition,[32] the Benelux Extradition Convention,[33] the Arab League Extradition Agree-

28. See Alona E. Evans, "The New Extradition Treaties of the United States," *American Journal of International Law* 59 (1965), 351–362.

29. The treaties are listed in Abbell and Ristau, *International Judicial Assistance*, 4:9. See also *Worldwide Review of Status of U.S. Extradition Treaties and Mutual Legal Assistance Treaties: Hearing Before the House Committee on Foreign Affairs*, 100th Cong., 1st Sess. (1987), 17–25.

30. See Appendix F, in which the countries represented by the 1931 treaty are noted with the superscript "c." See also Abbell and Ristau, *International Judicial Assistance*, 5:A-146.

31. See U.N. Division of Narcotic Drugs, *Extradition for Drug-Related Offenses* (New York: United Nations, 1985), 17–19. The principal author of the report is Robert Linke.

32. European Treaty Series (ETS), No. 24 (Dec. 13, 1957). See also the additional protocol of Oct. 15, 1975, at ETS No. 86 and the protocol of Mar. 17, 1978, at ETS 98. See the discussion of these treaties in Dominique Poncet and Paul Gully-Hart, "The European Model," in M. Cherif Bassiouni, ed., *International Criminal Law*, vol. 2, *Procedure* (Dobbs Ferry, N.Y.: Transnational Publishers, 1986), 461–503 (the texts of the treaty and protocols are reprinted at 505–522).

33. The Benelux Extradition Convention, which also covers mutual assistance in criminal matters, was signed by Belgium, Luxembourg, and the Netherlands on June 27, 1962, and entered into force in 1967. It is modeled on the European convention but contains provisions authorizing even closer cooperation among the three Benelux states. See B. de Schutter, "International Criminal Law in Evolution: Mutual Assistance in Criminal Matters Between the Benelux Countries," *Netherlands Journal of International Law* 114 (1967), 382. See the text at 616 UNTS 8893 and at *Benelux Publicatieblad* (1960–62), 22.

ment,[34] the 1981 Inter-American Convention on Extradition[35] and its predecessor the Montevideo Convention,[36] and the Convention on Judicial Cooperation of the Organization Communale Africaine et Malgache (OCAM).[37] In addition, the Nordic Treaty members[38] and the members of the Commonwealth[39] had each agreed during the 1960s on schemes to enact reciprocal extradition legislation, and the Soviet bloc countries had worked out their own comprehensive scheme, including mutual assistance in criminal matters, based on separate but nearly identical bilateral treaties with one another.[40]

U.S. officials generally demonstrated little interest in the multilateral conventions, although the United States' accession in 1985 to the Council of Europe's Convention for the Transfer of Prisoners suggested a growing interest in the benefits of such treaties.[41] A U.S. delegate had signed the Inter-American Treaty for the Extradition of Criminals and for Protection Against Anarchism in Mexico City in 1902, but it had never been put into force for the United States.[42] The United States has yet to sign the Inter-American Convention on Extradition adopted by the Organization of American States in 1981, nor has it made much use of the 1933 Montevideo Convention, of which it is a member.[43] Only when the the supreme court of Colombia declared the 1979 extradition treaty between the United States and Colombia invalid did U.S. officials attempt to employ—albeit to little effect—the somewhat forgotten convention of an earlier era. U.S. officials also reacted warily to efforts

34. The Arab League Extradition Agreement was approved by the Council of the League of Arab States on Sept. 14, 1952; an English translation is in *British and Foreign State Papers* 159, p. 606, and in League of Arab States, *Collection of Treaties and Agreements*, No. 95 (1978). It is briefly discussed in Shearer, *Extradition in International Law*, (supra n. 20), 52–53.

35. OAS Treaty Series No. 60 (OEA/Ser. A/36 [SEPF]).

36. 49 Stat. 3111; TS 882; 3 Bevans 152; 165 LNTS 45. Signatories of this convention are listed in Appendix F marked with a superscript "b."

37. The agreement was signed on Sept. 12, 1961.

38. The Nordic Treaty of July 1, 1962, can be found at 434 UNTS 145.

39. The Scheme Relating to the Rendition of Fugitive Offenders Within the Commonwealth, signed in 1966, can be found at HMSO, London, Cmnd. 3008.

40. See the discussion of the Soviet bloc system in Lech Gardocki, "The Socialist System," in Bassiouni, ed., *International Criminal Law*, 2:133–149; and Karin Schmid, "Extradition and International Judicial and Administrative Assistance in Penal Matters in East European States," *Law in Eastern Europe* 34 (1987), 167–182.

41. Convention on the Transfer of Sentenced Prisoners, TIAS 10824. See also U.S. Senate Treaty Doc. 98-23 (1984).

42. See *American Journal of International Law* 29 (Supp.) (1935), 278–282.

43. 49 Stat. 3111; TS 882; 3 Bevans 152; 165 LNTS 45.

initiated by the Council of Europe in the late 1980s to negotiate a new European extradition convention, fearing that it would undermine the accomplishments of the United States' bilateral treaties with member states. The long-standing American resistance to multilateral extradition conventions can be explained in part by the relative complexity of the U.S. legal system, with its common law traditions, federal distribution of jurisdiction, and highly intricate rules of evidence, none of which has been particularly well suited to multilateral extradition arrangements with the majority of foreign states in which civil law traditions dominate. But much of the resistance can also be attributed to the tendency of multilateral arrangements to settle on the minimum common denominators of cooperation. Bilateral treaties, by contrast, provide an opportunity to push each negotiating partner to include the provisions that are of greatest interest and advantage to the United States. The only exceptions to this aversion for multilateral extradition treaties (all of which date back no further than 1970) have been the multilateral conventions directed at hijacking and other crimes involving aircraft, terrorism, crimes against diplomats, hostage taking, and illicit drug trafficking, each of which contains provisions regarding extradition.[44]

The years since 1970 can best be characterized as the modern era of U.S. extradition treaty negotiations. U.S. negotiators have sought to maximize the number of offenses for which a treaty partner will extradite; to narrow as much as possible the "political offense" exception, especially in negotiations with close allies; to accommodate the extraterritorial reach of U.S. and foreign criminal laws and jurisdictional notions; to persuade foreign governments to extradite their nationals, or else ensure vicarious prosecution at the request of the U.S. government; to reconcile U.S. capital punishment laws with the insistence of foreign governments that fugitives delivered by them not be executed; and, more generally, to clear up confusions and eliminate needless obstacles that had hobbled extradition relations under the older treaties. Multilateral conventions—such as the 1972 Protocol to the 1961 Single Convention on Narcotic Drugs and the 1988 United Nations Convention Against Illicit Traffic in Narcotic Drugs and Psychotropic Substances—have filled in some of the gaps in the older treaties, most notably the omission of

---

44. See *Treaties in Force* (supra n. 1), and Abbell and Ristau, *International Judicial Assistance* (supra n. 1), 5:A-1075–1114.

drug law violations as grounds for extradition, but they have proven too limited in scope to negate the general need for new extradition treaties.[45] During the early 1980s, the treaty negotiations were supplemented by efforts in Congress, stimulated in good part by State and Justice Department officials, to modernize the extradition laws, which had last been substantially revised in 1882. The judiciary committees responded favorably, but political opposition involving the "political offense" exception scuttled the attempt to overhaul the extradition statute.[46]

Dual Criminality and Extraditable Offenses

A chronological examination of U.S. extradition treaties reveals both the trend toward ever-increasing breadth and inclusiveness and the persistent need to eliminate and clarify ambiguities in the language of old treaties that had resulted in both U.S. and foreign courts, and executive branch officials, rejecting extradition requests. Beginning with the Jay Treaty's provision for the extradition of fugitives accused of murder and forgery, the list of extraditable offenses grew ever longer thereafter until it was simply replaced during the 1980s by a fairly open-ended "dual criminality" provision authorizing extradition for any crime punishable in both countries by imprisonment for at least one year. In 1845, just two years after the United States had signed with France its first full-fledged extradition treaty—which listed murder, attempted murder, rape, forgery, arson, and embezzlement by public officers as extraditable crimes—the two governments appended a supplementary treaty that added robbery and burglary to the list of such crimes (and carefully defined both terms). In 1858, a further supplement included counterfeiting and embezzlement by private persons. Beginning in the 1880s, treaty negotiators made sure to include embezzlement and other types of fraud, and also became more particular in listing specific types

45. See the discussion in U.N. Division of Narcotic Drugs, *Extradition for Drug-Related Offenses* (supra n. 31), 4–12.

46. See *Reform of the Extradition Laws of the United States: Hearings Before the Subcommittee on Crime of the House Committee on the Judiciary*, 98th Cong., 1st Sess., on H.R. 2643 (1983); *Extradition Reform Act of 1981: Hearings* (supra n. 5); and *Extradition Act of 1984: Report (98-998) submitted by the House Committee on the Judiciary*, 98th Cong., 2d Sess., on H.R. 3347 (1984).

of murder, forgery, counterfeiting, and other crimes previously included only as generic categories.[47] Bigamy and abortion were also added to the lists in the early 1880s. And a few treaties included crimes that were not repeated in any other—the treaty with Mexico, for instance, made specific mention of mutilation.[48] The additions to the lists continued throughout the twentieth century. During the worldwide economic depression of the 1930s, bankruptcy offenses were included in newly negotiated treaties. By 1980, the "Schedule of Offenses" appended to a new extradition treaty with the Netherlands included not only the familiar crimes listed one hundred years before but also antitrust violations, illicit currency transfers, tax evasion, hijacking of airplanes, governmental corruption, violations of securities and commodities laws, obstruction of justice, and criminal offenses involving firearms, incendiary devices, and nuclear materials.[49]

The reliance on lists of extraditable crimes in the treaties meant that new initiatives in criminalization were difficult to incorporate into preexisting treaties without going through the process of negotiating, ratifying, and effecting supplementary treaties. The governments of the United States and Canada, for instance, were obliged to negotiate one supplementary treaty after another in order to keep pace with changes in one another's laws and judicial rulings, notably those involving securities law violations and other frauds.[50] During the early 1970s, U.S. law enforcement officials found many of their efforts to extradite drug traffickers from Latin America and elsewhere stymied by the fact that thirty-six of their treaties, including most of those with Latin American governments, made no mention of drug law violations, having been negotiated mostly before World War I. The lacuna was partially ameliorated by including a provision in the multilateral 1972 Protocol to the 1961 Single Convention on Narcotic Drugs that provided the legal basis

47. John Bassett Moore, "Extradition" (1893), reprinted in *The Collected Papers of John Bassett Moore* (supra n. 1), 1:274–285.

48. Art. 3 of the 1861 extradition treaty between Mexico and the United States, concluded Dec. 11, 1861; ratifications exchanged at Mexico, May 20, 1862; proclaimed June 20, 1862.

49. See the appendix to the Treaty of Extradition Between the United States of America and the Kingdom of the Netherlands, signed at the Hague on June 24, 1980; entered into force Sept. 15, 1983 (TIAS 10733). See also U.S. Senate Treaty Doc. 97-7 (1981), TS 209, Bevans 817, 12 Stat. 1199.

50. See William H. Timbers and Irving M. Pollack, "Extradition from Canada to the United States for Securities Fraud: Frustration of the National Policies of Both Countries," *Fordham Law Review* 24 (1955), 301–325.

for signatory governments to incorporate drug law violations into their preexisting extradition treaties.[51] But many governments were slow to ratify the convention, and some were uncertain whether the language in the Protocol provided sufficient authority to extradite. Meanwhile, the negotiation of new bilateral treaties required the time and resources of a very small number of officials with experience in extradition matters.

Even with respect to those treaties that either supplemented or replaced their lists of extraditable crimes with liberal "dual criminality" provisions, the U.S. government encountered additional problems. Many foreign courts had long been confused by the language of federal criminal statutes, which provided for federal jurisdiction based on an individual's use of the mails, telephone, wire service, or other forms of interstate commerce to commit a crime. U.S. requests for extradition under the old treaties occasionally had been stymied when foreign courts ruled that it was not against their domestic law for someone to use a telephone or write a letter. As the federal government's role in law enforcement grew dramatically, and as federal rather than state prosecutors began to account for a majority of U.S. extradition requests, foreign confusions on this point became increasingly frustrating. Many foreign courts also looked suspiciously on extradition requests involving violations of two federal statutes created in 1970 to deal with drug trafficking and organized crime: the Racketeer Influenced and Corrupt Organizations Act (RICO) and the Continuing Criminal Enterprise (CCE) statute.[52] Similar skepticism greeted U.S. efforts during the 1980s to prosecute drug traffickers for violating U.S. tax laws and other statutes directed at drug-related money laundering. And at least a few foreign governments were wary of the increasingly extraterritorial drift of U.S. criminal statutes, which contrasted so starkly with U.S. jurisdictional notions before World War II. U.S. extradition treaty negotiators responded to all these developments and problems by combining liberal

51. TIAS 8118; 976 UNTS 3. See Nelson G. Gross and G. Jonathan Greenwald, "The 1972 Narcotics Protocol," *Contemporary Drug Problems* 2 (1973), 119–163.

52. Steven A. Bernholz, Martin J. Bernholz, and G. Nicholas Herman, "Problems of Double Criminality: International Extradition in CCE and RICO Cases," *Trial*, Jan. 1985, 59–63; idem, "International Extradition in Drug Cases," *North Carolina Journal of International Law and Commercial Regulation* 10 (1985), 353–382; Barbara Sicalides, "RICO, CCE, and International Extradition," *Temple Law Review* 62 (1989), 1281–1316; Michael J. Dinga, "Extradition of RICO Defendants to the United States Under Recent U.S. Extradition Treaties," *Boston University International Law Journal* 7 (1989), 329–354.

dual criminality provisions with specific clauses designed to avoid the distractions of different terminology and jurisdictional bases.

The Principle of Specialty

The principle of specialty, which requires that a fugitive not be tried for an offense other than that for which he or she was extradited, was one that complicated the first decades of U.S. extradition relations and that continues to arise in a substantial proportion of prosecutions subsequent to extradition.[53] The first dozen treaties concluded by the U.S. government contained no explicit limitation of this sort, but subsequent treaties, beginning with the Italian treaty of 1868, did incorporate the specialty principle. During the 1870s, extradition relations between the governments of Britain and the United States foundered on this issue. The extradition clauses in the 1842 Webster-Ashburton Treaty had made no reference to limitations on trial, but the British Extradition Act of 1870, which represented the culmination of Britain's first systematic consideration of extradition law and policy, incorporated the principle of specialty into British law. When Secretary of State Fish refused in 1876 to provide the British government with the assurances it requested on this issue, the latter responded by rejecting—albeit only temporarily—a number of extradition requests from the United States.[54] In 1886, the U.S. Supreme Court addressed the issue in *United States v. Rauscher* and came down firmly in favor of the British position.[55] Extradition treaties negotiated thereafter typically included both language reflecting the specialty principle as well as clauses providing for exceptions to the principle. By the 1980s, the exceptions to the principle allowed the requesting government substantially greater latitude in prosecuting offenders for crimes other than those for which they had specifically been extradited.[56] The *Rauscher* decision was also notable for its suggestion—developed thereafter in the lower courts—that a fugitive could raise the

---

53. The early history of the specialty principle in U.S. extradition law and practice is discussed in Moore, *Treatise on Extradition* (supra n. 3), 194–280.
54. Ibid., 196–240.
55. 119 U.S. 407 (1886).
56. Abbell and Ristau, *International Judicial Assistance* (supra n. 1), 4:76–80.

specialty principle as a defense even in the absence of a formal protest by the government that had extradited him to the United States.[57]

Extraterritorial Jurisdiction

Another issue that restricted the capacity of the U.S. government to respond favorably to foreign extradition requests was its reluctance to acknowledge the more expansive jurisdictional notions of civil law nations. In the 1873 case of a Prussian citizen, Carl Vogt (alias Stupp), the Prussian government requested his extradition by the United States so that he could be tried for certain heinous crimes committed in Belgium. (A request the previous year from the Belgian government for Vogt's extradition had been rejected—in the case that ruled New York's extradition statute unconstitutional—due to the absence of an extradition treaty between the United States and Belgium.[58]) Among the seventeen extradition treaties then in force, all but one referred to crimes committed "within the jurisdiction" of the requesting state by individuals "found within the territory" of the other. In keeping with their civil law traditions, most foreign governments defined the first term as including crimes committed by their citizens in other territories, and a few went so far as to extend their jurisdictional claims to extraterritorial crimes in which only the victims were their citizens. U.S. jurisprudence, by contrast, eschewed any claim to jurisdiction based on the nationality of either the criminals or the victims and largely limited its jurisdictional claims to acts committed within its own territorial boundaries. Few crimes committed abroad by Americans, with the exception of treason and international crimes such as piracy and slave-trading, were regarded as violations of U.S. laws. The Prussian extradition request was nonetheless approved by Judge Blatchford, but the Department of State then

57. See Jonathan George, "Toward a More Principled Approach to the Principle of Specialty," *Cornell International Law Journal* 12 (1979), 309–327. See *U.S. v. Levy*, 905 F.2d 326 (10th Cir. 1990), cert. denied 111 S.Ct. 759 (1991), and *U.S. v. Cuevas*, 847 F.2d 1417 (9th Cir. 1988), cert. denied, 489 U.S. 1012, 109 S.Ct. 1122 (1989). The standing of the defendant to assert the principle of specialty is questioned in *Demjanjuk v. Petrovsky*, 776 F.2d 571, cert. denied, 475 U.S. 1016 (1986).

58. *People v. Curtis*, 50 N.Y. 321, Nov. 19, 1872; discussed in Moore, *Treatise on Extradition*, 70.

submitted the question of jurisdiction to Attorney General George Williams, who held that the reference to jurisdiction in the treaty meant territorial jurisdiction.[59] The extradition request was thus rejected, Vogt was set free, and an extradition treaty was signed with Belgium the following year.[60]

This lack of complementarity in jurisdictional notions continued to hamper extradition relations for another century. Only in the 1960s did U.S. negotiators begin to address this problem. Much of the incentive arose from the enactment of new federal laws that extended U.S. criminal jurisdiction to acts committed entirely outside the United States that were deemed to have an undesirable effect within the United States. Based primarily on the principle of "objective territorial jurisdiction" or the "effects" doctrine, and secondarily on the "protective" principle of jurisdiction, these new laws (of which the Comprehensive Drug Abuse Prevention and Control Act of 1970 was by far the most significant) were the subject of an increasing number of U.S. extradition requests. Beginning in the 1960s, all new U.S. extradition treaties authorized extradition for offenses committed outside the territory of the requesting government if the U.S. government would have jurisdiction over such offenses in similar circumstances.[61] In the late 1970s, U.S. negotiators went a step further and included treaty provisions authorizing extradition in cases such as *In re Stupp,* where the foreign government's request involved a crime committed by a citizen outside its territory.[62] And by the mid-1980s, new U.S. extradition treaties virtually eliminated the obstacles posed by differing jurisdictional notions, providing for extradition so long as the dual criminality requirement had been met.[63] As the

59. Moore, *Treatise on Extradition,* 134–135; *In re \Stupp,* 11 Blatchford 124, 23 Fed. Cas. 281 (S.D.N.Y. 1873), 14 Op. 281, Williams, 1873; For. Rel., 1873, 80–85, 301.

60. The treaty is reproduced in Moore, *Treatise on Extradition,* 1080–1087. Vogt's extradition to Belgium was subsequently upheld by Judge Blatchford. See *In re Stupp,* 12 Blatchford 501, 23 Fed. Cas. 296 (S.D.N.Y. 1875). The same issue emerged in extradition treaty negotiations with the Russian government in 1874. Secretary of State Fish's refusal to acknowledge the extraterritorial claims of foreign states in that instance is reproduced in Wharton, *Digest of International Law* (supra n. 17), 2:800.

61. Abbell and Ristau, *International Judicial Assistance,* 4:64–65. See, e.g., the 1963 extradition treaty with Sweden, Art. 4, TIAS 5496; the 1964 treaty with Israel, Art. 3, TIAS 5476; the 1964 treaty with Brazil, Art. 4, TIAS 5691; and the 1976 treaty with Australia, Art. 4, TIAS 8234.

62. Ibid., 65–66. See, e.g., the 1980 treaty with Japan, Art. 4, TIAS 9625.

63. Ibid., 66. See, e.g., the 1984 treaty with Italy, Art. 3, TIAS 10837, and the 1984 treaty with Ireland, Art. 3, TIAS 10813.

problems generated by the lack of complementarity and reciprocity in jurisdictional claims faded, conflicts involving mutual claims of jurisdiction appeared increasingly likely.[64]

Capital Punishment

Another issue that emerged during the nineteenth century and that has continued to complicate extradition relations throughout the twentieth involves the death penalty. Governments that have abolished the death penalty in their own countries generally refuse to extradite fugitives to the United States and other nations that retain capital punishment unless assurances are provided that the death penalty will not be employed. This issue first emerged in U.S. extradition relations during the nineteenth century. It became a source of conflict with the Italian government during the first decades of this century, when the latter refused to extradite Italian-American members of the Black Hand who had been condemned in the United States to death in the electric chair.[65] And it reemerged during the late 1980s as a major impediment to U.S. extradition efforts. The U.S. government has preferred not to include any waiver of capital punishment in its treaties. The compromise that emerged early in the twentieth century was to include a provision in extradition treaties formally acknowledging the right of a requested state not to extradite a fugitive unless the U.S. government promised to forgo the death penalty.[66] What has complicated matters on this issue, as on many other extradition issues, is the sovereign power of states within the United States to enforce their own criminal laws in the absence of an explicit federal law or treaty to the contrary. In 1985, the Canadian government agreed to extradite Tony Ng, who was wanted for his involvement in the murders of thirteen people in a Chinese gambling club in Seattle, only after Washington State officials promised not to seek the death penalty.[67] In late 1989, however, the same government consented to extradite

64. See Blakesley and Lagodny, "Finding Harmony Amidst Disagreement" (supra n. 2).

65. Thomas Monroe Pitkin and Francesco Cordasco, *The Black Hand: A Chapter in Ethnic Crime* (Totowa, N.J.: Littlefield, Adams & Co., 1977), 215.

66. See J. S. Reeves, "Extradition Treaties and the Death Penalty," *American Journal of International Law* 18 (1924), 298–300.

67. John F. Burns, "With Death at Issue, Can Canada Wash Its Hands?" *New York Times*, Nov. 1, 1988, A4.

Charles Ng (no relation to Tony), who had been charged with the abduction and murder of a dozen people, to California despite the refusal of state officials to forgo the death penalty.[68] The government reportedly had received 100,000 letters insisting that Ng be extradited.[69] In another case in 1989 with greater implications for U.S. extradition efforts, the European Court of Human Rights held that the British government could not extradite a German national, Jens Soering, to the United States to face charges of murder in a Virginia court without a promise from U.S. or Virginian authorities that the death penalty would not be sought or imposed.[70] In the court's judgment, the prospect of the relatively young man spending many years on death row in a state prison with a reputation for interprisoner violence violated the provision in the European Convention on Human Rights prohibiting torture or inhuman or degrading treatment or punishment. The British government responded to the decision by extraditing Soering to the United States only on charges for which he could not receive the death penalty. Some months later, the supreme court of the Netherlands refused to approve the extradition of an American serviceman, Sergeant Charles Short, accused of killing his Turkish wife and trying to dispose of her remains, in the absence of an assurance from U.S. authorities that he would not be tried for a capital offense. Relying heavily on the *Soering* decision and the European Convention on Human Rights, the court stated that international human rights obligations overrode the obligation to extradite. Following a commitment by U.S. officials not to prosecute Short for a capital offense, the Dutch government delivered the American soldier, who had been based with a U.S. unit at the Dutch Soesterberg Air Force Base, to U.S. authorities.[71] The two cases, combined with the

68. Bruce Zagaris, "Canada Extradites Ng Without Seeking Death Penalty Assurances," *International Enforcement Law Reporter* 5 (1989), 420–422.

69. This and other extradition cases involving the death penalty are discussed in Andrea Sachs, "A Fate Better Than Death," *Time*, Mar. 4, 1991, 52.

70. *Soering v. United Kingdom* (161 Eur. Ct. H.R., ser. AO (1989)). See the discussion of the case in John Quigley and S. Adele Shank, "Death Row as a Violation of Human Rights: Is It Illegal to Extradite to Virginia?" *Virginia Journal of International Law* 30 (1989), 241–271; "*Soering v. United Kingdom*: Whether the Continued Use of the Death Penalty in the United States Contradicts International Thinking," *New England Journal on Criminal and Civil Confinement* 16 (1990), 339–368; Wilson Finnie, "Extradition and the Death Penalty," *The Scots Law Times*, Feb. 16, 1990, 53–57; Stephan Breitenmoser and Gunter E. Wilms, "Human Rights v. Extradition: The *Soering* Case," *Michigan Journal of International Law* 11 (1990), 845–886; and John Andrews and Ann Sherlock, "Extradition, Death Row, and the Convention," *European Law Review* 15 (1990), 87–92.

71. The *Short* case and related developments are discussed in *International Enforcement Law Reporter* 7 (1991), 313–315.

abolition of capital punishment in virtually all of Europe as well as in many other countries, suggested that capital offenses might well be the only area of extradition law and practice in which U.S. efforts to extradite fugitives were finding themselves more rather than less constrained than before.[72]

The "Political Offense" Exception

No extradition issue has attracted as much attention and controversy as the "political offense" exception, a clause included in all U.S. extradition treaties as well as in most other extradition treaties currently in force that circumscribes extradition in cases involving politically motivated crimes and prosecutions.[73] The notion of a "political offense" exception to extradition had arisen during the 1830s in Europe when popular opinion in France and Belgium rebelled at the notion of extraditing political refugees who had committed violent acts to the governments against which those acts had been directed.[74] In 1833, the French government began to include the clause in its new extradition treaties and to supplement its older treaties accordingly. A "political offense" exception clause was thus included in the first full-fledged extradition treaty signed by the United States—the 1843 treaty with France.[75] The extradition provision included in the Webster-Ashburton Treaty approved the previous year had not included such a clause, but the message of President Tyler submitting the treaty to the Senate had.[76] With a few

72. A similar conflict arose when the U.S. government asked Italian authorities to extradite Anthony Sciacca, an Italian citizen who had been accused of murder in New York when he was seventeen years old. Italian courts rejected the extradition request on the grounds that Sciacca would be treated as an adult under New York law and thus face a sentence of up to life in prison, while under Italian law he would be treated as a juvenile and probably accorded a lenient sentence. When subsequent efforts to have Sciacca vicariously prosecuted in Italian courts faltered because of a statute of limitations, the district attorney of Queens, John Santucci, flew to Italy with Justice Department officials to attempt to find a solution. See Joseph P. Fried, "Santucci to Go to Italy in Battle over a Slaying," *New York Times*, July 14, 1990, 24.

73. There is an extensive and continually growing legal literature on this question. See esp. Christine Van den Wijngaert, *The Political Offence Exception to Extradition* (London: Kluwer, 1980).

74. Lora L. Deere, "Political Offenses in the Law and Practice of Extradition," *American Journal of International Law* 27 (1933), 247–270.

75. The extradition treaty with France was concluded on Nov. 9, 1843; ratifications exchanged at Washington, Apr. 12, 1844; proclaimed Apr. 13, 1844; TS 89, 7 Bevans 830, 8 Stat. 580.

76. Ibid., 214, 305.

exceptions, notably the extradition treaty with Prussia and other German states, all subsequent U.S. extradition treaties made reference to the
"political offense" exception. During the 1850s, a controversy between
the governments of Belgium and France involving the latter's request for
the extradition of two Frenchmen who had attempted to blow up a train
carrying Napoleon III yielded a new provision, known as the *attentat*
clause, that excluded attempted assassinations of heads of state and their
families from the "political offense" exception.[77] The clause quickly
became a fixture of many extradition treaties. It was first included in the
United States' extradition treaty with Belgium in 1882, just shortly after
the assassination of President Garfield, and became a standard provision
during the twentieth century.

The first case in which an extradition request was rejected on account
of the "political offense" exception occurred in 1837, when Governor
Marcy of New York refused—pursuant to New York's 1822 extradition
statute—to extradite a Canadian, William Lyon McKenzie, who had led
a minor insurrection against Governor Head in Toronto. The crime
McKenzie had committed, Marcy pointed out, was in effect treason and
thus not susceptible to extradition.[78] Between 1880 and 1920, requests
from Mexico City for the extradition of revolutionaries were often
turned down on much the same grounds—although in 1896 the Supreme
Court approved the extradition of bandits operating along the border
who had claimed they were part of a revolutionary movement but failed
to show that their motives were primarily political.[79] In 1894, an
extradition request from the government of Salvador for the delivery of
General Antonio Ezeta—who had helped overthrow a previous regime
and then been ousted from office himself—as well as four of his
followers, was rejected by a U.S. magistrate. He relied heavily on a
British case decided three years earlier, *In re Castione*, in which Judge
Denman had refused to extradite the leader of an uprising in a Swiss
canton on the grounds that crimes committed in the course of, or
incident to, a revolution or uprising were political and hence nonextra-
ditable.[80] This formulation, known as the "incidence test," emerged in

77. Deere, "Political Offenses in the Law and Practice of Extradition," 252–253; Moore,
Treatise on Extradition, 308–311.
78. Moore, *Treatise on Extradition*, 313–315.
79. *Ornelas v. Ruiz*, 161 U.S. 502 (1896).
80. See *In re Ezeta*, 62 F. 972 (N.D. 1894); *In re Castione*, [1891] 1 Q.B. 149. See also
the discussion in John Bassett Moore, "The Case of the Salvadorean Refugees," *American Law
Review* 29 (1895), 1–20; and Barbara Ann Banoff and Christopher H. Pyle, " 'To Surrender

subsequent decades as the central determinant of whether a crime fell within the "political offense" exception.

The extradition cases that aroused the greatest public interest in the United States typically involved revolutionaries whose movements claimed substantial popular support in the United States. During the first decade of the twentieth century, requests from the czarist government for the extradition of two Russian revolutionaries accused of murder and other crimes were approved by U.S. commissioners but then rejected by the secretary of state in the wake of vocal public opposition.[81] The most controversial cases, however, involved Irish revolutionaries fighting British rule in Ireland. Beginning with the Lynchehaun case in 1903, U.S. refusals to extradite Irish revolutionaries who had committed violent acts have generated substantial tensions between the governments of Britain and the United States. Between 1979 and 1986, U.S. courts rejected four extradition requests from Britain for IRA members—in *McMullen*,[82] *Mackin*,[83] *Quinn*,[84] and *Doherty*[85]—who had been charged or convicted of murder and other violent crimes directed at British soldiers and other officials. The Reagan administration, which preferred to favor Britain's requests, responded in a variety of ways. Each case was appealed to higher courts, with the result that Quinn was extradited in 1986. Congressional bills narrowing the "political offense" exception were backed by the White House,[86] and a supplementary extradition treaty was negotiated with Britain, dramatically limiting the political offense exception.[87] Both encountered substantial opposition in the

---

Political Offenders': The Political Offense Exception to Extradition in United States Law," *New York University Journal of International Law and Politics* 16 (1984), 169–210.

81. Deere, "Political Offenses in the Law and Practice of Extradition," 267; Green Haywood Hackworth, *Digest of International Law* (Washington, D.C.: Government Printing Office, 1942), 4:49–50. See the debate over the political offense exception among J. Reuben Clark Jr., Frederic R. Coudert, and Julian W. Mack in *Proceedings of the American Society of International Law 1909*, 95–165.

82. The magistrate's denial of extradition can be found at No. 3-78-1099 (N.D. Cal. May 11, 1979), reprinted in *Congressional Record* S9146 (daily ed. July 16, 1986), 132.

83. 668 F.2d 122 (2d Cir. 1981).

84. 783 F.2d 776 (9th Cir. 1986), cert. denied 479 U.S. 882 (1986).

85. 786 F.2d 491 (2d Cir. 1986).

86. The proposed legislation is analyzed in M. Cherif Bassiouni, "Extradition Reform Legislation in the United States: 1981–1983," *Akron Law Review* 17 (1984), 495–574.

87. Supplementary Treaty to the Extradition Treaty of June 8, 1972, signed at Washington June 25, 1985, entered into force Dec. 23, 1986. See the text in U.S. Senate Treaty Doc. 99-8 (1985) and the analysis of the treaty in U.S. Senate Exec. Rept. 99-17 (1986). See also Terri Lee Wagner, "Expediting Extraditing: The United States–United Kingdom Supplemental Extradition Treaty of 1986," *Loyola of Los Angeles International and Comparative Law*

Congress and elsewhere.[88] The proposed extradition reform bill failed to make it through the Congress primarily because of this issue, and the first supplementary treaty submitted to the Senate required minor revisions before the Senate would approve it.[89] Similar treaty supplements were subsequently signed, however, with Germany,[90] Canada,[91] and Australia.[92] U.S. treaty negotiators had already begun, during the late 1970s, to include a clause explicitly authorizing the executive rather than the judicial branch to evaluate the motivations of the requesting state and, in a few cases, a clause to determine the applicability of the political offense exception[93]—but they were obliged to forgo the first clause in subsequent treaties as a result of the controversy in Congress. Determined to appease the British government, Justice Department officials instituted deportation proceedings against the three other IRA fugitives[94] and renewed their attempts to extradite McMullen and Doherty under the supplementary treaty.[95]

The IRA cases, however, represented more an aberration than a

---

Journal 10 (1988), 135–162; and Kathleen A. Basso, "The 1985 U.S.-U.K. Supplementary Extradition Treaty: A Superfluous Effort?" *Boston College International and Comparative Law Review* 12 (1989), 301–333.

88. See the fine discussion in Committee on Immigration and Nationality Law, "Report Recommending Reform of the Law of International Extradition," *Record of the Association of the Bar of the City of New York* 41 (1986), 587–614.

89. Steven V. Roberts, "Pact with Britain on Extraditions Backed by Senate," *New York Times,* July 18, 1986, A1.

90. *Supplementary Extradition Treaty with the Federal Republic of Germany,* U.S. Senate Treaty Doc. 100-6 (1987).

91. *Protocol Amending the Extradition Treaty with Canada,* U.S. Senate Treaty Doc. 101-17 (1990). See David K. Shipler, "U.S. and Canada Close Extradition Gap," *New York Times,* Jan. 12, 1988, A3.

92. *Protocol Amending the Treaty on Extradition Between the United States of America and Australia of May 14, 1974;* U.S. Senate Treaty Doc. 102-23 (1992).

93. See, e.g., the 1980 treaty with the Netherlands, TIAS 10733, U.S. Senate Treaty Doc. 97-7. The first clause can also be found in the 1983 treaty with Jamaica, U.S. Senate Treaty Doc. 98-18, and in the 1983 treaty with Ireland, TIAS 10813, U.S. Senate Treaty Doc. 98-19. The second clause is also in the 1978 treaty with Mexico, 31 UST 5059, TIAS 9656, and in the 1979 treaty with Colombia, U.S. Senate Treaty Doc. 9-8.

94. Desmond Mackin was deported to Ireland, with his permission, at the end of 1981. Litigation generated by efforts to deport Doherty to Ireland ultimately led to the Supreme Court. See *INS v. Doherty,* 112 S.Ct. 719 (1992). See also Michael J. Bowe, "Deportation as De Facto Extradition: The Matter of Joseph Doherty," *New York Law School Journal of International and Comparative Law* 11 (1990), 263–296. Efforts to deport McMullen are discussed in *In re McMullen,* 769 F.Supp. 1278 (S.D.N.Y. 1991).

95. Ronald Sullivan, "U.S. Court Blocks IRA Extradition," *New York Times,* Jan. 13, 1992, A7.

pattern of judicial intervention in extradition cases involving the "politi-cal offense" exception. In two cases involving attacks by Palestinian Arabs that had resulted in the deaths of Israeli civilians—the first in Tiberias, the second in the West Bank—federal courts rejected the defendants' attempts to invoke the exception.[96] U.S. courts also have hewed fairly close to the "rule of non-inquiry," according to which any inquiries into a foreign government's motives in making an extradition request as well as into the fairness of its judicial proceedings are reserved to the executive branch.[97] One exception to this rule arose in the latter of the Palestinian cases, *Ahmad v. Widen*, in which Judge Weinstein held a hearing to determine whether Ahmad would be accorded due process if extradited to Israel (and concluded that he would).[98]

The courts have similarly refrained from giving any sanctuary to Nazi war criminals who thought they had found a safe refuge in the United States. The one exception occurred in 1959, when a California federal court rejected a request from the government of Yugoslavia for the extradition of Andrija Artukovic, the former interior minister of the independent state of Croatia during World War II.[99] His alleged crimes, which included control over concentration camps and the murders of thousands of civilians, were viewed by the court as "political offenses" for which extradition could not be granted. Until well into the 1970s, moreover, the Immigration and Naturalization Service devoted few efforts to identifying and deporting Nazi war criminals. During the late 1970s, however, the chair of the House Judiciary Committee's Subcom-

96. See *Eain v. Wilkes*, 641 F.2d 504 (7th Cir. 1981), cert. denied, 454 U.S. 894 (1981), in which the defendant was accused of setting a bomb that exploded in an Israeli marketplace, killing two young boys and maiming or otherwise injuring more than thirty others. See also *Ahmad v. Wigen*, 910 F.2d 1063 (2d Cir. 1990), involving an attack on an Israeli civilian bus in the West Bank that resulted in the death of the bus driver. In the latter case, as in *Quinn*, the assertion of the "political offense" exception was acknowledged as a bar to extradition in the first judicial hearing, *In re Extradition of Atta*, No. 87-0551-M (E.D.N.Y. June 17, 1988) (Westlaw 1988 WL 66866), but then rejected in subsequent hearings. See the discussion in Sheryl A. Petkunas, "The United States, Israel, and Their Extradition Dilemma," *Michigan Journal of International Law* 12 (1990), 204–228.

97. The "rule of non-inquiry" is discussed in Michael P. Scharf, "Foreign Courts on Trial: Why U.S. Courts Should Avoid Applying the Inquiry Provision of the Supplementary U.S.-U.K. Extradition Treaty," *Stanford Journal of International Law* (1989), 257–288, and in Abraham Abramovsky, "The Political Offense Exception and the Extradition Process: The Enhancement of the Role of the U.S. Judiciary," *Hastings International and Comparative Law Review* 13 (1989), 1–24.

98. *Ahmad v. Wigen*, 726 F.Supp. 389 (E.D.N.Y. 1989).

99. *U.S. ex rel. Karadzole v. Artukovic*, 170 F.Supp. 383 (S.D. Cal. 1959).

mittee on Immigration, Elizabeth Holtzman, pushed through legislation requiring the Justice Department to assume responsibility for Nazi war crime cases.[100] Attorney General Griffen Bell responded in 1979 by creating an Office of Special Investigations (OSI) dedicated to finding Nazi war criminals and arranging for them to be extradited or deported to face charges in foreign courts.[101] Its efforts were aided by the widespread repudiation of the 1959 *Artukovic* decision by most commentators and all federal courts.[102] By 1991, the OSI's investigations had resulted in seventy-five extraditions and deportations,[103] including the 1986 extradition of Artukovic to Yugoslavia, where he died before his sentenced execution; the 1983 extradition of Hermine Braunsteiner-Ryan, a former SS member and Majdank concentration camp guard, to West Germany, where she was sentenced to life imprisonment for multiple murders; the 1984 deportation of Feodor Fedorenko, a Ukranian guard in the Treblinka concentration camp, to the Soviet Union, where he was executed for his crimes; the 1987 deportation of Karl Linnas, an Estonian who supervised the killing of Jews in the concentration camps at Tartu, to the Soviet Union, where he died while awaiting action on an appeal for a pardon;[104] and the 1986 extradition of John Demjanjuk, a Ukranian who had gained a reputation as "Ivan the Terrible" while serving as an SS guard at the Treblinka and Sobibor death camps, to Israel, where he was sentenced to death for his crimes.[105]

The transformation in the U.S. government's view of the "political offense" exception could also be seen in the evolving response to hijackers fleeing communist states. In 1950, the U.S. government had rejected, on "political offense" grounds, a request from the Czechoslo-

100. See Rena Hozore Reiss, "The Extradition of John Demjanjuk: War Crimes, Universality Jurisdiction, and the Political Offense Doctrine," *Cornell International Law Journal* 20 (1987), 281–315.

101. See Alan A. Ryan Jr., *Quiet Neighbors: Prosecuting Nazi War Criminals in America* (New York: Harcourt Brace Jovanovich, 1984).

102. See *Eain v. Wilkes*, 641 F.2d 504 (7th Cir. 1981), cert. denied 454 U.S. 894 (1981).

103. Jennifer Combs, "Time Running Out for Nazi War Criminals," *Reuter Library Report*, Sept. 4, 1991.

104. Damon J. Borrelli, "The Legacy of Nuremburg: Disguised Extradition and Karl Linnas," *Suffolk Transnational Law Journal* 11 (1987), 277–286.

105. These and other cases are listed in Michael Hedges, "U.S. Nazi Hunters Railroaded 'War Criminal,' Experts Say," *Washington Times*, Sept. 24, 1990, A1. The Demjanjuk case is analyzed in Reiss, "The Extradition of Demjanjuk" (supra n. 100); and in Steven Lubet and Jan Stern Reed, "Extradition of Nazis from the United States to Israel: A Survey of Issues in Transnational Criminal Law," *Stanford Journal of International Law* 23 (1986), 1–65.

vakian government for the extradition of eight Czech citizens who had hijacked a Czechoslovak Airlines plane to the U.S. Occupation Zone in Germany.[106] In 1951, another request involving a Czechoslovak train that had been hijacked to the U.S. zone was similarly rejected.[107] By the early 1970s, however, sentiments had shifted as the Cold War mellowed somewhat and as a rash of airplane hijackings prompted two multilateral conventions—signed in the Hague in 1970 and Montreal in 1971— directed at airplane bombing and hijacking, as well as an agreement between Cuba and the United States to cooperate in suppressing further incidents.[108] Most U.S. extradition treaties signed after 1978 accordingly included clauses that explicitly precluded violators of the multilateral conventions from asserting the "political offense" exception in their defense.[109]

The vast majority of extradition cases involving the political offense exception have involved requests to the United States. Among the few exceptions was a U.S. request to the Mexican government for the extradition of William Morales, a leader of the Puerto Rican independence group known as the Armed Forces of National Liberation (FALN) who had escaped from custody in the United States. Morales had been implicated in more than fifty terrorist attacks in the United States, including a 1975 bombing of an airplane in New York that killed four people and wounded sixty, and had been sentenced to up to ninety-nine years in prison. In 1988, the Mexican government chose to release Morales, who had been incarcerated in Mexico in 1983 following a shootout in which a Mexican policeman had been killed, and allow him to go to Cuba. The State Department responded to the Mexican government's invocation of the "political offense" exception by recalling its ambassador in protest. The Mexican decision, which bypassed any judicial evaluation, was motivated, many believed, by the government's desire to stir up nationalist sentiments in advance of the upcoming election.[110]

---

106. Marjorie M. Whiteman, *Digest of International Law* (Washington, D.C.: Government Printing Office, 1968).

107. Ibid., 811–813.

108. See Alona E. Evans, "The Apprehension and Prosecution of Offenders: Some Current Problems," and "Aircraft and Aviation Facilities," in Alona E. Evans and John F. Murphy, eds., *Legal Aspects of International Terrorism* (Lexington, Mass.: Lexington Books, 1978).

109. Abbell and Ristau, *International Judicial Assistance* (supra n. 1), 4:110–111.

110. Larry Rohter, "Mexicans Reject Criticism from U.S.," *New York Times*, July 1, 1988, A3; Elaine Sciolino, "U.S. Recalls Mexico Envoy over Militant's Release," *New York Times*, June 29, 1988, A3.

In many respects, the shift in U.S. perspectives on the "political offense" exception reflected less a rejection of the notion than a fairly explicit politicization of its application. Whereas it initially had been interpreted quite broadly by both the courts and the State Department to require denials of extradition requests even from governments with which the U.S. government was on friendly terms, by the 1980s the State Department and other executive branch departments increasingly insisted that the "political offense" exception could not provide a defense against an extradition request from a government that was both friendly and democratic. They also appeared increasingly willing to act favorably on extradition requests from governments not known for the rectitude or due process of their judicial institutions. Their efforts—in litigation, treaty negotiations, and proposed legislation—to minimize the role of the courts in deciding the applicability of the exception reflected this desire to transform the notion from one of principle to one of political expedience. The tension between the two perspectives was, of course, nothing new. But what had changed—in this domain of extradition as in others—was the perspective of the State Department. Where once it had routinely rejected extradition requests even for fugitives who had committed quite heinous crimes in the name of their revolutions, it increasingly perceived its role as representative of foreign government requests and defender of the foreign policy interests of the U.S. government.[111] It was determined, as never before, to interpret the "political offense" exception solely in terms of its bilateral relationship with the requesting government. Consideration would still be given to the question of whether the fugitive could expect a fair trial, but little if any regard would be given to motives for acts of violence.[112]

The Extradition and Non-extradition of Nationals

The source of greatest frustration in U.S. efforts to prosecute foreign violators of its laws in American courts has been the refusal of most governments to extradite their own citizens.[113] The legal traditions of

111. John G. Kester, "Some Myths of United States Extradition Law," *Georgetown Law Journal* 76 (1988), 1441–1493, esp. 1476–1489.

112. See the comments by Yoram Dinstein in "Major Contemporary Issues in Extradition Law," *Proceedings of the 84th Annual Meeting of the American Society of International Law, 1990*, 389–407, esp. 404.

113. See the excellent, if somewhat dated, analysis of this issue by Robert W. Rafuse, *The*

most civil law countries, as well as some common law countries, regard the nonextradition of their citizens as an important principle deeply ingrained in their legal traditions. They justify the principle on various grounds, including the state's obligation to protect its citizens, lack of confidence in the fairness of foreign judicial proceedings, the many disadvantages defendants confront in trying to defend themselves in a foreign country before a strange legal system, as well as the additional disadvantages posed by imprisonment in a foreign jail where family and friends may be distant and the chances of rehabilitation are significantly diminished.[114] By contrast, the legal traditions of the United States and most other common law nations reject the exception for nationals as an illegitimate relic of nationalist sentiments and argue that justice is most fully and conveniently served by trying defendants where they committed their crimes. Victims, witnesses, and evidence are most likely and easily found in the vicinity of the *locus delicti*, and common law rules of evidence present obstacles to the collection and admission of evidence from foreign countries that civil law prosecutors and judges do not confront. Yet despite the strong arguments against excepting nationals from extradition, the principle of nonextradition has evolved since the nineteenth century from a mere rule of custom to an emotionally charged conviction.

Historically, the U.S. government, like many other governments of common law countries, has been willing both in practice and principle to extradite its nationals abroad for crimes committed elsewhere. The first U.S. extradition agreements—with Great Britain, France, Hawaii, and Switzerland—made no exception for nationals, although the French government steadfastly refused to extradite its citizens, and the Swiss did so only once before insisting that the treaty be renegotiated. American insistence that nationals not be excepted from extradition was singularly responsible for delaying the conclusion of the first extradition treaties with Prussia, Belgium, and the Netherlands[115]—and it explained much of the U.S. hesitance to conclude extradition treaties with most Latin

---

Extradition of Nationals, Illinois Studies in the Social Sciences, No. 24 (Urbana: University of Illinois Press, 1939).

114. Shearer, *Extradition in International Law* (supra n. 20), 98, 118–125.

115. Moore, *Treatise on Extradition* (supra n. 3), 159–162. See also the extended defense of the extradition of nationals in the 1890 correspondence from Secretary of State Blaine to the Italian minister, Baron Falva, reprinted in John Bassett Moore, *Digest of International Law* (Washington, D.C.: Government Printing Office, 1906), 4:290–298.

American countries until the turn of the century. U.S. officials ultimately conceded the point, however, and agreed to a provision in their treaties with civil law and other similarly minded governments that allowed each party to refuse to extradite its nationals. Within the United States, the principal reservations against extraditing U.S. citizens were of two sorts. The first, debated since the origins of U.S. extradition practice, was the question of whether the U.S. government could and should extradite its citizens to governments that were unable or unwilling to reciprocate. The stress placed on formalistic notions of reciprocity in extradition relations during the nineteenth century generally favored nonextradition of U.S. citizens to such countries, although exceptions were made in numerous cases. In 1913, the Supreme Court repudiated the emphasis on reciprocity when it held, in *Charlton v. Kelly*, that the Italian government's failure to extradite its own citizens to the United States under a treaty that made no exception for nationals did not prevent the U.S. government from extraditing its own citizens.[116]

The second reservation emerged during the latter part of the nineteenth century in response to debate over the meaning of a provision included in many U.S. extradition treaties providing that "neither of the contracting parties shall be bound to deliver up its own citizens or subjects under the stipulations of this convention."[117] A supplementary clause, first included in the 1886 extradition treaty with Japan, appended the words "but they shall have the power to deliver them up if in their discretion it be deemed proper to do so." Debate focused on whether the unappended provision, which had been designed to accommodate the wishes of governments unable or unwilling to extradite their nationals, prevented the U.S. government from extraditing its own citizens. Between 1874 and 1891, Secretaries of State Fish, Frelinghuysen, Bayard, and Blaine each adopted the view that the extradition treaty with Mexico, which contained only the unappended provision, precluded the extradition of nationals.[118] Frelinghuysen and Bayard each refused to

---

116. *Charlton v. Kelly*, 229 U.S. 447 (1913). See also "The Charlton Extradition Case," *American Journal of International Law* 5 (1911), 182–192.

117. Rafuse, *Extradition of Nationals*, 31.

118. James Wilford Garner, "Non-Extradition of American Citizens: The Neidecker Case," *American Journal of International Law* 30 (1936), 480–486. Frelinghuysen, Garner notes, subsequently expressed "serious doubt as to the correctness of his interpretation [and] gave instructions that, if [the fugitive] were re-arrested, the President would not object to his extradition, or that of other American citizens, on the grounds of citizenship, provided they were informed that they were entitled to a hearing before the Supreme Court upon the question of his power under the treaty to surrender them."

deliver an American to Mexico, while Fish and Blaine refused to ask the Mexican government to extradite a Mexican citizen for crimes committed in the United States. That interpretation was also adopted in 1891 by a Texas federal court in *Ex parte McCabe*,[119] even though the supreme court of Mexico had held to the contrary in 1879.[120] The State Department responded to the *McCabe* decision by including the supplementary clause in six new treaties signed between 1896 and 1905, including a renegotiated treaty with Mexico.[121] Far more treaties, however, were signed without the appended phrase.[122]

In 1936, the Supreme Court resolved lingering disputes regarding this issue when it ruled, in *Valentine v. U.S. ex rel. Neidecker*, that the unappended provision (in the extradition treaty with France) did not permit the extradition of nationals.[123] The decision was heavily criticized on the grounds that the U.S. treaty negotiators had not intended the provision to forbid the extradition of U.S. citizens given the inability of the U.S. government to prosecute its citizens for violations of foreign laws—and that if the negotiators had so intended, they would have stated it explicitly.[124] The result of the decision, the critics pointed out, would be to create a nonreciprocal relationship in which foreign citizens of civil law nations could be prosecuted in their nation's courts for crimes committed in the United States but American citizens would be immune from prosecution for whatever crimes they committed abroad. Nonetheless, the "*Valentine* infirmity," as some Justice Department officials called it,[125] became law, with the result that many American fugitives from foreign justice found safe havens at home in the United States. In subsequent treaty negotiations, U.S. officials made sure to include both

119. 46 Fed. 363 (1891).

120. 1 Vallarta, *Cuestiones Constitucionales*, 1879, 35, and *Foreign Relations of the United States, 1878–1879*, 564ff., discussed in Garner, "Non-Extradition of American Citizens."

121. The other treaties were with Argentina (1896), 31 Stat. 1883, TS 6, Bevans 67; Orange Free State (1896), 26 Stat. 1508, TS 139, 12 Bevans 211; Guatemala (1902), 33 Stat. 2147, TS 425, 8 Bevans 482; Nicaragua (1905), 35 Stat. 1869, TS 462, 10 Bevans 356; and Uruguay (1905), 35 Stat. 2028, TS 501, 12 Bevans 979.

122. The treaties are listed in Rafuse, *Extradition of Nationals*, 31. See also Arthur K. Kuhn, "Extradition from the United States of American Citizens Under Existing Treaties," *American Journal of International Law* 31 (1937), 476–480. I have not been able to uncover the reasons for the omission of the appended phrase.

123. *Valentine v. U.S. ex rel. Neidecker*, 299 U.S. 5 (1936).

124. See Garner, "Non-Extradition of American Citizens," and Kuhn, "Extradition from the United States. . . ."

125. Author's interviews with treaty negotiators in the OIA, Criminal Division, Department of Justice, Washington, D.C.

the appended provision first used in the treaty with Japan as well as a new provision authorizing each party (but in fact the other government) to prosecute the fugitive in its own courts if it refused to extradite on account of the fugitive's citizenship. Each of the extradition reform bills considered by Congress in the early 1980s included a provision designed to correct the "*Valentine* infirmity," but none were enacted into law for reasons unrelated to this issue.[126] In November 1990, Congress at last corrected the problem with an extradition reform law—first suggested by critics of the *Valentine* decision in 1937—directed at this issue alone.[127]

Any global trend in attitudes toward the nonextradition of nationals is difficult to discern. The view that nationals should not be excepted from extradition had been adopted by the Institute of International Law in 1880 as well as by the influential Draft Convention on Extradition produced by the Harvard Research Project on International Law in 1935.[128] Most common law countries continue to extradite their citizens willingly, although Israel reversed stride in 1978 when it amended its penal code to expand Israeli jurisdiction over extraterritorial offenses and forbid the extradition of its citizens.[129] Among the Commonwealth nations, Cyprus stands out as one of the few exceptions. Within Western Europe, Germany, France, and Switzerland are among the majority that absolutely refuse to extradite their nationals while Italy—which had angered U.S. officials in the late nineteenth century by refusing to extradite its citizens under the bilateral treaty—is the most conspicuous among the minority that now do so.[130] In most cases, the custom of nonextradition of nationals dates at least to the early 1800s, although few countries enacted it into law or their constitutions until late in the nineteenth century or early in the twentieth. In Switzerland's case, the legislation was prompted by the widespread criticism that attended the

126. Ibid. The extradition reform bills are analyzed in M. Cherif Bassiouni, "Extradition Reform Legislation in the United States: 1981–1983" (supra n. 86), 495–574.

127. See 18 U.S.C. 3196, Pub. L. 101-623, Sec. 11(a), Nov. 21, 1990, 104 Stat. 3356. The suggestion was advanced in Kuhn, "Extradition from the United States. . . ." (supra n. 118).

128. See *American Journal of International Law* 29 (1935), Supp., 123–136, 236–238, 300–301.

129. C. Shachor-Landau, "Extra-territorial Penal Jurisdiction and Extradition," *International and Comparative Law Quarterly* 29 (1980), 274–295.

130. Shearer, *Extradition in International Law* (supra n. 20), 102–110. The change of heart on the part of the Italian government was confirmed in an exchange of notes with the U.S. government in 1946; TIAS 1699, 9 Bevans 192, 61 Stat. 3687. See Whiteman, *Digest of International Law* (supra n. 106), 6:872–873.

extradition of a Swiss citizen to the United States in 1890 under the terms of a bilateral 1850 extradition treaty that did not except nationals.[131] In France, the rule of nonextradition of nationals dates back to the 1840s, but it was not included in the 1843 extradition treaty with the United States and not incorporated into domestic legislation until 1927, when France enacted its first extradition law.[132] The Netherlands, by contrast, signed an extradition treaty with the United States in 1980 that authorizes the extradition of nationals provided both countries are also bound by a prisoner transfer treaty.[133] That condition was met as of 1985, when the United States became a party to the European Convention on the Transfer of Sentenced Prisoners.[134] Presumably, the Dutch negotiators regarded the lack of any means to have a Dutch offender serve his or her sentence in the Netherlands as the most important remaining justification for the nonextradition of nationals rule. The possibility exists that this feature of the U.S.-Netherlands extradition treaty will provide a model for other nations that so far have adhered strictly to the principle of nonextradition of nationals. The Europeans have compensated for their inability to extradite their citizens by improving their capacity for successful vicarious prosecution and by negotiating, under the auspices of the Council of Europe, a multilateral convention on transfer of criminal proceedings.[135]

In extradition negotiations with Latin American governments, U.S. officials have urged flexibility on this issue, stressing the importance of prosecuting drug traffickers wherever possible. Most governments, however, have refused to concede on the issue of extraditing their citizens, insisting that they will comply instead with U.S. requests to prosecute fugitives in their own courts. Among the few exceptions was the government of Colombia, which signed a new extradition treaty with the United States in 1979 that provided for the extradition of nationals.[136] This was neither the first nor the only Colombian extradition treaty to

131. Rafuse, *Extradition of Nationals*, 120–122; Moore, *Digest of International Law* (supra n. 115), 4:298–300.

132. Ibid., 75–92.

133. The treaty, signed at the Hague on June 24, 1980, entered into force Sept. 15, 1983 (TIAS 10733).

134. Done at Strasbourg Mar. 21, 1983 (TIAS 10824).

135. Julian Schutte, "Transfer of Criminal Proceedings: The European System," in Bassiouni, ed., *International Criminal Law* (supra n. 32), 2:319–335.

136. See the fascinating account in Guy Gugliotta and Jeff Leen, *Kings of Cocaine* (New York: Simon & Schuster, 1989).

approve such exchanges, but it did represent somewhat of an exception to Colombia's extradition traditions.[137] The treaty was ratified by the Colombian government and formally entered into force in 1982,[138] but it was not used to extradite a Colombian to the United States until 1984, when President Belisario Betancur activated the treaty in response to the assassination of his justice minister, Rodrigo Lara Bonilla, by Colombia's increasingly powerful and brazen drug traffickers. During the following two years, more than a dozen Colombians were extradited to the United States, as well as three Americans to Colombia. Throughout this period, the leading drug traffickers, calling themselves "The Extraditables," mounted an increasingly effective campaign of public relations, bribery, intimidation, and murder to shift public and official opinion against the treaty. Their first priority, they declared, was the recission of the extradition treaty with the United States, and in particular the provision permitting their own extradition.[139] Most Colombians recognized that their own judicial system was not capable of bringing the traffickers to justice and that only the U.S. judicial system could successfully prosecute and imprison the traffickers. Even so, many Colombians agreed in principle with the traffickers' criticism of the treaty. Under substantial pressure by the U.S. government, the administration of President Virgilio Barco refused to back away from the treaty. In December 1986, however, the Colombian supreme court, in what many perceived as a capitulation not to the traffickers' legal arguments but to their violence and threats, declared the treaty no longer valid because of a petty and arguably irrelevant technicality.[140] Barco thereupon took steps suggested by the court's opinion to correct the technical problems and was able to extradite one of the most famous traffickers, Carlos Lehder, when he was arrested by Colombian police in February 1987.[141] But in June 1987, the court once again declared the treaty invalid, thereby blocking any future extraditions to the United States.[142]

137. See, e.g., Art. 4 of the extradition treaty between Colombia and Chile, signed Nov. 16, 1914, ratified Aug. 4, 1928, which states that "extradition of their own nationals is not compulsory" (LNTS 82 at 244).

138. Signed at Washington Sept. 14, 1979; entered into force Mar. 4, 1982 (the treaty appears to have never received a TIAS number).

139. Gugliotta and Leen, *Kings of Cocaine*, 241–250.

140. See the fine discussion of these events in Bruce M. Bagley, "Colombia and the War on Drugs," *Foreign Affairs* 67 (Fall 1988), 70–92.

141. Gugliotta and Leen, *Kings of Cocaine*, 241–250. See also *U.S. v. Lehder Rivas*, 668 F.Supp. 1623 (M.D. Fla. 1987).

142. The Colombian supreme court's decision, translated into English, is reproduced at

In August 1989, President Barco responded to the assassination of the leading presidential candidate in the upcoming election, Senator Luis Carlos Galán, by invoking his state-of-siege powers under the constitution and renewing the summary extradition of Colombian traffickers without judicial review.[143] Much to the surprise of many observers, on October 4, the Colombian supreme court upheld the president's emergency action. During the following year, more than two dozen Colombian traffickers and money launderers—though none on the "most wanted list"—were extradited to the United States, with the Colombian president and supreme court continuing to stand by the extradition process.[144] Numerous public opinion polls, however, indicated that many Colombians had wearied of the war against the "extraditables" and wanted to seek alternative solutions.[145] When President Barco was succeeded in July 1990 by César Gaviria Trujillo, the new president quickly extradited a few more traffickers but decreed simultaneously that any major drug traffickers who surrendered to the government would not be extradited. His offer was taken up by the leading drug traffickers of Medellín, who had been responsible for most of the violence, and President George Bush indicated that he was prepared to give President Gaviria's strategy a chance to prove itself.[146] In 1991, the option of extraditing Colombian citizens to foreign countries was effectively eliminated when Colombia adopted a new constitution that explicitly prohibited any future extraditions of its citizens.[147] In Bolivia, meanwhile, the Colombian policy of offering immunity from extradition

International Legal Materials 27 (1988), 492–511. See Mark Andrew Sherman, "United States International Drug Control Policy, Extradition, and the Rule of Law in Colombia," *Nova Law Review* 15 (1991), 661–702.

143. Andres Oppenheimer, "Colombia Offers to Extradite Cocaine Trafficker," *Miami Herald*, Aug. 23, 1989, 8A; *Latin American Regional Reports: Andean Group*, Oct. 5, 1989, 1–5; Bruce Michael Bagley, "Dateline Drug Wars: Colombia: The Wrong Strategy," *Foreign Policy* 77 (1989–90), 154–171.

144. Eugene Robinson, "Colombia Says Extraditions to Continue," *Washington Post*, Oct. 25, 1989, A38; "Colombian Drug Suspect Extradited," *Washington Post*, Oct. 25, 1989, A20.

145. Joseph B. Treaster, "Colombians, Weary of the Strain, Are Losing Heart in the Drug War," *New York Times*, Oct. 2, 1989, A1; Michael Getler and Eugene Robinson, "Colombia's War on Drugs Zeroes in on Just Two Men," *Washington Post*, Oct. 29, 1989, A1.

146. Rensselaer W. Lee III, "Colombia's Cocaine Syndicates," in Alfred W. McCoy and Alan A. Block, eds., *War on Drugs: Studies in the Failure of U.S. Narcotics Policy* (Boulder, Colo.: Westview Press, 1992), 93–124.

147. See Sherman, "United States International Drug Control Policy" (supra n. 142). See also Mark Andrew Sherman, "Colombian Constitutional Assembly Endorses Ban of Extradition of Nationals," *International Enforcement Law Reporter* 7 (1991), 174–178.

to traffickers who surrendered was adopted by the Paz Zamora government.[148]

Most governments that refuse to extradite their nationals, however, are willing, at least in principle, to prosecute them for crimes committed elsewhere, provided the violation of foreign law would also be considered a violation of domestic law if committed within their borders. Unlike the United States, most civil law countries are able to adhere to the principle of *aut dedere, aut iudicare* because they interpret the nationality principle underlying their criminal jurisdiction far more broadly than the United States does—as extending to virtually all crimes committed by their citizens abroad that would also constitute a violation of domestic laws if committed at home. In a number of countries, the notion of vicarious administration of justice even extends to trying foreign citizens for certain crimes committed in their homeland or another foreign territory. In one mid-1980s case, for instance, German authorities agreed to prosecute a Hungarian national for crimes committed in Hungary once it became evident that German law did not permit him to be extradited.[149] By contrast, U.S. law only authorizes the prosecution of Americans or foreign citizens for crimes committed abroad that violate either multilateral conventions or the proliferating statutes that specifically criminalize extraterritorial acts perceived as harmful to U.S. citizens or interests.[150]

The more recent extradition treaties between the United States and governments that refuse to extradite their nationals include provisions making prosecution mandatory when extradition is denied on grounds of nationality. But the principle of *aut dedere, aut iudicare* tends to lose much of its force in practice, which explains in part why the U.S. government refused to incorporate the notion into its extradition treaties until well into the twentieth century.[151] Governments that refuse to

148. Michael Isikoff, "Bolivia Offers No-Extradition Deal to Traffickers," *Washington Post*, July 19, 1991, A13; "Questions About Surrender Policy: Politicians and Media Suspect More Than Meets the Eye," *Latin America Weekly Report*, Aug. 8, 1991, 4.

149. Reported by Paul Wilkitzki, director of office of international criminal law enforcement matters, Federal Ministry of Justice, Bonn, Germany, at the Harvard Law School Conference on International Cooperation in Criminal Matters, Cambridge, Massachusetts, June 16–18, 1988.

150. Christopher L. Blakesley, "A Conceptual Framework for Extradition and Jurisdiction over Extraterritorial Crimes," *Utah Law Review* 4 (1984), 685.

151. See the 1924 correspondence from Secretary of State Hughes to the French ambassador regarding this issue in Hackworth, *Digest of International Law* (supra n. 81), 4:58–59.

extradite their nationals often assign lower priority to requests for vicarious prosecution than they do to either domestic prosecutions or extradition requests for nonnationals. Requesting governments similarly lose interest in many such cases, no doubt in part because the personal and bureaucratic incentives of the prosecutor do not favor pursuing vigorously such vicarious prosecutions. Significant obstacles also arise from the difficulties involved in trying an individual for a crime committed in another country. The investigating judge must travel abroad to prepare the case according to his own country's judicial procedures, witnesses must be persuaded to travel to another country, and so on. Consequently, most requests to prosecute offenders for crimes committed abroad prove unsuccessful.[152] The principal exceptions are cases in which high-level U.S. officials express a strong and repeated interest in seeing the fugitive prosecuted.

No government has so frustrated U.S. law enforcement authorities with its refusal to extradite its nationals as the government of Mexico. Despite the renegotiation of the extradition treaty folllowing the *McCabe* case, the Mexican government fairly consistently refused to extradite its citizens to the United States[153]—although it did respond favorably, if irregularly, to U.S. requests for prosecution of the fugitives in Mexico. The U.S. response to Mexican requests for the extradition of U.S. citizens was mixed. In 1960, the State Department's legal adviser was able to point to at least nine cases in which American citizens had been extradited to Mexico, but more often than not, Mexican requests were rejected on grounds of lack of reciprocity despite the inability of the U.S. government to prosecute the offenders in American courts.[154] In 1976, the U.S. government responded to the continuing Mexican policy and the growing number of Mexican fugitives wanted on drug trafficking charges by creating Operation JANUS, a systematic effort to encourage and assist Mexican criminal justice officials in vicariously prosecuting Mexican drug traffickers for violations of U.S. drug laws.[155] Strongly

152. Wilkitzki comments at Harvard Law School Conference, 1988 (supra n. 149).

153. Moore, *Digest of International Law* (supra n. 115), 4:301–304; Hackworth, *Digest of International Law* (supra n. 81), 4:59–62.

154. Hackworth, *Digest of International Law*, 4:59–62; and Note, "Executive Discretion in Extradition," *Columbia Law Review* 62 (1962), 1313–1329, esp. 1322.

155. The program is briefly described in *Departments of State, Justice, Commerce, the Judiciary, and Related Agencies Appropriations for 1979: Hearings Before a Subcommittee of the House Committee on Appropriations*, 95th Cong., 2d Sess., Part 6 (1978), 969. See also James Mills, *The Underground Empire* (Garden City, N.Y.: Doubleday, 1986), 390, 1088.

backed at first by the Mexican attorney general, the operation initially appeared successful, but it was phased out within a few years, having largely failed to bring Mexican violators of U.S. laws to justice in Mexican courts.[156] Although the Mexican government continued to prosecute Mexican violators of U.S. drug laws in its courts, particularly when pressured strongly by U.S. officials, persistent U.S. frustrations in this regard ultimately contributed to more direct action by U.S. law enforcement agents, about which more below.

Alternatives to Extradition

The history of U.S. rendition of fugitives from abroad by means other than those provided for in extradition treaties dates back even further than that of extradition. When extradition treaties have been either unavailable or inadequate to accomplish the rendition of a fugitive, U.S. officials often have relied on foreign extradition and deportation laws as well as the occasional willingness of foreign officials to deliver fugitives to the United States by less formal means not explicitly sanctioned by their laws. U.S. law enforcement officials also have become increasingly involved in orchestrating and even managing the apprehension of fugitives from abroad. They have provided foreign authorities with the tactical intelligence needed to find and arrest fugitives on their territory. They have worked directly with foreign agents in apprehending fugitives abroad and arranging their transport to the United States, often via third countries. They have employed various ruses, both unilaterally and in cooperation with foreign police, to lure fugitives to the United States (where a sealed indictment awaits them) or to other countries from which their rendition can be more readily arranged, or into international waters where they can be seized and returned to U.S. territory. And they have relied on private agents, including informants, private detectives, bail bondsmen, and bounty hunters, to accomplish many of the same

156. *Worldwide Review of U.S. Extradition Treaties and MLATs: Hearings* (supra n. 29), 67–69. In 1985, the DEA reported that only seven defendants, none of whom was a major violator, had been prosecuted in Mexico on the basis of evidence and witnesses from the United States provided by the DEA. See *International Narcotic Control: Hearing Before the Subcommittee on Foreign Assistance and Related Programs of the Senate Committee on Appropriations*, 99th Cong., 1st Sess., S. Hrg. 99-90 (1985), 189.

tasks. These methods have acquired many names: "irregular rendition," "de facto extradition," "informal expulsion," and even "extradition Mexican-style," in deference to the long-standing arrangement by which fugitives are "pushed over the border" by Mexican police into the hands of U.S. law enforcement agents. Some Justice Department officials have claimed that the most common term, "irregular rendition," is largely a misnomer because rendition of fugitives by means other than an extradition treaty is neither illegal nor unusual. Nonetheless, the phrase has prevailed ever since John Bassett Moore so named the practice in his classic 1891 treatise on extradition.

U.S. government options for delivering fugitives to foreign governments have been relatively limited in comparison. Apart from one infamous incident in 1864—when U.S. officials summarily delivered to Spanish authorities in Cuba an army officer, Don José Augustin Arguelles, who had illegally sold a seized cargo of slaves in the United States[157]—the U.S. government has refrained from delivering fugitives to foreign governments without first allowing them to appeal the rendition in court. Without an extradition treaty, the only alternatives available to the U.S. government in responding to an extradition request have involved exclusion and deportation proceedings—the former with respect to fugitives apprehended as they attempt to enter the United States, the latter when fugitives are arrested within U.S. territory. Although both procedures are designed principally for purposes of immigration control, each has been relied upon to expel fugitives and other criminals both at the request of foreign governments and, far more frequently, at the initiative of the U.S. government. Such tactics have been used since the early 1900s to expel Italian-born mafiosi and, more recently, Nazi war criminals, IRA fugitives, and Latin American and Caribbean drug dealers.

U.S. courts have imposed virtually no restrictions on how U.S. officials obtain custody over fugitives. Under the Supreme Court's long-standing *Ker-Frisbie* rule, it is even legal under U.S. law to abduct fugitives from a foreign country[158]—although U.S. agents risk being charged with violations of foreign laws against kidnapping if they do so without the consent of host country officials. Courts have imposed only two restric-

157. Moore, *Treatise on Extradition* (supra n. 3), 33–35.
158. See *Ker v. Illinois*, 119 U.S. 436, 7 S.Ct. 225, 30 L.Ed. 421 (1886), and *Frisbie v. Collins*, 342 U.S. 519, 72 S.Ct. 509, 96 L.Ed. 541 (1952), which held that a court need not examine how a defendant had been brought within its jurisdiction.

tions on the rendition of fugitives by means other than extradition treaties. The first, imposed by a New York federal court in 1974 (in *U.S. v. Toscanino*) and rendered largely ineffectual since then, is that jurisdiction cannot be legally obtained by an abduction involving "the infliction . . . of grossly cruel and inhumane treatment by or at the direction of American officials or agents."[159] The second restriction, imposed by a federal judge in California in 1990 but rejected by the Supreme Court in 1992, is that any defendant apprehended abroad from a country with which the United States has an extradition treaty must be released if the foreign government formally protests the violation of the treaty.[160] This issue is discussed in greater depth below.

Most irregular renditions have involved Canada and Mexico, whose long borders with the United States have presented temptations both to fleeing fugitives and to those interested in obtaining custody over them. Until well into the twentieth century, few fugitives were deemed sufficiently important to invest substantial resources in procuring them by means other than extradition. The few exceptions were those who had attained some substantial notoriety. One unusual case, in that it involved a foreign territory where the U.S. government exercised extraterritorial rights, was the 1866 rendition from Alexandria, Egypt, of John Surratt, accused of participation in the assassination of President Lincoln.[161] In a 1934 effort to gain custody of Samuel Insull, a major Chicago financier who had engineered a substantial fraud and then fled abroad, the State Department first tried to extradite him from Greece, then pressured the Greek government to deport him following a court's rejection of the extradition request, and ultimately persuaded Turkish police to seize the fugitive aboard a Greek vessel in Turkish territorial waters.[162] And in

159. See *U.S. v. Toscanino*, 500 F.2d 267 (2d Cir. 1974); and *U.S. ex rel. Lujan v. Gengler*, 510 F.2d 62 (2d Cir.) cert. denied, 421 U.S. 1001, 95 S.Ct. 2400, 44 L.Ed.2d 668 (1975). The quotation is taken from *U.S. v. Orsini*, 424 F.Supp. 229, 231 (E.D.N.Y. 1976). The *Toscanino* case involved an Italian drug trafficker, Francisco Toscanino, who was seized by a special Uruguayan police unit operating under the direction of a U.S. drug enforcement agent. Toscanino was then driven over the border to Brazil, where he was kept for three weeks while the Brazilian police interrogated him under torture. He was then put on a commercial airline flight to the United States, where he was indicted and prosecuted. Although dozens of defendants have since pointed to the *Toscanino* case in an effort to invalidate their abduction, none has succeeded in showing a sufficiently direct and heinous involvement by U.S. officials to invoke the *Toscanino* exception.

160. *U.S. v. Alvarez-Machain* 112 S.Ct. 857 (1992).

161. Moore, *Treatise on Extradition*, 104–105.

162. See *Foreign Relations of the United States 1934*, 2:566–583; and Charles Cheney

1951, the FBI worked with Mexican security agents to arrest and deliver to the United States Morton Sobell, who had been charged with conspiring with the Rosenbergs to commit espionage against the United States.[163]

Before the 1970s, most irregular renditions were initiated by federal, state, and local police working near the borders. The few exceptions involving more distant nations were typically engineered by private detectives and bounty hunters. But the growing desire, beginning in the early 1970s, to collect dozens of drug traffickers from Latin America— in particular the Corsican criminals who had created the Southern Cone dimension of the heroin trafficking scheme known as the French Connection—provided the impetus for a more coordinated and systematic rendition effort initiated by the Bureau of Narcotics and Dangerous Drugs. Efforts to extradite many of these traffickers by more formal means were seriously hampered by the inadequacies of the extradition treaties, which mostly dated back to the turn of the century and thus contained no references to drug law violations or to extraterritorial violations of U.S. laws. In some cases, the fact that a Latin American government had signed the 1972 Protocol to the Single Convention on Narcotic Drugs rectified the omission. Even so, the challenges of processing the extradition requests through Latin American courts unfamiliar with U.S. legal notions as well as past judicial and executive officials susceptible to the bribes and intimidations of the drug traffickers proved daunting.

The U.S. response to these limitations was labeled "Operation Springboard." During the early 1970s, U.S. drug enforcement agents worked closely with specially created police units in Latin America to apprehend and expel almost five dozen major drug traffickers to the United States without resort to formal extradition procedures.[164] The willingness of the governments to cooperate was facilitated by the fact that most of the targets were not citizens of their countries. In the aftermath of the coup in Chile against President Allende, however, General Pinochet demonstrated his gratefulness to the United States by summarily deporting to

---

Hyde, "The Extradition Case of Samul Insull Sr. in Relation to Greece," *American Journal of International Law* 28 (1934), 307–312.

163. *U.S. v. Sobell*, 142 F.Supp. 515 (2d Cir. 1956).

164. See Robert Solomon, "The Development and Politics of the Latin American Heroin Market," *Journal of Drug Issues* 9 (1979), 363–364.

the United States about twenty Chileans whom the DEA had identified as major cocaine traffickers.[165] The expulsion, labeled Operation Grab-Bag, was significant for two reasons: it virtually eliminated Chile as a major refiner and exporter of cocaine, and it pointed out the hazards of resorting to such methods, when one of those expelled by the government turned out to be a case of mistaken identity.[166]

One fugitive rendition that appeared irregular despite its reliance on an extradition treaty and judicial proceedings involved a 1971 request to Paraguay for the extradition of a leading Corsican drug trafficker, Auguste Ricord. Although U.S. officials ultimately succeeded in bringing the trafficker to justice in a federal court in New York, the trip north was delayed for more than a year by a combination of legal obstacles and intra-Paraguayan political wrangles. The initial U.S. request was rejected by a Paraguayan district court on the grounds that the 1913 extradition treaty did not include drug law violations among the list of extraditable offenses, that Ricord had never entered the United States, and that the "dual criminality" requirement was not met because Paraguayan law included no counterpart to the U.S. statutes under which Ricord was charged.[167] With little confidence that the appellate court would reverse the lower court, the Nixon administration applied a heavy dose of diplomatic pressure. When the U.S. ambassador, Ray Ylitalo, failed to persuade the Paraguayan president, Alfredo Stroessner, of the importance of handing over Ricord, he was replaced. Shortly thereafter, President Nixon sent Nelson Gross, the senior narcotics official in the State Department, to Paraguay to threaten a cutoff in the $11 million of

165. Art. 24 of the Chilean constitution gives the government broad powers to expel Chilean citizens. The Pinochet government used those powers frequently to expel opponents of the regime. But the same article also provided the U.S. government with grounds to request that the Pinochet government expel two former high-level intelligence agents who had been implicated in the 1976 murder of President Allende's foreign minister, Orlando Letelier, in Washington. A previous effort to have the agents extradited was rejected by the Chilean supreme court in 1979. See Shirley Christian, "Chile Indicates It Won't Turn over Two to the U.S. in Letelier Case," *New York Times*, June 15, 1987, A10.

166. Pete Axthelm with Anthony Marro, "The Drug Vigilantes," *Newsweek*, Aug. 16, 1976, reprinted in *The Global Connection: Heroin Entrepreneurs: Hearings Before the Subcommittee to Investigate Juvenile Delinquency of the Senate Committee on the Judiciary*, 94th Cong., 2d Sess. (Vol. 1, 1976), 70–72.

167. John Patrick Collins, "Traffic in the Traffickers: Extradition and the Controlled Substances Import and Export Act of 1970," *Yale Law Journal* 83 (1974), 706–744, esp. 706–707.

annual U.S. aid and U.S. support for loans from the World Bank and the Inter-American Development Bank.[168] Stroessner protested that the matter was up to the courts and sent Gross to meet with both the solicitor general and the Chief Justice of the Supreme Court.[169]

Stroessner's real concerns, however, appeared to involve a power struggle between Ricord's protectors and those who preferred to see him extradited. On Ricord's side were three powerful figures who had first made their fortune smuggling whiskey and cigarettes in the early 1960s but who had expanded into drug smuggling with Ricord's assistance: General Andrés Rodríguez, whose power was reported to be second only to that of Stroessner (and who would eventually assume the presidency himself following a nonviolent coup in early 1989), General Patrício Colmán, "one of Stroessner's oldest and dearest friends"; and Pastor Coronel, the chief of the secret police.[170] On the other side were Interior Minister Sabino Montanaro and the chief of police, General Francisco Brítez, neither of whom had ever been linked to the drug traffic.[171] Although Stroessner had not been personally tied to Ricord, few doubted that the president was aware of Ricord's connections and high-level involvement in drug trafficking. His reluctance to hand the trafficker over to the United States was attributed to either loyalty to or fear of Colmán, Rodríguez, and Coronel. A week after Gross's visit, Colmán suddenly became ill and died shortly thereafter. Just before he died, the Paraguayan court of appeals unanimously granted the extradition request. A few weeks later, the supreme court also gave its approval, and Ricord soon after found himself in New York.[172] The courts' decisions, many believed, reflected more the interventions by powerful Paraguayan officials who preferred not to anger the United States government on

168. In a recent foreign aid act passed by Congress, the president had been authorized to cut off aid to any government that refused to cooperate against international drug trafficking.

169. See Evert Clark and Nicholas Horrock, *Contrabandista!* (New York: Praeger Publishers, 1973), 177–231, for an extensive description of the U.S. effort to extradite Ricord.

170. Paul Lewis, *Paraguay Under Stroessner* (Chapel Hill: University of North Carolina Press, 1980), 135–137.

171. Ibid.

172. The events preceding the extradition attracted substantial media attention. See, e.g., *Newsweek*, Jan. 24, 1972, 24–26; *Time*, Aug. 28, 1972, 24; *Latin America*, June 9, 1972, 188, and Aug. 25, 1972, 269. During this period, Jack Anderson devoted a number of columns to berating official Paraguayan involvement in drug trafficking. See *Washington Post*, Apr. 22, 1972, F11; Apr. 30, 1972, M1; May 24, 1972, B15; July 26, 1972, B15.

this issue, and less any substantive disagreements with the lower court's reasoning.

Operation Springboard and the other irregular renditions of the 1970s attracted substantial commentary in the law journals but not much excitement elsewhere. They did suggest, however, a change in American attitudes regarding the issue. For perhaps the first time, federal police officials, occasionally joined by federal prosecutors, began to devote substantial time and energy to concocting schemes to get foreign drug traffickers into U.S. courts. Their efforts were encouraged and facilitated not just by the *Ker-Frisbie* doctrine, with its virtually carte blanche invitation to engage in such operations, but by the newly established presence of U.S. drug enforcement agents in dozens of foreign countries and by clear indications of political support from the White House. Where federal law enforcement officials had previously assumed that extradition represented more or less the only possibility of obtaining custody of a fugitive from abroad, they began instead to consider a wide range of options apart from the procedures set down in the extradition treaties. This change in attitude quickly became conventional wisdom within the DEA, and thereafter took hold in the FBI and the U.S. Marshals Service, both of which were increasingly involved in the apprehension of fugitives from abroad.

Virtually all of these renditions, it should be stressed, were conducted in cooperation with law enforcement officials in the countries from which the fugitives were being deported or abducted. With rare exceptions, U.S. officials have never acted entirely unilaterally in abducting fugitives from foreign countries without the permission of host government officials. Abductions such as the 1960 kidnapping of the Nazi war criminal Adolf Eichmann from Argentina to face trial in Israel were viewed warily by U.S. officials. But the regularization of irregular rendition during the 1970s revealed the ambiguities inherent in conducting such operations, particularly when they appeared to flout foreign laws or targeted criminals with powerful protectors. Many renditions required that DEA and other U.S. law enforcement agents work closely with foreign police and military officials and at the same time keep secret their rendition plans from other officials who might disapprove either because they disagreed with the tactics or because they had been corrupted by the targeted fugitive. The fact that high-level foreign officials often disagreed regarding such renditions meant that it could be difficult to discern afterward whether "the government" had approved or disapproved of the operation. And the desire of many top police and military officials in foreign countries to retain a measure of plausible deniability and avoid assuming official responsibility for the renditions only heightened the degree of ambiguity. In many cases, moreover, the State Department and its representatives abroad were "cut out of the loop" by U.S. law enforcement officials who feared that their more diplomatic colleagues would undermine or veto renditions that might generate political problems.

These ambiguities became significant, from the perspectives of U.S. law and diplomacy, only when the renditions were met with public and diplomatic protests after the fact. A U.S. drug enforcement agent who had been prominently involved in Operation Springboard told me that the Uruguayan interior minister had approved the BNDD's irregular rendition plan only on condition that his consent would not be publicly revealed if anything went wrong. Indeed, he told the agent, he would be among the first to publicly condemn the entire operation if any backlash resulted. In other cases, U.S. law enforcement officials were given permission by top foreign officials to proceed with their operations and told that a formal—but otherwise meaningless—protest might thereafter be filed by their government. In the case of Operation Springboard, dozens of irregular renditions were accomplished with relatively few legal or diplomatic problems, apart from the brief concerns raised by the *Toscanino* decision. The same tactics continued to be used thereafter, often with even greater creativity and aggressiveness, but sometimes with greater problems as well.

Most irregular renditions involve cooperative endeavors by U.S. and local police agents to seize a fugitive and get him or her on a plane out of the country as fast as possible. The precise tactics, however, vary substantially. In some cases, U.S. agents have arranged for fugitives to be arrested during trips to foreign countries or even when their flights have stopped briefly in another country en route to the fugitive's destination. For instance, in 1975, DEA agents arranged for Dominique Orsini, a drug trafficker based in Argentina, to be arrested by Senegalese police and thereafter deported to the United States, when the flight on which he was traveling from Buenos Aires to Nice stopped briefly in Dakar.[173] Many irregular rendition schemes have required U.S. law enforcement agents to lure fugitives from their foreign havens to other

173. *U.S. v. Orsini*, 424 F.Supp. 229 (E.D.N.Y. 1976).

countries in which cooperative law enforcement officials would then arrest them and extradite or deport them to the United States. In a fairly typical case, in 1977, a DEA agent based in Venezuela tricked a drug trafficker into flying to Panama, where he was arrested and interrogated by the Panamanian police before being deported to the United States.[174] Similarly, in 1973 Julio Lujan, an Argentine pilot charged with heroin trafficking, was lured from Argentina to Bolivia by a DEA informant, where he was then seized by local police working for the DEA and put on a plane to the United States without ever being charged or extradited under Bolivian law.[175] And in 1982, a former CIA agent, Edwin Wilson, who had been charged with selling weapons to the Qaddafi regime in Libya, was lured by an undercover informant from his Libyan haven to the Dominican Republic, where he was seized by local police and put on a plane to the United States.[176] Each of these cases was typical of many others, not only in the tactics employed but also in their reliance on local police in Bolivia, Panama, and the Dominican Republic—in each of which DEA and other U.S. agents have often been able to work out informal rendition arrangements based on money, friendship, and professional understandings.

A variation of this tactic has been to lure a fugitive onto a sea vessel and then arrest him in international waters. In 1983, DEA and FBI agents operating out of Miami planned to do just that to a Bahamian cabinet minister, Kendal Nottage, who was strongly suspected of laundering money for drug traffickers; the operation was vetoed, however, by the local U.S. ambassador because he feared its consequences for other aspects of the U.S.-Bahamian relationship.[177] More successful was an undercover operation in September 1987 by the FBI, the DEA, and the CIA that lured Fawaz Younis, a Lebanese Shiite suspected in the June 1985 hijacking of a Jordanian airliner, from his Lebanese haven onto a yacht in the Mediterranean, where he was arrested in international waters.[178] Similarly, in early 1991, FBI agents lured two suspected money

174. *Di Lorenzo v. U.S.*, 496 F.Supp. 79 (S.D.N.Y. 1980).

175. *U.S. ex rel. Lujan v. Gengler*, 510 F.2d 62 (2d Cir.) cert. denied, 421 U.S. 1001.

176. The abduction is discussed in *U.S. v. Wilson*, 565 F.Supp. 1416 (1983). See also Peter Maas, *Manhunt* (New York: Random House, 1986), 254–268.

177. Reginald Stuart, "U.S.-Bahamian Relations Are Straining Under Drug Investigations," *New York Times*, Sept. 28, 1983, A21.

178. *U.S. v. Yunis*, 681 F.Supp. 909 (D.D.C. 1988) rev'd, 859 F.2d 953 (D.C. Cir. 1988). *Washington Post*, Sept. 18, 1987, A1; *Washington Post*, Sept. 19, 1987, A18. See the discussion in D. Cameron Findlay, "Abducting Terrorists Overseas for Trial in the United States: Issues of International and Domestic Law," *Texas International Law Journal* 23 (1988), 1–53; G.

launderers from Colombia to a private yacht off the Caribbean coast, where they were then arrested, transferred to a Coast Guard cutter, and sent to Los Angeles to await trial.[179]

Another common tactic has been to lure fugitives directly into U.S. territory, where a sealed indictment may await them. In one 1971 case, for instance, the corrupt and well-connected Panamanian chief of air traffic control, Joaquim Him Gonzales, was invited to a softball game in the Canal Zone, where he was arrested by U.S. police and soon after flown to the United States.[180] His irregular rendition, which the resident BNDD agents had planned without notifying the U.S. ambassador, briefly generated serious tensions in U.S. relations with the Torrijos regime. In March 1985, undercover DEA agents arrested the chief minister of the Turks and Caicos as well as one of his cabinet ministers in Miami after they agreed to ensure safe passage for cocaine and marijuana transiting their islands in return for a $20,000 payment.[181] A few weeks later, another DEA undercover operation lured a former Belizean cabinet minister to Miami and arrested him for conspiracy to import marijuana into the United States.[182] And in 1986, undercover DEA agents in Miami arrested Etienne Bourenveen, commander of the Suriname army and reportedly the second most powerful man in the country, when he agreed to provide protection for shipments of drugs and ether through his country.[183]

During the late 1980s, the Justice Department and U.S. law enforcement agencies adopted a far more aggressive attitude regarding irregular rendition. The reasons were numerous. A lingering reluctance to risk

Gregory Schuetz, "Apprehending Terrorists Overseas Under United States and International Law: A Case Study of the Fawaz Younis Arrest," *Harvard International Law Journal* 29 (1988), 499–531; and Abraham Abramovsky, "Extraterritorial Jurisdiction: The United States' Unwarranted Attempt to Alter International Law in *United States v. Yunis*," *Yale Journal of International Law* 15 (1990), 121–161.

179. David Johnston, "FBI Arrests 2 Drug Suspects on High Seas," *New York Times*, Feb. 22, 1991, A16; and *Money Laundering Alert* 2 (1991), 2.

180. See Clark and Horrock, *Contrabandista!* (supra n. 169), 193–198; and John Dinges, *Our Man in Panama* (New York: Random House, 1990), 53–58.

181. Jon Nordheimer, "U.S. Arrests Atlantic Islands' Leader in Drug Plot," *New York Times*, Mar. 6, 1985, A1; Liz Balmaseda, "Drug Net Snares Island Ministers," *Miami Herald*, Mar. 6, 1985, 1A.

182. Jon Nordheimer, "U.S. Accuses Ex-Minister from Belize in Plot to Import Marijuana," *New York Times*, Apr. 9, 1985, A15.

183. Brian Duffy, "Chief of Suriname Army Denies He Smuggled Drugs," *Miami Herald*, Apr. 5, 1986, 3A; and "Suriname Official Held in Drug Case," *New York Times*, Mar. 27, 1986, B13.

offending foreign governments by conducting quasi-unilateral law enforcement operations abroad—reflected in a legal opinion issued by the Justice Department's Office of Legal Counsel during the last year of the Carter administration—had faded considerably.[184] The boom in the international cocaine market, combined with the rapidly growing U.S. drug enforcement campaign mounted by the White House and Congress, meant that law enforcement officials had both the additional incentives and the necessary resources to pursue an ever growing number of drug traffickers abroad. Moreover, Congress had eased the way in 1985 and 1986 by carving out exceptions to the 1976 Mansfield Amendment that had prohibited U.S. law enforcement agents abroad from participating in arrests of drug traffickers.[185] Similarly, many officials in both branches of government were determined to take more aggressive action against Middle Easterners and others involved in hostage takings, airplane hijackings, assassinations, bombings, and other terrorist acts directed at U.S. citizens and interests abroad. The increasingly proactive stance of the FBI, the U.S. Marshals Service, and the CIA, as well as new federal legislation extending U.S. jurisdiction to terrorist acts committed abroad, were both reflections of this new attitude. Even though officials in the Justice Department and the State Department's Legal Adviser's Office had succeeded in renegotiating a number of outdated extradition treaties, irregular rendition options typically promised to be faster and less cumbersome, as well as less susceptible to circumvention by targeted fugitives. The fact that extradition requests had to be processed through the fairly small and incredibly busy Office of International Affairs in the Justice Department also provided something of an incentive to develop alternative measures. U.S. courts, meanwhile, had repeatedly held that the existence of an extradition treaty between the United States and another government did not bar the use of other means to obtain custody over a criminal located abroad.[186]

The changing perspective was formalized in 1989 in a legal opinion

---

184. The legal opinion is reproduced in Margaret Colgate Love, ed., *Opinions of the Office of the Legal Counsel of the U.S. Department of Justice* 4B (1980), 543–557, and in *FBI Authority to Seize Suspects Abroad: Hearing Before the Subcommittee on Civil and Constitutional Rights of the House Committee on the Judiciary*, 101st Cong., 1st Sess., Serial No. 134 (1989), 75–90.

185. The evolution of the Mansfield amendment is reviewed in Andrew B. Campbell, "The *Ker-Frisbie* Doctrine: A Jurisdictional Weapon in the War on Drugs," *Vanderbilt Journal of Transnational Law* 23 (1990), 385–433, esp. 422–428.

186. See, e.g., *U.S. v. Reed*, 639 F.2d 896 (2d Cir. 1981).

produced by William Barr, the assistant attorney general in charge of the Office of Legal Counsel, who would subsequently succeed Richard Thornburgh as attorney general, that explicitly repudiated the 1980 opinion.[187] Whereas the first opinion had determined that customary international law imposed absolute restrictions on the authority of the U.S. government to take extraterritorial action, and thus barred U.S. law enforcement agencies from conducting extraterritorial arrests contrary to customary international law norms, the 1989 opinion stated that the President and the FBI did in fact possess such authority under the Constitution. In testimony before Congress, both Barr and the State Department's legal adviser, Abraham Sofaer, tempered the significance of the opinion by emphasizing that it reflected neither a substantial change in actual policy nor any statement of intention to ignore the many political and practical constraints on conducting unilateral arrests on foreign soil.[188]

The single most important catalyst for the new policy was the abduction, torture, and murder of Enrique Camarena, a DEA agent stationed in Guadalajara (as well as a Mexican contract pilot employed by the DEA), by Mexican drug traffickers and corrupt police officials in 1985. When U.S. efforts to investigate the incident faced not just resistance on the part of Mexican authorities but also substantial evidence that top Mexican officials had been involved in both the abduction and the subsequent cover-up, DEA and Justice Department officials reacted with fury. Determined to send a powerful message that "no one could kill a DEA agent and get away with it," the drug enforcement agency combined with federal prosecutors and Justice Department officials in an all-out effort to track down those involved in Camarena's murder and to ensure that they were brought to trial. Most of the major Mexican drug traffickers were ultimately arrested by Mexican police and tried and convicted in Mexican courts in the wake of powerful pressures from the U.S. government. One of the most notorious, Rafael Caro Quintero, was arrested in Costa Rica in a joint operation mounted by resident DEA agents and local police and then expeditiously deported, with the

187. The legal opinion—which the attorney general refused to make public, or even to turn over to Congress until the House Judiciary Committee subpoenaed a copy—is summarized in Michael Isikoff, "U.S. 'Power' on Abductions Detailed," *Washington Post*, Aug. 14, 1991, A14, and in William Barr's testimony to Congress. See *FBI Authority to Seize Suspects Abroad: Hearing* (supra n. 184), 2–21, 59–71.

188. *FBI Authority: Hearings.*

approval of the Costa Rican president, to Mexico (since he had not yet been indicted in the United States).[189] A number of those involved in the Camarena abduction, however, were brought by one means or another into the United States to face criminal charges.

The most important of the traffickers involved in the Camarena abduction to be recovered by U.S. officials was Juan Ramón Matta Ballesteros—a Honduran citizen who had worked closely with the Colombian drug traffickers, acting as their liaison with Mexican traffickers based in Guadalajara, and who had emerged as one of Honduras' leading philanthropists. Efforts to extradite Matta from Honduras had been precluded both by Matta's influence with powerful Honduran officials and by Honduras' prohibition on extraditing its citizens. So agents of the DEA and the U.S. Marshals Service worked quickly and discreetly with selected Honduran officials to devise a plan whereby Matta would be quickly arrested and flown out of the country and thus deprived of any opportunity either to appeal to the courts or to contact his powerful protectors within the government. In April 1988, Matta was arrested at his home in Tegucigalpa by Honduran military officials, forced into a van driven by a U.S. marshal, taken to the airport, and flown to the United States.[190] The rendition was hardly the first from a Central American nation to be pulled off in such a manner, but it was the first of such a major figure. When news of the abduction became public the following day, a Honduran mob, incensed at the apparent affront to Honduran sovereignty and perhaps incited as well by drug trafficker funding, attacked the U.S. embassy and succeeded in setting part of it on fire.[191] Despite protests from a few Honduran congressmen, no formal protest was made by the Honduran president, foreign ministry, or congress.[192]

More significant, from the perspectives of U.S. law and policy, were the renditions of two Mexican fugitives, Rene Martin Verdugo-Urquidez and Dr. Humberto Alvarez-Machain, in January 1986 and April 1990, respectively. Both were apprehended and deported to the United States

189. Elaine Shannon, *Desperados: Latin American Drug Lords, U.S. Lawmen, and the War America Can't Win* (New York: Viking, 1988), 245–257.

190. *Matta-Ballesteros*, 697 F.Supp. 1040 (S.D. Ill. 1988), aff'd 896 F.2d 255 (7th Cir. 1990).

191. See Mark B. Rosenberg, "Narcos and Politicos: The Politics of Drug Trafficking in Honduras," *Journal of Interamerican Studies and World Affairs* 30 (Summer-Fall 1988), 143–166; and *Matta-Ballesteros ex rel. Stolas v. Henman*, 896 F.2d 255 (7th Cir. 1990).

192. *Matta-Ballesteros*, 697 F.Supp. 1040, 1044.

by Mexican police at the behest of the DEA, which paid rewards for their renditions. What distinguished these two renditions from most of the dozens that had preceded them were the formal protests by the Mexican government that followed. In the first case, Mexico lodged what it termed "a formal complaint regarding the kidnapping of" Verdugo by agents of the U.S. government and asked that the "U.S. judicial authorities" be informed of its position.[193] The latter case—which involved a fairly prominent Mexican gynecologist and occurred just a few months after the Mexican government had been embarrassed by the airing of an NBC mini-series based upon the Camarena murder and the ensuing investigation—occasioned a much stronger response.[194] The Mexican embassy presented three diplomatic notes to the State Department between April and July 1990. The first requested a detailed report on U.S. involvement in the abduction. The second stated the Mexican government's view that the abduction constituted a violation of the extradition treaty and demanded Alvarez-Machain's return to Mexico. And the third requested the provisional arrest and extradition of both the informant and the DEA agent who had played a role in the abduction.[195] Even more significant, a federal judge in California, Edward Rafeedie, ruled in both cases that the Mexican government's protest provided the defendants with standing to invoke the violation of the extradition treaty as grounds for their repatriation to Mexico.[196] The fact that the Mexican government had formally protested the violation of the treaty, the court ruled, distinguished these two cases from *Ker v. Illinois* and other cases of irregular rendition. Judge Rafeedie's rulings were upheld by the Court of Appeals for the Ninth Circuit[197] but rejected by a 6 to 3 majority of the Supreme Court in June 1992.[198] Neither the formal Mexican government protest nor the fact that the abduction had been engineered by U.S. agents, Chief Justice Rehnquist wrote, were sufficient to distinguish the Alvarez-Machain case from *Ker v. Illinois*.

193. *International Legal Materials* 30 (1991), 1197ff.

194. The miniseries, entitled "Drug Wars: The Camarena Story," aired on NBC on Jan. 7, 8, and 9, 1990. It was based on Shannon, *Desperados* (supra n. 189). See also Larry Rohter, "Mexicans React Furiously to an NBC Drug Series," *New York Times*, Jan. 18, 1990, A13.

195. See *U.S. v. Caro-Quintero*, 745 F.Supp. 599 (C.D. Cal. 1990), aff'd 946 F.2d 1466 (9th Cir. 1991).

196. Ibid.

197. *U.S. v. Verdugo-Urquidez*, 939 F.2d 1341 (9th Cir. 1991); *U.S. v. Alvarez-Machain*, 946 F.2d 1466 (9th Cir. 1991).

198. *U.S. v. Alvarez-Machain*, 112 S.Ct. 857 (1992).

Without any provision in the extradition treaty explicitly prohibiting abductions, the defendant lacked any right under U.S. law to invoke the treaty in his defense. The ruling was met with howls of official protest in Mexico and elsewhere, to which the Bush adminstration quickly responded with assurances that it had no intention of either increasing or institutionalizing the practice of extraterritorial abductions. Six months later, in December 1992, the Justice Department was deeply embarrassed when Judge Rafeedie acquitted Alvarez-Machain on all charges and rebuked the prosecution for presenting a case based on flimsy evidence.[199] The Mexican Attorney General's Office responded by renewing its call for the extradition of the two DEA agents who reportedly had orchestrated the abduction.[200]

The two abduction cases were not the first in which a foreign government had lodged a formal protest or requested the extradition of those involved in the rendition. In the case of Britain and Canada, such protests dated back to the first part of the nineteenth century, and in the case of Mexico to the 1880s.[201] The U.S. government had also had numerous occasions to protest abductions from its territory by agents of Britain, Canada, Mexico, and Spain[202]—as well as the 1952 abduction by Soviet agents of Dr. Walter Linse from the U.S. sector of Berlin to the Soviet sector. Some cases had involved unilateral actions, such as the 1841 seizure by a British military detachment of a fugitive from his home in Albury, Vermont,[203] or a variety of incidents in which Texan sheriffs and posses crossed into Mexico to recover a fugitive. Others bore a greater resemblance to the cases of Verdugo and Alvarez-Machain in that they involved unofficial cooperation between police officials and/or private detectives of both nations. In most of these, the protests had led to the release of the person seized, although in a few cases the protesting government had indicated that an apology would be sufficient. And in a

---

199. Lou Cannon, "U.S. Judge Acquits Mexican in DEA Agent's '85 Killing," *Washington Post*, Dec. 15, 1992, A1; and Seth Mydans, "Judge Clears Mexican in Agent's Killing," *New York Times*, Dec. 15, 1992, A20.

200. Tod Robberson, "Mexico Seeks DEA Agents on Charges of Kidnapping," *Washington Post*, Dec. 16, 1992, A10.

201. Moore, *Treatise on Extradition* (supra n. 3), 281–302; Moore, *Digest of International Law* (supra n. 115), 4:328–332; Hackworth, *Digest of International Law* (supra n. 81), 224–228.

202. Moore, *Treatise on Extradition*, 281–302; Moore, *Digest of International Law*, 4:328–332; Hackworth, *Digest of International Law*, 224–228.

203. Moore, *Treatise on Extradition*, 282–283.

few instances involving abductions by bounty hunters and other nongovernment agents, the abductors had been prosecuted or extradited at the request of the protesting government.

U.S.-Mexican relations regarding the rendition of fugitives, however, have always diverged from the norms of extradition practice between the United States and most other nations. In 1905–6, the U.S. government responded to the abduction from Mexico of a Mexican fugitive, Antonio Martinez, by another Mexican citizen, Antonio Felix, by extraditing the latter to Mexico to face charges of kidnapping but rejecting a Mexican government request that Martinez be returned to Mexico.[204] In 1934, another incident occurred that bore a strong resemblance to the Verdugo and Alvarez-Machain abductions. Luis Lopez, a bond defaulter charged with violating the Harrison Narcotic Act, had been abducted in Mexico by a U.S. informant and some Mexican soldiers and delivered at the border to Edward Villareal, a constable of Webb County, Texas, who had orchestrated the rendition in order to claim the reward of $750. The Mexican government responded by protesting the violation of its jurisdiction and the failure to make use of the extradition treaty, asking that Lopez be returned to Mexico and charging Villareal and the informant, Tom Hernandez, with the crime of kidnapping and requesting their extradition. The extradition request was pursued by the Justice Department and approved by a federal district court and court of appeals, but subsequently rejected by the secretary of state. Lopez was tried and convicted. In contrast with the Verdugo and Alvarez-Machain cases, the district court judge ruled that he lacked jurisdiction to determine whether the irregularity of Lopez's abduction or the protest by the Mexican government required his release. When the Mexican embassy pursued the matter, the attorney general refused to order Lopez's release, noting that although Lopez's rendition had been irregular, his trial and imprisonment had been lawful.[205] In an interesting twist, however, the State Department suggested that Lopez might be returned if the Mexican government dropped its extradition request for Hernandez.[206]

204. *Foreign Relations of the United States, 1906*, 2:1121–1122.

205. *Ex parte Lopez*, 6 F.Supp. 342 (S.D. Texas 1934), *Villareal v. Hammond*, 74 F.2d 503 (5th Cir. 1934); and Hackworth, *Digest of International Law* (supra n. 81), 4:224–225.

206. Department of State Ms. File No. 211.12 Hernandez, Tomas/135, referred to in Alona E. Evans, "Acquisition of Custody over the International Fugitive Offender: Alternatives to Extradition: A Survey of United States Practice," *British Yearbook of International Law* 40 (1966), 77–104 (see 89).

In contrast to the abductions from Mexico, an abduction of an American fugitive from his home in Canada by a bail bondsman and a professional bounty hunter in 1981 led to a very different result. The fugitive, a Florida land developer named Sidney Jaffe, who had violated Florida's Land Sales Act, was tried and convicted in a Florida court and sentenced to thirty years in prison as well as an additional five for jumping bail. The Canadian government protested forcefully and demanded both that Jaffe be released and that the two abductors be extradited. The Justice Department responded by seeking Jaffe's release, which was first rejected by Florida authorities but then allowed when his sentence for illegal land sales was overturned. Federal prosecutors also pursued the extradition request, which was approved by a federal judge, and the bail bondsman and the bounty hunter were delivered to Canada.[207] When the governments of Canada and the United States signed a protocol revising their extradition treaty in 1988, a note was attached explicitly reassuring the Canadians of U.S. cooperation in preventing and punishing any future abductions by bounty hunters.[208] The willingness of the U.S. government to respond so favorably to Canadian protests reflected the fact that the abductors had not been official government agents and the recognition that such tactics should not be permitted with respect to Canadian territory.[209]

One infamous fugitive who eluded U.S. rendition efforts throughout the 1980s was Luis Arce Gómez, who had served in 1980–81 as the interior minister of the short-lived Bolivian military junta under General Luis García Meza and gained a reputation as the "minister of cocaine."[210] Efforts to extradite him from Argentina, where he had fled following the junta's downfall, proved unsuccessful. When Arce Gómez returned to Bolivia during the mid-1980s, he had reason to believe that he was safe from U.S. extradition efforts, given the Bolivian government's ban on extraditing nationals. In December 1989, however, he was arrested by the U.S.-trained paramilitary drug enforcement unit, UMO-PAR, and placed immediately on a plane to the United States.[211] This

207. See *Kear v. Hilton*, 699 F.2d 181 (4th Cir. 1983). See also Wade A. Buser, "The *Jaffe* Case and the Use of International Kidnapping as an Alternative to Extradition," *Georgia Journal of International and Comparative Law* 14 (1984), 357–376.

208. *Protocol Amending the Extradition Treaty with Canada*, U.S. Senate Treaty Doc. 101-17, 101st Cong., 2d Sess. (1990).

209. The history of irregular renditions between Canada and the United States is briefly reviewed in C. V. Coles, "Extradition Treaties Abound but Unlawful Seizures Continue," *International Perspectives*, Mar.–Apr. 1975, 40–44.

210. "Ex-Bolivian Minister Held on Drug Charges," *New York Times*, Dec. 14, 1989, A27.

211. "Extradition Causes Institutional Crisis: Judge Accuses President of Assault on Judicial

rendition differed from most other comparable efforts in three respects: the fugitive was not only a Bolivian citizen but also a former cabinet minister; the deportation was personally approved by the president, Jamie Paz Zamora; and the incident almost led to the downfall of the government. The Bolivian ambassador in Washington publicly stated that Arce Gómez had been deported "because of the scant confidence the government has in Bolivia's judicial system"—which led the chief justice of Bolivia's supreme court to accuse Paz Zamora of engaging in illegitimate action. That was followed by the initiation of impeachment proceedings against the president by an opposition deputy in the Bolivian Congress on grounds that Paz Zamora had violated the constitution with his deportation order.[212] The Bolivian president survived the attacks, however, and Arce Gómez was prosecuted and convicted in Fort Lauderdale.[213] In October 1990, Arce Gómez's special assistant, Herland Echeverría, met the same fate when he was seized by Bolivian police and immediately flown to the United States.[214]

The increasingly proactive stance of the U.S. government was motivated, I have suggested, by concern with terrorists as well as drug traffickers. The 1987 sting operation that netted Fawaz Younis in the Mediterranean represented the first extraterritorial arrest of a suspected terrorist by U.S. law enforcement agents, although it followed the October 1985 incident in which U.S. fighters intercepted a plane carrying the hijackers of the *Achille Lauro* and forced it down in Italy.[215] Both operations occurred in the midst of a fairly extensive debate within the National Security Council and other agencies of the executive branch over proposals for arresting terrorists abroad.[216] Although William Barr's legal opinion indicated that the Republican administration was ready to take such proposals seriously, both his comments and those of

Power," *Latin America Regional Reports: Andean Group*, Feb. 1, 1990, 3; and "Colonel Luis Arce Departs at Dawn: Extradition on Drugs Charges Triggers Row with Judiciary," *Latin America Weekly Report*, Jan. 18, 1990, 2.

212. "Judiciary Triggers Conflict of Powers: Behind Impeachment Row, a Clear Political Agenda," *Latin America Weekly Report*, Dec. 6, 1990, 4.

213. "Escalating Conflicts of Power in Bolivia," *Latin America Regional Reports: Andean Group*, Dec. 20, 1990, 4, and "Cocaine Minister Guilty," in ibid., Jan. 31, 1991, 8.

214. "Alleged Bolivian Drug Trafficker Sent to U.S. for Trial," *Reuter Library Report*, Oct. 26, 1990.

215. See the legal analysis of the incident in Jordan J. Paust, "Extradition and United States Prosecution of the *Achille Lauro* Hostage-Takers: Navigating the Hazards," *Vanderbilt Journal of Transnational Law* 20 (1987), 235–257.

216. Stephen Engelberg, "U.S. Is Said to Weigh Abducting Terrorists Abroad for Trials Here," *New York Times*, Jan. 19, 1986, 1.

Abraham Sofaer suggested that there were abundant reasons not to act hastily. The rendition of Younis represented an ideal operation precisely because it refrained from infringing directly on any other government's sovereignty.

The focus on extraterritorial arrests of terrorists represented, moreover, only one dimension of a much broader antiterrorist campaign promoted by the U.S. government that included everything from more intensive exchange of information among police and intelligence agencies, and pressures on foreign governments to enact tougher counterterrorism policies, to the bombing of Libyan territory by U.S. warplanes. Where other governments—notably those of Greece and France— seemed to dread the prospect of prosecuting Middle Eastern terrorists in their courts,[217] U.S. officials proudly proclaimed their desire to see such offenders prosecuted in American courts. When German police arrested Mohammed Ali Hamadei—a Lebanese who had been accused of participating in the hijacking of TWA Flight 847 to Beirut and the killing of a U.S. Navy diver on board—at the Frankfurt airport in early 1987, the U.S. government applied substantial (albeit ultimately fruitless) pressure on the German government to extradite him to the United States.[218] The Greek government was subjected to even stronger pressures when its police acted on a tip from U.S. law enforcement officials and arrested Mohammed Rashid, a Palestinian accused of planting a bomb in a Pan Am jet flying between Tokyo and Honolulu in 1982. The U.S. request for Rashid's extradition was approved by the Greek supreme court but then rejected by Prime Minister Constantine Mitsotakis. In the subsequent trial in Athens, which ended in Rashid's conviction on charges of premeditated murder, the prosecutors relied largely on evidence provided by the U.S. government, including the testimony of three FBI agents and a former accomplice of Rashid who had entered the U.S. witness protection program.[219] And in May 1987, U.S. officials obliged

217. The reluctance of many European governments to extradite Middle Eastern terrorists is discussed in Malcolm Anderson, *Policing the World: Interpol and the Politics of International Police Co-operation* (Oxford: Clarendon Press, 1989), 133–140; Juliet Lodge, "The European Community and Terrorism: From Principles to Concerted Action," in Juliet Lodge, ed., *The Threat of Terrorism* (Brighton, Sussex: Wheatsheaf Books, 1988), 229–264; and Richard Bernstein, "The Terror: Why France? Why Now?" *New York Times Magazine*, Oct. 19, 1986, 31ff.

218. David M. Kennedy, Torsten Stein, and Alfred P. Rubin, "The Extradition of Mohammed Hamadei," *Harvard International Law Journal* 31 (1990), 5–35.

219. William D. Montalbano, "Palestinian Guilty of Bombing U.S. Jet," *Los Angeles Times*, Jan. 9, 1992, A4.

the Israeli government by arranging for a Palestinian-American, Mahmoud El-Abed Ahmad, whom the Israelis had charged with participating in an attack on a civilian bus in the West Bank, to be deported from Venezuela to the United States and then extradited to Israel.[220]

Any analysis of irregular rendition of fugitives by the U.S. government cannot conclude without noting the arrest of General Manuel Noriega following the invasion of Panama in December 1989 by more than 25,000 U.S. troops. The White House justified the invasion, coined "Operation Just Cause," as an act of self-defense in response to a "pattern of aggression" by the Noriega government that included the general's declaration of war and the murder of a U.S. officer the previous weekend. In his speech to the nation, President Bush declared that the invasion had been intended "to safeguard the lives of Americans, to defend democracy in Panama, to combat drug trafficking, and to protect the integrity of the Panama Canal Treaty." The overriding objective, however, appeared to be the removal of Noriega (and his henchmen in the Panamanian Defense Forces) as the de facto leader of Panama by either capturing or killing him. When Noriega finally surrendered after ten days of hiding in the Nunciature, he was taken into custody not by U.S. soldiers—indeed, General Maxwell Thurman deliberately refused to allow him to make a military surrender—but by agents of the U.S. Marshals Service, who flew him to Howard Air Force Base.[221] There he was handed over to waiting DEA agents, who accompanied him on a flight to Miami to face charges on an indictment for drug trafficking and conspiracy charges handed down twenty-three months earlier.

The invasion was widely criticized as a violation of international law and the principle of nonintervention by foreign governments, in resolutions passed by the Organization of American States and the U.N. General Assembly, and by most international law scholars.[222] Much

220. The absence of an extradition treaty between Venezuela and Israel precluded Ahmad's direct extradition to Israel. See the analysis of the U.S. role in Andreas F. Lowenfeld, "Ahmad: Profile of an Extradition Case," *New York University Journal of International Law and Politics* 23 (1991), 723–749; and Robert E. Ryals, "*Ahmad v. Wigen* Extradition: Weapon Against International Terrorism or Violation of Due Process?" *George Mason University Civil Rights Law Journal* (1991), 133–148.

221. Margaret E. Scanlon, *The Noriega Years: U.S.-Panamanian Relations, 1981–1990* (Boulder, Colo.: Lynne Rienner Publishers, 1991), 207.

222. See Neil Lewis, "Scholars Say Arrest of Noriega Has Little Justification in Law," *New York Times*, Jan. 10, 1990, A12; and the three essays by Ved P. Nanda, Tom J. Farer, and Anthony D'Amato in "Agora: U.S. Forces in Panama: Defenders, Aggressors, or Human Rights Activists?" *American Journal of International Law* 84 (1990), 494–524.

criticism also focused on the fact that the brief conflict had left 10,000 to 20,000 civilian Panamanians homeless and at least several hundred dead. The Bush administration, however, had taken steps during the preceding months to provide the domestic legal authority and justification for an intervention such as Just Cause. The Barr opinion had alleviated one set of obstacles. Following a failed coup attempt against Noriega in October 1989, the office of the Army judge advocate general had drafted a new ruling that "significantly" expanded the scope of legal military operations against terrorists, drug traffickers, and other fugitives abroad.[223] And in November, the Justice Department's Office of Legal Counsel had produced another legal opinion that reinterpreted the Posse Comitatus statute to authorize arrests of fugitives abroad by U.S. military personnel.[224] Viewed in retrospect, the three legal opinions appeared to be not merely fortuitously timed but also a discreet foreshadowing of the invasion to come.

It is possible, in certain respects, to characterize the rendition of Noriega in terms of some of the renditions and other law enforcement actions, both successful and unsuccessful, that preceded it. General Pershing's pursuit of Pancho Villa into Mexican territory in 1917 provided the precedent of a military intervention into a foreign territory in order to apprehend a foreign political leader who had violated U.S. laws—although that case involved a relatively small military force pursuing a revolutionary who lacked any control over the central government. The undercover operation that culminated in the arrest of the chief minister of the Turks and Caicos in Miami in 1985 provided something of a precedent for the arrest of a foreign head of state to face drug trafficking charges in the United States—although that action took place on U.S. territory. The bombing of Libya in 1986 provided a rough precedent for responding to extraterritorial violations of U.S. law by a foreign leader with military force in an operation involving the deaths of substantial numbers of foreign civilians—although that attack did not appear to seek the apprehension of a foreign leader to face criminal charges in an American court. And the prosecution of German and Japanese officials following their apprehension or surrender at the end of World War II offered a precedent for trying foreign leaders on

223. Scanlon, *Noriega Years*, 193.
224. Ibid.; Isikoff, "U.S. 'Power' on Abductions Detailed" (supra n. 187). See also Jessica W. Julian, "Noriega: The Capture of a State Leader and Its Implications on Domestic Law," *Air Force Law Review* 34 (1991), 153–190.

criminal charges subsequent to a military conquest—although the tribunals at Nuremberg and Tokyo were not concerned with violations of a single nation's criminal laws. There was, in short, no close precedent for the manner and circumstances in which Noriega was apprehended and brought to trial in the United States.

Conclusion

The process of immobilizing criminals is both driven and bounded by law. Unlike waging war, it focuses on individuals not as representatives of foreign governments but as individuals *qua* individuals who are singularly and entirely responsible for their actions. It thus precludes the sacrifice of innocents in pursuit of any greater objective—hence the sense of discomfort among those who see the U.S. invasion of Panama as motivated primarily by the desire to apprehend a notorious criminal fugitive. Unlike covert operations, moreover, which occasionally seek to "immobilize" individuals by killing them, the immobilization efforts of law enforcement agents seek to bring fugitives before a court of law.

Nonetheless, what most distinguishes the international rendition of fugitives from other types of international law enforcement action and most domestic criminal justice activities is the tremendous extent to which it is unbounded by legal constraints. Both Congress and the courts have afforded the executive branch extensive latitude in bringing criminal fugitives before American courts. Like all other treaties, extradition treaties are regarded as the law of the land, but they also are viewed correctly as political, intergovernmental compacts that afford defendants few if any legal rights. The existence of a treaty is not viewed—under the laws of the United States and most other nations—as a prohibition against resorting to measures outside the treaty. And the absence of an extradition treaty does not preclude a wide array of other types of rendition tactics. The constraints on international fugitive rendition are primarily political and practical in nature, not legal, and the principal legal constraints involve foreign rather than domestic laws.

The principal intrusions of law on the international rendition process affect not the collection of fugitives but their delivery. Although the U.S. government has employed its powers of deportation and exclusion with increasing facility and frequency to deliver fugitives to foreign governments, its powers of extradition still remain largely dependent upon the existence of an extradition treaty. That requirement resulted in the negotiation of dozens of extradition treaties during the nineteenth century, and it accounts for the fact that the United States is now a party to more than 100 bilateral extradition treaties. Those treaties have provided the essential source of authority to comply with foreign government requests for fugitives, but the language and judicial interpretations of their clauses also have constrained the capacity of the Departments of State and Justice to accommodate foreign requests as much as they would have liked.

The evolution of U.S. extradition treaties and practice can best be understood as one of ever more encompassing treaty language and ever more accommodative institutions and procedures. Where once American views regarding extradition were shaped principally by perceptions of the United States as a haven for those fleeing the injustices of foreign political and criminal justice systems, contemporary Americans regard it as an essential component of U.S. and international efforts to suppress crime. And where once extradition treaties were negotiated with a keen sense of their intended limits, today they are increasingly designed to be highly open-ended. Legal obstacles that had hampered extradition relations for many decades—including substantive provisions, such as the political offense exception, and more legalistic hindrances, such as the "*Valentine* infirmity," the inevitably limited "Schedule of Offenses," and rigid notions of reciprocity—have been reduced or eliminated. Similarly, institutional handicaps, notably the relative lack of government officials or any government office with expertise in extradition matters, have evaporated with the creation and expansion of the OIA in the Justice Department's Criminal Division and the LEI in the State Department's Legal Adviser's Office.

The evolution of U.S. government involvement in the international rendition of fugitives has much in common with the evolution of U.S. involvement in international evidence-gathering efforts. Until well into the twentieth century, both types of international law enforcement action were seriously hampered by much the same obstacles: skepticism of foreign systems and requests; the cumbersome requirements of transmitting requests for assistance through slow and often neglectful diplomatic bureaucracies; the dominance of State Department officials who often had insufficient knowledge of criminal procedure and criminal justice systems; a general reluctance on the part of prosecutors, courts, and legislators to accommodate the peculiar requirements of international (as distinct from municipal) law enforcement, notably those involving foreign civil law systems; and the absence of any specialized office in the government with expertise in international law enforcement matters. Beginning in the 1970s, both domains of international law enforcement witnessed dramatic progress both in the numbers of requests forwarded and received and in the capacity of U.S. and foreign officials to provide and obtain what they needed. In both cases, the principal demands and conflicts were generated far more by U.S. initiatives than by those of foreign governments. U.S. officials devoted substantial efforts to negotiating ever more encompassing extradition and mutual legal assistance treaties. These and other officials developed and perfected a variety of more proactive and aggressive measures intended to obtain fugitives or evidence in specific cases and to pressure foreign governments to be more accommodating in the future. And in the vast majority of cases, these tactics were simultaneously or subsequently approved by most federal courts and reflected in the influential *Third Restatement of the Foreign Relations Law of the United States*. The evolution of U.S. international fugitive rendition capabilities, like the evolution of evidence-gathering capabilities, could well be compared to the development of an ever more powerful and efficient vacuum cleaner.

There are, however, significant differences as well between the evolution of U.S. rendition of fugitives and that of U.S. collection of evidence. The history of the former is both far more substantial and far more laden with controversy. Relatively free of the many constitutional, evidentiary, and other legal requirements that complicate international evidence-gathering efforts, U.S. rendition efforts have benefited from their capacity for informal action. On the other hand, the option of entirely unilateral action involving extraterritorial infringements on foreign sovereignty has been severely circumscribed. With relatively few exceptions, entirely unilateral actions by U.S. agents have limited themselves to luring fugitives from their havens into U.S., foreign, or international territories where they could be seized. By contrast, although U.S. evidence-gathering efforts have generally refrained from unilateral actions to collect evidence physically abroad, the contemporary history of those efforts is replete with *Bank of Nova Scotia* subpoenas, *Ghidoni* waivers, and other tactics viewed by foreign governments as unjustifiable infringements on their sovereignty. Unlike the more aggressive U.S. rendition efforts, moreover, which have been confined largely to Latin

America, unilateral evidence-gathering efforts have been directed at a great variety of nations, including many advanced industrialized nations.

In emphasizing the extent to which the U.S. government has enhanced its capacity to obtain fugitives from abroad, I have not meant to suggest that a substantial majority of fugitives are in fact apprehended and brought to justice in U.S. courts. Powerful legal notions such as the "political offense" exception and the prohibition on extraditing nationals continue to block rendition efforts directed at terrorists and drug traffickers respectively. Fears of retaliation by terrorist organizations and their discreet government sponsors, as well as powerful drug trafficking and other criminal organizations, have frequently persuaded foreign governments to reject extradition requests from the United States and other governments. And the time, expense, and hassle of locating, arresting, and extraditing fugitives who have fled abroad have ensured that most U.S. rendition efforts are limited to the more notorious criminals. Many thousands of fugitives wanted on criminal charges in the United States remain relatively free and safe in their foreign havens. Yet the fact remains that the number of fugitive renditions processed each year has increased more than tenfold since the 1970s.

It is also important to stress that many of the more irregular renditions of fugitives from abroad have been criticized extensively and severely by legal scholars both within and without the United States.[225] They have pointed out that *Ker v. Illinois*, the 1886 Supreme Court decision that gave a stamp of approval to irregular rendition, "was decided before it was so clear to us that arbitrary arrest is a fundamental wrong."[226] But the chief criticisms have focused on the violations of international law in cases such as the seizure of Noriega or the Mexican doctor involved in the Camarena killing. Imagine, the critics have suggested, how Americans would respond to abductions by agents of foreign governments of fugitives from U.S. territory. Their point is well taken, for even as the U.S. government has demonstrated a substantial willingness to accommodate foreign rendition requests, whether by extradition or deporta-

225. The more prominent and prolific critics include Abraham Abramovsky, M. Cherif Bassiouni, Lea Brilmayer, Richard Falk, Louis Henkin, Andreas Lowenfeld, Ved Nanda, and Ruth Wedgwood. See the references to their works cited in various footnotes here. A useful discussion among a number of international law scholars, including Henkin and Wedgwood, conducted shortly after the invasion of Panama, is in *Proceedings of the 84th Annual Meeting of the American Society of International Law, 1990,* 236–256.

226. Comment of Ruth Wedgwood, in *Proceedings, American Society of International Law, 1990,* 241.

tion, even in the absence of reciprocal capabilities, it has not been confronted with the sorts of aggressive and quasi-unilateral actions employed with increasing frequency by U.S. agents. Early in 1990, Robert Friedlander, the minority counsel of the Senate Foreign Relations Committee, observed with respect to international criminal law enforcement matters that "it seems to be the *practice* of the United States to do what it wants to do; it has long been so and probably will continue to be so."[227] It may well be that only when the United States finds itself on the receiving end of such practices will the government's tactics change.

Themes of regularization, accommodation, and homogenization pervade the evolution of U.S. rendition efforts. Although U.S. officials have devoted some efforts to persuading foreign governments to adopt U.S. approaches to extradition, most efforts have focused on seeking pragmatic approaches to fugitive rendition and making the most of the potential of foreign systems to complement the U.S. system. Rigid notions of reciprocity, for instance, have yielded to more pragmatic notions of fugitive immobilization motivated by the need to accommodate the legal and political constraints on foreign governments. Evidence of the regularization of fugitive rendition abounds: the creation of the OIA, the development of Interpol's "wanted notice" system, the enhancement of the capacity of the DEA, the FBI, and the U.S. Marshals Service to arrange fugitive renditions from abroad, and the inevitable familiarization with fugitive rendition procedures, both formal and informal, that has accompanied the great increase in the numbers of fugitives being collected and delivered each year. And the proliferation of criminal statutes directed at money laundering, insider trading, and other "white-collar" crimes has created an increasingly homogeneous, and hence receptive, international environment for U.S. fugitive rendition efforts. As in other domains of international law enforcement, the distinguishing features of U.S. rendition efforts have been their aggressiveness and their scope.

227. Ibid., 254.

Chapter Eight

The Transformation of U.S. International Law Enforcement

There has always been a criminal justice dimension to U.S. foreign policy and an international dimension to American criminal justice. The first secretaries of state forwarded and responded to requests for the rendition of fugitives. Customs agents crossed U.S. borders to collect intelligence on smuggling ventures destined for the United States. Federal and state officials as well as private citizens tracked down black men and women who had fled into foreign territories to escape their enslavement in the United States. Military and police officials patrolled the borders and occasionally pursued bandits across U.S. borders. U.S. naval forces and coast guard cutters searched for pirates and slavers in the Caribbean and the Atlantic. U.S. consular officials abroad collected intelligence on matters of potential interest to municipal law enforcers. And top police officials in New York City and other metropolitan centers kept in touch with fellow officers in foreign capitals.

By the end of the nineteenth century and the beginning of the twentieth, law enforcers no longer concerned themselves with fugitive slaves, slavers, and pirates. Transnational banditry across the Canadian border was no longer a concern either. But the southwestern border with Mexico had emerged as a hotbed of criminal and law enforcement activity. Military units, Rangers, local sheriffs, and citizen posses had their hands full with cattle rustlers, horse thiefs and bandits of all sorts, Indian bands resisting pacification, and Mexican revolutionaries plotting and hiding on U.S. territory. Smuggling persisted across both borders as well as along U.S. shores. The Chinese Exclusion Acts of 1882 and 1904 required enforcement, as did the Smoking Opium Exclusion Act of 1909. Prohibition during the 1920s introduced a wave of smuggling unlike anything the country had witnessed before. Treasury agents stationed around the world investigated violations of U.S. prohibition and tariff laws, and special agents were sent on missions to conduct operations of particular import. The delegation of hundreds of thousands of troops during World War I created a need for military investigative units abroad. Agents of the Secret Service and the Bureau of Investigation were called upon to perform espionage and counterespionage activities both inside and outside the United States. By the end of the 1930s, the first FBN and FBI agents could be found in foreign posts.

The modern era of international criminal law enforcement emerged in three stages following World War II. During the late 1940s and 1950s, hundreds of military criminal investigative agents were assigned to foreign posts to police the hundreds of thousands of U.S. military personnel stationed abroad. The assumption of global security responsibilities invited creation of a substantial police training program. The Customs Service reasserted its presence overseas, the FBI opened twenty offices, the Federal Bureau of Narcotics gradually expanded its presence, and the Secret Service opened an office in Paris. The second stage began during the 1960s, with the emergence of crime as a national political issue and the rapid nationalization of law enforcement within the United States. It took off in the early 1970s, with President Nixon's declaration of a "war on drugs" and the internationalization of U.S. drug enforcement activities. The Bureau of Narcotics and Dangerous Drugs and its successor agency, the Drug Enforcement Administration, rapidly emerged as the first (nonimperial) transnational police organization in world history.

The third stage of the modern era began during the late 1970s and blossomed during the 1980s. The Justice Department, the State Department, and the Securities and Exchange Commission each created offices to handle international criminal law enforcement matters. These grew rapidly in size and responsibility, as did the U.S. national central bureau of Interpol. More than a dozen mutual legal assistance treaties (MLATs) were negotiated and signed, as well as a host of agreements to improve cooperation in drug and securities law enforcement. All of the federal police agencies expanded their extraterritorial presence and activities. Foreign police agencies began to station their own attachés in Washington, D.C., and other U.S. cities. U.S. military forces reassumed international criminal law enforcement responsibilities for the first time since the antislaver patrols of the pre–Civil War era. Police training programs were reinstituted on a significant scale. Dozens of federal criminal statutes were modified and enacted to cover extraterritorial offenses against U.S. citizens and other interests abroad. Prosecutors devised, and federal judges approved, a variety of innovative techniques to compel foreign banks and corporations to provide evidence located abroad. And the U.S. attorney general revealed that he often spent more than 50 percent of his day dealing with international criminal law enforcement matters.

A prime example of the blossoming of U.S. international criminal law enforcement could be found in Italy. During the 1980s, the two governments signed and put into force both an updated extradition treaty and an innovative mutual legal assistance treaty, both of which were quickly put to use by U.S. and Italian law enforcement officials. An Italian-American Working Group on Organized Crime was created, and its sessions were frequently attended by the U.S. attorney general and top officials of the FBI and other federal law enforcement agencies. By the late 1980s, the law enforcement group within the U.S. embassy included representatives of the DEA, the FBI, the Secret Service, Customs, the IRS, the INS, the Naval Investigative Service, the Army Criminal Investigative Division, the Air Force Office of Special Investigations, and the first federal prosecutor stationed abroad, Richard Martin.[1] An Italian Office of International Affairs grew rapidly, and its chief, initially hostile to many U.S. initiatives, evolved into a vigorous proponent of closer law enforcement relations with the United States. The Italian Parliament enacted new legislation bringing its own drug laws and regulation of

1. Richard Martin was the lead prosecutor in the "Pizza Connection" case from 1985 to 1987. During his tenure in Rome (1987–90), his various titles included Special Representative of the U.S. Attorney General, Department of Justice Attaché, and Senior Counsel for International Law Enforcement.

financial and securities transactions more in line with U.S. norms.[2] And Italian criminal investigative methods increasingly resembled those employed by the DEA and other U.S. police agencies.

There is, clearly, no one explanation for the internationalization of U.S. criminal law enforcement. The perennial concerns with controlling the nation's borders, suppressing smuggling, collecting revenues, and renditing criminal fugitives have remained constant even as the energies, personnel, resources, and international agreements devoted to these tasks have multiplied. What have changed, however, are many of the criminal laws requiring extraterritorial enforcement efforts. Police and prosecutors today no longer need worry about fugitive slaves, illicit slavers, rum runners, and cross-border Apache raids. But unlike their counterparts a hundred years ago, they have their hands full with illicit heroin and cocaine smugglers, securities law violators, high-tech smugglers, money launderers, and tax offenders. As we contemplate the future of U.S. involvement in international criminal law enforcement matters, we do well to keep in mind the potential for current laws to be repealed, for new criminal laws to emerge, and for enforcement priorities to change. New laws justify the creation of new international law enforcement capabilities, which in turn invite additional laws and other new initiatives. Changing perceptions of U.S. national security interests, as well as changing markets and morals, have radically transformed the nature and objectives of U.S. international law enforcement efforts in the past and are certain to do so in the future.

That being said, I must stress the dominant role that drug enforcement has played in the evolution of U.S. international law enforcement since the late 1960s. The "war on drugs" proclaimed by the Nixon administration in 1969, and renewed on an even more ambitious scale during the 1980s, provided the crucial impetuses for a host of actions and agreements that otherwise would never have occurred. It was not just the transformation of a relatively small federal police agency into a substantial transnational police organization with agents stationed in more than sixty foreign cities. Over and above that significant development, the "war on drugs" provided a reason for other federal police agencies, including the FBI and Customs, to extend their efforts abroad. It accounted for roughly 70 percent of the 16,300 fugitives sought by the

2. Lawrence J. Fassler, "The Italian Penal Procedure Code: An Adversarial System of Criminal Procedure in Continental Europe," *Columbia Journal of Transnational Law* 29 (1991), 245–278.

U.S. Marshals Service in 1993. It led to the modification of the Posse Comitatus Act to allow U.S. military forces to play a role in civilian law enforcement. It provided the impetus for creation of paramilitary enforcement groups composed of U.S. military and police officials to target drug trafficker facilities in South America. It prompted the negotiation and renegotiation of dozens of extradition treaties as well as a number of mutual legal assistance treaties. It accounted for much of the business pursued by the Justice Department's Office of International Affairs. It led to a new role for the CIA and other intelligence agencies in criminal law enforcement matters.[3] It helped stimulate the negotiation of a number of global drug enforcement conventions, including a 1988 U.N. convention that dramatically increased the level of international law enforcement cooperation expected of governments. It exercised a profound influence on the nature of criminal investigation in dozens of foreign countries. It compelled dozens of foreign governments to change their financial and corporate secrecy laws. It provided a central justification for the military invasion of Panama. And it offered a powerful foot in the door with which to weaken domestic and foreign resistance to a range of other international criminal law enforcement endeavors. In short, there can be no question that but for the U.S. "war on drugs" the extent of U.S. involvement in international law enforcement matters would be far less developed than it is today.

My principal aim throughout much of this book has been to explain *how* U.S. law enforcement agents have responded to the challenges of internationalization—in particular, the need to collect from abroad the information, evidence, and bodies required to "immobilize" transnational criminals. The principal obstacles, I noted, are of three sorts: the loss of sovereign police powers outside U.S. borders; the foreign, international, and domestic political frictions that inevitably hamper most domains of foreign policy; and the frictions generated by the need to interact with alien law enforcement systems. My analysis accordingly focused on explaining how U.S. law enforcers have dealt with these obstacles.

The dominant theme in the evolution of U.S. international law enforcement is one of progress toward an ever more powerful capacity to immobilize transnational criminals. Extradition and mutual legal assis-

3. See William J. Broad, "Charting Drug Trade from the Skies," *New York Times*, Oct. 14, 1989, 6; and Jeff Gerth, "C.I.A. Shedding Its Reluctance to Aid in Fight Against Drugs," *New York Times*, Mar. 25, 1990, A1.

tance treaties have proliferated and become more and more inclusive. Prosecutors have devised an increasing array of techniques for acquiring evidence from abroad. Growing numbers of agencies and people have developed expertise in handling international law enforcement matters. The number of U.S. agents stationed abroad has steadily increased. Congress and the federal courts have consistently reduced and eliminated domestic legal obstacles to effective international law enforcement action and enhanced the legal powers of U.S. law enforcement officials. And foreign governments and law enforcement agencies have mostly worked at common purposes with U.S. officials to reduce the frictions that emanate from their own criminal justice systems. By contrast, the obstacles generated by Congress, U.S. courts, and foreign governments have been relatively few and brief. It is fair to say that U.S. international law enforcement capabilities have advanced three steps forward for every step backward. They are now more powerful and more streamlined than ever before.

The internationalization of U.S. law enforcement has proceeded in tandem with the internationalization and harmonization of foreign law enforcement systems. The evolutionary process has been both dynamic and interactive, involving efforts by U.S. law enforcers and foreign counterparts to regularize relations, to accommodate domestic systems to the requirements of foreign systems, and to homogenize criminal justice norms across borders. Most of these efforts have occurred at the transgovernmental level, where low- and middle-level officials, primarily in the Justice Department but also in smaller numbers in the Departments of State and Treasury and the intelligence agencies, have established relations with foreign counterparts. Many U.S. law enforcers involved in international law enforcement matters on a regular basis now perceive themselves both as representatives of the U.S. government and as members of a transnational subculture based on common functions and objectives. Indeed, it is this transnational identity—based on the notion that a cop is a cop, and a criminal is a criminal, no matter what their respective nationalities—that provides the oil and glue of contemporary international law enforcement. Where once U.S. law enforcers barely perceived a commonality of identity with foreign police and prosecutors, they now represent quite active and conscious developers of this transnational subculture.

U.S. law enforcers generally see the internationalization of criminal justice as relatively free of costs or trade-offs. The negotiation of extradition treaties has not required U.S. agents to forgo less-formal means of rendition. The negotiation of mutual legal assistance treaties have required relatively few concessions in terms of abstaining from *Bank of Nova Scotia* subpoenas, *Ghidoni* waivers, and other unilateral means of compelling the production of evidence. And the fairly operational activities of U.S. agents in foreign countries only rarely have led to demands that foreign police agents be permitted to do likewise in the United States.

There are three explanations for the relative absence of costs or trade-offs. The first is simply that many apparent concessions by the U.S. government have not been perceived as such by most law enforcement officials and other citizens. Unlike citizens of most civil law countries and many others as well, Americans have long been accustomed to the notion that U.S. citizens should be extradited to foreign countries for crimes committed abroad. Unlike citizens of countries that have experienced humiliating occupations and dominations by foreign powers, Americans have rarely been bothered by the presence of foreign law enforcement officials on U.S. territory. Most Americans regard undercover operations, wiretapping, the employment of informants, and the practice of recruiting informants with financial and legal rewards as natural components of criminal investigation. They tend not to view financial and corporate secrecy with the same deference as many foreign citizens. And they generally view criminal laws and the criminal justice system as appropriate methods for curtailing and suppressing a great variety of undesirable activities. As a consequence, U.S. officials rarely feel compelled to say no to foreign requests for law enforcement assistance from other advanced industrial democracies, and only occasionally are obliged to reject requests from other countries.

The second explanation is that the harmonization of national criminal justice systems during this century, and particularly since the 1960s, has been powerfully shaped by the United States. Unlike the last decades of the nineteenth century and the first decades of the twentieth, when U.S. law enforcement officials looked to Europe for lessons in police methods and organization, the modern era of international law enforcement is one in which U.S. criminal justice priorities and U.S. models of criminalization and criminal investigation have been exported abroad. Foreign governments have responded to U.S. pressures, inducements, and examples by enacting new criminal laws regarding drug trafficking, money laundering, insider trading, and organized crime and by changing financial and corporate secrecy laws as well as their codes of criminal procedure to better accommodate U.S. requests for assistance. Foreign police have adapted U.S. investigative techniques, and foreign courts and legislatures have followed up with the requisite legal authorizations. And foreign governments have devoted substantial police and even military resources to curtailing illicit drug production and trafficking. By contrast, the demands of foreign law enforcement systems have required remarkably few responses by Congress or accommodations by U.S. courts, prosecutors, and police. The threefold processes of regularization, accommodation, and homogenization by which states transcend the frictions of international law enforcement have hardly been equal or reciprocal. By and large, the United States has provided the models, and other governments have done the accommodating. It thus would be quite fair, in describing the evolution of drug enforcement and many other domains of law enforcement around the world since the 1960s, to substitute the word "Americanization" for "harmonization."

The third explanation is that Americans have not yet had to deal with the sorts of pressures and interventions that the U.S. government imposes on others. The U.S. government has little reason to fear the consequences of rejecting an extradition request from a foreign government. Only a small number of fugitives from foreign justice have been abducted from U.S. territory, and almost all of those occurred before World War I. The extensive presence of Mexican agents north of the border during the Mexican revolution has not been repeated by the Mexican or any other government since. U.S. corporations and banks only rarely have to deal with the sorts of sanctions levied by U.S. courts that want to obtain documents located abroad. And the United States generally has not been subjected to anything resembling the pressures it has exerted in promoting the war on drugs to foreign governments. Foreign governments that prohibit the sale of alcohol, or the importation of firearms, or the export of capital, or the pollution of the environment in ways that remain legal in the United States, lack the power to require the United States to submit to their own criminal norms. Should that balance of power shift, or should foreign governments impatient with U.S. criminal procedures decide to act more unilaterally on U.S. territory, the attitudes of American citizens and the U.S. government regarding international law enforcement may well undergo a striking change.

The fact that U.S. law enforcers still regard most dimensions of the internationalization process as cost-free does not mean that others share their perspective. It is important to keep in mind that the internationalization of law enforcement since the 1960s has coincided with a fairly persistent expansion of criminal justice systems in the United States and abroad, as well as quite extensive enhancements in the powers of law enforcement officials. Apart from a brief period during the mid-1970s, when Congress circumscribed the powers of federal law enforcement officials within and without the United States, both Congress and the courts have preferred to broaden the latitude and powers of law enforcement officials. Civil libertarians, criminal defense lawyers, and many others who oppose new extensions of police powers have decried the apparent evisceration of the "political offense" exception, the Supreme Court's refusal to apply Fourth Amendment standards to extraterritorial searches by U.S. law enforcement agents and its legitimation of extraterritorial abductions, the insistence of the State and Justice Departments on extraditing U.S. citizens to foreign countries that do not recognize American standards of due process, and the efforts of extradition and mutual legal assistance treaty negotiators to monopolize the benefits of the treaties for prosecutors. Banking and corporate interests both in the United States and abroad have regarded with concern the growing regulation of transnational money movements, the increasing criminalization of violations of those regulations, and the apparent willingness of U.S. law enforcement officials to provide information on capital flight to foreign governments that restrict exports of capital. In many foreign countries, the adoption of DEA-style investigative techniques has been viewed warily by citizens who recall the outrages perpetrated by *agents provocateurs* and secret police earlier in the century. DEA agents know that many drug trafficking suspects arrested in foreign countries on the basis of information provided by the DEA are tortured by local police. And critics of drug prohibition within and without the United States insist that current policies are no more successful, and even more costly and counterproductive, than the alcohol prohibition policies of the 1920s.

It is extremely difficult to gauge the impact of U.S. international law enforcement efforts on levels of crime. Law enforcement agencies can provide fairly reliable statistics on drug seizures and drug trafficker arrests, but they can only guess at the number of drug shipments and traffickers that are not detected. No one knows how many times U.S. securities and money laundering laws are violated each year, whether in the United States or abroad. Estimates of the number of illegal immigrants entering the United States vary dramatically as well. New laws transform activities that were once legal into criminal activities, thereby suddenly and often quite dramatically increasing the total amount of transnational crime. And some international law enforcement initiatives backfire, as when successes in immobilizing amateur criminals benefit more professional and organized criminals, or when successes in suppressing marijuana trafficking end up stimulating cocaine trafficking.

The internationalization of U.S. law enforcement can be judged a success, however, in at least one important respect. By and large, the odds that U.S. law enforcers will succeed in immobilizing a particular transnational criminal they have targeted have increased substantially since the 1960s. The number of havens in which transnational criminals can elude apprehension have diminished substantially. Foreign financial secrecy jurisdictions no longer provide quite the same protection for criminal assets and money movements. And the resources and expertise committed to U.S. international law enforcement efforts have increased to the point that they can sustain expensive and complex multinational criminal investigations for as long as it takes to immobilize a wanted transnational criminal. By 1991, virtually all of the most notorious Latin American drug traffickers sought by U.S. officials during the 1980s were either dead or incarcerated in U.S. and foreign prisons. Although transnational criminals continue to take advantage of the frictions generated by conflicting sovereignties, political interests, and law enforcement systems, the streamlining and enhancement of U.S. international law enforcement has succeeded in narrowing the criminals' advantage.

International law enforcement endeavors are generally bilateral and cooperative in nature, reflecting states' recognition of mutual interests in crime control as well as principles of reciprocity and comity. Among the features that distinguish U.S. international law enforcement behavior from that of most other states, however, are the relatively high number of endeavors in which U.S. officials act unilaterally and coercively. No other government has acted so aggressively in collecting evidence from foreign jurisdictions, apprehending fugitives from abroad, indicting foreign officials in its own courts,[4] targeting foreign government corruption, and persuading foreign governments to change their criminal justice norms to better accord with its own. Nor has any other government

---

4. Jean E. Engelmayer, "Foreign Policy by Indictment: Using Legal Tools Against Foreign Officials Involved in Drug Trafficking," *Criminal Justice Ethics*, Summer/Fall 1989, 3–31.

devoted comparable diplomatic resources to pursuing its international law enforcement agenda during the past few decades. The U.S. government has, more than any other government, proven willing and able to intrude on the prerogatives of foreign sovereigns, to challenge foreign political sensibilities, and to circumvent and override foreign legal norms.

This aggressiveness has been successful in two respects. First, it has, in individual cases, resulted in the immobilization of transnational criminals who would otherwise have eluded immobilization. One need only recall the ways in which August Ricord, Joaquim Him, Edwin Wilson, Carlos Lehder, Juan Matta Ballesteros, Humberto Alvarez Machain, Fawaz Younis, Luis Arce Gómez, and Manuel Noriega were delivered to U.S. custody to appreciate the effectiveness of aggressive action. Much the same could be said of the ways in which financial documents and other evidence were obtained by resorting to *Bank of Nova Scotia* subpoenas, *Ghidoni* waivers, and other coercive mechanisms devised by U.S. prosecutors and backed by U.S. courts. Aggressive actions in most of these cases produced angry reactions by foreign governments and societies, including diplomatic protests, enactment of blocking statutes, and expulsions of U.S. law enforcement agents—but they accomplished their central objectives.

Second, U.S. aggressiveness has proved successful in pressuring foreign governments to be more forthcoming in the future. Combined with public and private pressures by Congress, the White House, and other top U.S. officials, these aggressive actions have helped persuade foreign governments to change their own laws, create law enforcement working groups and other cooperative arrangements with U.S. law enforcers, enter into extradition and mutual legal assistance treaty negotiations desired by U.S. officials, and generally play a more active role in vicariously representing U.S. criminal justice interests. The success of U.S. international law enforcement efforts has thus depended upon the willingness and ability of the U.S. government to offend foreign sovereignties and sensibilities in particular cases, as well as on the capacity to avoid future frictions and improve cooperation by harmonizing U.S. and foreign criminal justice systems over the long term.

The relative success of the U.S. government in pursuing its international law enforcement agenda can be attributed to at least three factors. The first, and most obvious, is the overall power of the United States and its government. Foreign governments know that the costs of defying the

United States may be substantial, particularly if they represent relatively vulnerable, less-developed, countries. Foreign banks and corporations know that defiance of U.S. court orders for documents may result in their de facto exclusion from American territory and markets. And transnational criminals know that the U.S. government is sufficiently powerful and wealthy to sustain a global police presence as well as far-reaching and long-term criminal investigations.

The second factor is the elevation of criminal justice officials, concerns, and objectives to the upper echelons of U.S. foreign policy formulation and implementation—a phenomenon that can be explained largely by the persistent prominence of "law and order" themes in American national politics since the late 1960s. The first significant elevation occurred during the Nixon administration, when White House officials insisted that the State Department and the CIA take international drug enforcement objectives seriously. During the 1980s, drug enforcement ranked among the top three concerns of U.S. ambassadors in well over a dozen countries and engaged growing numbers of officials in the military, the intelligence agencies, and the White House. It provided the occasion for two Andean Summit meetings of President Bush and Latin American leaders. And it emerged, together with terrorism and money laundering, on the agendas of the G-7 meetings and other notable gatherings of world leaders. Congressional committees charged with oversight of foreign affairs took an active interest in international drug control matters and other crime control issues. Attorney generals of the United States were increasingly drawn into foreign policy deliberations as well as international negotiations and travel. The net result was to empower—both intragovernmentally and transgovernmentally—police, prosecutors, and other officials involved in international criminal law enforcement.

The third factor is the ever-present but increasingly strident and pervasive sense of moralism associated with criminal justice efforts both domestically and internationally. Within the federal bureaucracy of the United States, the number of government officials willing to oppose an international law enforcement initiative that might be costly to other U.S. foreign policy objectives has diminished in recent decades, particularly as anti-Soviet and anticommunist objectives have lost their place at the pinnacle of the U.S. foreign policy agenda. Where once officials in the White House and the State Department felt secure in pushing criminal justice issues onto the back burners, they now know that they risk public embarrassment by Congress and the media if they are accused of treating criminal justice objectives with insufficient regard. One result is that indictments of transnational criminals initiated by lower-level prosecutors are increasingly likely to proceed unimpeded by higher-level officials even if they threaten to disrupt relations with foreign governments.[5] Similarly, foreign governments are increasingly wary of arousing the ire of the U.S. Congress and the American public by appearing to be insensitive to U.S. criminal justice concerns. Where once anticommunism represented the principal moral imperative of U.S. foreign policy, drug enforcement and other criminal justice objectives have emerged as the new moral imperatives.

It is both easy and quite accurate to describe the internationalization of U.S. law enforcement as a natural and inevitable response to the internationalization of crime. As the flow of people, goods, money, and just about everything else across U.S. borders has increased dramatically in recent decades, so too have the criminal violations associated with those transnational movements. The dramatic internationalization of the financial, securities, and commodities markets since the 1970s—to take the most prominent examples—inevitably was accompanied by a proliferation of transnational frauds on those markets. But the internationalization of U.S. law enforcement must also be understood as a consequence of criminalizations of previously licit transnational activities as well as extensions of U.S. jurisdiction to offenses committed abroad. The FBI derives much of the justification for its expanding role overseas from Congressional legislation during the mid-1980s that brought terrorist offenses against U.S. citizens and interests abroad under U.S. federal law. U.S. Customs similarly was able to justify its international expansion during the 1980s as a response to the criminalization of transnational money movements and the expansion of export controls on technologically advanced products. And even the invasion of Panama and arrest of Noriega were justified primarily by Noriega's extraterritorial violations of U.S. drug laws.

There has, in short, been something of a fusion (or perhaps re-fusion would be more accurate) of U.S. criminal justice and U.S. national security concerns. These two concerns overlapped at sea during the first decades of the nation's history, when naval patrols sought to suppress

5. See Philip Shenon, "The Justice Department Takes on Diplomatic Tasks Pursuing Foreign Targets," New York Times, Aug. 28, 1988, E5.

piracy, and along the U.S. borders until World War I, where posses, law enforcers, and military units confronted challenges to frontier stability. With the quieting of the borders, the two sets of concerns were more or less disentangled. During the decades following World War II, espionage and high-tech smuggling represented virtually the only issues implicating both concerns. During the 1980s, extraterritorial terrorism, traditionally a national security concern, was added to the criminal justice agenda by Congressional statutes, and drug trafficking, traditionally a criminal justice concern, was placed on the national security agenda by the White House, Congress, and, in a formal sense, a National Security Directive.[6] During the mid-1980s, both the U.S. military and the intelligence agencies reoriented their priorities, often reluctantly, to devote greater attention to drug trafficking, money laundering, and other criminal activities they previously had largely ignored. By the early 1990s, this reorientation had progressed substantially, driven both by the emergence of advocates within the military and intelligence bureaucracies and by the general search for new agendas and objectives to fill the void left by the collapse of the Soviet Union and the international communist threat. A fusion of criminal justice and national security concerns could also be perceived along the border with Mexico, where substantial efforts were under way to enhance the presence and role of the Border Patrol, federal law enforcement agencies, and even the U.S. military.

The fusion of the two sets of concerns could be explained in part by the inherent malleability of definitions of national security. Defining transnational drug trafficking as a national security threat jibed neatly with the rhetoric of the "war on drugs" during the 1980s. One can well imagine, in this vein, the depiction of illicit migration into the United States as a national security threat of the future. But the fusion also reflected the more general domestication of U.S. foreign policy during the 1980s and into the 1990s—by which I mean both the injection of traditionally domestic concerns and norms into the formulation and implementation of U.S. foreign policy, and a diminished capability and desire to continue assuming the traditional military and economic costs of global hegemony. Indeed, the internationalization of U.S. law enforcement during the 1980s can well be viewed as a form of hegemony on the cheap. The Cold War vision of the United States as the world's policeman

6. President Reagan signed National Security Decision Directive No. 221, entitled *Narcotics and National Security*, in April 1986.

has yielded to a new post–Cold War vision, one that more closely aligns the ordinary citizen's notion of policing with U.S. involvement in international politics. This vision is dramatically less expensive than the former one, even if it increasingly invites the use of military force to deal with extraterritorial violations of U.S. laws.

There is every reason to believe that the internationalization of U.S. law enforcement will continue apace into the foreseeable future. The international tentacles of U.S. criminal justice will become more numerous and diverse and extend further. The channels will become more streamlined and efficient. Multilateral treaties, conventions, and institutions will proliferate and strengthen. Other nation's law enforcement systems will increasingly reflect U.S. examples and norms, thereby enhancing their vicarious enforcement of U.S. laws. U.S. diplomats, soldiers, and intelligence officials will find more and more of their responsibilities determined by U.S. criminal laws. International crime control issues will increasingly be redefined as national security issues. And national security issues will increasingly be dealt with by police and prosecutors.

All these developments are part and parcel of the increasingly complex and multidimensional interdependence of states and societies. All governments today face the challenge of controlling growing domains of transnational activities that either ignore or take advantage of national borders, even as their own powers remain powerfully circumscribed by the political, geographical, and legal limitations that attend notions of national sovereignty. The internationalization of law enforcement represents one of the more substantial responses to this challenge by the U.S. government and by most others as well. States have expanded the reach of their criminal laws over transnational and extraterritorial transactions and affairs, and criminal justice systems have improved their capacity to enforce these laws both unilaterally and in cooperation with one another. No one has done more in this regard than the United States government. Both its global police presence and its activist approach to transnational criminality dwarf those of any other government. The United States has consistently taken the lead in promoting both criminal prohibitions and criminal justice cooperation among nations. It has succeeded in making its own criminal justice norms and concerns those of most other states as well. And it has demonstrated a unique willingness to act decisively and unilaterally in responding to transnational crimes of all sorts. In this arena, more than most others, the United States retains the title of global hegemon.

Appendixes

Appendix A: Foreign Offices of U.S. Federal Law Enforcement Agencies, 1992–1993

	DEA	FBI	Customs	Secret Service	INS	Commerce
North America						
Belize, Belize City	x					
Canada, Ottawa	x	x	x			
Montreal	x					
Costa Rica, San José	x					
El Salvador, San Salvador	x					
Guatemala, Guatemala City	x					
Honduras, Tegucigalpa	x					
Mexico, Mexico City	x	x	x		x	
Guadalajara	x				x	
Hermosillo	x		x			
Mazatlán	x					
Mérida	x		x			
Monterrey	x		x		x	
Tijuana					x	
Panama, Panama City	x	x	x		x	
Caribbean						
Bahamas, Nassau	x					
Freeport	x					
Barbados, Bridgetown	x	x				
Dominican Republic, Santo Domingo	x		x			
Haiti, Port-au-Prince	x					
Jamaica, Kingston	x					
Netherlands Antilles, Curaçao	x					
South America						
Argentina, Buenos Aires	x					
Bolivia, La Paz	x					
Cochabamba	x					
Santa Cruz	x					
Brazil, Brasília	x					
Chile, Santiago	x					
Colombia, Bogotá	x	x				
Barranquilla	x					

Appendix A   Continued

	DEA	FBI	Customs	Secret Service	INS	Commerce
South America (cont'd)						
Ecuador, Quito	x					
Guayaquil	x					
Paraguay, Asunción	x					
Peru, Lima	x					
Uruguay, Montevideo	x	x	x			
Venezuela, Caracas	x	x	x			
Maracaibo	x					
Europe						
Austria, Vienna	x		x		x	x
Belgium, Brussels	x	x	x			
Cyprus, Nicosia	x					
Denmark, Copenhagen	x					
France, Paris	x	x	x	x		
Marseilles	x					
Germany, Bonn	x	x	x	x		
Frankfurt	x				x	
Greece, Athens	x	x			x	
Italy, Rome	x	x	x	x	x	
Milan	x		x			
Netherlands, The Hague	x		x			
Spain, Madrid	x	x				
Sweden, Stockholm						x
Switzerland, Bern	x	x				x
Turkey, Ankara	x					
Istanbul	x					
United Kingdom, London	x	x	x	x	x	
Africa						
Egypt, Cairo	x					
Kenya, Nairobi					x	
Nigeria, Lagos	x					
Asia						
Hong Kong	x	x	x		x	
India, New Delhi	x				x	
Bombay	x					
Japan, Tokyo	x	x	x			
Korea, Seoul	x		x		x	
Malaysia, Kuala Lumpur	x					
Myanmar (Burma), Rangoon	x					
Pakistan, Islamabad	x					
Karachi	x					

Appendix A   Continued

	DEA	FBI	Customs	Secret Service	INS	Commerce
Asia (cont'd)						
Lahore	x					
Peshawar	x					
Philippines, Manila	x	x		TDY	x	
Singapore	x		x		x	
Thailand, Bangkok	x	x	x	x	x	
Chiang Mai	x					
Songkhla	x					
Udon	x					
Australia						
Australia, Canberra	x	x				
Total foreign offices	73	20	22	5	17	3
Total countries	50	20	18	5	14	3

SOURCES: Public affairs offices of each of the federal law enforcement agencies in early 1993.
NOTE: Not listed in the table are the Postal Inspection Service, which stationed a special agent in Wiesbaden, Germany, in 1993, and the Department of Justice, which has stationed an attaché (counsel, not special agent) in Rome since 1987.

Appendix B: BNDD and DEA Offices and Personnel Abroad (Authorized), 1969–1993

	1969	1970	1971	1972	1973	1974	1975	1976	1977	1983	1990	1993
Foreign regional offices	3	3	3	6	6	6	6	6	3			
Foreign district offices	12	17	20	39	41	52	64	62	63	61	68	73
Total authorized personnel	34	70	91	186	203	293	401	417	325	285	358	416
Agents	26	47	61	115	124	174	222	228	162	188	240	293
Other (professional, clerical & foreign nationals)	8	23	30	71	79	119	179	189	163	97	118	123

SOURCE: DEA Office of Public Affairs; annual editions of *Hearings Before the Subcommittee on Departments of State, Justice, Commerce, the Judiciary, and Related Agencies, Committee on Appropriations, U.S. House of Representatives.*

Appendix C: DEA Offices Abroad (Authorized), 1975 and 1993

	1975	1993
North America		
Belize, Belize City		x
Canada, Ottawa	x	x
Montreal	x	x
Vancouver	x	
Toronto	x	
Costa Rica, San José	x	x
El Salvador, San Salvador		x
Guatemala, Guatemala City	x	x
Honduras, Tegucigalpa		x
Mexico, Mexico City	x	x
Acapulco	x	
Guadalajara	x	x
Hermosillo	x	x
Mazatlán	x	x
Mérida	x	x
Monterrey	x	x
Veracruz	x	
Panama, Panama City	x	x
Caribbean		
Bahamas, Nassau		x
Freeport		x
Barbados, Bridgetown		x
Dominican Republic, Santo Domingo		x
Haiti, Port-au-Prince		x
Jamaica, Kingston	x	x
Netherlands Antilles, Curaçao		x
South America		
Argentina, Buenos Aires	x	x
Bolivia, La Paz	x	x
Cochabamba		x
Santa Cruz		x
Brazil, Brasília	x	x
Rio de Janeiro	x	
São Paulo	x	
Chile, Santiago	x	x
Colombia, Bogotá	x	x
Barranquilla		x
Cali	x	
Ecuador, Quito	x	x
Guayaquil	x	x
Paraguay, Asunción	x	x

Appendix C   Continued

	1975	1993
South America (cont'd)		
Peru, Lima	x	x
Uruguay, Montevideo	x	x
Venezuela, Caracas	x	x
Maracaibo		x
Europe		
Austria, Vienna	x	x
Belgium, Brussels	x	x
Cyprus, Nicosia		x
Denmark, Copenhagen	x	x
France, Paris	x	x
Marseilles	x	x
Nice	x	
Germany, Bonn	x	x
Frankfurt	x	x
Hamburg	x	
Munich	x	
Greece, Athens		x
Italy, Rome	x	x
Genoa	x	
Milan	x	x
Netherlands, The Hague	x	x
Spain, Madrid	x	x
Barcelona	x	
Switzerland, Bern	x	
Turkey, Ankara	x	x
Adana	x	
Istanbul	x	x
Izmir	x	
United Kingdom, London	x	x
Africa		
Egypt, Cairo		x
Morocco, Rabat	x	
Nigeria, Lagos		x
East Asia/Pacific		
Hong Kong	x	x
India, New Delhi	x	x
Bombay		x
Indonesia, Jakarta	x	
Japan, Tokyo	x	x
Okinawa	x	

Appendix C   Continued

	1975	1993
East Asia/Pacific (cont'd)		
Korea, Seoul	x	x
Laos, Vientiane	x	
Malaysia, Kuala Lumpur	x	x
Myanmar (Burma), Rangoon		x
Philippines, Manila	x	x
Singapore	x	x
Taiwan, Taipei	x	
Thailand, Bangkok	x	x
Chiang Mai	x	x
Songkhla	x	x
Udon		x
Vietnam, Saigon	x	
Southwest Asia/Near East		
Afghanistan, Kabul	x	
Iran, Tehran	x	
Lebanon, Beirut	x	
Pakistan, Islamabad	x	x
Karachi	x	x
Lahore		x
Peshawar		x
Australia		
Australia, Canberra		x

SOURCES: DEA Office of Public Affairs; annual editions of *Hearings Before the Subcommittee on Departments of State, Justice, Commerce, the Judiciary, and Related Agencies, Committee on Appropriations, U.S. House of Representatives.*

Appendix D: FBI Foreign Liaison Posts, 1965–1993

	1965	1973	1978	1985	1990	1993
North America						
Canada, Ottawa	x	x	x	x	x	x
Mexico, Mexico City	x	x	x	x	x	x
Nicaragua, Managua		x				
Panama, Panama City				x	x	x
Caribbean						
Barbados, Bridgetown					x	x
South America						
Argentina, Buenos Aires	x	x	x			
Bolivia, La Paz		x				
Brazil, Brasília		x				
Rio de Janeiro	x					
Colombia, Bogotá				x	x	x
Uruguay, Montevideo				x	x	x
Venezuela, Caracas		x	x			x
Asia						
Hong Kong		x	x	x	x	x
Japan, Tokyo	x	x	x	x	x	x
Philippines, Manila	x	x	x		x	x
Singapore		x				
Thailand, Bangkok						x
Europe						
Belgium, Brussels					x	x
Denmark, Copenhagen		x				
France, Paris	x	x	x	x	x	x
Germany, Bonn	x	x	x	x	x	x
Greece, Athens						x
Italy, Rome	x	x	x	x	x	x
Spain, Madrid		x	x			x
Switzerland, Bern	x	x	x	x	x	x
United Kingdom, London	x	x	x	x	x	x
Middle East						
Israel, Tel Aviv		x				
Lebanon, Beirut		x				
Australia						
Canberra				x	x	x
Total posts	11	20	13	13	16	20

SOURCE: FBI Office of Public Affairs; annual editions of *Hearings Before the Subcommittee on Departments of State, Justice, Commerce, the Judiciary, and Related Agencies, Committee on Appropriations, U.S. House of Representatives.*

Appendix E: Mutual Legal Assistance Treaties Signed by the United States, 1973–1992

Country	Signed	Entered into Force	Citations
Argentina	Dec. 4, 1990	Feb. 9, 1993	Treaty Doc. 102-18 Ex. Rpt. 102-33
Bahamas	June 12, 1987 Aug. 18, 1987	July 18, 1990	Treaty Doc. 100-17 Ex. Rpt. 100-3 Ex. Rpt. 101-12
Belgium	Jan. 28, 1988		Treaty Doc. 100-16 Ex. Rpt. 100-29 Ex. Rpt. 101-11
Canada	Mar. 18, 1985	Jan. 24, 1990	Treaty Doc. 100-14 Ex. Rpt. 100-28 Ex. Rpt. 101-10 24 *ILM* 1092
Colombia	Aug. 20, 1980		Treaty Doc. 97-11 Ex. Rpt. 97-35
Italy	Nov. 9, 1982	Nov. 13, 1985	Sen. Ex. 98-25 Ex. Rpt. 98-36
Jamaica	July 7, 1989		Treaty Doc. 102-16 Ex. Rpt. 102-32
Mexico	Dec. 9, 1987	May 3, 1991	Treaty Doc. 100-13 Ex. Rpt. 100-27 Ex. Rpt. 101-9 24 *ILM* 447
Morocco	Oct. 17, 1983		Sen. Ex. 98-24 Ex. Rpt. 98-35
Netherlands	June 12, 1981	Sept. 15, 1983	TIAS 10734 Treaty Doc. 97-16 Ex. Rpt. 97-36
Nigeria	Sept. 13, 1989		Treaty Doc. 102-26
Panama	Apr. 11, 1991		Treaty Doc. 102-15
Spain	Nov. 20, 1990	June 30, 1993	Treaty Doc. 102-21 Ex. Rpt. 102-35
Switzerland	May 25, 1973	Jan. 23, 1977	TIAS 8302 20 UST 2019 Ex. Rpt. 94-29 Ex. Rpt. F (1976)

Appendix E   Continued

Country	Signed	Entered into Force	Citations
Thailand	Mar. 19, 1986	June 10, 1993	Treaty Doc. 100-18 Ex. Rpt. 100-31 Ex. Rpt. 101-13
Turkey	June 7, 1979	Jan. 1, 1981	TIAS 9891 Exec. AA (1979)
United Kingdom (Cayman Isl.)	July 3, 1986	Mar. 19, 1990	Treaty Doc. 100-8 Ex. Rpt. 100-26 Ex. Rpt. 101-8 26 *ILM* 536
Uruguay	May 6, 1991		Treaty Doc. 102-16 Ex. Rpt. 102-34

SOURCE: Office of the Legal Adviser, U.S. Department of State.

NOTES: "Sen. Ex." (Senate Executive Print), "Ex. Rpt." (Executive Report), and "Treaty Doc." (Treaty Document) refer to documents published by the U.S. Senate. "TIAS" refers to *Treaties and Other International Acts Series*, issued singly in pamphlets by the Department of State. "UST" refers to *United States Treaties and Other International Agreements*. "*ILM*" refers to *International Legal Materials*.

Appendix F: Countries with Which the United States Has Extradition Treaties in Force (May 1, 1993)

Country	Signed	Entered into Force	Official Citation
Albania	Mar. 1, 1933	Nov. 14, 1935	49 Stat. 3313 TS 902 5 Bevans 22 53166 LNTS 195
Antigua & Barbuda[a]	June 8, 1972	Jan. 21, 1977	28 UST 227 TIAS 8468
Argentina[b]	Jan. 21, 1972	Sept. 15, 1972	23 UST 3501 TIAS 7510
Australia	May 14, 1974	May 8, 1976	27 UST 957 TIAS 8234
Protocol	Sept. 4, 1990	Dec. 21, 1992	Treaty Doc. 101-23 Ex. Rpt. 102-30
Austria	Jan. 31, 1930	Sept. 11, 1930	46 Stat. 2710 TS 822 5 Bevans 358 106 LNTS 379
Suppl.	May 19, 1934	Sept. 5, 1934	49 Stat. 2710 TS 873 5 Bevans 378 153 LNTS 247
Bahamas[c]	Dec. 22, 1931	June 24, 1935	47 Stat. 2122 TS 849 12 Bevans 482 163 LNTS 59
Exch. of Notes	Mar. 7, June 19, Aug. 17, 1978	Aug. 17, 1978	30 UST 187 TIAS 9185 1150 UNTS 99
Barbados[c]	Dec. 22, 1931	June 24, 1935	47 Stat. 2122 TS 849 12 Bevans 482 163 LNTS 59

Appendix F   Continued

Country	Signed	Entered into Force	Official Citation
Belgium	Oct. 26, 1901	July 14, 1902	32 Stat. 1894 TS 409 5 Bevans 566 164 LNTS 205
1st Suppl.	June 20, 1935	Nov. 7, 1935	49 Stat. 3276 TS 900 5 Bevans 566 164 LNTS 205
2nd Suppl.	Nov. 14, 1963	Dec. 25, 1964	15 UST 2252 TIAS 5715 522 UNTS 237
Belize[a]	June 8, 1972	Jan. 21, 1977	28 UST 227 TIAS 8468
Bolivia	Apr. 21, 1900	Jan. 22, 1902	32 Stat. 1857 TS 399 5 Bevans 735
Brazil	Jan. 13, 1961	Dec. 17, 1964	15 UST 2093 TIAS 5691 532 UNTS 177
Add. Protocol	June 18, 1962	Dec. 17, 1964	15 UST 2112 TIAS 5691 532 UNTS 198
Bulgaria	Mar. 19, 1924	June 24, 1924	43 Stat. 1886 TS 687 5 Bevans 1086 26 LNTS 27
Suppl.	June 8, 1934	Aug. 15, 1935	49 Stat. 3250 TS 894 5 Bevans 1103 161 LNTS 409
Burma[c]	Dec. 22, 1931	Nov. 1, 1941	47 Stat. 2122 TS 849 5 Bevans 482 163 LNTS 59

Appendix F   Continued

Country	Signed	Entered into Force	Official Citation
Canada	Dec. 3, 1971	Mar. 22, 1976	27 UST 983 TIAS 8237
Protocol	Jan. 11, 1988	Nov. 26, 1991	Treaty Doc. 101-17 Ex. Rpt. 102-2 27 *ILM* 422
Exch. of Notes	June 28, 1974 July 9, 1974	Mar. 22, 1976	27 UST 983 TIAS 8273
Chile[b]	Apr. 17, 1900	June 26, 1902	32 Stat. 1850 TS 407 6 Bevans 543
Colombia[b]	Sept. 14, 1979	Mar. 4, 1982	Treaty Doc. 97-8 Ex. Rpt. 97-34
Congo	Jan. 6, 1909	July 27, 1911	37 Stat. 1526 TS 561 7 Bevans 872
1st Suppl.	Jan. 15, 1929	May 19, 1929	46 Stat. 2276 TS 787 7 Bevans 972 92 LNTS 259
2nd Suppl.	Apr. 23, 1936	Sept. 24, 1936	50 Stat. 1117 TS 909 7 Bevans 995 172 LNTS 197
Costa Rica	Dec. 4, 1982	Oct. 11, 1991	Treaty Doc. 98-17 Ex. Rpt. 98-30
Croatia	Oct. 25, 1901	June 12, 1902	32 Stat. 1890 TS 406 12 Bevans 1238
Cuba	Apr. 6, 1904	Mar. 2, 1905	33 Stat. 2265 TS 440 6 Bevans 1128
Add. Protocol	Jan. 14, 1926	June 18, 1926	44 Stat. 2392 TS 737 6 Bevans 1136 61 LNTS 363

Appendix F   Continued

Country	Signed	Entered into Force	Official Citation
Cyprus[c]	Dec. 22, 1931	June 24, 1935	47 Stat. 2122 TS 849 12 Bevans 482 163 LNTS 59
Czech Republic	July 2, 1925	March 29, 1926	44 Stat. 2367 TS 734 6 Bevans 1247 50 LNTS 143
Suppl.	Apr. 29, 1935	Aug. 28, 1935	49 Stat. 3253 TS 895 6 Bevans 1283 162 LNTS 83
Denmark	June 22, 1972	July 31, 1974	25 UST 1293 TIAS 7864
Dominica[a]	June 8, 1972	Jan. 21, 1977	28 UST 227 TIAS 8468
Dominican Republic[b]	June 19, 1909	Aug. 2, 1910	36 Stat. 2468 TS 550 7 Bevans 200
Ecuador[b]	June 28, 1872	Nov. 12, 1873	18 Stat. 199 TS 79 7 Bevans 321
Suppl.	Sept. 22, 1939	May 29, 1941	55 Stat. 1196 TS 972 7 Bevans 346
Egypt	Aug. 11, 1874	Apr. 22, 1875	19 Stat. 572 TS 270 10 Bevans 642
El Salvador[b]	Apr. 18, 1911	July 10, 1911	37 Stat. 1516 TS 560 7 Bevans 507
Estonia	Nov. 8, 1923	Nov. 15, 1924	43 Stat. 1849 TS 703 7 Bevans 602 43 LNTS 277

Appendix F   Continued

Country	Signed	Entered into Force	Official Citation
Fiji[c]	Dec. 22, 1931	June 24, 1935	47 Stat. 2122 TS 849 12 Bevans 482 163 LNTS 59
Exch. of Notes	July 14, 1972 Aug. 17, 1973	Aug. 17, 1973	24 UST 1965 TIAS 7707
Finland	June 11, 1976	May 11, 1980	31 UST 944 TIAS 9626 1203 UNTS 165
France	Jan. 6, 1909	July 27, 1911	37 Stat. 1526 TS 561 7 Bevans 872
Suppl.	Feb. 12, 1970	Apr. 3, 1971	22 UST 407 TIAS 7075 791 UNTS 273
Gambia[c]	Dec. 22, 1931	June 24, 1935	47 Stat. 2122 TS 849 12 Bevans 482 163 LNTS 59
Germany	June 20, 1978	Aug. 29, 1980	32 UST 1485 TIAS 9785 1220 UNTS 269
Suppl.	Oct. 21, 1986	Mar. 11, 1993	Treaty Doc. 100- Ex. Rpt. 102-28
Ghana[c]	Dec. 22, 1931	June 24, 1935	47 Stat. 2122 TS 849 12 Bevans 482 163 LNTS 59
Greece	May 6, 1931	Nov. 1, 1932	47 Stat. 2185 TS 855 8 Bevans 353 138 LNTS 293
Protocol	Sept. 2, 1937	Sept. 2, 1937	51 Stat. 357 EAS 114 8 Bevans 366 185 LNTS 408

Appendix F   Continued

Country	Signed	Entered into Force	Official Citation
Grenada[c]	Dec. 22, 1931	June 24, 1935	47 Stat. 2122 TS 849 12 Bevans 482 163 LNTS 59
Guatamala[b]	Feb. 27, 1903	Aug. 15, 1903	33 Stat. 2147 TS 425 8 Bevans 482
Suppl.	Feb. 20, 1940	Mar. 13, 1941	55 Stat. 1097 TS 963 8 Bevans 528
Guyana[c]	Dec. 22, 1931	June 24, 1935	47 Stat. 2122 TS 849 12 Bevans 482 163 LNTS 59
Haiti	Aug. 9, 1904	June 28, 1905	34 Stat. 2858 TS 447 8 Bevans 653
Honduras[b]	Jan. 15, 1909	July 10, 1912	37 Stat. 1616 TS 569 8 Bevans 892
Suppl.	Feb. 21, 1927	June 5, 1928	45 Stat. 2489 TS 761 8 Bevans 903 85 LNTS 491
Hungary	July 3, 1856	Dec. 13, 1856	11 Stat. 691 TS 9 5 Bevans 211
Iceland	Jan. 6, 1902	Apr. 16, 1902	32 Stat. 1096 TS 405 7 Bevans 38
Suppl.	Nov. 6, 1905	Feb. 19, 1906	34 Stat. 2887 TS 449 7 Bevans 43
India[c]	Dec. 22, 1931	Mar. 9, 1942	47 Stat. 2122 TS 849 12 Bevans 482 163 LNTS 59

Appendix F   Continued

Country	Signed	Entered into Force	Official Citation
Iraq	June 7, 1934	Apr. 23, 1936	49 Stat. 3380 TS 907 9 Bevans 1 170 LNTS 267
Ireland	July 13, 1983	Dec. 15, 1984	TIAS 10813
Israel	Dec. 10, 1962	Dec. 5, 1963	14 UST 1707 TIAS 5476 484 UNTS 283
Exch. of Notes	Apr. 4 & 11, 1967		18 UST 382 TIAS 6246
Italy	Oct. 13, 1983	Sept. 24, 1984	TIAS 10837
Jamaica	June 14, 1983	July 7, 1991	Treaty Doc. 98-18 Ex. Rpt. 98-31
Japan	Mar. 3, 1978	Mar. 26, 1980	31 UST 892 TIAS 9625 1203 UNTS 225
Kenya[c]	Dec. 22, 1931	June 24, 1935	47 Stat. 2122 TS 849 12 Bevans 482 163 LNTS 59
Exch. of Notes	May 14, 1965 Aug. 19, 1965	Aug. 19, 1965	16 UST 1866 TIAS 5916 574 UNTS 153
Kiribati[a]	June 8, 1972	Jan. 21, 1977	28 UST 227 TIAS 8468
Latvia	Oct. 16, 1923	Mar. 1, 1924	43 Stat. 1738 TS 677 9 Bevans 515 27 LNTS 371
Suppl.	Oct. 10, 1934	Mar. 29, 1935	49 Stat. 3131 TS 884 9 Bevans 554 158 LNTS 263

Appendix F   Continued

Country	Signed	Entered into Force	Official Citation
Lesotho^c	Dec. 22, 1931	June 24, 1935	47 Stat. 2122 TS 849 12 Bevans 482 163 LNTS 59
Liberia	Nov. 1, 1937	Nov. 21, 1939	54 Stat. 1733 TS 955 9 Bevans 589 201 LNTS 151
Liechtenstein	May 20, 1936	June 28, 1937	50 Stat. 1337 TS 915 9 Bevans 683 157 LNTS 491
Lithuania	April 9, 1924	Aug. 23, 1924	43 Stat. 1835 TS 699 9 Bevans 655 51 LNTS 191
Luxembourg	Oct. 29, 1883	Aug. 13, 1884	23 Stat. 808 TS 196 9 Bevans 694
Suppl.	Apr. 24, 1935	Mar. 3, 1936	49 Stat. 3355 TS 904 9 Bevans 707 168 LNTS 129
Macedonia	Oct. 25, 1901	June 12, 1902	32 Stat. 1890 TS 406 12 Bevans 1238
Malawi^c	Dec. 22, 1931	June 24, 1925	47 Stat. 2122 TS 849 12 Bevans 482 163 LNTS 59
Exch. of Notes	Dec. 17, 1966 Jan. 6, 1967 April 4, 1967	April 4, 1967	18 UST 1822 TIAS 6328 692 UNTS 191
Malaysia^c	Dec. 22, 1931	July 31, 1939	47 Stat. 2122 TS 849 12 Bevans 482 163 LNTS 59

Appendix F   Continued

Country	Signed	Entered into Force	Official Citation
Malta^c	Dec. 22, 1931	June 24, 1935	47 Stat. 2122 TS 849 12 Bevans 482 163 LNTS 59
Mauritius^c	Dec. 22, 1931	June 24, 1935	47 Stat. 2122 TS 849 12 Bevans 482 163 LNTS 59
Mexico^b	May 4, 1978	Jan. 25, 1980	31 UST 5059 TIAS 9656
Monaco	Feb. 15, 1939	Mar. 28, 1940	54 Stat. 1780 TS 959 9 Bevans 1272 202 LNTS 61
Nauru^c	Dec. 22, 1931	Aug. 30, 1935	47 Stat. 2122 TS 849 12 Bevans 482 163 LNTS 59
Netherlands^d	June 24, 1980	Sept. 15, 1983	TIAS 10733
New Zealand	Jan. 12, 1970	Dec. 8, 1970	22 UST 1 TIAS 7035 791 UNTS 253
Nicaragua^b	Mar. 1, 1905	July 14, 1907	35 Stat. 1869 TS 462 10 Bevans 356
Nigeria^c	Dec. 22, 1931	June 24, 1935	47 Stat. 2122 TS 849 12 Bevans 482 163 LNTS 59
Norway	June 9, 1977	Mar. 7, 1980	31 UST 5619 TIAS 9679 1220 UNTS 221
Pakistan^c	Dec. 22, 1931	Mar. 9, 1942	47 Stat. 2122 TS 849 12 Bevans 482 163 LNTS 59

Appendix F   Continued

Country	Signed	Entered into Force	Official Citation
Panama[b]	May 25, 1904	May 8, 1905	34 Stat. 2851 TS 849 10 Bevans 673
Papua New Guinea[c]	Dec. 22, 1931	Aug. 30, 1935	47 Stat. 2122 TS 849 12 Bevans 482 163 LNTS 59
Paraguay	May 24, 1973	May 7, 1974	25 UST 967 TIAS 7838
Peru	Nov. 28, 1899	Feb. 22, 1901	31 Stat. 1921 TS 288 10 Bevans 1074
Poland	Nov. 22, 1927	July, 1929	46 Stat. 2282 TS 789 11 Bevans 206 92 LNTS 101
Suppl.	Apr. 5, 1935	June 5, 1936	49 Stat. 3394 TS 789 11 Bevans 265 170 LNTS 287
Portugal	May 7, 1908	Nov. 14, 1908	35 Stat. 2071 TS 512 11 Bevans 314
Romania	July 23, 1924	Apr. 7, 1925	44 Stat. 2020 TS 713 11 Bevans 391
Suppl.	Nov. 10, 1936	July 27, 1937	50 Stat. 1349 TS 916 11 Bevans 423 181 LNTS 177
Saint Kitts & Nevis[a]	June 8, 1972	Jan. 21, 1977	28 UST 227 TIAS 8468
St. Lucia[a]	June 8, 1972	Jan. 21, 1977	28 UST 227 TIAS 8468
St. Vincent & the Grenadines[a]	June 8, 1972	Jan. 21, 1977	28 UST 227 TIAS 8468

Appendix F   Continued

Country	Signed	Entered into Force	Official Citation
San Marino	Jan. 10, 1906	July 8, 1908	35 Stat. 1971 TS 495 11 Bevans 440
Suppl.	Oct. 10, 1934	June 28, 1935	49 Stat. 3198 TS 891 11 Bevans 446 161 LNTS 149
Seychelles[c]	Dec. 22, 1931	June 24, 1935	47 Stat. 2122 TS 849 12 Bevans 482 163 LNTS 59
Sierra Leone[c]	Dec. 22, 1931	June 24, 1935	47 Stat. 2122 TS 849 12 Bevans 482 163 LNTS 59
Singapore[c]	Dec. 22, 1931	June 24, 1935	47 Stat. 2122 TS 849 12 Bevans 482 163 LNTS 59
Exch. of Notes	Apr. 23, 1969 June 10, 1969	June 10, 1969	20 UST 2764 TIAS 6744 723 UNTS 201
Slovak Republic	July 2, 1925	Mar. 29, 1926	44 Stat. 2367 TS 734 6 Bevans 1247 50 LNTS 143
Suppl.	Apr. 29, 1935	Aug. 28, 1935	49 Stat. 3253 TS 895 6 Bevans 1283 162 LNTS 83
Slovenia	Oct. 25, 1901	June 12, 1902	32 Stat. 1890 TS 406 12 Bevans 1238
Solomon Islands[a]	June 8, 1972	Jan. 21, 1977	28 UST 277 TIAS 8468
South Africa	Dec. 18, 1947	Apr. 30, 1951	2 UST 884 TIAS 2243 148 UNTS 85

Appendix F   Continued

Country	Signed	Entered into Force	Official Citation
Spain	May 29, 1970	June 16, 1971	22 UST 737 TIAS 7136 796 UNTS 245
Suppl.	Jan. 25, 1975	June 2, 1978	29 UST 2283 TIAS 8938
2nd Suppl.	Feb. 9, 1988	July 2, 1993	Treaty Doc. 102-24 Ex. Rpt. 102-31
Sri Lanka^c	Dec. 22, 1931	June 24, 1935	47 Stat. 2122 TS 849 12 Bevans 482 163 LNTS 59
Surinam	June 2, 1887	July 11, 1889	26 Stat. 1481 TS 256 10 Bevans 47
Extension	Jan. 18, 1904	Aug. 28, 1904	33 Stat. 2257 TS 436 10 Bevans 53
Swaziland^c	Dec. 22, 1931	June 24, 1935	47 Stat. 2122 TS 849 12 Bevans 482 163 LNTS 59
Exch. of Notes	May 13, 1970 July 28, 1970	July 28, 1970	21 UST 1930 TIAS 6934 756 UNTS 103
Sweden	Oct. 24, 1961	Dec. 3, 1963	14 UST 1845 TIAS 5496 494 UNTS 141
Suppl.	Mar. 14, 1983	Sept. 24, 1984	TIAS 10812
Switzerland	May 14, 1900	Mar. 29, 1901	31 Stat. 1928 TS 354 11 Bevans 904
1st Suppl.	Jan. 10, 1935	May 16, 1935	49 Stat. 3192 TS 889 11 Bevans 924 159 LNTS 243
2nd Suppl.	Jan. 31, 1940	Apr. 8, 1941	55 Stat. 1140 TS 969 11 Bevans 938

Appendix F   Continued

Country	Signed	Entered into Force	Official Citation
Tanzania[c]	Dec. 22, 1931	June 24, 1935	47 Stat. 2122 TS 969 12 Bevans 482 163 LNTS 59
Exch. of Notes	Nov. 30, 1965 Dec. 6, 1965	Dec. 6, 1965	16 UST 2066 TIAS 5946
Thailand	Dec. 14, 1983	May 17, 1991	Treaty Doc. 98-16 Ex. Rpt. 98-29
Tonga[c]	Dec. 22, 1931	June 24, 1935	47 Stat. 2122 TS 849 12 Bevans 482 163 LNTS 59
Exch. of Notes	Mar. 14, 1977 Apr. 13, 1977	Apr. 13, 1977	28 UST 5290 TIAS 8628 1087 UNTS 289
Trinidad & Tobago[c]	Dec. 22, 1931	June 24, 1935	47 Stat. 2122 TS 849 12 Bevans 482 163 LNTS 59
Turkey	June 7, 1979	Jan. 1, 1981	32 UST 3111 TIAS 9891
Tuvalu[a]	June 8, 1972	Jan. 21, 1977	28 UST 227 TIAS 8468
United Kingdom[a]	June 8, 1972	Jan. 21, 1977	28 UST 227 TIAS 8468 1049 UNTS 167
Suppl.	June 25, 1985	Dec. 23, 1986	Treaty Doc. 99-8 Ex. Rpt. 99-17
Uruguay	Apr. 6, 1973	Apr. 11, 1984	TIAS 10850
Venezuela	Jan. 19 & 21, 1922	Apr. 14, 1923	43 Stat. 1698 T.S. 675 12 Bevans 1128 49 LNTS 435
Yugoslavia	Oct. 25, 1901	June 12, 1902	32 Stat. 1890 T.S. 406 12 Bevans 1238

Appendix F   Continued

Country	Signed	Entered into Force	Official Citation
Zambia^c	Dec. 22, 1931	June 24, 1935	47 Stat. 2122
			T.S. 849
			12 Bevans 482
			163 LNTS 59

SOURCE: U.S. Department of State, *Treaties in Force* (Washington, D.C.: Government Printing Office, 1992); Michael Abbell and Bruno A. Ristau, *International Judicial Assistance* (Washington, D.C.: International Law Institute, 1990), vol. 5, appendix A-135 to A-145; Office of the Legal Adviser, U.S. Department of State.

NOTES: "Ex. Rpt." (Executive Report) and "Treaty Doc." (Treaty Document) refer to documents published by the U.S. Senate. "TIAS" refers to *Treaties and Other International Acts Series*, issued singly in pamphlets by the Department of State. "UST" refers to *United States Treaties and Other International Agreements*. "*ILM*" refers to *International Legal Materials*. Other abbreviations used are as follows: "Stat." = United States Statutes at Large; "TS" = Treaty Series, issued singly in pamphlets by the Department of State (until replaced in 1945 by the TIAS); "EAS" = Executive Agreement Series, issued singly in pamphlets by the Department of State (until replaced in 1945 by the TIAS); "Bevans" = Treaties and Other International Agreements of the United States of America 1776–1949, compiled under the direction of Charles I. Bevans; "LNTS" = League of Nations Treaty Series; "UNTS" = United Nations Treaty Series.

ªExtradition relations governed by 1972 Treaty with United Kingdom (28 UST 277; TIAS 8468).

ᵇAlso a signitory of the multilateral 1933 Convention on Extradition adopted by the Seventh International Conference of American States (the Montevideo Extradition Treaty), signed Dec. 26, 1933, entered into force Jan. 25, 1935. 49 Stat. 3111; TS 882; 3 Bevans 152; 165 LNTS 45.

ᶜExtradition relations governed by 1931 Treaty with United Kingdom (47 Stat. 2122; TS 849).

ᵈApplicable to Aruba and the Netherland Antilles.

ᵉApplicable to all U.K. territories, Channel Isl., Isle of Man, Bermuda, British Indian Ocean Territory, British Virgin Isl., Cayman Isl., Falkland Isl. and dependencies, Gibraltar, Hong Kong, Montserrat, Pitcairn, Henderson, Ducie and Oeno Isl., Anguilla, St. Helena and dependencies, Sovereign Base Areas of Akrotiri and Dhekelia in the Island of Cyprus, and Turks and Caicos Isl.

Index